The New American Commentary

Volume 26

General Editor
DAVID S. DOCKERY

Consulting Editors

L. RUSS BUSH	PAIGE PATTERSON
DUANE A. GARRETT	ROBERT B. SLOAN
KENNETH A. MATHEWS	CURTIS VAUGHAN
RICHARD R. MELICK, JR.	LARRY L. WALKER

THE NEW AMERICAN COMMENTARY

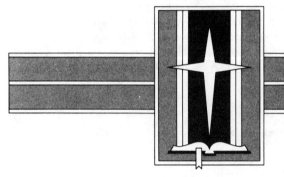

Volume
26

ACTS

John B. Polhill

BROADMAN PRESS
NASHVILLE, TENNESSEE

© Copyright 1992 • Broadman & Holman Publishers
All rights reserved
4201-26
ISBN: 0-8054-0126-1
Dewey Decimal Classification: 226.6
Subject Heading: BIBLE. N.T. ACTS
Library of Congress Catalog Card Number: 91-21660
Printed in the United States of America
06 05 04   7 6 5

Library of Congress Cataloging-in-Publication Data

Polhill, John B.
  Acts / John B. Polhill.
    p. cm. — (The New American commentary ; v. 26)
  Includes indexes.
  ISBN 0-8054-0126-1
  1. Bible. N.T. Acts—Commentaries. I. Title. II. Series.
BS2625.3.P65 1992
226.6'077—dc20

To *Nancy*

who has been

for 25 years

my constant

inspiration in

faith, hope, and love

Editors' Preface

God's Word does not change. God's world, however, changes in every generation. These changes, in addition to new findings by scholars and a new variety of challenges to the gospel message, call for the church in each generation to interpret and apply God's Word for God's people. Thus, THE NEW AMERICAN COMMENTARY is introduced to bridge the twentieth and twenty-first centuries. This new series has been designed primarily to enable pastors, teachers, and students to read the Bible with clarity and proclaim it with power.

In one sense THE NEW AMERICAN COMMENTARY is not new, for it represents the continuation of a heritage rich in biblical and theological exposition. The title of this forty-volume set points to the continuity of this series with an important commentary project published at the end of the nineteenth century called AN AMERICAN COMMENTARY, edited by Alvah Hovey. The older series included, among other significant contributions, the outstanding volume on Matthew by John A. Broadus, from whom the publisher of the new series, Broadman Press, partly derives its name. The former series was authored and edited by scholars committed to the infallibility of Scripture, making it a solid foundation for the present project. In line with this heritage, all NAC authors affirm the divine inspiration, inerrancy, complete truthfulness, and full authority of the Bible. The perspective of the NAC is unapologetically confessional and rooted in the evangelical tradition.

Since a commentary is a fundamental tool for the expositor or teacher who seeks to interpret and apply Scripture in the church or classroom, the NAC focuses on communicating the theological structure and content of each biblical book. The writers seek to illuminate both the historical meaning and the contemporary significance of Holy Scripture.

In its attempt to make a unique contribution to the Christian community, the NAC focuses on two concerns. First, the commentary emphasizes how each section of a book fits together so that the reader becomes aware of the theological unity of each book and of Scripture as a whole. The writers, however, remain aware of the Bible's inherently rich variety. Second, the NAC is produced with the conviction that the Bible primarily belongs to the church.

We believe that scholarship and the academy provide an indispensable foundation for biblical understanding and the service of Christ, but the editors and authors of this series have attempted to communicate the findings of their research in a manner that will build up the whole body of Christ. Thus, the commentary concentrates on theological exegesis, while providing practical, applicable exposition.

THE NEW AMERICAN COMMENTARY's theological focus enables the reader to see the parts as well as the whole of Scripture. The biblical books vary in content, context, literary type, and style. In addition to this rich variety, the editors and authors recognize that the doctrinal emphasis and use of the biblical books differ in various places, contexts, and cultures among God's people. These factors, as well as other concerns, have led the editors to give freedom to the writers to wrestle with the issues raised by the scholarly community surrounding each book and to determine the appropriate shape and length of the introductory materials. Moreover, each writer has developed the structure of the commentary in a way best suited for expounding the basic structure and the meaning of the biblical books for our day. Generally, discussions relating to contemporary scholarship and technical points of grammar and syntax appear in the footnotes and not in the text of the commentary. This format allows pastors and interested laypersons, scholars and teachers, and serious college and seminary students to profit from the commentary at various levels. This approach has been employed because we believe that all Christians have the privilege and responsibility to read and to seek to understand the Bible for themselves.

Consistent with the desire to produce a readable, up-to-date commentary, the editors selected the New International Version as the standard translation for the commentary series. The selection was made primarily because of the NIV's faithfulness to the original languages and its beautiful and readable style. The authors, however, have been given the liberty to differ at places from the NIV as they develop their own translations from the Greek and Hebrew texts.

The NAC reflects the vision and leadership of those who provide oversight for Broadman Press, who in 1987 called for a new commentary series that would evidence a commitment to the inerrancy of Scripture and a faithfulness to the classic Christian tradition. While the commentary adopts an "American" name, it should be noted that some writers represent countries outside the United States, giving the commentary an international perspective. The diverse group of writers includes scholars, teachers, and administrators from almost twenty different colleges and seminaries, as well as pastors, missionaries, and a layperson.

The editors and writers hope that THE NEW AMERICAN COMMENTARY will be helpful and instructive for pastors and teachers, scholars and students, for men and women in the churches who study and teach God's Word in various settings. We trust that for editors, authors, and readers alike, the commentary will be used to build up the church, encourage obedience, and bring renewal to God's people. Above all, we pray that the NAC will bring glory and honor to our Lord, who has graciously redeemed us and faithfully revealed himself to us in his Holy Word.

SOLI DEO GLORIA
The Editors

Author's Preface

This commentary is the culmination of twenty years of teaching the Book of Acts in the twin settings of the seminary classroom and the local church. It has been written with these two groups in mind. The basic commentary is designed for the use of pastors and laity in the preaching and teaching ministries of the church. Its focus is on the meaning and message of the biblical text. The footnotes are aimed at the student, discussing such matters as translation and alternative interpretations and providing bibliography that covers the range of scholarly opinion for the student's further research. If I have not always succeeded in balancing these two levels of treatment, I would wish to have erred to the advantage of the former setting. The ultimate goal of biblical scholarship should be the application of the text in the witness and ministry of the church.

I have not sought to break any new ground in the interpretation of Acts but rather to preserve the insights of both past and present scholarship. More akin to Luke's experience in writing his Gospel than his Acts (for which he had no predecessors), I have had "many" to go before me (Luke 1:1). There is a rich heritage of commentary by Baptists reaching back to the classic missionary treatment of W. O. Carver and the thorough Greek exegesis of A. T. Robertson in the third volume of his *Word Pictures in the New Testament.* Frank Stagg's emphasis on the "unhindered gospel" has strongly made its impression, both through his commentary and his influence as my teacher. Charles Talbert's emphasis on Acts as a literary text has likewise had its impact. A particularly fruitful source have been the doctoral students at the Southern Baptist Theological Seminary who have written dissertations on various subjects in Acts. I have often drawn from their insights and cited their work where possible in the footnotes.

I would be remiss should I fail to acknowledge my heavy indebtedness to the wider guild of Acts scholars. These include the now-classic works of such as William Ramsay, Henry Joel Cadbury, and Kirsopp Lake. The massive commentaries of G. Schneider and R. Pesch have consistently proved their value. I have drawn regularly from many others, and these will be readily apparent from their frequent citation in the footnotes. Two deserve particular mention. The commentary by E. Haenchen has had a strong influence on my work. He and I often disagree on judgments about the historical reliability of Acts traditions, but his constant challenges to old assumptions provoke a reexamination which is of value in itself. Of greatest help, however, have been Haenchen's careful examination of the literary flow of the Acts narrative and his exposition of its major themes, matters which in no way depend on historical judgments one way or the other.

More compatible with my own viewpoint has been the extensive work of F. F. Bruce on Acts. His *New International Commentary* on Acts is regularly cited in the footnotes. Fortunately, Bruce completed his major revision of his commentary on the Greek text of Acts (third edition) before his death this past fall. The book was released a few months later and serves as a suitable memorial to this scholar who devoted a lifetime to the study of Acts. Although the published form of his commentary became available only after the manuscript of this commentary was completed, Eerdmans graciously furnished me with the galleys some two years previous to final publication. Consequently, the influence of Bruce's Greek commentary on the present work is more pervasive than the footnotes might indicate.

A final note of appreciation should be expressed for the many who have encouraged and assisted me in this undertaking. I am especially indebted to President Roy Lee Honeycutt and the Trustees of Southern Seminary for granting me a sabbatical leave the spring and summer of 1990 to complete this project. By continuing my full salary on leave and furnishing the typist, the seminary virtually underwrote the commentary. My typist, Ms. Keitha Brasler, was always prompt and accurate, even in deciphering long, hand-written German references and in catching many of my errors. It would be difficult to express my gratitude for her industry, support, and cheerful spirit through even the worst of it. My colleagues at Southern Seminary have been uniformly supportive, and for their understanding I am most grateful. This is especially true of Dean Larry McSwain and Provost Willis Bennett, who made adjustments in schedules and assignments to allow the completion of the commentary.

The editorial staff at Broadman Press have gone beyond the call of duty in preparing the published form of this commentary. Mike Smith, the editor of the series in its early stages and a former student in my Acts class at the seminary, played a major role in my invitation to furnish this volume. David Dockery has served as editor during the final publication phase. I would be hard-pressed to express adequate appreciation for his careful oversight of editing, his enthusiastic support, and his accommodation to a somewhat unwieldy manuscript.

It is generally customary to express gratitude to one's spouse for moral support during such a "birthing" process as this has been. In this case, however, more than the custom is in order. In many ways my wife Nancy was literally co-author of this commentary. She did all the "leg work," spending many days running down books at the seminary library, looking up journal articles and duplicating them, bringing everything home and freeing me from the many days of time that these duties entail. Without her assistance, the commentary could not have been completed within its deadline.

A word of appreciation should be expressed for the students in my classes at Southern Seminary. They often endured excurses on Acts when that wasn't the subject for the day, always patiently, generally supportively. And finally there are the millions of Southern Baptists who have through the years supported the Cooperative Program and with it the seminary where I teach, allowing me to pursue God's calling for my life. Many of them will never visit a seminary. Perhaps this book will give them some glimpse into the ministry they support with their offerings.

Abbreviations

Bible Books

Gen	Isa	Luke
Exod	Jer	John
Lev	Lam	Acts
Num	Ezek	Rom
Deut	Dan	1, 2 Cor
Josh	Hos	Gal
Judg	Joel	Eph
Ruth	Amos	Phil
1, 2 Sam	Obad	Col
1, 2 Kgs	Jonah	1, 2 Thess
1, 2 Chr	Mic	1, 2 Tim
Ezra	Nah	Titus
Neh	Hab	Phlm
Esth	Zeph	Heb
Job	Hag	Jas
Ps (*pl.* Pss)	Zech	1, 2 Pet
Prov	Mal	1, 2, 3 John
Eccl	Matt	Jude
Song of Songs	Mark	Rev

Commonly Used Reference Works

AB	*Anchor Bible*
ACNT	Augsburg Commentary on the New Testament
AJT	*American Journal of Theology*
AnBib	Analecta biblica
ATR	*Anglican Theological Review*
ATRSup	*Anglican Theological Review Supplemental Series*
AUSS	*Andrews University Seminary Studies*

BAGD	W. Bauer, W. F. Arndt, F. W. Gingrich, and F. Danker, *Greek-English Lexicon of the NT*
Bib	*Biblica*
BibSac	*Bibliotheca Sacra*
BJRL	*Bulletin of the John Rylands Library*
BK	*Bibel und Kirche*
BR	*Biblical Research*
BT	*The Biblical Translator*
BTB	*Biblical Theology Bulletin*
BZ	*Biblische Zeitschrift*
CJT	*Canadian Journal of Theology*
CBQ	*Catholic Biblical Quarterly*
CTM	*Concordia Theological Monthly*
DSB	*Daily Study Bible*
DownRev	Downside Review
EBC	*Expositor's Bible Commentary*
ExpTim	*Expository Times*
ETC	*English Translation and Commentary*
ETL	*Ephemerides theologicae lovanienses*
EvQ	*Evangelical Quarterly*
EvT	*Evangelische Theologie*
FM	*Faith and Mission*
GNC	*Good News Commentary*
Her	*Hermenia*
HTKNT	Herders theologischer Kommentar zum Neuen Testament
HTR	*Harvard Theological Review*
IBS	*Irish Biblical Studies*
ICC	International Critical Commentary
INT	*Interpretation: A Bible Commentary for Preaching and Teaching*
Int	*Interpretation*
JAAR	*Journal of the American Academy of Religion*
JAOS	*Journal of the American Oriental Society*
JETS	*Journal of the Evangelical Theological Society*
JBL	*Journal of Biblical Literature*
JJS	*Journal of Jewish Studies*
JRS	*Journal of Roman Studies*
JR	*Journal of Religion*
JSNT	*Journal for the Study of the New Testament*
JSOT	*Journal for the Study of the Old Testament*
JSS	*Journal of Semitic Studies*
JTS	*Journal of Theological Studies*
LCL	Loeb Classical Library
LouvSt	*Louvain Studies*

LThQ	*Lexington Theological Quarterly*
MDB	*Mercer Dictionary of the Bible*
MNTC	Moffatt NT Commentary
NAC	New American Commentary
NCB	*New Clarendon Bible*
NIC	New International Commentary
NovT	*Novum Testamentum*
NRT	*La nouvelle revue théologique*
NTD	Das Neue Testament Deutsch
NTM	*New Testament Message*
NTS	*New Testament Studies*
NTM	*The New Testament Message*
PC	Proclamation Commentaries
Proc	*Proclamation Commentaries*
PRS	*Perspectives in Religious Studies*
Pol *Phil*	*Polycarp's Epistle to the Philippians*
RB	*Revue Biblique*
RelSRev	*Religious Studies Review*
RevThom	*Revue thomiste*
RHPR	*Revue d'histoire et de philosophie religieuses*
RSPT	*Revue des sciences philosophiques et théologiques*
RSR	*Recherches de science religieuse*
RTL	*Revue théologique de Louvain*
RTP	*Revue de théologie et de philosophie*
RTR	*Reformed Theological Review*
SBLMS	Society of Biblical Literature Monograph Series
SJT	*Scottish Journal of Theology*
SPCK	Society for the Promotion of Christian Knowledge
ST	*Studia theologica*
TB	*Tyndale Bulletin*
TBT	*The Bible Today*
TDNT	G. Kittel and G. Friedrich, eds., *Theological Dictionary of the New Testament*
TNTC	*Tyndale New Testament Commentaries*
TLZ	*Theologische Literaturzeitung*
TRu	*Theologische Rundschau*
TS	*Theological Studies*
TSK	*Theologische Studien und Kritiken*
TZ	*Theologische Zeitschrift*
VC	*Vigiliae christianae*
UBSGNT	United Bible Societies *Greek New Testament*
WP	Word Pictures in the New Testament, by A. T. Robertson
WTJ	*Westminster Theological Journal*

ZNW	*Zeitschrift für die neutestamentliche Wissenschaft*
ZRGG	*Zeitschrift für Religions- und Geistesgeschichte*
ZTK	*Zeitschrift für Theologie und Kirche*

Contents

Acts

INTRODUCTION

Our knowledge of early Christianity would be greatly impoverished had Luke not conceived of his "second book to Theophilus," which tradition has designated "The Acts of the Apostles." Acts is unique among the New Testament writings that deal with the life and mission of the Christian community in the age of the apostles. The Gospels, of course, were written during this period; and Luke contributed his own. The Gospels, however, deal with the ministry and teaching of Jesus and are only at best an indirect witness to the life of the churches during the period of their writing.

Likewise, the epistolary literature of the New Testament comes in large part from this period; but it too provides no real framework for reconstructing the life and growth of the church. Constantly one is driven back to Acts. Take Paul, for instance. Although it has sometimes been advocated, no one has ever succeeded in producing a convincing portrait of the apostle and his missionary activity on the basis of his epistles alone, not to mention the early Jewish Christian church. What would we know about the Jerusalem church without Acts? But Acts is far more than mere history. It contains much solid theology. This is particularly to be found in the speeches, which comprise nearly one-third of its total text. The many episodes from the lives of the apostles present more than a bare chronicling of events. They are rich testimonies in narrative form of the faith of the community and the driving force behind its mission.

In the following introduction, the first six sections are provided to orient the user of the commentary to the "external" matters that assist in interpreting the text, such as traditions about authorship, date, and the like. The final six sections take a more "internal" look at the book and treat such matters as Luke's characteristics as a writer and the main themes recurring throughout his writing.

1. Acts in the Early Tradition

Our earliest witnesses to the Book of Acts are for the most part fairly late, dating from the latter part of the second century. These are of two types: (1) works that appear to be aware of Acts and draw from its content and (2) specific references to the book in the writings of the early church fathers.

(1) Earliest Use of Acts

Echoes of Acts possibly are in the Apostolic Fathers. For instance, Clement of Rome, writing ca. A.D. 95–100, spoke of "giving more gladly than receiving" (1 Clem 2:1), which may be an allusion to Acts 20:35 but is more likely an independent quote from the oral tradition of Jesus' sayings. The same can be said of his reference to the "pouring out of the Spirit" in the very next verse (1 Clem 2:2). This could reflect an awareness of Acts 2:17, but more likely it is an independent quote from Joel. Ignatius, whose writings date from the first decades of the second century, used the phrase "to go to his own place" (Ign. *Magn.* 5:1), which recalls Peter's words about Judas in Acts 1:25. The phrase is a common Greek idiom, however, and probably reflects no use of Acts. The phrase "you shall not say anything is your own" is found in Barnabas 19:8 and Didache 4:8, both from the early second century. The phrase is reminiscent of Acts 4:32 but is again a common Greek expression and may simply reflect an independent tradition of the early Christian practice. Other examples could be cited from the Apostolic Fathers,[1] but they are all too sporadic, brief, and too "traditional" in nature to establish dependence on Acts. One seems to be on firmer ground with Justin Martyr (ca. A.D. 130–150). In his *First Apology* (39:3) he referred to the apostles as "illiterate, of no ability in speaking" (cf. Acts 4:13). In his *Second Apology* 10 he seems to have reflected an acquaintance with Paul's Areopagus speech in referring to "the unknown God" (cf. Acts 17:23). Clearest of all, however, is the following statement from his *First Apology* 50:12:

> And afterwards, when he had risen from the dead and appeared to them, and had taught them to read the prophecies in which all these things were foretold as coming to pass, and when they had seen him ascending into heaven, and had believed, and had received power sent by him upon them, and went to every race of men, they taught these things, and were called apostles.

This is basically a precis of Acts 1 as well as a general summary of the remainder of the book. It thus seems that by the middle of the second century, Acts was known and being used.

---

[1] The phrase "judge of the living and the dead" is found in Pol. *Phil.* 2:1 and *Barn.* 7:2 (cf. Acts 10:42). Ign. *Smyrn.* 3:3 refers to Jesus' "eating and drinking" with the apostles after his resurrection (cf. Acts 10:41). *Diog.* 3:34 (ca. A.D. 150) uses language similar to Acts 17:24f., and the term παῖς is applied to Jesus in *Did.* 9:2 and 10:2 (cf. Acts 3:13, 26).

(2) Explicit References to Acts

From the end of the second century come the first explicit references to the Book of Acts and its Lukan authorship.[2] In his book *Against Heresies* (3.14.1) Irenaeus, bishop of the church of Lyons in Gaul, discussed the authorship of both the third Gospel and Acts, stating that both were by Luke, the physician, the traveling companion of Paul. He went into detail in describing those passages beginning at Acts 16:10, where the first-person plural appears in the narrative of Acts, thus establishing the writer as Paul's associate. He further cited 2 Tim 4:10f. and Col 4:14, which point to Luke as Paul's companion.

Dating from the same period, the Muratorian canon, an early canonical list generally believed to have come from the church at Rome, also gives testimony to the common authorship of Luke and Acts. Like Irenaeus, it depicts the author as Luke the physician, the traveling companion of Paul, and adds the note that Acts does not relate the deaths of Peter and Paul because Luke restricted his account only to those matters where he was himself present. It also gives the rather strange detail that Luke served as Paul's legal counsel, something attested nowhere else in the early tradition. Later witnesses confirm the basic testimony of Irenaeus and the Muratorian canon to Luke-Acts being by Luke, Paul's traveling companion. An occasional additional detail is added, and these tend to become more fanciful with time. Thus Origen (ca. A.D. 230) suggested that Luke was the "brother who is praised by all the churches" Paul mentioned in 2 Cor 8:18. Eusebius (*Hist. eccl.* 3.4.6), writing in the early fourth century, is the earliest extant witness to the tradition that Luke came from Antioch. In the latter half of the fourth century, Jerome repeated the view of Luke's Antiochene origin and added that Luke was with Paul during his two-year house arrest in Rome and wrote Acts from that city. He likewise stated that Luke's tomb was located in Constantinople (*De Vir. Ill.* 6). Generally reputed as the best Christian linguist of his day, it is significant that he commended Luke's grammar for its eloquence and considered it to be the most educated Greek of the four Evangelists' (*Comm. on Isa* 3:6). In the preface to his commentary on Matthew, he discussed the Gospel of Luke and cited a tradition that it was written in the districts of Boetia and Achaia.

Still later traditions add further details, all of which seem to be primarily speculative. For example, the Monarchianist Prologue to Luke claims that Luke had no wife or son, that he lived to age seventy-four, and that

---

[2]For a full treatment of the early tradition with quotes in the original language, see F. J. Foakes-Jackson and K. Lake, eds., *The Beginnings of Christianity*, vol. 2, *Prolegomena and Criticism* (London: Macmillan, 1922), 209-64.

he died in Bithynia. Adamantius, seeking to give him more direct apostolic status, maintained that he was one of the seventy disciples of Luke 10:1; and a marginal note found in several ancient manuscripts identified him as the companion of Clopas and the one who walked with the risen Jesus on the road to Emmaus (Luke 24:13-35).

In summary, the information listed in the earliest witness (Irenaeus) has the most claim to reliability—that Luke the physician of Col 4:14, the traveling companion of Paul, was the author of the third Gospel and Acts. Some credence can perhaps be given to the tradition that links Luke with Antioch, but that could well have come about as an attempt to find some explicit mention of Luke in his writings (note the Lucius of Cyrene found among the leaders in Antioch in Acts 13:1).

Before leaving the early witnesses, a word should be said about the traditional title "Acts of the Apostles." Whatever its original title, if any, the work seems to have had no fixed name in the second-century's earliest witnesses. Irenaeus described it as "Luke's witness to the apostles" (*Lucae de apostolis testificatio*). Tertullian referred to it as "Luke's Commentary" (*Commentarius Lucae; de jejunio* 10). Perhaps closest to our present title is that of the Muratorian canon—*The Acts of All the Apostles* (*Acta omnium apostolorum*). Although of disputed date, the "anti-Marcionite" Prologue to Luke may be our earliest Greek witness to the familiar name "Acts of the Apostles" (*praxeis apostolōn*).[3] In any event, by the third century that title seems to have become fixed in the tradition.

2. The Author of Acts

Scholars of all persuasions are in agreement that the third Gospel and the Book of Acts are by the same author. There are always a few dissenting voices on any issue, and some would argue for separate authorship of the two volumes.[4] The evidence is decidedly against them. Not only is there the unanimous voice of the tradition from Irenaeus on, but the internal evidence of the two books points to their common authorship.

---

[3]F. F. Bruce, *The Acts of the Apostles: The Greek Text*, 3rd ed. rev. (Grand Rapids: Eerdmans, 1990), 1. If the anti-Marcionite Prologue to Luke is dated later than the second century, Clement of Alexandria would be the earliest witness to the Greek title πράξεις ἀποστόλων.

[4]A. C. Clark argued for separate authors in his commentary, *The Acts of the Apostles* (Oxford: Clarendon, 1933), 393-408. Clark argued that Acts uses different words (synonyms) for the same concepts when compared with Luke. His view was revived in more recent years by A. W. Argyle, "The Greek of Luke and Acts," *NTS* 20 (1973-74): 441-45. See the rebuttal of this argument by B. E. Beck, "The Common Authorship of Luke and Acts," *NTS* 23 (1976-77): 346-52.

(1) Relationship to Gospel of Luke

For one, a common style and vocabulary run throughout the two books.[5] Many common themes also bind the two volumes together (cf. section 11). Above all is the claim of the author himself as reflected in the prefaces to each of the books. Both Luke and Acts are dedicated to the same person, Theophilus (Luke 1:3; Acts 1:1); and Acts 1:1 refers to his "former book," which dealt with "all that Jesus began to do and to teach"—namely, the Gospel of Luke.

Finally, the conclusion to Luke's Gospel provides an introduction to the Book of Acts. Jesus' final words to his disciples are a virtual summary of the main themes of the first chapters of Acts—the waiting in Jerusalem until clothed with the power of the Spirit, the preaching to all the nations beginning with Jerusalem, and the fulfillment of the Scriptures in the death and resurrection of the Messiah, which is the central topic of Peter's sermons in Jerusalem (Luke 24:44-49). Then there is the ascension. In all the New Testament the ascension narrative is related only in Luke and Acts, though several passages in the epistles refer to Jesus seated at God's right hand (e.g., Heb 1:3). It closes the Gospel of Luke and opens the Acts of the Apostles, binding Luke's two volumes together.

(2) "We" Narratives

Beginning with Irenaeus, the tradition has maintained that this single author, whose two volumes comprise nearly 27 percent of the entire New Testament, was Luke. For Irenaeus the occurrence of the first-person plural in the later chapters of Acts pointed to the author of the book as having been a traveling companion of Paul. Often referred to as the "we" narrative, the passages involved are 16:10-17, which relates Paul's voyage from Troas to Philippi; then 20:5–21:18, covering Paul's journey from Philippi to Jerusalem; and finally 27:1–28:16, involving the journey from Caesarea to Rome. This "we" has always been a crux in the debate over Lukan authorship. Those who follow the traditional view concur with Irenaeus in seeing it as an indication that the author of Luke-Acts was present with Paul on these occasions. Others argue that the "we" is an indication only that the author of Luke-Acts used a source from a traveling associate of Paul (see section 5).

(3) Medical Theory

Who was Luke? Very little is said about him in the New Testament. He is mentioned three times, all in the "greetings" sections of Paul's

---

[5]See the comparative word statistics in J. C. Hawkins, *Horae Synopticae*, 2nd ed. rev. (Grand Rapids: Baker, 1968), 174-89. See also E. J. Goodspeed, "The Vocabulary of Luke and Acts," *JBL* 31 (1912): 92-94.

epistles. In Col 4:14 Paul sent greetings from Demas and "our dear friend Luke, the doctor." In Philemon he is again linked with Demas in the sending of greetings.[6] In 2 Tim 4:11, in something of a despondent mood, Paul lamented that everyone had either deserted him or gone to minister elsewhere and noted that "only Luke is with me." All the direct New Testament testimony to Luke yields but scant information. He was an associate of Paul.[7] He was with him when Colossians, Philemon, and 2 Timothy were written—periods of imprisonment for Paul. Finally, he was a physician, which would indicate a person of some education and social standing.

Luke's status as a physician became the basis for an elaborate argument which was first proposed by W. Hobart in the late nineteenth century.[8] The subtitle to his volume is perhaps the best commentary on the purpose of his work: "A proof from internal evidence that the Gospel according to St. Luke and the Acts of the Apostles were written by the same person and that the writer was a medical man." Drawing from the Greek medical writers, particularly Galen and Hippocrates, Hobart sought to demonstrate that the author of Luke-Acts used the same "technical" medical terminology and was thus a doctor. In this way he sought to undergird the traditional authorship of Luke and Acts. His work was taken up and refined by one of the leading German scholars of the day, A. Harnack.[9] In this country the "medical theory" was strongly advocated by A. T. Robertson.[10] The argument, however, was flawed. Hobart and Harnack had failed to examine the frequency of the alleged "medical" terminology in the nonmedical Greek writers. H. J. Cadbury undertook such a comparison and found that all these terms occur in nonmedical writers, such as Josephus, Plutarch, Lucian, and even in the Septuagint. In

---

[6]This is scarcely "additional information" since Colossians and Philemon were most likely both written and delivered at the same time.

[7]It can be argued that Irenaeus arrived at the name *Luke* by a process of elimination. Assuming from the "we" narrative that Acts was written by a Pauline associate, one could go through Paul's epistles and note all who are mentioned as companions of the apostle. Assuming that the author of Acts is a Gentile because of his elevated Greek style, all Jewish associates can be eliminated as well as all those who are mentioned in Acts, who would be distinct from the authorial "I." Others like Crescens and Demas can be eliminated as no longer present with Paul in his imprisonment (2 Tim 4:10). Finally, only Luke remains. For this argument see R. Pesch, "Die Zuschreibung der Evangelien an apostolische Verfasser," *ZTK* 97 (1975): 56-71. The only response to this kind of argument is that Irenaeus must have done his job well. No one has ever come up with a more suitable candidate in the debate over authorship.

[8]W. K. Hobart, *The Medical Language of St. Luke* (London: Longmans Green, 1882).

[9]A. Harnack, *Luke the Physician*, trans. J. R. Wilkinson (New York: Putnam's, 1907).

[10]A. T. Robertson, *Luke the Historian in the Light of Research* (New York: Scribner's, 1920).

a close investigation of portions of Lucian, he found the frequency of the "medical" words to be twice that found in Luke-Acts. His conclusion was that Luke used the language of the best Hellenistic writers, not the technical vocabulary of a physician.[11] He was quick to point out that this in no way disproved that Luke was a physician. It might be added that for one who assumes the traditional Lukan authorship, it perhaps also demonstrates that Luke was more concerned with communicating his message to as wide a circle as possible than with impressing through his expertise.

A large group of German and American scholars do not find the traditional authorship of Luke-Acts tenable, generally on the grounds that the Paul of Acts is so different from the Paul of the epistles that a companion of the apostles could not possibly have written it. These scholars point out (1) that the Paul of Acts is presented as a miracle worker and a skilled orator, contrary to Paul's epistles; (2) that the theology of Acts is lacking the central tenets of Paul's theology, such as justification and the atoning death of Christ; and (3) that the title of "apostle" is denied Paul in Acts, the title he clearly preferred to use for himself.[12] Some also argue that the "law-abiding" Paul of Acts who circumcised Timothy and took Nazirite vows was totally incompatible with the grace-centered Paul of the epistles. Likewise, specific incidents recounted in Acts such as the Jerusalem Conference of Acts 15 are seen to be in conflict with Paul's allusions to the same events in his epistles.[13] (Each of these arguments is treated in the commentary at the appropriate places where the issues arise.)

Two things need to be noted in the discussion, however. One is simply that Luke was not Paul, nor was he addressing the same issues Paul treated in his epistles. One would hardly expect Luke's view of Paul to be the same as Paul's or Luke's theological emphases to be the same as those of the apostle. Not even Paul's own epistles reflect the same emphases one from another—the particular situation directs the emphases. One would never guess Paul's emphasis on justification as found in Galatians from reading 1 Corinthians. The second point is that those who point to the differences between Acts and Paul's epistles rarely note the many remarkable coincidences between the two. Again this is pointed

---

[11]H. J. Cadbury, *Style and Literary Method of Luke*, Part 1 (Cambridge: Harvard University Press, 1920). See his more tongue-in-cheek article "Lexical Notes on Luke-Acts: v. Luke and the Horse-Doctors," *JBL* 52 (1933): 55-56. A recent attempt to revive the medical theory on other than linguistic grounds has not met with much success: W. G. Marx, "Luke, the Physician, Reexamined," *ExpTim* 91:6 (1980), 168-72.

[12]For a full development of these arguments, see E. Haenchen, *The Acts of the Apostles: A Commentary*, trans. B. Noble and G. Shinn (Philadelphia: Westminster, 1971), 114-16. Particularly influential has been the article by P. Vielhauer, "On the 'Paulinism' of Acts," *Studies in Luke-Acts*, ed. L. Keck and J. Martyn (Nashville: Abingdon, 1966), 33-50.

[13]See H. Windisch, "The Case Against the Tradition," *Beginnings* 2:298-348.

out regularly in the commentary.[14]

Traditional Lukan authorship is assumed throughout this commentary. Having said this, can we know more about the author than the bare bones that he was a physician and a traveling companion of Paul by the name of Luke? The answer is "not much." A good guess is that he was a Gentile, judging from the quality of his Greek. It has sometimes been suggested that he may have been a freedman, since physicians were often drawn from the slave class; and the name Luke (*Loukanos/Lucius*) was a common name among slaves. From the time of Jerome on, the tradition that he came from Antioch has been strong. The Western reading of Acts 11:28 introduces "we" into the narrative, which, if genuine, would place Luke in Antioch at the beginning of Paul's missionary career and would link up quite nicely with the Lucius in the Antioch church at Acts 13:1.[15] But a weakly attested Western reading and a Cyrenian by the Latin name of Lucius are a rather slim basis for elaboration of the tradition surrounding Paul's Greek-named associate Luke. Further, judging from the "we" narrative, the evidence seems to point to Luke's joining Paul somewhere in the vicinity of Troas (Acts 16:10). A better case could perhaps be made for Luke's coming from Pisidian Antioch (Rackham) or Macedonia (Ramsay).[16] Judging from the external evidence, not much can be said about Luke apart from shaky later tradition and the realm of pure speculation. Internally, a great deal can be known about him because he revealed much about himself, his community, and his faith in the legacy of his writings. (Cf. section 7.)

3. The Date of Acts

The opinion among scholars about the date when Acts was written varies greatly, ranging all the way from as early as A.D. 57/59 to A.D. 150.[17] Though someone represents nearly every point on this ninety-year

---

[14]At base the discussion on authorship is closely tied to the question of the historical reliability of Acts. On this see section 8. For a positive comparison between the Paul of Acts and the Paul of the epistles, see F. F. Bruce, "Is the Paul of Acts the Real Paul?" *BJRL* 58 (1975-76): 282-305.

[15]For the problems with the Western text of Acts, see section 6. Lucius is a Latin name; Luke (*Loukanos*) is Greek, but there is some inscriptional evidence that the forms were interchangeable. See H. J. Cadbury, "Lucius of Cyrene," *Beginnings 5: Additional Notes*, 489-96.

[16]Cited in Robertson, *Luke the Historian*, 16-29.

[17]F. Blass represents the earliest dating (A.D. 57–59) and H. Koester the latest (A.D. 135) in a list of sixty-nine scholars and their dating for Acts provided by C. Hemer, *The Book of Acts in the Setting of Hellenistic History* (Tübingen: Mohr/Siebeck, 1989), 367-70. The name of J. T. Townsend should be added to Hemer's list as the latest extreme—A.D. 150: "The Date of Luke-Acts," *Luke-Acts: New Perspectives from the SBL Seminar*, ed. C. Talbert (New York: Crossroad, 1984), 47-62.

spectrum, there are in general three distinct viewpoints. First, a large group of scholars date Acts before A.D. 64. This view is always combined with the traditional Lukan authorship and is primarily advanced in an attempt to explain the ending of Acts, which mentions a two-year house arrest of Paul in Rome but says nothing about the outcome of Paul's arrest (Acts 28:30f.). The abrupt ending would be explained if Luke wrote Acts at precisely this point—two years after Paul's arrival in Rome and before his case came to trial.[18] All this fits quite well, since the "we" narrative has brought Luke to Rome (cf. 27:1–28:16); and the epistles to Colosse and Philemon, which have traditionally been ascribed to Paul's Roman imprisonment, both mention Luke as being present with Paul during this period. Luke is thus seen to have written Acts at precisely this point and concluded his story after "two whole years" in Rome.

Advocates of this view appeal to other features of Acts, such as the primitive theology of Peter's speeches, the fact that the Neronic persecution (A.D. midsixties) is nowhere alluded to, and that Luke showed no acquaintance with Paul's epistles.[19] None of these would preclude a later date, however, and the most attractive feature of the early dating remains its giving an explanation for the ending of Acts. This, however, should not be the determining factor in deciding on the date of Acts. Perhaps Luke ended Acts as he did because he had fulfilled his purposes.[20]

The relationship to the Gospel of Luke has led many scholars to opt for a later dating of Acts.[21] These can be described as those advocating a "middle-dating" position. The spectrum runs from A.D. 70 to A.D. 90,

---

[18]A. Harnack, who had originally dated Acts in the 80s, later changed to the early dating (A.D. 62) on the basis that it alone provided a satisfactory explanation of the ending of Acts: *The Date of Acts and of the Synoptic Gospels*, trans. J. R. Wilkinson (New York: Putnam's, 1911), 90-135.

[19]See the arguments for the early date in J. Munck, *The Acts of the Apostles*, rev. W. F. Albright and C. S. Mann, AB (Garden City: Doubleday, 1967), xlvi-liv. Hemer (*Acts in Hellenistic History*, 365-410) suggests a date before A.D. 65 but possibly after Paul's release, seeing Luke as exercising discretion about Paul's whereabouts because of his enemies. For the argument that Luke would not have failed to give the outcome of Paul's trial, whether favorable or unfavorable, see A. J. Mattill, Jr., "The Date and Purpose of Luke-Acts: Rackham Reconsidered," *CBQ* 40 (1978): 335-50.

[20]See commentary on Acts 28:30f. A less likely solution postulates that Luke proposed to write a third volume to deal with Paul's subsequent experiences. See W. Ramsay, *St. Paul the Traveller and Roman Citizen* (Grand Rapids: Baker, 1978), 27f.; J. de Zwaan, "Was the Book of Acts a Posthumous Edition?" *HTR* 17 (1924): 106-10; W. L. Knox, *The Acts of the Apostles* (Cambridge: University Press, 1948), 59.

[21]A few scholars, noting the problems with the early date in relationship to the Gospel of Luke, have circumvented these by arguing that Acts was written before the Gospel of Luke. As an example, see H. G. Russell, "Which was Written First, Luke or Acts?" *HTR* 48 (1955): 167-74. A variation of this view argues that Luke wrote an early form of his Gospel

with most falling about midway. Luke wrote his two volumes in sequence, which is the most natural assumption and certainly the indication of the preface to Acts ("my former book" means the Gospel of Luke, Acts 1:1). It follows that Acts must be dated subsequent to Luke. Two problems exist with dating the Gospel as early as A.D. 62. First, Luke's Gospel quite possibly reflects an awareness of the fall of Jerusalem, which took place in A.D. 70. In the Gospel of Luke are three predictions of the judgment that was to befall Jerusalem (19:41-44; 21:20-24; 23:28-31). That Jesus predicted the destruction of the city is related in the other Gospels as well (cf. Mark 13:14), so it is not a question of Luke having introduced something "after the event," as has often been maintained.[22] It is a matter of an emphasis unparalleled in the other Gospels. Luke chose to include in his Gospel a sizable body of oracles against Jerusalem from the tradition of Jesus' words. The stress they are given lends the impression that Luke had a vivid recollection of the fall of the city and how tragically true the Lord's predictions had proved to be.[23] This remains a matter of impression and in no way could stand on its own as a decisive argument for a date after A.D. 70.

The second consideration that speaks against an early date for the Gospel of Luke is the likelihood that Luke used the Gospel of Mark as one of his sources. In his preface (Luke 1:1), Luke referred to many who had undertaken to compile a gospel narrative before him. Since nearly all of Mark is paralleled in Luke's Gospel, Mark was likely one of those to whom Luke was referring.[24] Irenaeus indicated that Mark wrote his Gospel based on the memoirs of Peter and after the death of Peter.[25] Tradition links Peter and Paul together as martyrs during the Neronic persecution in

---

(called "Proto-Luke") in A.D. 60–62 before Mark wrote his Gospel, then Acts after the two years of Paul's house arrest (early date, ca. A.D. 62), then the final form of his Gospel after he obtained a copy of Mark and incorporated it (A.D. 65–70). As will be seen, this solves the problems for the early date of Acts in relation to Luke's use of Mark but only at the expense of postulating the purely hypothetical "Proto-Luke." See P. Parker, "The 'Former Treatise' and the Date of Acts," *JBL* 84 (1965): 52-58.

[22] Many have argued that the references to the destruction of Jerusalem in the Gospels are all *vaticinia ex eventu*, given "after the fact." C. H. Dodd has shown that all the predictions are drawn from allusions in the OT prophetic literature, need not be seen as recollections of the Roman siege of Jerusalem, and thus can be viewed as authentic predictions of Jesus: "The Fall of Jerusalem and the 'Abomination of Desolation,'" *JRS* 37 (1947): 47-54.

[23] F. F. Bruce, who in his earlier commentaries had argued for the early date, in his later commentary changed to a "middle-date" position (ca. A.D. 80), largely on the basis of the Jerusalem oracles and the relationship to Mark: *Acts: Greek Text*, 12-20.

[24] A. T. Robertson argues strongly for Luke's use of Mark: *Luke the Historian*, 37-39. He opts for the early date of Luke and Acts and consequently dates Mark early—ca. A.D. 61–63.

[25] Irenaeus, *Against Heresies* 8.1.1. Irenaeus refers to Peter's "departure," which is most likely a euphemism for his death.

Rome in the midsixties. This thus places the Gospel of Mark sometime after A.D. 65. It is possible that Luke had immediate access to Mark and composed his Gospel shortly after Mark. More likely some time elapsed between the two Gospels. Combining this consideration with the first possibility that the Jerusalem oracles point to a date after the destruction of Jerusalem, the Gospel of Luke seems best dated after A.D. 70. There is no reason to believe that Acts did not follow shortly after it. Of those who advocate a "middle date," scholars who follow traditional authorship generally date the book toward the earlier end of the spectrum, during the decade of A.D. 70–80.[26]

Those who would opt for a "late" dating of Acts are in a decided minority. These fall into two groups. First are those who date the book around 95–100. Usually these scholars believe that Luke was dependent on the *Antiquities* of the Jewish historian Josephus published in A.D. 93. Acts is believed to show dependence on Josephus mainly in the speech of Gamaliel in 5:35-39, the story of Herod's death in 12:20-23, and Lysias's reference to the "Egyptian" in 21:38. None of these passages, however, shows the least literary dependence on Josephus; and at most they reflect commonly known Jewish events. It has also been argued that the apologetic emphasis in Acts reflects a situation of persecution such as that of Domitian in the nineties.[27] In fact, the picture of the favorable relationship between Christians and the Roman authorities would point in the opposite direction—to an earlier period before imperial persecutions had begun. Other proponents of a late date tend to place Acts between A.D. 125 and 150. These scholars are impressed by language that Acts has in common with the Apostolic Fathers,[28] or they see its emphasis on the Jewish roots of Christianity as a polemic against Marcion.[29]

In Acts too many evidences exist of an earlier period to be convinced by those who would date it later—the primitive Jewish-Christian Christology of Peter's sermons, the simple organization of the churches, the concern with Christianity's relationship to Judaism. Of course, it can always be argued that Luke had access to good early sources. More likely the freshness of Luke's account is due to his own involvement in and proximity to the matters he related in his account of the early Christian

---

[26]As an example, see D. J. Williams, *Acts*, GNC (San Francisco: Harper & Row, 1985), 26. He dates Acts in the mid-70s. Interestingly, W. Ramsay, who argued strongly for traditional authorship, dated Acts in the 80s (*Paul the Traveller*, 386-89).

[27]D. W. Riddle, "The Occasion of Luke-Acts," *JR* 10 (1930): 545-62.

[28]J. C. O'Neill, *The Theology of Acts in Its Historical Setting* (London: SPCK, 1970).

[29]J. Knox, "Acts and the Pauline Letter Corpus," *Studies in Luke-Acts*, 279-87. J. T. Townsend (see n. 17) dates Acts at A.D. 150 because of certain affinities he sees with the pseudo-Clementine writings.

witness. There are solid reasons for dating the book after A.D. 70 but no convincing reason for dating it later than sometime during that decade.

4. The Provenance and Destination of Acts

Where did Luke write from, and to whom did he write? These questions probably are unanswerable. Luke dedicated the book to Theophilus, and Theophilus is a Greek name. Did Luke then write primarily to Gentiles? If so, why did he concern himself so much with Jewish questions? Why the elaborate messianic proofs of Peter's sermons in Acts 2 and 3 if not to provide his readers with a pattern for witness to Jews? The most likely answer is that Luke intended his work for Christian communities that included both Jews and Gentiles—mixed congregations such as those we encounter frequently in Paul's epistles.

Can we be more specific and pinpoint an area? Late tradition links Luke with Antioch. Eusebius, writing in the early fourth century A.D., was the first to attest it. As noted under the section "The Author of Acts," it has much going for it. The remarkable information Acts provides on the Antioch church would be understandable if Luke had roots there.[30] But for whom did Luke write? Did he write for the churches in the area of Syrian Antioch? J. Jervell thinks he did, pointing to the strong emphasis in Acts on Jewish Christians and noting that Jewish Christianity was strong in Syria in the period of A.D. 70–80 when Luke most likely wrote Acts.[31]

Other scholars see Acts as intended for the Christians of Rome. After all, the book ends with Paul preaching in that city. From 19:21 on, the whole narrative of Acts focuses on Paul's being led to witness in the imperial capital. F. J. Foakes-Jackson and K. Lake show how much the ideas of the Roman apostles' creed are reflected in the speeches of Acts, and they suggest that this might point to a Roman provenance for Acts.[32]

Antioch and Rome have been the two usual suggestions for the provenance of Acts. Recently, however, P. Esler has taken an entirely different approach, seeking to determine from the recurring emphases in Acts the sort of social setting for which it seems designed. He concludes that Luke was written for mixed Jewish-Gentile churches in the Roman east in a

---

[30]M. Wilcox notes the many similarities in confessional language between Acts and the writings of Ignatius of Antioch and suggests that this might be a further indication of Luke's Antiochene origin: *The Semitisms of Acts* (Oxford: Clarendon, 1965), 183.

[31]J. Jervell, "Paulus in der Apostelgeschichte und die Geschichte des Urchristentums," *NTS* 32 (1986): 378-92.

[32]*Beginnings* 2:199-204. H. Conzelmann concurs: "Luke's Place in the Development of Early Christianity," *Studies in Luke-Acts*, 298-316. For a Roman provenance, see also J. Roloff, "Die Paulus-Darstellung des Lukas," *EvT* 39 (1979): 510-31.

primarily urban setting.[33] "Roman east" is a rather sweeping designation
and could refer to anywhere from the Aegean to Syro-Palestine. But perhaps we need not get more specific than that. For the later church Acts
has been without boundary in its appeal. Perhaps Luke wanted it so from
the beginning. Esler's suggestions of an "urban" destination for Acts is
worthy of consideration. We have been so accustomed to focusing on
Paul's "journeying" in Acts that we perhaps get the picture his main mission thrust was in the highways and hedges. Not so the picture of Acts.
Most of Paul's time was devoted to the large urban centers like Corinth,
Ephesus, and Rome—where the masses were.

5. The Sources of Acts

Where did Luke gather his materials for Acts? Did he have available
to him written sources, or was he primarily dependent on oral reports for
matters he himself did not witness? The history of investigation in Acts
has often preoccupied itself with elaborate source theories. Only the main
lines of research and the evidence for Luke's use of sources will be noted
here. Source theories have been of four types: (1) the search for written
sources, mainly in chaps. 1–15; (2) the specific question of whether an
Aramaic original stands behind chaps. 1–15; (3) theories connected with
the "we" narrative of chaps. 16–28; and (4) the possibility that Luke used
primarily oral sources and isolated bits of local tradition.

(1) Written Sources

Around the turn of the twentieth century extensive scholarly attention
was given to the question of whether written sources could be detected
within the text of Acts. It was a natural assumption since Luke seems to
have indicated his use of the writings of predecessors in the preface to his
Gospel and since source criticism had been carried on for some time in
the first three Gospels. But source criticism in the Gospels is an altogether different matter. The first three ("Synoptic") Gospels all have
extensive material in common, and a comparative analysis can be made
between them to see if one can detect any sort of source relationship in
their use of common material. This is simply not possible for Acts. With
no parallels available for comparative study, Acts is unique among the
New Testament narratives. Those who undertook a source analysis of
Acts were consequently forced to postulate a more subjective methodology for the detection of Luke's possible sources. Various criteria were
established. The centrality of certain places in the narrative was seen as
possibly indicative of a source originating in that locale. Another possible

---

[33]P. F. Esler, *Community and Gospel in Luke-Acts* (Cambridge: University Press, 1987),
30-45.

pointer to a source was the recurrence of the same character. Sometimes differences in the theological emphases in various portions of Acts were seen as indicative that Luke was using sources.[34] For some scholars, however, the most certain hint of a source is the occurrence of supposed "doublets," or duplicated material, in the text.

Exemplary of the heyday of source criticism in Acts is A. Harnack's elaborate theory of the sources Luke used in the composition of Acts 1–15.[35] Harnack was a strong defender of the traditional authorship of Luke-Acts and argued that as Paul's traveling companion Luke had his own participation to draw from in the events covered in Acts 16–28. Since the "we" narrative would indicate that Luke did not participate in the events prior to Troas (Acts 16:10), Harnack assumed Luke would have been forced to use sources for all the prior material of Acts.

Using a combination of criteria involving places, characters, and "doublets," Harnack detected several strands of sources behind Acts 1–15. First, he saw an "Antioch" source behind the material related to that city that came from written records of the Antioch church. This included the traditions about Stephen (6:1–8:4) and the narratives centering in Antioch and its mission (11:19-30; 12:25; 13:1–15:35). A second source is the account of Paul's conversion (9:1-28), which Harnack saw as based on a separate written tradition. A third source is Harnack's "Jerusalem Caesarean" tradition, representing the accounts of the Christian mission in Judea and possibly stemming from the Caesarean church. It included the work of Philip (8:5-40), Peter's witness in the plain of Sharon and the conversion of Cornelius (9:29–11:18), and Peter's escape from prison (12:1-23).

Harnack's most controversial source was his "Jerusalem source," which he divided into two parts, postulating two sources from the Jerusalem church that covered the same events. One he considered reliable, the other legendary and unreliable. It was here that his "doublet" theory came into play. The "unreliable" source, which he called Jerusalem B, contained the account of Pentecost (Acts 2) and the apostles' second trial before the Sanhedrin (Acts 5:17-42). The reliable Jerusalem A source was seen to cover the events of Acts 3:1–5:16. Harnack considered these two sources to be duplicative of the same events. The outpouring of the Spirit narrated in Acts 4:23-31 (source A) was seen as a doublet of Pentecost (source B). The appearance of the apostles before the Sanhedrin in Acts

---

[34]For instance, W. Bousset argued that the manner in which the title κύριος appears in the text can be used as a criterion for delineating sources, "Der Gebrauch des Kyriostitels als Kriterium für die Quellenscheidung in der ersten Halfte der Apostelgeschichte," *ZNW* 15 (1914), 141-62.

[35]For his source theory, see A. Harnack, *The Acts of the Apostles*, trans. J. R. Wilkinson (London: Williams & Norgate, 1909), 162-202.

5:17-42 (which involves a miraculous escape from prison) was relegated to the unreliable source B and seen as a duplication of the Sanhedrin appearance narrated in 4:5-22 (the historically valuable source A). Frankly one is at a loss to see how Acts 4:23-31 could ever be seen as a doublet of Acts 2. All the passages have in common is the outpouring of the Spirit, and the Spirit "comes" in special outpourings often in Acts. Likewise the two appearances before the Sanhedrin are altogether likely on historical grounds and not "doublets," as J. Jeremias has shown.[36]

Harnack's source-critical reconstruction of Luke's "sources" in Acts 1–15 has been given at some length to illustrate the basically subjective nature of such attempted reconstructions. A hidden agenda is clearly notable in his two Jerusalem sources. The "doublet" theory betrays his rationalist presuppositions, allowing him to excise the miraculous elements of the Pentecost narrative and the apostles' escape in Acts 5:17-23. Beyond that, even the sources he considered reliable are not convincing. Such criteria as the centrality of places and characters are simply not adequate for postulating written sources. Luke's information could as well have come to him through oral tradition. To establish written sources behind the text, one would have to indicate differences in vocabulary and style in portions in Acts, and this has not been done convincingly in any source-critical investigation. A uniformity of Lukan style runs throughout Luke-Acts. If Luke used sources in Acts, he reworked them into his own style so skillfully that it is no longer possible for us to detect them.[37]

One of Harnack's sources, however, continues to have a sizeable following—his Antioch source. It was picked up by Jeremias in an article of 1937;[38] and in his summary of source-critical research in Acts, J. Dupont judged it as the most viable of Harnack's suggested sources.[39] Perhaps the most surprising advocacy has been that of R. Bultmann, who suggested that it might have been quite a bit more extensive than Harnack suggested and that the author of Acts may have obtained it from the written archives of the Antioch church.[40] The centrality of Antioch, however, could be

---

[36]Jeremias pointed out that the two appearances follow the proper legal procedure—the first constituting a warning and establishing culpability, the second involving the apostles' transgression of the interdiction established in the first hearing: "Untersuchungen zum Quellenproblem der Apostelgeschichte," *ZNW* 36 (1937): 205-13.

[37]For an attempt to verify Harnack's Jerusalem A and B sources through computer analysis, see A. Q. Morton and G. H. C. MacGregor, *The Structure of Luke and Acts* (New York: Harper & Row, 1964). The fallacy of the procedure is that the differentiation the computer found was programmed into it from the start.

[38]Jeremias, "Untersuchungen zum Quellenproblem," 213-21.

[39]J. Dupont, *The Sources of Acts*, trans. K. Pond (London: Darton, Longman & Todd, 1964), 62-72.

[40]R. Bultmann, "Zur Frage nach den Quellen der Apostelgeschichte," *Exegetica* (Tübingen: Mohr, 1967), 412-23.

explained on grounds other than a written source—the tradition that connects Luke himself with Antioch or the possibility that Luke received oral reports from that congregation. That there existed a written document from Antioch would have to be established on stylistic grounds, and that has yet to be demonstrated.

In summary, the quest for written sources in Acts has been basically a dead-end. Luke followed the usual practice of Hellenistic historiographers by never explicitly citing any sources he used in Acts.[41] He may well have had access to some, but he so incorporated them into his narrative that it is unlikely they could be recovered.[42] Still, in two specific areas scholars tend to argue for Luke's use of sources—the possibility of a Semitic source in Acts 1–15 and of a source behind the "we" passages of chaps. 16–28.

(2) Semitic Source Theory

A more substantial basis for delineating sources in Acts was suggested by C. C. Torrey, who argued that an Aramaic source lay behind Acts 1–15.[43] Torrey pointed to a number of difficult Greek constructions in Acts, which he argued were most readily explainable as mistranslations from Aramaic. Others, he reasoned, are best seen as overly literal translations from an Aramaic original. He saw this Aramaic substratum as running homogeneously throughout chaps. 1–15 of Acts but to be totally absent in chaps. 16–28. His conclusion: an original Aramaic document lay behind the first fifteen chapters of Acts. The response to Torrey's theory has generally not been favorable. H. J. Cadbury pointed out that the Semitic style of the early portions of Acts is probably due to Luke's skill as a writer, to his deliberate imitation of Palestinian style.[44] Others have noted that many of Torrey's alleged Aramaisms are really Septuagintalisms and that the overall style in chaps. 1–15 is the same uniform Lukan style that runs throughout Luke-Acts.[45]

Many of the Semiticisms may reflect the language of the Christian churches, a sort of "synagogue Greek" deriving from their Jewish

---

[41]Greek historiographers rarely cited their sources and seldom quoted them directly. See H. J. Cadbury, *The Making of Luke-Acts* (New York: Macmillan, 1927), 155-68.

[42]This is the final judgment of Dupont after his thorough investigation of source criticism in Acts: *The Sources of Acts*, 166-68.

[43]C. C. Torrey, *The Composition and Date of Acts* (Cambridge: Harvard University Press, 1916). See also his defense against his critics in "Fact and Fancy in Theories Concerning Acts," *AJT* 23 (1919): 61-86, 189-212.

[44]H. J. Cadbury, "Luke-Translator or Author," *AJT* 24 (1920): 436-55.

[45]H. F. D. Sparks, "The Semitisms of Acts," *JTS*, n.s. 1 (1950): 16-28; P. F. Payne, "Semitisms in the Book of Acts," *Apostolic History and the Gospels*, ed. W. Gasque and R. Martin (Grand Rapids: Eerdmans, 1970).

roots.[46] In his thorough study of the Semiticisms in Acts, M. Wilcox concludes that there is simply no evidence for an Aramaic source in Acts.[47] Small "knots" of Semiticisms are found in the Old Testament material in Acts that do not seem derivative from the Septuagint. These are particularly found in Stephen's speech and Paul's address in Pisidian Antioch. They may reflect the Aramaic Targumic traditions. In short, room remains for further examination of the Scripture materials found in the speeches of Acts. The theory of an Aramaic source in Acts, however, has been largely abandoned.[48]

(3) "We" Source Theory

In general, there are four views relative to the passages in Acts 16–28 where the first-person plural occurs. Those who assume the traditional authorship of Acts view the "we" as indicative of Luke's presence with Paul at the points where it occurs (cf. section 2.2). Some, who do not maintain that the final author of Acts was a traveling companion of Paul, argue that the author incorporated a source that was from such a traveling companion and from which the "we" derives. A third group believes that the author of Acts utilized a diary or an itinerary from a Pauline traveling associate but rejects the idea of a "we" source. A fourth group accepts neither a source nor a diary and maintains that the "we" is merely a literary device of the author of Acts.

The idea of a "we source" in Acts is not new. Scholars of the "Tübingen school," who argued that Acts was written in the second century and was as a whole historically tendentious and unreliable,[49] nevertheless appealed to the "we passages" to argue that the later author of Acts utilized in these places a reliable historical source from a traveling companion of Paul. This "we-source" theory continued long after the excesses of the Tübingen hypothesis were dead.[50] A. Harnack, however, pointed out that the style of the "we passages" is the same style that runs throughout all of Luke-Acts, and it is more natural to conclude that the author of the "we passages" is the same author as the final author of

---

[46]F. L. Horton, Jr., "Reflections on the Semitisms of Luke-Acts," *Perspectives on Luke-Acts*, ed. C. Talbert (Edinburgh: T & T Clark, 1978), 1-23.

[47]Wilcox, *Semitisms of Acts*, 180-85.

[48]An exception is an attempt to bolster Torrey's thesis by arguing for Aramaic influence on the syntax of Acts 1–15 and Luke 1–2 by R. A. Martin: "Syntactical Evidence of Aramaic Sources in Acts I-XV," *NTS* 10 (1964-65): 38-59.

[49]On the "Tübingen school," see section 8 on Luke as historian.

[50]For instance, the influential German commentator on Acts, H. H. Wendt, not only embraced the idea of a "we source" but even argued for extending it beyond chaps. 16–28 to include the Stephen material (6:1–8:4), the Antioch narrative of 11:19-28, and the first missionary journey (13–14) ("Die Hauptquelle der Apostelgeschichte," *ZNW* 24 [1925]: 293-305).

Luke-Acts.[51] Harnack was defending the traditional view of Luke as both Paul's traveling companion and the author of Luke-Acts. The same was true of Cadbury, who argued that Luke's reference to having "carefully investigated everything" in the preface to his Gospel (Luke 1:3) is best seen as his indication that he participated in some of the events he was narrating, namely, those where the "we" occurs.[52]

A modification of the "we-source" theory holds that the author of Acts incorporated a diary from a travel companion of Paul, not an extensive source. Various persons have been suggested for the diarist, Timothy being the most popular.[53] Silas[54] and Epaphroditus[55] have also been proposed. M. Dibelius advocated a modified version of the "diary" view, maintaining that it was in no sense a connected narrative but only an "itinerary," a collection of travel notes on length of journeys, places visited, ports of call, and the like.[56] The diary view is open to the same objections raised by Harnack with regard to the full "we-source" view; namely, that regarding the unity of style of Acts, it would be more natural to assume that the author of the whole book was including himself in the "we"—not incorporating a source.

Those who argue that the "we" is a literary device would agree with the last statement—only they would not see it as an indication of the author's presence with Paul. Some see it as a literary device used by Greek historians to lend an appearance of veracity to their accounts.[57] Others point to the fact that the narrative first-person plural is found primarily in the voyage narratives of chaps. 16; 20–21; and 27–28. It is noted that the "we" style is commonplace in Greco-Roman voyage accounts and that Luke seems to have been following this literary convention in Acts. [58]

---

[51]Harnack, *Luke the Physician*, 26-120.

[52]H. J. Cadbury, "'We' and 'I' Passages in Luke-Acts," *NTS* 3 (1956-57): 128-33.

[53]First suggested by F. Schleiermacher and recently advocated by S. Dockx, "Luc, a-t-il été le compagnon d'apostolat de Paul?" *NRT* 103 (1981), 385-400.

[54]Suggested by E. A. Schwanbeck as cited in Dupont, *Sources*, 79.

[55]James A. Blaisdell, "The Authorship of the 'We' Sections of the Book of Acts," *HTR* 13 (1920): 136-58.

[56]M. Dibelius, "The Acts of the Apostles in the Setting of the History of Early Christian Literature," *Studies in the Acts of the Apostles*, trans. M. Ling (London: SCM, 1956), 192-205.

[57]E. Plumacher, "Wirklichkeitserfahrung und Geschichtsschreibung bei Lukas: Erwägungen zu den Wir-Stücken der Apostelgeschiche," *ZNW* 68 (1977): 2-22. A similar viewpoint is taken by G. Schille, "Die Fragwürdigkeit eines Itinerars der Paulusreisen," *TLZ* 84 (1959): 165-74.

[58]V. K. Robbins, "The We-Passages in Acts and Ancient Sea Voyages," *BR* 20 (1975): 5-18; idem., "By Land and by Sea: The We-Passages and Ancient Sea Voyages," *Perspectives in Luke-Acts*, 215-42.

Some of the conclusions drawn in these studies are open to serious question.[59] For instance, for many Greek historians the first-person style is not employed as a convention but is only used when the writer was actually present. Likewise, ancient sea narratives occur in third person as frequently as they do in first person. Further, the first person is not used with regularity in the sea narratives of Acts, which would seem to be the case where it is merely a stylistic convention. The studies in the literary use of the first-person plural in Greek literature may, however, prove of value ultimately even for those who advocate traditional Lukan authorship. If Luke's use of "we" is to some extent influenced by literary considerations, such as its frequency in his travel narratives, then it follows that one cannot rigidly assume he was present only where the "we" occurs. He clearly prefers the narrative third person and only shifts to first-person plural in those contexts where "comradery" is an element, such as the "community" aspect of travel narratives. Given that observation, he may well have been present on many occasions in Paul's missionary activity where third-person narrative occurs.

(4) Oral Sources and Local Tradition

If written sources for Acts cannot be established, what sources are left for Luke's work? Even if he were present on a large part of Paul's missionary activity, what was the basis of his account for the history of the early Jerusalem church, the mission of Philip, the conversion of Cornelius, the apostolic conference in Jerusalem, and the many other events of Acts 1–15? The answer must surely be that he had access to the local traditions of the Christian communities, perhaps eyewitness reports and reminiscences that were cherished and passed down in the churches.[60] As an example, a "we" passage in Acts 21:8 relates that Paul and his fellow travelers stayed in Caesarea with Philip the evangelist. On such an occasion Luke could have heard the story of Philip's work among the Samaritans and the Ethiopian eunuch. From the Caesarean Christians he may have heard of Cornelius's conversion. If one assumes that Luke was the traveling companion of Paul who accompanied the apostle to Jerusalem (21:1-18, "we" narrative) and two years later from Caesarea to Rome (27:1–28:16, "we" narrative), he would have had ample opportunity for exposure to all the traditions recorded in Acts.[61]

---

[59]See the critiques offered by C. J. Hemer, "First Person Narrative in Acts 27–28," *TB* 36 (1985): 79-109, and S. M. Praeder, "The Problem of First Person Narration in Acts," *NovT* 29 (1987): 193-218.

[60]Dibelius suggested that Luke had access to such isolated bits of local tradition, *Studies in Acts*, 102-08. Haenchen (*Acts*, 32f.), though considerably skeptical about their historical reliability, acknowledges the same.

[61]Hemer (*Acts in Hellenistic History*, 335-64) suggests that Luke may have gathered

In considering Luke's information base, one question remains as yet untreated. Did Luke have access to Paul's letters? Did he use them at all in Acts? The answer to this question seems to be no.[62] No quotes from Paul's epistles occur in Acts. There is an undeniable overlap in material—Paul's conversion, his churches in Macedonia and Achaia, his desire to visit Rome. Paul's speeches in Acts are often reminiscent of elements in Paul's epistles, particularly the "farewell address" of Acts 20. But there is no indication that Luke derived any of this information from Paul's epistles. Perhaps Paul's epistles had not yet been collected together and were still at the churches to which he sent them. As Paul's associate, Luke would surely have been aware of Paul's letter-writing activity. He evidently either did not have immediate access to them or did not consider them germane to his purposes. Paul's epistles were mainly occasional letters, addressed to specific problems within individual congregations. Luke had a broader purpose—to tell the story of Paul to the church at large. In any event, Acts and Paul's epistles are independent witnesses to the apostle. The commentary regularly notes the points at which the two overlap.

6. The Text of Acts

In the history of the text of the New Testament, Acts poses a special problem. The early witnesses for the text of Acts diverge more than those of any other New Testament writing. Basically, we have two ancient texts for Acts that are generally referred to as the Alexandrian (or "Egyptian") text and the "Western" text. The "Western" text of Acts differs significantly from the Alexandrian, being almost 10 percent longer. The differences are not apparent in the English translations of Acts. Modern translations of Acts are all based on the Alexandrian witnesses. Likewise, earlier English translations such as the KJV were based on the "majority" (or "Byzantine") textual tradition, which also tended to follow the Alexandrian text. One would never guess the radically different readings found in the Western text from reading modern versions of Acts. The

---

most of his material for the early chapters of Acts by visiting the churches of Judea during the two years of Paul's Caesarean imprisonment. Even if one assumes a more skeptical stance toward Luke's involvement in the events, W. Gasque points to the evidence from Paul's epistles that information was exchanged among the early Christian churches to a greater extent than is sometimes assumed ("Did Luke Have Access to Traditions about the Apostles and the Early Churches?" *JETS* 17 [1974]: 45-48).

[62] This is the judgment of most scholars, including C. K. Barrett, "Acts and the Pauline Corpus," *ExpTim* 78 (1976-77): 2-5. A few scholars, however, vigorously argue that Acts shows some dependence on the Pauline Epistles. See M. S. Enslin, "Luke and Paul," *JAOS* 58 (1938): 81-91; W. O. Walker, Jr., "Acts and the Pauline Corpus Reconsidered," *JSNT* 24 (1985): 3-23.

ancient witnesses, however, provide ample evidence for the longer Western text of Acts from a very early date. The most important witness to the
Western text is a major uncial, codex Bezae (designated by text critics as
D), a diglot manuscript containing both the Greek text and a Latin translation of the New Testament in parallel columns. Both the Greek and
Latin texts in Bezae follow the Western tradition in Acts.[63] A number of
other Greek witnesses also reflect Western readings. Some are early
papyri ($\mathfrak{P}^{38}$, $\mathfrak{P}^{48}$); others are later minuscules (33, 81, 1175). Among the
early versions the Old Syriac and Old Latin are the most significant
Western witnesses. Early church fathers show familiarity with the Western tradition, among them Irenaeus, Tertullian, Cyprian, and Augustine.
In short, the Western tradition is well-attested in very early witnesses,
some of which date back to the second century. In fact, based on the date
of its witnesses, the Western text has as much claim to antiquity as the
Alexandrian.

There are good reasons, however, for seeing the Western text as secondary and derivative from the shorter Alexandrian tradition. Apart from
the time-honored text-critical principle that the shorter text is more likely
to be the original, the Western text shows many evidences of being an
"improved" or harmonizing text. Gaps in the narrative are filled in. Thus
in chap. 3, when the setting jumps from the temple (v. 8) to Solomon's
Colonnade (v. 11), the Western text provides the missing link, adding that
they "exited [the Temple]." Sometimes one's curiosity is satisfied by the
Western text. If one should wonder what happened to the other prisoners
at Philippi, the Western text adds to 16:30 that the jailer secured them
before exiting with Paul and Silas. Sometimes the Western text reflects a
greater emphasis on God's leading. An example is 19:1, where it refers to
the Holy Spirit directing Paul to Ephesus, an emphasis lacking in the
Alexandrian reading. Finally, the Western text tends to introduce certain
biases to the text, among which are a pronounced anti-Semitic element[64]
and a tendency to downplay the role of women in the narrative.[65] When
all such things are taken into account, however, there still remain a number of Western readings that are not obvious harmonizings or indicative
of any bias but only the provision of additional details not found in the
Alexandrian text. Such, for instance, is the additional note in the Western

---

[63]The most ready access to the Western text of Acts is the third volume of *The Beginnings of Christianity*, which is entirely devoted to the text of Acts and contains the entire
Greek and Latin texts of Bezae as well as other Western witnesses, such as the marginalia of
the Harclean Syriac (*The Text of Acts* [London: Macmillan, 1926]).

[64]E. J. Epp, "The 'Ignorance Motif' in Acts and Antijudaic Tendencies in Codex Bezae,"
HTR 55 (1962): 51-62.

[65]B. Witherington, "The Anti-Feminist Tendencies of the 'Western' Text in Acts," *JBL*
103 (1984): 82-84.

reading of 28:16 that the centurion turned Paul over to the "stratopedarch" in Rome. In such cases there is the distinct possibility that such details might have dropped out in the Alexandrian tradition through scribal error with the Western preserving the original reading.

The general consensus among text critics today is that the Alexandrian text is the more reliable text.[66] In some instances the Western witnesses may preserve an original reading. For this reason an "eclectic" method is recommended, calling for an examination of each variant on its own merits and not making a blanket *a priori* decision to go with any one text.[67] Since the unique Western readings are not available in any English translation, the commentary regularly points to the more significant of these at the appropriate places or in the footnotes.

7. Luke as a Writer

One of the most significant emphases in research into Luke-Acts over the past half century has been a focus on Luke's own contribution in his two-volume work. One of the pioneers in this area was H. J. Cadbury, who, in his *Making of Luke-Acts* (1927), set the pattern of study by comparing Luke's writings with those of his contemporaries and noting the idiosyncrasies of Luke's style and interests in both Luke and Acts. The emphasis was furthered by the work of H. Conzelmann, who in 1953 emphasized the theological emphases in Luke's work and started a whole spate of work on "Luke the theologian."[68] Cadbury portrayed Luke as a conscious writer with a deliberate literary purpose. Conzelmann engendered consideration of Luke as a theologian, a person of faith. Both emphases are important for obtaining the full benefit from Luke and Acts. The first will preoccupy our attention in this section; the latter, in the next.

---

[66]A minority of scholars have argued for the originality of the Western text. A. Clark argued that it was the original text on the dubious principle that the longer text should be preferred. F. Blass argued that both the Alexandrian and Western texts were by Luke and that the Western text represents his original draft with the Alexandrian being a later refined edition: "Die Textüberlieferung in der Apostelgeschichte," *TSK* 67 (1894): 86-119. Blass's theory has been recently revived in a more complicated theory involving four stages of revision on Luke's part: M. E. Boismard, "Le Texte Occidental des Actes des Apôtres (à Propos de Actes 27, 1-13)," *ETL* 63 (1987): 48-58.

[67]For advocates of the "eclectic" method, see A. F. J. Klijn, "In Search of the Original Text of Acts," *Studies in Luke-Acts*, 103-10; G. D. Kilpatrick, "Western Text and Original Text in the Gospels and Acts," *JTS* 44 (1943): 24-36; K. and S. Lake, "The Acts of the Apostles," *JBL* 53 (1934): 34-45.

[68]H. Conzelmann, *The Theology of St. Luke*, trans. G. Buswell (New York: Harper & Row, 1960).

(1) Genre of Acts

Luke obviously set out to produce a two-volume work. His dual prefaces amply testify to this (Luke 1:1-4; Acts 1:1). The Gospel genre had already been established. Luke had his predecessors like Mark and referred to them in his preface (Luke 1:1). But what was his pattern for Acts? For his story of the early Christian mission, he had no predecessor as far as we know. In a real sense his work was without parallel; yet characteristics of his writing link him with other literary currents.

Acts has much in common with other Greek forms of literature. The device of a literary preface with a formal dedication is without precedent in biblical literature; it is a formality of Greek literature. There is certainly a biographical interest in Luke's Gospel, and to a certain extent this has been carried over into Acts in the treatment of Peter and Paul.[69] Most who have studied the genre of Luke-Acts feel that it has more in common with Greek historiography. The use of formal speeches, of voyages, and the episodic style all link Acts with the Hellenistic historical monograph.[70]

Greek literature, however, was not the only influence on the form of Acts. The Old Testament seems to have had an even more profound impact. Not only does Acts quote the Old Testament extensively, but the form of much of the Acts narrative is based on Old Testament precedents, like the call of the prophets and the divine commissioning narratives. The overall perspective of the book is not that of the Hellenistic histories with their concepts of fate and destiny but the biblical view that all of history is ultimately under the direction of a sovereign God.[71]

A final form that likely influenced Luke in his conception of Acts was the Gospel form itself. The parallels between the life of Jesus as pictured in Luke's Gospel and the careers of Peter and Paul in Acts have often been noted. Sometimes they are quite striking—parallel miracles, parallel defenses, parallel sufferings. In some sense Luke saw a continuation of the story of Jesus in the lives of the apostles. What Jesus began to do and teach is continued by his faithful witnesses (Acts 1:1). For Luke the Gos-

---

[69]C. Talbert suggests that Luke patterned both his Gospel and Acts on the biographical "succession narrative" type in which the biography of the founder of a philosophical school is followed by short biographies of the founder's successors: *Acts*, KPG (Atlanta: John Knox, 1984), 1-3. D. Barr and J. Wentling suggest that Luke-Acts is not so much a succession narrative (these are usually much briefer in the Greek writings than in Acts) but rather a "serial biography": "The Conventions of Classical Biography and the Genre of Luke-Acts," *New Perspectives*, 63-88.

[70]Cadbury, *Making Luke-Acts*, 133f.; E. Plumacher, "Die Apostelgeschichte als historische Monographie," *Les Actes des Apôtres*, ed. J. Kremer (Gembloux: Duculot, 1979), 457-66.

[71]G. Krodel, *Acts*, PC (Philadelphia: Fortress, 1981), 2. For a similar view see R. Maddox, *The Purpose of Luke-Acts* (Edinburgh: T & T Clark, 1982), 16.

pel and Acts represent two stages of the same story.

(2) Language and Style of Acts

Luke has been described as "the most Greek of the New Testament writers."[72] Certainly the vocabulary of Luke-Acts would indicate his proficiency in the language. His vocabulary is the largest of any New Testament writer and one that exceeds some secular Greek writings, such as those of Xenophon.[73] He wrote in good Hellenistic Greek and often employed constructions from the classical writers, those "Atticisms" so prized by first-century writers, like an occasional use of the optative mode, of the future infinitive, and of the future participle. He used Greek figures of speech, having an especial love for litotes. Still his language is not that of the neoclassicists, but it is instead good literary koine Greek.

Luke's writings are steeped in the language of the Old Testament. A full 90 percent of his vocabulary is found also in the Septuagint. There are, in addition, a number of Semiticisms not found in the Greek Old Testament. N. Turner suggests that these may be "Jewish Greek," expressions that would have been common in the Jewish Diaspora.[74] Most frequent in the infancy narratives of Luke 1–2 and in the "Jewish" portions of Acts, chaps. 1–15, these probably indicate Luke's skill as a writer. Throughout Acts there is a verisimilitude in the narrative. Jews speak with a Jewish accent, Athenian philosophers speak in Atticisms, and Roman officials speak and write in the customary legal style. Luke showed not only a familiarity with such linguistic idiosyncrasies but also the ability to depict them through his style of writing.

(3) Speeches of Acts

One of the most characteristic features of Acts is the presence of many speeches interspersed throughout the narrative. Altogether these comprise nearly a third of the text of Acts, about 300 of its approximately 1,000 verses.[75] In all there are twenty-four of these—eight coming from Peter, nine from Paul, and seven from various others.[76] Of the twenty-

---

[72]J. de Zwaan, "The Use of the Greek Language in Acts," *Beginnings* 2:65.

[73]Cadbury, *The Style and Literary Method of Luke*, 2-4. See also Cadbury's "Four Features of Lucan Style" in *Studies in Luke-Acts*, 87-102. For Luke's Atticisms, see G. D. Kilpatrick, "The Historic Present in the Gospels and Acts," *ZNW* 68 (1977): 285-362.

[74]N. Turner, "The Quality of the Greek of Luke-Acts," *Studies in New Testament Language and Text* (Leiden: Brill, 1976), 387-400. See also Turner's treatment in vol. 4 of J. H. Moulton's *Grammar of New Testament Greek* (Edinburgh: T & T Clark, 1976), 45-63.

[75]W. G. Kümmel, *Introduction to the New Testament*, 17th ed. rev., trans. H. C. Kee (Nashville: Abingdon, 1975), 167.

[76]J. Dupont, "Les discours de Pierre," *Nouvelles Etudes sur les Actes des Apôtres* (Paris: Cerf, 1984), 58. See also "Le discourse à l'Aréopage," *Nouvelles Etudes*, 382-84.

four, ten can be described as "major" addresses: three "missionary" sermons of Peter (chaps. 2; 3; 10); a trilogy of speeches from Paul in the course of his mission (chaps. 13; 17; 20), three "defense speeches" of Paul (chaps. 22; 24; 26), and Stephen's address before the Sanhedrin (chap. 7).

The trilogy of Pauline mission speeches is particularly striking, with one major address for each phase of the mission, each addressed to a different group. On the first journey Paul addressed the Jews in the synagogue of Pisidian Antioch (chap. 13). On the second he addressed the pagans in his famous Areopagus speech (chap. 20). On the third he spoke to the Christian leaders of the Ephesian congregation in the address at Miletus (chap. 20). Luke presented a balanced variety of speeches with regard to both occasion and listeners.

In recent years a major scholarly debate over the speeches of Acts has focused primarily over the question of whether they are wholly Lukan compositions or whether they are based on historically reliable traditions. One consideration involves the manner in which speeches were employed by Hellenistic historiographers. For his Gospel, Luke had the oral tradition and predecessors like Mark for the words of Jesus, which existed primarily in the form of short sayings. There was likely no such "sayings of the apostles" tradition available to Luke; and for Acts he presented their teachings in the form of extended discourses or speeches.[77] This speech form links him with the convention of Greek historiographers, who often depicted their characters making major addresses at crucial junctures, such as the eve of a battle. If Luke followed this precedent in his account of the early Christian mission, it is natural to inquire about how the historiographers went about gathering the material for their speeches. Did they employ sources? Did they compose their speeches totally from their own judgment about what might be appropriate to the occasion?

Actually, the evidence from Greek historiography is quite mixed. Speech composition was a major element in ancient rhetorical training. For some historiographers the correctness of form and elegance of the speech was more important than its basis in accurate historical reminiscence; for others, however, this practice was roundly condemned. Polybius, for instance, strongly criticized his predecessors for freely inventing speeches; and in his treatise on history writing, Lucian insisted on facts, fidelity, and accurate reporting.[78] Perhaps the most relevant statement is that of Thucydides, who described his procedure in providing speeches in

---

[77]A. Schlatter, *Die Apostelgeschichte* (Stuttgart: Calwer, 1948), 11.

[78]W. W. Gasque, "The Speeches of Acts: Dibelius Reconsidered," *New Dimensions in New Testament Study*, ed. R. Longenecker and M. Tenney (Grand Rapids: Zondervan, 1974), 244-46; C. J. Hemer, "Luke the Historian," *BJRL* 60 (1977-78): 29-34.

his historical narrative. He remarked that he was unable to reproduce exactly the words delivered on a given occasion either from his own memory when he had been present or from the reports given him from eyewitnesses but that he had endeavored as closely as possible "to give the general purport of what was actually said."[79] It has often been suggested that Luke may have followed the same procedure, gathering information from eyewitnesses, relying on his own memory where possible, and providing as accurately as he could the "gist" of what was said.[80]

It would be hard to deny that Luke provided the speech material in his own words. Even for the longest of them, the Acts speeches are quite short, taking only a few minutes to read aloud. This is one of the ways they differ from those of the Greek historiographers. The latter are generally quite long, many times longer than the speech of Stephen, the longest speech in Acts. The speeches in Acts are a summary, an example of the things said, not a full report of the address. For example, Peter's speech in the temple square evidently began around three in the afternoon (3:1) and lasted until sundown (4:3); but Luke provided only a seventeen-verse précis of the sermon.[81]

Another indication of Luke's literary contribution in the speeches is that the basic vocabulary and style of the speeches is the same uniform style that runs throughout Acts.[82] Likewise, the speeches all tend to follow a common outline and structure.[83] Then there is an interdependence among the speeches.[84] Peter's remarks at the Apostolic Conference refer to the account of the conversion of Cornelius; Paul alluded to texts in his Pisidian Antioch address that are only fully expounded in Peter's sermon at Pentecost. Luke assumed the reader is familiar with the earlier accounts and felt no need to give a fuller treatment. As the author of Acts,

---

[79] *History of the Peloponnesian War* (1.22.1), as cited in Bruce, *Acts: Greek Text*, 34. Thucydides's statement τῆς ξυμπάσης γνώμης τῶν ἀληθῶς λεχθέντων is open to interpretation. Dibelius, for instance, argued that Thucydides only referred to the "appropriateness" of the speech to the occasion, not to the facticity of its content: "The Speeches in Acts and Ancient Historiography," *Studies in the Acts of the Apostles*, 138-85. For a balanced treatment of the various viewpoints on Thucydides's statement among scholars of the classics, see S. E. Porter, "Thucydides 1.22.1 and Speeches in Acts: Is There a Thucydidean View?" *NovT* 32 (1990): 121-42.

[80] F. F. Bruce, "The Speeches in Acts—Thirty Years After," *Reconciliation and Hope*, ed. R. Banks (Exeter: Paternoster, 1974), 53-68.

[81] Luke often pointed to a speech being interrupted (cf. 2:40; 4:1-7; 7:54f.; 10:44-46). This is perhaps a device for indicating that the speech is a summary. See G. H. R. Horsley, "Speeches and Dialogue in Acts," *NTS* 32 (1986): 609-14.

[82] See E. Richard, *Acts 6:1-8:4—The Author's Method of Composition* (Ann Arbor: Edwards, 1978).

[83] E. Schweizer, "Concerning the Speeches in Acts," *Studies in Luke-Acts*, 208-16.

[84] J. T. Townsend, "The Speeches in Acts," *ATR* 42 (1960): 150-59.

Luke provided the speeches—in his words, in his selection of material. But does this mean that he created them and that they are not reliable reports of what was actually said?

Is there evidence that the speeches in Acts are based on reliable traditions?[85] A number of indications point in that direction. One is the sheer variety of the speeches themselves. One can indeed detect a common structure in many of the speeches, but the content and argument often run in quite different directions. The three missionary speeches to Jews have the most in common (chaps. 2; 3; 13)—Jesus as Messiah, the extensive Old Testament citations, the emphasis on the resurrection. Peter's speech to the God-fearer Cornelius (chap. 10) follows the same basic pattern. C. H. Dodd long ago argued that the common structure of these sermons reflects the early preaching or "kerygma" of the church.[86] Within Peter's speeches in Acts 2–3 are elements of a very early Christology—unusual titles for Jesus, such as "servant," "Righteous One," "prophet like Moses," and the concept of Jesus as being "designated" by God as Messiah. Such concepts reflect Jewish-Christian thought and testify to the primitiveness of these speeches.[87]

Stephen's speech is unique. His emphasis on God's revelation outside the Holy Land and his temple critique are totally unparalleled in any other speech of Acts. His unusual Scripture traditions are equally without parallel. Such considerations may indicate that Luke was using some sort of Hellenist source—if not a written source, at least an accurate account of their thought gleaned from Hellenist circles.[88] The Areopagus speech of Acts 17 and the words to the pagans at Lystra (14:15-17) with their "natural theology" and appeal to Greek philosophical thought are altogether different from the sermons to Jews. The Miletus address is strongly reminiscent of the Pauline Epistles, having particularly much in common with the Pastorals. Suffice it to say, the speeches in Acts are suited to

---

[85]A number of scholars maintain that the speeches in Acts reflect the preaching of the later Gentile church. Among them are U. Wilckens, *Die Missionsreden der Apostelgeschichte* (1963); and C. F. Evans, "The Kerygma," *JTS*, n.s. 7 (1956): 25-41. F. G. Downing argues that they reflect Christianity's appeal to pagan ethical monotheism: "Ethical Pagan Theism and the Speeches in Acts," *NTS* 27 (1981) 544-63.

[86]C. H. Dodd, *The Apostolic Preaching and Its Developments* (London: Hodder & Stoughton, 1936).

[87]See W. F. Lane, "The Speeches of the Book of Acts," *Jerusalem and Athens* (Phillipsburg, N.J.: Presbyterian and Reformed, 1971), 260-72; J. Schmitt, "Les discours missionaires des Actes et l'histoire des traditions prépauliniennes," *RSR* 69 (1981): 165-80; E. E. Ellis, "Midrashic Features in the Speeches of Acts," *Mélanges Bibliques*, ed. A. Descamps and A. de Halleux (Gembloux: Duculot, 1970), 303-12.

[88]M. Simon, *St. Stephen and the Hellenists in the Primitive Church* (London: Longmans Green, 1958). Cadbury likewise sees a case for tradition standing behind Stephen's speech, the Areopagus speech, and the Miletus address (*Making Luke-Acts*, 184-90).

their various contexts; and one need not doubt that Luke based them on reliable traditions and indeed succeeded in giving the "general purport of what was actually said."

(4) Other Forms in Acts

Luke utilized other forms of material in his narrative of the early Christian witness. One form Acts has in common with the Gospels is that of the miracle story. In Acts the apostles continued the work of Jesus in performing the same kinds of miracles—healings of the lame, exorcisms, raising the dead. A major difference was that Jesus healed by his own authority; the apostles healed through the power of the Spirit "in the name of Jesus." Unique to Acts are the so-called "punitive" miracles, where someone suffers punishment for resisting, lying to, or attempting to manipulate the Spirit. The tremendous power of the Holy Spirit behind the advance of the Christian witness has its negative side: one simply does not tamper with the divine Spirit. On the positive side the miracles in Acts are always shown serving God's word. Whether it be the tongues of Pentecost or the healing of a lame man in the temple compound, the miracle prepares the way for the preaching of the word and the "greater miracle" of commitment to Christ.

Another type of material found throughout Acts is the travel narrative. Jesus is often depicted as traveling in the Gospels, but the travelogues are of a different nature in Acts with their extensive notes of cities visited, stopping places, and locations sighted from a ship. On the surface many of these "travel notes" seem almost superfluous, adding no content to the story. This is particularly true of those found in the account of Paul's mission. The notes, however, play their role in the story of Acts. For one, they are quite accurate and give a certain stamp of reliability, as from one who was actually a participant in the events being related. Second, they picture movement and progress. Many of the travel notes are a form of summary depicting how the gospel first reached a new area, whether it be Azotus and Caesarea (8:40), or the cities such as Lydda (9:32) or Joppa (9:36) on the Plain of Sharon (9:32), or the cities of the Phoenician coast (11:19). The constant note of travel enhances the impression of movement as the Christian mission reached out in ever-widening circles.

A third type of material found throughout Acts is the edifying story. Much of the text consists of short episodes. In fact, a great deal of the account of the progress of the Christian witness is told by means of stories. Chapter 19 might serve as an example. We are told that Paul's ministry in Ephesus lasted for three years (20:31), and yet only the briefest account is given of Paul's actual witness in the synagogue and lecture hall (19:8-10). The major portion of the chapter is devoted to a series of episodes, individual encounters with some disciples of John the Baptist

(vv. 1-7), some itinerant Jewish exorcists (vv. 13-16), those who had practiced magical arts (vv. 17-19), and the shrine-makers' guild of Ephesus (vv. 23-41).

One might ask what sort of account this is of a major three-year mission. The answer is that it is a rather full account. Luke chose to illustrate the success of Paul's mission through these episodes. There are first disciples of John the Baptist—those with an incomplete and inadequate understanding of Christ. Paul led them to a full commitment. Then there were the charlatans and the magical papyri—the marks of pagan superstition. The charlatans were exposed, and the charm books were burned. And finally even those with economic interests in town were thwarted in their effort to overturn Paul's witness.

Luke has taught us quite a bit about Paul's work in Ephesus and about Christian witness in general—in its encounter with inadequate understanding, fraudulence, popular religion, and powerful forces in society. The theme in all instances is that truth prevails, and the gospel triumphs; Paul only had to remain true to his witness. Throughout Acts, Luke used this episodic style to portray the dynamic of the Christian witness. He conveyed the inner force of the Christian mission through the medium of these stories. Acts does not chronicle mere events; it is "narrative theology" at its best.[89]

A final form that characterizes Acts is the summary. Sometimes these summaries are quite brief and point only to the growth of the Christian community (cf. 6:7; 9:31; 12:24). Others point to the inner life of the community—its prayer life (1:14), the hallmarks of its fellowship (2:42-47), its community of sharing (4:32-35), and the healing ministry of the apostles (5:12-16). In form these might be described as the antitheses of the episodes. The episodes teach by means of specific incidents. The summaries generalize, giving a broad impression of the main characteristics of the Christian community. The long summaries are the three found in chaps. 2; 4; 5. They thus belong to the first days of Christianity after the burst of the Spirit at Pentecost. They portray a community marked by mutual prayer and devotion, a total sharing of selves and substance, complete trust in one another, a passion for witness, a sense of the Spirit's power among them, and a unity of commitment and purpose. They portray an ideal Christian community—the "roots" of the fellowship.[90]

---

[89]R. Pervo has recently drawn attention to this element in Acts and linked it with the popular Hellenistic romance. I would not agree with this classification of the genre of Acts or with Pervo's skepticism about the historical base of the Acts episodes, but he has rightly drawn attention to the impact that such an episodic style has in conveying a message: *Profit with Delight* (Philadelphia: Fortress, 1987).

[90]H. Zimmermann, "Die Sammelberichte der Apostelgeschichte," *BZ* 5 (1961): 71-82.

These summaries are some of the most valuable material Luke provided in his story of the early church.

(5) Luke's Personal Interests

Before leaving the consideration of Luke as a writer, note a few characteristics of his personality reflected in his writing. Obviously Luke was a good storyteller. The account of Peter's escape from prison (chap. 12) with little Rhoda leaving him at the gate is a masterpiece of suspense and irony. The same can be said of Philip's conversion of the eunuch (chap. 8), of Eutychus's fall from the window (chap. 20), and the narrow escape from the storm at sea (chap. 27).

The latter account illustrates another trait of Luke—his eye for detail. In the storm scene every nautical procedure is carefully described, but this very detail only serves to heighten the suspense of the story. Some of Luke's details can only be attributed to his own personal idiosyncrasies. He must have traveled a great deal because he showed a decided interest in lodging, whether it be Peter with Simon the tanner (9:43) or Paul with Lydia (16:15), Priscilla and Aquila (18:2), Philip (21:8), Mnason (21:16), or Publius (28:7).[91]

Another Lukan interest seems to have been shared meals. Note how often Jesus is shown at meals in Luke's Gospel, and the same continues in Acts. The story begins with Jesus eating with the apostles in the upper room (1:4) and continues right on to the end, with Paul sharing a meal with his pagan shipmates in the storm at sea (27:33f.). One of the hallmarks of the early Christians is described as their breaking bread together and doing so with "glad and sincere hearts" (2:46). And Peter's acceptance of Cornelius is illustrated by his sharing at table with him (11:3). Perhaps this is the key to Luke's emphasis. He knew that one of the surest marks of one's acceptance of fellow human beings is the willingness to share with them at table. This indeed was one of the central issues at the conference in Jerusalem (chap. 15)—making it possible for Jewish and Gentile Christians to express their unity in Christ in table fellowship.[92]

Luke had other interests as well. In general he had a concern for people who are oppressed and downtrodden—people like Samaritans and eunuchs. He likely made it a special point to include Philip's activity as he selected his material for Acts. He cared about the poor also, and that interest is amply exemplified in his Gospel. It too carries over into Acts. Part of his portrait of the ideal early community is one in which those who have share with those who have not, where "there were no needy persons

[91]H. J. Cadbury, "Luke's Interest in Lodging," *JBL* 45 (1926): 305-22.
[92]Cadbury, *Making Luke-Acts*, 234-51.

among them" (4:34). There is a concern for women also in Acts. True,
Luke was a child of his day and often spoke in "male" language, but he
did not fail to show the prominence of women in the early church—the
women in the upper room who participated in Pentecost (1:14); Sapphira,
who was on "equal terms" in receiving her judgment; Lydia, Priscilla,
and the "noble women" of Macedonia (17:4,12).[93] One of Luke's main
concerns in Acts was to portray a church without human barriers, a community where the gospel is unhindered and truly inclusive.[94]

8. Luke the Historian

It has often been argued that Acts is not a reliable historical docu-
ment.[95] This opinion seems to have first flowered with the so-called
Tübingen school in the midnineteenth century. Its name derives from the
German university where F. C. Baur, the leader of this school of thought,
taught. Baur attempted a full-scale historical reconstruction of early
Christianity in which he argued that the first Christian century was
marked by a sharp conflict between Jewish and Gentile Christian factions.
The Jewish Christians rallied around Peter as their leader and were legal-
ists, maintaining that Christians should live in strict accordance with the
Jewish law. The other faction considered Paul their leader and advocated
his law-free, grace-centered gospel.

Obviously, if Baur's reconstruction was at all accurate, Acts could not
qualify as a document from this period. Throughout Acts, Peter and Paul
are shown to be on good terms. In fact, Peter was the staunchest defender
of Paul's law-free Gentile mission at the Jerusalem Conference (15:7-11).
In Acts, Paul is depicted as a law-abiding Jew and well received by the
Jerusalem church. This simply does not fit Baur's reconstruction. Baur
and his disciples concluded that Acts could not have come from the early
Christian period but was rather an eirenicon, a text concerned with
resolving differences in the church, and thus a tendentious document
coming from the second-century church when the struggle was long over.
The second-century church was labeled the "early catholic" church and
was seen as being concerned with unity, peace, and conformity of doctrine. Baur maintained that this second-century Christianity produced
Acts—to give the impression that the unity and harmony of its own day

---

[93]R. Beck, "The Women of Acts: Foremothers of the Christian Church," *With Steadfast
Purpose*, ed. N. Keathley (Waco: Baylor University, 1990), 279-307.

[94]F. Stagg, *The Book of Acts: The Early Struggle for an Unhindered Gospel* (Nashville:
Broadman, 1955).

[95]For a contemporary advocate of the historical unreliability of Acts, see E. Haenchen,
"The Book of Acts as Source Material for the History of Early Christianity," *Studies in
Luke-Acts*, 258-78.

had existed in the earlier apostolic period. Acts was thus historically invalid as a document for early Christianity.[96]

The Tübingen hypothesis was eventually discredited. The British scholar J. B. Lightfoot, more than any other, was responsible for this. He demonstrated the late date of the pseudo-Clementine literature, the main documents Baur had used in support of this thesis of the Jewish-Gentile Christian battle in the first century. About the same time another British scholar, Sir Wm. Ramsay, began to rehabilitate the historical credibility of Acts. Ramsay had himself been inclined toward the Tübingen reconstruction of early Christian history and had originally advocated a second-century dating for Acts. However, as a result of his extensive archaeological excavations in Asia Minor, he became increasingly impressed with the accuracy of detail in the Acts account—the names of local officials, place names, and the like. He became convinced that Acts was so accurate in such details that the whole had to be historically trustworthy.[97] The more recent work of W. Gasque and C. Hemer has continued to support historical reliability of Luke's account through careful scholarship.[98] Of special note is the judgment from the German scholar M. Hengel that Luke measures up well to the best canons of reliable Hellenistic historiography.[99]

Luke seems to have seen himself as something of a historian. His use of the prefaces and the speech form link him with Hellenistic historiography. Of all the Gospel writers he is the only one who consciously connected the story of Jesus with *world* history (cf. 2:1f.; 3:1f.). This interest continues in the Book of Acts. An occasional note connects the story of the church with the Roman emperor and events of the empire (cf. 11:28; 18:2). Lesser rulers have an important role, like Herod Agrippa I, Agrippa II, and Gallio, the procurator of Achaia. At the end of the story line Paul was set in Rome for his appearance before no lesser figure than the emperor himself. Luke surely was not interested in history for its own sake, but he was interested in world events where they intersected the young Christian movement. He was above all interested in showing that

---

[96]For full treatments of the Tübingen hypothesis, see S. Neill, *The Interpretation of the New Testament, 1861-1961* (New York: Oxford, 1966), 19-60; W. G. Kümmel, *The New Testament: The History of the Investigation of Its Problems*, trans. S. M. Gilmour and H. C. Kee (Nashville: Abingdon, 1970), 120-84.

[97]Ramsay, *Traveller and Roman Citizen*, 7-10. See also Ramsay's *The Cities of St. Paul* (Grand Rapids: Baker, 1979); W. W. Gasque, "The Historical Value of the Book of Acts," *TZ* 28 (1972): 177-96.

[98]W. W. Gasque, *A History of the Criticism of the Acts of the Apostles* (Grand Rapids: Eerdmans, 1975); Hemer, *Acts in Hellenistic History*.

[99]M. Hengel, *Acts and the History of Earliest Christianity*, trans. J. Bowden (Philadelphia: Fortress, 1979).

Christianity is of worldwide significance, that the events which transpired in Jesus Christ had not been done "in a corner" (26:26). They are worthy of the note of Gentiles, kings, even emperors; for Christ is Savior of all. Surely something of the historian's interest is in this; but more than that, the Evangelist was concerned to share the Savior of the world *with* the world.

9. Luke the Theologian

If Luke can be called a historian, he is equally qualified for the designation of theologian. All good historians are interpreters of the events they treat. Through selection, emphasis, and analysis they seek meaning in the events. Luke was no exception. He viewed early Christian history through the eyes of faith and saw constant traces of the divine providence that guided those events. In this respect he was also a theologian. He wrote from the perspective of faith. This in no way detracts from his stature as a historian. He wrote his history "from within," from the viewpoint of faith, and was thus both historian and theologian.

Since the release of H. Conzelmann's book on Lukan theology in the early fifties, extensive scholarly investigation of the Lukan theological perspective has been underway. The following treatment is designed as a bare introduction to that discussion and is divided into two subsections. The first will deal with two special areas that have dominated the discussion. The second will give an overview of some of the theological distinctives of Acts.

(1) "Salvation History" and "Early Catholicism"

In his seminal work Conzelmann suggested that Luke's main theological emphasis was that of portraying a divine history of salvation. Taking Luke-Acts together, he saw Luke as dividing holy history into three distinct epochs—that of Israel (the old people of God), that of Christ (the center of all history), and that of the church (the new people of God).[100] He maintained that Luke wrote in a time when the original eschatological expectation of the imminent return of Christ had waned, when Christians were settling down to a long wait and needed to come to terms with their existence in the world. Appealing to Acts 1:6-8, Conzelmann saw Luke as replacing the original eschatological fervor with the agenda of the mission of the church. The Spirit then became tied to the history of the church. In all of this are the seeds of institutionalism and a fall from the immediacy of the individual experience of justification through grace in

---

[100]Conzelmann, *Theology*, 16, 150.

the Spirit which marked Paul's theology. Justification has been replaced by salvation history.

Many of Conzelmann's conclusions are questionable. First, the idea of the "delayed Parousia" has been greatly overplayed. Acts often evidences that the original eschatological fervor of the Christian community had not waned.[101] The mission of the church was itself born out of the conviction that Christians were the people of God of the end time and were to be the "light to the nations" who bore the message of God's decisive redemptive act in Christ. Second, it is simply not true that the Spirit is tied to the church in Acts. The Spirit is always transcendent in Acts. The true salvation-historical perspective of Luke-Acts is not that of a three-part periodization of *earthly* history but a two-part scheme where God in his Spirit continues *from transcendence* to work among his people on the earthly, historical level.[102]

Finally, Conzelmann set up an unnecessary either/or. The church exists in the world, in history, and it must come to terms with that reality. Yet the church mediates the living, convicting word of God.[103] The church only fails when it is no longer open to the *living* word, to the convicting, judging, leading Spirit of God but instead ties both word and Spirit to its own dogma and institutions. There is no evidence that this was true of the Christians in Acts. The opposite was the case—their assumptions were constantly challenged anew by their openness to the Spirit at work among them.

E. Käsemann would disagree with that last statement. He sees strong marks of the institutionalized church in Acts. Somewhat reminiscent of the old Tübingen hypothesis, he labels this "early catholicism," meaning by this the early manifestations of tendencies that eventually developed into the full-blown "Catholic" church with its elaborate hierarchy and dogma. The "catholic" tendencies Käsemann saw as being present in Acts include such things as the formation of hardened dogma; apostolic succession and transmitted authority; a distinction between clergy and laity; an authoritative tradition of scriptural interpretation; sacramentalism; a concern for unity and consolidation; and a historical, institutional perspective.[104] Käsemann's "early Catholic" thesis has generally not

---

[101]R. Hiers, "The Problem of the Delay of the Parousia in Luke-Acts," *NTS* 20 (1973-77): 145-55; A. J. Mattill, Jr., "Näherwartung, Fernerwartung and the Purpose of Luke-Acts: Weymouth Reconsidered," *CBQ* 34 (1972): 276-93.

[102]H. Flender, *St. Luke: Theologian of Redemptive History*, trans. R. H. and I. Fuller (Philadelphia: Fortress, 1967). See also R. H. Smith, "The Theology of Acts," *CTM* 42 (1971): 527-35.

[103]E. Lohse, "Lukas als Theologue der Heilsgeschichte," *EvT* 14 (1954): 256-75.

[104]E. Käsemann, *New Testament Questions for Today*, trans. W. J. Montague (Philadelphia: Fortress, 1969), 214, 236-51; Käsemann, "Ephesians and Acts," *Studies in Luke-Acts,* 288-97.

been well received by the scholarly community.[105] There simply is no evidence for dogmatism, successionism, sacramentalism, traditionalism, and institutionalism in Acts.

(2) Theological Aspects of Acts

To speak of a "theology" in Acts in any systematic sense probably would not be proper. If one assumes that Luke's speeches reflect their actual settings, one would expect a certain theological diversity. This does seem to be the case—the primitive Christology in Peter's speeches to Jews, the "natural theology" in Paul's addresses to pagans, the cultic-reform element in Stephen's speech.

Two observations with regard to treatments of the theology of Acts are noteworthy. First, it might be well to drop the hyphen in Luke-Acts and concentrate on each of Luke's two writings separately in dealing with Luke's theology, as M. Parsons has suggested.[106] A common procedure has been to run an analysis of the theological themes in the Gospel of Luke and then search for confirmation of these in Acts. The result has often been a lopsided picture that omits many of the major emphases in Acts. Acts has a different historical setting from Luke and utilizes different literary genres. It should stand on its own. The second observation relates closely to the first: a theology of Acts should derive primarily from its narrative movement. Acts is basically narrative, and its "theology" is to be found primarily there. What are the recurrent themes in the episodes? What motifs dominate in the movement of the story line? This is where the "theology" of Acts really lies. It is a "narrative theology." As such, it will be primarily considered in section 11 under the themes of Acts.

A few theological distinctives in the more traditional sense, however, have often been observed in Acts and should be considered. The Christology of Acts might best be described as a "messianic Christology." Most of the Christological statements occur in the speeches to Jews where the emphasis is on convincing them from the Old Testament Scriptures that Jesus is the promised Messiah. Closely tied to this is the emphasis on the resurrection. Throughout Acts the decisive act of Christ is described in

---

[105]Conzelmann, "Luke's Place in Early Christianity," 298-316; I. H. Marshall, "'Early Catholicism' in the New Testament," *New Dimensions*, 217-31; U. Luz, "Erwägungen zur Entstehung des 'Fruhkatholizismus.' Eine Skizze," *ZNW* 65 (1974): 88-111; L. Morris, "Luke and Early Catholicism," *WJT* 35 (1972-73): 121-36; K. Giles, "Is Luke an Exponent of 'Early Protestantism'? Church Order in the Lukan Writings," *EvQ* 54 (1982): 193-205 and 55 (1983), 3-20; J. H. Elliott, "A Catholic Gospel: Reflections on 'Early Catholicism' in the New Testament," *CBQ* 31 (1969): 213-23.

[106]M. C. Parsons, "The Unity of the Lukan Writings: Rethinking the *Opinio Communis*," *With Steadfast Purpose*, 29-53.

terms of his resurrection.[107] The resurrection is the event that demonstrates Christ is Messiah. The messianic emphasis likely explains why atonement is not a major emphasis in Acts. By the resurrection God confirmed the messianic status of Jesus. Less emphasis falls on the death of Jesus. The atonement is present to a limited extent in Acts—in Paul's reference to Christ's death according to the Scriptures (13:27-29) and in his description of the church as being "purchased through his own blood" (20:28). It is probably implicit in the "servant" terminology of Peter's sermon in the temple square as well as in the strong stress on repentance found throughout Acts (cf. 2:38; 26:20).[108]

Luke is often faulted for not including the idea of justification in the Pauline portions of Acts. The idea is not wholly missing (cf. 13:38f.), and it should be noted that the terminology of justification does not occur in all of Paul's own epistles, including the Corinthian letters. Still, Acts reveals much in common with Paul's thought with respect to receiving salvation. It is never through works. Peter's words about the yoke of the law and his insistence on salvation through God's grace (15:10f.) could hardly be closer to the thought of Paul.[109] Luke was no systematic theologian, and nowhere in Acts is a clear soteriology worked out; but throughout there is a simple gospel that salvation comes by no other name than Jesus (cf. 2:38f.; 4:12; 16:31), a salvation brought by the work of God and solely as a gift.[110]

10. The Purpose of Acts

In any consideration of an author's purpose, the logical starting point would be his own statement on the matter. Luke did in fact provide such a statement in the preface to his Gospel. If the preface was intended to introduce both volumes, as is likely the case, then v. 4 provides Luke's intent.[111] The preface is very general: "that you may know the certainty

---

[107]I. H. Marshall, "The Resurrection in the Acts of the Apostles," *Apostolic History and the Gospel*, 92-107.

[108]I. H. Marshall, *Luke: Historian and Theologian* (Grand Rapids: Zondervan, 1971), 188-202. R. Tannehill sees atonement as being implicit in the servant emphasis of the eucharistic account in Luke's Gospel: "A Study in the Theology of Luke-Acts," *ATR* 43 (1961): 195-203.

[109]On the complex issue of the law in Acts, see E. Larsson, "Paul: Law and Salvation," *NTS* 31 (1985): 425-36.

[110]The concept of "grace" in Acts is connected more with Christian witness than with salvation. It is a gift of divine power granted to the faithful (cf. 4:33; 6:8; 7:10; 14:3,26; 15:40). See J. Nolland, "Luke's Use of *Charis*," *NTS* 32 (1986): 614-20.

[111]For a general introduction to the issues involved in relating the prefaces to the general purpose of Luke-Acts, see S. Brown, "The Role of the Prologues in Determining the Purpose of Luke-Acts," *Perspectives on Luke-Acts*, 99-111.

(*asphaleian*) of the things you have been taught" (Luke 1:4).[112] The preceding verses have described how he went about reaching this goal—by closely following the events as they had come down to him through eyewitnesses and servants of the word and by arranging them in an orderly fashion. The emphasis on literary predecessors, eyewitnesses, and careful investigation would indicate a historian's interest—to present the events in an accurate and well-arranged manner.[113] The emphasis on "certainty" (literally "firm foundation") would point to his "theologian's" interest—to give a solid grounding in the faith. His reference to "the things you have been taught" would indicate that he was writing to someone who had already received some instruction in the Christian traditions. To give "Theophilus" a solid grounding in the faith by means of an orderly account was Luke's stated purpose.[114] Can we know more?

Some have seen a clue to a more specific purpose in Luke's "addressee," Theophilus. The name is a well-established Greek name. Since its etymology yields "lover of God," it has often been concluded that Luke intended the name symbolically, perhaps referring to those "God-fearers" who were associated with the synagogues, Gentiles who shared with the Jews their faith in God but who had not undergone full proselyte procedure and converted to Judaism.[115] E. Goodspeed suggested that Theophilus may have been Luke's publisher and that the inclusion of his name would indicate that Luke intended his work for the secular book market.[116] B. H. Streeter postulated that Theophilus must have been an influential Roman official since the title "most excellent" is reserved elsewhere in Acts for high-ranking officials. He suggested that Theophilus may have been Flavius Clemens, the cousin of the emperor Domitian, who may have been a secret Christian.[117] Recently Agrippa II has been suggested.[118] Perhaps the most popular "Theophilus Theory"

---

[112]D. J. Sneen suggests that ἀσφάλεια should be taken in a Christological sense—to know the firm basis in Christ: "An Exegesis of Luke 1:1-4 with Special Regard to Luke's Purpose as an Historian," *ExpTim* 83 (1971-72): 40-43.

[113]L. C. A. Alexander's research indicates that the references to "eyewitnesses" (αὐτόπται) and accuracy link Luke's prologue more to Greek scientific manuals than to historiography: "Luke's Preface in the Context of Greek Preface-Writing," *NovT* 28 (1986): 48-74. For καθέξης, see G. Schneider, "Der Zweck des lukanischen Doppelwerks, *BZ* 21 (1977): 45-66.

[114]I. I. du Plessis, "Once More: The Purpose of Luke's Prologue (Luke 1:1-4)," *NovT* 16 (1974): 259-71.

[115]On the basis of a reader-response methodology, R. Creech has recently concluded that Theophilus represents a God-fearer who is open to Christianity: "The Most Excellent Narratee: The Significance of Theophilus in Luke-Acts," *With Steadfast Purpose*, 107-26.

[116]E. J. Goodspeed, "Was Theophilus Luke's Publisher?" *JBL* 73 (1954): 84.

[117]B. H. Streeter, *The Four Gospels: A Study of Origins* (London: Macmillan, 1924), 535.

[118]W. G. Marx, "A New Theophilus," *EvQ* 52 (1980): 17-26.

has been that he was Paul's legal counsel in Rome, and Luke-Acts was written as a brief for the preparation of his case.[119]

Of all these theories, the God-fearer suggestion has the most to commend it. Luke's reference to the things Theophilus had been taught as well as the specifically Christian detail of Luke and Acts was surely intended for those who had significant acquaintance with Christianity and were either strongly inclined toward it or were already (as seems most likely) Christian. It is difficult to conceive of a Roman official or Gentile pagan sorting through all of Luke-Acts for the material of interest.

Some have argued that Luke-Acts was written to counter a particular false teaching. Most often suggested has been Gnosticism.[120] Any evidence for Luke fighting Gnosticism in his books is indirect at best. In Acts the threat to the church is not from within the fellowship but always from without.[121] The same can be said for Marcion. The emphasis on Christianity's roots in Judaism can be better explained on other grounds than as a polemic against Marcionism.[122] We are thus finally left with Luke's general statement of purpose. Does Acts offer any more specific indication of Luke's purpose through its recurring themes? The evidence points to an affirmative answer and to a multiplicity of "purposes."

11. The Themes of Acts

In speaking of an author's "purpose," two problems arise. One is that this assumes we can pick the author's brain. I am not sure that we can. We only know him through his works and can ultimately only speak of the emphases that seem to stand out in his writings. The second problem is that attempts to delineate a single purpose of a writing tend to become overly focused and to omit other significant motifs. It seems better to speak of themes and to acknowledge a multiplicity of them in Acts. None of them is distinct. They all interweave and overlap with one another to furnish together the rich tapestry that is the story of Acts.

(1) World Mission

If Luke gave an explicit clue to his purpose anywhere in Acts, it would be the thematic 1:8. In answer to the disciples' question about the restoration of the kingdom, Jesus set before them a mission to the world. They were to be witnesses in Jerusalem, all Judea, Samaria, and to the

---

[119]Munck, *Acts*, 55-56.

[120]C. H. Talbert, *Luke and the Gnostics: An Examination of the Lucan Purpose* (Nashville: Abingdon, 1966).

[121]J. Knox, *Marcion and the New Testament* (Chicago: University of Chicago Press, 1942).

[122]W. C. van Unnik, "Die Apostelgeschichte und die Hëresien," *Sparsa Collecta* I (Leiden: Brill, 1973), 402-09.

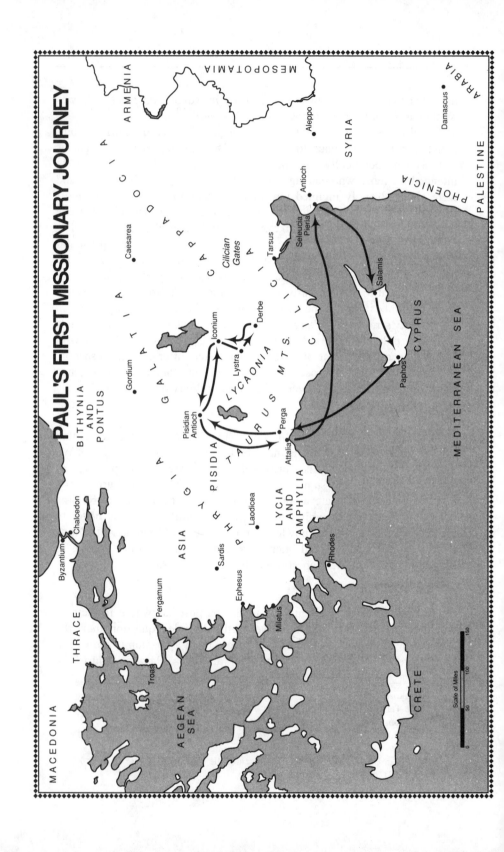

PAUL'S FIRST MISSIONARY JOURNEY

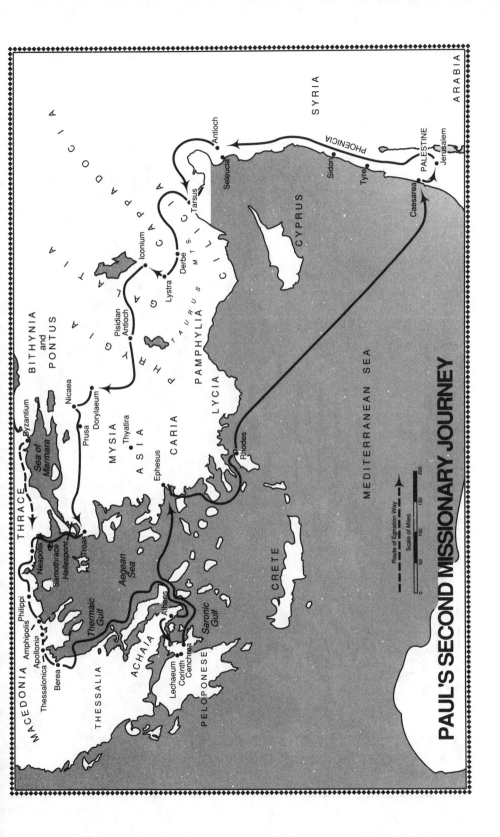

PAUL'S SECOND MISSIONARY JOURNEY

Route of Egnatian Way
Scale of Miles

MACEDONIA
THRACE
Byzantium
Sea of Marmara
Amphipolis
Neapolis
Apollonia
Philippi
Thessalonica
Samothrace
Berea
Hellespont
Troas
THESSALIA
Aegean Sea
Athens
ACHAIA
Lechaeum
Corinth
Cenchrea
Saronic Gulf
PELOPONESE
CRETE
Thermaic Gulf

BITHYNIA and PONTUS
Nicaea
Prusa
Dorylaeum
MYSIA
Thyatira
ASIA
CARIA
Ephesus
Rhodes
LYCIA
PAMPHYLIA
TAURUS MTS.
Iconium
Pisidian Antioch
Lystra
Derbe
Tarsus
CILICIA
CAPPADOCIA
GALATIA

MEDITERRANEAN SEA

CYPRUS

SYRIA
Antioch
Seleucia
Sidon
Tyre
PHOENICIA
Caesarea
PALESTINE
Jerusalem
ARABIA

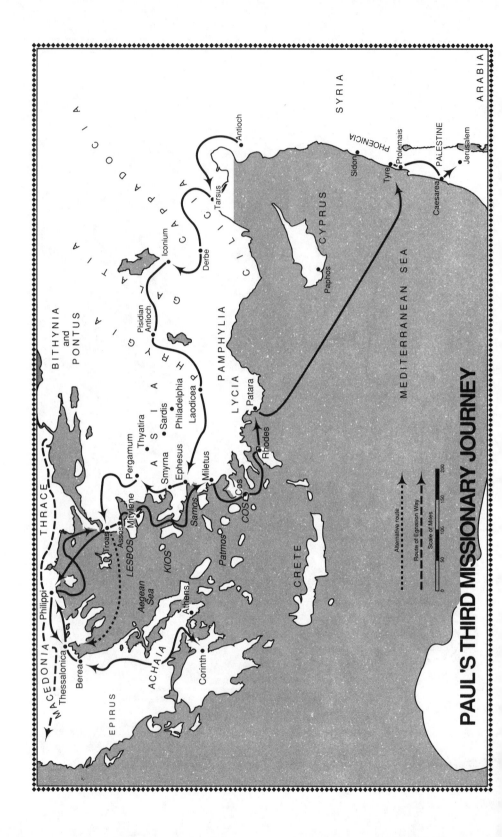

PAUL'S THIRD MISSIONARY JOURNEY

PAUL'S JOURNEY TO ROME

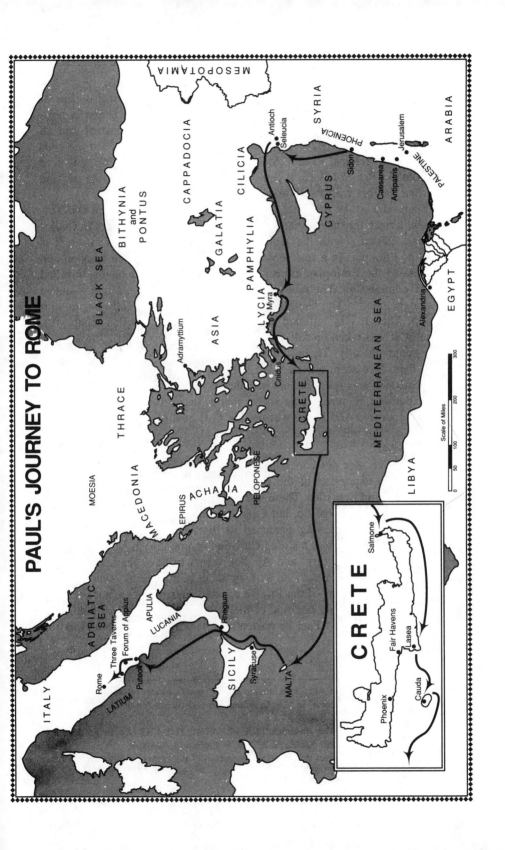

ITALY

ADRIATIC SEA

Rome
Three Taverns
Forum of Appius
LATIUM
Puteoli
APULIA
LUCANIA
Rhegium
SICILY
Syracuse
MALTA

MOESIA

THRACE

MACEDONIA
EPIRUS
ACHAIA
PELOPONESE

BLACK SEA

BITHYNIA and PONTUS

CAPPADOCIA

GALATIA

ASIA

Adramyttium

LYCIA
Myra
Cnidus

PAMPHYLIA

CILICIA

Antioch
Seleucia

SYRIA

PHOENICIA
Sidon

CYPRUS

Caesarea
Antipatris

PALESTINE
Jerusalem

ARABIA

Alexandria

EGYPT

MEDITERRANEAN SEA

LIBYA

MESOPOTAMIA

Scale of Miles
0 50 100 200 300

CRETE

CRETE

Salmone
Fair Havens
Lasea
Cauda
Phoenix

ends of the earth.[123] This verse presents a rough geographical outline of
the spread of the Christian mission as depicted in Acts. It began in Jerusalem (chaps. 1–5), then it started moving out from Jerusalem into all
Judea and Samaria (chaps. 6–8), and finally with Paul went "to the ends
of the earth" (chaps. 13–28). Since the term "ends of the earth" was used
of Rome in *Pss. Sol.* 8:16, it generally has been assumed that the mission
reached its goal with Paul's arrival in Rome.

Such may not be the case. The term "ends of the earth" is an Old Testament phrase for the ultimate limits of civilization and appears in Greco-
Roman literature with the same connotation.[124] In some literature it is
used of Ethiopia. In a real sense Philip, with his Samaritan mission and
witness to the Ethiopian eunuch, could be described as having fulfilled
Jesus' commission. The mission in Acts tends to move in circles—not in
a straight line.[125] The Gentile mission, for instance, actually began with
Philip. Then it was initiated anew by Peter with Cornelius (chap. 10).
Finally, it was taken up fully by the Antioch church (11:20). The same is
true geographically. There was an apparent ever-increasing circle of witness from Jerusalem outward, but it had a way of doubling back. Paul's
third mission was spent mainly in Ephesus. There was no new geographical expansion, no territory he visited that he had not already visited on his
second journey. And Rome was not the final goal of Acts in a geographical sense. The mission had reached there already—long before Paul (cf.
18:2; 28:14f.).

That Luke was not concerned with giving a complete history of the
mission and expansion of the early church is amply evidenced also by
consulting Paul's epistles. There was a Pauline congregation at Colosse as
we know from that epistle, but Luke did not mention Paul's work there.
Paul spoke of his having preached in Illyricum (Rom 15:19). Acts is
silent on this. There was a strong Christian community in North Africa by
the early second century, and Apollos seems to have learned of Christ
there (Acts 18:24f.). Luke said nothing about it, nor did he relate the missionary activity of any of the Twelve apostles outside Judea, not even that
of Peter. He gave only one line of the mission thrust—that of Paul. And
through his picture of Paul he presented a paradigm of Christian mission
for all time.

---

[123]M. Hengel describes Acts as "a mission history" and "a history of the Pauline mission
with an extensive introduction" in "Die Ursprünge der christlichen Mission," *NTS* 18 (1971-
72): 15-38.

[124]W. C. van Unnik, "Der Ausdruck ΈΩΣ 'ΕΣΧΑΤΟΥ ΤΗΣ ΓΗΣ (Apostelgeschichte 1,
8) und sein altestamentlicher Hintergrund," *Sparsa Collecta*, I, 386-401.

[125]S. M. Praeder describes this as a dual "progressive" and "repetitive" itinerary in Acts:
"From Jerusalem to Rome," *TBT* 24 (1986): 79-84.

The ends of the earth are never reached in Acts. The mission goal is never completed. It remains open, yet to be fulfilled. Paul continued bearing his witness in Rome. The abrupt ending of the book is open-ended. There are many "completed" missions in Acts. Each of Paul's has a sort of closure with his return to Antioch or Jerusalem.[126] But each ending is the starting point for a new beginning. Perhaps that is the missionary message of Acts. The story remains open. There must always be new beginnings. The "ends of the earth" are still out there to receive the witness to Christ.

(2) Providence of God

That the mission of the church is under the direct control of God is perhaps the strongest single theme in the theology of Acts. One of the primary ways in which it is set is through the use of Scripture in a promise-fulfillment pattern. Acts makes extensive use of Old Testament Scripture, particularly the prophets and psalms.[127] The quotations are often presented with the formula "the Scripture had to be fulfilled" (cf. 1:16). These Old Testament quotations occur at almost every juncture of the church's life. They establish the necessity for replacing Judas (1:16-21), provide the basis for the miracle at Pentecost (2:16-21), and prove the necessity of the death (2:25-28) and resurrection of Jesus (2:34-35). Scripture establishes the Gentile witness (13:47) and the Gentile inclusion in the people of God (15:16-18). The examples could be multiplied. Acts 26:22 summarizes this emphasis. All is according to Scripture, and all is in the divine purpose. The point is that the Scriptures legitimate the entire activity of the Christian community—its faith in Christ and its witness.[128] The Scriptures establish that these things *must be* fulfilled. They attest to the divine purpose, and their fulfillment is a certain sign that God is behind the events.

It is not only with regard to Scripture that one finds this emphasis on the "divine necessity" (Greek, *dei*) in Acts.[129] The suffering of Paul as

---

[126]The concept of missionary "journeys" is not always an accurate description of Paul's work and seems to have been of late origin: J. Townsend, "Missionary Journeys in Acts and European Missionary Societies," *ATR* 68 (1986): 99-104.

[127]Many of the quotations in Acts likely reflect the early Christian use of collections of prophetic proof texts or "testimonia." See B. Lindars, *New Testament Apologetic: The Doctrinal Significance of the Old Testament Quotations* (Philadelphia: Westminster, 1961); J. R. Harris, *Testimonies*, 2 vols. (Cambridge: University Press, 1916 and 1920); C. H. Dodd, *According to the Scriptures* (London: Nisbet, 1952); R. Longenecker, *Biblical Exegesis in the Apostolic Period* (Grand Rapids: Eerdmans, 1975), 79-103.

[128]C. H. Talbert, "Promise and Fulfillment in Lucan Theology," *New Perspectives*, 91-103. The fulfillment of Scripture assures the church that all is under God's control. See D. L. Tiede, *Prophecy and History in Luke-Acts* (Philadelphia: Fortress, 1980).

[129]C. H. Cosgrove, "The Divine ΔEI in Luke-Acts," *NovT* 26 (1984): 168-90.

Christ's faithful witness was part of the divine purpose (9:16), as was his destiny to appear before Caesar (19:21; 23:11; 27:24). The miracles likewise attest to the divine providence behind the entire life and witness of the Christian community in Acts.[130] This aspect of God's providence is most apparent in the activity of the Spirit.

(3) Power of the Spirit

The role of the Holy Spirit is part of the emphasis on God's providence in Acts. It is primarily through God's Spirit that the community was aware of the divine power at work among them. So central was the work of the Spirit in Acts that some have suggested that a more appropriate title for the book would be "The Acts of the Holy Spirit." The Spirit is not even mentioned in eleven chapters of Acts, but the Spirit does not have to be named to have been present in Acts. Luke gave enough clues in the earlier chapters of Acts for readers to realize that references to the Christians speaking "boldly" and the like indicate that the Spirit was with them. Such indications occur to the last verse of Acts.

In a real sense, the church was born of the Spirit at Pentecost (chap. 2) just as the infancy narrative of Luke's Gospel shows how Jesus was born of the Holy Spirit. The parallel does not end there. Just as the Spirit descended upon Jesus at his baptism (Luke 3:22) and continued to abide with him throughout his ministry (Luke 4:18), so the Spirit was the constant companion in the life of the young church.[131] The Holy Spirit is a gift to every believer (Acts 2:38) and comes as a special endowment of power in times of crisis to enable a bold witness (cf. 4:8). The Holy Spirit inspired the Scriptures that the Christian community saw being fulfilled in its own time (cf. 4:25).

As the divine power at work in the community, the Spirit also possesses an awesome capacity of judgment, as Ananias and Sapphira experienced when they were guilty of lying to the Spirit (5:1-11). It is striking that the Spirit is not linked directly to the healing narratives in Acts. Generally healings are performed "in the name of Jesus." The name of Jesus, however, represents his presence and his power, and the presence of Jesus is experienced in the church through the Spirit. The Spirit is the abiding presence of Jesus; the Holy Spirit *is* the Spirit of Jesus (cf. "Holy Spirit" and "Spirit of Jesus" in 16:6-7).

---

[130]G. W. H. Lampe, "Miracles in the Acts of the Apostles," in *Miracles* (London: Mowbray, 1965), 165-78.

[131]G. W. H. Lampe, "The Holy Spirit in the Writings of St. Luke," *Studies in the Gospels* (Oxford: Basil Blackwell, 1955), 193-98; J. H. E. Hull, *The Holy Spirit in the Acts of the Apostles* (New York: World, 1968).

The most characteristic role of the Spirit in Acts is his activity in the Christian mission. Every major breakthrough in mission occurs through the guidance of the Spirit. Sometimes this is explicitly stated, as when the Spirit called the church at Antioch to set apart Paul and Barnabas for a mission (13:3f.) and when the Spirit prevented Paul from working in Bithynia and Asia and literally forced him to the first mission on European soil at Philippi (16:6-10). Sometimes the Spirit's activity is more subtly depicted in story form. Philip's pioneering witness to the Ethiopian eunuch is a good example. The Spirit is explicitly mentioned in 8:29,39; but his presence is felt at every point of the narrative, directing Philip's every step and providentially setting the stage with every possible "coincidence" (the perfect Scripture, a pool of water at just the right time) for the conversion of the Ethiopian. An important activity of the Spirit is his "legitimation" of new groups in the Christian outreach—the Samaritans (8:17-25), Cornelius and his fellow Gentiles (10:44-48), the disciples of John the Baptist at Ephesus (19:6f.). Each of these events marked a new breakthrough, a new level of outreach in the Christian mission; and each was accompanied by a special, outwardly demonstrable evidence that the Spirit had come upon them and God had accepted them.

Scripture, miracles, angelic visions, the activity of the Spirit: such are the constant accompaniment of the Christian mission in Acts. Such were the sure evidences to the young community that their endeavors were within the purposes and under the direction of God.

(4) Restored Israel

Much of Acts concerns the Christian witness to the Jews. The first five chapters center in Jerusalem and are preoccupied with the preaching to the Jews of the city. Four of the major speeches of Acts are addressed to Jewish audiences (chaps. 2; 3; 7; 13). Paul always began his witness in a new locality by entering the synagogue. A mixed picture of the Jewish response to the gospel, however, emerges. Growing success—3,000 converts at Pentecost (2:41), a total of 5,000 in the Jerusalem church only shortly thereafter (4:4), the conversion of priests (6:7), and "many thousands" of believers in the Jerusalem church by the time of Paul's last visit there (21:20)—paralleled a growing rejection of the Christian message by the Jews. This began with the Jewish officials, particularly the Sanhedrin, who arrested and tried the apostles twice (chaps. 4–5), whipped them on the latter occasion (5:40), and eventually killed Stephen (7:57-60). A massive persecution followed, led by the Jewish Zealot Saul (8:3); but even Saul's conversion did not end the Jewish resistance. Paul became the persecuted.

The pattern of his rejection by the Diaspora synagogues is set in Pisidian Antioch (13:44-47) and continued throughout his ministry all the way to the Jews of Rome (28:23-28). Yet even there some Jews believed Paul's witness to Christ (28:24). Still, the Jewish resistance to Paul was fairly complete by the end of Acts. Beginning with the mob scene in the temple square (21:27), the "whole crowd" of Jews attempted to lynch the apostle; and this strong Jewish opposition kept Paul confined under Roman custody and forced his appeal to Caesar. It stands behind the remainder of the story of Acts.

What is one to make out of this picture of the mixed response of the Jews to the Christian message? The positive response should not be overlooked. A successful witness in Jerusalem resulted in a Jewish Christian community containing thousands of converts. But the picture is one of only limited success. Most of the Jews did not accept Christ. There was no question of Judaism becoming Christian in any official sense.[132] The Sanhedrin and the synagogues rejected and even persecuted the messengers of Christ.

Stephen's speech in Acts 7 is programmatic in this whole development. It has two major themes, and both point to the Jewish rejection of the Christian message. Stephen's first theme showed from Israel's history that the people had always rejected their divinely appointed leaders. What was true in the past should only be expected in their rejection of Christ at that time. Second, Stephen showed that the official Jewish manner of worship had likewise failed. The temple should have been a place of genuine worship. It had instead become a man-made institution, tying God down to a particular people and place. It could no longer remain the worship center for the true people of God. Stephen's speech thus set down the theological agenda for the Jewish rejection of Christ. The temple could no longer remain in the center for the worship of God, nor could Jerusalem continue as the "holy city."

At the beginning of Acts, Jerusalem was at the center. Everything radiated from Jerusalem—the first witnesses went out from there; Paul always returned there after each mission. All this changed with Paul's final journey to Jerusalem. In the temple, the center of official Jewish worship, Paul was mobbed by the crowd. The gates of the temple were shut (21:30), and they never again are reopened in the narrative of Acts. From this point on, the movement was away from Jerusalem and toward

---

[132]A major contemporary issue is whether Acts depicts the Jews as being totally excluded from God's people. Among those who hold this view that Acts comes from a wholly Gentile Christianity that has rejected any mission to the Jews is J. T. Sanders, "The Salvation of the Jews in Luke-Acts," *New Perspectives*, 104-28; R. Maddox, *Purpose of Luke-Acts*, 42-52; J. B. Tyson, "The Jewish Public in Luke-Acts," *NTS* 30 (1984): 574-83. The evidence of Acts would point more to mixed Jewish-Gentile Christian congregations, excluded from the synagogues, but not having given up on witness to individual Jews. For further bibliography, see chap. 10, nn. 91-92.

Rome, the center of the Gentile world.[133]

Clearly Judaism as a whole, Judaism in any "official" sense, did not
accept Christ; Luke underlined this reality in Paul's concluding quote
from Isaiah to the Jews of Rome, a prophetic text that pointed to precisely
this "calloused" heart on the part of Israel (28:27). In Romans 9–11 Paul
pointed to the same experience of the Jewish rejection of the gospel. But
this is not the whole story. It is a question of who at that point constituted
the true people of God.[134] Throughout Acts, Christians are clearly the
people of God, the true or "restored" Israel. Acts begins with the disciples' question about when the kingdom would be restored to Israel (1:6).
Jesus rejected their question of time, but he did not reject the question of
Israel's restoration. Indeed, the mission he gave the disciples was closely
related to the question of God's people. God's people are now the people
of the Messiah, i.e., a people on mission, a light to the nations (13:47).
The extensive use of the Old Testament in the early speeches of Acts
points to this. They establish that God has fulfilled his promises in his
final decisive act of "raising up" Christ as the Messiah. The people of the
Messiah are the true people of God, the "restored" Israel. This reality is
depicted in the language used throughout Acts for Christians. They are
described as "brothers," the favorite self-designation among Jews. They
are "believers"—those who believe in God's Messiah, the promised Messiah *to Israel*. They are "the way," the true way within the people of God.
The true people of God are not coterminus with the historical, ethnic Jewish nation. They are in direct continuity with the people of God of the old
covenant, the Israel of the Messiah, the people of the promises. In Acts
the church is not Israel but a new, restored Israel not confined to one
people or place.

(5) Inclusive Gospel

If Acts gives a picture of massive Jewish rejection of the gospel and
their resulting exclusion from the people of God, it also gives the other
side as well—the inclusion of Gentiles in the people of God. It is not a
matter of the exclusion of one, inclusion of the other. As we have seen,
Acts depicts great success among the Jews and a sizable Jewish-Christian
congregation. It is rather the story of how these early Jewish-Christians

---

[133]F. V. Filson, "The Journey Motif in Luke-Acts," *Apostolic History and the Gospel*,
74-75; F. D. Weinert, "The Meaning of the Temple in Luke-Acts," *BTB* 11 (1981): 85-89;
A. C. Winn, "Elusive Mystery: The Purpose of Acts," *Int* 13 (1959): 144-56.

[134]I am in basic agreement with J. Jervell that Acts presents Christianity as the restored
Israel, although he has perhaps exaggerated the Jewish-Christian influence in Luke's church.
See his *Luke and the People of God* (Minneapolis: Augsburg, 1972). For a similar view, see
H. C. Kee, *Good News to the Ends of the Earth: The Theology of Acts* (Philadelphia: Trinity,
1990).

were led by God to the vision of a more inclusive people of God, a church
that transcended all barriers of human discrimination and prejudice. As
F. Stagg pointed out, it is a question of the struggle for an "unhindered
gospel."[135] For Jewish Christians the idea of accepting Gentiles into the
people of God would not have come easy, particularly accepting Gentiles
without first requiring that they convert to Judaism. Judaism already had
a procedure for admitting Gentile proselytes, and it involved circumcision
and agreeing to live by the Jewish Torah. It is nothing short of remarkable that the early Jewish Christians were able to overcome this understanding and conclude that only belief in Jesus as the Messiah qualifies
for membership in the people of God.[136]

Chapters 6–15 largely concern this story of the inclusion of the Gentiles. Beginning with Stephen's vision of a God not tied to locale or cult,
the first steps were taken by Philip in his outreach to the "half-Jewish"
Samaritans and the Gentile Ethiopian (chap. 8). The central place is occupied by Peter's being led through divine vision to preach to the God-
fearing Cornelius and his Gentile friends (chap. 10). The gift of the Spirit
to the Gentiles convinced Peter that God accepted them with no further
qualifications, and the basic principle was established. A witness to Gentiles was undertaken by the Antioch church (11:20), and it was that congregation that sent Paul and Barnabas forth on mission.

In the course of this mission, Paul turned from the Jews to the Gentiles
at Antioch of Pisidia. He pointed to the words of Isaiah, which provide
the scriptural base for the witness to the Gentiles (13:47). The great success among the Gentiles both in Antioch and on Paul and Barnabas's mission prompted the major conference in Jerusalem over the matter of
Gentile inclusion (chap. 15). There the issue was settled: Gentiles were to
be accepted into God's people without the requirements of the Torah. The
restored people of God were to be an inclusive community—Jew *and*
Gentile.[137]

The inclusive message of Acts goes far beyond racial inclusiveness. It
extends to economic levels, as is evidenced by the early church's practice
of sharing so as not to permit any needy person among them. It extends to
physical barriers: the lame beggar at the temple gate and the Ethiopian
eunuch were no longer excluded from full participation in the people of

---

[135]Stagg, *Acts: The Early Struggle for an Unhindered Gospel.*

[136]G. Dix, *Jew and Greek: A Study in the Primitive Church* (Westminster: Dacre, 1953),
19-60.

[137]A number of interpreters, who see Luke as writing primarily from a Gentile Christian
perspective, see the emphasis on the Jewish-Christian roots of Christianity directed toward
the question of the legitimacy of the Gentile church. For this view see R. L. Brawley, *Luke-
Acts and the Jews: Conflict, Apology, and Conciliation* (Atlanta: Scholars Press, 1987);
Maddox, *Purpose of Luke-Acts*, 183-86.

God. Women like Lydia and Priscilla were given a leading role in the young Christian fellowship, which is quite remarkable for that time and culture. The inclusiveness extends in every direction—the gospel was preached to governors, kings, perhaps even the emperor. It has no bounds but is an *inclusive* gospel.

Another side to inclusiveness is unity. Honest inclusiveness implies genuine acceptance. The "Apostolic Decrees" of chap. 15 probably are to be seen in this light, as cultic provisions designed to enable table fellowship between Jewish and Gentile Christians.[138] F. C. Baur notwithstanding, the issue of Christian fellowship and unity was central for the early church, since many of the congregations undoubtedly consisted of a mix of Jewish and Gentile members. The issue of mutual acceptance and genuine unity was vital. An expanding mission and a truly inclusive gospel demand a unity of fellowship where no barriers exist.

(6) Faithful Witnesses

The concept of "witness" is the term that links the two halves of Acts together. For the most part, Luke reserved the title "apostle" for the Twelve, indicating by it their unique role as witnesses to the ministry, death, and resurrection of Jesus (1:21f.). The term "witness" (martys) links the work of the Twelve (1:8) with Stephen (22:20) and with Paul (10:39-41; 13:31; 22:15; 26:16). All in their own way were witnesses to the risen Lord (26:16), but their primary role was to bear their faithful testimony (martyria) to his word.[139]

In Acts the role of witness is closely linked to that of discipleship. A true disciple is a faithful witness, not only willing to bear testimony to Christ but even to suffer for him. The word "witness" came in the later church to have just that connotation: a true witness is one who carries his or her testimony to the death. Our word "martyr" derives from this later usage of the Greek word for "witness" (*martys*). Whether the word carries such a connotation in Acts is doubtful, though its application to Stephen (22:20) comes close. That a faithful witness must be willing to suffer is expressed throughout Acts, particularly in the parallels drawn between the experiences of Jesus, Peter, Stephen, and Paul. These have often been noted, and the more striking of them are regularly pointed out in the commentary.[140] Peter's healings parallel those of Jesus in the Gospel of Luke.

---

[138]Esler (*Community and Gospel*, 71-109) points to the centrality of the issue of table fellowship in Luke-Acts.

[139]J. Dupont, "L' Apôtre comme intermédiaire du salut dans les Actes des Apôtres," *RTP* 112 (1980): 342-58; P. B. Mather, "Paul in Acts as 'Servant' and 'Witness,'" *BR* 30 (1985): 23-44.

[140]See A. J. Mattill, Jr., "The Jesus-Paul Parallels and the Purpose of Luke-Acts: H. H. Evans Reconsidered," *NovT* 17 (1975): 15-26.

Stephen's martyrdom bears striking resemblance to the trial and crucifixion of Jesus. Paul's final journey to Jerusalem, the mob in the temple square, the charges brought against him, and the trial scenes all have their counterparts in the passion narrative of Luke's Gospel. The careers of Peter and Paul even share links within Acts—similar miracles, escapes from prison, and the like. Luke seems to have brought his materials together and emphasized them in such a fashion as to highlight the correspondences—to present a sort of discipleship succession narrative. An overarching theme binds them all together: The true prophet, the faithful witness can expect suffering and rejection.[141] Stephen experienced firsthand the truth of this theme of his speech. But so did Peter and Paul, the other faithful witnesses in Acts. Perhaps this was Luke's way of illustrating the truth of Jesus' words: "A student . . . will be like his teacher" (Luke 6:40).

(7) Relationship to the World

The last half of Acts emphasizes the relationship of Christians to the Roman political authorities by two recurring patterns. First, the constant note that Paul was innocent of breaking any law is acknowledged by the magistrates of Philippi, declared by Gallio in Corinth, Lysias in Jerusalem, and in turn by Felix, Festus, and Agrippa II. The latter sums up the matter: Paul could have been released had he not appealed to Caesar (26:32). All the officials agreed that Paul had not broken any Roman law, and any charges the Jews had brought against him were solely a matter of internal Jewish religious disputes (cf. 18:15; 23:29; 25:19). Second, in many instances Roman officials stepped in to deliver Paul from Jewish threats to his life—Gallio at Corinth, Lysias from the temple mob and the plot of the forty zealots to ambush Paul, eventually Caesar himself with the right of appeal, which rescued Paul from the prospect of an unjust trial in Jerusalem. Many interpreters have seen in these emphases an apologetic motive—an appeal to the Roman authorities to acknowledge Christian innocence of any political crimes and to secure their tolerance and protection. It has sometimes been argued that the Romans had a list of legal and illegal religions and that this apologetic motif was designed to secure Christian recognition as a sect of Judaism and protection under Judaism's status as a legal religion (religio licita).[142] There are serious problems with this view. For one, no evidence demonstrates that the

---

[141]D. Moessner traces this "rejected prophet" emphasis to the Deuteronomistic tradition, "'The Christ Must Suffer': New Light on the Jesus-Peter, Stephen, Paul Parallels in Luke-Acts," *NovT* 28 (1986): 220-56.

[142]For the *religio licita* view, see B. S. Easton, *Early Christianity: The Purpose of Acts and Other Papers* (London: SPCK, 1955), 41-57.

Romans had such a list.[143] Second, it is doubtful that this emphasis in Acts was directed to Roman officials. The Romans are simply not depicted in an altogether favorable light. Felix was controlled by his avarice. Festus could not live by his own standards of justice but was willing to compromise them out of favoritism to the Jews. If Luke had really wanted to appeal to the Romans, he would scarcely have pictured them in so unflattering a light.

More likely this emphasis in Acts is directed to Christian readers as a realistic assessment of the political situation. Paul exemplified how to relate to the system. He experienced considerable injustice at the hands of Roman justice, being held in prison for an undue length of time by officials who had already acknowledged his innocence. But Paul never gave up. He made use of the legal rights he possessed—using his citizenship rights, appealing to Caesar. And Paul was careful not to transgress a law. Clearly whatever he suffered at the hands of the political authorities was not due to any civil crime on his part but solely to his witness for Christ (cf. 1 Pet 4:15f.). Another side to the "Roman" emphasis is the favorable action of the Roman officials toward the Christians, which showed them as possible candidates for witness. It was not by accident that Paul witnessed to Roman officials like Sergius Paulus and Felix. Through Paul's example Luke set forth a realistic political agenda for his Christian readers: give no grounds for charges against you, use what legal rights you have, be willing to suffer for your faith, and bear your witness where you can. Even Rome could be won to Christ.[144]

(8) Triumph of the Gospel

The story of Acts can perhaps be summarized in the single phrase "the triumph of the gospel." It is a triumphant story of how the early Christian community in the power of the Spirit saturated their world with the message of God's salvation in Jesus Christ. It was not an easy path. There were obstacles from within. Old assumptions were challenged. Opinions had to be revised and prejudices overcome as the Spirit led to an ever more inclusive people of God. There were abundant obstacles from without—imprisonments, beatings, martyrdoms, storms at sea and angry mobs on land. But the faithful witnesses continued their testimony. The word of God grew, bearing ever more fruit among both Jews and Gentiles. The Spirit of God was behind it all, and the gospel triumphed.

---

[143]Maddox, Purpose of Luke-Acts, 91-93.

[144]On the political perspectives of Luke-Acts, see also P. W. Walaskay, "'And so we came to Rome': The Political Perspective of St. Luke" (Cambridge: University Press, 1983); R. J. Cassidy and P. J. Scharper, eds., Political Issues in Luke-Acts (Maryknoll, N.Y.: Orbis, 1983); R. J. Cassidy, Society and Politics in the Acts of the Apostles (Maryknoll, N.Y.: Orbis, 1988).

A danger in such triumph is the arrogance of a lopsided "theology of glory." The picture of the faithful witnesses in Acts must be placed alongside that of the triumphant word.[145] There is no arrogance there—only persecution, suffering, even death. The witnesses do not triumph—the *word* triumphs, and the word only triumphs when the witnesses are faithful servants. Only in being open to the Spirit of God were the witnesses of Acts able to fulfill the divine commission. Often the Spirit almost had to override their will, as in Peter's struggle to understand how God could include Cornelius and his fellow Gentiles. There is no room for arrogance here—only humility and openness to God's direction.

The Book of Acts is in a real sense a book for renewal. It calls the church back to its roots—to the early church in the upper room in its undivided devotion to prayer, to its missionary fervor, its fellowship and sharing, its mutual trust and unity. It sets a pattern for faithful discipleship, for a witness that walks in the footsteps of the Master, a wholehearted commitment with a willingness to sacrifice and even to suffer. It speaks to us when discouraged, reminding us that all time is in God's hands, reassuring us of the reality of his Spirit in our lives and witness. It challenges us to open our hearts to the power of the Spirit that we might be faithful witnesses to the word and come to experience anew its triumph in our own time.

12. The Structure of Acts

Acts falls naturally into two divisions: the mission of the Jerusalem church (chaps. 1–12) and the mission of Paul (chaps. 13–28). Each of these may be subdivided into two main parts. In the Jerusalem portion chaps. 1–5 treat the early church in Jerusalem; chaps. 6–12, the outreach beyond Jerusalem. In the Pauline portion 13:1–21:16 relates the three major missions of Paul; 21:27–28:31 deals with Paul's defense of his ministry. The following outline has been subdivided still further for convenient chapter length. Chapters I and II cover the Jerusalem portion of Acts. Chapters III and IV relate the breakthrough to the Gentile mission. Chapters V-VII are each devoted to one of Paul's three major mission periods. Chapter VIII relates Paul's arrest in Jerusalem and his defense speeches. Chapter IX concludes with Paul's voyage and arrival in Rome.

---

[145]J. Roloff, "Die Paulus-Darstellung des Lukas," *EvT* 6 (1979): 510-31. R. Brown warns of the opposite danger that a declining congregation might become discouraged by the picture of the triumphant word in Acts: *The Churches the Apostles Left Behind* (New York: Paulist, 1984), 61-74.

———————— *OUTLINE OF THE BOOK* ————————

I. The Spirit Empowers the Church for Witness (1:1–2:47)
   1. Literary Prologue (1:1-2)
   2. Instructions Preparatory to Pentecost (1:3-5)
   3. Christ's Legacy: The Call to Witness (1:6-8)
   4. The Ascension of Christ (1:9-11)
   5. Preparation in the Upper Room (1:12-14)
   6. Restoration of the Apostolic Circle (1:15-26)
      (1) Judas's Defection (1:15-20a)
      (2) Matthias's Installation (1:20b-26)
   7. Miracle at Pentecost (2:1-13)
      (1) The Gift of the Spirit (2:1-4)
      (2) The Witness to the Spirit (2:5-13)
   8. Peter's Sermon at Pentecost (2:14-41)
      (1) Scriptural Proof Concerning the Pentecost Experience (2:14-21)
      (2) Scriptural Proof Concerning Christ's Messiahship (2:22-36)
      (3) Invitation and Response (2:37-41)
   9. The Common Life of the Community (2:42-47)
II. The Apostles Witness to the Jews in Jerusalem (3:1–5:42)
   1. Peter's Healing a Lame Beggar (3:1-11)
   2. Peter's Sermon from Solomon's Colonnade (3:12-26)
   3. Peter and John before the Sanhedrin (4:1-22)
      (1) Arrested and Interrogated (4:1-12)
      (2) Warned and Released (4:13-22)
   4. The Prayer of the Community (4:23-31)
   5. The Common Life of the Community (4:32-37)
   6. A Serious Threat to the Common Life (5:1-11)
   7. The Miracles Worked by the Apostles (5:12-16)
   8. All the Apostles before the Council (5:17-42)
      (1) Arrest, Escape, and Rearrest (5:17-26)
      (2) Appearance before Sanhedrin (5:27-40)
      (3) Release and Witness (5:41-42)
III. The Hellenists Break Through to a Wider Witness (6:1–8:40)
   1. Introduction of the Seven (6:1-7)
   2. Stephen's Arrest and Trial (6:8–7:1)
   3. Stephen's Speech before the Sanhedrin (7:2-53)
   4. Stephen's Martyrdom (7:54–8:1a)
   5. Persecution and Dispersal of the Hellenists (8:1b-3)
   6. The Witness of Philip (8:4-40)
      (1) The Mission in Samaria (8:4-25)
      (2) The Witness to the Ethiopian Treasurer (8:26-40)

――――――――――――― *SECTION OUTLINE* ―――――――――――――

I. THE SPIRIT EMPOWERS THE CHURCH FOR WITNESS (1:1–2:47)
   1. Literary Prologue (1:1-2)
   2. Instructions Preparatory to Pentecost (1:3-5)
   3. Christ's Legacy: The Call to Witness (1:6-8)
   4. The Ascension of Christ (1:9-11)
   5. Preparation in the Upper Room (1:12-14)
   6. Restoration of the Apostolic Circle (1:15-26)
      (1) Judas's Defection (1:15-20a)
      (2) Matthias's Installation (1:20b-26)
   7. The Miracle at Pentecost (2:1-13)
      (1) The Gift of the Spirit (2:1-4)
          The Setting (2:1)
          The Event (2:2-4)
      (2) The Witness to the Spirit (2:5-13)
          The Gathering of the Crowd (2:5-8)
          The Composition of the Crowd (2:9-11a)
          The Response of the Crowd (2:11b-13)
   8. Peter's Sermon at Pentecost (2:14-41)
      (1) Scriptural Proof Concerning the Pentecost Experience
          (2:14-21)
      (2) Scriptural Proof Concerning Christ's Messiahship (2:22-36)
      (3) Invitation and Response (2:37-41)
   9. The Common Life of the Community (2:42-47)

――――――――――― **I. THE SPIRIT EMPOWERS** ―――――――――――
THE CHURCH FOR WITNESS (1:1–2:47)

The first two chapters of Acts revolve around the miracle of Pentecost.
Everything in chap. 1 is related to that event. The risen Jesus instructed
the apostles to wait in Jerusalem for the coming of the Holy Spirit (1:4-
5). Immediately prior to his ascension, he commissioned them for a
worldwide mission and promised that they would be empowered for this
by the Holy Spirit (1:8). Following the ascension, the apostles returned to
Jerusalem to the upper room and engaged in fervent prayer, awaiting the
promised Spirit (1:12-14). But it was necessary that the apostolic circle of
witnesses be complete so that all might experience the gift of the Spirit,
and Matthias was chosen to replace Judas (1:15-26). Then the Spirit came
with great power (2:1-5). The Spirit-filled apostles began to witness to a

large crowd, which represented "every nation under heaven"; and all in the crowd heard this in their own native languages (2:6-13). As spokesman for the apostles, Peter seized the opportunity to deliver his first sermon in Acts (2:14-40), and 3,000 were convicted and baptized (2:41). The newborn "church" consolidated by developing a close community of learning, worshiping, and sharing; and the Spirit of the Lord continued to bless their witness by adding to their numbers daily (2:47). The entire narrative of Acts that follows will show the ever-increasing scope of their witness as they were directed and empowered by the Holy Spirit.

1. Literary Prologue (1:1-2)

[1]In my former book, Theophilus, I wrote about all that Jesus began to do and to teach [2]until the day he was taken up to heaven, after giving instructions through the Holy Spirit to the apostles he had chosen.

Of all the New Testament writers, only Luke used the form of a literary prologue.[1] Such prologues were a convention with the writers of his day, and the use of them suggests that Luke saw himself as a producer of literature for the learned public.[2] Acts begins with a "secondary prologue," a device used for introducing new segments to works consisting of more than one book. Luke's, of course, was a two-volume work; and Luke 1:1-4 is the "primary preface" for his entire work, including Acts.[3] In Hellenistic literature a secondary preface usually consisted of a brief summary of the prior volume followed by a short introduction to the matter to be covered in the new volume. The preface of Acts gives a summary of the Third Gospel: "All that Jesus began to do and to teach until the day he was taken up." There is, however, no introduction to the content of the new

---

[1]Commentators differ about the extent of the prologue. G. Schneider sees the prologue as vv. 1-3, *Die Apostelgeschichte*, HTKNT (Freiburg: Herder, 1980), 1:187-88. H. Conzelmann sets the prologue at vv. 1-4: *Acts of the Apostles*, trans. J. Limburg, A. Kraabel, and D. Juel, Her (Philadelphia: Fortress, 1987), 3-4. F. F. Bruce treats vv. 1-5 as the prologue: *Commentary on the Book of Acts*, NIC (Grand Rapids: Eerdmans, 1977), 30. (Hereafter referred to as *Acts*: NIC.) E. Haenchen takes vv. 1-8 as the prologue: *The Acts of the Apostles*, trans. B. Noble and G. Shinn (Philadelphia: Westminster, 1971), 136-47. Since the literary convention appears only in vv. 1-2, it seems more natural to limit the prologue to them, as does B. Reicke, *Glaube und Leben der Urgemeinde: Bemerkungen zu Apg. 1-7* (Zurich: Zwingli, 1957), 9-11; and M. Dibelius, *Studies in the Acts of the Apostles*, ed. H. Greeven (London: SCM, 1956), 194.

[2]For a discussion of Hellenistic prologues, see H. J. Cadbury, *The Making of Luke-Acts* (New York: Macmillan, 1927), 194-204; V. K. Robbins, "Prefaces in Greco-Roman Biography and Luke-Acts," *Perspectives in Religious Studies* 6 (1979): 94-108.

[3]See R. Stein, *Luke*, vol. 24, NAC (Nashville: Broadman, forthcoming) for a full treatment of the Lukan preface. Luke's dependence on "eyewitnesses and servants of the word" as well as his desire to present "an orderly account" apply as much to Acts as to his Gospel.

volume.[4] The book is dedicated to Theophilus, without the formality of the title "most excellent" found in the first volume (Luke 1:3).[5]

1:1 Since the etymology of Theophilus yields "loved by God" or "lover of God," many attempts have been made to see the name as symbolic, a suggestion first made by Origen. As "lover of God" some would identify him with "God-fearers" like Cornelius (Acts 10), but Luke used a different terminology for them than "God-lover."[6] There is no need to see the name as symbolic since Theophilus is a good Greek name, well-documented from as early as the third century B.C. Neither is there warrant for identifying him with a specific Theophilus otherwise known or to speculate that he may have been Paul's defense lawyer before Caesar in Rome, with Luke-Acts being written as his legal brief.[7] One would assume that Theophilus was a Christian himself whom Luke was seeking to undergird with the "certainty of the things [he] had been taught" (Luke 1:4). Though Luke surely intended his work for the whole Christian community, Theophilus may have received the special dedication for being a patron who helped defray some of the costs of Luke's writing.

Luke referred to his Gospel as his "former book." The Greek text reads literally "first" book, but the NIV translators were surely correct in translating "former." In classical Greek the word "first" was used only in series that consisted of more than two, the word "former" being used for series of two. Some have used this observation to argue that Luke must have intended a third volume. Such a supposition might help alleviate the abrupt ending of Acts (the outcome of Paul's appeal is never related), but it cannot be based on the linguistic argument because the word "first" was the normal Greek word in Luke's day used in series of two.[8] There is no evidence Luke intended a third volume.

Luke summarized his Gospel with the utmost brevity—"all that Jesus began to do and to teach." The unusual construction "began to" has been noted by many. It may imply that the work is unfinished. The work and words of Jesus continue throughout Acts in the ministry of the apostles

---

[4]C. H. Talbert cites books 8 and 13 of Josephus's *Antiquities* as examples of other Hellenistic prefaces that lack the summary to the new volume: *Acts*, KPG (Atlanta: John Knox, 1984), 6.

[5]Probably no inferences should be drawn from the lack of the title in Acts other than its being in a secondary preface, briefer and less formal. Suggestions such as that Luke was treating him less formally because he had become a Christian between the writing of the two prefaces are unnecessary.

[6]His terms are *seboumenoi* and *phoboumenoi*.

[7]Bruce, *Acts*: NIC, 31, cites J. I. Still for the "legal brief" theory and B. H. Streeter for the suggestion that Theophilus was Titus Flavius Clemens, the cousin of the Emperor Domitian.

[8]K. Lake and H. J. Cadbury, *The Beginnings of Christianity*, Part I: *The Acts of the Apostles*, vol. 4, ETC (London: Macmillan, 1933), 2. (Hereafter cited as *Beginnings.*)

and other faithful Christian witnesses. It still goes on in the work of the church today.[9] The summary ends with a reference to the ascension, which marked the closure to the story of Jesus in Luke's Gospel (Luke 24:50f.). In Acts the ascension marks the beginning of the story of the church.[10]

1:2 In a real sense the summary ends and the new story begins in the last half of v. 2, where mention is made of Jesus' instructions to his disciples before his ascension.[11] In his Gospel, Luke already mentioned this period when Jesus instructed his disciples after the resurrection, opening their understanding of the Scriptures, commissioning them for a mission to all the nations, and promising the gift of the Spirit (Luke 24:44-49). This period of instruction and its closure at the ascension will receive fuller attention in the narrative of Acts that immediately follows (1:3-11). The period of instruction was a time of transition. In the Gospel it was the time when Jesus completed his earthly ministry. In Acts it was the time when Jesus prepared the apostles for theirs.

One interesting question remains in the last half of v. 2. How does the Holy Spirit fit in? The NIV translates "after giving instructions through the Holy Spirit." The account in Luke 24:44-49, however, has the risen Jesus personally instructing the disciples, as does Acts 1:3-8. The Greek order is somewhat ambiguous in verse 2b and could also be translated "after giving instructions to the apostles whom he had chosen through the Holy Spirit."[12] Either translation shows a close connection of Jesus with the Holy Spirit, and this is fully in accord with the picture in Luke's Gospel. During Jesus' ministry, there is no reference to the Holy Spirit being upon anyone except Jesus. The Spirit descended upon him at his baptism (Luke 3:22), filled him as he returned from the Jordan (Luke 4:1), led him both in and out of the wilderness (Luke 4:1,14), and rested upon him in his programmatic sermon at Nazareth (Luke 4:18).[13] The introduction of

---

[9]A point well emphasized by D. J. Williams, *Acts*, GNC (San Francisco: Harper & Row, 1985), 2.

[10]For a literary analysis of Luke's closure of his Gospel and opening of Acts, see M. C. Parsons, "The Ascension Narratives in Luke-Acts," Ph.D. diss., Southern Baptist Theological Seminary, 1985.

[11]The time of the ascension has long created problems, since it takes place forty days after the resurrection in Acts and seemingly on the day of the resurrection in Luke 24:51. The Western text seems to have attempted to solve the problem by omitting the references to the ascension in both Luke 24:51 and Acts 1:2. Lake, however, argues in favor of the Western omission at Acts 1:2, "The Preface to Acts and the Composition of Acts," *Beginnings*, vol. 5: *Additional Notes*, 1-7.

[12]Schneider (*Apostelgeschichte* 1:192) lists T. Zahn, A. Loisy, and R. Pesch as being in agreement with him in connecting the Spirit with the *selection* of the apostles.

[13]The sermon at Nazareth has long been recognized as programmatic for Luke-Acts. It sets the theme for the Jewish rejection of Jesus and the "witnesses" of Acts as well as that

the Spirit in Acts 1:2 is probably not incidental for Luke. He emphasized that the same Spirit who rested upon Jesus in his ministry would empower the apostles for witness. And the same Jesus who taught them during his earthly life would continue to instruct them through the presence of the Spirit once they experienced the Spirit through the presence of Jesus. Formerly they had experienced the Spirit through the presence of Jesus. After Pentecost they would experience Jesus through the presence of the Spirit.

2. Instructions Preparatory to Pentecost (1:3-5)

³After his suffering, he showed himself to these men and gave many convincing proofs that he was alive. He appeared to them over a period of forty days and spoke about the kingdom of God. ⁴On one occasion, while he was eating with them, he gave them this command: "Do not leave Jerusalem, but wait for the gift my Father promised, which you have heard me speak about. ⁵For John baptized with water, but in a few days you will be baptized with the Holy Spirit."

1:3 In vv. 3-5 Luke delineated some of the instructions to the disciples referred to in v. 2. As there, the setting was the period after Jesus' death and resurrection.[14] He began by providing them with "many convincing proofs that he was alive" (3a). The word for "proofs" (*tekmēriois*) is a technical term from logic, meaning "demonstrative proof, evidence."[15] Luke had already given vivid examples of these proofs in his Gospel: on the Emmaus road (24:13-32), to Peter (24:34), and to the disciples (24:36-43). The appearances to the apostles are absolutely essential for their primary role in Acts of being witnesses to his resurrection (1:22; 2:32; 3:15; 5:32; 10:39-41; 13:31).[16]

The appearances lasted "over a period of forty days" (see n. 16). The picture is that of a continual coming and going of the risen Lord rather than of one extended stay. In all the New Testament, this is the only reference that explicitly delimits the period of appearances to forty days.[17] It

---

of the inclusion of the Gentiles.

[14]The NIV translates the phrase μετὰ τὸ παθεῖν αὐτὸν as "after his suffering," which refers to the whole passion event, including both death and resurrection.

[15]*Beginnings* 4:4. See also D. L. Mealand, "The Phrase 'Many Proofs' in Acts 1, 3 and in Hellenistic Writers," *ZNW* 80 (1989): 134-35.

[16]The long list of appearances in 1 Cor 15:5-8 would seem to allow for an extended time of appearances. Luke, however, would probably quibble with Paul over his experience being of the same order as the others. In Acts the resurrection appearances stop with the ascension.

[17]It is often noted that this seems to conflict with Luke 24:51, where the ascension took place on the same day as the resurrection. Some would resolve this by seeing the reference in Luke 24:51 as only a temporary departure during the period of appearances, but the language ("borne up into heaven") and the setting (Bethany, on Mount of Olives) point to an ascension. One could, of course, opt for the Western text and omit the phrase altogether. The

is a time frame with rich biblical associations—the period in the wilderness, the time Moses spent on Sinai receiving the law, the period of Elijah's sojourn on Mt. Horeb. Most of all it evokes the period of Jesus' temptation in the wilderness (Luke 4:2). Just as it was a time when Jesus prepared for his ministry, so for forty days the risen Jesus prepared his followers for theirs.[18] From the viewpoint of chronology it should also be noted that the forty days fit the dating of Pentecost: resurrection on the third day, appearances for forty days, approximately a week in the upper room (1:12-14), and then Pentecost, fifty days from the crucifixion (2:1).

Not only did Jesus give the apostles proof of his resurrection, but he also continued to instruct them in the "kingdom of God" (v. 3a), just as he had done during his earthly life. The kingdom, always with the meaning of God's reign or rule, had been the main subject of Jesus' teaching. In Acts the terms are much less common than in the Gospels, occurring only five more times (8:12; 19:8; 20:25; 28:23, 31).[19] Other words like "gospel" naturally replace the phrase in Acts, since in light of the resurrection one enters the kingdom by responding to the good news about Christ. In spite of the sparse references, God's kingdom is a central concern of Acts, and it is interesting to note that the book begins (1:3) and ends (28:31) on that theme.

1:4 Verse 4 speaks of one of the occasions when the risen Jesus appeared to his disciples. He is said to have been "eating with them." This translates a Greek verb that does not occur elsewhere in this exact form. The word has several possible derivations, and translations differ accordingly: (1) *assemble, gather together with*; (2) *lodge or spend the night with*; (3) *share salt*, i.e., *eat with*.[20] The NIV has gone with the third alternative. It fits in well with Jesus' appearance to his disciples in Luke 24:43, where he ate in their presence. On this occasion Jesus commanded

---

most likely solution is to consider Luke's literary purpose. The ascension in the Gospel serves to give closure to the Gospel. Luke was not concerned to deal extensively with the ascension in his Gospel. He would do that in Acts. He only wanted to give a suitable closure to the story of Jesus, and the ascension was the logical point of closure. Chronology was not his concern. His only connecting links between pericopes are a vague δε (vv. 44,50). Anyone familiar with Luke's linking devices and chronological notes should know that those δε's could represent almost any period of time. In point of fact, Luke 24:44-53 is almost a summary of the first chapter of Acts and probably should be interpreted by it.

[18] See G. Lohfink, *Die Himmelfahrt Jesu* (München: Kosel, 1971), 176-86; J. F. Maile, "The Ascension in Luke-Acts," *TB* 37 (1986): 53. Later Gnostic systems lengthened the period of resurrection appearances considerably to allow for Jesus' esoteric instruction of their group—eighteen months for the Valentinians, 550 days in the *Ap. Jas.* (Conzelmann, *Acts*, 6). Some suggest that Luke's strict delimitation of the forty days may have been directed at such Gnostic speculation (e.g., Schneider, *Apostelgeschichte*, I, 194).

[19] A. T. Robertson, *WP* 3:7.

[20] Robertson, *WP* 3:7, opts for "assemble." For "spending the night," see *Beginnings* 5:5.

his disciples to remain in Jerusalem and await the gift of the Father. The Greek construction can be rendered quite literally, "Stop departing from Jerusalem," implying that at this point the disciples had been coming and going from the Holy City.[21] They were to remain there and await the Father's promise. That promise has already been introduced in Luke 24:49 ("clothed with power from on high") and is made explicit in the following verse in Acts ("you will be baptized with the Holy Spirit").

1:5 The promise of the Spirit is specified in v. 5 with a reminder of the tradition attributed to John the Baptist in the Gospels: "He will baptize you with the Holy Spirit and with fire" (Luke 3:16; cf. Mark 1:8; Matt 3:11; John 1:33). The reference is to the unique, unrepeatable event at Pentecost when the Holy Spirit was poured out on the disciples in a visible form like fire (2:3). John's was a baptism of repentance, and the church would continue to use the outward form of his water baptism as a confession of the name of Jesus on entry into the community of believers (2:38a). Unlike John's baptism, the new converts would also receive the presence and power of the Holy Spirit (2:38b). Throughout Acts new converts experienced repentance, baptism, and the gift of the Spirit. All three are essential elements of the conversion experience. The succeeding narrative of Acts shows no set pattern in which these various elements appear. The Spirit can come before baptism (10:47), in conjunction with baptism (2:38), or some time after baptism (8:16). The Spirit's presence in the lives of believers is also evidenced in less dramatic ways such as the Ethiopian's joy (8:39), Lydia's hospitality (16:15), and the Philippian jailer's offer of first-aid (16:33). Although the Spirit cannot be tied to a mechanistic pattern, these patterns show that repentance and the gift of the Spirit are essential to the conversion experience.[22]

3. Christ's Legacy: The Call to Witness (1:6-8)

[6]So when they met together, they asked him, "Lord, are you at this time going to restore the kingdom to Israel?"

[7]He said to them: "It is not for you to know the times or dates the Father has set by his own authority. [8]But you will receive power when the Holy Spirit comes on you; and you will be my witnesses in Jerusalem, and in all Judea and Samaria, and to the ends of the earth."

---

[21]Lake (*Beginnings* 5:7-16) suggests that the disciples had been spending the night at Bethany, as Jesus had done during his days in Jerusalem prior to the passion. That they may have been departing from Jerusalem also allows for the Galilean appearance traditions, which are not otherwise mentioned in the Lukan appearance narratives. See Reicke, *Glaube und Leben* 14-15, for the intriguing suggestion that Luke's silence on the Galilean appearances may have been due to the "revolutionary" associations of Galilean Judaism.

[22]This point is convincingly demonstrated by J. D. G. Dunn in *Baptism in the Holy Spirit* (Philadelphia: Westminster, 1970), *passim.*

1:6-8 Verses 6-8 are closely tied together. In v. 6 the disciples asked Jesus about the time of the kingdom. In v. 7 Jesus rejected speculation about "times" altogether and in v. 8 replaced this with the relevant subject—the Christian task in the interim period before the kingdom's coming.

The setting of the disciples' question is rather vague, "when they met together" (v. 6). The verses that follow clarify that this was the last time Jesus appeared to them, just prior to his ascension (v. 9), and that the location was the Mount of Olives (v. 12). It is not surprising from Jesus' prior remarks about the coming of the Spirit and the fulfillment of God's promises (v. 5) that the disciples concluded the final coming of God's kingdom might have been imminent. In Jewish thought God's promises often referred to the coming of Israel's final salvation, and this concept is reflected elsewhere in Acts (cf. 2:39; 13:23, 32; 26:6).[23] Likewise, the outpouring of the Spirit had strong eschatological associations. Such passages as Joel 2:28-32 were interpreted in nationalistic terms that saw a general outpouring of the Spirit on Israel as a mark of the final great messianic Day of the Lord when Israel would be "restored" to the former glory of the days of David and Solomon.

Jesus corrected the disciples by directing them away from the question about "times or dates" (v. 7).[24] These are matters wholly within God's own purposes and authority. During his earthly life Jesus had denied such knowledge even for himself (Mark 13:32).[25] In denying such knowledge to the disciples, the hope in the Parousia is not abandoned.[26] If anything, it is intensified by the vivid picture of Jesus returning on the clouds of heaven in the same mode as his ascension (Acts 1:11). Neither did Jesus reject the concept of the "restoration of Israel."[27] Instead, he "depoliti-

---

[23]J. Munck, *The Acts of the Apostles*, rev. W. F. Albright and C. S. Mann, AB (Garden City: Doubleday, 1967), 4.

[24]Probably no great distinction is intended here between the words "times" (χρόνους) and "dates" (καιρούς).

[25]The Western text of Acts reads "no one can know" instead of "it is not for you to know," which Lake and Foakes-Jackson prefer as the *lectio difficilior*, *Beginnings* 4:8.

[26]Many scholars see Acts 1:7-8 as Luke's attempt to deal with the delayed Parousia. Luke replaced the expectation of the Lord's imminent return with a "salvation history" (Haenchen, 143; Conzelmann, 6-7). More likely Luke shared the prophetic view that the final times depended on the successful Gentile mission.

[27]The question of the Jews in Luke-Acts is a thorny one, with radically divergent viewpoints among the scholars. For the view that Luke totally wrote off the Jews, see J. T. Sanders, *The Jews in Luke-Acts* (Philadelphia: Fortress, 1987). For the view that Luke-Acts was written primarily from a Jewish perspective, see J. Jervell, *Luke and the People of God* (Minneapolis: Augsburg, 1972). That the prophetic concept of a restored Israel is central to Luke-Acts is argued by D. L. Tiede, "The Exaltation of Jesus and the Restoration of Israel in Acts 1," *HTR* 79 (1986): 278-86. See also idem., *Prophecy and History in Luke-Acts* (Philadelphia: Fortress, 1980).

cized it" with the call to a worldwide mission.[28] The disciples were to be the true, "restored" Israel, fulfilling its mission to be a "light for the Gentiles" so that God's salvation might reach "to the ends of the earth" (Isa 49:6). In short, to speculate on times and dates is useless. The Lord's return does not revolve around such speculation but around God's own purposes, and those purposes embrace the salvation of the world. The surest route to the Parousia is the evangelization of the world.

Verse 8 places the disciples' question in proper perspective. The "restoration of the kingdom" involves a worldwide mission. Jesus promised the disciples two things: power and witness. The future tense here has an imperatival sense: "you *will* [must] receive power"; "you *will* be my witnesses." Luke stressed this commission from the risen Lord at the close of his Gospel (24:47-49).[29] All the same elements are there—the witness, the call to the nations, the power of the Spirit. The power they were to receive was divine power; the word is *dynamis*, the same word used of Jesus' miracles in the Gospels. It is the *Spirit's* power (2:1-21). The endowment with the Spirit is the prelude to, the equipping for, mission. The role of the apostles is that of "witness" (*martys*).[30] In Acts the apostles' main role is depicted as witnessing to the earthly ministry of Jesus, above all to his resurrection (cf. 1:22; 2:32; 3:15; 5:32; 10:39,41). As eyewitnesses only they were in the position to be guarantors of the resurrection. But with its root meaning of *testimony*, "witness" comes to have an almost legal sense of bearing one's testimony to Christ. In this way it is applied to Stephen (22:20) and to Paul (22:15; 23:11; 26:16). The background to this concept is probably the servant psalms of Isaiah, where God called on his servant to be a witness (Isa 43:10; 44:8).[31] L. Keck notes the close connection between the Spirit's power and the witness to Jesus, observing that what was true of those first apostolic witnesses is still true of witnesses today: "The less Jesus is the core of witness, the less power we have."[32]

The geographical scope of Acts 1:8 provides a rough outline of the entire book: Jerusalem (1-7), Judea and Samaria (8-12), the ends of the

---

[28]R. Pesch, *Die Apostelgeschichte*, Teilband I: *Apg. 1-12* (Zurich: Benziger, 1986), 70-71.

[29]J. Dupont, *Nouvelles Etudes sur les Actes des Apôtres*, Lectio divina 118 (Paris: Cerf, 1984), 49-52.

[30]The Greek word μαρτυς ("witness") came to have in later Christian literature the sense of "martyr," one who bore testimony even to death. The only place it could possibly have such a meaning in Acts is 22:20 in connection with Stephen.

[31]W. O. Carver, *The Acts of the Apostles* (Nashville: Southern Baptist Sunday School Board, 1916), 15.

[32]L. E. Keck, "Listening to and Listening for: From Text to Sermon (Acts 1:8)," *Int* 27 (1973): 197.

earth (13–28). As such it can well be considered the "theme" verse of Acts. It is not by accident that Jerusalem came first. In Luke's Gospel, Jerusalem was central, from the temple scenes of the infancy narrative to the long central journey to Jerusalem (9:51–19:28), to Jesus' passion in the city that killed its prophets (13:34). The story of Jesus led *to* Jerusalem; the story of the church led *from* Jerusalem. Judea and Samaria are probably to be taken together; Judea was understood in the sense of the Davidic kingdom, which would include the coastal territories and Galilee as well.[33] Samaria would be included within Judea in this broader sense, but it is mentioned separately because of its non-Jewish constituency. The "ends of the earth" are often taken as referring to Rome, since the story of Acts ends in that city.[34] The phrase is often found in the prophets, however, as an expression for distant lands; and such is the meaning in Isa 49:6, which may well lie behind Acts 1:8. In fact, the final verse in Acts (28:31), with Paul preaching "without hindrance" in Rome, suggests that the story has not reached its final destination—the witness continues.

4. The Ascension of Christ (1:9-11)

⁹After he said this, he was taken up before their very eyes, and a cloud hid him from their sight.
¹⁰They were looking intently up into the sky as he was going, when suddenly two men dressed in white stood beside them. ¹¹"Men of Galilee," they said, "why do you stand here looking into the sky? This same Jesus, who has been taken from you into heaven, will come back in the same way you have seen him go into heaven."

1:9-11 The ascension is related with the utmost brevity (v. 9), with the emphasis again being on the instruction to the disciples, this time by two heavenly messengers (vv. 10-11).

The ascension tradition is unique to Luke-Acts, in all the New Testament being found only here, in Acts 1:2, and in Luke 24:51, though it is implied in John 20:17. It is, however, closely related to the many New Testament texts that speak of Jesus' exaltation to the Father, such as 1 Tim 3:16; 1 Pet 3:21f.[35] What is unique to Luke's ascension narratives is that he depicted in pictorial form the final departure of the resurrected Lord from the earth, thus marking an end to the forty-day period of resurrection appearances. One should not get the picture that the ascended

---

[33] A. Schlatter, *Die Apostelgeschichte* (Stuttgart: Calwer, 1948), 6.

[34] *Pss. Sol.* 8:16 refers to Pompey's coming from the ends of the earth, which happened to be Rome; but even there the phrase seems to follow the Old Testament meaning of "distant lands" rather than reflecting a set epithet for Rome. In a recent article D. R. Schwartz argues that "end of the earth" refers only to the extreme borders of Israel ("The End of the Γῆ," *JBL* 105 [1986]: 669-76).

[35] I. H. Marshall, *The Acts of the Apostles*, TNTC (Leicester: Inter-Varsity, 1980), 60.

Christ was no longer active among believers. He continued to reveal himself to such as Stephen (7:56) and Paul (9:5). These visions, however, were not on the same order as the appearances over the forty days. These close with the ascension, and Jesus will not return to earth until the Parousia (v. 11).

The ascension narrative evokes rich biblical reminiscences—the translations of Enoch and Elijah, the cloud that enveloped Mt. Sinai. Indeed, clouds are often associated with theophanies.[36] One particularly thinks of the transfiguration narrative of Luke 9:28-36. The picture in Acts 1:9 is that of a cloud enveloping Jesus as he disappeared from sight, just as in Luke 9:34-36 the appearance of the cloud led to the disappearance of Moses and Elijah. The vivid pictorial depiction of Jesus' ascension into heaven serves to give tangible form to the apostles' testimony to the exaltation of Christ. Indeed, Luke stressed this by referring to their seeing and looking intently no fewer than five times in vv. 9-11, and he returned to the importance of their eyewitness in v. 22.

Luke did not dwell on the ascension. He quickly shifted the apostles' gaze back to earth (v. 10). Two men suddenly appeared beside them. They were angels, heavenly messengers, as their white garb indicated.[37] Angels often accompanied heavenly visitations as interpreters of the event, such as those who interpreted the significance of the empty tomb (Luke 24:4-9). Indeed, a striking parallel exists between the women who were rebuked for seeking "the living among the dead" (Luke 24:5) and the disciples who stood there "looking into the sky" (Acts 1:11) for one who had just returned to God's eternity beyond all creaturely bounds of earth and space. The angels addressed the apostles as "Men of Galilee" (literally, "Men, Galileans").[38] That their Galilean origin was highlighted may not be incidental. A strong Galilean witness motif is in Luke-Acts. The women of Galilee witnessed the crucifixion (Luke 23:49,55); at this point the men of Galilee became the apostolic witnesses to the ascension.[39]

The apostles' gaze into the sky is understandable after witnessing such a miracle. The angelic rebuke, however, is necessary. Moments of high

---

[36]For a thorough treatment of the ascension narrative, see Lohfink, *Himmelfahrt*. See also R. F. O'Toole, "Luke's Understanding of Jesus' Resurrection-Ascension-Exaltation," *BTB* 9 (1979): 106-14; J. A. Fitzmyer, "The Ascension of Christ and Pentecost," *TS* 45 (1984): 409-40. See also Parsons, *Ascension Narratives*.

[37]Compare Matt 28:3; John 20:12; Luke 24:4; also see Luke 9:29. The motif also appears in extrabiblical literature: 2 Macc 3:26, 11:8; *T. Levi* 8:2. See Lohfink, *Himmelfahrt*, 199-200.

[38]This striking double-noun form is a common Hellenistic form of address found in Thucydides, Plato, and Plutarch, among many others. See P. van der Horst, "Hellenistic Parallels to the Acts of the Apostles: 1:1-26," *ZNW* 74 (1983): 22.

[39]Lohfink, *Himmelfahrt*, 270.

spiritual experience are never ends in themselves. It was time to come down from the mountain and witness to what they had seen. The angelic rebuke was followed by a promise: "This same Jesus . . . will come back in the same way you have seen him go into heaven." It was a strong affirmation of Jesus' return—not just a promise but a reality concretized and affirmed by the ascension they had just witnessed.[40]

5. Preparation in the Upper Room (1:12-14)

[12]**Then they returned to Jerusalem from the hill called the Mount of Olives, a Sabbath day's walk from the city.** [13]**When they arrived, they went upstairs to the room where they were staying. Those present were Peter, John, James and Andrew; Philip and Thomas, Bartholomew and Matthew; James son of Alphaeus and Simon the Zealot, and Judas son of James.** [14]**They all joined together constantly in prayer, along with the women and Mary the mother of Jesus, and with his brothers.**

The apostles returned to Jerusalem in compliance with the Lord's command to wait there for the Spirit (cf. v. 4).[41] There they joined the other Christians in an upper room where they devoted themselves to fervent prayer (vv. 13-14).

1:12 In v. 12 we learn the setting of the ascension—the Mount of Olives.[42] Olivet lies to the east of Jerusalem on the opposite side of the Kidron Valley. The distance of their walk was a "Sabbath day's walk," which was the longest distance one could walk without breaking the Sabbath.[43] The rabbinic tradition set this at 2,000 cubits, i.e., about three-fourths of a mile, as the NIV note indicates. It is not necessary to conclude from this that the ascension took place on a Sabbath.[44] More likely Luke placed the ascension in close proximity to Jerusalem, the holy city

---

[40]Pesch, *Apostelgeschichte* 1:74, notes that Luke's treatment of the Parousia in Luke 21 links it closely to the success of the Gentile mission (cf. vv. 24,27).

[41]It is, of course, possible that some of the larger groups of disciples witnessed the ascension, but Luke seems to have implied that his narrative to this point had primarily involved only the eleven (v. 2). The subsequent narrative confirms this impression by linking the apostles with the ascension (v. 22).

[42]According to Luke 24:50 the ascension took place "in the vicinity of Bethany," which was on the opposite side of the Mount of Olives and several miles from Jerusalem. Williams suggests that the Greek of Luke 24:50 (ἕως πρὸς Βηθανίαν) should be taken quite literally—on the road *toward* Bethany: D. J. Williams, *Acts*, 17. The setting on the Mount of Olives may have had significance in light of Zech 14:4, according to which the Messiah will descend from heaven at Olivet.

[43]This was calculated by interpreting Exod 16:29 ("stay where he is") by Num 35:5, which measures the limits of a city at 2,000 cubits. One could thus not leave his "place" (city), i.e., go beyond its limits. See *Beginnings* 4:10.

[44]First suggested by Chrysostom according to R. B. Rackham, *The Acts of the Apostles* (London: Methuen, 1901), 9.

where Jesus died and rose, where the Spirit would be given, where the Christian witness would begin.

1:13 Upon their arrival in Jerusalem, the apostles went "upstairs to the room where they were staying." It is tempting to see this as the room where the last supper was held, but this is far from certain. Luke used different words for the two rooms (*katalyma*, Luke 22:11; *hyperōon*, Acts 1:13). There is even less basis for connecting it with the house of John Mark's mother, Mary (Acts 12:12). The upper room of Acts 1:13 seems to refer to the top floor of a large Palestinian house. Such rooms were usually on the third floor and reached by outside steps. They were often used as dining rooms, as study places for students, or were sublet to poorer people.[45] The list of disciples in v. 13 is identical with that of Luke 6:13-16, although in differing order and with the omission of Judas Iscariot. The reordering of the first names is possibly deliberate. Andrew was moved from second place in the Gospel to fourth place in Acts, and John was moved to second place. This gives prominence to Peter, John, and James, the only apostles who have any individual role in the narrative of Acts.

1:14 Verse 14 mentions others who were present in the upper room—"the women," Mary, and Jesus' brothers. The women may have included the wives of the apostles and certainly the women who accompanied Jesus from Galilee and witnessed his crucifixion (Luke 8:2; 23:55; 24:10).[46] Mary may have accompanied the beloved disciple (John 19:26), but it is likely she was a member of the believing community in her own right. Like Jesus' brothers, she was confused by Jesus' ministry (Mark 3:11; John 7:5). Like them she may have experienced an appearance from the risen Jesus. Paul mentioned such an appearance to James, the oldest of the brothers (1 Cor 15:7). According to Mark 6:3, Jesus had four brothers—James, Judas, Joseph, and Simon. There is no reason to take Mark's words in any other sense than that they were Jesus' half-brothers, the natural offspring of Mary and Joseph after the birth of Jesus.[47] James assumed the leadership of the Jerusalem church in the latter portion of Acts (12:17; 15:13; 21:18), and according to tradition Judas later assumed the same position and authored the Epistle of Jude.

---

[45]F. J. Foakes-Jackson, *The Acts of the Apostles*, MNTC (New York: Harper, 1931), 6.

[46]The Western witness codex Bezae replaces "the women" with "their wives and children."

[47]Some early church fathers, under the strong influence of a celibate ideology, suggested that they were of a different relationship to Jesus. Epiphanius maintained that they were Joseph's children by a previous marriage, thus protecting the "perpetual virginity" of Mary. Jerome argued that they were Jesus' cousins, the children of Mary's sister, thus protecting the virginity of Joseph as well. For a full discussion see J. H. Ropes, *The Epistle of St. James*, ICC (Edinburgh: T & T Clark, 1916), 53f.

Verse 14 is often viewed as the first of the "summaries" in Acts, those passages where Luke gave a generalized review of the activity of the Christian community. The primary characteristic that marked their life together in this period was prayer, as they anticipated together the promised gift of the Spirit. Prayer was a hallmark of the church in its early days (cf. 1:24; 2:42; 3:1; 4:24; 6:6).[48] The time before Pentecost was a time for waiting, a time spent in prayer undoubtedly for the promised Spirit and for the power to witness. There is no effective witness without the Spirit, and the way to spiritual empowerment is to wait in prayer.[49]

6. Restoration of the Apostolic Circle (1:15-26)

This entire section, devoted to the replacement of Judas Iscariot, is carefully constructed in two main parts. After an introductory verse (v. 15), the first part (vv. 16-19) deals with the vacancy created by the demise of Judas. The second treats Judas's replacement (vv. 21-26). Joining the two sections is v. 20, which contains two scriptural proofs from the Psalms, the first relating to the prior section (Judas's death); the second, to the following (his replacement).[50]

Judas's Defection (1:15-20a)

[15]In those days Peter stood up among the believers (a group numbering about a hundred and twenty) [16]and said, "Brothers, the Scripture had to be fulfilled which the Holy Spirit spoke long ago through the mouth of David concerning Judas, who served as guide for those who arrested Jesus—[17]he was one of our number and shared in this ministry."

[18](With the reward he got for his wickedness, Judas bought a field; there he fell headlong, his body burst open and all his intestines spilled out. [19]Everyone in Jerusalem heard about this, so they called that field in their language Akeldama, that is, Field of Blood.)

[20]"For," said Peter, "it is written in the book of Psalms,

" 'May his place be deserted;
let there be no one to dwell in it,' "

---

[48]A number of interpreters see the phrase "devoted themselves to prayer" (RSV) (προσκαρτεροῦντες . . . τῇ προσευχῇ) as a technical term for attending formal worship in the temple and synagogue. This is based on synagogue inscriptions that deal with manumitted slaves for whom the proviso is made that they must continue to attend synagogue worship, using this exact phraseology. See *Beginnings* 4:10-11 and T. C. G. Thornton, "'Continuing Steadfast in Prayer,' New Light on a New Testament Phrase," *ExpTim* 83 (1971): 23-24.

[49]For further exposition on this theme, see W. Willimon, *Acts*, INT (Atlanta: John Knox, 1988), 21.

[50]This analysis is indebted to J. Dupont, "La destinée de Judas prophetisée par David (Actes 1, 16-20)," *Etudes sur les Actes des Apôtres*, Lectio divina 45 (Paris: Cerf, 1967), 309-20.

1:15 "In those days" marks a transition to a new section.[51] During this period of prayer and waiting, one essential item of business had to be considered by the young Christian community—the reconstitution of the apostolic circle of Twelve. Significantly, Luke made the parenthetical remark that the group numbered about 120 "believers." "Believers" is a correct rendering of the Greek ("brothers"), since the term was not gender specific and would include female as well as male members of the community. The number is also significant. In rabbinic tradition 120 was the minimum requirement for constituting a local Sanhedrin.[52] Peter assumed leadership among the apostles and convened the assembly. Throughout Acts, Peter played this role. He was the spokesman, the representative apostle. The other apostles were present and active, but Peter was their mouthpiece.[53]

1:16 Addressing the assembly,[54] Peter referred to the Scripture that the Holy Spirit inspired through David.[55] Peter said here that "the Scripture *had to* be fulfilled," using the *past* tense of the verb for necessity (*edei*, "it was necessary"). The Scripture he was referring to is Ps 69:25, which is quoted in v. 20a. Peter saw that psalm as pointing to the desertion of Judas's place, which had already been fulfilled. In v. 20b, Ps 109:8 is quoted, which points to another person assuming his place of leadership. This had not been fulfilled yet, so Peter used the present tense of the verb for necessity in v. 21, "it *is* necessary" (*dei*). The fulfillment of that Scripture constituted the main agenda item for the assembly. This use of the verb for necessity in connection with Scripture reflects a view that runs throughout Acts: Scripture that has a prophetic emphasis must come to fulfillment.[56]

1:17 In v. 17 Peter introduced the business at hand, the replacement of Judas. In language filled with Old Testament allusions (cf. Ps 41:9), he

---

[51]This Greek phrase marks off a new division at Acts 6:1 ("in those days"); 11:27 ("during this time"). This could be an indication that with v. 14 the introductory narrative ends (all of 1-14 has its parallel in Luke 24), and at v. 15 the new story begins.

[52]One member of the council for each ten males (*m. Sanh.* 1:6). The Christian assembly with twelve apostles as leaders would thus consist of 120. There is not a perfect analogy to the Jewish pattern since the Christian group also included females (v. 14).

[53]This role is perhaps anticipated in Luke 22:32.

[54]Peter addressed them as Ἄνδρες, ἀδελφοί. The occurrence of ἄνδρες would seem to indicate that only males took part, but there is some evidence in Acts that even ἄνδρες like ἄνθρωποι can include women. See 17:34, where "a woman named Damaris" was among the believing ἄνδρες.

[55]When referring to Scripture, "David" pointed to the psalms in Acts, indicative of the Jewish association of the psalms with King David (cf. 2:25, 34). Sometimes "Psalms" is specified (cf. 1:20).

[56]C. H. Cosgrove, "The Divine *dei* in Luke-Acts: Investigations into the Lukan Understanding of God's Providence," *NovT* 26 (1984): 168-90.

reminded the other apostles that Judas was a full member of their circle and shared their ministry.[57] Verses 18-19 are not a part of Peter's speech but constitute an "aside" that Luke provided for his readers, as indicated by the parentheses in the NIV.[58] Peter's train of thought was thus: Judas was a member of the Twelve (v. 17); his place was now vacant (v. 20a) and needed to be filled (v. 20b).

1:18-19 Luke provided us with the story of Judas's demise in vv. 18-19. Judas purchased a field (literally, "an estate or farm") with "the reward he got for his wickedness." The reference is clearly to the money the temple officials agreed to pay Judas for leading them to Jesus (Luke 22:5). The language is more obscure in the remainder of v. 18: "And becoming prone, he burst in the middle, and all his entrails poured out" (literal translation). The NIV probably is right in interpreting the strange phrase "becoming prone" as "fell headlong."[59] The picture is that of a fall so severe as to open his body cavity and cause his inner organs (*splanchna*) to spill out. In consequence of this gory death the field became known by Jerusalem locals as Akeldama. For his non-Semitic readers, Luke translated the Aramaic word—"that is, Field of Blood." Matthew gave a fuller account of Judas's death. Despite significant differences in detail, the main emphases are the same in the two accounts—the purchase of a field with Judas's blood money, the grisly death of the betrayer, the naming of the field "Field of Blood."[60] For Peter the recollection of Judas's gruesome end must have been a grim reminder of his

---

[57]Literally "shared the lot κλῆρον of this ministry." The word refers to the small stone used in casting lots, as it is used in 1:26. It came to have the derivative meaning of the office or rank so obtained and then simply "rank," regardless of the manner obtained, as is the usage in 1:17. Today it refers to ecclesiastic rank and is found in the words "cleric, clergy."

[58]In current scholarship these are referred to as "narrative asides." See S. Sheeley, "Narrative Asides in Luke-Acts," Ph.D. diss., Southern Baptist Theological Seminary, 1987. Obviously the apostles needed no reminder of the recent events with Judas. Luke's readers did.

[59]Evidence exists that some of the early versions of Acts took πρηνὴς ("prone") as πρησθείς ("swollen"); for the Syriac, Georgian, and Armenian versions translate it as "having swelled up." Perhaps this was an early attempt to explain how a headlong fall could lead · to rupture. There may be some connection with a later tradition of Judas's death, attributed to Papias by Apollinarius of Laodicea, according to which Judas became ill and swelled up to such enormous proportions that even an ox cart could not negotiate past him in a narrow street. See *Beginnings* 5:22-30. One should also not overlook the parallel with the death of Antiochus Epiphanes in 2 Macc 9:8.

[60]The most significant difference between the two accounts is that Judas hung himself in the Matthean version. An early attempt to deal with this is found in the early Latin Vulgate, where "prone" is translated "suspended." Augustine likewise suggested that the rope by which Judas hung himself broke, causing him to fall headlong and burst open. For a harmonization of all the differences between the two accounts, see C. W. Carter and R. Earle, *The Acts of the Apostles* (Grand Rapids: Zondervan, 1959), 20-21; A. B. Gordon, "The Fate of

own denial of his Lord as he now sought to lead the assembly to fill the abandoned post.

(2) Matthias's Installation (1:20b-26)

And,
" 'May another take his place of leadership.'
[21]Therefore it is necessary to choose one of the men who have been with us the whole time the Lord Jesus went in and out among us, [22]beginning from John's baptism to the time when Jesus was taken up from us. For one of these must become a witness with us of his resurrection."
[23]So they proposed two men: Joseph called Barsabbas (also known as Justus) and Matthias. [24]Then they prayed, "Lord, you know everyone's heart. Show us which of these two you have chosen [25]to take over this apostolic ministry, which Judas left to go where he belongs." [26]Then they cast lots, and the lot fell to Matthias; so he was added to the eleven apostles.

1:20b-22 In vv. 21-22 Peter laid down the qualifications for Judas's replacement. He had to be one who had witnessed the entire ministry of Jesus from the time of his baptism by John to the ascension. Above all he had to have witnessed the resurrection appearances. Here we have the basic understanding of the apostles' role in Acts. They were primarily "witnesses" to Jesus, eyewitnesses who could share his teaching and confirm his resurrection and ascension. As such, the role of apostle was limited to the Twelve. It was a unique, irreplaceable office (Eph 2:20; Rev 21:14). There could be no apostolic succession, since there were no further eyewitnesses to succeed them. Note that James was not replaced after his martyrdom (12:2). It was necessary to replace Judas because he had abandoned his position. His betrayal, not his death, forfeited his place in the circle of Twelve. Even after death James continued to be considered an apostle.

Luke 22:28-30 speaks of the apostles' unique role of sitting in the kingdom and judging the twelve tribes of Israel. Their number corresponds to the tribes of Israel, for in a real sense they represent the restored Israel, the people of God. The continuity with Israel necessitates the restoration of the full number of twelve. Because the church is built on the foundation of these Twelve as representatives of the true Israel, the people of God of the messianic times, their number had to be completed before the coming of the Spirit and the "birth of the church." Throughout Acts this unique circle of the Twelve eyewitnesses is characteristically

Judas According to Acts 1:18," *EvQ* 43 (1971): 97-100. For the view that the Judas tradition originated as a midrash on *Akeldama*, see M. Wilcox, "The Judas Tradition in Acts 1:15-26," *NTS* 19 (1973): 438-42; F. Manns, "Un Midrash Chrétien: Le Recit de la mort de Judas," *RSR* 54 (1980): 197-203.

designated as "the apostles."[61]

1:23 The assembly put forward two candidates who met the qualifications, Joseph and Matthias (v. 23). Joseph is described as also having been called Barsabbas, "son of the Sabbath." Jews and proselytes often bore Gentile nicknames, among which "Justus" was common (cf. Acts 18:7; Col 4:11). Nothing more is known of Joseph except for a later tradition cited by Eusebius that as a result of his missionary work he was forced to drink poison and suffered no ill effects.[62] Matthias, whose name means *gift of God*, is merely mentioned with no further fanfare. Later tradition speculated that he became a missionary to the Ethiopians or that his bones were buried in Germany at Treves.[63] In the Acts text Joseph is given such prominence that one would expect *him* to have been chosen, perhaps a reminder that God's ways are not always man's ways.[64] The assembly did turn the matter over to God by praying for divine direction (v. 24).

1:24-25 Perhaps a further requirement of a strong inner faith on the part of the one to be chosen is implicit in the address to God as the one who "know[s] everyone's heart."[65] The prayer concludes with the specific need to replace Judas's ministry, which he had abandoned "to go where he belongs" (v. 25). The Greek phrase is a little softer, literally "to his own place," and could also be taken as "place of his own choosing." Despite the reticence of the phraseology, most would already have in mind where that place would be. As the assembly prayed for God's direction in the selection of the twelfth apostle, it was following a precedent already set by Jesus, who also prayed before he chose the original Twelve (Luke 6:12f.).

---

[61]Luke restricted the term apostles to the Twelve, with the sole exception of chap. 14 (vv. 4,14), where Paul and Barnabas were given the designation. The word has a much broader usage elsewhere in the NT, especially in Paul's writings. He differentiated between the Twelve and another group of apostles that included James, the brother of Jesus (1 Cor 15:5,7). He also included Andronicus and Junias among the apostles (Rom 16:7). For Paul the term seems to have denoted those who like himself had received a special commission from the risen Lord. On the whole question see K. H. Rengstorf, "Ἀποστέλλω . . . ἀποστολή," *TDNT*, 1:398-447; W. Schmithals, *The Office of Apostle in the Early Church*, trans. J. Steeley (Nashville: Abingdon, 1969).

[62]From the second century on, there are many such traditions about the other apostles that seem primarily to be later attempts to fill in the gaps left by Acts. They are usually fanciful and offer little historical credibility. Eusebius (*Hist. Eccl.* 3:39) attributes the Joseph tradition to one of Philip's prophesying daughters. See C. S. C. Williams, *The Acts of the Apostles*, HNTC (New York: Harper, 1957), 61.

[63]For Ethiopia see Bruce, *Acts*: NIC, 51; for Germany see Haenchen, *Acts*, 162. Other traditional speculations were that Matthias is another name for Zacchaeus (according to Clement of Alexandria) or Barnabas (*The Clementine Recognitions*): *Beginnings* 4:14-15.

[64]Schneider, *Apostelgeschichte* 1:120.

[65]D. J. Williams, *Acts*, 17.

1:26 The prayer concluded, they then "cast lots" (v. 26). The Greek text reads literally "they gave lots to them." The meaning seems to be that they *assigned* lots for them. The method was likely the one depicted in the Old Testament. Marked stones were placed in a jar and shaken out. The one whose stone fell out first was chosen (cf. 1 Chr 26:13f.). Some have wanted to see Matthias selected by vote of the church,[66] but the text points more to the ancient procedure of lot-casting. One should not be put off by the "chance" element. In the Old Testament the outcome was always seen to be determined by God. That was probably the consideration in this case. Before Pentecost, before the presence of the Spirit to lead it, the church sought the direction of God and used the Old Testament procedure of securing divine decision. After Pentecost the church in Acts made its own decisions under the direction of the Spirit. In this particular instance it was all the more important that the decision be the Lord's, not theirs. Like his first selection of the Twelve, its constituency was his to determine.[67]

7. The Miracle at Pentecost (2:1-13)

Everything in chap. 1 is preparatory to the great outburst of the Spirit who poured upon the praying band of believers at Pentecost. Over a period of forty days they had listened to the teaching of their Lord (1:3). They had received his commission to be worldwide witnesses, and they had been given his promise that the Holy Spirit would be granted them as empowerment for that mission (1:5; 1:8). With the Lord's final departure in his ascension, nothing was left to do but to wait and pray for the fulfillment of that promise (1:14). In chap. 2 their prayer was answered in a mighty way.

Pentecost has often been referred to as "the birth of the church." A significant parallel between Pentecost and the Lukan infancy narrative is the prominent role of the Spirit in both. John was to be filled with the Spirit for his role as witness to Christ (Luke 1:15), as were the various other witnesses to the significance of the child Jesus in God's saving purposes—Elizabeth (1:41), Zechariah (1:67), and Simeon (2:25-35). Above all, Jesus was conceived of the Holy Spirit (1:35). Just as through the Spirit God and humanity were perfectly united in Christ, so through the same Spirit God was united with his church at Pentecost.[68] Perhaps even more striking was the prominent role of the Spirit in equipping Jesus for his ministry. The Spirit descended upon Jesus at his baptism "in bodily form" (Luke 3:22). Likewise in its "baptism" of the Spirit (Acts 1:5), the

---

[66]Munck (*Acts*, 10) argues for casting by ballot.
[67]Reicke, *Glaube und Leben*, 26.
[68]Carver, *Acts*, 23.

church received the Spirit in visible form (2:3). Endowed with the Spirit (Luke 4:1,14), Jesus delivered his "inaugural address" at Nazareth, the keynote speech that set the pattern for his entire ministry (4:18).[69] The Nazareth sermon announced the fulfillment in his own ministry of the messianic prophecies and, with its examples from Elijah and Elisha, pointed beyond the boundaries of Israel to the worldwide scope of his messianic mission. With this point the congregation at Nazareth was enraged and rejected him. The "inaugural address" at Pentecost was Peter's speech (Acts 2:14-40). It too was delivered through the power of the Spirit, which had just come upon him. It too dealt with the fulfillment of the messianic times. It too assumed a worldwide outreach (2:39), and it too would be rejected by a large part of the Jewish community according to the unfolding story of Acts.

Acts 2 forms a unity around the gift of the Spirit at Pentecost. It falls into three main parts: (1) the miracle at Pentecost (vv. 1-13), (2) Peter's sermon and its tremendous results (vv. 14-41), and (3) a picture of the life held in common by the greatly enlarged community of believers in Jerusalem (vv. 42-47). The first segment falls into two main parts: (a) the coming of the gift of the Spirit on the band of believers (2:1-4) and (b) the manifestation of this gift to the Jewish crowd (2:5-13).

(1) The Gift of the Spirit (2:1-4)

[1]When the day of Pentecost came, they were all together in one place. [2]Suddenly a sound like the blowing of a violent wind came from heaven and filled the whole house where they were sitting. [3]They saw what seemed to be tongues of fire that separated and came to rest on each of them. [4]All of them were filled with the Holy Spirit and began to speak in other tongues as the Spirit enabled them.

THE SETTING (2:1). **2:1** The time was the day of Pentecost, which Luke noted with a phrase that is literally translated "when the day of Pentecost was fulfilled." The "fulfillment" language bears more weight than mere chronology as the fulfillment of the time of the divine promise for the gift of the Spirit (1:4f.).[70] The time of waiting was over. Luke was much more vague in his reference to the place. They were all together "in one place" (*epi to auto*). The next verse specifies that it was a "house" in which they were sitting. But where was the house? Was it a room in the

---

[69]There are many interesting points of contact between the initial sermons of Jesus (Luke 4), Peter (Acts 2), and Paul (Acts 13). For a thorough comparison, see R. I. Garrett, Jr., "The Inaugural Addresses of Luke-Acts," Ph.D. diss., The Southern Baptist Theological Seminary, 1980.

[70]Compare Luke 9:51, where the same construction marks an important stage in salvation history. The time had come for Jesus to go to Jerusalem and face his destiny there. See E. Lohse, "Die Bedeutung des Pfingstberichtes im Rahmen des lukanischen Geschichtswerkes," *EvTh* (1958): 422-36.

temple? That would certainly explain how a large crowd could have been so quickly attracted to the scene. Luke, however, usually referred to the temple by the normal designation *hieron*, never by the word "house"; and there was really no room in the temple where a gathering of laypeople could "sit." The most likely place for the gathering is the upper room where they had been praying. Perhaps it was near the temple, where large crowds would assemble on a feast day.

Who were the people gathered in the upper room? On whom did the Spirit descend? Was it the 120 mentioned in 1:15 or only the Twelve apostles? In 2:14 Luke mentioned only the Twelve, but there it probably was to connect them with Peter's speech, which appealed to their special role as eyewitnesses to the resurrection (2:32). The presence of the large crowd testifying to the witness of the Spirit-filled Christians (2:6-11) would indicate that the full 120 were involved, as would the text Peter quoted from Joel that refers to women as well as men prophesying (2:17-18).

Pentecost was the second of the three great harvest festivals of Judaism, coming between Passover and Tabernacles. In the New Testament (cf. 1 Cor 16:8) it is referred to as "Pentecost," which means *fiftieth* in Greek. In the Old Testament it is referred to as the Festival of Weeks or of the Firstfruits, the first term referring to its coming a "week of weeks" after Passover, the second to the fact that an offering of two loaves prepared from the wheat harvest was made on this day. Although there was a difference among the Sadducees and the Pharisees over the precise reckoning of the day, the Pharisaic procedure seems to have been followed in the period prior to A.D. 70 in which Pentecost was reckoned as coming exactly fifty days after the first day of the Passover.[71] It was a day of "solemn assembly," and all work ceased. It was also one of the most popular pilgrim festivals, even more so than Passover, which was likely due to the improved weather conditions by the time of Pentecost.

THE EVENT (2:2-4). **2:2** The coming of the Spirit is described in three carefully constructed parallel statements, each pointing to an aspect of the event: a *sound* came . . . and it filled the house (v. 2); *tongues* appeared . . . and one sat on each of them (v. 3); they were filled with the Holy Spirit . . . and *began to speak* in other tongues (v. 4). The emphasis is on the objectivity of the event. It was audible, visible, and manifested itself in an outward demonstration of inspired speech. The audible manifestation is described as coming suddenly from heaven. The picture is of a blowing blast of wind, like the roar of a tornado.[72] Wind phenomena often accompany an appearance by God in the Old Testament (cf. 1 Kgs

---

[71]For a full discussion, see E. Lohse, "πεντηκοστή" *TDNT* 6:44-53.

[72]Robertson, *WP* 3:20.

19:11; Isa 66:15).[73] In Greek *pneuma* has the double connotation of both wind and Spirit, and that connection is to be seen here. As in Ezekiel the wind, the breath of Yahweh, is God's Spirit, which brings life in the vision of the dry bones (Ezek 37:9-14).

2:3 The same sort of double meaning is found in v. 3 in the reference to the "tongues." Much as in English, the Greek word *glōssa* can refer to the physical organ of the tongue. It also has the metaphorical meaning of what is spoken by the tongue, spoken *language*. So here, the lapping flames that had the visible likeness to tongues enabled the believers to speak in inspired language. Again it was a question of a heavenly manifestation. Throughout the Old Testament fire phenomena are used to depict the presence of God (cf. Exod 3:2; 19:18; 1 Kgs 18:38-39; Ezek 1:27). Here the fire is described as "separated." The picture is that of one great flame representing the Spirit, which separates into many tongues of flame with one resting on each individual.[74] Luke was well aware that he was using metaphorical language in these verses by carefully employing adverbs of comparison: "like the blowing of a violent wind" (v. 2), "what seemed to be tongues" (literally, "tongues as of fire," v. 3). He was dealing with the transcendent, that which is beyond ordinary human experience and can only be expressed in earthly analogies.

2:4 Verse 4 gives the result of the Spirit's coming on those gathered in the upper room. They were "filled with the Holy Spirit," and this led them to "speak in other tongues." From this point on in Acts, the gift of the Spirit became a normative concomitant of becoming a Christian believer (2:38). The expression of this differs; in 9:17 Saul is said to have been "filled" with the Spirit, as here. Sometimes this experience is described as a "baptism" in the Spirit (1:5; 11:16). In other instances the word "poured out" is used (2:17f.; 10:45) or "came upon" (8:16; 10:44; 11:15) or simply "receive" (2:38; 10:47). All these instances refer to new converts and point to the Spirit's coming in various ways, not always signified by tongues, as a permanent gift to every believer. This should be distinguished from other references to "filling," where the Spirit comes upon one who is already a believer in a time of special inspiration and testimony to the faith (cf. 4:8,31; 7:55; 13:9).

What is one to make of their speaking in "other tongues"? Does this refer to their speaking in languages other than their own native tongue, or does it refer to the phenomenon of glossolalia, speaking in tongues, the ecstatic "Spirit language" Paul dealt with in 1 Cor 12-14? Or does it

---

[73]Schneider, *Apostelgeschichte* 1:248.

[74]There is a curious shift of number in v. 3 from plural ("separated tongues") to singular "it sat." The NIV obscures any shift: "tongues . . . separated and came." The missing singular antecedent is surely *ad sensum*: "tongues of flame, and [one] sat on each of them."

refer to a miracle of hearing as well? A good case can be made for each of these views. Those who consider the miracle to be speaking in tongues can point to its being a well-attested, early Christian phenomenon (1 Cor 12–14) as well as to its seeming appearance elsewhere in Acts (10:46; 19:6). It is described as "declaring the wonders of God" in v. 11, and this could be likened to Paul's description of tongue-speaking as speaking to God and speaking mysteries in the Spirit (1 Cor 14:2). Above all, the charge of some of the bystanders that the Christians were "drunk" could be linked to the ecstatic nature of tongue-speaking. Paul likewise worried that outsiders might consider the Corinthian tongue-speakers to be "out of [their] mind" (1 Cor 14:23).[75]

There are strong reasons, however, for questioning whether the Pentecost experience could have been the sort of ecstatic language Paul dealt with at Corinth. From Paul's treatment the glossolalia there was clearly not rational discourse but an ecstatic "praise language," edifying to the individual tongue-speaker, but not to the church (1 Cor 14:1-5). It was as meaningless to others as indistinct musical notes or a language totally foreign to them (1 Cor 14:6-12). For the church Paul preferred to speak "five intelligible words" ("with my mind," RSV) than ten thousand "in tongues" (1 Cor 14:19). The Pentecost experience did seem to involve intelligible communication to those in the Jewish crowd.

The word "tongue" may be ambiguous in v. 4, but the word "dialect," or "language" (*dialektos*), in vv. 6,8 is not. It can only refer to a known language or dialect. Luke used the expression "to speak in other [*heteros*, "different"] tongues [languages]" in v. 4, thus making a distinction from tongue-speaking (which he did know and referred to in 10:46). Likewise, in v. 4b he used an uncommon Greek word in the phrase "as the Spirit enabled them." This rare word means *to utter, to declare, to speak with gravity* and is used in the Greek translation of the Old Testament for prophesying (cf. 1 Chr 25:1; Ezek 13:9; Mic 5:12). Finally, the long list of nations in vv. 9-11 is sandwiched between references to people who marvel at hearing the Christians in their own language (vv. 8,11b). The list obviously illustrates the breadth of the languages that were spoken.[76] Awareness of this has led some scholars to postulate

---

[75]For the view that Pentecost involved glossolalia, see I. J. Martin III, "Glossolalia in the Apostolic Church," *JBL* 63 (1944): 123-30; W. Neil, *The Acts of the Apostles*, NCB (Grand Rapids: Eerdmans, 1973), 73; C. S. C. Williams, *Acts*, 63. There are many modifications to this view such as that of Bruce, *Acts*: NIC, 56-58, who sees it as the sort of glossolalia that contains many foreign phrases, as attested by Pentecostals. Unlikely is the theory of W. S. Thomson that the Christians repeated the ecstatic praise language of the pilgrims, whom they had earlier heard worshiping in the temple: "Tongues at Pentecost," *ExpTim* 38 (1926-27): 284-86.

[76]Exemplary of many who argue for a foreign language phenomenon is E. F. Harrison,

a miracle of "hearing." The usual form of this view assumes that the Christians experienced glossolalia, but the crowd understood this as their own language through a miracle of hearing. This would emphasize the word "hear" in vv. 6,11b: "each one heard them speaking in his own language."[77] The major problem with this view is that it presupposes the reception of the Spirit on the part of the crowd. Indeed, if the miracle was in the crowd's hearing rather than in the believers' speaking, one wonders why it was even necessary for Luke to tell of the Spirit's coming so powerfully upon them.

When one's attention is focused on Luke's story of Pentecost, the flow of the narrative does seem to favor the view of a miracle of foreign speech. Filled with the Spirit, the Christians began to speak in tongues different from their own (v. 4). A crowd was attracted and utterly amazed to hear these Galileans speaking their languages (v. 7), a crowd that represented the greater portion of the entire Jewish Diaspora (vv. 9-11). Certainly it was an ecstatic experience. The disciples were brim-full of the Spirit. They praised God; they magnified his name (v. 11);[78] they prophesied (v. 17). The members of the crowd were bewildered. It had to be a sign, but what did it mean (v. 12)? As in every crowd, there were scoffers (v. 13). Still the inspired speech of the Christians demonstrated the spiritual power present that day. All were prepared to hear Peter's explanation.

(2) The Witness to the Spirit (2:5-13)

[5]Now there were staying in Jerusalem God-fearing Jews from every nation under heaven. [6]When they heard this sound, a crowd came together in bewilderment, because each one heard them speaking in his own language. [7]Utterly amazed, they asked: "Are not all these men who are speaking Galileans? [8]Then how is it that each of us hears them in his own native language? [9]Parthians, Medes and Elamites; residents of Mesopotamia, Judea and Cappadocia, Pontus and Asia, [10]Phrygia and Pamphylia, Egypt and the parts of Libya near Cyrene; visitors from Rome [11](both Jews and converts to Judaism); Cretans and Arabs— we hear them declaring the wonders of God in our own tongues!" [12]Amazed and perplexed, they asked one another, "What does this mean?"

[13]Some, however, made fun of them and said, "They have had too much wine."

Interpreting Acts (Grand Rapids: Zondervan, 1986), 59-62. A modification of this view found in the more radical critics is that Luke was responsible for the foreign language motif, having altered an original experience of glossolalia, e.g., Conzelmann, *Acts*, 15-16.

[77] This was suggested by Lake, *Beginnings* 5:111-21. A somewhat modified view that involves the ecstatic utterance of Scripture is that of R. O. P. Taylor, "The Tongues of Pentecost," *ExpTim* 40 (1928-29): 300-03.

[78] Several scholars who see the miracle as one of speaking in foreign languages emphasize that it probably consisted primarily of praise. See Dupont, *Salvation of Gentiles*, 48-50; Kremer, *Pfingstbericht*, 122.

THE GATHERING OF THE CROWD (2:5-8). **2:5** The constituency of the Pentecost crowd is given in v. 5. They were pious Jews "from every nation under heaven." The NIV describes them as "God-fearing," but "pious" would be a less confusing translation. "God-fearing" is a term used elsewhere in Acts for Gentiles who, like Cornelius (10:2), worshiped God and supported the synagogue but had not become full converts to Judaism. The word used here is *eulabeis*, which means *pious* and in Luke-Acts is always used of Jews, never of Gentiles (cf. Luke 2:25; Acts 8:2; 22:12). These devout Jews are described as "staying" (or "dwelling," RSV) in Jerusalem. The word usually implies residency, making it unlikely that these were merely pilgrims who had come to the feast. They were rather Diaspora Jews who had returned to the city of the temple to dwell there. A large contingency of these in Jerusalem has been well documented from inscriptions and excavated graves.[79] The "Synagogue of the Freedmen" in which Stephen debated was likely comprised of them (6:9). A few manuscripts omit the reference to Jews in v. 5, and some scholars opt for so doing who want to see here the beginning of the Gentile mission.[80] It is most unlikely that the omission is the correct reading and even more unlikely that the Gentile mission began here. The Gentile mission was a hard-won battle in Acts and only began in earnest with Peter's witness to Cornelius (chap. 10).

Some have objected that to see these as Jews living in Jerusalem would render meaningless the witness of the Christians in foreign tongues, since they would surely have some proficiency in the Aramaic dialect spoken in Jerusalem. That, however, is to miss altogether the point of the speech miracle. The miracle was a demonstration of the Spirit's power and presence: these Diaspora Jews heard their own tongue spoken (not Aramaic or Greek) and realized that this should have been impossible for the "Galileans." This "sign" prepared them for Peter's speech, which probably was in Aramaic and which they indeed understood. The note that they represented "every nation under heaven" is perhaps a bit of poetic license but a not altogether inaccurate description of the extent of the Jewish Diaspora.

2:6-8 The crowd is said to have come together at the "sound." What sound, that of the rushing wind or that coming from the Spirit-filled Christians? One cannot be certain, since Luke left out more detail than he told. The inspired Christians doubtless left the upper room and rushed forth, most likely to the temple precincts. Only there would be found sufficient room for a crowd of 3,000 plus. There also the crowds were to be found, assembled for the Pentecost festivities. Most likely the inspired

---

[79]Schneider, *Apostelgeschichte* 1:251.
[80]For example, Lake, *Beginnings* 5:111-21.

cries of the Christians attracted the onlookers.[81] Certainly the inspired speech perplexed them "because each one heard them speaking in his own language." Luke heaped up words to describe the crowd's perplexity. They were "utterly amazed" ("astounded and amazed," author's translation, v. 7), not at what the Christians said but that such simple Galileans would know their languages. The label "Galilean" need not imply that all 120 were from Galilee, though a sizable band of disciples had accompanied Jesus from there to Jerusalem (cf. Luke 8:1-3; 10:1-17; also see 23:49).[82] Verse 8 basically repeats v. 6, with the added note that it was in their "native" tongue, the language group into which they were born, that they were hearing these "Galileans." This prepares for vv. 9-11, which list the various areas of the Diaspora represented.

THE COMPOSITION OF THE CROWD (2:9-11a). **2:9-11a** Verses 9-11a are a part of the direct discourse spoken by the crowd, but likely they are a note from Luke enumerating the various nationalities present. The list has long intrigued scholars. It begins in what is present-day Iran (Parthia) and then proceeds across the Middle East (Mesopotamia), then southward to Judea, then north to central Turkey (Cappadocia), to northern Turkey (Pontus), eastward to the Aegean coast of Turkey (Asia), inland to Phrygia, then south to the Mediterranean coast of Turkey (Pamphylia). To this point, with the exception of Judea, which seems strangely out of place, the progress is a more-or-less regular curve, from southeast to north to southwest. After Pamphylia no real pattern is discernible. The catalog covers North Africa (Egypt, Libya, Cyrenaica), then north and west all the way to Rome, then southeast to the Mediterranean island of Crete, and finally much farther east and southward to Arabia. There are some striking omissions, areas of particular prominence in Acts, like Syria, Galatia, Macedonia, and Achaia. Then there are the "problem" references, such as Judea. From ancient times interpreters have emended the text to give a more natural reference than the Judeans, who were scarcely foreigners in Jerusalem. Tertullian suggested Armenia, for example, and Chrysostom India.[83] The most natural explanation would be that Judea is included in

---

[81]Bruce, *The Acts of the Apostles: The Greek Text*, 3rd ed., rev. (Grand Rapids: Eerdmans, 1990), 165. (Hereafter referred to as *Acts*: GT.)

[82]Bruce notes that Galilean diction was quite distinct by "its confusion or loss of laryngals and aspirates," *Acts*: NIC, 59, n. 15.

[83]G. D. Kilpatrick, "A Jewish Background to Acts 2:9-11?" *JJS* 26 (1975): 48-49. Kilpatrick's own suggestion is that the list came from the Jewish community of Rome and enumerated the places of origin of its members, which would explain the presence of Judea as well as its ending with the resident Jews and proselytes of Rome. Another suggestion is that Judea should be emended to Iberia, the ancient name for modern Georgia: J. M. Ross, "'Judaea' in Acts 2:9," *ExpTim* 96 (1985): 217. Reicke, *Glaube und Leben*, 35-36, sees the list as originating in Antioch, which would explain both the presence of Judea as well as the absence of Syria.

the widest sense as the extent of the Davidic Empire, from the Euphrates to Egypt. It would thus come naturally after Mesopotamia and would include Syria as well.[84] Reference is often made to an astrological chart of the fourth century A.D. from Paulus Alexandrinus that links various nations to the signs of the Zodiac. A number of scholars have argued that Luke used an earlier form of Paulus's list in his catalog.[85] B. Metzger has shown rather convincingly that Luke's list has little in common with Paulus's chart.[86]

Most attempts at uncovering the source of the Lukan list have either been unconvincing or demanded radical surgery, such as the elimination of Judea or Rome or Cretans and Arabians, often with the desire to end up with a neat list of twelve (one for each apostle or one for each sign of the Zodiac). It seems prudent to stick with the list as it is and view it in line with Luke's purposes in providing it. The territories Luke listed all had extensive Jewish communities.[87] Parthia, Medea, Elam, Mesopotamia had large groups of Jews from the time of the exile on. There was a large Jewish contingent in North Africa, Philo noting that two of the five wards of Alexandria were comprised of Jews. Acts witnesses to the Jewish representation in Phrygia and Asia, and their presence in Pontus and Cappadocia is amply evidenced. The Jewish population in Rome is well-known. The single exception to the resident Jews at Pentecost may be the Romans, who are described as "visitors" in verse 10b.[88] The verse division at v. 11 is somewhat disconcerting. The phrase "both Jews and converts to Judaism" probably refers to Roman Jews and Gentiles who converted to Judaism by embracing circumcision and the Jewish law, as well as by providing for a sacrifice in the temple.[89] The reference to Cretans and Arabians comes at

---

[84]Bruce, *Acts:* NIC, 62.

[85]This has been argued in an article by S. Weinstock (*JRS* 38 [1948]: 43-46), and it has been more recently advanced by J. A. Brinkman, "The Literary Background of the 'Catalogue of Nations' (Acts 2:9-11)," *CBQ* 25 (1963): 418-27. A very different approach is advocated by E. Guting, "Der geographische Horizont der sogenannten Volkerliste des Lukas (Acta 2:9-11)," *ZNW* 66 (1975): 149-69. Guting sees Luke as responsible for composing the list, which was based on the languages of his day along the lines of a similar linguistic enumeration in Strabo.

[86]B. Metzger, "Ancient Astrological Geography and Acts 2:9-11," in *Apostolic History and the Gospel*, ed. W. Gasque and R. Martin (Grand Rapids: Eerdmans, 1970), 123-33. Metzger shows that at most there are five agreements between the lists, which is no more than coincidence.

[87]For an excellent summary of the evidence for Jewish settlement in these regions, see D. J. Williams, *Acts*, 28-29.

[88]"Romans" possibly refers to Roman citizens of the wider empire, such as Paul, as Cadbury and Lake argue in *Beginnings* 4:20. In the context of this list, however, it more likely is a geographical reference to actual residents of the city of Rome.

[89]Possibly also by undergoing proselyte baptism, although this practice is not documented with certainty before the second century A.D. See G. F. Moore, *Judaism in the First*

the end of the list, almost as an afterthought. There were Jewish communities on Crete as well as in Arabia, which most likely refers to the Nabatean kingdom that extended the length of the Arabian peninsula from the Red Sea to the Euphrates. Perhaps the mention of these two locales was Luke's way of rounding off his list—not only mainlanders but islanders and desert dwellers as well. In all he gave a rather representative picture of the Jewish Diaspora and its presence at Pentecost.

THE RESPONSE OF THE CROWD (2:11b-13). **2:11b-13** Verse 11b picks up the narrative, once again expressing the amazement of the Jewish crowd.[90] This time the content of the Christians' speaking is given, the only hint in the entire narrative about what they were saying. They were declaring the "wonders" of God. Their testimony was the language of praise. They may even have burst forth in song, for such can be a natural expression when one is filled with the Spirit (Eph 5:18-19). They were "utterly amazed" (cf. v. 7a) and wondered, "What does this mean?" (v. 12). They had observed the miracle of the Christians speaking in their own language, but there had as yet been no interpretation about the meaning of this sign. They were thus prepared for the explanation Peter would soon provide. Others, however, were more skeptical—"no spiritual power here, just people who've had too much to drink" (author's paraphrase, v. 13).[91] Here for the first time appears a motif that runs throughout Luke-Acts—in itself, without the element of personal faith and experience, even the most profound aspects of the good news are not self-confirming but can lead to skepticism and even rejection (cf. Luke 24:11; Acts 17:32; 26:24).

Overview. Before turning to Peter's speech, it would be well to take a last overview of the Pentecost narrative and summarize its major themes. One of the most commonly cited interpretive keys for understanding Acts 2:1-13 has been to compare it with the giving of the law at Sinai. This comparison is based on rabbinic sources which show that later Judaism celebrated the giving of the law at Sinai as a part of their Pentecost lit-

---

Centuries of the Christian Era (Cambridge: Harvard University Press, 1927), 1:327-38.

[90]The Western text understood vv. 9-11 as Luke's comment and so reads "they hear" instead of "we hear" in 11, to make this clear.

[91]The word used for wine here is γλεῦκος, which usually refers to "new wine." Following the usual chronology of Pentecost, there would have been no "new wine" available, the grape harvest still being nearly two months in the future. Most interpreters deal with this by observing that new wine was often kept fresh (and thus "new" or "sweet") for as long as a year by immersing it in water. An interesting suggestion is that Qumran seems to have kept three "Pentecosts," each separated by fifty days, to celebrate the wheat, wine, and oil harvests, respectively. The association here would thus be with the second, wine Pentecost, which came 100 days after Passover. See J. A. Fitzmyer, "The Ascension of Christ and Pentecost," *TS* 45 (1984): 434-36.

urgy. If this was so, we can conclude that Luke wanted to show that the Spirit, not the law, is the mark of the new dispensation in Christ.[92] Two problems exist with this view. The first is the lateness of the sources. Although it is beyond dispute that second-century Judaism celebrated the giving of the Torah as part of its Pentecost liturgy, no clear first-century references support such a connection.[93] More important is that Luke himself did not make any such connection explicit. The superiority of the Spirit over the law is certainly a major Pauline theme (cf. 2 Cor 3:6-18), but nowhere in Luke's account of Pentecost is any allusion made to the Torah: not in the narrative and not in Peter's speech. Luke's emphases lay along different paths.

Another common interpretation sees Acts 2:1-13 as depicting the "reversal of Babel."[94] This view sees the disunity of humanity that resulted from the many languages of Babel being overcome by a new language of the Spirit, which brings a new unity. Jewish tradition maintained that all people, and even the animals, spoke one common language in Eden. It was lost by the animals in Eden and by humans at Babel but will be restored at the end time.[95] Certainly the reversal-of-Babel understanding is an attractive, and to some extent legitimate, interpretation of Pentecost. Luke, however, did not seem to have made the connection. Nothing in the text of Acts 2 recalls Gen 11:1-9. When Luke saw connections with an Old Testament tradition, he usually gave echoes from the Old Testament text, and these are lacking here. This is not to say that it is illegitimate to make such an application when expounding on the miracle at Pentecost. It is certainly not contrary to the meaning of the event. The

---

[92]For a "classic" presentation of this view, see W. L. Knox, *The Acts*, NCB (Oxford: Clarendon, 1967), 80-84. See also N. Snaith, "Pentecost, the Day of Power," *ExpTim* 43 (1931-32): 379-80.

[93]Often cited is a tradition in Philo (*De. Dec.*, 9.11) of a speech miracle at Sinai where the Torah is said to have rested on the Israelites in the form of fiery tongues and endowed them with a gift of speech. Philo, however, never connected Sinai with Pentecost, nor did any other first-century source. See Lohse "πεντηκοστή," *TDNT* 6:48-49. Some evidence in *Jub.* and 1QS suggests that some Jewish sectarian circles celebrated Pentecost as a covenant renewal, but whether they also connected this with the giving of the Torah is uncertain. See I. H. Marshall, "The Significance of Pentecost," *SJT* 30 (1977): 347-69. Dupont, *Salvation of the Gentiles*, 34-45, has attempted to link Acts 2:1-13 by pointing to the number of words it has in common with the LXX text of Exod 19. Most of the parallel vocabulary, however, consists of stock theophany terminology rather than any dependence of Acts on the Sinai text: Schneider, *Apostelgeschichte* 1:246.

[94]For representatives of this view, see J. G. Davies, "Pentecost and Glossolalia," *JTS*, n.s. 3 (1952): 228-31; Rackham, *Acts*, 19. Rackham considered the list of nations in Gen 10, followed by the account of Babel in Gen 11:1-9, as "most obvious" evidence that Luke intended to connect his account with Babel.

[95]This tradition is found in Josephus (*Ant.* 1.1.4), in Philo (*De Confus. Ling.* 3.405), and in other first-century sources. See *Beginnings* 5:115-16.

Spirit does unify humanity around the lordship of Christ, and that is a major message of Acts and even of this immediate context (cf. 2:41-47). One thing should be kept in mind when expounding this theme, however. It would be contrary to the text to speak of the Spirit giving a new common language. The opposite is rather the case. The Spirit gave the Christians many languages, all the languages represented by the nationalities listed in vv. 9-11. And is this not how the Spirit continues to work? He empowers Christian witnesses to take the gospel to the many different languages of the world to create a worldwide people of God, united by a common confession in the lordship of Christ.[96]

What, then, are the emphases Luke expounded in his treatment of Pentecost? First, his major emphasis doubtless was that the church has now been empowered for its mission. Everything in chap. 1 has anticipated this event (1:5,8). With the coming of the Spirit, the witness began. It began with the enthusiastic praise of the Spirit-filled Christians and the inspired sermon of Peter, and it resulted in the immediate harvest of 3,000 converts to Christ (2:41). And there is certainly a second, closely related theme of the text. Just as Pentecost was the festival of the firstfruits, so these are the "firstfruits" of the harvest in the Spirit.[97] This connects with a third emphasis of the text: the spiritual harvest did not culminate at Pentecost. It began there and continued in ever-widening circles, from Jerusalem to Samaria to Antioch, from Cyprus to Asia Minor, from Greece to Rome, from Jews to Samaritans, from God-fearers to Gentiles.

The worldwide scope of the Christian witness is anticipated at Pentecost in the roll call of nations (vv. 9-11). To be sure, it was a question of only Jews and Jewish proselytes at this point, but they were Diaspora Jews and represented "every nation under heaven" (v. 5). Already the national barrier had been overcome. The racial barriers would be overcome, and the gospel would be shared with "every *people* under heaven" (alternate rendering of the Greek *ethnos*). Pentecost foreshadowed the worldwide mission. Finally, the pouring out of the Spirit has eschatological significance. It inaugurated the final period in God's plan of salvation. He acted decisively and definitely in Jesus Christ to create a people for his own. The Spirit is the sign of these final times. This central emphasis comprised a major part of Peter's sermon.

---

[96]Dupont, *Nouvelles Etudes*, 196-98.

[97]Fitzmyer, "Ascension and Pentecost," 439. See also the useful summary of the themes in the Pentecost narrative by A. T. Lincoln, "Theology and History in the Interpretation of Luke's Pentecost," *ExpTim* 96 (1985): 204-09.

8. Peter's Sermon at Pentecost (2:14-41)

Peter's sermon comprised the first of the "missionary addresses" of Acts. C. H. Dodd popularized the view that these addresses, such as the one here and those in chaps. 10 and 13, represented the early "kerygma" of the church, the primitive form of gospel preaching, usually consisting of scriptural proofs concerning the Messiah, some reference to Jesus' ministry, an emphasis on his death and resurrection, and a call to repentance.[98] Although Dodd's structure may be too "pat"—there is considerable variance in pattern among the speeches—nonetheless he has isolated the major recurring elements in the missionary addresses to Jews in Acts.

In this, Peter's first sermon, the element of scriptural proof dominates. Three major texts form the framework of the speech: Joel 2:28-32; Ps 16:8-11; 110:1. Echoes of other texts and Old Testament traditions occur as well. The sermon falls into three main divisions. First, the full citation of the Joel text serves to connect the sermon with the immediate occasion of the Spirit-filled Christians (2:14-21). The central section of the speech establishes that Jesus is the Messiah, with Ps 16:8-11 pointing to his resurrection and Ps 110:1 to his exaltation (2:22-36). Finally, there is a call to repentance, with a final allusion to the text of Joel to "round off" the sermon and a report of the response of the Jewish crowd (2:37-41).[99]

(1) Scriptural Proof Concerning the Pentecost Experience (2:14-21)

[14]**Then Peter stood up with the Eleven, raised his voice and addressed the crowd: "Fellow Jews and all of you who live in Jerusalem, let me explain this to you; listen carefully to what I say.** [15]**These men are not drunk, as you suppose. It's only nine in the morning!** [16]**No, this is what was spoken by the prophet Joel:** [17]**" 'In the last days,' God says,**

'I will pour out my Spirit on all people.
Your sons and daughters will prophesy,
your young men will see visions,
your old men will dream dreams.
[18]**Even on my servants, both men and women,**
I will pour out my Spirit in those days,
and they will prophesy.

---

[98]C. H. Dodd, *The Apostolic Preaching and Its Developments* (London: Hodder & Stoughton, 1936). Many recent critics have challenged the primitive nature of these Acts speeches, seeing them as more reflective of Luke's own Christology; e.g., R. F. Zehnle, *Peter's Pentecost Discourse: Tradition and Lukan Reinterpretation in Peter's Speeches of Acts 2-3*, SBLMS 15 (Nashville: Abingdon, 1971).

[99]There are many variations on this outline, with many scholars separating vv. 22-36 into two sections: vv. 22-28 giving the scriptural proof of the resurrection, and vv. 29-36 the connection of this to Pentecost; e.g., Schneider, *Apostelgeschichte* 1:265 (cf. Pesch, *Apostelgeschichte* 1:116). A rather original chiastic structure is suggested by G. Krodel, *Acts*, ACNT (Minneapolis: Augsburg, 1986), 83.

¹⁹**I will show wonders in the heaven above**
   and signs on the earth below,
      blood and fire and billows of smoke.
²⁰**The sun will be turned to darkness**
   and the moon to blood
      before the coming of the great and glorious day of the Lord.
²¹**And everyone who calls**
   on the name of the Lord will be saved.'"

2:14-16 Verses 14-16 form the introduction to Peter's sermon, marking the transition from the Spirit-filled utterance of the Christians to Peter's explanation of the event. Peter stood up along with the eleven other apostles. The eleven are not incidental to the narrative. As the Twelve, the apostles were the witnesses to the resurrection, which would be the central subject of Peter's sermon. As always in the early chapters of Acts, Peter was their representative, the spokesman for the testimony of all Twelve. Peter "raised his voice," a common Semitic expression for beginning to speak. He "addressed" the crowd. The verb means *to speak seriously, with gravity*, a word often used for prophetic, inspired utterance.[100] He most likely spoke in the Aramaic dialect used in Jerusalem, which all these residents of Jerusalem would have understood (cf. 2:5, *katoikountes*, "residents" [author's translation]). "Fellow Jews" and "all of you who live in Jerusalem" refer to the same group. Such parallel expression typifies Semitic style, as also the expression "give ear to my words" (NIV: "listen carefully to what I say"). Luke's writing skill is apparent by his preservation of the Semitic flavor of Peter's language.

Nine a.m. (v. 15) was a customary prayer hour (literally, "the third hour"), and Jews would only eat after that—at the fourth hour.[101] Probably this is an example of the sort of humor that runs throughout Acts: "Folks don't get drunk first thing in the morning . . . that comes later in the day" (author's paraphrase). That would be especially true of a solemn feast day like Pentecost when the celebrating would only begin in earnest in the evening. Often the speeches in Acts begin with a correction of a misunderstanding (cf. 3:12; 14:15), a natural attention-getting device. Here, after having obtained the crowd's attention, Peter explained the real basis behind all the ecstatic behavior at Pentecost: the outpouring of the Spirit predicted by the prophet Joel (v. 16).[102]

---

[100] Ἀποφθέγγομαι: The same word used of the Spirit-filled Christians in 2:4.

[101] That Jews were required to pray three times a day is well-established. There is some question, however, whether the hours were set at definite times in the first century. See Haenchen, *Acts*, 178, n. 8.

[102] The Western text lacks the specific reference to Joel, and some commentators would follow that reading; e.g., *Beginnings* 4:21.

2:17-21 Peter gave the relevant passage in Joel in full. Luke reproduced this for his readers in the Greek translation of the Old Testament, the Septuagint. The Septuagint of Joel 2:28-32 (LXX, 3:1-5) is followed faithfully with only a few minor, though perhaps significant, differences. Joel's prophecy was originally given after a locust plague had ravaged the land, creating a severe famine. Joel called the people to repentance, promising the restoration of their prosperity and going on to foresee the coming of the Day of the Lord, the dawn of the messianic age, when the Spirit would be poured out on all of Israel.

Peter could not miss its applicability to Pentecost. Joel began his prophecy by saying "and afterward." Peter's version refers more specifically to "in the last days," reflecting his conviction that the messianic age had already dawned in the resurrection of Christ, that we are indeed already living in the final days of God's saving history. Peter's conviction was very much in keeping with the rabbinic consensus that the Spirit no longer rested on all Israel but would return as a universal gift at the end time. For Peter the universal pouring out of the Spirit on the whole Christian group was demonstration that the end time had come. Perhaps the clearest indication that the entire 120 received the Spirit at Pentecost is Joel's inclusion of daughters as well as sons—*all* were prophesying. Joel undoubtedly had seen the Spirit's outpouring only as a gift to Israel, and perhaps many of those Jewish-Christians at Pentecost saw it the same way. The remainder of Acts clarifies that the promise applies to the Gentiles as well: it is indeed poured out on "all people."

Verse 18 is probably best understood as being parallel to v. 17. "My servants, both men and women" are the same as the sons and daughters, young and old of v. 17, with the added refinement that those who received God's gift of the Spirit are indeed his servants.[103] The final phrase in v. 18 expands the text of Joel, reiterating the point made in v. 17, "They will prophesy." Whatever the actual phenomenon at Pentecost, Peter emphasized here that it was prophecy, inspired utterance from the Lord.

The signs referred to in vv. 19-20 have often perplexed interpreters. Did Peter see them as having transpired at Pentecost, or did he relegate them to the final times, to the period of the second coming? Did he perhaps include them only in order to get to the crucial v. 21 with its reference to salvation, which would become the final appeal of his sermon? A key may perhaps be found in the little words "above" and "below," which have been added to the Septuagint of Joel. D. Arichea has suggested that we may have a chiastic *a-b-b-a* pattern here with *a* comprising the signs above: the darkened sun, the blood-colored moon. The signs below are the blood, fire, and thick smoke, which could more easily be

---

[103]D. C. Arichea, Jr., "Some Notes on Acts 2:17-21," *BT* 35 (1984): 442-43.

related to the events in Jesus' passion and at Pentecost.[104] In any event the signs in v. 19 are standard apocalyptic language and almost certainly refer to the final cosmic events preceding the Parousia.

Verse 21 was the most important verse for Peter: "Everyone who calls upon the name of the Lord will be saved." For Peter the "Lord" in the context of this sermon was Jesus Christ. Everything that followed in the sermon—Christ's death, his resurrection, his exaltation—pointed in the same direction. Whoever calls on his name, whoever confesses him as Lord, will be saved. Appropriately, Peter concluded his appeal with this same theme of calling (v. 39).[105]

(2) Scriptural Proof Concerning Christ's Messiahship (2:22-36)

[22]"Men of Israel, listen to this: Jesus of Nazareth was a man accredited by God to you by miracles, wonders and signs, which God did among you through him, as you yourselves know. [23]This man was handed over to you by God's set purpose and foreknowledge; and you, with the help of wicked men, put him to death by nailing him to the cross. [24]But God raised him from the dead, freeing him from the agony of death, because it was impossible for death to keep its hold on him. [25]David said about him:

" 'I saw the Lord always before me.
    Because he is at my right hand,
    I will not be shaken.
[26]Therefore my heart is glad and my tongue rejoices;
    my body also will live in hope,
[27]because you will not abandon me to the grave,
    nor will you let your Holy One see decay.
[28]You have made known to me the paths of life;
    you will fill me with joy in your presence.'

[29]"Brothers, I can tell you confidently that the patriarch David died and was buried, and his tomb is here to this day. [30]But he was a prophet and knew that God had promised him on oath that he would place one of his descendants on his throne. [31]Seeing what was ahead, he spoke of the resurrection of the Christ, that he was not abandoned to the grave, nor did his body see decay. [32]God has raised this Jesus to life, and we are all witnesses of the fact. [33]Exalted to the right hand of God, he has received from the Father the promised Holy Spirit and has poured out what you now see and hear. [34]For David did not ascend to heaven, and yet he said,

" 'The Lord said to my Lord:
    "Sit at my right hand
[35]until I make your enemies
    a footstool for your feet." '"

---

[104]Ibid.

[105]The text of Joel seems to have influenced the entire text of Acts 2:1-16 to some extent. See C. A. Evans, "The Prophetic Setting of the Pentecost Sermon," *ZNW* 74 (1983): 148-50.

[36]"Therefore let all Israel be assured of this: God has made this Jesus, whom you crucified, both Lord and Christ."

Acts 2:22-36 is the heart of Peter's sermon. It begins with an introductory summary of God's action in the ministry, death, and resurrection of Christ (vv. 22-24). A scriptural proof from Ps 16:8-11 then shows that Christ is indeed the expected Messiah, as his resurrection proves (vv. 25-31). A further scriptural proof from Ps 110:1 depicts how the risen Christ is now both Messiah and Lord exalted to the right hand of the Father (vv. 32-36).

Many interpreters feel that these verses incorporate the most primitive form of the Christian kerygma, in which the death of Christ is closely linked to his resurrection. The basic form of this confession is found throughout Acts and runs: "Jesus of Nazareth whom you killed . . . but God raised."[106] Here Peter expanded on the basic kerygmatic formula by referring briefly to the earthly ministry of Jesus.

2:22 Jesus is introduced as "Jesus of Nazareth," a designation found frequently in Acts, which merely identifies Jesus by naming his hometown.[107] Jesus is further identified as "a man accredited by God to you by miracles, wonders and signs, which God did among you through him" (v. 22). Here perhaps is found a very early Jewish-Christian Christology in which Jesus is depicted as the Messiah-designate. Undue stress should probably not be placed on the term "man," which merely stresses his personhood rather than betraying a primitive adoptionism.[108] The key term is "accredited" (*apodedeigmenon*), a semitechnical term often found in Greek papyri and inscriptions for office holders. It can either be used of those who already hold office or for those who have received appointment but have not yet entered into active service in the office. The latter sense seems to fit the context here. Peter depicted Jesus in his earthly ministry as being designated by God as Messiah but as only entering into the active function of that role upon his death and resurrection.[109]

The proof that Jesus was God's appointed Messiah is to be seen in the "miracles, signs, and wonders" he performed during his earthly ministry.

---

[106]Compare Acts 3:15; 4:10; 5:30; 10:39-40; 13:28-30. See Schneider, *Apostelgeschichte* 1:271.

[107]There have been many attempts to find messianic links to the term "Nazarene," such as deriving it from the Hebrew *nazer* for "root, shoot"; but it was a common Jewish practice to designate persons by means of their place of origin. That seems to be the function of "Nazarene" in connection with Jesus throughout Acts (cf. Acts 3:6; 4:10; 6:14; 22:8; 26:9; Luke 18:37). The sole exception is Acts 24:5, where the term is used of the Christian group as a whole, the sect of the Nazarenes (i.e., those connected with Jesus). See *Beginnings* 5:356-57.

[108]H. K. Mouton, "Acts 2:22, 'Jesus, a man approved by God'?" *BT* 30 (1979): 344-45.

[109]*Beginnings* 4:23.

The dominant word is "miracles" (*dynameis*), the "mighty acts" of Jesus, the characteristic term used in the Gospels to depict his miracles. These are further defined as "wonders" (*terata*) and "signs" (*sēmeia*), things that point beyond themselves to a deeper reality. Throughout Acts the term "wonders" only occurs in conjunction with "signs," a testimony to the fact that mere marvels have no value in themselves except as they point beyond themselves to the divine power behind them and so lead to faith.[110] Peter stressed that the Jerusalem Jews should have read the meaning of these signs and recognized Jesus as the appointed Messiah: "You yourselves know these things; you witnessed Jesus' miracles" (author's paraphrase, v. 22b). This portion of Peter's speech established the guilt of the Jewish crowd, put them under conviction, and so led them to repentance and faith.

2:23 Far from seeing in Jesus God's designated Messiah, they rejected him and gave him over to "wicked men" to be crucified (v. 23). All of this was, however, according to God's plan and foreknowledge. Peter carefully balanced the elements of God's divine purposes and the human responsibility for the crucifixion of Jesus.[111] In the paradox of divine sovereignty and human freedom, Jesus died as the result of deliberate human decision made in the exercise of their God-given freedom of choice. The Jewish crowd at Pentecost could not avoid their responsibility in Jesus' death. Nonetheless, in the mystery of the divine will, God was working in these events of willful human rebellion to bring about his eternal purposes, bringing out of the tragedy of the cross the triumph of the resurrection. The Jews were not alone in their responsibility for Jesus' death, however. They worked through the agency of "lawless men" ("wicked," NIV), a term used by Jews to designate Gentiles. Jesus died on a Roman cross;[112] Gentiles too shared the guilt. Peter carefully balanced all the participants in the drama of Jesus' death—the guilt of Jew and Gentile alike, the triumphal sovereignty of God.

2:24 Verse 24 supplies the second member of the early Christian kerygma. True, humans nailed Jesus to a cross, but God raised him from the dead. This is further defined in an unusual manner: literally, "loosing him from the birth pangs [*ōdinas*] of death" ("freeing him from the agony of death"). "Birth pangs" seems an unusual metaphor to apply to death, and there may be a Hebrew translation variant behind the text here, with

---

[110]Carter and Earle, *Acts*, 36.

[111]This double dimension of divine purpose and human responsibility runs throughout Luke-Acts. On the one hand, Jesus' death follows the divine purpose: Luke 9:22; 17:25; 22:37; 24:26; 24:44,46; Acts 17:3. On the other, guilt of the people is strongly emphasized in the passion narrative: Luke 23:2,4-5,20-23,25,51.

[112]At v. 23b the Greek text reads simply "nailing him." Obviously the reference is to the cross, which must be supplied. See Robertson, *WP* 3:29.

an original meaning of "cords, bonds," which would go naturally with loosing: Jesus was loosed from the cords of death that bound him.[113] Still, one could perhaps see some appropriateness in the metaphor of "birth pangs," since resurrection in a real sense is a new birth from death.[114]

2:25-28 Having set forth the basic Christian confession that Jesus is God's appointed Messiah, Peter sought to support this with scriptural proof from Ps 16:8-11. Luke reproduced the psalm exactly as it appears in the Septuagint (vv. 25-28). The attribution of the psalm to David is particularly important in this instance, since its application to Jesus is based on the Davidic descent of the Messiah.[115] Originally the psalm seems to have been a plea of the psalmist that God would vindicate him and that he might escape death and Sheol. Peter applied the psalm messianically, seeing in it a prophecy of David that could not ultimately apply to himself.[116] Verse 27 is the key, in which David is seen to have expressed his confidence that he would not be abandoned to the grave, that God would not allow his holy one to suffer decay. The phrases are parallel, both expressing David's hope that God would not abandon him to death. The NIV has wisely translated the Greek word *Hades* as "the grave." The reference is to *Sheol*, the realm of the dead, and thus to death; and this is the sense in which Peter applied it.[117] "Holy One" could apply to David as the anointed king, but for Peter it was even more appropriate as a designation for Christ. Verse 28 continues the quotation with v. 11 of Ps 16. One wonders why Peter included it since it adds nothing to his argument about the resurrection. Perhaps it was because of the reference to the "paths of life." Christ is the "author of life" (cf. Acts 3:15), the leader in the path to new life by virtue of his resurrection.

In vv. 29-31 Peter applied the psalm to Christ. His reasoning was straightforward. It is well known that David died, so the psalm could not apply to him (v. 29). The psalm is thus a prophecy of David intended for a descendant who would sit on the Davidic throne (v. 30). The psalm

---

[113]The variation would be due to a confusion of חֵבֶל ("pangs") with הֶבֶל ("cord"). Such a variant is found in Ps 18:5, where the Hebrew text has "cords of death" but which was translated "pangs of death" in the Septuagint. See Marshall, *Acts*, 75f.

[114]D. J. Williams, *Acts*, 34; Rackham, *Acts*, 29.

[115]In first-century Judaism all the psalms were attributed to David, and this understanding is followed faithfully throughout Acts (cf. 1:16; 2:34).

[116]The Septuagintal form of the psalm has a decidedly eschatological slant. Such variants from the Hebrew text as the reading "in hope" (v. 26) instead of "securely" and "to see corruption" (v. 27) instead of "decay" allow an interpretation in terms of resurrection and immortality. See A. Schmitt, "Ps. 16, 8-11 als Zeugnis der Auferstehung in der Apg.," *BZ* 17 (1973): 229-48.

[117]Some have wanted to see a reference to Christ's descent into hell here, but Hades cannot bear that meaning and in this context simply means *death*. See Robertson, *WP* 3:31.

applies to Christ, who indeed has risen and is thus the messianic descendant of whom David spoke (v. 31). The psalm is not used to prove the resurrection but rather the messianic status of Jesus. The proof of the resurrection is the eyewitness report of the disciples (v. 32). The psalm depicts David's vision that the Messiah would not be bound by death. Since Christ alone has burst the bonds of death by virtue of his resurrection, then he alone is the Messiah whom David foresaw.[118]

2:29 Some unusual ascriptions are given to David in these verses. "Patriarch" (v. 29) was a term generally reserved for Abraham, Isaac, Jacob, and his twelve sons; but there is some evidence that by Peter's day the term had been extended to include David and others.[119] Equally unusual is the inclusion of David among the prophets in v. 30, but again there is first-century evidence that the term was occasionally applied to him.[120] The site of David's tomb mentioned in v. 29 is no longer certain but was probably on the south side of the southeast hill of Jerusalem near the pool of Siloam. Josephus said that John Hyrcanus looted the tomb of 3,000 talents of silver during the siege of Jerusalem in 135/134 B.C. and that Herod attempted the same. According to Josephus, Herod's attempt was thwarted when two of his men were killed by a sudden burst of flame upon entering the tomb. Having second thoughts, Herod abandoned the project and built a white marble portico over the tomb.[121]

2:30-31 Behind the oath referred to in v. 30 stands Nathan's prophecy (Ps 132:11; 2 Sam 7:12-13) that God would establish an eternal kingdom with one of David's descendants, a prophecy that had come to be understood messianically.[122] Peter's application of the original Davidic psalm to Christ may seem somewhat strained but was very much in line with Hebrew thought, which saw a close link between individuals and their descendants. The Greek expresses this concept quite graphically with the phrase "from the fruit of his loins" ("one of his descendants," NIV).[123] Since David died, Peter had to have been speaking of a descendant, a descendant who fulfilled the words of David by not being abandoned in the grave or suffering the decay of death (v. 31). Only one has ever conquered the grave, so David must have foreseen the resurrection of the Messiah. Jesus' resurrection links him to David's prophecy. It follows that Jesus is the Messiah.

---

[118]Dupont, *Salvation of the Gentiles*, 106-10.

[119]Pesch, 1:123, cites Sir 47 as an example of the broader usage.

[120]Josephus (*Ant.* 6.8.2) describes David as "prophesying," as does 11QPss. See J. A. Fitzmyer, "David, 'Being Therefore a Prophet' . . . (Acts 2:30)," *CBQ* 34 (1972): 332-39.

[121]*Antiquities* 13.249 and *War* 1.61. See *Beginnings* 4:24.

[122]There is evidence from the Qumran writings (4QFlor) that 2 Sam 7:10-16 was interpreted messianically. See Marshall, *Acts*, 77.

[123]Compare the same line of reasoning in Heb 7:9-10.

2:32-35 From resurrection Peter then proceeded to the exaltation of Christ. Christ is indeed the Messiah, for God has raised him, fulfilling the prophecy of David. The proof of Jesus' resurrection is the eyewitness report of the apostles (v. 32). The exaltation has already been implicitly mentioned by the reference to the enthronement of David's descendant in v. 30. Now it becomes explicit in v. 33. God has exalted Christ to his right hand and given him the gift of the Holy Spirit, which has now been poured out. Just as the apostles were witnesses to Jesus' resurrection, so the Jewish crowd itself was witness to the exaltation of Christ as they had witnessed the gift of the outpoured Spirit at Pentecost.[124] Only the one exalted to God's right hand can dispense the Spirit.

The Spirit has been poured out, as "you now see and hear." It follows that the Christ has been exalted. But again Peter used a scriptural proof to back up this assertion, again a psalm of David (Ps 110:1). The reasoning is much the same as before. David spoke of one being exalted to God's right hand. David did not ascend into heaven, so he could not have been speaking of himself. It follows, implicitly this time, that David must have spoken of his messianic descendant. The conclusion is the same as before. The outpouring of the Spirit testifies to the ascent of the Messiah since David predicted this ascent. Thus Christ is Messiah.

Psalm 110:1 was a favorite text for the early church. According to Mark 12:35-37, it was first used of the Messiah by Jesus himself to attack the usual political understanding of a Davidic Messiah. It reappears throughout the New Testament, in 1 Cor 15:25; Heb 1:13; 10:13 and with strong allusions in Rom 8:34; Eph 1:20,22; Col 3:1; Heb 1:3; 8:1; 10:12; 12:2; 1 Pet 3:22. Originally it may have been an enthronement psalm acknowledging the earthly king as God's representative. For the early Christians it became the basis for the affirmation that Jesus has been exalted to God's right hand. For Peter it served as a natural transition from the confession of Jesus as Messiah, the dominant concept to this point, to the ultimate confession that Jesus is Lord.

2:36 Verse 36 provides the climax to Peter's sermon and returns full circle to its beginning point, the affirmation of Jesus as Lord (v. 21). In fact, every point to this conclusion of the sermon harks back to its beginning. "God has made this Jesus . . . Lord and Christ" is reminiscent of the Messiah-designate language of v. 22. "Whom you crucified" returns to the theme of the Jewish guilt in Jesus' death (v. 23). Peter's whole use of

---

[124]A connection between the exaltation of Christ and the outpouring of the Spirit is found by many exegetes by appealing to an early Christian use of Ps 68:18 in the form found in Eph 4:8. See J. Dupont, "Ascension du Christ et don de l'Espirit d'après Actes 2, 33," *Christ and the Spirit in the New Testament*, 219-28. Allusions to Ps 68:18, however, are simply not apparent in Acts 2:33.

the psalms had been to establish the messianic status of Jesus for his Jewish audience. Now, with the prompting of Ps 110:1, he moved them to call upon the name that is above every name (Phil 2:9) and confess Jesus as Lord, leading back to his original text of Joel 2:32.[125]

(3) Invitation and Response (2:37-41)

[37]When the people heard this, they were cut to the heart and said to Peter and the other apostles, "Brothers, what shall we do?"

[38]Peter replied, "Repent and be baptized, every one of you, in the name of Jesus Christ for the forgiveness of your sins. And you will receive the gift of the Holy Spirit. [39]The promise is for you and your children and for all who are far off—for all whom the Lord our God will call."

[40]With many other words he warned them; and he pleaded with them, "Save yourselves from this corrupt generation." [41]Those who accepted his message were baptized, and about three thousand were added to their number that day.

2:37-39 Peter's Jewish crowd got his point. They were guilty of rejecting, even crucifying, the Messiah. Luke said they were "cut to the heart," an uncommon word Homer used to depict horses stamping the earth with their hooves (v. 37).[126] Peter's response was almost programmatic in that he presented them with four essentials of the conversion experience (v. 38): repentance, baptism in the name of Jesus Christ, forgiveness of sins, and receipt of the Spirit.[127] These four generally form a single complex throughout Luke-Acts. They are the normative ingredients of conversion. There is no set, mechanistic pattern by which the various components come into play, particularly baptism and the receipt of the Spirit. The connection of the Spirit with baptism is depicted in various sequences through Acts. Here the Spirit seems to be promised immediately following or as a concomitant of baptism, whereas in 10:44-48 the coming of the Spirit seems to have preceded water baptism. The Ethiopian eunuch was baptized, but receipt of the Spirit was not mentioned (8:38), though his resulting joy was a gift of the Spirit. Baptism and the gift of the Spirit are separated by some interval of time for the Samaritans (8:12,17). The disciples of John at Ephesus were rebaptized and immedi-

---

[125]In the original context of Joel 2:32, κύριος refers to Yahweh. Very early it came to apply to Christ as well, which reflects a high Christology. Although it has often been argued that κύριος came into Christian usage via Hellenistic cults (e.g., W. Bousset, *Kurios Christos* [Göttingen: Vandenhoeck und Ruprecht, 1921]), the occurrence of the Aramaic phrase *marana-tha* ("Lord, come") in 1 Cor 16:22 and in *Did.* 10:6 (also *translated* in Rev 22:20) points more in the direction of an early Jewish-Christian application of the normal appellation for God to Jesus as well.

[126]Robertson, *WP* 3:34.

[127]For the view that these form a complex of associated ideas that appear in various formulations, see S. New, in *Beginnings* 5:121-40. The same viewpoint is argued by J. D. G. Dunn, *Baptism in the Spirit*.

ately received the Spirit (19:5-6). The Spirit cannot be tied down to a set pattern. Clearly, however, both baptism and receipt of the Spirit are normative to the experience of becoming a Christian believer.[128]

The connection of baptism with the forgiveness of sins in v. 38 has often been a matter of controversy. A literal rendering of the verse runs: "Repent, and let each of you be baptized in the name of Jesus Christ *for/ on the basis of* the forgiveness of your sins." The disputed word is the preposition *eis*, which could indicate purpose and thus be taken to mean that baptism is the prerequisite for the forgiveness of sins. There is ample evidence in the New Testament, however, that *eis* can also mean *on the ground of, on the basis of*, which would indicate the opposite relationship—that the forgiveness of sins is the basis, the grounds for being baptized.[129] Perhaps more significant, however, is that the usual connection of the forgiveness of sins in Luke-Acts is with repentance and not with baptism at all (cf. Luke 24:47; Acts 3:19; 5:31).[130] In fact, in no other passage of Acts is baptism presented as bringing about the forgiveness of sins. If not linked with repentance, forgiveness is connected with faith (cf. 10:43; 13:38f.; 26:18).[131] The dominant idea in 2:38 thus seems to be repentance, with the other elements following. Repentance leads to baptism, the forgiveness of sins, and the gift of the Spirit. The essential response Peter called from the Jewish crowd is the complete turnabout that comprises true repentance, to turn away from their rejection of the Messiah and to call upon his name,[132] receive baptism into his community, and share the gift of the Spirit they had just witnessed so powerfully at work in the Christians at Pentecost. Peter concluded his appeal with a promise, the promise of Joel 2:32 (cf. v. 21): "Everyone who calls on the name of the Lord will be saved." The universal scope of the promise is emphasized. Salvation is not only for the group of Jews present at Pentecost but for future generations ("your children") as well. It is not only for Jews but for Gentiles, for those "who are far off."[133]

---

[128]For a comprehensive survey of research in Acts on the connection between baptism and the Spirit, see M. Quesnel, *Baptisés dans l'Espirit: Baptême et Espirit Saint dans les Actes des Apôtres*, Lectio divina 120 (Paris: Cerf, 1985).

[129]A. T. Robertson, *A Grammar of the Greek New Testament in the Light of Historical Research* (New York: Doran, 1914), 592; also *WP* 3:35.

[130]See *Beginnings* 4:26.

[131]B. Sauvagnat, "Se repantir, etre baptisé, recevoir l'Espirit: Actes 2:37ss.," *Foi et Vie* 80 (1981): 77-89.

[132]There seems to be no distinction between the prepositions ἐπί, ἐν, and εἰς in the baptismal formulas of Acts. The meaning seems to be the same in every case: calling upon the name is to invoke the power of Jesus and commit oneself to his rule.

[133]The allusion is probably to Isa 57:19, which Paul also employed with reference to God's inclusion of the Gentiles (Eph 2:14,17).

2:40-41 Luke's note that Peter warned them "with many other words" was his way of indicating that he had only been able to give a portion of Peter's sermon. His reference to a "corrupt generation" (*skolias*, "crooked, perverse") is Old Testament language for a generation that is stubborn and rebellious and not faithful to God (Ps 78:8; cf. Deut 32:5; Phil 2:15). The Jews at Pentecost were part of such a generation, a generation that witnessed the coming of the Messiah and rejected him.[134] So Peter's final word was an appeal to "save" themselves from the lot of such a generation. And they were saved; about 3,000 accepted Peter's invitation that day, were baptized, and were added to the 120.[135]

9. The Common Life of the Community (2:42-47)

[42]They devoted themselves to the apostles' teaching and to the fellowship, to the breaking of bread and to prayer. [43]Everyone was filled with awe, and many wonders and miraculous signs were done by the apostles. [44]All the believers were together and had everything in common. [45]Selling their possessions and goods, they gave to anyone as he had need. [46]Every day they continued to meet together in the temple courts. They broke bread in their homes and ate together with glad and sincere hearts, [47]praising God and enjoying the favor of all the people. And the Lord added to their number daily those who were being saved.

2:42 This section comprises the first extensive "summary" in Acts.[136] Luke perhaps provided two summaries here: v. 42 pictures the community life in itself and has much in common with the more extensive treatment beginning in v. 43. Quite possibly v. 42 should be viewed separately, as a conclusion to the Pentecost narrative.[137] Thus viewed, it provides a glimpse into the manner in which the new converts were incorporated into the believing community. Verses 43-46 thus would appear to introduce a new section that deals with the life of the whole Christian community and

---

[134]Often Jesus used the term "this generation" with reference to the stubbornness and refusal to heed his words on the part of those who witnessed his ministry: Mark 8:12,38; Luke 9:41; 11:29-32,50f.; 17:25; Matt 16:4.

[135]Some have fretted about numbers—3,000 would have been too many in proportion to the small population of Jerusalem, would have necessitated too many baptisms in the arid Judean climate, would have been too large a crowd for the temple area to accommodate. None of these presents insurmountable problems. Jerusalem had an ample water supply, the temple area was vast and would accommodate 200,000 or more (so Harrison, *Acts*, 72), and the resident population of Jerusalem has been estimated at 55,000, swelling to 180,000 during pilgrim festivals: J. Jeremias, *Jerusalem at the Time of Jesus*, trans. F. H. and C. H. Cave (Philadelphia: Fortress, 1989), 83.

[136]For the Lukan summaries, see comments on 1:14.

[137]This division is suggested by Schneider, *Apostelgeschichte* 1:287. Pesch (*Apostelgeschichte* 1:180) also argues for two summaries but sees the first as including both vv. 42 and 43 and built around the subject of "apostles," with the second summary (vv. 44-47) built around the phrase ἐπὶ τὸ αὐτό.

to prepare for the narratives of the witness in Jerusalem that follow in chaps. 3–5. That this is so is supported by the fact that the latter summary begins with a reference to the apostolic miracles (v. 43), one of which follows immediately after the summary (3:1-10).

In v. 42 the believers are said to have "devoted themselves" to four practices in their new life together. First was the teaching of the apostles. Just as the apostles had been instructed by Jesus, so they passed along that instruction to the new Christians. In keeping with Jesus' teaching to them (chap. 1), this would have included such subjects as his resurrection, the Old Testament Scriptures, the Christian witness, and surely their own reminiscences of Jesus' earthly ministry and teachings.[138] The second activity to which they devoted themselves was "the fellowship." The Greek word used here (*koinōnia*) is one Paul often employed, but it appears only here in all of Luke-Acts. Its basic meaning is "association, communion, fellowship, close relationship."[139] In secular Greek it could involve the sharing of goods, and Paul seems to have used it this way in 2 Cor 9:13. It was also used of communion with a god, especially in the context of a sacred meal; and Paul used it in that sense in 1 Cor 10:16.[140] Since it appears in a list in Acts 2:42, it is not easy to determine its exact nuance in this context. The key may be to see the terms "breaking of bread" and "prayer" in apposition to "fellowship." The meaning would then be that they devoted themselves to a fellowship that was expressed in their mutual meals and in their prayer life together.[141] If this is so, then the meaning of the third element, "the breaking of bread," would be further clarified. Joined with fellowship, it would likely carry the cultic sense of sharing a meal with the Lord, participating in the Lord's Supper.[142] It probably also involved as well their participation in a main *agapē* meal together.[143] The fourth and final element of their life together, another expression of their fellowship, was "the prayers" (RSV). The presence of the article in the Greek text before prayers has

---

[138]Harrison, *Acts*, 73, suggests that it may also have included instruction in ethics, interpersonal relationships, facing persecution, and the other types of material covered in the paraenetic portion of the NT epistles.

[139]BAGD, 439.

[140]F. Hauck, "κοίνης, κ.τ.λ.," *TDNT* 3:805.

[141]Pesch, *Apostelgeschichte* 1:130.

[142]It is often debated whether "breaking of bread" (κλάσις) is a technical term for the eucharist in Luke-Acts. The noun form only occurs here and in Luke 24:35, but the verbal expression "to break bread" is more frequent (cf. Luke 22:19; 24:30; Acts 2:46; 20:7,11; 27:35). Bruce argues that the symbolism of broken bread in connection with Christ's body would definitely point to eucharistic associations (*Acts*: NIC, 79).

[143]For a good discussion of the association of eucharist with an *agapē* meal, see R. Michiels, "The 'Model of Church' in the First Christian Community of Jerusalem: Ideal and Reality," *LouvSt* 10 (1985): 309-10.

led some interpreters to see this as a reference to their keeping the formal prayer hours of Judaism in the temple.[144] They may well have done so to some extent, for their faithfulness in attending temple worship is noted in 2:46 and 3:1. The reference, however, is probably much broader and involves primarily their sharing in prayer together in their private house worship.

2:43 The longer summary gives a fuller description of the life of the entire Christian community. It begins in v. 43 by referring to the miracles performed by the apostles. The miracles are described with the character-istic combination "signs" and "wonders."[145] The same phrase continues to be used of the apostles' miracle-working in 4:30 and 5:12 and is applied to others as well: Jesus (2:22), Stephen (6:8), Moses (7:36), Philip (8:13), and Paul and Barnabas (14:3; 15:12). It is interesting to note that the phrase is no longer used after chap. 15, although Paul con-tinued to work miracles.[146]

An example of one such miraculous sign is given in 3:1-10. Luke's summary statement would indicate that this healing story is only one example of many miracles worked by the apostles in this early stage of their ministry. The response of the people is a reverent fear (*phobos*, "awe," NIV). "Everyone" probably refers to those outside the Christian community who were awed by apostolic miracles (cf. 5:12-13).

2:44-45 Verse 44 elaborates on the fellowship enjoyed by the Chris-tians. The word *koinōnia* is not used, but other terms express the same reality. First, they are said to have been "together" (*epi to auto*). This Greek phrase is notoriously difficult to translate, occurring five times in Acts (1:15; 2:1, 44,47; 4:26). It seems to depict the gathered community, with a strong emphasis on their unity.[147] This unity is further expressed by their holding "everything in common" (which is described in v. 45 as selling their goods for the benefit of others whenever a need arose).

Here two ideals for a community of goods seem to be combined. First is the Greek ideal of a community in which everything is held in common and shared equally. It is a basically utopian concept, which can be traced

---

[144]Basing his argument on a technical usage of προσκαρτεροῦντες (devoting themselves) in synagogue inscriptions with the meaning of worship, Jeremias claimed that 2:42 depicts the four elements of the formal worship service for the early Christians: (1) teaching, (2) table fellowship, (3) Eucharist, and (4) prayers. See *The Eucharistic Words of Jesus*, trans. N. Perrin (London: SCM, 1966), 118-21.

[145]For the relationship between these two words, see comments on 2:22.

[146]Perhaps this is reflective of Luke's subtlety as a writer. "Signs and wonders" is a com-mon OT phrase and so is employed in the earlier chapters of Acts, where the witness was primarily to Jews. In the later portions of Acts, with their Greek setting, Paul used less "biblical" terminology (cf. 19:11).

[147]For a full treatment of the phrase see J. Dupont, *Nouvelles Etudes*, 308-09.

as far back as the Pythagorean communities and is often expressed by the
same phrase Luke employed in v. 44, "holding all in common" (*echein
hapanta koina*).[148] Verse 45, however, speaks against the early Christian
community adopting a practice of community ownership. The imperfect
tense is used, indicating that this was a recurrent, continuing practice:
their practice was to sell their property and goods[149] and apportion the
proceeds whenever a need arose.[150] This is much more in keeping with
the Old Testament ideal of community equality, of sharing with the needy
so that "there will be no poor among you" (Deut 15:4f.).

2:46-47 Verse 46 sets forth the dual locale of their life together. They
remained faithful to their Jewish worship, devoting themselves "with one
accord" ("together") in the temple. The word translated "with one
accord" (*homothymadon*) is commonly used in Acts to express unity of
purpose and particularly applies to the "one heart and mind" (4:32) of the
Christian fellowship (cf. 1:14; 2:1; 4:24; 5:12; 15:25). F. Stagg, however,
points out that single-mindedness is not always a good thing. The same
word is used of the angry mobs that rushed upon Stephen (7:57) and Paul
(19:29).[151] For the Christian community, fellowship and unity of purpose
are salutary only when rooted in fellowship with Christ and in the unity
of his Spirit. The structure of Acts should remind us of this—the unity of
the Christian community derives from and is guided by the gift of the
Spirit that lies at the heart of its life together.

The Christian presence in the temple testifies not only to their remaining faithful to their Jewish heritage but also evidences their zeal for witness. In Jerusalem the temple was the primary place where crowds would
be found, and there the Christians went to bear their witness (3:11-12;
5:21,42). If the temple was the place of witness, homes were the place for
fellowship.[152] In the intimacy of the home setting, a common meal was
shared together, probably including the Lord's Supper as well. It was a
time marked by rejoicing in their fellowship with one another and with

---

[148]For references in the Hellenistic literature, see P. W. van der Horst, "Hellenistic Parallels to the Acts of the Apostles (2:1-47)," *JSNT* 25 (1985): 59-60. For a comparison with
the community of goods practiced at Qumran, see the comments on Acts 4:32-35 and
J. Downey, "The Early Jerusalem Christians," *TBT* 91 (1977): 1295-1303.

[149]Two types of property are probably to be seen in v. 45, possessions in general
(ὑπάρξεις) and real estate (κτήματα).

[150]This practice is described in greater detail in 4:32-35. See the comments on that passage.

[151]F. Stagg, *The Book of Acts: The Early Struggle for an Unhindered Gospel* (Nashville:
Broadman, 1955), 67-70.

[152]The Greek phrase κατ' οἶκον can be translated "at home" or "from house to house."
The latter is probably preferable, depicting the Christians as individually opening their
homes to the larger fellowship. With such a large membership, the picture is probably that of
a number of home fellowships.

the Spirit and by their own openness and sincerity (*aphelotēs*). On the giving end, they expressed their joy by praising God for his presence in their life together (v. 47). On the receiving end, they experienced the favor of the nonbelieving Jewish community in Jerusalem.[153] God responded to their faith and blessed the young community, adding new converts daily.[154] Indeed, as with the young Jesus, so it was for the growing church—favor with God and favor with humanity (Luke 2:52).[155]

Verses 43-46 give an ideal portrait of the young Christian community, witnessing the Spirit's presence in the miracles of the apostles, sharing their possessions with the needy among them, sharing their witness in the temple, sharing themselves in the intimacy of their table fellowship. Their common life was marked by praise of God, joy in the faith, and sincerity of heart. And in it all they experienced the favor of the nonbelievers and continual blessings of God-given growth. It was an ideal, almost blissful time marked by the joy of their life together and the warmth of the Spirit's presence among them. It could almost be described as the young church's "age of innocence." The subsequent narrative of Acts will show that it did not always remain so. Sincerity sometimes gave way to dishonesty, joy was blotched by rifts in the fellowship, and the favor of the people was overshadowed by persecutions from the Jewish officials. Luke's summaries present an ideal for the Christian community which it must always strive for, constantly return to, and discover anew if it is to have that unity of spirit and purpose essential for an effective witness.

---

[153]Λαός refers to the Jewish people as a whole, just as in the normal usage of the Septuagint.

[154]The present participle σῳζομένους should not be seen as referring to a gradual process of salvation for the believers but rather as a reference to the gradual process of God's addition of new converts to the community: *Beginnings* 4:30. Robertson summarizes the picture as being "a continuous revival, day by day" (*WP* 3:40).

[155]The most troublesome appearance of ἐπὶ τὸ αὐτό occurs at the end of v. 47. After "And the Lord added those who were being saved day by day," the Greek phrase is ἐπὶ τὸ αὐτό. The NIV translates it "to their number." The "unity" emphasis of the phrase would favor a translation such as "to the fellowship/unity of the existing community." See E. Delebecque, "Trois simples mots, chargés d'une lumière neuve," *RevThom* 80 (1980): 75-85. The scribes had trouble with the phrase. Some added the words "to the church" in v. 47, while others moved ἐπὶ τὸ αὐτό to the next verse, thus reading "Peter and John together."

SECTION OUTLINE

II. THE APOSTLES WITNESS TO THE JEWS IN JERUSALEM (3:1–5:42)

True to the mandate of Acts 1:8, the witness that began with Pentecost was pursued vigorously in Jerusalem. The events of chaps. 3–5 are set entirely within the holy city. At this point the Christian community was wholly Jewish in membership. These first believers were true to their Jewish heritage and committed to the task of winning their fellow Jews to Jesus the Messiah. As a result their activity in these chapters is set in their home fellowships, the temple, and the Jewish Sanhedrin. Their home meetings were the place for renewal; the temple was the place for witness; the Sanhedrin, the place for defense. The first two locales are familiar from chaps. 1–2. The latter is new to this section and sets an ominous note, the opposition to the gospel that would dog the Christian witnesses throughout the whole of Acts.

This portion of Acts begins with a rather tightly knit section running from 3:1–4:31. It begins with Peter's healing a lame beggar in the temple precincts (3:1-11), which attracted a crowd and prompted a sermon from Peter (3:12-26). This led to his and John's arrest by the temple guard and a hearing before the Jewish ruling council (4:1-21). At the center of their interrogation was the subject of the lame man's healing (4:9,16,22). The section ends with the community's prayer of praise to God for the apostles' release and their petition for more signs and wonders, a final closure to the healing episode and its aftermath (4:23-31).

The narrative now turns to a further glimpse into the community's life together, particularly focusing on their sharing of goods. This comprises 4:32–5:11, which depicts the practice at its best (4:32-37) and its tragic worst (5:1-11). A summary statement on the continuing miracles performed by the apostles (5:12-16) is followed by their arrest and a second appearance before the Sanhedrin (5:17-42), much as Peter's miraculous healing of the beggar provoked the first arrest.

1. Peter's Healing a Lame Beggar (3:1-11)

[1]One day Peter and John were going up to the temple at the time of prayer—at three in the afternoon. [2]Now a man crippled from birth was being carried to the temple gate called Beautiful, where he was put every day to beg from those going into the temple courts. [3]When he saw Peter and John about to enter, he asked them for money. [4]Peter looked straight at him, as did John. Then Peter said, "Look at us!" [5]So the man gave them his attention, expecting to get something from them.

[6]Then Peter said, "Silver or gold I do not have, but what I have I give you. In the name of Jesus Christ of Nazareth, walk." [7]Taking him by the right hand, he helped him up, and instantly the man's feet and ankles became strong. [8]He jumped to his feet and began to walk. Then he went with them into the temple courts, walking and jumping, and praising God. [9]When all the people saw him walking and praising God, [10]they recognized him as the same man who used to sit begging at the temple gate called Beautiful, and they were filled with wonder and amazement at what had happened to him.

[11]While the beggar held on to Peter and John, all the people were astonished and came running to them in the place called Solomon's Colonnade.

Of the many miracles recounted in Acts, none has more formal resemblance to the miracles of Jesus in the Gospels than this one. There is one major difference—Jesus healed by His own authority; Peter healed by the "name" of Jesus, which was indeed by Jesus' authority at work through the agency of the apostles. Perhaps more striking still are the parallels between this story, Jesus' healing of a paralytic (Luke 5:17-26), and Paul's healing of a lame man at Lystra (Acts 14:8-11). Indeed, in Acts most of the miracles of Peter have their counterpart in similar works of

Paul in the latter half of the book.[1] In this way Luke showed that the work of Christ begun in his earthly life (cf. Acts 1:1) continued in the work of the young Christian community. In Acts the miracles were always in the service of the word, confirming God's presence in the spread of the gospel or as a sign that enabled faith. Nowhere is that more evident than in this healing of the blind beggar.

3:1 The first two verses provide the setting. Peter and John were going up to the temple at the time of prayer. They were often together in the early portion of Acts (3:1,3,11; 4:13,19; 8:14).[2] Peter did all the speaking and acting, with John merely standing in the background.

John's presence is sometimes explained as based on the Jewish law that at least two witnesses are necessary to confirm any testimony (cf. 2 Cor 13:1). The practice may be traced to Jesus' sending his disciples out on mission by pairs (Luke 10:1), a practice that still retains its wisdom and validity. Peter and John are said to have gone *up* to the temple. There were various accesses to the temple, some of which involved a descent. Whether one actually ascended or descended to the temple, the customary idiom was to "go up" for worship there. The word Luke used for the temple throughout this narrative is *hieron*, i.e., the broad term for the entire temple complex.

The time of the apostles' visit was the "ninth" hour, three in the afternoon, i.e., the hour of prayer. It was also the time of the evening *Tamid*, one of the two sacrifices held daily in the temple.[3] These had become prescribed times of prayer, and people would come to the temple at the sacrifice times to observe the ceremony and pray. The largest crowds would thus have been found at the times of sacrifice, as Peter and John must have been well aware; for they went to the temple for prayer and for witness.

---

[1] For a treatment of the miracles in Acts, see the excurses in G. Schneider (*Die Apostelgeschichte*, HTKNT [Freiburg: Herder, 1980], 1:304-10) and R. Pesch (*Die Apostelgeschichte*, Teilband I: Apg. 1-12 [Zurich: Benziger, 1986], 141-48). See also P. J. Achtemeier, "The Lukan Perspective on the Miracles of Jesus: A Preliminary Sketch," *JBL* 94 (1975): 547-62; F. Neirynck, "The Miracle Stories in the Acts of the Apostles," in *Les Acts des Apôtres: Tradition, rédaction, theologie*, ed. J. Kremer (Gembloux: Duculot, 1979), 169-213; J. A. Hardon, "The Miracle Narratives in the Acts of the Apostles," *CBQ* 16 (1954): 303-18.

[2] John was almost certainly the disciple John, the son of Zebedee. Some interpreters have identified him with John Mark, based on the testimony of Papias that he was the disciple and interpreter of Peter (Eusebius, *Hist. Eccl.* 3.39). When Luke introduced him to the narrative in Acts, however, he was careful to distinguish him as "that John who is also called Mark" (Acts 12:12). Assuming John was the "beloved disciple," the Fourth Gospel is an independent witness to this pairing of Peter and John (13:23-25; 20:2-8; 21:20-22).

[3] Josephus recorded that the two daily sacrifices took place in the morning and at the ninth hour (*Ant.* 14.65; cf. Num 28:4). There also was a third time of prayer, probably at sunset. See O. Holtzmann, "Die Taglichen Gebetsstunden im Judentum und Urchristentum," *ZNW* 12 (1911): 90-107.

3:2 Verse 2 introduces the one who would be healed. He is described as "crippled [*chōlos*, lame] from birth [literally, 'from his mother's womb']." The fact that he was born lame makes his healing all the more remarkable (cf. 4:22). This man was no recent "psychosomatic" cripple but one who was congenitally lame. When Peter and John arrived at one of the temple gates, this man was in the process of being carried and placed there to beg for alms from those entering the temple.

That he would have been carried there so late seems strange, for the afternoon *Tamid* was the final stage of the daily temple worship; the crowds would soon have been gone for the day. Still, it was one of the two major periods of worship, and many would have come to the temple at precisely this time to express their devotion to God. It was prime time for receiving alms. The rabbis taught that there were three pillars for the Jewish faith—the Torah, worship, and the showing of kindness, or charity.[4] Almsgiving was one of the main ways to show kindness and was thus considered a major expression of one's devotion to God. With their minds set on worship, those who entered the temple for the evening sacrifice and prayer would be particularly disposed to practice their piety by generously giving alms to a lame beggar.

Where did all this take place? Luke described the gate as the "gate called Beautiful." Unfortunately Jewish literature has no reference to a gate called "beautiful." From the third century on, it has been identified with the Shushan gate, which was located on the eastern wall of the temple precincts and was the main access for those approaching the temple from the Kidron Valley. There are serious problems with this identification, however. It was primarily an access for those coming to the temple from the east outside Jerusalem, and Acts has given the picture that the apostles were no longer residing at Bethany, east of the city, but were staying in Jerusalem (cf. 1:14; 2:1). Further, access to the Shushan gate was extremely steep and treacherous because it was located on the eastern wall at the top of the precipitous cliff overlooking the Kidron valley. Few would have chosen such a hazardous entrance to the temple, and it would not have been a good spot for begging.[5] A more likely identification thus seems to be one of the gates that led into the sanctuary proper. Josephus spoke of ten gates in the sanctuary. Nine, he said, were overlaid with silver and gold; but the tenth "was of Corinthian bronze and far

---

[4]*M. Abot* 1:2.

[5]The Shushan gate provided immediate access to Solomon's Colonnade where Peter delivered his speech (v. 11). This observation offers plausible grounds for identifying it as the place where the healing took place. For arguments favoring the Shushan gate, see K. Lake and H. J. Cadbury, *The Beginnings of Christianity, The Acts of the Apostles*, 4:32 and D. Hamm, "Acts 3:1-10: The Healing of the Temple Beggar as Lucan Theology," *Bib* 67 (1986): 305-19.

exceeded in value those plated with silver and set in gold."[6] So massive was this gate that when it was closed each evening, it "could scarcely be moved by twenty men."[7] This seems to be the same gate identified in the rabbinic literature as the Nicanor gate.

There is some discrepancy between the sources about the exact location of this gate. Josephus placed it at the far eastern access to the sanctuary, leading from the court of the Gentiles (the outer courtyard) into the court of the women. The rabbinic sources place it at the eastern access to the court of the men of Israel, thus between the court of the women and that of the men. Many scholars see Josephus as giving the correct location, since he was writing from living memory, whereas the rabbinic writings date from a period long after the destruction of the temple.[8] This seems to be the most likely spot for Peter's encounter with the lame man. He lay at the beautiful gate with its magnificent doors of Corinthian bronze, begging at the entrance to, but still definitely outside, the sanctuary.

3:3-5 Verses 3-5 relate Peter and John's encounter with the lame man. "Alms, alms," he begged, like a stuck phonograph record, as he would have uttered hundreds of times a day. This time the response was different. Typically, donors would flip a coin in his direction as they hastened into the temple, scarcely giving him a glance. This time the would-be benefactors stopped in their tracks. Peter fixed his gaze on him (*atenizō*). "Look [*blepō*] at me," he said. This obviously was not going to be a chance encounter, so the man responded by giving his total attention (*epechō*) to Peter.[9] Perhaps he expected a display of unusual generosity. Would this be his day? Yes, it would be, but not as he might think.

3:6a Verse 6 is the heart of the passage, the one detail that sets this story apart from the usual narrative: "I have no silver or gold." Peter perhaps cast his glance up at the magnificent doors that towered above the poor beggar. They had no silver or gold either, with their beautiful craftsmanship in solid Corinthian bronze. They were too precious to be marred with an overlay that would only detract from their beauty. All the other gates of the sanctuary were gilded. Not this one. Some things are more precious than silver or gold. The beggar was soon to learn this lesson of the "Beautiful" gate.

---

[6]Josephus, *War* 5.201 (cf. 5.198, 201-06; 2.411).

[7]Ibid., 6.293.

[8]G. Schrenck, "ἱερός, κ.τ.λ." *TDNT* 3:236; E. Schürer, "Die *Thura* oder *Pulē* Horaia Acts. 3, 2 und 10," *ZNW* 7 (1906): 51ff. The view that the rabbinic location (between courts of women and men) is correct is argued by E. Stauffer, "Das Tor des Nikanor," *ZNW* 44 (1952-53): 44-66. For a full discussion of the issues, see K. Lake, *Beginnings* 5:479-86.

[9]Hamm, "Acts 3:1-10," 314-15, suggests that this concentration of words for "fixing one's attention" points to the deeper significance of the healing narrative in its total context. The miracle sets the stage for the gospel (3:12-26), which is the truest basis of "healing" in a spiritual sense.

3:6b-10 That more precious something is related in vv. 6b-8, the gift of healing. "In the name of Jesus" Peter commanded the man to walk. The reference to "the name" is not incidental. In the biblical sense a name is far more than a label. It represents a person and is an extension of that person's being and personality. To invoke the name of Jesus is to call upon his authority and power.[10] In a real sense, then, Jesus through Peter continued his healing ministry. With a healing touch common to miracle narratives, Peter grasped the man's right hand and lifted him up. It is almost as if at this point the man needed all the encouragement he could get.[11] The man felt the new strength surging through his feet and ankles.[12] He jumped to his feet and began to walk. With his increasing awareness of the miracle that had happened to him, he entered the sanctuary with Peter and John. Before, as the lame beggar, he sat in the court of the Gentiles at the gate to the sanctuary. Day by day he sat there at the threshold to the place of worship, but he could not enter. He was lame, blemished, and denied access to the inner courts (cf. Lev 21:17-20; 2 Sam 5:8).[13] At this time not only had he received physical healing, but he had found spiritual acceptance as well. For the first time he was deemed worthy to enter the house of worship. This theme will repeat itself in Acts. Those who were rejected as unworthy for worship in the old religion of Israel found full acceptance in the name of Jesus, whether a lame beggar, an Ethiopian eunuch, a woman, or a Gentile.

No wonder the man was filled with such joy. He began walking, jumping, and praising God. For the first time he could really praise God in the place of praise, in God's house. Luke perhaps gave a veiled reference to the man's healing being a sign of the messianic times that had come in Jesus. He used a rare word (*hallomai*) for the man's jumping, a word found in the Septuagint text of Isa 35:6 with reference to the messianic age: "Then will the lame leap like a deer." The people who were present at the temple witnessed the transformation. They knew the man for the lame beggar he had been and saw what he had become as he leapt about

---

[10] "The name" represents many aspects of the authority and presence of Christ in Acts: healings and miracles (3:6,16; 4:7,10,30), baptism into his lordship (2:38; 8:16; 10:48; 19:5), forgiveness of sins (10:43), the power for witness (4:17f.; 5:28,40), even persecutions (5:41; 9:16; 15:26). The "name" represents the abiding presence of Christ in the community of believers. See W. Willimon, *Acts*, INT (Atlanta: John Knox, 1988), 45. Commitment to Christ is essential to invoking the power of Jesus' name. There is no magical efficacy to it, as Acts 19:13-22 illustrates.

[11] A. T. Robertson, *WP* 3:42.

[12] Verse 7 has often been used to support the "medical language" theory for Lukan authorship. The terms used here, however, are more literary vocabulary than technical medical language. See *Beginnings* 4:34.

[13] See B. Reicke, *Glaube und Leben der Urgemeinde: Bemerkungen zu Apg. 1-7* (Zurich: Zwingli, 1957), 64-65.

in the temple praising God. They were filled with awe and amazement at what they saw, and that wonder prepared them for Peter's explanation.

3:11 Verse 11 is transitional, linking the healing narrative in the temple with Peter's sermon from Solomon's Colonnade. Solomon's Colonnade lay along the eastern wall and thus across the court of the Gentiles and some distance from the sanctuary.[14] Although Luke did not mention any exit from the sanctuary, one has to assume that the group exited the temple by way of the beautiful gate, traversed the court of the Gentiles, and reassembled at Solomon's portico.[15] The scene was now set for Peter's speech. The healed man was there as living evidence of the miracle, holding fast to Peter and John. The crowd likewise came running to the scene with a mixture of curiosity and awe. Peter was not about to miss this opportunity for witness.

2. Peter's Sermon from Solomon's Colonnade (3:12-26)

[12]When Peter saw this, he said to them: "Men of Israel, why does this surprise you? Why do you stare at us as if by our own power or godliness we had made this man walk? [13]The God of Abraham, Isaac and Jacob, the God of our fathers, has glorified his servant Jesus. You handed him over to be killed, and you disowned him before Pilate, though he had decided to let him go. [14]You disowned the Holy and Righteous One and asked that a murderer be released to you. [15]You killed the author of life, but God raised him from the dead. We are witnesses of this. [16]By faith in the name of Jesus, this man whom you see and know was made strong. It is Jesus' name and the faith that comes through him that has given this complete healing to him, as you can all see.

[17]"Now, brothers, I know that you acted in ignorance, as did your leaders. [18]But this is how God fulfilled what he had foretold through all the prophets, saying that his Christ would suffer. [19]Repent, then, and turn to God, so that your sins may be wiped out, that times of refreshing may come from the Lord, [20]and that he may send the Christ, who has been appointed for you—even Jesus. [21]He must remain in heaven until the time comes for God to restore everything, as he promised long ago through his holy prophets. [22]For Moses said, 'The Lord your God will raise up for you a prophet like me from among your own people; you must listen to everything he tells you. [23]Anyone who does not listen to him will be completely cut off from among his people.'

[24]"Indeed, all the prophets from Samuel on, as many as have spoken, have foretold these days. [25]And you are heirs of the prophets and of the covenant God made with your fathers. He said to Abraham, 'Through your offspring all peoples

---

[14]Although a part of the Herodian temple, the colonnade was attributed to Solomon because he was the first to fortify the eastern wall and erect a colonnade inside it. See Josephus, *War* 5.185. Christians evidently often gathered there (cf. Acts 5:12), and Jesus was found there in the Fourth Gospel (John 10:23).

[15]The Western text solved this problem by adding the participle ἐκπορευομένου to v. 11, thus noting that they "exited" the temple.

on earth will be blessed.' ²⁶When God raised up his servant, he sent him first to you to bless you by turning each of you from your wicked ways."

Comparison of this sermon with Peter's sermon at Pentecost reveals many of the same elements. The elements in common are the address ("Men, Israelites"), beginning the sermon by correcting a false impression, reference to God's "glorifying" Jesus, a contrast of Jesus' death with his resurrection, reference to the apostles' witness to the resurrection, the responsibility of the Jerusalemites for Jesus' death, extensive proofs from the prophets, references to Jesus' exaltation and God's divine purposes, and an appeal for repentance. The two sermons contain significant differences as well. For example, the scriptural proofs in the Pentecost sermon aim at establishing the messianic status of Jesus. Those in this sermon are aimed at the need for the Jews to repent and accept Jesus as the one sent from God. A far greater proportion of this sermon is devoted to the appeal. Also there are new elements in this sermon: an emphasis on faith, a softer treatment of the Jewish responsibility for Jesus' death, and a number of striking, perhaps early Jewish-Christian titles for Jesus, such as Servant, Holy and Righteous One, Author of life, and Prophet-like-Moses.[16] The speech itself falls into two main portions. First, Peter established the relationship between the healing of the lame man and the basic Christian proclamation of the death and resurrection of Christ (3:12-16). Then he appealed to the Jews to repent and accept Christ as the Messiah sent from God (3:17-26).[17]

3:12 Verses 12 and 16 go closely together. Verse 12 raises the question about the power behind the man's healing. Verse 16 provides the answer. In between is inserted the basic kerygma of the death and resurrection of Christ and the Jewish responsibility in those events. The basic function of vv. 13-15 is to establish the Jewish guilt in rejecting Jesus. The remainder of the sermon is basically an appeal to repent and affirm Christ.

Peter began by seeking to correct any misunderstanding that he or John had healed the man by their own power or piety. No, it was faith in the name of Jesus that healed the man (v. 16). But how could the name of Jesus have such power? Verses 13-15 answer that question. The power is his by virtue of his glorification (v. 13) and his resurrection (v. 15). The "God of Abraham, Isaac and Jacob" had glorified his servant Jesus, raising him from the dead (v. 15). The patriarchal formula was a familiar one

---

[16]On the whole subject see R. F. Zehnle, *Peter's Pentecost Discourse: Tradition and Lukan Reinterpretation in Peter's Speeches of Acts 2 and 3*, SBLMS 15 (Nashville: Abingdon, 1971).

[17]Adapted from J. Schlosser, "Moise, Serviteur du Kerygme apostolique d'après Ac.3, 22-26," *RSR* 61 (1987): 17-31.

in Judaism (cf. Exod 3:6). It is perhaps not by accident that the same formula appears in Luke 20:37, a passage that deals with the resurrection.
God is the God of the living. The glorification refers to Christ's exaltation
to God's right hand. As the glorified, risen One, Christ has the power to
grant healing in his name.

3:13-15   One is struck by the unusual title "servant" (*pais*) applied
here to Jesus. It is not a common title for Jesus in the New Testament,
occurring only here and in v. 26 and twice in chap. 4 (vv. 27,30).[18] The
usage seems to be basically liturgical in chap. 4, for it is applied there to
David as well as Christ (v. 25). Here in chap. 3, particularly in a context
dealing with the *death* of Jesus, it is tempting to see an allusion to Christ
as the suffering servant of Isaiah. This becomes even more likely when
one considers the possible allusions to the servant psalms that run
throughout vv. 13-14, in the references to "glorification" (Isa 52:13), the
"righteous one" (Isa 53:11), and being "handed over" or "delivered up"
(*paradidomi*, twice in LXX of Isa 53:12).[19]

Finally, the most likely prophecies of Christ's suffering, referred to in
3:18, would be those of Isa 52:13–53:12, the passage quoted in Acts
8:32-33. The suffering servant concept is prominent throughout the New
Testament. Perhaps the reason the title only occurs in the early chapters
of Acts is that the Greek word used in Isaiah for servant (*pais*) can be
translated "son" as well and so was assimilated into the more familiar
"son of God" confession in the Greek-speaking church. Indeed, that very
tendency appears in the *King James Version* of Acts 3:13,26. The emphasis in the use of a servant Christology in Acts 3:13,26 is not on the vicar-
ious death but on the election of Christ as servant. God has chosen him,
sent him, and exalted him. The Jewish guilt lies in their rejection and
denial of God's chosen servant.

Even though God glorified Jesus, the Jerusalemites did the opposite,
handing him over to death and disowning him before Pilate (v. 13b). The
best commentary on this statement is the passion narrative in Luke 23:13-
25. There Pilate is shown to have attempted to release Jesus three times,
each being rebuffed by the Jews. So here Pilate is said to have decided to

---

[18]Though the title παῖς θεοῦ is confined to Acts, the servant psalms are quoted throughout the NT (Matt 8:17; 12:18-21; Luke 22:37; John 12:38; Acts 8:32f; Rom 10:16; 15:21)
and perhaps alluded to in significant places such as Jesus' baptism (Mark 1:11 and parallels),
Jesus' "ransom" saying (Mark 10:45), and the last supper (Mark 14:24). There are many
additional places where the concept of Jesus' suffering servanthood appears, notably in 1 Pet
2:22-25; 3:18. See J. D. Williams, *Acts*, GNC (San Francisco: Harper & Row, 1985), 59;
Beginnings 5:364-70; J. Jeremias, "παῖς θεοῦ," *TDNT* 5:677-717.

[19]See J. E. Menard, "*Pais Theou* as Messianic Title in the Book of Acts," *CBQ* 19
(1957): 83-92; J. Dupont, *Salvation of the Gentiles*, trans. J. Keating (New York: Paulist,
1979), 142.

let him go. Both here and in the Gospel, Pilate was primarily a witness to the guilt of the Jerusalem Jews. He "surrendered Jesus to their will" (Luke 23:25). Likewise the Jewish request for Barabbas, a "murderer," is fully set forth in Luke 23:18-19,25. One should not miss the irony in v. 14. The Jerusalemites requested that a murderer be released to them, for they were themselves murderers. They killed "the author of life" (v. 15). But the seeming defeat of the cross ended in victory: "God raised him from the dead." Peter and John were themselves witnesses to the reality of his resurrection. The guilt of the Jerusalem Jews was well established. Their real guilt was, however, not so much in their delivering God's chosen one to death as in their denial of Jesus (vv. 13-14). Peter continued to emphasize this in the remainder of his sermon. God sent the Christ to bless them, the sons of the covenant (v. 25), but they disowned him.

In vv. 14-15 three additional terms are applied to Christ—the Holy One, the Righteous One, and the Author of life. The Holy One is a title in the Old Testament applied to Elisha (2 Kgs 4:9) and Aaron (Ps 106:16, RSV). In the New Testament it appears to be a messianic term. Demons (Mark 1:24) and men (John 6:69) confessed Jesus as "Holy One of God." It occurs also in 1 John 2:20 ("holy one") and in Rev 3:7 ("him who is holy") as a designation for Christ. There is some evidence for the messianic use of Righteous One prior to Christianity; it appears as a title for the Messiah in *1 Enoch* 38:2; 46:3; 53:6 and *Pss. Sol.* 17:35. In Zech 9:9, a Christian *testimonium* (cf. Matt 21:5), the messianic King is described as "righteous." The title appears also in Acts 7:52 and 22:14. Finally there is the term "author [*archēgos*] of life." The term occurs only here, in 5:31, and twice in Hebrews (2:10; 12:2). The word has a double nuance, meaning either leader/pioneer or author/originator. In this passage either meaning could be applied. Christ is either the author, the originator and source of life, or he is the leader in the resurrection-life, the firstborn from the dead (cf. 26:23). The term is not a messianic title as such but an apt summary of the work of Christ in a context that deals with resurrection.

3:16 Having established that Christ has been exalted by God in light of his resurrection, and consequently that he is now in the position to dispense the divine Spirit and power, Peter answered his original question about the power behind the lame man's healing (v. 16). The Greek is complex and somewhat obscure, but the NIV probably renders it as clearly as it can be by separating it into two parallel statements, both of which emphasize two things active in the man's healing—faith and the name of Jesus. Ultimately the name, the power of Jesus, healed the man—not Peter's or John's power. But the power of Jesus worked through faith. Whose faith? That of the apostles or that of the man? Perhaps Luke deliberately left it open. Surely Peter worked by faith. But what about the man? If he had little faith to begin with, the miracle that led him to this point—clinging as he did to the apostles (v. 11)—was already bringing about in him the greater miracle of faith in Christ, the Author of life. Perhaps this is what Luke wanted us to see by emphasizing faith alone rather than the possessor of faith. For after all, faith is the greatest miracle of all, and that miracle stood open to all in Solomon's Colonnade that day.

The concluding portion of Peter's sermon can be divided into two parts, both relating to the need for the Jews to repent. Verses 17-21 give the basic call to repentance and the blessings God will grant them as a result. Verses 22-26 give scriptural support for the appeal.

3:17-18 One is struck by the conciliatory tone of vv. 17-18. The Jews in Jerusalem acted "in ignorance" when they did not recognize Jesus as the Holy and Righteous One, the anointed Servant of God. In actuality he was the author of life for them, but they sent him to his death. This was a sin of ignorance. Had they known him for who he truly was, "they would not have crucified the Lord of glory" (1 Cor 2:8). Such sins were considered by the Jews as forgivable sins and were distinguished from conscious, intentional sins, which the Old Testament describes as those done "with a high hand" (RSV). Means of atonement were available for sins of ignorance, but not for intentional, deliberate sins (cf. Num 15:27-31). Jesus himself had recognized their ignorance in crucifying him and had already prayed for their forgiveness (Luke 23:34). Thus, Peter was offering the Jerusalem Jews a second chance. Once they had disowned the Christ. It was, however, a rejection in ignorance. Now they could accept Christ and be forgiven. Should they fail to do so once Peter gave them a full understanding of Christ's true identity, it would be a wholly different matter, a deliberate, "high-handed" rejection.

In these passages that deal with the Jewish responsibility for Jesus' death, it should be borne in mind that there are four mitigating emphases. One is this emphasis on ignorance. A second is that Acts nowhere contains a blanket condemnation of the Jews: only the Jerusalem Jews are given responsibility in Jesus' death. In Paul's speeches to the Jews of the dispersion, he never charged them with any guilt in Jesus' crucifixion but made clear that only the Jerusalemites were responsible (cf. Acts 13:27-28; cf. Luke 13:33-34). Third, the Gentiles are shown to have shared in the culpability ("lawless men," 2:23; Pilate, 3:13). Finally, the suffering of the Messiah was bound up with God's own divine purposes (v. 18): God foretold it, the prophets had spoken it, and the death of Christ fulfilled it. The mystery of the divine sovereignty worked through the tragedy born of human freedom to bring about God's eternal purposes for the salvation of humanity (cf. 2:23f.). God took the cross, the quintessence of human sin, and turned it into the triumph of the resurrection. But where did the prophets predict this suffering of Christ? Luke referred to such predictions often (cf. Luke 24:46; Acts 17:3; 26:22f.; significantly also 1 Pet 2:21f.). The servant psalm of Isa 52:13–53:12 immediately comes to mind, but the early Christians did not fail to note many other Old Testament passages as finding their ultimate realization in the passion of Christ (e.g., Jer 11:19; Zech 12:10; 13:7; Pss 22; 31; 34; 69).

3:19-20 Peter gave the call to repentance (v. 19) with two expressions: "repent" (*metanoeō*) and "turn to God" (*epistrephō*). The Jerusalem Jews were to have a complete change of mind, turning from their rejection of Christ and turning, or "returning," to God. In rejecting God's Messiah they had rejected God's purpose for them. Accepting the Messiah would thus be a return to God. In vv. 19b-20 Peter gave the threefold result of their repentance: (1) their sins would be forgiven, (2) the "times of refreshing" would come upon them, and (3) God would send the Messiah whom he had appointed for them. The forgiveness of sins is clear enough.[20] Throughout Acts repentance is closely connected with forgiveness; indeed it is the basis for forgiveness (cf. 2:38).

The main sin Peter laid upon the Jerusalem Jews was their sin of ignorance in rejecting the Messiah. True forgiveness could only have come from their turning to God by accepting his Messiah. Then only would "the times of refreshing" come from the Lord. The phrase "times of refreshing" (*anapsyxis*) is difficult. The basic meaning of the word is the cooling off that comes from blowing, like the refreshment of a cool breeze. This rare biblical word occurs only here and once in the Septuagint (Exod 8:11), where it refers to the relief that came to Egypt after the plague of frogs ceased. It appears in the Jewish apocalypse 4 Ezra 11:46, where it refers to the final messianic times of Israel's redemption. What is unclear is whether it indicates a temporary period of respite during the period of messianic woes preceding the end time or whether it pictures the final time itself. Probably the latter is intended. The term is likely synonymous with the concept of "restoration" in v. 21[21] and reflects Jewish messianic expectation. It was particularly appropriate to Peter's sermon to the Jews in the temple square. The same can be said for the third result of their repentance—God's sending the Messiah to them (v. 20). This seems to reflect a common Jewish expectation that the Messiah would only come on the repentance of Israel. The reference is surely to the Messiah, as the presence of the articles indicates, "*the* Christ," the Anointed One. He is described as having been "appointed for you," i.e., "you Jews."

3:21 Verse 21 concludes Peter's appeal with an explanation for why the Messiah was not then present. He must remain in heaven until the

---

[20]Here forgiveness is expressed as "wiping out" (ἐξαλείφω), a word used in a similar sense in Col 2:14 of the wiping out of a debt or IOU.

[21]See E. Schweizer, "ἀνάψυξις," *TDNT* 9:664-65.

final time when God will restore everything.[22] The best commentary on this concept is to be found in 1:6-11. The concept of restoration is basically the same as that about which the disciples questioned in 1:6. The Messiah's present location in heaven presupposes the ascension and return at his Parousia (1:9-11). The question still remains: does 3:19-21 presuppose a Jewish messianic concept that understood the first coming of the Messiah as being predicated upon the repentance of Israel? The passage could surely be so viewed if taken in isolation from its context.[23] In the context of Peter's sermon, however, something quite different is expressed. The difference lies in the reference at the opening of his sermon to Jesus' death and resurrection. The Messiah indeed has come as the glorified Servant, the Holy and Righteous One of God. But the Jerusalem Jews did not receive him as Messiah; they disowned him. He is indeed the Messiah appointed by God, but they failed to recognize and receive him as their Messiah. The Messiah will come again to restore his kingdom to Israel (Rom 11:25-26). Whether that will be a time of refreshing for Israel depends very much on their repentance and reception of Jesus as the Messiah.[24] What was true for the Jews in Solomon's Colonnade still holds true today. Only in receiving the Christ of God by repentance and turning to him is there forgiveness, refreshing, and restoration.

3:22-23 Still continuing his appeal, Peter then gave the negative side. Jesus is depicted as the "prophet like Moses" whom God will "raise up"

---

[22]The word "restoration" (ἀποκατάστασις) can also mean *establishment* of something formerly envisioned or agreed upon, such as the payment of money due. With such a meaning, the phrase could be rendered "the establishment of all the things which the prophets predicted." This seems the more likely since "all the things written/spoken" is a standard phrase used in Luke-Acts when referring to prophecy (Luke 18:31; 21:22; 22:37; 24:44; Acts 13:29; 24:14). See G. Lohfink, "Christologie und Geschichtsbild in Apg. 3:19-21," *BZ* 13 (1969): 223-41.

[23]Verses 19-21 do appear to reflect a very old Jewish-Christian Christology. J. A. T. Robinson describes it as an "embedded fossil": "The Most Primitive Christology of All?" *JTS*, n.s. 7 (1956). O. Bauernfeind suggests that it is based on a Jewish messianism that saw Elijah coming as forerunner to the Day of the Lord, an expectation that entered Christianity by way of Baptist circles: *Kommentar und Studien zur Apostelgeschichte* (Tübingen: Mohr-Siebeck, 1980), 65-69; "Tradition und Komposition in dem Apokatastasis Spruch Apg. 3, 20f.," *Abraham unser Vater* (Leiden: Brill, 1963), 13-23. See also C. H. H. Scobie, who sees a Samaritan theology here: "The Use of Source Material in the Speeches of Acts III and VII," *NTS* 25 (1979): 399-421. For opposing viewpoints see D. L. Jones, "The Title *Christos* in Luke-Acts," *CBQ* 32 (1970): 71-73 and C. F. D. Moule, "The Christology of Acts," *Studies in Luke-Acts*, ed. L. Keck and J. L. Martyn (Nashville: Abingdon, 1966), 168-69.

[24]Whether or not one should speak of a "new Israel" or a "restored Israel" in the theology of Acts is an issue of heated scholarly debate. What is certain is that Acts depicts Christianity as being in full continuity with Israel. It is comprised of those who accept Jesus as Lord and Messiah, including Gentiles. Only those Jews who hear and respond in faith to Christ (3:22-23) have membership in the people of God.

and the people must heed (v. 22). Whoever does not listen to him will be utterly rooted out from the people (v. 23). This is basically a quotation of Deut 18:15,19, supplemented by Lev 23:29. The passage in Deuteronomy gives Moses' promise that after he is gone God will continue to speak to Israel by raising up prophets who will speak his word.

Already before the coming of Christ, this passage was being interpreted messianically in some Jewish circles. Evidence exists, for instance, that the Qumran community expected a prophet like Moses as a part of their messianic expectation, and the Samaritans hoped in a prophet-messiah called the Taheb.[25] In his Gospel, Luke often likened Jesus to a prophet (cf. Luke 4:24; 7:16,39; 24:19), and in Stephen's speech the Mosaic-prophetic typology is treated in detail (cf. Acts 7:37).

Two motifs in the tradition of Deuteronomy were particularly applicable to Christ. One was the prophetic motif. A new prophet would come, a newer and greater prophet than Moses—one whom the people must hear. The second was the reference to God's "raising up" (*anistēmi*) this prophet. In the original context of Deuteronomy the word simply meant *to bring forth*, but in application to Christ it was sure to be seen as a reference to his resurrection. Most significant of all, use of this text shows Moses himself to have been one of the prophets who witnessed to Christ. Leviticus 23:29 originally dealt with those in Israel who refused to observe the Day of Atonement. They were to be "rooted out," totally "cut off" from the community. The application to Christ means that those who do not listen to him and turn to him in repentance will no longer be a part of the people of God (v. 23b; cf. Heb 2:3).

3:24-25 Moses was not the only prophet who predicted the Christ. "All the prophets from Samuel on" did so (v. 24).[26] Samuel was considered the first prophet after Moses, with Moses being the very first (cf. 13:20). Thus all the prophets foretold these days, i.e., the days of salvation, the coming of Christ. For whom did the prophets speak if not for Israel? The Jews themselves were "the heirs of the prophets" (v. 25). With their fathers God established his covenants. To take comfort in their privileged position was easy. John the Baptist had already warned them of the danger of relying on their descent from Abraham and membership in the covenant community (Luke 3:8). Here Peter reminded them of the content of the covenant with Abraham: "Through your offspring all peoples on earth will be blessed." It was not Peter's concern to emphasize the

---

[25] 4QTestim 5-8; 1QS 9:11. See J. de Waard, "The Quotation from Deuteronomy in Acts 3, 22, 23 and the Palestinian Text: Additional Arguments," *Bib* 52 (1971): 537-40.

[26] The Greek is obscure. One possible translation is to take the καὶ before κατήγγειλαν as intensive: "All the prophets who spoke, from Samuel on, also proclaimed these days" (i.e., in addition to Moses).

missionary imperative implicit in this promise to Abraham (Gen 12:3).[27] At this point he probably was largely unaware of it himself; God had to prod him pretty hard to witness to Cornelius (chap. 10). What Peter was concerned to do was to convince his Jewish hearers that God's covenant with Abraham was fully realized in Jesus.

3:26 The word "offspring" is singular here. Much as in Gal 3:16, the Abrahamic covenant is related to Christ. He is that sole offspring in whom blessing would come. First and foremost, he was Israel's Messiah. God sent him "first to you" (v. 26). Verse 26 serves as a suitable closure to the sermon because it recapitulates various earlier themes: the servant role of Christ (v. 13); God's "raising him up," with its overtone of resurrection (vv. 15,22); the need for the Jews to repent and "turn" (v. 19). God sent his servant to them, to fulfill God's blessing to Abraham by turning each of them from their evil ways.[28] There is significance in the little word "first," just as there is in Abraham's blessing extending to "all peoples on earth." It may have taken the apostles some time to fully realize the implications of the missionary imperative, but there it is. Peter was primarily concerned with the Jews. The gospel was preached to them first. Soon it would reach far beyond the boundaries of Judaism "to all the peoples on earth."

3. Peter and John before the Sanhedrin (4:1-22)

Up until this point in Acts, there had been no resistance to the Christians on the part of the Jews. Indeed, the picture has been that of the general acceptance and favor accorded them by the people (cf. 2:47). In chap. 4 the picture changes. Not, however, with the people. They still were responding favorably to the message of the apostles, indeed, in an overwhelming way (cf. 4:4). It was the officials who turned against the apostles, and not even all of them. The primary enemy was the priestly Sadducean aristocracy for whom the Christians were a serious threat to the status quo. Twice they arrested the apostles. The first time occurred here, as they descended upon Peter and John in the course of their witness in the temple square. This time the two apostles were given a "preliminary hearing" in their proclamation of Christ. Because the apostles did

---

[27]Of significance is that the Hebrew version of Gen 12:3 is followed here in giving "families" (πατριαὶ) rather than "tribes" (φύλαι), which is found in the Septuagint. The Septuagint reading can be taken to refer only to the tribes of Israel. Acts follows the tradition that relates the blessing to all the peoples of the earth.

[28]The ἐν τῷ clause of 3:26b could be either transitive (God turning each) or intransitive (each turning from). The NIV follows the transitive alternative and rightly so: conversion itself is a gift of God.

not heed this warning and preached Christ all the more, the Sadducees were enraged, and they arrested and tried all the apostles (5:17-42).[29]

This section falls into two natural divisions, corresponding to the arrest of the apostles (4:3) and their release (4:21). The first section treats the arrest, interrogation, and defense of Peter and John (4:1-12). The second relates the deliberations of the court, the warning to the apostles, their response, and their release (4:13-22).

(1) Arrested and Interrogated (4:1-12)

¹The priests and the captain of the temple guard and the Sadducees came up to Peter and John while they were speaking to the people. ²They were greatly disturbed because the apostles were teaching the people and proclaiming in Jesus the resurrection of the dead. ³They seized Peter and John, and because it was evening, they put them in jail until the next day. ⁴But many who heard the message believed, and the number of men grew to about five thousand.

⁵The next day the rulers, elders and teachers of the law met in Jerusalem. ⁶Annas the high priest was there, and so were Caiaphas, John, Alexander and the other men of the high priest's family. ⁷They had Peter and John brought before them and began to question them: "By what power or what name did you do this?"

⁸Then Peter, filled with the Holy Spirit, said to them: "Rulers and elders of the people! ⁹If we are being called to account today for an act of kindness shown to a cripple and are asked how he was healed, ¹⁰then know this, you and all the people of Israel: It is by the name of Jesus Christ of Nazareth, whom you crucified but whom God raised from the dead, that this man stands before you healed. ¹¹He is

"'the stone you builders rejected,
    which has become the capstone.'
¹²Salvation is found in no one else, for there is no other name under heaven given to men by which we must be saved."

THE ARREST (4:1-4). **4:1** Peter's sermon was suddenly interrupted by an official contingency comprised of priests, the captain of the temple guard, and Sadducees, who "descended upon" the apostles.[30] That Luke used the plural "while *they* were speaking" is interesting. It was Peter's sermon that was interrupted. As always he was the spokesman, but the

---

[29]Scholars have often felt that the trial scenes in Acts were redundant and perhaps based on separate sources of a single trial. (For a recent adaptation of this view see Reicke, *Glaube und Leben*, 55-114.) An alternative explanation maintains that in certain cases it was necessary for Jewish courts to give persons a preliminary hearing in which they were apprised of the culpability of their actions and warned against continuing them. If they failed to heed the warning, they were formally tried. That well fits the picture of the two trials in Acts 4–5. See I. H. Marshall, *The Acts of the Apostles*, TNTC (Leicester: Inter-Varsity, 1980), 97.

[30]NIV "came up to" is too mild. The Greek ἀφίστημι is a stronger word—"come upon suddenly, descend upon."

plural shows that John was not silent. Like all the apostles, he also was bearing his witness to Christ.

The priests who were present in the arresting company were perhaps those who were on duty that day for the evening sacrifice.[31] The captain of the temple (*stratēgos*) was probably the official whom the *Mishna* designates the *sagan*. The *sagan* had extensive duties, which included assisting the high priest in all ceremonies and serving as his alternate in such capacities. Ranking second in the priestly hierarchy, he was always chosen from one of the families of the priestly aristocracy. Indeed, serving as *sagan* was viewed as a stepping-stone to appointment as high priest. The *sagan's* involvement in this scene is particularly appropriate since he had ultimate responsibility for order in the temple grounds and had the power to arrest.[32] His linkage with the Sadducees here is also quite natural. Representing the priestly aristocracy, he belonged to their ranks.

The Sadducees were clearly the powers behind the arrest of the two. Josephus listed them as one of the three "schools of thought" among the Jews of the first century, along with the Pharisees and Essenes (*Ant.* 13.171). The origin of their name is disputed but may go back to Zadok, the high priest in Solomon's day.[33] The Sadducees of the first century represented the "conservative" viewpoint. They rejected the oral traditions of the Pharisees and considered only the written Torah of the Pentateuch as valid. They considered the concepts of demons and angels, immortality and resurrection as innovations, believing in no life beyond this life.

More important than their theology, however, was their political orientation. Coming largely from the landed aristocracy, they were accommodationists with regard to the Roman occupation of Israel. Possessing considerable economic interests, their concern was to make peace with the Romans, preserve the status quo, and thus protect their own holdings. In return the Romans accorded the Sadducees considerable power, invariably appointing the high priest from their ranks, who was the most powerful political figure among the Jews in that day. The prime concern of the Sadducean aristocracy, of whom the high priest was the chief spokesman, was the preservation of order, the avoidance at all costs of any confrontation with the Roman authorities.

4:2 The Sadducees' annoyance at Peter and John's witness to the resurrection was not so much theological as political, as was generally the

---

[31]The temple police as such were Levites. These may be included here under a generalized meaning of "priests." See J. Jeremias, *Jerusalem at the Time of Jesus*, trans. F. H. and C. H. Cave (Philadelphia: Fortress, 1989), 209-10.

[32]Ibid., 161-63.

[33]The Sadducees were certainly not Zadokites. The last legitimate Zadokite priest fled to Leontopolis in Egypt in the second century B.C. All the high priests from then on were non-Zadokite. See R. Meyer, "Σαδδουκαῖος," *TDNT* 7:35-54.

case with the Sadducees. Note the wording in v. 2: not "they were proclaiming the resurrection of Jesus" but "they were proclaiming in Jesus the resurrection of the dead." The idea of a general resurrection was an apocalyptic concept with all sorts of messianic overtones. Messianic ideas among the Jews of that day meant revolt, overthrow of the foreign overlords, and restoration of the Davidic kingdom. There had been such movements before (cf. 5:36-37), and the Romans had put them down. There would be many more in the future. In fact, the worst fears of the Sadducees were indeed realized when war broke out with the Romans in A.D. 66, with terrible consequences for the Jews.[34] Here, with the large crowds surrounding Peter and John, their fears were aroused. The notes of Peter's sermon alarmed them: resurrection, Author of life, a new Moses. These were revolutionary ideas. The movement must not spread. It must be nipped in the bud.

4:3 So they arrested Peter and John and placed them "in jail" until next morning.[35] The Jewish high court, the Sanhedrin, had jurisdiction over matters of temple violation. It met regularly each day, with the exception of Sabbaths and feast days. Since it was now already evening and the Sanhedrin had already recessed, Peter and John would have to be detained until the court reconvened in the morning.

4:4 Verse 4 comes almost as an intrusion in the narrative. It is not so. The interruption had been the arrest. Luke returned to Peter's temple sermon. Despite adversities the sermon was no failure. Many did respond and place their faith in the Author of life. So much was this the case that the total number of Jewish Christians came to 5,000.[36] Not only does this serve as a suitable climax to the sermon of chap. 3, but it also serves as an introduction to the trial scene of 4:5-22. The Sadducees tried their best to stop the witness of the apostles. They did not succeed. The Christian message was finding too much acceptance with the people. The rulers raged, but it was all in vain (4:25).

THE COUNCIL'S INQUIRY (4:5-7). **4:5** The next morning the council convened to hear the apostles, just as they had tried Jesus in a morning

---

[34]F. J. Foakes-Jackson, *The Acts of the Apostles*, MNTC (New York: Harper, 1931), 32.

[35]The Greek εἰς τήρησιν is ambiguous and could mean either *in detention* or *in the keep* ("in jail," NIV). The Jews did not punish by imprisonment, but prisoners could be detained in jail pending trial.

[36]Notice the steady progression from 120 (1:15) to 3,000 (2:41) to 5,000 (4:4) to "many thousands" (21:20). Many commentators (e.g., E. Haenchen, *The Acts of the Apostles* [Philadelphia: Westminster, 1971], 220) would see this as referring to male converts only (ἄνδρες), but we have already shown that this term in Acts does not necessarily exclude women. See chap. I, n. 54; also Robertson, *WP* 3:50. As to the population of Jerusalem being sufficient to include so many converts, see chap. I, n. 135. Hanson estimates the population as being perhaps a quarter million: R. P. C. Hanson, *The Acts*, NCB (Oxford: Clarendon, 1967), 76f. (n. 4).

session (Luke 22:66). At this point Luke did not use the term Sanhedrin, but it appears at v. 15. The term was also used of minor, local courts; but the reference here was to the supreme court of the land, which held the jurisdiction over the temple area. Exactly where it met is uncertain. Josephus indicated that it met outside the temple precincts and just to the west of it, while the rabbinic sources placed it within the temple area in a room especially designated for it on the south side of the forecourt.[37] Its origin seems to date to Hellenistic times when Israel was a client-nation and no longer had a king as its supreme political authority.

Matters regarding local jurisdiction were entrusted by the Hellenistic overlords to a council of Jews, which developed into the Sanhedrin of New Testament times. It seems to have consisted of seventy-one members, based on Num 11:16, counting the seventy elders mentioned there plus Moses as presiding officer. The presiding officer in the New Testament period was the high priest. At first the Council seems to have consisted primarily of the leading priests and lay elders from the aristocracy. From the time of Queen Alexandra (76–67 B.C.), however, Pharisees were admitted on the Council. Probably always in the minority, the latter still had considerable clout because of their popularity with the people (cf. Josephus, *Ant.* 13.298).

The picture of the assembly here in v. 5 comports well with the known composition of the body. It consisted of the ruling priests, the elders, and the scribes. Luke used the term "rulers," but this almost certainly refers to the priestly representation on the Sanhedrin. Verse 6 mentions four of these plus an unspecified additional number of members from the high-priestly families.[38] The "elders" were the lay members from the Jewish aristocracy, probably comprising the bulk of the entire body and being of Sadducean persuasion. The "teachers" were the scribes, students of the law and responsible for interpreting it before the body. Most scribes were of Pharisaic outlook, so it was likely in this group that the Pharisees were represented on the Sanhedrin.

4:6 In v. 6 Luke gave an "aside" that mentions by name several of the high-priestly group represented on the Council. Annas is named as high priest. Actually, Annas was high priest from A.D. 6–15, and at this time (early A.D. 30s) his son-in-law Caiaphas was the reigning high

---

[37]*Beginnings* 5:477f. On the Sanhedrin site, cf. also E. Lohse, "συνέδριον," *TDNT* 7:860-71; E. Schürer, *History of the Jewish People in the Age of Jesus Christ*, new rev. English version, ed. G. Vermes, F. Millar, and M. Black (Edinburgh: T & T Clark, 1974), 2:199-226.

[38]Jeremias suggested that these "high priests" on the Sanhedrin were not only ex-high priests like Annas but also the high-ranking temple officials like the *sagan*, the gate-keeper, the captains of the courses, and the treasurer. Such a usage would explain the frequent use of the plural term "high priests" (64 times) in the NT when technically there was only one high priest at a time: *Jerusalem*, 175-81.

priest.[39] Luke's attribution of the title to Annas may reflect the actual state of affairs. Annas was the most powerful political figure among the Jews at that time. Five of his sons, one grandson, and a son-in-law all acquired the rank of high priest. He may well have been the power behind the scenes, calling all the shots.[40] Caiaphas, Annas's son-in-law, was high priest from A.D. 18–36, the longest tenure of any high priest during New Testament times. He seems to have struck it off well with Pilate, since he survived the entire period of the latter's term of office. He and his father-in-law were instrumental in the conviction of Jesus (John 11:49f.; 18:13f.).[41] At this time they were considering a pair of his followers whom they probably saw as equally threatening to the peace and consequently to their own considerable interests.

There is no known John among those who held the office of high priest. Codex Bezae, however, reads "Jonathan" in this verse. If one follows that variant, he would then be the Jonathan, son of Annas, who served as high priest in A.D. 36–37. No record exists of an Alexander who served as high priest in the New Testament period. He may have belonged to one of the families of the priestly aristocracy.

4:7 The interrogation began with the apostles being brought before the Council. The Greek says literally "in the middle" (v. 7), which comports well with the rabbinic statement that the Sanhedrin sat in a semicircle: "The Sanhedrin was arranged like the half of a round threshing-floor so that they might all see one another. Before them stood the two scribes of the judges, one to the right and one to the left, and they wrote down the words of them that favored acquittal and the words of them that favored conviction."[42] The question was then posed to the apostles: "By what power or what name did you do this?" The verb is plural, as if the Court asked the question in unison; but one would assume that the high priest, as presiding officer, served as spokesman in beginning the interrogation. Some interpreters assume that the question has to do with the man's healing, but the main reason for the arrest had been the preaching of the apostles (v. 2). They were concerned about the source of the disciples' teaching and the possibility that their emphasis on the resurrection could

---

[39]Compare Luke 3:2, where the same coupling occurs: "During the high priesthood of Annas and Caiaphas." High priests retained their title and membership on the Sanhedrin for life, even after removal from office (Jeremias, *Jerusalem*, 157).

[40]Annas had a considerable economic empire as well, both inside and outside the temple. See P. Gaechter, "The Hatred of the House of Annas," *TS* 8 (1947): 3-34.

[41]Some have argued that there were two Sanhedrins at this time, one religious and one political. According to this view it was the political, not the religious, leaders who tried both Jesus and the apostles; e.g., S. Zeitlin, *Who Crucified Jesus?* (New York: Harper & Brothers, 1942), 68-83, 180-88.

[42]*M. Sanh* 4:3.

lead to a major messianic insurrection with serious political repercussions. They were concerned about authority, proper accreditation, law and order, keeping the peace.[43]

PETER'S RESPONSE (4:8-12). **4:8** The question as to the "name" behind their preaching was a question of accreditation and authorization, but Peter could not let this one get by. The lame man was healed by the name of Jesus. If the Sanhedrin wanted to know about that name, he would tell them all about it. Instead of the expected defense, Peter gave them a sermon.[44] In fulfillment of Jesus' promise (Luke 12:11f.), he was given a special endowment of the Holy Spirit to bear his witness with boldness.[45]

Verses 9-12 comprise a minisermon on "the name that brings salvation." It begins with the reference to the name raised by the Sanhedrin and repeated by Peter (vv. 7,10), which is linked to the word "saved" with regard to the healing of the man (v. 9). These two concepts are brought back together at the conclusion, with the reference to salvation in no other name (v. 12). The crux of the sermon is a play on the Greek word *sōzō*, which means both physical "salvation" in the sense of healing (v. 9) as well as the spiritual, eschatological sense of salvation (v. 12).[46] The physical "salvation" of the lame man through the name of Jesus is thus a pointer to the far greater salvation that comes to all who call upon his name in faith.

4:9 In many ways Peter's testimony before the Sanhedrin is a condensed form of his address in Solomon's Colonnade. It began with a reference to the healing of the lame man (v. 9). The crowd in the temple wondered about the source of the lame man's healing, and Peter pointed to the name of Jesus. The Sanhedrin wanted to know about the name, and Peter pointed them to the healing of the lame man. The two go together: wholeness, salvation, is in the name of Jesus; the name of Jesus brings wholeness. Peter's words contain a bit of irony. The rulers were worried about the political dangers of the "name" the apostles were preaching. "This name is not destructive," said Peter; "it brings good things; it

---

[43]B. Reicke, *Glaube und Leben*, 76f.

[44]C. W. Carter and R. Earle (*The Acts of the Apostles* [Grand Rapids: Zondervan, 1959], 59) note how Peter scarcely fit the normal defendant before the Sanhedrin, whom Josephus described as submissive and wearing a black mourning garment (*Ant.* 14.172).

[45]The aorist participle πλησθείς is used for special moments of inspiration as here (cf. Luke 1:15,41,67; Acts 13:9). It is to be distinguished from the reception of the Spirit, which abides on every believer (2:38), as well as from the adjective form πλήρης ("full of the Spirit") used of especially spiritual persons (Jesus, Luke 4:1; Stephen, Acts 6:5; 7:55; Barnabas, 11:24).

[46]For full treatments see Hamm, "Acts 3:1-10," 306; I. Foulkes, "Two Semantic Problems in the Translation of Acts 4:5-20," *BT* (1978): 124-25.

brings wholeness" (author's paraphrase). Peter underlined his point. "Be very sure of this," he said, "you and everyone else in Israel."[47]

4:10-11 Peter was ready to preach to all, even the Sanhedrin. But like the crowd in the Colonnade, the judges in the Sanhedrin rejected the *name* that could bring them salvation. Peter repeated the familiar kerygmatic formula: "Whom you crucified, but whom God raised." Indeed, it is by the very fact that God has exalted him that the power had come for healing the man. The themes are the same as before: the healing name of Jesus, which proves his resurrection and points to his salvation, the guilt of the Jews who rejected him. Also, as before, there is a proof from Scripture, this time from Ps 118:22. It establishes the guilt of the Sanhedrin. They were the "builders," the leaders of the nation,[48] who rejected the very rock on which God's people are to be built.[49] Very early Ps 118:22 came to be viewed by the Christians as pointing to Christ, the one rejected by his own people, whom God made the crowning stone of his people.[50] This text also appears in Luke 20:17 as well as in 1 Pet 2:7 and in both passages is linked to other Old Testament texts that incorporate a "stone" motif. Many see this as evidence that the early Christian community made collections of Old Testament texts that were applied to Christ.[51]

4:12 All Peter's sermons to this point ended with an appeal, but there seems to be none here. The appeal, however, is present implicitly. If there is salvation in no other name (v. 12), then obviously one must make a commitment to that sole name that brings salvation. But the appeal is even stronger than that. Peter switched to the first person at the end of the verse, "by which we must be saved," amounting to a direct appeal to the Sanhedrin. Peter had been bold indeed. He had come full circle. They asked for the name in whom his authority rested. He answered their question. It was the name, the power of Jesus. He directed the charges. The Council had rejected the one who bore this powerful name. The ultimate verdict rested with them. Would they continue to reject the one whom God had placed as the final stone for his people, the only name under

---

[47]The phrase γνωστὸν ἔστω is emphatic, aimed at getting one's attention (cf. 2:14; 13:38; 28:28).

[48] "Builders" is used in rabbinic writings for teachers, and in the Qumran writings it is used for leaders of the community.

[49]Verse 11 is not an exact quote from the LXX. The verb ἐξουθενέω is used instead of the LXX's ἀποδοκιμάζω. Ἐξουθενέω has a nuance of rejecting despitefully, with contempt, thus making for a sharper application to the crucifixion. Likewise, ὑμῶν ("you") has been introduced before "builders," making for a more direct reference to the Sanhedrin.

[50]The κεφαλὴ γωνίας (v. 11) can be either the final stone (capstone) that completes a building or the cornerstone around which the whole building is erected. NIV follows the influential article by J. Jeremias ("γωνία," *TDNT* 1:791-93) in rendering "capstone."

[51]These are usually referred to as "testimonia." See J. R. Harris, *Testimonies* (Cambridge: University Press, 1916).

heaven in which they would find their own salvation? The final verdict would rest in their own decision.

(2) Warned and Released (4:13-22)

[13]When they saw the courage of Peter and John and realized that they were unschooled, ordinary men, they were astonished and they took note that these men had been with Jesus. [14]But since they could see the man who had been healed standing there with them, there was nothing they could say. [15]So they ordered them to withdraw from the Sanhedrin and then conferred together. [16]"What are we going to do with these men?" they asked. "Everybody living in Jerusalem knows they have done an outstanding miracle, and we cannot deny it. [17]But to stop this thing from spreading any further among the people, we must warn these men to speak no longer to anyone in this name."

[18]Then they called them in again and commanded them not to speak or teach at all in the name of Jesus. [19]But Peter and John replied, "Judge for yourselves whether it is right in God's sight to obey you rather than God. [20]For we cannot help speaking about what we have seen and heard."

[21]After further threats they let them go. They could not decide how to punish them, because all the people were praising God for what had happened. [22]For the man who was miraculously healed was over forty years old.

4:13-14 Peter had borne his testimony. It was now time for the Council to deliberate. They assessed the evidence (vv. 13-14). First, there was the courage, the sheer freedom with which Peter spoke.[52] They hardly expected this from men who had no formal education in matters of the law, who were ordinary laymen.[53] Then there was the fact that they had been with Jesus. He too had been just a "commoner" but also with an amazing boldness and knowledge beyond his training. But he too had been a dangerous person, a threat to their peace; and they consequently had condemned him to death. Finally, there was the healed man, standing with them before the Tribunal. Whether he was there voluntarily in support of Peter and John or whether he had been summoned as a witness, we are not told. In any event there he was, standing there, "exhibit A," a "known sign" (v. 16). He was hard to overlook. It was hardly a clear-cut case. The Council sat in silence. At this point there was nothing they could say. Indeed, Jesus' promise was being fulfilled before the apostles' eyes (Luke 21:15).[54] The irony can scarcely be missed—the accused

---

[52]NIV "courage"; the Greek word παρρησία means *boldness, openness, freedom in speaking.*

[53]NIV "unschooled," ἀγράμματος, often has the meaning *illiterate* but came to mean merely *uneducated,* which is the likely meaning here. The other word is ἰδιῶται ("ordinary," NIV), meaning *private person, a layperson, nonprofessional.*

[54]There is likely a conscious parallel here, since Luke used the same verb (ἀντειπεῖν, "answer back") both here (v. 14) and in Luke 21:15.

spoke with utter boldness and freedom; their accusers sat in stony silence.

4:15-17 When the Sanhedrin ordered Peter and John out of the court-room (v. 15), they were following normal procedure. Their custom after hearing the witnesses was to dismiss them in order to have as clear and open a discussion among themselves as possible.[55] In this instance they were at something of a loss. They really had no charge to lay upon them. Further, the accused were popular with the people, for the news about healing of the lame man had already spread throughout Jerusalem. There was only one thing they could do—they could threaten. They would warn the apostles to no longer speak "in this name" (v. 17).

4:18-19 Although only implicit at this point, this would also establish culpability should the apostles decide to transgress the interdiction of the court (cf. 5:28). So the apostles were brought back into the court and given the warning. They were no longer "to speak and teach in the name of Jesus" (v. 18). The warning was given in narrative style rather than in direct speech, perhaps Luke's way of underlining the timidity of the Council on the whole matter. The response of Peter and John was in direct discourse; it was bold and almost defiant: "Judge for yourselves whether it is right in God's sight to obey you rather than God."

4:20-22 The response was much the same as that given by Socrates to his Athenian accusers who warned him to desist from his teaching. The saying had become quite proverbial, however, and was widely used by Jews and Greeks.[56] It would seem a bit ironic if these unlearned and com-mon men (v. 13) were throwing the words of the Greek philosopher at them. The stronger irony, however, is in the boldness of the apostles and the timidity of their accusers. The apostles could only speak of what they had seen and heard (v. 20). They were the eyewitnesses of Jesus' entire ministry (1:21f.), the witnesses to his resurrection (2:32; 3:15). Peter and John had no choice but to defy the court's order, for it had "stepped in between the conscience and God."[57] The court had no alternative but to threaten them further and release them (v. 21). They could find no grounds for punishing them at this point, and they feared the apostles' popularity with the populace.[58] The man, born lame, was over forty years old (v. 22),

---

[55]Reicke, *Glaube und Leben*, 73-76. As to how Luke had access to such information on a closed session, one could readily deduce their discussion from the decision rendered the two apostles. G. Stählin (*Die Apostelgeschichte*, NTD 5 [Göttingen: Vandenhoeck & Ruprecht, 1962], 74) reminds us that the Christians may well have had friends on the Sanhedrin such as Nicodemus or Joseph of Arimathea. Even Paul could have been present, since students of the law had access to deliberations of the court.

[56]Plato, *Apol.* 29d. Compare similar statements in 2 Macc 7:2; 4 Macc 5:16-21; and Jose-phus, *Ant.* 17.158f.

[57]Robertson, *WP* 3:53.

[58]The NIV is somewhat misleading. The Sanhedrin was not at a loss about "how"

so the miracle was particularly striking; and the people took it for what it was, an act of God, a sign. The little word "sign" should not be overlooked in the Greek text of v. 22. That is what the man's healing had been—a sign to the temple crowd in Solomon's Colonnade that attracted them to the gospel and ultimately to faith. It had been a sign to the Sanhedrin as well, a pointer to the sole name in which salvation (ultimate "healing") is to be found. There is no record of response for Peter's appeal to the Sanhedrin, as there was for his temple sermon (v. 4). Here for the first time is found a theme that will recur throughout Acts—the rejection of the Messiah by the Jews. For many of them, particularly their official leadership, he was, and continued to be, the stone rejected by the builders.

4. The Prayer of the Community (4:23-31)

[23]**On their release, Peter and John went back to their own people and reported all that the chief priests and elders had said to them.** [24]**When they heard this, they raised their voices together in prayer to God. "Sovereign Lord," they said, "you made the heaven and the earth and the sea, and everything in them.** [25]**You spoke by the Holy Spirit through the mouth of your servant, our father David:**

"'Why do the nations rage
 and the peoples plot in vain?
[26]**The kings of the earth take their stand**
 and the rulers gather together
against the Lord
 and against his Anointed One.'
[27]**Indeed Herod and Pontius Pilate met together with the Gentiles and the people of Israel in this city to conspire against your holy servant Jesus, whom you anointed.** [28]**They did what your power and will had decided beforehand should happen.** [29]**Now, Lord, consider their threats and enable your servants to speak your word with great boldness.** [30]**Stretch out your hand to heal and perform miraculous signs and wonders through the name of your holy servant Jesus."**
[31]**After they prayed, the place where they were meeting was shaken. And they were all filled with the Holy Spirit and spoke the word of God boldly.**

Peter's first sermon, at Pentecost, was followed by a glimpse into the common life of the Christians in Jerusalem (2:42-47). Here, after Peter's witness before the crowd in the temple square and before the Sanhedrin, we are again given a glimpse into the life of the Christian community. Just as chap. 2 spoke of their common prayer life (2:42), here again the prayer of the Christians is emphasized, with the major difference being that what was mentioned in summary fashion in the former passage is here related concretely with an example of their prayers.

---

they should be punished. It could not find the grounds, the basis, the charges necessary for punishing them at all.

4:23 Verse 23 provides the setting and the linkage with the preceding narrative. After their release Peter and John returned "to their own people." Many interpreters see this as referring only to the other apostles, viewing vv. 24-30 as the apostles' prayer for boldness in their witness.[59] The apostles, however, were not the only bold witnesses in Acts. Note Stephen (6:10) and Philip (8:5), to mention only the next two major witnesses in Acts. The whole community was involved in the proclamation of the word, and the community gathered for prayer when the apostles were in difficulty (cf. 12:12). That is the picture here—the Christians gathered to pray for the deliverance of the two apostles from the Sanhedrin. When Peter and John arrived on the scene, they informed them of the warning given by "the chief priest and elders."[60] The fellowship responded with praise to God for delivering the apostles (vv. 24-28) and a petition for courage to continue their bold witness in the face of such opposition (vv. 29-30).

4:24-28 Together they lifted their voices in praise to God. That they offered an occasional prayer of this nature in unison is unlikely. Luke was simply expressing that the whole community joined together in this prayer.[61] God was addressed as "Sovereign Lord," a common designation for God in the Old Testament and appropriate to this gathering of Jewish Christians.[62] God was further addressed as Creator, Maker of heaven, earth, the seas and all that dwell in them, again in language thoroughly steeped in Old Testament phraseology (cf. Exod 20:11). More than that the whole form of the prayer has Old Testament precedents. Compare Hezekiah's prayer in Isa 37:16-20, where the same elements appear: God was addressed as Lord and Creator, there followed a reference to the threat of Israel's enemies, and the prayer concluded with a petition. It is in the petition that the major difference from the Christians' prayer appears. Hezekiah prayed for deliverance. The Christians prayed for courage.

---

[59]J. Dupont, *Nouvelles Etudes sur les Actes des Apôtres*, Lectio divina 118 (Paris: Cerf, 1984), 51-52; R. B. Rackham, *The Acts of the Apostles* (London: Methuen, 1901), 60; E. F. Harrison, *Interpreting Acts* (Grand Rapids: Zondervan, 1986), 95.

[60]Note that the scribes are not mentioned, who represented the Pharisaic viewpoint on the Sanhedrin. It was the chief priests and the lay aristocracy, the *Sadducees*, who threatened the apostles and constituted the real opposition to the Christian witness at this point in the narrative. The same would hold true for the trial scene in chap. 5.

[61]Marshall (*Acts*, 103) suggests they may have followed the Jewish liturgical procedure of using a leader who prayed a phrase at a time, with the others repeating phrase by phrase.

[62]The Greek word here (δεσπότης) is applied to God some twenty-five times in the Septuagint but only three times in the NT (cf. Luke 2:29; Rev 6:10). It is applied to Christ three more times (2 Tim 2:21; 2 Pet 2:1; Jude 4). It is quite common in the Apostolic Fathers. Perhaps the reticence of the NT writers to use it was due to its negative overtones of arbitrary rule, as the English cognate "despot" also bears.

In the community's prayer the reference to the threat of enemies is given in the form of a scriptural proof. The Scripture is in the exact Septuagintal rendering of Ps 2:1-2 and is presented as a prophecy, spoken by God through David under the inspiration of the Holy Spirit.[63] Most likely originally relating to God's triumph over Israel's enemies through the anointed king, the Christians came to see it as in a real sense prophetic of Christ.[64] All the details of these first verses of the psalm were applicable to the passion of Christ, and the Christians did so in their prayer (v. 27). The raging nations represented the Gentile rulers and their cohorts, the soldiers who executed Jesus. The people of Israel were those who plotted in vain.[65] Herod represented the "kings of the earth"; Pilate, the "rulers";[66] and Christ, the "anointed" of God.[67] Here again as in chap. 3 the title "servant" is applied to Jesus. Here in a prayer the term is primarily liturgical and is applied to David as well in v. 25.[68] The theme of v. 28 is by now familiar. All the plotting against God's anointed is in vain because God has already predetermined the outcome (cf. 2:23; 3:18). In the paradox of human freedom and divine sovereignty, despite all the raging of humanity, God's purposes prevail. They did so in Christ. They did so with the apostles before the Sanhedrin.

4:29-30 The community turned to its petition: "Now, Lord, consider their threats." Whose threats? The Sanhedrin's, of course. Just like the threats, plots, and rages against Jesus, the community viewed itself in

---

[63]The Greek of Acts 4:25a is extremely difficult, being primarily a string of genitives with only the preposition διὰ before πνεύματος ἁγίου. For an intriguing solution see H. W. Moule, "Acts IV, 25," *ExpTim* 51 (1939-40): 396. Despite the grammatical difficulties, the meaning seems fairly evident. Two agencies are expressed: God spoke through the Spirit; the Spirit in turn spoke through David. (Codex Bezae construed it thus, placing a second διὰ before David.)

[64]There is evidence that Ps 2 was already viewed messianically in some Jewish circles prior to Christ (cf. *Pss. Sol.*, 17:25-27). See Jones, "*Christos*," 69-76.

[65]How would the phrase "in vain" apply? Marshall (*Acts*, 105) suggests that the opening of the prayer provides the answer. God is Creator (v. 24). He spoke these words of the psalm through David long before they came to bear in Christ. It was fruitless for them to scheme against a God who was their Creator and who even knew in advance of their scheming.

[66]The reference to Herod Antipas's involvement in Jesus' passion is only found in Luke among the Gospels (23:7-12).

[67]The term "anointed" as applied to Christ most likely refers to his being anointed with the Spirit at his baptism (Luke 3:22; 4:10; cf. Acts 10:38, the only other passage in Luke-Acts where Jesus is described as "anointed").

[68]The term is used throughout the OT in the sense of one who is at God's disposal, is his servant, much as Paul used the term δοῦλος ("slave, servant") to describe his own relationship to Christ. A "servant Christology" does not therefore seem as evident in chap. 4 as in chap. 3, although the passion setting of 4:27 may lend to such an interpretation. See J. Jeremias, "παῖς θεοῦ," *TDNT* 5:702-03. In the later Christian literature the term is common, especially in the Apostolic Fathers, and always in a liturgical rather than a Christological context.

much the situation he had experienced.[69] The authorities had raged against him, and God made him to triumph in the power of his resurrection. So now the same temporal powers had raged and plotted against the apostles. Like Christ, God had delivered them. The Christians realized that the opposition was not over. The Sanhedrin continued to threaten them. One would expect them to ask God for further deliverance. They did not. Instead, they asked for more of the same, requesting of him boldness in witness and further miraculous signs. The request for miracle was not a request for power over their enemies. It was closely related to the request for boldness in witness.

In Acts the miracles are always in the service of the word. They are "signs" in the sense that they point beyond themselves to the ultimate power of the gospel message of Christ's resurrection and the salvation that is in him (4:12). That was amply illustrated in the miracle they experienced. The healing of the lame man started the whole train of events that took them before the Sanhedrin. The healing did not deliver them from danger; if anything, it provoked it. On the other hand, the healing first attracted those who listened to Peter's sermon in Solomon's Colonnade and responded to the word in faith. This is what the community prayed for—more signs to undergird the word, more boldness to proclaim it. They surely knew what the result would be—more persecution.

4:31 Their prayer was answered by the shaking of the house. Perhaps a shaking from thunder or a quaking of the earth, it gave them a tangible sense of God's presence and his response to their prayer.[70] And their prayer was fulfilled at once. Immediately they were filled with the Holy Spirit and began to speak the word with boldness, just as they had petitioned. This was not a "second Pentecost."[71] They had already received the Spirit. The Spirit had helped Peter and John in a mighty way before the Sanhedrin. It was a fresh filling, a renewed awareness of the Spirit's power and presence in their life and witness. This was not an ephemeral ecstatic manifestation but a fresh endowment of power for witness that would continue (cf. 4:33).

---

[69]There is an interesting lesson in hermeneutics here. The community continued to see the fulfillment of the psalm, not solely in Christ but in the continuing experience of the church. For this linkage between the experience of Christ and that of the church, see D. Hamm, "You Are Precious in My Sight," *The Way* 18 (1978): 193-203, and B. R. Gaventa, "To Speak Thy Word with All Boldness, Acts 4:23-31," *FM* 3 (1986): 76-82.

[70]For shaking phenomena signifying the presence of God, see Isa 6:4; Exod 19:18; 4 Ezra 6:15,29. Elijah's experience was not to find God in the usual expressions of theophany—wind, fire, and earthquake (1 Kgs 19:11-12).

[71]Some of the older source critics argued that this is a parallel account of Pentecost due to a separate source treating the event. This passage is too different from the Pentecost narrative and too closely linked to the previous trial scene for such a suggestion to merit serious consideration.

5. The Common Life of the Community (4:32-37)

[32]All the believers were one in heart and mind. No one claimed that any of his possessions was his own, but they shared everything they had. [33]With great power the apostles continued to testify to the resurrection of the Lord Jesus, and much grace was upon them all. [34]There were no needy persons among them. For from time to time those who owned lands or houses sold them, brought the money from the sales [35]and put it at the apostles' feet, and it was distributed to anyone as he had need.

[36]Joseph, a Levite from Cyprus, whom the apostles called Barnabas (which means Son of Encouragement), [37]sold a field he owned and brought the money and put it at the apostles' feet.

The previous episode exemplified the prayer life of the community with an actual incident. Luke returned to his summary style to further picture the life together, much as he did in 2:42-47. Many of the themes are the same, but there is considerable development of one theme in particular, the sharing of goods within the fellowship.

4:32-33 The opening two verses are almost identical with 2:43-44, only in reverse order. Together they characterize the community life as marked by four things: their unity in mind and heart (v. 32a), their sharing of their possessions (v. 32b), the power and witness of the apostles (v. 33a), and the grace of God, which rested upon them (v. 33b). The overarching concept was their unity, their being "one in heart and mind," their fellowship in the Spirit (cf. *koinōnia* in 2:42).[72] This served as the basis of their sharing of their possessions. The latter is described in two ways. First, "no one claimed that any of his possessions was his own." The picture is one of unqualified sharing, of not claiming owner's rights, of saying "what's mine is yours." The second expression is "they shared everything they had." The Greek literally reads "everything was in common with them." Taken by itself, this could refer to shared ownership; but in conjunction with the first expression, it also refers to a practice of freely sharing one's goods with another.

Many interpreters have seen Luke's description of the Christian practice here as reflecting Greek ideals, particularly in such phrases as "one mind" (*psychē mia*) and "all in common" (*hapanta koina*). The Greeks shared a common myth that in primitive times people lived in an ideal state in which there was no ownership but everything was held in common. Some attributed such a practice to the Pythagoreans, and Plato envisioned his ideal republic as one devoid of all private ownership. It is

---

[72]"Heart and mind" is an OT expression, not found in Greek. In Hebrew thought the "heart" is the center of the will. Cf. Deut 4:29; 6:5; 11:18. B. Gerhardsson suggests that Deut 6:5 lies behind the whole of v. 32, with "might" taken in the common Hebraic sense as *means*: "Einige Bemerkungen zu Apg. 4, 32," *ST* 24 (1970): 142-49.

doubtful such a utopian ideal was ever realized among the Greeks, but for some Greeks communal ownership was a major part of their dream of a "Golden Age."[73]

More common than this myth was the Greek ideal of friendship according to which true friends held everything in common (*panta koina*) and were of "one mind" (*mia psychē*).[74] Aristotle is reputed to have defined a friend as "one soul dwelling in two bodies."[75] Such expressions became commonplace and are found in Roman writers such as Cicero as well as the Hellenistic Jew Philo. Luke's description would have evoked an immediate response in his Gentile readers. What they esteemed as an ideal had become a reality in the young Christian community. They were of one mind, for they shared freely with one another, truly common both in soul and in means. The main business of the community was, of course, the witness for Jesus; and this the apostles continued to do "with great power" (*dynamis*, v. 33). This power likely refers to their continuing performance of miracles, a further testimony to God's answering their prayer (v. 30; cf. 5:12-16). "Much grace was upon them all," primarily in God's blessing on their lives and witness. On this note Luke's general summary of the Christian life together ends (cf. 2:47). He then turned to a more thorough discussion of one particular aspect of their common life—their sharing of goods.

4:34-35 If v. 32 depicted the Christian sharing in terms of Greek ideals, verse 34a sets forth the Old Testament ideal: "There were no needy persons among them." This is the ideal God established for Israel. According to Deut 15:4f., Israel was to keep God's commands; and God would bless them; there would be no poor among them.[76] There is evidence that in New Testament times the text of Deut 15:4 was seen as a reference to the ideal final times when Israel would be fully faithful to the law and there would be no poverty in the land.[77] The Christians saw themselves as the people of God of the final times (cf. 2:17), they were experiencing God's blessing (4:33), and they were striving to realize the ideal of a people of God with no poor among them.

---

[73]For a full discussion with references, see Dupont, *Salvation of the Gentiles*, 85-102; H. J. Degenhardt, *Lukas Evangelist der Armen* (Stuttgart: Katholisches Bibelwerk, 1965), 168-72, 181-83; D. L. Mealand, "Community of Goods and Utopian Allusions in Acts II-IV," *JTS*, n.s. 28 (1977): 96-99.

[74]Aristotle, *Eth. Nic.* 9.8.2.

[75]Diogenes Laertius, *Lives of Eminent Philosophers*, 5:20.

[76]L. T. Johnson, *The Literary Function of Possessions in Luke-Acts* (Missoula, Mont.: Scholar's, 1977), 200. In Johnson's view Luke used the motif of the community of goods to depict the Christians as the faithful Israel.

[77]This interpretation is reflected in the *Jerusalem Targum I* according to Dupont, *Salvation of the Gentiles*, 92.

Verses 34b-35 depict the means by which they sought to realize this ideal. Those who had lands or houses would sell them, bring the proceeds, and lay them at the apostles' feet. The proceeds were then distributed to the needy among them. Repeated attempts have been made to see this as an early Christian experiment in community ownership. Sometimes a specific pattern has been suggested, such as the common ownership practiced by the Qumran covenanters.[78] There are many reasons to reject such suggestions. Every evidence is that the early Christian practice was wholly voluntary.

First, there was no transfer of ownership, no control of production or income, no requirement to surrender one's property to the community. The voluntary nature of the Christian practice is evidenced by the consistent use of the iterative imperfect tense throughout vv. 34b-35. This is how they "used to" do it. They "would sell" their property and bring it to the apostles as needs arose.

Second is the example of Barnabas in vv. 36-37. His sale of property would hardly be a sterling example if surrender of property were obligatory.

Third, in the example of Ananias and Sapphira, Peter clarified for Ananias that his sin was in lying about his charity. The land remained his to do with as he pleased; he was under no obligation to give the proceeds to the church (5:4).

Fourth, the picture of the central fund for the widows in 6:1-6 is clearly not an apportioning of each one's lot from a common fund but a charity fund for the needy.

Finally, there is the example of Mary in 12:12f. She still owned a home and had a maid. The Christians enjoyed the hospitality of her home. This was clearly no experiment in common ownership.[79]

But what of the practice of laying the proceeds at the apostles' feet? The gesture was one of submission to another. At this point the Twelve were the representatives appointed by Christ as the foundation of the true people of God. The submission was not to them but to the one they represented. To lay one's gift at their feet was to offer it to Christ. The apostles certainly did not consider this an enviable role. They were all too glad to turn the responsibility over to others (cf. 6:2).

---

[78] There is really no comparison to be made between the obligatory surrender of one's property upon initiation into the Qumran monastery and the voluntary Christian practice. See J. Fitzmyer, "Jewish Christianity in the Light of the Qumran Scrolls, *Studies in Luke-Acts* (Nashville: Abingdon, 1966), 242-44; D. L. Mealand, "Community of Goods at Qumran," *TZ* 31 (1975): 129-39.

[79] See D. P. Seccombe, *Possessions and the Poor in Luke-Acts* (Linz: Studien zum Neuen Testament und seiner Umwelt, 1982), 207-09.

4:36-37 Luke concluded his treatment of the early Christian sharing with two specific examples—one to be followed (Barnabas) and one to be avoided (Ananias and Sapphira). Barnabas sold a field and placed all the receipts at the apostles' feet. Of more interest to us are the little details told about Barnabas here.

Luke had a way of taking characters who played a major role later in the book and introducing them early, but only briefly and in passing, as is the case with Barnabas here. His name was Joseph, and he was given the nickname Barnabas by the apostles. This was not insignificant in itself because the granting of a nickname was often seen as a sign of respect. (Compare Jesus giving Simon the nickname of Peter/Rock.) The problem is that Luke said the name meant *Son of Encouragement*. Now *bar* does mean *son* in Aramaic, but no scholar has ever been able to give a convincing derivation of "encouragement" (*paraklēsis*) from *nabas*.[80]

Etymologies aside, the important thing is how well the by-name fits the picture of Barnabas in Acts. He was the encourager, the advocate, the *paraklete* par excellence of all the characters in Acts. When the Christians in Jerusalem shied away from Paul after his conversion, Barnabas interceded and introduced him to them (9:26f.). When Paul refused to take Mark on his second missionary journey, Barnabas took up for Mark (15:36-39). When the Christians of Jerusalem became concerned over the orthodoxy of the Antiochene Christians in their witness to Greeks, Barnabas again served as intercessor, saw the gracious work of the Antiochene Christians, and encouraged them (11:20-23). Indeed, 11:24 well sums up the portrait of this "Son of Encouragement": "He was a good man, full of the Holy Spirit and faith."

We also learn that Barnabas was a Levite from Cyprus. Levites were officials in the temple cultus, subordinate in rank to the priests. Prohibited from offering sacrifices and barred entrance to the holy place, they served in such capacities as policing the temple grounds, keeping the gates, and providing the music at sacrifices and on ceremonial occasions.[81] According to ancient provisions (Deut 10:9; Num 18:20,24), Levites were not supposed to own land, but that no longer seemed to apply in Barnabas's day. (Indeed, Jeremiah, a priest, owned land [Jer 32:6-15].)

---

[80] All sorts of conjectures have been suggested, such as Bar-nabi (son of a prophet), or Bar-nawha (son of refreshment), or Bar-nebo (son of the pagan god Nebo), or Bar-menahem (son of consolation). Obviously the last suggestion fits best, but there is no way one can derive *nabas* from *menahem*. Scholars who make this suggestion assume that Luke confused Barnabas with the Manaen whose name is listed along with his in Acts 13:1, but this is grasping at a straw. For further treatment see S. Brock, "Barnabas, Huios Paraklēseos," *JTS* 25 (1974): 93-98; A. Deissmann, *Bible Studies* (Edinburgh: T & T Clark, 1901), 308-10.

[81] R. Meyer, "Levites," *TDNT* 4:239-41.

We are not told where the field was located, whether in Judea or his native Cyprus. Nothing was made of Barnabas's Levitical status in Acts.[82] He may never have served as a Levite. Such service was in no way compulsory for one of Levitical lineage.[83] Just how strong were Barnabas's Cypriot roots we also are not told. Luke simply said here that he was a Cypriot by birth. His family may have moved to Jerusalem when he was quite young, and it is in and around Jerusalem where we find Barnabas active in the early chapters of Acts. On the other hand, it is probably not by chance that Paul and Barnabas's mission work together began on the island of Cyprus.

6. A Serious Threat to the Common Life (5:1-11)

[1]Now a man named Ananias, together with his wife Sapphira, also sold a piece of property. [2]With his wife's full knowledge he kept back part of the money for himself, but brought the rest and put it at the apostles' feet.

[3]Then Peter said, "Ananias, how is it that Satan has so filled your heart that you have lied to the Holy Spirit and have kept for yourself some of the money you received for the land? [4]Didn't it belong to you before it was sold? And after it was sold, wasn't the money at your disposal? What made you think of doing such a thing? You have not lied to men but to God."

[5]When Ananias heard this, he fell down and died. And great fear seized all who heard what had happened. [6]Then the young men came forward, wrapped up his body, and carried him out and buried him.

[7]About three hours later his wife came in, not knowing what had happened. [8]Peter asked her, "Tell me, is this the price you and Ananias got for the land?" "Yes," she said, "that is the price."

[9]Peter said to her, "How could you agree to test the Spirit of the Lord? Look! The feet of the men who buried your husband are at the door, and they will carry you out also."

[10]At that moment she fell down at his feet and died. Then the young men came in and, finding her dead, carried her out and buried her beside her husband. [11]Great fear seized the whole church and all who heard about these events.

If Barnabas was a positive example of the community's sharing, the story of Ananias and Sapphira provides a sharp contrast. They too sold a piece of property, pledging the proceeds to the community of believers. But they held back part of the proceeds; and a terrible judgment followed, resulting in both their deaths. Perhaps no passage in Acts raises more serious difficulties for Christian readers. The judgment on these two seems so harsh, so nonredemptive, so out of keeping with the gospel. It

---

[82]Luke may have seen some symbolical significance in Barnabas's being a Levite. Levites were the subordinates in the temple cultus, and Barnabas was consistently depicted in Acts as being in the service of others, humble, and self-effacing.

[83]Jeremias, *Jerusalem*, 213.

will be necessary to return to this question; but in order to make an accurate assessment, it would be wise first to look at the passage itself and examine what it seems to say and what it does not say.

The passage falls into two natural divisions: the confrontation of Ananias (vv. 1-6) and the strikingly parallel confrontation with Sapphira (vv. 7-11). In both sections Peter, as the spokesman for the apostles, to whom the community funds were entrusted (4:35), did the confronting. It is striking that "equal time" is given to both the man and the woman. In both his Gospel and in Acts, Luke paired women with men, particularly in contexts of witness and discipleship. Here perhaps he was showing that along with discipleship goes responsibility; and this applies to all disciples, female as well as male. This would have been particularly noteworthy in the Jewish culture of the early Jerusalem church, where a woman's religious status was largely tied up with her father or husband and depended on his faithful execution of the religious responsibilities.[84]

Ananias was the first to be confronted. Although the first two verses refer to Sapphira's complicity and are in that sense introductory to both parts of the passage, the verbs are singular—he "sold a piece of property . . . he kept back part of the money." There is a mild irony even in Ananias's name, whose etymology is "God is gracious." In light of the fearsome judgment that befell his own actions, the grace of God was surely his only hope.

5:1 Ananias had evidently sold a piece of land,[85] like Barnabas, and also like Barnabas had pledged the full proceeds to the community. This can be assumed from the use of a rare Greek verb (*nosphizomai,* v. 2) to describe his action in holding back part of the money. The verb means *to pilfer, to purloin, to embezzle.* One does not embezzle one's own funds but those of another, in this instance those that rightfully belonged to the common Christian fund. Significantly, the same rare verb occurs in the Greek version of Josh 7:1-26, the story of Achan, who took from Jericho some of the booty "devoted" (i.e., set aside for God) for sacred use. Achan received a judgment of death from God himself, and Luke may well have seen a reminder of his fate in the similar divine judgment that came upon Ananias and Sapphira. They too had embezzled what was sacred, what belonged to the community in whom the Holy Spirit resided. One must assume either that the practice of the community was always to pledge the full proceeds of a sale or that Ananias and Sapphira had made such a pledge with regard to the sale of the field.[86]

---

[84]Ibid., 359-76.

[85]Verse 1 is ambiguous, referring to κτῆμα, a possession; but v. 3 clarifies that it was a field, landed property (χωρίου).

[86]J. D. M. Derrett suggests that what the couple held back was Sapphira's *ketubah,* the

5:2-3 In any event, when Ananias placed the reduced portion at the apostles' feet, Peter confronted him with his duplicity (v. 3). How Peter knew it was an incomplete sum the text does not say. The emphasis on the Spirit throughout the passage would indicate that it was inspired, prophetic insight on Peter's part, just as the Spirit inspired Elisha to see his servant Gehazi's duplicity in accepting money from Naaman the leper (2 Kgs 5:26).[87] Peter knew that Ananias's gesture was a lie. He had not given his pledge but only a part. "Why have you embezzled ["kept for yourself," NIV] a portion of the sale price? Why have you allowed Satan to enter your heart?" One must remember that the community was "of one heart and mind" (4:32). This spiritual unity lay behind their not claiming their possessions as their own, their sharing everything they had. They were the community of the Holy Spirit, and in this community they placed all their trust, found their identity and their security. But this was not so with Ananias. His heart was divided. He had one foot in the community and the other still groping for a toehold on the worldly security of earthly possessions. To lie with regard to the sharing was to belie the unity of the community, to belie the Spirit that undergirded that unity.[88] That is why Peter accused Ananias of lying to the Spirit. The Greek expression is even stronger than that—he "belied," he "falsified" the Spirit.[89] His action was in effect a denial, a falsification of the Spirit's presence in the community.[90] All this had happened because he had allowed the archenemy of the Spirit, Satan, to enter his heart. Satan "filled" Ananias's heart just as he had Judas's (cf. Luke 22:3). Like Judas, Ananias was motivated by money (cf. Luke 22:5). But in filling the heart of one of its members, Satan had now entered for the first time into the young Christian community as well.

---

portion belonging to her as her bridal rights, which could come to her in the event she was divorced or widowed. This would explain her own involvement in the transaction ("Ananias, Sapphira, and the Right of Property," DownRev 89 (1971): 225-32.

[87] Note also that Gehazi experienced a punishment-miracle by being struck with Naaman's leprosy (2 Kgs 5:27).

[88] L. Johnson, *Literary Function*, 207-8. F. F. Bruce notes that this concept of the ideal community being totally indwelt by the Spirit is found in Qumran texts that deal with the community of the end time: "The Holy Spirit in the Acts of the Apostles," *Int* 27 (1973): 166-83.

[89] F. Stagg, *The Book of Acts: The Early Struggle for an Unhindered Gospel* (Nashville: Broadman, 1955), 83.

[90] Many have sought to see the reference to Ananias's lying to the Spirit as indicating the "unforgivable sin" of blasphemy against the Spirit (Mark 3:28-29), but Ananias was not guilty of that, which is to attribute the works of God to Satan. Ananias was guilty of duplicity, lying, greed, hypocrisy—but not of blasphemy. See P. Menoud, "La Mort d'Ananias et de Saphira (Acts 5, 1-11)," *Aux Sources de la Tradition Chrétienne: Melanges offerts à M. Maurice Goguel* (Neuchatel: Delachaux et Niestlé, 1950), 146-54.

5:4 Peter reminded Ananias that he had been under no compulsion (v. 4). He did not have to sell his land. Even if he sold it, he still could have retained the proceeds. The act of dedicating the land to the community was strictly voluntary. Once pledged, however, it became a wholly different matter.[91] It had been dedicated to the community. In lying about the proceeds, he had broken a sacred trust. Ultimately, he had lied to God. Not that he had not betrayed the community. Not that he had not lied to the Spirit. Rather, to betray the community is to lie to the Spirit that fills the community, and to falsify the Spirit of God is an affront to God himself.

5:5-6 When Ananias heard these words, "he fell down and died" (v. 5). How did he die? Was it from shock from overwhelming guilt and remorse upon the exposure of his sin? Was he struck down by God?[92] The text does not say. The note about the fear that came upon all who heard about it, however, would indicate that they at least saw the hand of God in it all. The manner in which his funeral was handled would like-wise indicate that a divine judgment was seen in the whole affair. The young men arose,[93] wrapped up his body,[94] and carried him outside the city to bury him.[95] They wasted no time in ceremony, for they were back in three hours (vv. 7,10). This was most unusual procedure. Burials were often fairly hasty in Palestine, but not that hasty, not, that is, except for death under unusual circumstances, such as suicides and criminals—and judgments from God.[96]

5:7 About three hours later Sapphira appeared on the scene. Just where the scene was we are not told. Luke told the story with the greatest economy. We are also not told who was present. Were all the apostles

---

[91]F. Scheidweiler emends the οὐχὶ to οὐκ ὁ, thus changing the question to a declaration: "What remained was not yours, nor when sold was it at your disposal" ("Zu Act. 5:4," *ZNW* 49 [1958]: 136-37). B. Capper argues that the phrase ἐν τῇ σῇ ἐξουσίᾳ is a terminus techni-cus and indicates that the early church had a practice much like Qumran of holding a nov-ice's funds in trust until he became a full member and the funds would be merged into the common fund ("The Interpretation of Acts 5:4," *JSNT* 19 [1983]: 117-31).

[92]Derrett ("Ananias, Sapphira," 229-31) speaks of the rabbinic category of death "at the hands of heaven," special cultic offenses which were not covered by specific laws and pun-ishments but which were seen to come under divine retribution; and he suggests that Ananias and Sapphira may fall in this category. He adds that such deaths were often viewed as having atoning efficacy for the sin involved and in no way excluded one from the life to come.

[93]Some see in the Greek word for young men (νεώτεροι) a reference to a special order of "youngers" as opposed to "elders." There is no evidence in the NT for such an order, and the "elders" do not appear in Acts until 11:30.

[94]"Wrapped up" seems the most likely translation of συστέλλω, which could also be translated "snatch up" or "carry away."

[95]Only prophets and kings were buried within Jerusalem and few of those. Burial was generally outside the walls, where the corpse was laid in a cave, which explains why the young men could complete the procedure so quickly.

[96]So Derrett, "Ananias, Sapphira," 230.

there? Only Peter is mentioned. How many of those upon whom fear came (v. 5) were actually present to hear the confrontation? We must assume that at least the young men were there with Peter and Ananias (v. 6). For all we are told, in this scene it may have been a matter of only Peter and Sapphira. Where had she been all this time? Why had she not been informed of her husband's death? Why did she now appear; was she looking for her husband?

Luke was not interested in such details. His only goal was to point to the grim outcome of her duplicity with her husband. She joined him in the conspiracy with the funds. She would join him in death.

5:8 Peter confronted her about the sale price, just as he had confronted Ananias. "Is this the price you . . . got for the land?" he asked her (v. 8). "Yes," she replied. We are again left with questions. Did Peter mention the actual sale price or the reduced sum Ananias had brought? In giving an affirmative answer, was Sapphira conforming her guilt by continuing the lie? That is the most likely event, and most interpreters so take it. Yet if Peter had mentioned the actual full sale price, then her response would have been an admission of guilt, a confession.

5:9-10 In any event, with neither Ananias nor Sapphira did Peter pronounce a curse. His questioning of Sapphira left her the opportunity of repentance, and one can probably assume the same for Ananias. Peter's role was to confront—not to judge. The judgment came from God. But Peter had to lay before her the consequences of her action. She had joined with her husband in "testing" the Spirit of the Lord. This time the expression was not of lying to the Spirit but of testing him, to see how far he would go in his tolerance.[97] Not very far, was Peter's answer: "The feet of the men who buried your husband are at the door, and they will carry you out also." This was the first Sapphira had heard of her husband's death, and she fell down immediately at Peter's feet, dead.

Peter's words scarcely sound redemptive. He was fulfilling the prophetic role of the divine mouthpiece, pronouncing God's judgment on her for her complicity with her husband. She may have died of shock; but if so, it was inevitable, for Peter already knew and informed her that her doom was sealed. One can scarcely miss the irony of the situation. Now she lay at Peter's feet, in the place of her money. She had joined her husband in conspiracy. Now she would join him in the grave.[98]

5:11 Sapphira's story is bracketed by the same epitaph as that of her husband (cf. v. 5b): "Great fear seized the whole church and all who

---

[97]Seccombe (*Possessions*, 213) points out that the expression "testing the Spirit" with one exception (Isa 7:12) always in the OT refers to Israel's putting God to test in the wilderness: Exod 17:2; Deut 6:16; Pss 78:18,41,56; 95:8f. Is there an implicit wilderness motif for the "new people of God" in the Ananias and Sapphira story?

[98]L. Johnson, *Literary Function*, 209.

heard about these events." The repetition is not by chance: it is the whole point of the story. The church is a holy body, the realm of the Spirit. By the power of this spiritual presence in its midst, the young community worked miracles, witnessed fearlessly, and was blessed with incredible growth. The Spirit was the power behind its unity, and its unity was the power behind its witness. But just as with God there is both justice and mercy, so with his Spirit there is also an underside to his blessing. There is his judgment. This Ananias and Sapphira experienced. The Spirit is not to be taken lightly. As the Spirit of God he must always be viewed with fear in the best sense of that word (*phobos*), reverent awe and respect. It might be noted that this is the first time the word "church" (*ekklēsia*) occurs in Acts, which denotes the people of God gathered as a religious community. Perhaps it is not by accident that it occurs in the context of this story. The church can only thrive as the people of God if it lives within the total trust of all its members. Where there is that unity of trust, that oneness of heart and mind, the church flourishes in the power of the Spirit. Where there is duplicity and distrust, its witness fails.

Overview. There have been numerous approaches to dealing with the severity of this passage. One has been to note the various parallels to this story elsewhere. In form this story can be classified as a "penalty miracle," or miracle of divine judgment; and such stories are common in the Old Testament.[99] To those of Achan and Gehazi, one could add the incident of Nadab and Abihu in Lev 10:1f., who were consumed by the same "unauthorized fire" that they laid upon the censor, or the devastating judgment on Jeroboam delivered to his disguised wife by Abijah the prophet (1 Kgs 14:1-18). Even closer is the unhappy fate of the two elders whose lie about Susanna led to their own death rather than hers (Sus). The most apt Old Testament parallel is the provision for Israel's purity, which one encounters frequently in Deuteronomy: "Root out the evil one from your midst" (author's translation).[100] A number of recent interpreters have sought a closer parallel in the punishment the Qumran community enforced on those who held back goods from the common fund. As has already been noted, this is not a real parallel, since the early church seems to have had a voluntary system of sharing and not an enforced monastic community of goods like Qumran. What happened to Ananias and Sapphira is quite remote from the punishment meted to the Qumran member who failed to surrender all his property on entrance to the com-

---

[99] G. Theissen classifies this as a "rule miracle" and notes that it is the only example in the NT of a community rule enforced negatively by means of a punishment (*The Miracle Stories of the Early Christian Tradition*, trans. F. McDonagh [Philadelphia: Fortress, 1983], 109).

[100] Deut 13:5; 17:7,12; 19:19; 21:21; 22:21,24; 24:7. Cf. 1 Cor 5:13.

munity. Such violators were excluded from the common meal for a period of a year and had their food rations cut by a quarter.[101]

Other suggestions have sought to alleviate the judgmental note in the story of Ananias and Sapphira. It is often argued that their "lying to the Spirit" was the sin Jesus declared to be "unforgivable."[102] It has already been noted that Acts 5:1-11 simply does not depict Ananias and Sapphira's sin in terms of blaspheming the Spirit, attributing the work of the Spirit to Satan.[103] Often it is said that the pair died of psychological fright. This can be neither proved nor disproved from the text, and it well may have been the case; but it does not alleviate the strong judgmental note of the text. Peter knew and told Sapphira beforehand that she was about to be carried feetfirst out the door. Luke's emphasis on the fear of the people would likewise indicate that they saw divine judgment in the incident, not just a couple's panic in being caught with the goods.[104]

When all is said and done, there is no "comfortable" solution to the passage. It is a unique story. There is nothing like it elsewhere in Acts,[105] or for that matter in the New Testament. But nowhere in the story are Ananias and Sapphira condemned to eternal perdition. Their death did not necessarily involve their loss of salvation.[106] Still, the judgment that befell Ananias and Sapphira was severe, and one is all too aware that today's churches would be much emptier if such standards were consistently applied. It is part and parcel of Luke's ideal portrait of the early church in Acts. None of the standards fit the church of our experience— "one in heart and mind," no one "claimed that any of his possessions was his own." Luke depicted it as a unique period, the new people of God in Christ, filled with the Spirit, growing by leaps and bounds. There was no room for distrust, for duplicity, for any breach in fellowship.

The same Spirit that gave the community its growth also maintained its purity. This seems to have been Luke's point, for the Ananias and

---

[101]J. A. Fitzmyer, "Jewish Christianity," 243.

[102]So J. Munck, *The Acts of the Apostles*, rev. by W. F. Albright and C. S. Mann, AB (Garden City: Doubleday, 1967), 41; Robertson, *WP* 3:61.

[103]See n. 90.

[104]The same can be said for P. Menoud's view ("La Mort d'Ananias et Sapphira," see n. 90) that the story developed from the first deaths in the church and the consternation this created for the Christians who expected to still be alive at the Parousia. Luke's concern was not with deaths but with breach of fellowship, and the text must be dealt with in that light, i.e., in its context.

[105]There are other penalty miracles in Acts, but none are so severe. Elymas the magician lost his sight but only "for a time" (13:11); the sons of Sceva took a beating and lost their clothing, but that is all (19:16), though Herod's death and worm-eaten state could possibly be considered a penalty miracle (12:19b-23).

[106]Paul attributed deaths within the Corinthian community to a breach of fellowship and did not imply any loss of salvation (1 Cor 11:30).

Sapphira story is bracketed by an emphasis on the unity of the community (4:32-35) and the power of the Spirit in its midst (5:12-16).

One must not pass the story off, however, as a unique phenomenon of the primitive church or an adjunct to Luke's ideal portrait of the church. If the incident makes us uncomfortable, it should. For one, it deals with money. Luke, who as a physician probably had known personally the pitfalls of wealth, of all the Gospel writers gave the strongest treatment of money's dangers. Ultimately the temptations of money ensnared Judas (Luke 22:5; Acts 1:18), the rich young man (Luke 18:18-23), and the rich fool (Luke 12:15-21). The same quest for material security trapped Ananias and Sapphira. Not only was it their undoing, but it also threatened the church. Then, and now, the mark of any Christian fellowship is the relationship of its members to material matters. That is where its real heart and mind are revealed. This story reminds us of a further truth. The church, when it *is* the church, is a holy community, the temple of the Holy Spirit (1 Cor 3:16f.). Disunity, duplicity, and hypocrisy always "belie" the Spirit and hinder his work. If the church is to have genuine spiritual power in its life and witness, it must be an environment of the Spirit, devoted to maintaining its sanctity and purity.

7. The Miracles Worked by the Apostles (5:12-16)

[12]The apostles performed many miraculous signs and wonders among the people. And all the believers used to meet together in Solomon's Colonnade. [13]No one else dared join them, even though they were highly regarded by the people. [14]Nevertheless, more and more men and women believed in the Lord and were added to their number. [15]As a result, people brought the sick into the streets and laid them on beds and mats so that at least Peter's shadow might fall on some of them as he passed by. [16]Crowds gathered also from the towns around Jerusalem, bringing their sick and those tormented by evil spirits, and all of them were healed.

This third summary statement in Acts comes close on the heels of the second. That one emphasized the community of sharing practiced by the church (4:32-35). This one emphasizes the healing ministry of the apostles and bears out the divine response to their prayer for signs and wonders in 4:30. In structure the first statement, about the signs and wonders done by the apostles (v. 12a), connects directly with v. 15 and constitutes the main new emphasis in the summary statements—the healing ministry. Verses 12b-14 are a sort of parenthesis, continuing emphases that have been made in all the summaries—the effectiveness of the Christians' witness and their favor with the people (cf. 2:47; 4:33). The whole passage, with its focus on the healing ministry and the growing acclaim of the people, prepares for the renewed concern of the Sadducees and their arrest of the apostles, just as the healing of the lame man (3:1-10) led to the first arrest (4:1-22).

5:12-14 Verses 12-13 are deceptively clear in the NIV. The Greek text is far more ambiguous. The first statement is clear enough: "The apostles performed signs and wonders among the people." An example of such a sign has already been given with Peter's healing the lame man (3:1-10). Now all the apostles were shown to be doing miraculous works. The miracles were performed among the Jewish populace (*laos*) and were "signs" that pointed to and prepared the way for the witness to the word. The Greek of v. 12b says that "they all" were accustomed to meet together in Solomon's Colonnade. The NIV clarifies by adding "believers." Some interpreters would see the "all" of v. 12b as referring only to the apostles and then see "no one else" in v. 13 as referring to none of the other Christians. This has the advantage of solving the seeming contradiction between vv. 13-14, where no one dared join the Christians, yet many new converts were added. It, however, raises the rather serious question of why the other Christians wouldn't join the apostles in Solomon's Colonnade. Were they afraid of their power after what happened to Ananias and Sapphira? Were they afraid of being arrested by the temple authorities? Such timidity is scarcely likely for the community that prayed so boldly in 4:23-31. It is probably best, and the most likely reading, to follow the NIV and see v. 12b as referring to the other Christians joining the apostles in Solomon's Colonnade. Peter had preached there after the healing of the lame man (3:11), and it was likely the customary gathering place for the Christians. Other references to their preaching in the temple may well have been in this place just inside the eastern wall (cf. 5:20f., 25,42).

The people were awed by the power of the apostles, seeing the miracles worked through their hands,[107] and perhaps having heard the report about Ananias and Sapphira. They did not run up and join the Christian band in the colonnade but kept a healthy distance (v. 13a).[108] Nevertheless they held the Christians in the highest regard. Luke was working with a paradox here. It is the same two-sidedness of the Spirit's power that had just been demonstrated in Ananias and Sapphira. The power of the miracles

---

[107]Verse 12a reads literally, "Many signs and wonders happened *through the hands of the apostles.*" Luke's wording was carefully chosen. Peter made clear that he himself did not heal the lame man (3:12); the apostles were merely the agents through whom God worked his miracles.

[108]A number of scholars have wanted to see "the rest" of v. 13 as referring to the Jewish officials, emending λοιπῶν to "Levites" (Hilgenfeld) or "elders" (C. C. Torrey), or "rulers" (M. Dibelius). Often this is combined with the view that κολλᾶσθαι should be translated "seize," giving the meaning that they dared not arrest the Christians for fear of their popularity with the people. See C. C. Torrey, "The 'Rest' in Acts v. 13," *ExpTim* 46 (1934-35): 428-29; D. Schwarz, "Non-Joining Sympathizers (Acts 5, 13-14)," *Bib* 64 (1983): 550-55.

attracts. The awesome power of the Spirit that judges also demands commitment and responsibility. Before that power the crowd kept its distance
with healthy respect, unless they were willing to fully submit to that
power and make a commitment. Many did, Luke said, making it clear this
time that men and women became disciples and were added to the growing
community of believers (v. 14).

5:15 Verse 15 returns to the main theme of the summary, the healing
ministry of the apostles. Again Peter was the representative. So widespread was the fame of his healing powers that people would bring their
sick friends and relatives into Peter's presence in the hope that even his
shadow might fall upon them. One is reminded of the woman who shared
a similar hope that the fringe of Jesus' garment might heal her (Luke
8:44). In the ancient world a person's shadow was the subject of much
superstition and was believed to represent his or her power and personality, to literally be an extension of their person.[109] Whether or not they
were healed by Peter's shadow Luke did not explicitly say, but the note
underlines the strength of the apostle's healing reputation.

5:16 In any event, crowds came from all the surrounding villages to
Jerusalem to be healed by the apostles. One is reminded of Jesus' own
healing ministry as recorded in Mark 6:53-56 and the similar response of
the people.[110] At this point the apostles were still confined to Jerusalem.
The people came to them from the outlying villages. Only later would
they go forth from Jerusalem and take their gospel and their healing ministry into the villages of Judea (cf. 9:32-43).

8. All the Apostles before the Council (5:17-42)

As in 3:1—4:5, the apostles' healing led to their arrest by the temple
authorities and to a hearing before the Jewish Sanhedrin. Many similarities exist between this section and other portions of Acts, especially the
twofold trial scenes of 4:5-22 and 5:27-40 and the escape scenes of 5:17-
26 and 12:6-11. This has led many scholars to postulate Luke's use of
different sources that covered the same events,[111] but this tends to overlook the real progression that takes place in the narrative. The conflict
between the Christians and the Jews steadily intensified.[112] With the
growing success of the Christian witness, there is a heightened reaction

---

[109]P. W. van der Horst, "Peter's Shadow: The Religio-Historical Background of Acts
v. 15," *NTS* 23 (1977): 204-12.

[110]This Markan pericope is not paralleled in Luke's Gospel.

[111]Any source analysis of Acts tends to be fairly subjective since there are no parallel
sources to be compared with it as is the case with the Synoptics. See the discussion in the
introduction.

[112]This stress on the narrative development rather than on sources is effectively made by
E. Haenchen, *Acts*, 254-56.

on the part of the Jewish authorities—at first only a hearing, warning, and release (4:5-22). Now those on the Council would impose the death penalty (5:33) and were only thwarted in their intentions by the sage advice of a Pharisee (5:34-39). The apostles were again released, but this time the Council had them whipped before so doing (5:40). The conflict became even stronger with the killing of Stephen (6:8—8:2) and the resulting persecution of the Christians in Jerusalem (8:1); and it reached its apex in chap. 12, where the execution of James and the attempt to do the same to Peter found the support not only of the Jewish officials but the populace as well (12:3).

This second encounter with the Sanhedrin can be divided into three main parts: the initial arrest and its almost ludicrous result (5:17-26), the hearing before the Sanhedrin (5:27-40), and the release of the apostles with their continued witness (5:41-42).

(1) Arrest, Escape, and Rearrest (5:17-26)

[17]Then the high priest and all his associates, who were members of the party of the Sadducees, were filled with jealousy. [18]They arrested the apostles and put them in the public jail. [19]But during the night an angel of the Lord opened the doors of the jail and brought them out. [20]"Go, stand in the temple courts," he said, "and tell the people the full message of this new life."

[21]At daybreak they entered the temple courts, as they had been told, and began to teach the people.

When the high priest and his associates arrived, they called together the Sanhedrin—the full assembly of the elders of Israel—and sent to the jail for the apostles. [22]But on arriving at the jail, the officers did not find them there. So they went back and reported, [23]"We found the jail securely locked, with the guards standing at the doors; but when we opened them, we found no one inside." [24]On hearing this report, the captain of the temple guard and the chief priests were puzzled, wondering what would come of this.

[25]Then someone came and said, "Look! The men you put in jail are standing in the temple courts teaching the people." [26]At that, the captain went with his officers and brought the apostles. They did not use force, because they feared that the people would stone them.

5:17-18 As before, the Sadducees were enraged by the apostles' preaching. They were described as being "filled with jealousy," undoubtedly over the tremendous success of the Christian witness (5:15-16). The word translated "jealousy" can also mean *zeal*, and there may well have been an element of zeal in their determination to stamp out this growing messianic movement before its increasing popularity aroused the concern of the Roman authorities and led to severe reprisals. The high priest was again the spokesman.[113] He was ultimately responsible for the proper

---

[113]One Old Latin manuscript reads *Annas* for the participle ἀναστὰς, which begins v. 17,

maintenance of the temple precincts and its cultus, and so it was very much on his turf where the Christians were having all their success (cf. v. 12b). His cohorts in the local party[114] of Sadducees would have shared his concern for preserving the peace against such popular movements and supported him in putting the apostles in the public jail (v. 18).[115] One should not miss the irony of their being placed in the public jail, i.e., openly and for everyone to see. Soon they would be unable to find these very ones who were so openly placed in jail.

5:19-21a The miraculous escape of the apostles is told with the greatest economy here. In vv. 21b-26 it will be retold in far greater detail. The emphasis is placed on the total helplessness of the Jewish authorities. In this way the lesson of Gamaliel's speech is illustrated vividly beforehand—"If it is from God, you will not be able to stop these men" (v. 39).

An "angel" of the Lord appeared to the imprisoned apostles at night, opened the prison doors,[116] and led them out (v. 19). The angel gave the apostles God's instructions. They were to return to the temple and speak "the full message of this new life."[117] They were to resume their witness, preaching the gospel that leads to life, the message of salvation.[118] The apostles went and did as the angel bade them, early in the morning when the crowds would be gathering in the temple to observe the morning sacrifice. They obviously were not concerned for their safety. They returned to the very spot where they had been arrested, preaching the same words of life for which they were arrested. Perhaps there is irony in their deliverance by the angel. Sadducees did not believe in angels.

5:21b-24 Now the interesting part of the story begins. The scene shifts to the Council chambers where the Sanhedrin had gathered for its

---

thus rendering "Annas the High Priest," and Moffatt follows that variant in his translation. This is very much in keeping with Luke's designation of Annas as high priest in 4:6, but it is too poorly attested to adopt.

[114] Josephus used the term "philosophies" to describe the three major parties within contemporary Judaism—the Pharisees, Sadducees, and Essenes (*Ant.* 18.11). The rather awkward phrase "the existing sect" (ἡ οὖσα αἵρεσις) appears in v. 17, which seems to mean *the local sect* in accordance with the usage elsewhere in Acts for ἡ οὖσα (cf. 14:13; 28:17).

[115] Τηρήσει δημοσίᾳ could refer either to the "public jail" or to their being put "in jail publicly."

[116] If it was the same prison in which Peter was later confined, two doors were involved (12:10).

[117] The Greek word ἄγγελος means *messenger*. In Acts angels are *God's* messengers, speaking his words, performing his acts of deliverance—cf. 8:26; 10:3; 12:7,23. Note also how consistently in Acts miraculous escapes from prison took place at night—12:6; cf. 16:25.

[118] In Acts the terms "salvation" and "life" are virtually synonymous. Cf. "life" in 3:15; 11:18; 13:46 with "salvation" in 4:12; 11:14; 15:11; 16:17,30f.

morning session.[119] The first item on the agenda was the interrogation of the apostles; so officers were sent to the jail to fetch them. But they were not there. The officers hastened back to deliver the startling news. The prison doors were securely locked. The guards were duly *standing* at their posts (and thus evidently awake). Yet there was no one inside. How in the world did they get out through locked gates, past the guards? The Council was at a total loss.

5:25-26 Finally someone arrived with the good news, or was it bad news? The prisoners hadn't totally escaped. They were on the temple grounds, back to their old tricks, teaching the people. Now the captain, the *sagan*, decided he had better handle the matter personally. After all, he was second in rank to the high priest himself and ultimately responsible for order on the temple grounds. Unusual circumstances like this had best not be left to lesser officials. So he went with his officers to gently persuade the apostles to accompany him to the Council chambers. He personally might have desired their execution by the usual procedure of stoning, but at this point he was more concerned about being stoned to death himself by the people, who held the apostles in the highest regard (cf. v. 13). One must not miss the irony in this entire fiasco.

The Sanhedrin was totally thwarted in its designs, totally helpless to control the situation. All was in God's hands. The only reason the apostles finally appeared before the Council was their own willingness to do so. And they were willing to do so because the events of the night had convinced them once more that they were very much in God's hands.

(2) Appearance before Sanhedrin (5:27-40)

[27]**Having brought the apostles, they made them appear before the Sanhedrin to be questioned by the high priest. [28]"We gave you strict orders not to teach in this name," he said. "Yet you have filled Jerusalem with your teaching and are determined to make us guilty of this man's blood."**

[29]**Peter and the other apostles replied: "We must obey God rather than men! [30]The God of our fathers raised Jesus from the dead—whom you had killed by hanging him on a tree. [31]God exalted him to his own right hand as Prince and Savior that he might give repentance and forgiveness of sins to Israel. [32]We are witnesses of these things, and so is the Holy Spirit, whom God has given to those who obey him."**

[33]**When they heard this, they were furious and wanted to put them to death. [34]But a Pharisee named Gamaliel, a teacher of the law, who was honored by all the people, stood up in the Sanhedrin and ordered that the men be put outside**

---

[119]Luke used two expressions for the council in 21b, the "Sanhedrin" and the "full assembly (γερουσία) of the elders of Israel." Some scholars argue that Luke referred here to two separate judicial bodies, but the terms are most likely parallel expressions for a single body, as the NIV indicates by the use of dashes.

for a little while. [35]Then he addressed them: "Men of Israel, consider carefully what you intend to do to these men. [36]Some time ago Theudas appeared, claiming to be somebody, and about four hundred men rallied to him. He was killed, all his followers were dispersed, and it all came to nothing. [37]After him, Judas the Galilean appeared in the days of the census and led a band of people in revolt. He too was killed, and all his followers were scattered. [38]Therefore, in the present case I advise you: Leave these men alone! Let them go! For if their purpose or activity is of human origin, it will fail. [39]But if it is from God, you will not be able to stop these men; you will only find yourselves fighting against God."

[40]His speech persuaded them. They called the apostles in and had them flogged. Then they ordered them not to speak in the name of Jesus, and let them go.

This second appearance before the Sanhedrin is significantly different from the first (4:5-22). That one only involved two apostles, Peter and John. Here all the apostles stood before the Council. There was no formal charge leveled against Peter and John; the questions mainly regarded their authorization (4:7). The apostles now were confronted with violation of the Council's interdiction (5:28). The possibility of a verdict of death was not raised before, but at this point it became explicit (5:33). Most significant of all, there was no particular spokesperson for the Christians. Now there was, and he was a Pharisee (5:34-40). The trial scene falls into two rather balanced parts, focusing on the witness of the Christians (5:27-32) and the intercession of Gamaliel (5:33-40).

5:27-28 The trial began with the apostles being brought before the Sanhedrin. The Greek text has them "stood up" (*estēsan*) before the body, and this was the usual procedure, the defendants standing, the judges sitting. The high priest as presiding officer began the interrogation, charging the apostles with two offenses. First, they had broken the interdiction of the Sanhedrin and continued to preach "in this name." Second, they were determined to lay the guilt for "this man's blood" on them, the Jewish leaders.

What the high priest did not say is perhaps more significant than what he did say. He made absolutely no reference to the apostles' escape. Was this out of total embarrassment? Further, he scrupulously avoided mentioning Jesus by name. Does this reflect that already at this early stage mentioning the name of Jesus was considered in some circles as blasphemous?[120] In any event, there were formal charges this time. The apostles had been duly warned by the court not to continue further witness, and the interdiction had been fully ignored. They were unmistakably

---

[120]In the period after the fall of Jerusalem (post A.D. 70), Christians were placed by Pharisaic orthodoxy under a formal curse or ban (the *birkat ha minim*), and uttering the name of Jesus was indeed considered blasphemy. It was scrupulously avoided in the rabbinic writings.

culpable.[121] The high priest's concern about being charged with responsibility for Jesus' "blood" may have had more significance than appears at first sight. To "lay someone's blood" on someone is an Old Testament expression for a charge of murder and in accordance with the *ius Talionis* demanded the death of the guilty party.[122] In essence the high priest was saying, "You are trying to get us killed for responsibility in this man's death" (author's paraphrase).

5:29 Peter, of course, was not trying to get the leaders killed but rather to get them saved. As in the first trial, his response was more of a witness than a defense. As then, he referred to the basic principle of obeying God rather than man (cf. 4:19), this time the form being even closer to that of Socrates' famous quote in Plato's *Apology* 29d. This principle underlies this entire section of Acts. Where God's will lay in this instance was fully demonstrated in the escape with its command to resume the preaching in the temple. Not impeding God's purposes would be the main thrust of Gamaliel's speech. Peter had no choice. He had to remain true to the divine leading. His saying has continued to be used by Christians throughout the centuries, by Christian martyrs making the ultimate sacrifice in obedience to their Lord, and by power-hungry medieval popes exerting their influence over the secular rulers.[123] It is a dangerous saying, subject to abuse and misappropriation; and one should be as clear as Peter was about what God's purposes really are before ever using it.

5:30-32 Peter's witness before the Sanhedrin was basically a summary of the Christian *kerygma*, as it had been at his first trial (4:10-12). The basic elements are all there—the guilt of the Jewish leaders for crucifying Jesus, the resurrection and exaltation, repentance and forgiveness in his name, the apostolic witness. There are some differences in detail. Jesus' crucifixion is described as "hanging on a tree," probably in allusion to Deut 21:23, an Old Testament text the early Christians saw as pointing to Christ.[124]

---

[121]Jeremias's theory for the necessity of a preliminary trial informing the defendant of his culpability has been critiqued by B. Reicke (*Glaube und Leben*, 105ff.), who pointed out that such a law applied only in capital offenses. However, Jeremias's main point still seems to apply. In the first trial the Sanhedrin had no formal charges to make. In the second they did—the apostles had transgressed their interdiction. See J. Jeremias, "Untersuchungen zum Quellenproblem der Apostelgeschichte," *ZNW* 36 (1937): 208-13.

[122]R. Pesch, *Apostelgeschichte* 1:216.

[123]An excellent summary of the use and abuse of this saying throughout Christian history is given by Pesch (ibid., 1:222-24).

[124]Peter did not here use Deut 21:22f. to develop the idea of Christ's becoming a curse for us, although that idea seems to be present in 1 Pet 2:24 and is fully developed by Paul in Gal 3:13. Compare further uses in Acts 10:39; 13:29. For the form of text behind the citations, see M. Wilcox, "Upon the Tree—Deut. 21:22-23 in the New Testament," *JBL* 96 (1977): 85-99.

In v. 31 the exalted Christ is described as "Prince" and "Savior." Neither term was new to Peter's sermons. The first term occurred in his temple sermon (3:15), where it had the nuance of author or originator of the resurrection life. Here it has the sense of "leader" or "prince" but still in close connection with the new life he brings through repentance and forgiveness of sins. It is thus closely connected with the title "Savior," which Peter had not used before. The concept of the salvation in his name, however, was at the very heart of his previous witness before the Sanhedrin (cf. 4:12). Here as there Peter's purpose was the same—to demonstrate that Christ is indeed the risen Savior and to urge repentance and commitment to his name. Peter was issuing an invitation to the Sanhedrin. They had indeed sinned in hanging Jesus on the cross, but there is forgiveness and salvation for Israel in him. If they needed further proof that he is their deliverer, risen and exalted to God's right hand, the apostles could bear eyewitness testimony to these realities (v. 32).

The pouring out of the Holy Spirit, so evident in all the miraculous works that were being accomplished, was bearing his own witness. Then as now, the Spirit is granted to all who obey God. Peter had been obedient, obeying God rather than man. Now his implicit appeal was that the Sanhedrin follow him in the same obedience.

5:33-34 The Jewish leaders were not the least inclined to respond to Peter's appeal. Their reaction was quite the opposite. They were infuriated (*dieprionto*; lit., "sawn in two"). Some called for the death penalty, undoubtedly the Sadducees on the Council. Theologically they were not inclined to be convinced by Peter's appeal to the resurrection, and politically Peter's messianic message only served to further confirm that this was a dangerous, rabble-rousing group. They might have passed the verdict then and there had not a voice been raised urging moderation. It was a voice from the Pharisaic minority on the Council.

One wonders how much of a part politics played in the Sanhedrin's decision on this particular occasion. Josephus said that the Sadducean officials usually yielded to the recommendations of the Pharisees because the latter enjoyed the support of the masses.[125] Gamaliel may have used this occasion as another opportunity to assert this Pharisaic ascendancy over the Sadducees. As a Pharisee he would have had more sympathy with the Christians theologically.[126] Pharisees believed in a coming Messiah, in the resurrection, and in a life after death, none of which the Sad-

---

[125]*Antiquities* 18.17.

[126]In Acts the Pharisees are generally depicted as fairly sympathetic toward the Christians, in marked contrast to the picture in the Gospels, though in Luke the Pharisees played no real role in the crucifixion of Jesus. In Acts the Sadducees were the ones who mounted the real opposition, as here. See J. T. Sanders, *The Jews in Luke-Acts* (Philadelphia: Fortress, 1987), 94-101.

ducees accepted. The Pharisees also had an oral tradition of interpretation of the Torah that gave them considerable flexibility and openness to change. Not so the Sadducees, who accepted only the written Torah and were far more rigid and conservative in attitude. Such differences must have contributed considerably to Gamaliel's more tolerant stance toward the apostles.[127]

The Gamaliel in question here was Gamaliel I, who is referred to in several places in the rabbinic literature, though surprisingly sparsely for a man of his stature. He was the son or grandson of the famous Hillel and seemed to have been at the prime of his influence from about A.D. 25–50. Rabbinic tradition gives him the title of Nasi, or president of the high court, and has his son Simeon follow him in that role. His grandson Gamaliel II held the presidency after A.D. 90,[128] when the court met at Jamnia. Perhaps nowhere is the esteem in which he was held better expressed than in the following statement of the *Mishna*: "When Rabban Gamaliel the Elder died, the glory of the Law ceased and purity and abstinence died."[129] For Christians he is best known through his pupil, Paul (Acts 22:3).

5:34-39 Gamaliel's power in the Sanhedrin is subtly reflected in his ordering the apostles to be removed "for a little while." Such matters were generally the prerogative of the high priest, and his reference to "a little while" reflects his confidence that it wouldn't take him long to sway the court. He began by urging the court to "consider carefully" what they were about to do to the apostles. Considering that the death penalty had just been suggested, he was implying that this might be a bit rash and bring unfortunate results down on them, particularly given the Christian popularity with the masses. There was a better way. Simply leave the movement alone. Leave it to God. If he was not in it, it would fizzle out (vv. 38-39).

5:36-37 To make his point, Gamaliel cited two examples of similar messianic movements in recent Jewish history. His reasoning was simple. Neither movement succeeded—God was not in them. The examples he chose, however, raise serious historical problems. These revolve primarily around the first example—Theudas. According to Gamaliel, this Theudas appeared "some time ago," claiming to be somebody (cf. 8:9), raised a following of about 400 men, and was killed. With his death the followers scattered in every direction, and the whole movement ended. The only other Theudas during this period of whom there is record is mentioned in

---

[127]On the origins of the parties, see T. W. Manson, "Sadducee and Pharisee—The Origin and Significance of the Names," *BJRL* 22 (1938): 144-59.

[128]*Beginnings* 4:60.

[129]*M. Sota* 9:15.

Josephus's *Antiquities* (20.97-99). According to Josephus, this Theudas raised a considerable following from the masses, persuading them to take along all their possessions and join him at the Jordan River. Claiming to be a prophet, he insisted that at his command the waters of the Jordan would part (as in the days of Joshua). Getting wind of the movement, the Roman procurator arrived on the scene with a squadron of cavalry, took many prisoners, and beheaded Theudas, taking the trophy to Jerusalem (for a public object lesson).

If Luke and Josephus were talking about the same Theudas, there is a serious anachronism, for Josephus's Theudas is dated during the procuratorship of Fadus, whose term began in A.D. 44, some ten to fifteen years later than the time when Gamaliel would have delivered this address. To make matters worse, Gamaliel then gave the example of Judas the Galilean, who he said arose after Theudas, when in fact Judas's rebellion occurred in A.D. 6, nearly forty years earlier than Theudas's movement.

Many approaches have been taken in dealing with this problem,[130] but basically three possibilities emerge: (1) either Josephus was in error, (2) or Luke was responsible for the anachronisms, or (3) they refer to two different Theudases. It is unlikely that Josephus would have made such an error. He lived in Palestine during the period of Fadus and would have had personal recollection of such events as the movement under Theudas. This leads many scholars to attribute the anachronism to Luke.[131] Obviously for those who are impressed with Luke's general historical accuracy elsewhere and who are not disposed to according him such a mistake, the third option remains the most viable route.

Although it is an argument from silence, there is solid basis for arguing that the Theudas of Acts may be a different person from the one mentioned by Josephus. For one, the Acts account is very brief and could be applied to any number of messianic pretenders. Apart from the name Theudas and the fact of his death, it has little in common with Josephus's account. All the colorful highlights are missing—the parting of the Jordan, the arrival of the cavalry, the beheading. Acts gives the modest fol-

---

[130]Josephus spoke of the sons of Judas the Galilean in the paragraph immediately following his account of Theudas (*Ant.* 20.102). It is sometimes argued that Luke used this section of Josephus and confused the sons with the father. This solves the problem of sequence between Theudas and Judas but raises others, not least of which would be a very late date for Acts. (*Ant.* was published in A.D. 93.) Though it often has been maintained, it is not likely Luke used Josephus. Where their matter overlaps, no literary relationship can be shown. For an entirely different solution, which would move the historical setting of Gamaliel's speech to chap. 12 (ca. A.D. 44), see J. W. Swain, "Gamaliel's Speech and Caligula's Statue," *HTR* 37 (1944): 341-49.

[131]E.g., E. Haenchen, *Acts*, 257; H. Conzelmann, *Acts of the Apostles*, trans. J. Limburg, A. Kraabel, and D. Juel, *Her* (Philadelphia: Fortress, 1987), 42.

lowing of 400 men; Josephus spoke of "the majority of the masses" following Theudas. Acts says they were dispersed; Josephus, that many were arrested.

A second consideration is that the name Theudas may be a nickname or a Greek form of a common Hebrew name. In such a case the Theudas of Acts may be identified elsewhere by a different, Hebrew name.[132] Finally, Josephus spoke of innumerable tumults and insurrections that arose in Judea following the death of Herod the Great (4 B.C.).[133] Though he mentioned no leaders of these movements by name, this would be a plausible context for the Theudas incident mentioned in Gamaliel's speech.

Gamaliel's second example is less problematic. He referred to Judas the Galilean who arose "in the days of the census." This is almost surely the same Judas who is referred to by Josephus in both his *Jewish War* and his *Antiquities*.[134] He started a major rebellion in protest of the census under Quirinius (A.D. 6–7), which was undertaken for purposes of taxation. Josephus did not mention his death, but Gamaliel referred to his being killed and all his followers being scattered. Although the original rebellion under Judas was stifled by the Romans, such was not the case with the general movement begun by Judas. According to Josephus, he laid the foundations of the Zealot movement within Judaism, a movement that would grow to such proportions that in less than twenty-five years after Gamaliel's speech, it would initiate all-out war with the Romans.

5:38-39 Gamaliel's point is clear (vv. 38-39). God will work out his will. A movement that has his backing will prevail. Otherwise it will abort. So leave these men alone, lest you find yourselves fighting God. At this point in time Gamaliel might also have been concerned about their finding themselves fighting the Jewish populace. In any event he enunciated a sound rabbinic principle: "Any assembling together that is for the sake of Heaven shall in the end be established, but any that is not for the sake of Heaven shall not in the end be established."[135] Gamaliel's advice was sound and yet also a bit ironical. Already his counsel was

---

[132]Theudas is most likely a shortened form of a Greek name such as Theodotus or Theodosius, meaning *Gift of God*. Jews often adopted such Greek names that corresponded etymologically to their given Hebrew names. Hebrew names corresponding to Theodotus would be such common ones as Jonathan, Nathaniel, and Matthias. See C. J. Hemer, *The Book of Acts in the Setting of Hellenistic History* (Tübingen: Mohr-Siebeck, 1989), 162-63, n. 5. A similar argument sees Theudas as a possible Aramaic nickname meaning *witness*; P. Winter, "Miszellen zur Apostelgeschichte. 1. Acta 5, 36: Theudas," *ExpTim* 17 (1957): 398-99.

[133]*Antiquities* 17.269, 285.

[134]*Antiquities* 18.4-10; 18.23; 20.102; *War* 2.433; 7.253. See M. Black, "Judas of Galilee and Josephus's 'Fourth Philosophy,'" *Josephus-Studien* (Göttingen: Vandenhoeck und Ruprecht, 1974), 45-54.

[135]*M. Abot* 4:11.

finding fulfillment—in the growing Christian community, in their signs and wonders, in their escape from jail just the night before. It had become obvious whose side God was on. Already the Council were finding themselves fighters against God.

5:40 The Sanhedrin concurred with Gamaliel's advice. Again they released the apostles, but this time with a flogging. The flogging referred to was the customary punishment used as a warning not to persist in an offense. It consisted of thirty-nine lashes, often referred to as the forty less one (cf. 2 Cor 11:24). Based on the provision for forty stripes given in Deut 25:3, the practice had developed of only giving thirty-nine in the event of miscounting, preferring to err on the side of clemency rather than severity. It was still a cruel punishment. With bared chest and in a kneeling position, one was beaten with a tripled strap of calf hide across both chest and back, two on the back for each stripe across the chest. Men were known to have died from the ordeal.[136] As before, the apostles were warned not to continue their witness in Jesus' name. This time the warning was reinforced with somewhat stronger persuasion.

(3) Release and Witness (5:41-42)

41The apostles left the Sanhedrin, rejoicing because they had been counted worthy of suffering disgrace for the Name. 42Day after day, in the temple courts and from house to house, they never stopped teaching and proclaiming the good news that Jesus is the Christ.

5:41-42 The apostles were not persuaded. They would continue to obey God rather than men. In fact, they rejoiced at having suffered for the name, very much in accord with the beatitude of their Lord (Luke 6:22f.). And the witness to the name continued—publicly in the temple and privately in the homes of the Christians. Luke seems to have used a common Greek rhetorical construction in v. 42 called a chiasm, which is most easily pictured as an A-B-B-A pattern. In the temple (A) and in homes (B), the apostles taught (B) and preached the gospel (A). Teaching was the task within the Christian fellowship, preaching the public task in the temple grounds. If there is any significance to his using such a device, it would be to give emphasis to the beginning and concluding elements. Their witness, their preaching of the gospel, was their primary task and occupation.

---

[136]*M. Mak.* 3:10-14. In some instances less than thirty-nine stripes were prescribed, with the sole provision that the number had to be divisible by three (in order to get the proportion of chest to back stripes to come out right). There is no reason to see less than the customary thirty-nine being given to the apostles.

―――――――――――――― *SECTION OUTLINE* ――――――――――――――

―――――――― **III. THE HELLENISTS BREAK THROUGH** ――――――――
TO A WIDER WITNESS (6:1–8:40)

The first five chapters of Acts have presented the picture of a Christian
community in Jerusalem that was still closely bound to Judaism. The outreach effort of this group was strictly to the Jews. There was no conscious
breach with Judaism, and the temple was itself the major site for the

church's evangelistic efforts.[1] These first chapters thus comprise a development of Jesus' injunction in Acts 1:8: "You will be my witnesses in Jerusalem." Chapters 6–12 pick up this theme, showing the further realization of the commission—"in all Judea and Samaria." The ministry of Paul in chaps. 13–28 extends its fulfillment "to the ends of the earth." Chapters 6–8 may thus be described as transitional. They show Christianity breaking out from the bounds of its Jewish heritage, taking a first step toward its mission to the wider world. This is more than a story of the geographical spread of Christianity. It is much more the story of the gospel becoming a truly universal gospel, breaking the racial, national, and religious barriers in which it was born and carrying out a genuinely worldwide witness. It is the triumphant story of the inclusive gospel.[2]

Paul was the key figure in Acts for the Christian witness to the wider world, but the story of his mission to the Gentiles does not begin in earnest until chap. 13. His mission was not fully recognized by the whole Christian community until the Jerusalem conference related in chap. 15. The development of the worldwide mission was a gradual one according to the picture of Acts. It involved controversy, resistance, and some hard lessons along the way. But ultimately the vision triumphed because the Spirit of God was in it. That Luke made infinitely clear.

The first decisive steps take place in chaps. 6–8, and they seem to have been taken by a particular group within the Christian community in Jerusalem whom Luke called "the Hellenists" (Greek, *Hellēnistai*). The name does not seem to have been a technical term, and Luke only employed it twice in all of Acts (6:1; 9:29). The NIV translates the term "Grecian Jews," and all evidence points to the correctness of this rendering. They seem to have been Greek-speaking Jews in contrast to the Jews who spoke the native Aramaic dialect of Jerusalem (*Hebraioi*, 6:1).[3] Acts 9:29

---

[1] See Acts 2:46; 3:1-3,11f.; 5:12,25,42.

[2] Luke developed the theme of the universal gospel in his Gospel as well as in Acts. See F. Stagg, *The Book of Acts: The Early Struggle for an Unhindered Gospel* (Nashville: Broadman, 1955), 12-17, 28-34, et passim.

[3] The identity of the Hellenists has been widely debated. H. J. Cadbury argued that the term means "Greeks" (*The Beginnings of Christianity*, vol. 5, *Additional Notes* [London: Macmillan, 1933], 59-74), but it is most unlikely that Greek Gentile converts were already in the church at this point given the difficulty Peter had in accepting the witness to the Gentile Cornelius (chap. 10). O. Cullmann has argued that the Hellenists were heterodox Jews with viewpoints in common with the Samaritans and the Qumran Essenes: "The significance of the Qumran texts for research into the beginnings of Christianity," *JBL* 74 (1955): 213-26; cf. *The Johannine Circle*, trans. J. Bowden (Philadelphia: Westminster, 1975). The Samaritan thesis has been elaborately developed by A. Spiro (appendix 5 in J. Munck's *The Acts of the Apostles*, rev. W. F. Albright and C. S. Mann, AB [Garden City: Doubleday, 1967], 285-300), who argues that Stephen was a Samaritan and that the term *Hebraioi* refers to the Samaritan element within the Jerusalem church.

describes the recently converted Paul as having disputed with Hellenists/
Grecian Jews, but their attempt to kill him indicates they were certainly
not Christians. Acts 6:9 refers to a dispute between Stephen and those
who belonged to the "Synagogue of the Freedmen" and lists the various
areas of the Diaspora from which it drew its membership.

Putting this together, "Hellenists" would seem to indicate Greek-
speaking Jews of the Diaspora who were living in Jerusalem.[4] The seven
Hellenists of Acts 6:1-7 would have been Christian converts who came
from this Greek-speaking Jewish community and had possibly themselves
belonged to a synagogue in Jerusalem composed of Diaspora Jews, such
as those with whom Stephen (6:9) and, later, Paul (9:29) disputed. That
there would have been many such Diaspora converts in the Jerusalem
Christian community is altogether likely, given the large number of them
who were present at Pentecost (2:5-11). Although an integral part of the
Jerusalem Christian community, their common language and upbringing
in the wider Hellenistic world probably gave them some sense of cohe-
siveness as a group and a predisposal toward a more worldwide witness.[5]

In any event these Greek-speaking, Diaspora Jewish Christians, who
are the main characters in chaps. 6–8, seem to have been instrumental in
first taking the Christian witness beyond Jerusalem. The story begins with
the selection of the seven Hellenist "deacons" in 6:1-6. Among these
were Stephen and Philip (6:5). Stephen debated with his fellow Diaspora
Jews in their synagogue, was strongly opposed by them, arrested, brought
before the Sanhedrin, and stoned to death (6:15–8:1a). He never left Jerusalem, and yet he was instrumental in the Christian mission outside Jerusalem that followed his martyrdom.

Stephen's influence is exemplified in two ways. First, his speech
before the Sanhedrin (7:2-53) was programmatic for the wider Christian
mission, providing a critique of the Jewish resistance to the Christian
gospel and an inclusive outlook on the promises of God. Second, his

---

[4]The most thorough argument for the Hellenists being Diaspora Jews is that of M. Hengel, "Zwischen Jesus und Paulus: Die 'Hellenisten,' die 'Sieben' und Stephanus (Apg. 6:1-15;
7:54-8:3)," *ZTK* 72 (1975), 151-206.

[5]A number of scholars maintain that the term "Hellenist" probably involves an orientation toward Hellenistic culture as well as speaking the Greek language: E. Larson, "Die Hellenisten und die Urgemeinde," *NTS* 33 (1987): 205-22; W. Grundmann, "Das Problem des
hellenistischen Christentums innerhalb der Jerusalemer Urgemeinde," *ZNW* 38 (1939): 45-
73; H. Windisch, "῞Ελλην . . . ῾Ελληνιστί," *TDNT* 2:512-13. The likelihood of there being
some group mentality among the Hellenists is argued by R. Pesch, E. Gerhart, and F. Schilling in "'Hellenists' und 'Hebraer,' zu Apg. 9, 29 und 6, 1," *BZ* 23 (1979): 87-92. C. F. D.
Moule believes that the term Hellenists implies that they spoke *only* Greek: "Once more,
who were the Hellenists?" *ExpTim* 70 (1958): 100-02. That they were all Gentile proselytes
to Judaism (like Nicolas, 6:5) is argued by E. C. Blackman, "The Hellenists of Acts vi, 1,"
ExpTim 48 (1937): 524-25.

martyrdom precipitated a general persecution of the Christians, which forced them to leave Jerusalem (8:1b). Every evidence is that the primary target of this persecution was the Hellenist group.

In any event Philip, the second in the list of 6:5, was one of those forced to flee Jerusalem. He first went to Samaria and carried on an effective ministry there (8:4-13), thus fulfilling the witness to that territory commissioned by Jesus (1:8). Then he was led to the Gaza strip, where he led an Ethiopian eunuch to the Lord (8:26-40). This is the first explicit incident in Acts that treats the conversion of a non-Jew, or perhaps more precisely a non-Semite. Philip began the mission outside Jerusalem and beyond the confines of witness solely to Jews. He effectively put into action the program that was implicit in the speech of his fellow-Hellenist Stephen. It had been a Hellenist breakthrough. The wider witness had begun.

1. Introduction of the Seven (6:1-7)

(1) The Problem (6:1-2)

¹In those days when the number of disciples was increasing, the Grecian Jews among them complained against the Hebraic Jews because their widows were being overlooked in the daily distribution of food. ²So the Twelve gathered all the disciples together and said, "It would not be right for us to neglect the ministry of the word of God in order to wait on tables.

6:1 Luke introduced the new section with a rather vague "in those days." Luke generally was not concerned with giving precise chronological references, but from later data in Acts it may be concluded that this incident took place in the early to midthirties, perhaps five years or so after Pentecost.[6] The Jerusalem Christian community had witnessed considerable growth; and as is so often the case with rapid increase, administrative problems developed. The particular difficulty involved a complaint from the Greek-speaking Christians against the native Aramaic-speaking Christians that their widows were being neglected in the daily distribution of food (literally, "the daily ministry"). We may assume that at this point the Christian community consisted exclusively of Jews. The only exceptions would be the "proselytes," like Nicolas (v. 5), who were Gentiles who had converted to Judaism. The Gentile mission as such had not yet begun. Yet even though it could be considered a purely Jewish Christian community, the Jerusalem church was not fully homogeneous, as this

---

[6]Particular data in Acts that are datable from other sources include the conversion of Paul (chap. 9), which is variously dated on the basis of chronological references in his epistles between A.D. 31 and 35. The death of Herod Agrippa I (12:20-23) took place in A.D. 44, according to Josephus.

mention of the "Hellenists" and Aramaic-speakers indicates.[7] The Hellenists ("Grecian Jews," NIV) were more than likely Jews who had come from the Jewish dispersion and settled in Jerusalem. Their language and probably many of their ways were Greek. They had their own synagogues (cf. v. 9), and funerary inscriptions excavated in Jerusalem attest to their extensive presence there. As so often with ethnic groups, they tended to associate with those who shared their language and cultural background. As the church increased and came to include more and more of these "Hellenist" converts, it is only natural that they would have formed close associations with one another, perhaps even meeting in home fellowships together. There is no reason to picture a breach or separation in the total Christian community—only the sort of "distancing" created by natural linguistic and cultural differences.[8] Where the "distancing" manifested itself was in the very practical matter of the community's charity. The Hellenist widows were being overlooked—certainly not deliberately neglected but inadvertently left out. There may have been a considerable number of such widows. Dorcas (9:39) probably was one of them, and 1 Tim 5 attests to the large numbers of them in the Pauline congregations.

In Jewish society widows were particularly needy and dependent, and the Old Testament singles them out along with orphans as the primary objects of charitable deeds.[9] The Hellenist widows may have been a particularly sizable group. Diaspora Jews often moved to Jerusalem in their twilight years to die in the holy city. When the men died, their widows were left far from their former home and family to care for them and were thus particularly in need of charity.[10] Many of them may have been attracted to the Christian community precisely because of its concern for the material needs of its members.

The Christian concern that "there be no needy among them" has already been referred to in Acts (2:44f.; 4:32,34f.). The administration of community charity seems to have been in the hands of the apostles (4:35). As the church grew, they must have entrusted distribution to others, whom this text would indicate came primarily from the Aramaic-speaking

---

[7]For the view that the widows were "Greeks," see J. B. Tyson, "Acts 6:1-7 and Dietary Regulations in Early Christianity," *PIRS* 10 (1983): 145-61. Along the same lines is the view of A. Strobel that non-Christian foreign widows were the objects of the church's charity: "Armenfleger 'um des Friedens willen' (zum Verständnis von Act 6, 1-6)," *ZNW* 63 (1972): 270-76.

[8]This development into two more-or-less separate communities is argued by J. Dupont, *Nouvelles Etudes sur les Actes des Apôtres*, Lectio divina 118 (Paris: Cerf, 1984), 151-55. See also N. Walter, "Apostelgeschichte 6.1 und die Anfänge der Urgemeinde in Jerusalem," *NTS* 29 (1983): 370-93.

[9]Cf. Exod 22:22; Deut 10:18; 14:29; Ps 146:9; Jas 1:27.

[10]See E. Haenchen, *The Acts of the Apostles: A Commentary* (Philadelphia: Westminster, 1971), 261.

constituency. Language barriers being what they are, it is easy to picture how some of the Greek-speaking widows were overlooked. In its charity the church may have followed somewhat the precedents already set in contemporary Judaism, which had a double system of distribution to the needy. The Jews had a weekly dole for resident needy, called the *quppah*. It was given out every Friday and consisted of enough money for fourteen meals. There was also a daily distribution, known as the *tamhuy*.[11] It was for nonresidents and transients and consisted of food and drink, which were delivered from house to house where known needy were dwelling. The Christian practice seems to have embraced elements of both Jewish systems. Like the *tamhuy* it was daily, and like the *quppah* it was for the resident membership.

6:2 To solve the problem, the Twelve gathered all the disciples together. Even though the Hellenists had the main grievance, the problem involved the entire congregation; and the apostles wanted total participation in its resolution. This is not a bad precedent, particularly in matters where money is involved. As the spiritual leaders of the congregation and the ultimate administrators of the community funds, the apostles' duty was to solve the problem. This is what is meant by their statement in v. 2 about it not being right for them to neglect God's word to wait on tables. To oversee the distribution to the Hellenist widows would distract them from their primary responsibility of witness. The phrase "it would not be right" really means "not pleasing in God's eyes." Modern ministers sometimes misuse this statement as a biblical warrant for refusal to do the mundane administrative tasks in the church.

In context this passage deals with the apostles and their unique role. They alone in all of Christian history were the witnesses to the life, death, and resurrection of Jesus. Their witness was unique, unrepeatable, and absolutely foundational for the Christian movement. Surely it was not fitting for anything to limit their bearing their witness. But what did they mean by "wait on tables"? Does the phrase permit a closer definition of the church's charitable procedure? Actually, it is somewhat ambiguous. The word "table" was characteristically used as a metaphor for a meal or for a table from which money was distributed.[12] Either practice could have been followed by the church, just as both are found in the *tamhuy* (food) and *quppah* (money) of Judaism.

---

[11] J. Jeremias, *Jerusalem at the Time of Jesus*, trans. F. H. and C. H. Cave (Philadelphia: Fortress, 1989), 131-33. For the Roman practice of distributing baskets of food to the needy (*spartulae*), see F. J. Foakes-Jackson, *The Acts of the Apostles*, MNTC (New York: Harper & Row, 1931), 52-53.

[12] G. Schneider, *Die Apostelgeschichte*, HTKNT (Freiburg: Herder, 1980), 1:425.

(2) The Solution (6:3-4)

[3]Brothers, choose seven men from among you who are known to be full of the Spirit and wisdom. We will turn this responsibility over to them [4]and will give our attention to prayer and the ministry of the word."

6:3-4 As the leaders of the community, the apostles proposed that the members choose seven men from among them to administer the charity to the Hellenist widows. The context suggests that the seven men were to be Hellenists. The system had broken down with their group, and they would know better who the needy widows were and be better able to communicate with them. The apostles, however, laid down basic qualifications which the seven had to meet. First, they were to be "full of the Spirit," i.e., they were to have manifested a special degree of allowing the Spirit to work in them. Then they were to be known for their "wisdom," probably referring to the kind of practical know-how necessary for the proper management of the charitable funds. One would assume that the seven would take over the administration of the charity among the Hellenist Christians and the apostles would continue to do so among the others. Verse 4 concludes the apostolic proposal. By selecting the seven, the apostles were free to carry out their primary responsibilities of preaching and bearing witness to Christ.

(3) Selection and Installation (6:5-6)

[5]This proposal pleased the whole group. They chose Stephen, a man full of faith and of the Holy Spirit; also Philip, Procorus, Nicanor, Timon, Parmenas, and Nicolas from Antioch, a convert to Judaism. [6]They presented these men to the apostles, who prayed and laid their hands on them.

6:5 The solution proposed by the apostles was pleasing to the whole group, which made its selection. It is important to note that the congregation made the selection. The apostles assumed the leadership in making the proposal, but they left final approval of the plan and selection of the seven to congregational decision. That they were all Hellenists is likely, given the nature of the problem and the fact that all seven names listed in v. 5 are Greek. Stephen was named first. He met the qualifications (v. 3), being full of faith and the Holy Spirit. That Luke listed him first is no accident. He would be the primary character in the following narrative (6:8–8:4).

Next came Philip. He too would be a major figure in the story of the expanding Christian witness (8:5-40).[13] The other five play no further

---

[13]A. Ehrhart argues that the Philip of Acts 6:5 and 8:5-40 is the same Philip as the apostle, an identification that is found frequently in the early church fathers (*The Acts of the Apostles: 10 Lectures* [Manchester: University Press, 1969], 38-39). A close reading of Acts

role in Acts, and we have no reliable additional information on any of them. Early tradition connects Procorus with the apostle John, maintaining that he was John's amanuensis in writing the Fourth Gospel, that he later became the bishop of Nicomedia in Bithynia, and that ultimately he was martyred in Antioch. We know nothing further on Nicanor, Timon, and Parmenas. Interestingly, Luke gave the additional note on Nicolas that he was a proselyte from Antioch. Some scholars feel he may have been Luke's primary source of information about the Hellenists, who later seem to have centered around Antioch (11:19-21). The later Gnostic sect of Nicolaitans seems to have borrowed his name to gain authority for their teaching, but there is no evidence that he himself had any connection with them.[14]

6:6 The selection of the seven is followed by their installation. The congregation chose them and presented them to the apostles. The apostles confirmed the congregational decision by laying their hands on them.[15] It is best not to read our current practices of ordination back into the text of Acts with regard to this gesture of hand-laying. In the Old Testament the laying on of hands deals with the transfer of some personal characteristic or responsibility from one person to another, as from Moses to Joshua (Num 27:16-23).[16] The gesture is used in several ways in Acts: in healings (9:17), the gift of the Spirit (9:17; 8:18), and in commissioning to a task (6:6; 13:3). Even in the commissionings the emphasis is not so much on appointment to an office as to designation for a task.[17] Often the present passage is seen to be the initiation of the diaconate. The word "deacon" (*diakonos*) never occurs in the passage. The word "ministry" (*diakonia*) does occur several times, but it is applied to both the ministry of the daily distribution (v. 2) and the ministry of the word, the apostolic witness (v. 4). In fact, the word "deacon" never occurs in Acts. The office generally referred to is "elder" (Acts 11:30; 14:23, et passim).[18] If one is

---

will show differently. The disciple Philip was one of the Twelve "apostles"; the Hellenist Philip was "the evangelist, one of the seven" (21:8).

[14]N. Brox, "Nikolaos and Nikolaiten," *VC* 19 (1963): 23-30.

[15]The Greek of v. 6 could be construed to mean that the congregation laid hands on the seven, but the apostles are the most likely antecedent both grammatically and contextually.

[16]On the laying on of hands, see *Beginnings* 5:137-40; M. Dibelius and H. Conzelmann, *The Pastoral Epistles, Her* (Philadelphia: Fortress, 1972), 70-71.

[17]The real background to this passage is the OT commissioning accounts, in which the following elements appear, as they do in Acts 6:1-6: (1) the problem, (2) the proposed solution, (3) the qualifications for the candidates, and (4) the installation of the new leaders. Cf. the selection of the seven with Moses' appointment of the judges (Exod 18:13-26; Deut 1:9-18), with the selection of the seventy elders (Num 11:10-25), and with the installation of Joshua (Num 27:16-23).

[18]C. S. C. Williams argues that Stephen and Philip better fit the role of presbyter (*The Acts of the Apostles*, HNTC [New York: Harper, 1957], 97). See also J. T. Leinhard "Acts

inclined nevertheless to see the diaconate in this passage, that person should take a cue from Stephen and Philip. In the rest of Acts, nothing is made of their administrative duties. What one finds them doing is bearing their witness, even to martyrdom.

(4) Summary and Transition (6:7)

[7]So the word of God spread. The number of disciples in Jerusalem increased rapidly, and a large number of priests became obedient to the faith.

6:7 With the problem of the Hellenist widows solved, the community was once more at peace. The apostles were freed for their witness, and the word of God spread/grew. The strangeness of expression in describing the *word* as growing has often been noted. Perhaps the parable of the sower lies in the background.[19] Here "the word of God" points to the proclaimed word as it was preached in wider and wider areas. The "word" grows when it is faithfully proclaimed and falls on fertile soil. In this instance it grew on unexpected soil—among the Jewish priests. There were many poor priests in Palestine, perhaps as many as 8,000.[20] They received little support from the temple cult, had to support themselves primarily with their own hands, and had little in common with the Sadducean priestly aristocracy. From their ranks came these Christian converts. Luke's mentioning them at this point in the narrative may be significant. The next event would be Stephen's arrest and his stirring critique of the temple. Some of these priestly "insiders" may have shared the same viewpoint and longed for a purer worship of God.

2. Stephen's Arrest and Trial (6:8–7:1)

The narrative about Stephen constitutes a major turning point in Acts. It ends a series of three trials before the Sanhedrin. The first ended in a warning (4:21), the second in a flogging (5:40), and Stephen's in his death. The Stephen episode is the culmination in the witness to the Jews of Jerusalem, which has been the major subject of Acts 2–5. To this point a growing opposition toward the Christians from the Jewish leaders had been thwarted by the favor of the people toward the young movement. Then the picture changed. The people joined in the resistance to Stephen. With the death of Stephen and the dispersal of his fellow Hellenists, the focus would no longer be on Jerusalem but on Samaria and all of Palestine and, finally, with Paul on the further reaches of the Roman Empire.

6:1-6: A Redactional View," *CBQ* 37 (1975): 228-36.

[19]J. Kodell, "'The Word of God Grew'—The Ecclesial Tendency of *Logos* in Acts 6:7; 12:24; 19:20," *Bib* 55 (1974): 505-19.

[20]Jeremias's estimate (*Jerusalem*, 204). He added that there were probably 10,000 Levites as well.

Stephen is thus a key figure in the narrative of the wider Christian mission, and the lengthy treatment of his martyrdom is no coincidence. The account begins with his arrest and trial (6:8–7:1). There follows a lengthy speech of Stephen (7:2-53), which, though set in the context of his defense before the Sanhedrin, was more a critique of his contemporary fellow Jews than a defense. As a result, he was stoned to death by his enraged audience (7:54–8:1a). Stephen thus set the scene for Philip's work in Samaria.

(1) Stephen's Debate with the Hellenist Synagogue (6:8-10)

[8]Now Stephen, a man full of God's grace and power, did great wonders and miraculous signs among the people. [9]Opposition arose, however, from members of the Synagogue of the Freedmen (as it was called)—Jews of Cyrene and Alexandria as well as the provinces of Cilicia and Asia. These men began to argue with Stephen, [10]but they could not stand up against his wisdom or the Spirit by whom he spoke.

6:8-10 Luke began by telling us that Stephen was "full of God's grace and power." We have been well prepared for this. As one of the seven he met the qualification of being filled with the Spirit and wisdom (v. 3) and was personally described as full of faith and the Holy Spirit (v. 5). Faith, wisdom, grace, power, and above all the presence of the Spirit were the personal qualities that equipped him for the ultimate witness he would soon bear. The Spirit and power are closely linked and led him to perform signs and wonders among the people. He was the first other than the apostles to be described as working miracles. He quite naturally witnessed in the synagogue of his fellow Greek-speaking Jews.[21] Luke named it the Synagogue of the Freedmen, which indicates that many of its members formerly may have been slaves or were the descendants of former slaves. Its membership included Jews from the north African and Asian Diaspora. There is ample literary and inscriptional evidence for Cyrenian Jews settling in Jerusalem, and the rabbinic writings mention an Alexandrian synagogue in Jerusalem.[22] Paul himself was a Cilician Jew who had come to live in Jerusalem, and it was Asian Jews who later would accuse him of having violated the temple (Acts 21:27f.). In fact, Paul himself may have attended this synagogue, and it

---

[21]The Greek of v. 9 is notoriously obscure and could refer to as many as five synagogues. In fact, there are scholars who represent every point on the spectrum between one and five. Content suggests one synagogue (named "Freedmen") with the four national constituencies in its membership, although grammatically two synagogues has strong support—(1) Freedmen, with Alexandrians and Cyrenians, and (2) a synagogue of Asians and Cilicians. A poorly attested textual variant reads "Libyan" instead of "Freedmen" (*Libystinōn for Libertinon*), and Moffatt's translation adopts it, but its authenticity is highly unlikely.

[22]*Beginnings* 4:68.

may be there where he debated his fellow Greek-speaking Jews after becoming a Christian (Acts 9:29). In any event, they were unable to refute Stephen. He was too filled with the Spirit and wisdom (cf. v. 3).[23]

(2) The Frame-up (6:11-12)

[11]Then they secretly persuaded some men to say, "We have heard Stephen speak words of blasphemy against Moses and against God."
[12]So they stirred up the people and the elders and the teachers of the law. They seized Stephen and brought him before the Sanhedrin.

6:11-12 Unable to resist Stephen's persuasive power and his logic, the Hellenist Jews resorted to underhanded methods. They "hatched a frame-up." The Greek word (hypoballō) is really stronger than the NIV's "secretly persuaded," usually implying that one "puts someone else up to" something, giving them the words to say. In this case the words were to the effect that Stephen had spoken blasphemy against Moses and against God. This charge reappeared in slightly different terms when Stephen was taken before the Sanhedrin. This time the opposition was more formidable. The scandalous charges were spread all over town— Stephen, the blasphemer. This time the populace was moved against Stephen, the first time in Acts they came into active opposition against the Christians. Likewise, the elders of Jerusalem and the scribes became alarmed. The former represented the Sadducees, the latter the Pharisees. Both had their representatives on the Sanhedrin. The stage was set. Stephen was arrested and taken to the Sanhedrin.

It may come as something of a surprise that the Diaspora Jews were so incensed at Stephen. As Hellenistic Jews, would they not have been more tolerant, more receptive of his new ideas, less nationalistic? No, the evidence is that exactly the opposite was the case. The Jews who came from the Diaspora were usually highly nationalistic Jews, having left their homes in the dispersion to migrate to the holy city, the temple city. They were highly zealous for both law and temple. B. Reicke, with considerable justification, labels them "Zionists."[24] They would not at all have been open to Stephen's prophetic critique of their religion and worship. They were wrong in their charge of blasphemy, but blind zealotism is incapable of taking even the most constructive critique.

---

[23]The Western text of Acts adds "because they were refuted by him with all boldness. Therefore, they were not able to look straight at the truth." Some Western witnesses have an even longer reading.
[24]Glaube und Leben der Urgemeinde: Bemerkungen zu Apg. 1-7 (Zurich: Zwingli, 1957), 124-26. J. Jervell argues that this zeal for the law actually belonged to a later, post-70 Judaism: "The Acts of the Apostles and the History of Early Christianity," ST 37 (1983): 17-32.

(3) The Trial (6:13–7:1)

[13]They produced false witnesses, who testified, "This fellow never stops speaking against this holy place and against the law. [14]For we have heard him say that this Jesus of Nazareth will destroy this place and change the customs Moses handed down to us."

[15]All who were sitting in the Sanhedrin looked intently at Stephen, and they saw that his face was like the face of an angel.

[1]Then the high priest asked him, "Are these charges true?"

6:13-14 Before the Sanhedrin the plotters presented the charges against Stephen. He is described as speaking "against this holy place" and "against the law." These are really the same as the original charges of blasphemy against Moses and against God made in v. 11. Moses was identified in their minds with the receipt of the law at Sinai and its transmission in the Pentateuch. To speak against Moses was thus to attack the law itself. "This holy place" was the temple, which was considered by contemporary Jews as the dwelling place of God, containing his very presence in the holy of holies. To attack the temple was seen as a direct affront to God himself. The charges are given a third time in v. 14, this time in a more polemical form: Stephen was accused of saying that Jesus would destroy the temple and change the customs handed down by Moses. This time the charges were more threatening, not just blasphemy but destruction of the temple, alteration of the law. In the background to v. 14 stands the charge of blasphemy directed against Jesus at his own trial when he was accused of threatening to destroy the temple (Mark 14:57-58). Luke did not include that tradition in the narrative of Jesus' trial in his Gospel, but its inclusion here is highly significant. It put Jesus back on trial once again.[25] Stephen had only been faithful in his witness to the teaching of Jesus. To reject the testimony of Stephen was ultimately to reject Jesus. That is what his trial was all about. The violent rejection of Stephen represented a rejection of Jesus the Messiah. Ultimately it was not Stephen but the Sanhedrin on trial that day.

6:15–7:1 All attention then turned to Stephen to see how he would respond to the charges. What they saw was a visage transfigured, a face like that of an angel.[26] It is a picture of the martyr inspired by the heav-

---

[25]Note that as in Mark 14:57, "false witnesses" leveled the charges against Stephen (v. 13), just as they had against Jesus. The point that Jesus was put on trial here is made by J. Kilgallen, *The Stephen Speech: A Literary and Redactional Study of Acts 7:2-53, AnBib* 67 (Rome: Biblical Institute, 1976), 32-33.

[26]The radiant face of Stephen recalls that of Moses when descending from Sinai (Exod 34:29-35) and of Jesus on the mount of transfiguration (Luke 9:29). A later apocryphal work (*The Acts of Paul* 3) describes Paul also as having a visage "like that of an angel." In the later acts of the martyrs the picture of the heavenly inspired martyr becomes a standard descriptive feature at the beginning of the martyr's testimony (cf. *Martyrdom of Polycarp*, 9:1ff.).

enly vision, filled with the Spirit and empowered for fearless testimony before his accusers.[27] As presiding officer in the Sanhedrin, the high priest followed the proper protocol and allowed the accused to respond to the charges—"Are these charges true?" "How do you plead, guilty or innocent?" (author's translation).

3. Stephen's Speech before the Sanhedrin (7:2-53)

Stephen's speech, the longest of the many speeches in Acts, presents a real challenge to scholars. In its context it is often seen to be totally irrelevant to the charges against Stephen.[28] It is certainly true that Stephen's speech is more a testimony and a polemic than a defense; but, as we shall see, the charges were subtly addressed throughout the speech and were ultimately redirected toward his accusers.

Other scholars have occupied themselves with the background to the thought found in the speech, viewing it variously as a weakly Christianized Jewish document[29] or seeing its basis in the world of Qumran,[30] or the Samaritans,[31] or sectarian Judaism,[32] or Alexandrian Judaism.[33] Others have argued that it accurately represents the distinctive theology of Stephen and his fellow Hellenist Christians.[34] This latter view appears to be more on target, bearing in mind that the views of the Hellenists may not have been all that different from those of the non-Hellenist Christians. There are many links between Stephen's critique of his Jewish contemporaries and that directed against them in the speeches of Peter earlier in Acts.

---

[27]It has often been argued that 6:15 connects directly with 7:55, both treating the martyr's vision, and that the speech of Stephen (7:1-53) is consequently an insertion that breaks the context of an original martyrdom account: cf. M. Dibelius, *Studies in the Acts of the Apostles* (London: SCM, 1956), 168-69. This, however, is to miss the altogether different functions of 6:15 and 7:55; 6:15 depicts the martyr's inspiration for his defense; 7:55, the divine affirmation of that defense.

[28]F. J. Foakes-Jackson, *Acts*, 65. See also his article, "Stephen's Speech in Acts," *JBL* 49 (1930): 283-86.

[29]W. Grundmann, "Hellenistischen Christentums," 61-63.

[30]A. F. J. Klijn, "Stephen's Speech—Acts VII, 2-53," *NTS* 4 (1957): 25-31.

[31]C. H. H. Scobie, "The Use of Source Material in the Speeches of Acts III and VII," *NTS* 25 (1979): 399-421.

[32]T. L. Donaldson, "Moses Typology and the Sectarian Nature of Early Christian Anti-Judaism: A Study in Acts 7," *JSNT* 12 (1981): 27-52.

[33]L. W. Barnard, "St. Stephen and Early Alexandrian Christianity," *NTS* 7 (1960): 31-45.

[34]M. Simon, *St. Stephen and the Hellenists in the Primitive Church* (New York: Longmans, Green, & Unwin, 1953); see also his article, "St. Stephen and the Jerusalem Temple," *JETS* 2 (1951): 127-42. W. Manson notes the affinities of Stephen's speech with major themes of Hebrews, such as the pilgrim people and the temple critique, and suggests that Hebrews may have been written by a Hellenist: *The Epistle to the Hebrews* (London: Hodder & Stoughton, 1951), 25-46.

The crucial issue is the content of the speech. On the surface it appears to be a rather detached survey of Old Testament history from Abraham to David. A distinctive polemical note does not seem to appear until the mention of Solomon's temple in v. 47 and continues to run to the speech's abrupt conclusion in v. 53. What is the function of the historical survey in vv. 2-46, the lion's share of the speech? A careful reading of the survey, with attention to the Old Testament traditions Stephen chose and the linkages between his treatment and the earlier speeches of Acts, shows a definite "slant" in Stephen's interpretation of Jewish history. Stephen was leading his Sanhedrin audience in a definite direction, which prepared them for the more direct polemic in the final part of the speech. It is anything but a "detached" survey.

Two recurring themes stand out.[35] The first is that God can never be tied down to one land or place and correspondingly that his people are closest to him when they are a "pilgrim people," a people on the move.[36] The second major theme is that of Israel's pattern of constantly resisting and rejecting its God-appointed leaders. The second theme has accompanying it a subtle Christological emphasis, which is ultimately the main goal of the speech. Israel's past points to the present. The pattern of rejection in the past foreshadows the ultimate rejection of God's appointed Messiah in the present. Other themes are related to this major one, even the explicit temple critique in vv. 47-50. The fulfillment of Israel's true worship is in the Messiah, and in rejecting him they were rejecting what ultimately the temple was all about.

The form of Stephen's speech has ample Old Testament precedents, in those places where a leader challenges Israel to the correct behavior toward God through a recital of the history of the past, always referring to God's merciful deliverance and often reminding them of the failures of past generations.[37] In structure the speech falls into five sections: (1) the promises to Abraham (vv. 2-8), (2) the deliverance through Joseph (vv. 9-16), (3) the deliverance through Moses (vv. 17-34), (4) the apostasy of Israel (vv. 35-50), and (5) the rejection of the Messiah (vv. 51-53).[38]

---

[35]These two themes are delineated by a great number of interpreters. See *Beginnings* 4:70; F. F. Bruce, *Commentary on the Book of Acts*, NIC (Grand Rapids: Eerdmans, 1977), 141-42; B. Reicke, *Glaube und Leben*, 134.

[36]For the Christological interpretation of the speech see R. B. Rackham, *The Acts of the Apostles* (London: Methuen, 1901), 92-106; R. P. C. Hanson, "Ye Stiffnecked and Uncircumcised in Heart and Ears," *Theology* 50 (1947): 142-45; J. J. Scott, Jr., "Stephen's Defense and the World Mission of the People of God," *JETS* 21 (1978): 131-41; C. S. C. Williams, *Acts*, 104-11.

[37]Examples are Deut 26:5-10; Josh 24; Neh 9; Ezek 20.

[38]This outline is based on that of J. Dupont, who notes that Stephen's speech corresponds to the form of classical rhetoric, vv. 2-34 being the *narratio* (leading dispassionate preparatory discourse), vv. 35-50 moving to the *argumentatio* (more direct application of the lessons

(1) The Promises to Abraham (7:2-8)

²To this he replied: "Brothers and fathers, listen to me! The God of glory appeared to our father Abraham while he was still in Mesopotamia, before he lived in Haran. ³'Leave your country and your people,' God said, 'and go to the land I will show you.'
⁴"So he left the land of the Chaldeans and settled in Haran. After the death of his father, God sent him to this land where you are now living. ⁵He gave him no inheritance here, not even a foot of ground. But God promised him that he and his descendants after him would possess the land, even though at that time Abraham had no child. ⁶God spoke to him in this way: 'Your descendants will be strangers in a country not their own, and they will be enslaved and mistreated four hundred years. ⁷But I will punish the nation they serve as slaves,' God said, 'and afterward they will come out of that country and worship me in this place.' ⁸Then he gave Abraham the covenant of circumcision. And Abraham became the father of Isaac and circumcised him eight days after his birth. Later Isaac became the father of Jacob, and Jacob became the father of the twelve patriarchs.

7:2-5 Stephen began his speech with great deference to his hearers, reminding them that they were his fellow Jewish "brothers" and showing respect to the elders on the Sanhedrin by referring to them as "fathers." He quickly moved into his survey of patriarchal history by quoting Gen 12:1, God's call to Abraham to leave land and relatives and travel to a land to which he would direct him.[39] Although Gen 12:1 is set in the context of Abraham's residency in Haran, Stephen placed the call in an earlier context when Abraham lived in Ur before ever leaving for Haran, a conclusion one could draw from Gen 15:7. By thus stressing that the call came to Abraham at the very beginning, Stephen implicitly made the point that God was in control of Abraham's entire movement.[40]

The reference to God as "the God of glory" may also be a subtle touch. God revealed himself to Abraham in his full glory, even in a pagan land.[41] From Haran, God called Abraham into "this land where you are

---

to be drawn from the narrative portion), and vv. 51-53 the *peroratio* (polemical application of the lesson to the present hearers) ("La Structure oratoire du discours d'Etienne [Actes 7]," *Bib* 66 [1985]: 53-67).

[39] Stephen consistently quoted from the Septuagint, the Greek translation of the Old Testament, which would be natural for a Greek-speaker like himself as it was also for the Gentile Luke. There are many variants in the scriptural traditions cited by Stephen when compared with the Hebrew Scriptures. Many of these are due to variations already present in the Septuagint as well as to considerable fluidity within the Septuagintal textual tradition itself.

[40] J. Kilgallen, *The Stephen Speech*, 42-43.

[41] F. F. Bruce, *The Acts of the Apostles: The Greek Text* (Grand Rapids: Eerdmans, 1990), 263.

now living" (v. 4).[42] Yet Abraham was given no inheritance in Canaan, not so much as "a foot of ground" (v. 5). This latter statement was Stephen's emphatic way of stating that father Abraham had no possession in the "promised land" at all, and yet God was with him.[43] In fact, it was to this landless Abraham that God gave the promises to Israel.[44] The promise of the land was truly a promise, since at the time it was given, Abraham had neither the land nor an heir to possess it (v. 5).

7:6-7 Verses 6-7 provide the pattern for the fulfillment of the promise, combining Gen 15:13-14 with Exod 3:12. Abraham's descendants would be sojourners in a foreign land, would be enslaved and mistreated for 400 years, would be delivered through God's judgment of their foreign lords, and then finally would come and worship God "in this place."[45] These verses provide the promise-fulfillment pattern for the entire historical sketch Stephen drew in his speech. God ever renews his promise despite the constant failures of his people, who reject his chosen leaders like Joseph and Moses.[46] It reaches the temple itself, which should have led to the fulfillment of the promised goal "to worship God in this place."

There is no mistaking what Stephen meant by "this place."[47] The *temple* had been the sole meaning of the word throughout his trial (cf. 6:13-14). According to v. 7b, the real goal of God's promise to Abraham was not the land at all. It was instead the freedom to render true worship and devotion to God. Stephen would go on to show that even the temple had not realized this purpose. The promise remains yet unfulfilled. It is only fulfilled in Christ.

---

[42]The reference to Abraham's leaving Haran after Terah's death seems to conflict with the Genesis account, where Terah was seventy at Abraham's birth (Gen 11:26) and lived to age 205 (11:32), while Abraham was seventy-five when he left Haran (12:4), making Terah 145 at that time with sixty years to go. Philo (*De Migr. Abrahami* 177) and the Samaritan Pentateuch of Gen 11:32, however, give Terah's lifespan as 145, and Stephen seems to have been following that textual tradition.

[43]The reference to "not a foot" may derive from Deut 2:5, where it applies to Edom.

[44]"Land" is a major subject of the Abraham portion of Stephen's speech. In fact, the entire subject could be described as "the promise came, apart from the land." See W. D. Davies, *The Gospel and the Land* (Berkeley: University of California, 1974), 270; D. W. Hager, "Wealth and the Jerusalem Community: The Old Testament Influence on Luke's Portrayal in Acts," Ph.D. diss., The Southern Baptist Theological Seminary, 1987, 110-13.

[45]There was apparent discrepancy in the Jewish tradition over the time span between the birth of Isaac and the Exodus, Gen 15:13 having 400 years; and Exod 12:40, 430 years. Stephen followed the tradition in Gen 15:13. Cf. Gal 3:17.

[46]N. Dahl, "The Story of Abraham in Luke-Acts," *Studies in Luke-Acts* (Nashville: Abingdon, 1966), 139-48.

[47]Stephen reapplied the reference to "on this mountain" (i.e., Sinai) of Exod 3:12 to "in this place," connecting the promise of Israel's freedom to worship God more specifically to the temple.

7:8 Verse 8 is a transition verse, showing the beginnings of the fulfillment of God's promises to Abraham and leading into the history of the patriarchs. The covenant of circumcision (Gen 17:10-14) implies the birth of children, and the circumcision of Isaac confirms that God kept his promise to give descendants to Abraham (Gen 21:4). Stephen moved quickly through the patriarchal history using the motif of circumcision, from Isaac to Jacob to the twelve patriarchs.[48] The stage was now set for the next step in Stephen's promise-fulfillment pattern, the story of Joseph.

(2) The Deliverance through Joseph (7:9-16)

⁹"Because the patriarchs were jealous of Joseph, they sold him as a slave into Egypt. But God was with him ¹⁰and rescued him from all his troubles. He gave Joseph wisdom and enabled him to gain the goodwill of Pharaoh king of Egypt; so he made him ruler over Egypt and all his palace.
¹¹"Then a famine struck all Egypt and Canaan, bringing great suffering, and our fathers could not find food. ¹²When Jacob heard that there was grain in Egypt, he sent our fathers on their first visit. ¹³On their second visit, Joseph told his brothers who he was, and Pharaoh learned about Joseph's family. ¹⁴After this, Joseph sent for his father Jacob and his whole family, seventy-five in all. ¹⁵Then Jacob went down to Egypt, where he and our fathers died. ¹⁶Their bodies were brought back to Shechem and placed in the tomb that Abraham had bought from the sons of Hamor at Shechem for a certain sum of money.

7:9-10 Drawing at various points from the Joseph tradition of Gen 37–46 without quoting any passage directly, Stephen told the story of Joseph's being sold into Egypt by his brothers, his rise to power in Egypt, the two visits of his brothers in the time of famine, and finally the descent of Jacob's whole clan into Egypt (vv. 9-15a). Again the selectivity of his material is significant. A sharp contrast existed between Joseph and his brothers. God was with Joseph (v. 9). The Genesis narrative has much to say about Joseph's suffering, but Stephen chose not to dwell on this. Instead he stressed God's presence with Joseph. God fulfilled his promises through Joseph, delivering Israel from famine by his hand. God granted him "favor and wisdom" (RSV).

Note how the same characteristics are used of Stephen himself (6:3,8, 10). Wisdom is a particular sign of God's favor to his faithful disciples and would characterize Moses as well later in Stephen's speech (7:22). God gave Joseph favor with people which allowed him to rise in the eyes of Pharaoh, who established him as ruler over Egypt and the royal household (v. 10). The main part of Stephen's summary, however, does not dwell on Joseph at all but assumes his hearers' knowledge of the story.

---

[48]The word "patriarchs" does not occur in extant Greek literature before Acts, and the usage here and in v. 9 may constitute the earliest occurrences of it (*Beginnings* 4:72).

Attention is focused on Joseph's brothers. Though Joseph was characterized by wisdom and favor, his brothers were marked by jealousy, which
led them to sell their brother into Egypt (v. 9). Significantly, Stephen did
not identify them as Joseph's "brothers" but rather as "the patriarchs,"
the fathers of Israel. God was decidedly not with the jealous brothers.
They experienced famine and great distress and were unable to find sustenance (v. 11).

7:12-13 A certain judgmental note is in the language itself.[49] The
judgment was not final, however, for God delivered them through the
hand of Joseph (vv. 12-13). This is not explicit in Stephen's account, but
the Jews on the Sanhedrin knew the story well and could fill in the gaps.
What Stephen did emphasize, however, was the seemingly insignificant
detail that the brothers made two visits and only recognized Joseph on the
second. Why this emphasis? The same would be true of Moses later on in
Stephen's speech. His fellow Israelites did not recognize him either on his
first visit but rejected him (vv. 27-28). Only on his second visit did they
recognize him as the one God had sent to deliver them from Egypt
(vv. 35-36).

One is strongly tempted to see here a reference to the two "visits" of
Christ. The Jews had rejected him on his first coming. Would they now
accept him when confronted by Christ through Stephen's preaching? In
his temple sermon (3:17-23) Peter had made a similar appeal on the basis
of Christ's two comings, and Stephen could have been implicitly drawing
the same parallel with his references to the two visits to the Israelites by
their former deliverers, Joseph and Moses. Significantly, Israel's deliverance at this time did not occur in the "promised land." Indeed, only distress and famine were there. God delivered them in Egypt, where there
was food and where their brother was, their divinely appointed deliverer.
Indeed, all God's special acts of deliverance in Stephen's historical sketch
take place outside the borders of Israel.

7:14-16 The Joseph section of Stephen's speech ends with a reference
to the descent of Jacob's clan into Egypt and the burial of the patriarchs in
Shechem (vv. 14-16). The reference to the burial at Shechem is at some
variance with the Old Testament accounts, which give Hebron (Mamre)
as the burial place for Jacob (Gen 49:29-32; cf. Gen 23:19) and Shechem
as the burial place for Joseph (Josh 24:32).[50] Stephen's reference to the

---

[49]E. Richard, "The Polemical Character of the Joseph Episode in Acts 7," *JBL* 98
(1979): 255-67.

[50]According to Gen 49:29-32, Jacob requested burial in Hebron in the cave of Macpelah,
which Abraham bought from Ephron the Hittite (Gen 23:16f.). According to Josh 24:32,
Joseph was buried in the land Jacob purchased from the sons of Hamar. The burial of the
patriarchs is not related in the OT, but Josephus recorded a tradition of their burial in Hebron
(*Ant.* 2.199). One solution, suggested by Kilgallen (*The Stephen Speech*, 57), is to see only

burial site at Shechem, however, is clear enough. This too was outside the "holy" land, in hated Samaritan territory. In any event the stage was set for the Moses history. God had delivered Israel from famine and had brought them in peace to Egypt through the hand of Joseph.[51] God had remained true to his promises. Things would change with the coming of a new king to Egypt; and the cycle of oppression, rejection, and deliverance would begin all over again.

(3) The Deliverance through Moses (7:17-34)

[17]"As the time drew near for God to fulfill his promise to Abraham, the number of our people in Egypt greatly increased. [18]Then another king, who knew nothing about Joseph, became ruler of Egypt. [19]He dealt treacherously with our people and oppressed our forefathers by forcing them to throw out their newborn babies so that they would die.

[20]"At that time Moses was born, and he was no ordinary child. For three months he was cared for in his father's house. [21]When he was placed outside, Pharaoh's daughter took him and brought him up as her own son. [22]Moses was educated in all the wisdom of the Egyptians and was powerful in speech and action.

[23]"When Moses was forty years old, he decided to visit his fellow Israelites. [24]He saw one of them being mistreated by an Egyptian, so he went to his defense and avenged him by killing the Egyptian. [25]Moses thought that his own people would realize that God was using him to rescue them, but they did not. [26]The next day Moses came upon two Israelites who were fighting. He tried to reconcile them by saying, 'Men, you are brothers; why do you want to hurt each other?'

[27]"But the man who was mistreating the other pushed Moses aside and said, 'Who made you ruler and judge over us? [28]Do you want to kill me as you killed the Egyptian yesterday?' [29]When Moses heard this, he fled to Midian, where he settled as a foreigner and had two sons.

[30]"After forty years had passed, an angel appeared to Moses in the flames of a burning bush in the desert near Mount Sinai. [31]When he saw this, he was amazed at the sight. As he went over to look more closely, he heard the Lord's voice: [32]'I am the God of your fathers, the God of Abraham, Isaac and Jacob.' Moses trembled with fear and did not dare to look.

---

the patriarchs as the subject of v. 16 (and not Jacob), a possible construal from the Greek of v. 15b. This solves the problem of Jacob's burial. It does not solve the problem of the purchaser of the Shechem site (Jacob in Josh 24:32; Abraham in Acts 7:16). Perhaps Stephen "telescoped" the two burial-site accounts, as Bruce suggests (*Acts*: NIC, 149, n. 39).

[51] Verse 15 gives the number of Jacob's clan as seventy-five. This follows the Septuagint tradition of Gen 46:27; Exod 1:5 (cf. also the textual variant at Deut 10:22). The Hebrew text gives the number seventy. Philo recognized the problem and attempted to solve it through allegory, seeing seventy-five as the earthly/physical number and seventy as the spiritual number of those who had been purified of the five physical senses (*De Migr. Abrahami*, 199f.).

³³"Then the Lord said to him, 'Take off your sandals; the place where you are standing is holy ground. ³⁴I have indeed seen the oppression of my people in Egypt. I have heard their groaning and have come down to set them free. Now come, I will send you back to Egypt.'

The major portion of Stephen's historical sketch is devoted to the story of Moses, which is divided into three sections. Each covers forty years of Moses' life, based on the tradition that he lived to age 120 (Deut 34:7). The first forty years cover his upbringing in Pharaoh's house (vv. 17-22). The second forty years begin with his rejection by the contending Israelites and cover the period of his sojourn in Midian (vv. 23-29). The final forty years begin with God's call of Moses at the burning bush and cover the period of the Exodus and wilderness wandering. This final section continues until v. 45 with the reference to Joshua's entry into the promised land. The outline followed here, however, will limit the final section of the Moses history to vv. 30-34, considering v. 35 as the point at which Stephen departed from his more or less dispassionate recital of history and launched into a more pointed argumentative style.

7:17-22 If Israel's fathers enjoyed relative prosperity in the early days of their Egyptian sojourn, all that changed radically with the coming of a new king in Egypt, who was greatly alarmed at the ever-increasing numbers of Israelites (vv. 17-18).[52] The new king did not "know" Joseph (cf. Exod 1:10-11). The new king "dealt treacherously"[53] with the Israelites, enslaving them in forced labor and compelling them to "expose"[54] their children. Stephen greatly reduced the story of Moses' rescue, certain that the Sanhedrin members were familiar with it already, and focused on the essentials. Hidden for three months in his father's household and finally exposed when he could no longer be kept secret, Moses was adopted[55] by Pharaoh's daughter and reared as her own son (vv. 20-21). Moses is described as being "beautiful to God" (author's translation; the NIV translates "no ordinary child"), a description that prepares us early for his role as God's chosen deliverer of his people. Moses was thoroughly

---

[52]Compare the wording of v. 17b with the description of the church's growth in 6:7—the same words are used, αὐξάνω and πληθύνω, all of which is to say that Israel enjoyed God's favor in the early days in Egypt. It "grew and multiplied" (RSV).

[53]The verb translated "deal treacherously" (κατασοφίζομαι) also occurs in Exod 1:10 LXX, where Pharaoh said, "Let us deal shrewdly with [the Israelites]." It all depends on one's perspective: what was shrewd wisdom to Pharaoh was sheer treachery to the Jews.

[54]The technical term for "exposure," abandoning an infant to die, is used here and is described in terms of drowning them in the Nile in Exod 1:22.

[55]Verse 21 uses the Greek word ἀναιρέω for Pharaoh's daughter "taking up" Moses, which is the verb used in the LXX of Exod 2:10 for her "drawing him up" from the water. In Hellenistic Greek it was often used of formal adoption, and that meaning fits the usage in Acts 7:21.

trained in all the wisdom of Egypt (7:22).

This point is not made in Old Testament accounts of Moses but is a common motif in later Jewish works on his life. Philo, for example, related how the best teachers from Egypt and Greece were summoned to train the young Moses, who soon outstripped their own knowledge (*De Vita Mosis* 1:20-24). Other writers attributed to him the invention of the alphabet and even the whole of Egyptian civilization.[56] Such accounts are obvious exaggerations, but Stephen's pointing to Moses' upbringing in Egyptian wisdom was perhaps his reminder to the Sanhedrin that God could work through others than the Jews. He could use the wisdom of Egypt to prepare Moses as deliverer of his people. The reference to Moses' power in speech may come as something of a surprise, given his own protest that he was lacking in eloquence (Exod 4:10). Some have suggested that the reference may be to his skill in the written word.[57] In any event the stage had been set. Israel was oppressed, but God was true to his promises. He raised up a deliverer and had him trained for his future role. God was with Moses.

7:23-29 These verses treat the central forty-year period of Moses' career. Both of Stephen's central themes are emphasized—Israel's rejection of its divinely appointed leader and the "pilgrim" motif. The theme of rejection is given the major treatment and is developed in vv. 23-28, which relate the story of how two quarreling Israelites refused Moses' intercession in their dispute. Stephen's version follows fairly closely the account given in Exod 2:11-15 and quotes Exod 2:14 directly in vv. 27b-28.

The key to Stephen's understanding of the passage is found in the interpretive details he added in expounding it. By so doing he highlighted Moses' role as God's appointed deliverer of Israel. This begins in v. 23, where Moses decided to "visit" his fellow Israelites. The verb translated "visit" is used throughout Luke-Acts for God or his emissaries overseeing and caring for his people.[58] As God's emissary, Moses went forth to look after his fellow Israelites. Seeing an Israelite being mistreated by an Egyptian, he "went to his defense" and killed the Egyptian. The Old Testament account makes no reference to Moses "avenging" the Israelite. This was Stephen's interpretive comment. As God's emissary, Moses wreaked divine vengeance on the offending Egyptian. Verse 25 is totally unparalleled in Exod 2:11-15 and is Stephen's reflection on the account.

---

[56]Bruce, *Acts*: NIC, 150, n. 45.

[57]*Beginnings* 4:75.

[58]The verb ἐπισκέπτομαι is used of God visiting his people in Luke 1:68; 7:16; Acts 15:14, of the coming of the Messiah (Luke 1:78), of the Christian community's decision under divine guidance (Acts 6:3), and of Christian missionary leaders looking after the churches they established (Acts 15:36).

Moses assumed that the Israelites would recognize that God was "using him to rescue them."[59] The theme of Moses as God's deliverer for Israel continues in v. 26, where Moses is depicted as mediator between the two Israelites who were fighting with each other. He attempted to "reconcile" them. Again there is no mention of Moses being a reconciler in the Exodus account. This was Stephen's way of emphasizing Moses' role as God's representative. He was the divinely appointed mediator between Israel and God. Finally, Stephen saw in Exod 2:14 the explicit point he wanted to make and quoted it directly (vv. 27b-28), "Who made *you* ruler and judge over us?" (italics mine). By now Stephen had made the answer to this question infinitely clear—*God* did. Moses was God's divinely appointed leader.

Just as clearly as Stephen established the role of Moses as God's emissary, he depicted also the flat rejection of his leadership by the Israelites. This began with Stephen's interpretive comment in v. 25. The Israelites did not recognize Moses as their God-appointed deliverer and leader. The quote from Exod 2:14 underscores this (vv. 27b-28). The Israelite who was mistreating his brother refused Moses' intercession and firmly denied that Moses had any right to serve as leader and judge over him.[60] Stephen closed the account of the incident by continuing the direct quote from Exod 2:14, which shows the Israelite's awareness that Moses had killed the Egyptian. Hearing this, said Stephen, he immediately fled to Midian (v. 29).

A glance at Exod 2:15 will show that Moses' flight is attributed to Pharaoh's wrath upon hearing about the killing of the Egyptian. Exodus 2:14, however, clarifies that the Israelite's awareness of Moses' deed first alerted Moses that the word was out and his life was in danger. By concentrating on this and passing over the reference to Pharaoh, Stephen made even stronger the connection between Moses' flight and the Israelite rejection of him. They rejected their divinely chosen leader, put his life in danger, and forced him to flee.

Verse 29 closes the account of Moses' middle years, the sojourn in Midian.[61] Chronologically the years in Midian cover most of the forty-year period. Stephen was obviously not concerned with giving a complete historical picture but only in highlighting those events that advance his themes. The theme emphasized in v. 29 is that of sojourner, the pilgrim

---

[59]The Greek is even stronger in v. 25, "God was giving them deliverance [σωτηρίαν, 'salvation'] through his hand." Moses was thus Israel's redeemer, bringing them deliverance and salvation from their enemies (cf. 7:35).

[60]The reference to the Israelite's "pushing Moses aside" underscores the rejection of Moses. The Greek ἀπώσατο is a strong word with connotations of flat rejection (cf. 7:39).

[61]Midian is the area around the gulf of Aqabah. According to Gen 25:1-6, it was here in the "land of the east" where the children of Abraham's second wife, Keturah, settled.

motif. He was a sojourner, a foreigner in Midian.[62] The second son, Eliezer, is not mentioned until Exod 18:4. Moses had been rejected by his own people and forced to live in a strange land. But God was with him, and there in a foreign land God would reveal himself to Moses. By emphasizing Moses' pilgrim status, Stephen clarified that God cannot be tied down to a single place or people.

7:30-33 The final forty-year period of Moses' life began with God's appearance to him in the burning bush. It continued through the Exodus (vv. 36) and the wilderness period (vv. 36-38). Again Stephen scarcely gave a full picture of this final period of Moses' life but emphasized those events that advanced his themes. God's revelation to Moses on Mt. Sinai illustrates two of those themes—his revelation taking place outside the holy land and his choice of Moses as Israel's leader. Stephen's account of this is a rather straightforward presentation of the account in Exod 3:1-10, which quotes numerous portions of the Septuagint text directly and summarizes others.[63] God appeared to Moses in the desert region of Mt. Sinai through an angel in the flames of a burning bush (v. 30). Amazed at the sight, Moses approached the bush to examine the prodigy more closely and in doing so heard the voice of the Lord (v. 31). God revealed himself to Moses as the God of the patriarchs (v. 32a), and Moses, fearful, diverted his attention from the theophany (v. 32b). God commanded Moses to remove his sandals because he was standing on holy ground (v. 33). Stephen's inclusion of this detail may have been a subtle reminder to his hearers that there was holy ground elsewhere, far from the temple in Jerusalem.

7:34 Verse 34 concludes the account, giving God's promise to deliver his people from their Egyptian bondage through the hand of Moses. Following Stephen's treatment up to this point, the significance of this incident is clear. God remained true to his promises. He had looked upon their oppression and would deliver them. Moses was the one whom God had chosen as leader for Israel's deliverance. But the Israelites had already rejected him; they would continue to reject him.

---

[62]The reference to Moses' sons may be a subtle allusion to the "sojourner" theme. The first son, Gershom, was born of Zipporah; and the etymology of his name is "foreigner, sojourner" (Exod 2:22).

[63]Verse 30 quotes Exod 3:1b-2. Exodus has Horeb as the mountain, but Sinai and Horeb seem to refer to the same place in the OT tradition. Verse 31 summarizes Exod 3:3-4; v. 32a quotes Exod 3:6a; v. 32b summarizes Exod 3:6b; v. 33 quotes Exod 3:5. Note that the order of the command for Moses to remove his sandals and God's revelation of his identity are reversed in Exod 3:5-6 and Acts 7:32-33. Verse 34a quotes Exod 3:7-8a; v. 34b quotes Exod 3:10a, with minor modification.

(4) The Apostasy of Israel (7:35-50)

[35]"This is the same Moses whom they had rejected with the words, 'Who made you ruler and judge?' He was sent to be their ruler and deliverer by God himself, through the angel who appeared to him in the bush. [36]He led them out of Egypt and did wonders and miraculous signs in Egypt, at the Red Sea and for forty years in the desert.

[37]"This is that Moses who told the Israelites, 'God will send you a prophet like me from your own people.' [38]He was in the assembly in the desert, with the angel who spoke to him on Mount Sinai, and with our fathers; and he received living words to pass on to us.

[39]"But our fathers refused to obey him. Instead, they rejected him and in their hearts turned back to Egypt. [40]They told Aaron, 'Make us gods who will go before us. As for this fellow Moses who led us out of Egypt—we don't know what has happened to him!' [41]That was the time they made an idol in the form of a calf. They brought sacrifices to it and held a celebration in honor of what their hands had made. [42]But God turned away and gave them over to the worship of the heavenly bodies. This agrees with what is written in the book of the prophets:

" 'Did you bring me sacrifices and offerings
　　forty years in the desert, O house of Israel?
[43]You have lifted up the shrine of Molech
　　and the star of your god Rephan,
　　the idols you made to worship.
Therefore I will send you into exile beyond Babylon.'

[44]"Our forefathers had the tabernacle of the Testimony with them in the desert. It had been made as God directed Moses, according to the pattern he had seen. [45]Having received the tabernacle, our fathers under Joshua brought it with them when they took the land from the nations God drove out before them. It remained in the land until the time of David, [46]who enjoyed God's favor and asked that he might provide a dwelling place for the God of Jacob. [47]But it was Solomon who built the house for him.

[48]"However, the Most High does not live in houses made by men. As the prophet says:
[49]" 'Heaven is my throne,
　　and the earth is my footstool.
What kind of house will you build for me?
　　　　　　says the Lord.
Or where will my resting place be?
[50]Has not my hand made all these things?'

The style of Stephen's speech changes at v. 35. The treatment of Israel's history becomes more direct; the themes are applied with less subtlety. Even though continuing his survey in a more or less straight chronological fashion, the lessons of Israel's history are more explicitly drawn. Verses 35-38 treat the Exodus and wilderness period, with the emphasis not on the history but the person of Moses. Verses 39-43 deal with the apostasy in the wilderness, with the emphasis on the judgment of

God. Verses 44-50 deal with the entrance into the promised land and lead up to the time of Solomon and concentrate on the *temple* as an example of Israel's apostasy.

7:35-36 With the emphasis on Moses himself, his relation to Christ was more explicitly drawn.[64] Stephen reminded his hearers of the Israelites' rejection of his role as "ruler and judge" over them. They denied Moses, but God "sent" him (v. 35). It is a familiar pattern that already has appeared frequently in Peter's speeches with reference to Christ (cf. 3:13-15; 4:10-12; 5:30-31)—Israel rejected him, but God affirmed him.

The comparison to Christ becomes even stronger in the reference to Moses as "deliverer/redeemer" of Israel. It is the only occurrence in Luke-Acts of the noun "redeemer" (*lytrōtēs*); but the verbal form, "the one who was going to redeem Israel," is applied to Christ in Luke 24:21. The word "redeemer" is virtually equivalent to "Savior" (cf. 5:31), and the comparison to Christ is unmistakable. Moses was a type of Christ. Both were sent by God to deliver Israel. Both were denied, rejected by those they were sent to save. But the likeness does not end there. Moses performed "wonders and miraculous signs" in Egypt, the Red Sea, and in the wilderness (v. 36). The reference is surely to the plagues in Egypt, the parting of the waters, and the many miracles in the wilderness; but one cannot fail to remember how Jesus also performed signs and wonders (cf. 2:22) and that he had granted the same power to his apostles through his name (2:43; 4:30; 5:12; 6:8).

7:37-38 More than a foreshadowing of Christ took place with Moses. He predicted the coming of Christ, the prophet like himself whom God would raise up (v. 37). This prophecy (Deut 18:1) has already served as a major Christological proof in Peter's sermon in Solomon's Colonnade (3:22). With all these obvious overtones of Moses' likeness to Christ in vv. 35-37, one cannot help wondering whether they do not carry over into v. 38 with the references to Moses' being with the "assembly" in the wilderness and to his giving "living words" to the Israelites. The word for assembly, *ekklēsia*, is the normal word used in the Septuagint for the gathered community of Israel. The term also is one Christians used for their own assembly, the church. It is hard to resist the comparison between Moses standing in the assembly of Israel, mediating between the Israelites and the angel of God, and the presence of Christ in his church fulfilling the same role.

The reference to "living words" denotes the law Moses received on Mt. Sinai.[65] Is there an implicit comparison to the gospel, the word that

---

[64]For the many cross-references in these verses to other passages in Luke-Acts, see J. Via, "An Interpretation of Acts 7:35-37 from the Perspective of Major Themes in Luke-Acts," *PIRS* 6 (1979): 190-207.

[65]For references to the gospel as "word of life," cf. John 6:68; Heb 4:12; 1 Pet 1:23.

ultimately brings life (cf. 5:20)? The tradition that Moses received the
law through the mediation of angels is not found explicitly in the Old
Testament, but it is found elsewhere among New Testament writers (cf.
Gal 3:19).[66] Paul used this to argue the inferiority of the law: it did not
come directly from God but was mediated through angels. This was not
the case with Stephen. He did not in any sense criticize the law in any
part of his speech. The angelic presence only serves to enhance the law
and its status as the "living words" of God. The role of Moses was
strictly positive. He was the God-sent redeemer for Israel, the worker of
signs and wonders, the one who transmitted the living words of God. As
such he was a type of Christ. Also like Christ, he was rejected by his
people.

7:39-41 In this section Stephen highlighted Israel's apostasy in the
wilderness, particularly as illustrated by the golden calf. Just as the single
Israelite had pushed Moses aside in his attempt to mediate (v. 27), now in
the wilderness the entire nation refused to obey him and pushed him aside
("rejected," v. 39).[67] "In their hearts" they turned to Egypt. It was an
inward turning to the ways of Egypt, their minds already set on other
gods (cf. Ezek 20:8). Stephen directly quoted Exod 32:1, where the
people asked Aaron to make them gods. As for Moses, they did not know
what happened to him (v. 40). Compare v. 25, where the Israelites are
said not to have understood that God was using Moses to rescue them.
They committed the same sin of ignorance in the wilderness: To reject
God's messenger is to reject God. It was ultimately a lack of faith. So
they made a golden calf, offered a sacrifice to the idol, and rejoiced in this
work of their own hands. [68]

In summarizing the text of Exod 32:4-6, Stephen emphasized certain
points. The calf is described as an "idol" and as something made with
their own hands. Here he was being faithful to the prophetic tradition that
often criticized idolatry as the work of human hands.[69] The term will
recur with reference to the temple in v. 48. Here Stephen already was
moving in the direction of his temple critique. Already in the wilderness
the people along with Aaron the priest were moving in the direction of

---

[66]The tradition may have derived from Deut 33:2 LXX, which mentions angels accompanying God on Mt. Sinai.

[67]The same verb (ἀπώσατο) appears in vv. 27,39 for Israel's rejecting Moses, meaning literally *to push away.*

[68]Luke seems to have coined a word in v. 41, putting together the phrase ἐποίησεν . . . μόσχον ("he made a calf," Exod 32:4) into a single word (ἐμοσχοποίησαν, "they calf-made"), probably along the lines of χειροποιέω (to *hand-make*), a term often used of idolatry, which occurs in v. 48.

[69]Cf. Isa 40:19f.; 44:9-17; Ps 115:4; Hos 8:5.

the distortion of the pure worship of God, which marked the temple of Stephen's day.

7:42 Verse 42 describes how God handled the apostasy in the wilderness. God "gave them over" to their own desires. In Rom 1:24-28 Paul used the same word in a similar context of idolatry to describe how God "gave over" the Gentiles to such works of their hands and how this led to all kinds of sinful distortions. It is perhaps the most fearful judgment of all when God turns us over to ourselves and lets our own rebellious ways take their destructive natural course.

7:43 It was so for the Israelites in the wilderness, said Stephen. Their idolatrous calf led to the worship of the heavenly bodies, the gods of sun and moon and stars.[70] The reference to such astral worship may not have been the main subject Stephen wished to treat, but it was part of the text from Amos which he wanted to cite, a text which established the idolatrous practices of Israel in the wilderness. The text is that of Amos 5:25-27, which is quoted from the Septuagint version and is introduced as coming from "the book of the prophets," the customary Jewish designation for the twelve Minor Prophets, who are collected together in a single book in the Hebrew Bible. The Septuagintal version of Amos 5:25-27 differs considerably from the Hebrew version, and the references to the "shrine of Moloch" and the "star of your god Rephan" are difficult.[71] However, the main point Stephen wished to draw from the passage is clear: "Did you bring *me* sacrifices . . . in the desert, O house of Israel?" (v. 42, italics mine).[72] Stephen's implication was that they made sacrifices all right, to golden calves and heavenly bodies and the like, but *not* to God. Their wilderness days were days of apostasy. The result of the original apostasy of Israel was ultimately exile. God sent them "beyond Babylon."[73] Is there

---

[70]For Israel the worship of the heavenly bodies seems to have come into wide practice under Assyrian influence, though the practice is found as early as 1370 B.C. in Palestine. It is frequently referred to in the OT: Deut 4:19; 17:3; 2 Kgs 21:3-5; 23:4f.; 2 Chr 33:3, 5; Jer 7:18; 8:2; 19:13; Zeph 1:5. See Bruce, *Acts*: NIC, 156, n. 64.

[71]The Hebrew text speaks of Sakkuth your king and Kaiwan your star-god (cf. NIV margin). Sakkuth was the Akkadian god-king, the god of the planet Saturn. Kaiwan seems to be the Babylonian name for Saturn, so the two terms are parallel. The LXX is completely different. "Tent of Moloch" seems to derive from Sakkuth being translated as σκηνή ("tent") and *melek* ("king") being translated as Moloch, the Canaanite-Phoenician sun god. Rephan is totally uncertain but may come from Repa, the Egyptian name for Saturn. See Bruce, *Acts*: NIC, 155, n. 63.

[72]The Greek construction with μή anticipates a negative response. Literally it reads, "You did not bring me sacrifices, did you?"

[73]Amos referred to "beyond Damascus," since he was prophesying to the Northern Kingdom where the threat was from Assyria. The place of exile for the Southern Kingdom was Babylon, and Stephen may have "existentialized" the reference to better fit his Judean hearers' concept of exile.

an implicit suggestion that his contemporaries could expect little better themselves if they did not turn from the same apostasy and rejection of God's appointed Christ?

7:44-50 The final segment of Stephen's argument section begins with a reference to the "tabernacle of the Testimony," which seems to have little connection with the preceding, except for the words "tent" and "type" of v. 44 also being found in the preceding quote from Amos. A much closer connection, however, revolves around the emphasis on rejection, idolatry, and false worship, which were the main subjects of the wilderness section of the speech. They are still the subject in this section, but here the focus begins to narrow to a particular object of the false worship and rejection: namely, on the temple.

Verse 44 continues in the historical framework of the wilderness period. In the wilderness Israel's house of worship was a tent, the tent of the testimony. "Testimony" referred to the stone tablets of the law that were kept in the ark in the tabernacle. Now the tabernacle was provided by *God*. It was made precisely according to his guidelines, according to the pattern he laid down for Moses. The tabernacle remained the place of worship after the conquest under Joshua, and it remained in the land, passed down from generation to generation until the time of David (v. 45).

Everything seems to have been well as long as the tabernacle existed. A shift seems to have taken place with the mention of David's desire to build a "dwelling place" in v. 46. Who was this dwelling place for? A major textual problem occurs at this point, some manuscripts reading "a dwelling place for the house of Jacob," others, "a dwelling place for the God of Jacob." The NIV has chosen to follow the latter reading, but even the reading "house of Jacob" probably implies the same thing—a dwelling place (for God) for the house of Jacob (to worship him in). David only made the request. He did not build a temple. Second Samuel 7:1-17 tells the story of how God answered David's request through the prophet Nathan: God was perfectly content with the tabernacle; he did not want a house of cedar from David, but he would raise up a successor to David who would build such a house.[74] Solomon was that successor who built "a house" for God (v. 47). Stephen implied that all the trouble began here, for he immediately stated "the Most High does not live in houses made by men" (v. 48a) and backed this up with a quote from Isa 66:1f.,

---

[74]Verse 46 is extremely difficult. Its implications are not clear. M. Simon places great emphasis on the word σκήνωμα being used of David's request—"a dwelling place." Stephen, he believes, had no problems with a dwelling place for God, like the σκηνή, the tent of the wilderness. Solomon erred in building an οἶκος, a "house," a place for *confining* God ("La prophetie de Nathan et la Temple," *RHPR* 32 [1952]: 41-58 and "St. Stephen and the Jerusalem Temple," *JETS* 2 [1951]: 129-31).

which delineates the folly of building a house for the Creator-God who has all heaven and earth for his dwelling place (vv. 49-50).[75]

Scholarship is sharply divided over whether Stephen completely rejected the temple or whether he was offering a prophetic critique. In light of the overall picture of the temple in Luke-Acts and even in Stephen's speech itself, the latter seems the more likely. The theme of worshiping God in this place (i.e., in the Jerusalem temple) is set forth quite positively in the beginning of Stephen's speech (v. 7).[76] The emphasis, however, is on the worship—not the "place" of worship. Stephen did not reject the temple as such but the abuse of the temple, which made it into something other than a place for offering worship to God. His view is thus closely linked to that of Jesus, who also attacked the abuses of the temple cult and stressed its true purpose of being a "house of prayer" (Luke 19:46).

The particular abuse that Stephen addressed was the use of the temple to restrict, confine, and ultimately to try to manipulate God. This seems to have been the significance in his contrast between the tabernacle in vv. 44-46 and the temple in vv. 47-48. The tabernacle was designed (v. 44) and approved by God. It was a "dwelling place" for God, but not a "house" of God.[77] It is the concept of "house" to which Stephen objected. As a "house" the temple was conceived as a man-made edifice in which God was confined: "*This* is his house—*here* and nowhere else."

Stephen's reference to its being "made by men" (v. 48, literally, "hand-made") connects directly with the golden calf in the wilderness (v. 41) and is an implicit charge of idolatry. When a place of worship becomes a representation for God himself, it becomes a substitute for a living relationship to God. The man-made "house" is worshiped, not the living God; and that is idolatry. This seems to have been the point Stephen was driving at in his whole speech. God cannot be confined to one place or people. Israel's history demonstrates that. God revealed himself to Abraham in Mesopotamia, far from Jerusalem and its temple; indeed, the promises to Israel began there. He revealed himself to Moses

---

[75]The affinities between Heb 1–4 and Stephen's speech have often been noted. R. W. Thurston argues that this is in large measure due to a similar use of Isa 61:1-2 in both: "Midrash and 'Magnet' Words in the New Testament," *EvQ* 51 (1979): 22-39.

[76]Dahl argues that the promise of "worship in this place" made to Abraham (v. 7) is never actually fulfilled in Stephen's speech, but rather Stephen was implying that the true worship is only realized in the community of the Messiah, not in a man-made cult ("Story of Abraham," 145-47).

[77]Kilgallen argued that Stephen was criticizing not the temple as such but the false concept of the temple as a "house of God": *The Stephen Speech*, 94; cf. his "The Function of Stephen's Speech (Acts 7:2-53)," *Bib* 70 (1989): 173-93 and F. D. Weinert, "Luke, Stephen, and the Temple in Luke-Acts," *BTB* 17 (1987): 88-90.

not on Mt. Zion but in the wilderness of Mt. Sinai. His great act of deliverance for his people was set in Egypt, a foreign land. The tabernacle was the prototype of the true worship of God; for it symbolized God's movement with his people, a pilgrim people on the move, not tied down to land or place.

The concluding quotation from Isa 66:1f. caps off the entire argument. God is transcendent. He cannot be restricted to any "house," where one can say, "*This* is where God is to be found."[78] He is Creator of heaven and earth, and his presence is to be found in all his creation. Solomon himself was well aware of this, that his temple could scarcely contain the God of heaven and earth (1 Kgs 8:27). The temple was to be a house for Israel, not for God, a place for Israel to express their devotion to God. Stephen's critique was that it had become something else—not a house for Israel's worship but a house for God, a place where Israel sought to imprison their God and manipulate him according to their own concerns.

Stephen was a reformer, standing in a long line of prophets who criticized Israel's tendency to substitute man-made institutions for a living relationship to God. Had he "blasphemed" the temple as he was charged? Certainly not. Had he predicted its destruction? Probably so. Likely the most accurate of the Jewish charges leveled at Stephen's teaching on the temple was the reference to his propounding Jesus' prophecy of the temple's destruction (6:14; cf. Mark 13:2). Standing in the line of his Master's prophetic critique, Stephen saw that the temple of his day had become something other than a house of prayer. It had become a symbol of Jewish exclusivism and a rallying place for Jewish nationalism. Unless it recovered its true purpose as a house of prayer and devotion, it was ultimately doomed. As a Jew, Stephen offered a prophetic critique of the temple abuse.[79] As a Christian he was convinced that Israel would never find its true relationship to God, its true worship, apart from the Messiah, as the following verses (vv. 51-53) make clear. Tragically, his contemporaries heeded neither Stephen's temple critique nor his witness to the Messiah. The temple became more and more a seedbed of nationalism, the place where revolutionary movements began. Eventually this led to war with their Roman overlords, which resulted in their utter defeat. The Romans reduced the temple to rubble in A.D. 70; not one stone was left on another. The warnings of Jesus and of Stephen had not been heard.

---

[78]See D. D. Sylva, "The Meaning and Function of Acts 7:46-50," *JBL* 106 (1987): 261-75.

[79]T. C. G. Thornton points to a tradition found in a Jewish Targum that deals with Isaiah's temple critique (Isa 66:1f.) and links it directly to his being martyred ("sawn asunder"): "Stephen's Use of Isaiah LXVI, 1," *JTS* 25 (1974): 412-14.

(5) The Rejection of the Messiah (7:51-53)

[51]"You stiff-necked people, with uncircumcised hearts and ears! You are just like your fathers: You always resist the Holy Spirit! [52]Was there ever a prophet your fathers did not persecute? They even killed those who predicted the coming of the Righteous One. And now you have betrayed and murdered him—[53]you who have received the law that was put into effect through angels but have not obeyed it."

7:51-53 The final portion of Stephen's speech could be described in classical rhetorical terms as the "peroration," where the speaker applies the lessons learned from the previous material in his speech in a direct, frequently emotional appeal to his hearers to act. The aim was to secure their awareness of their own culpability in these matters and motivate them to take remedial action. It is an ancient form of argumentation found in both Greek rhetoric and Hebrew prophecy. The function of the peroration of Stephen's speech was not simply to malign his Jewish audience. In Christian terms his ultimate goal was their remedial action, their repentance.

The polemical nature of these verses is immediately evident in Stephen's switch from first to second person. Before now, Stephen had included himself in his references to the Jews. It was always "our fathers" (cf. vv. 19,38,39,44). Now it was "your fathers." It was no longer a question of Jewish history with which Stephen identified but a direct personal appeal to his hearers. Using the language of the prophets, he accused them of being "stiff-necked . . . , with uncircumcised hearts and ears," always resisting the Holy Spirit (v. 51).[80] His entire historical sketch has illustrated this point, the consistent pattern on Israel's part of rejecting its leaders. Stephen, who was "filled with the Spirit" (6:3,5), had already experienced their resistance (6:10). He would experience it in this instance as well (7:55-58). He reminded them of how they had always resisted and even killed their prophets—the very ones who in the Spirit spoke the words of the Lord.[81] More significantly these very prophets were the ones who predicted the coming of the Messiah (cf. 3:18, 24).[82] Stephen referred to the Messiah as the "Righteous One," a term

---

[80]For "stiff-necked" see Exod 33:3,5; 34:9; Deut 9:6,13. For "uncircumcised in heart and ears," see Lev 26:41; Jer 4:4; 6:10; 9:26; Ezek 44:7,9. Stubbornness and uncircumcision are combined in Deut 10:16. For resisting the Spirit, cf. Isa 63:10.

[81]The murder of prophets is not explicit in the OT, but numerous examples are found in the later Jewish traditions: e.g., Jeremiah being stoned to death, Isaiah sawn in two. Jesus likewise referred to the killing of the prophets (Luke 11:47-51; 13:34).

[82]G. D. Kilpatrick gives evidence for the term "coming" being a technical term in the Jewish prophetic pseudepigraphical literature for the coming of the Messiah ("Acts VII.52: Eleusis," *JTS* 46 [1945]: 136-45).

already employed by Peter in his temple sermon (3:14). Indeed, the linkages between the two sermons are even closer still, for Peter likewise accused his Jewish hearers of having betrayed and murdered the Righteous One (3:14-15).[83]

The whole purpose of Stephen's speech now becomes clear. His historical survey had illustrated Israel's constant rejection of God's chosen leaders. Moses, Joseph, the prophets are all types of and pointers to Christ; and Stephen pointed out to his hearers that they had already rejected and killed him. Is this a final condemnation? One is reminded of Peter's temple sermon with all its resemblances to this portion of Stephen's speech. For Peter it was not a final condemnation, but the door remained open to repent and receive the Christ at his second coming (3:19-21). Stephen already had shown how deliverance came for Israel on their second encounters with Joseph and Moses. Was there not an implicit second chance offered to his hearers here? Was Stephen making an appeal for them to take the needed remedial steps to their apostasy and repent?

Summary. It has often been stated that Stephen's speech does not address the charge that had been leveled against him, that of blasphemy against the temple and the law. Already we have seen that Stephen gave considerable attention to the temple charge. In effect, he turned back that charge on his accusers. They were the guilty parties in turning the temple into an object for human manipulation and distorting its true purpose of prayer and worship. He did virtually the same with the charge of blasphemy against the law. In his speech he never once criticized the law.[84] He gave only positive treatment of its provisions, such as circumcision (v. 8), and described it as "living words" (v. 38). No, it was not he but his Jewish accusers who were the real lawbreakers (v. 53). They were the apostates and idolaters who had constantly transgressed the first Commandments.

Overall one gets the impression that Stephen realized his defense was a lost cause from the start. He would never secure his acquittal without compromising his convictions. He determined to use the situation as one last opportunity to share those convictions, one last chance to appeal to his Jewish contemporaries to abandon their pattern of rejection and accept the Messiah God had sent them. This is why Luke made constant reference to his being filled with the Spirit (cf. Luke 21:12-15). It took courage and inspiration to do what he did. Ultimately his speech was not a defense at all but a witness.

---

[83]J. J. Scott, Jr., pointed out that the title "Righteous One" is always used in contexts where innocence and suffering are stressed, thus showing a possible linkage to the servant of Isa 53:11 ("Stephen's Defense and the World Mission of the People of God," *JETS* 21 [1978]: 131-41).

[84]For Stephen, the angelic mediation of the law is viewed positively. See comments on v. 38.

4. Stephen's Martyrdom (7:54–8:1a)

[54]**When they heard this, they were furious and gnashed their teeth at him.** [55]**But Stephen, full of the Holy Spirit, looked up to heaven and saw the glory of God, and Jesus standing at the right hand of God.** [56]**"Look," he said, "I see heaven open and the Son of Man standing at the right hand of God."**

[57]**At this they covered their ears and, yelling at the top of their voices, they all rushed at him,** [58]**dragged him out of the city and began to stone him. Meanwhile, the witnesses laid their clothes at the feet of a young man named Saul.**

[59]**While they were stoning him, Stephen prayed, "Lord Jesus, receive my spirit."** [60]**Then he fell on his knees and cried out, "Lord, do not hold this sin against them." When he had said this, he fell asleep.**

[1]**And Saul was there, giving approval to his death.**

7:54-55 Whether Stephen intended to give a direct appeal for his hearers to repent we will never know, for they abruptly broke him off. They were absolutely livid at Stephen's placing them on trial. Luke described their rage in terms of their being "cut to the heart" (*dieprionto*, cf. 5:33) and "grinding their teeth" (cf. Ps 35:16). Stephen's response to their rage certainly did nothing to assuage it. Looking into heaven, he had the beatific vision; he beheld the glory of the heavenly throne room and Jesus standing at God's right hand (v. 55).

7:56 Having first given this vision in narrative form, Luke underlined its importance by repeating it in direct discourse, as Stephen shared the experience with the infuriated Sanhedrin: "I see heaven open and the Son of Man standing at the right hand of God." Jesus had spoken similar words at his own appearance before the Sanhedrin (Luke 22:69), and what had been a prediction on his part became a reality for Stephen. Jesus is indeed now risen and exalted to his position of authority at God's right hand. The vision confirmed Stephen's testimony. His messianic claims for Jesus were verified in his vision of the exalted Son of Man. Significantly, Stephen referred to him as "the Son of Man," not simply as "Jesus," as in the narrative of v. 55.[85] This is the only instance in the New Testament where the term is spoken by another than Jesus himself. Even more striking is the reference to his standing. Generally the reference is to his being seated at God's right hand, as in Luke 22:69.[86] Scholarly opinion differs about the significance of the uncharacteristic standing position in Stephen's speech. Some see no significance other than a variation in expression.[87] Others see it as a reference to Christ having risen from his

---

[85]G. D. Kilpatrick has convinced few that the correct reading should be "Son of God" ("Again Acts vii 56: Son of Man?" *TZ* 34 [1978]: 232).

[86]Possibly under the influence of Ps 110:1.

[87]So M. Sabbe, "The Son of Man Saying in Acts 7:56," *Les Actes des Apôtres*, ed. J. Kremer (Gembloux: Duculot, 1979), 241-79.

seat to welcome the martyr Stephen.[88]

The view with the most far-reaching implications, however, is that Stephen's vision links up with the original Son of Man vision in Dan 7:13-14, where the Son of Man is depicted as standing before the Ancient of Days. The primary role of the Danielic Son of Man was that of judgment, and the New Testament consistently depicts Christ in this role of eschatological judge (cf. Matt 25:31-46). The standing position may thus depict the exalted Christ in his role of judge. If so, Stephen's vision not only confirmed his testimony, but it showed Christ rising to render judgment on his accusers.[89] They, not he, were the guilty parties. In Dan 7:14 the Son of Man was given dominion over "all peoples, nations, and men of every language." If this is a further implication of Stephen's Son of Man vision, it ties in well with his understanding of God as not being bound to one nation or people.[90] It is a vision of the boundless reign of Christ, which was soon to begin with the Samaritan mission of Stephen's fellow Hellenist Philip.

7:57-59 One can understand the furious response in the Sanhedrin at Stephen's testimony to his vision (v. 57). If he indeed had such a vision, they stood condemned. There was only one conclusion they could draw. Stephen was lying, claiming to have a vision of God. It was blasphemy! They put their fingers in their ears to shut out his words lest God come and consume them for listening to such blasphemy (v. 57). Screaming, they descended violently on him, threw him outside the city gates, and began to stone him. There was a certain irony in their action. Out of concern for the sanctity of the city, they performed their unholy deed outside its bounds. It has often been debated whether Stephen was "lynched" or condemned by formal verdict of the Sanhedrin, for which stoning was one of the chief manners of execution. In favor of the latter is the fact that Stephen was on trial before the Sanhedrin and was killed by stoning. Luke's account, however, gives more the picture of mob action.[91] There is also the question of whether the Sanhedrin had the legal right to carry out capital sentences during the Roman period. The evidence seems to indicate that they did not (cf. John 18:31).[92] Also the picture of Stephen's

---

[88] A useful summary of views is given in Haenchen, *Acts*, 292.

[89] Argued persuasively by R. Pesch, "Die Vision des Stephanus: Apg. 7:55-56," in *Rahmen der Apostelgeschichte* (Stuttgart: Katholisches Bibelwerk, 1966), 13-24. See also Schneider, *Apostelgeschichte* 1:475.

[90] Scott, "Stephen's Defense," 137-39; also Bruce, *Acts*: NIC, 166.

[91] The Western text solved the problem nicely by rendering the ambiguous "they" of v. 57 as "the people," thus making it a lynching mob rather than the Sanhedrin who stoned Stephen. See *Beginnings* 4:84.

[92] A. N. Sherwin-White gives a convincing case that Roman law delegated capital decisions solely to their own governing officials. The only exceptions were "free cities," and

stoning does not fit what is known of Jewish execution by stoning. According to the Mishna, *Sanhedrin* 6:1-6, stoning took place outside the city and the actual stoning was done by those who had witnessed against the condemned person.

These details fit the present scene, but they are about all that does. In formal stonings victims were stripped and pushed over a cliff ten- to twelve-feet high. They were then rolled over on their chests, and the first witness pushed a boulder (as large a stone as he could manage) from the cliff above. In the unlikely event the victim survived this first smashing, the second witness was to roll a second boulder from above. The picture of Stephen's stoning is radically different. He was not stripped. The witnesses stripped, evidently to give them greater freedom for throwing. It is doubtful Stephen could have knelt or uttered prayers after being pounded by a huge boulder from ten feet above. The picture in Acts is of an angry mob pelting Stephen with stones. His death was not instantaneous as was the case with Jewish executions. Whether the Sanhedrin participated in Stephen's "lynching" is another question. A later incident when Paul faced the Sanhedrin shows that body was not beyond forsaking decorum when sufficiently aroused (23:10).[93]

7:59-60 Stephen died as only one who was "full of the Holy Spirit" could (v. 55). He seems to have consciously followed the pattern of his Master as he faced his own death. His last words, "Lord Jesus, receive my spirit," echoed those Jesus prayed from the cross. This was the same basic commitment of his life to his Lord that Jesus made to the Father in his own dying moments (Luke 23:46). There is a certain trusting innocence in these dying words of Stephen and of Jesus. The words are an ancient Jewish prayer, based on Ps 31:5, which children were taught to pray at bedtime.[94] "Lord, do not hold this sin against them" reminds us of Jesus' prayer for the forgiveness of those who crucified him (Luke 23:34).[95] And so Stephen "fell asleep," perhaps in fulfillment of his

---

Jerusalem did not have this status. The picture of John 18:31 is therefore correct. (*Roman Society and Roman Law in the New Testament* [Oxford: Clarendon, 1963], 1-23, 38.) For the contrary view (that the Sanhedrin could punish capital cases involving religious matters under the Roman procurators), see P. Winter, *The Trial of Jesus* (Berlin: Walter de Gruyter, 1961), 75-90. Winter's view is based primarily on late rabbinical sources; Sherwin-White's, on Roman law. A different solution is that of P. Gaechter, who argues that the Sanhedrin used an interim period between Roman procurators as opportunity to pass their own sentence on Stephen: "The Hatred of the House of Annas," *TS* 8 (1947): 16-23.

[93] There are many interesting parallels between Stephen and Naboth. Both men were just, both were victims of a frame-up, both were stoned by a stirred-up crowd. See T. L. Brodie, "The Accusing and Stoning of Naboth (1 Kgs 21:8-13) as One Component of the Stephen Text (Acts 6:9-14, 7:58a)," *CBQ* 45 (1983): 417-23.

[94] Haenchen, *Acts*, 293.

[95] There is a major textual problem at Luke 23:34, some of the best manuscripts lacking

prayer in v. 59. The early Christians often used the concept of "sleep" for death, a confession of their assurance of resurrection. No one ever died with greater assurance than Stephen. He fell asleep with the vision of his risen Lord at God's right hand still fresh on his mind.

8:1a So ends the witness of Stephen. But there was another there that day whose story was just beginning. Luke introduced Saul for the first time at the stoning of Stephen. He was the young man who watched over the garments of the witnesses as they stoned Stephen (v. 58). There is no indication that Paul himself actually lifted a stone, but he was in total agreement with the action (8:1). Paul likely had a deeper involvement with the whole incident than appears in these brief references. He was himself a Greek-speaking Jew, a Cilician, who perhaps had argued with Stephen in the Hellenist synagogue in Jerusalem (6:9f.) We would like to know if he heard the speech. If he did, it would be eloquent testimony that Stephen's words did not fall only on deaf ears; for ultimately no one carried out more fully the implications of Stephen's words than did Paul. The incident of Stephen's martyrdom in any event surely had a profound effect as Paul himself later attested (Acts 22:20).

5. Persecution and Dispersal of the Hellenists (8:1b-3)

On that day a great persecution broke out against the church at Jerusalem, and all except the apostles were scattered throughout Judea and Samaria. [2]Godly men buried Stephen and mourned deeply for him. [3]But Saul began to destroy the church. Going from house to house, he dragged off men and women and put them in prison.

Acts 8:1b-3 is a transitional section, providing both a conclusion to the account of Stephen's martyrdom and an introduction to the witness of the Christians who were dispersed from Jerusalem as a result of the persecution following Stephen's death. At first sight the sequence of events seems somewhat out of order. First, the persecution and dispersal are mentioned (v. 1b). Then follows the notice about Stephen's burial (v. 2). Finally, Saul is designated as the prime persecutor (v. 3). One would have expected the more natural sequence to have been the burial of Stephen, the resulting persecution, the role of Saul, and the dispersal of the Christians. Luke's ordering of the events, however, is carefully constructed. By placing the burial of Stephen as the middle term between two references to the persecution, he emphasized the close connection between Stephen's

Jesus' prayer of forgiveness. There is no manuscript problem with Stephen's prayer. There is also no question of Acts 7:60 influencing the text of Luke 23:34—the wording of the two prayers is altogether different.

martyrdom and the persecution of the church.[96]

8:1b The reference to "that day" in v. 1b means that at that very time, following the death of Stephen, a great persecution arose against the Christians. The opposition to the Christians had been gaining momentum throughout chaps. 4–6. It came first from the Jewish officials in the arrest of the apostles and the two hearings before the Sanhedrin. The first resulted in a warning (4:21); the second, in a flogging (5:40). With the Hellenist Stephen came a third Sanhedrin trial, and this one resulted in death for the Christian witness (7:58-60). The new factor was that this time the officials had the backing of the people (6:12).

The opposition did not end with Stephen's death. If anything, his bold witness in both his Sanhedrin testimony and his death only served to fuel the flames. A violent persecution erupted, and the Christians were forced to flee Jerusalem—i.e., "all except the apostles." This note probably indicates that the real opposition was against Stephen's fellow Hellenists. The resistance began in the Hellenist synagogue (6:9) and was surely escalated by Stephen's prophetic critique of the Jewish worship and nationalistic religion. The Hellenist vision of an "unbounded God" was intolerable, particularly for the "Zionists" of the Diaspora-Jewish synagogues; and they unleashed their fury on these Greek-speaking Christian "radicals" in their midst. The apostles and their fellow Aramaic-speaking Christians had not taken such a radical stance but had remained faithful to the Jewish institutions; thus they were likely able to remain in Jerusalem unmolested. In any event, they were in the city throughout the subsequent narrative (cf. 8:14; 9:26-28; 11:22,27). Their Greek-speaking Hellenist brothers like Philip were persecuted and forced to flee the city (cf. 11:19-21). Luke's word for their dispersal (*diaspeirō*) comes from the Greek word for "seed." They were scattered like one scatters seed. But scattered seed grow, and the irony is that the persecution and scattering of the Christians only led to their further increase.[97] With the dispersal of the Hellenist Christians, the fulfillment of the second phase of Jesus' commission began—the witness to all Judea and Samaria (8:1b; cf. 1:8).

8:2 In between the references to persecution comes the closing note of the Stephen narrative (v. 2). In a real sense his martyrdom drew first

---

[96]It is thus unnecessary to see a time lapse between v. 1b and v. 2 as does Reicke. Assuming that Stephen died by verdict of the Sanhedrin, he argues that the burial in v. 2 refers to a later period when the bones of a criminal were allowed to be removed from the common burial ground for criminals and placed in an ossuary in the family burial ground, in accordance with the provisions of *m. Sanh.* 6:5-6; *Glaube und Leben*, 165, 169.

[97]The term διασπείρω also lies behind the designation "Diaspora" for the Jewish dispersion. With the persecution the Christian "diaspora" began, and with Paul it spread throughout the Jewish Diaspora. See C. H. Giblin, "A Prophetic Vision of History and Things (Acts 6:8-8:3)," *TBT* 63 (1972): 994-1001.

blood for the Jewish opposition, and they turned their fury on his Hellenist comrades. Stephen was given a proper burial by "godly men," probably some of his fellow Jewish-Christians.[98] It was an act of real courage on their part. Jewish law forbade funeral observances for a condemned criminal;[99] and even if Stephen had been the victim of mob violence, those who stoned him surely viewed him as a blasphemer and law breaker. One is reminded of the similar courage shown by Joseph of Arimathea and Nicodemus in the burial of Jesus.

8:3 Luke now turned his attention to Saul (v. 3), the third reference to him in six verses. The "escalation" of his opposition to the Christians is interesting. First, he was presented as a bystander at Stephen's martyrdom (7:58). Then we are informed that he gave full mental assent to the stoning of Stephen (8:1a). Then his consent led to full involvement. He became the church's worst enemy (v. 3). Indeed, he is portrayed as the persecution personified. He is described as attempting to "ravage" the church ("destroy"). The Greek word is *lymainō*, a strong expression that is used in the Septuagint for wild beasts, such as lions, bears, and leopards tearing at raw flesh. He is said to have gone "from house to house," possibly a reference to his breaking into their "house church" assemblies. In any event, his fury stopped at nothing. He turned against women as well as men, dragging them to court, throwing them in prison. The picture is totally consistent with his own testimony elsewhere in Acts (22:4f.; 26:10f.) and in his epistles (1 Cor 15:9; Gal 1:13,23; Phil 3:6; 1 Tim 1:13). So much did he embody the persecution in his own person that the church is described as experiencing "peace" upon his conversion (9:31).

6. The Witness of Philip (8:4-40)

Beginning with Acts 8:4, the story of the church's witness in all Judea and in Samaria unfolds. It extends throughout the whole of chaps. 8–11. Philip and the apostles witnessed to the Samaritans (8:1-25), and Philip witnessed to an Ethiopian at the Judean border and in the coastal cities (8:26-40). Paul was converted in Damascus, to which the Christian witness had already extended (9:1-31). Peter witnessed in the cities along the coast and to a Gentile God-fearer in Caesarea (9:32–10:48). The church in Antioch, established by Hellenists, began reaching out to the Gentile population (11:19-30). By the end of chap. 11 all of "Judea" in its broadest territorial sense of "land of the Jews" had been evangelized. Not only territorially but also ethnically, all the barriers had been crossed; and the stage was set for Paul's extensive witness to the Greco-Roman world.

---

[98] The term for "devout" (εὐλαβῆς) is used throughout Acts for pious Jews (2:5; 22:12; cf. Luke 2:25).

[99] *M. Sanh.* 6:5-6.

In a real sense the ministry of the "Hellenist" Philip foreshadowed this entire development and anticipated the fulfillment of Christ's commission (1:8). It was Philip who began the witness to Samaria (8:4-25), and his conversion of an Ethiopian in a real sense was a witness "to the ends of the earth" (8:26-40).

(1) The Mission in Samaria (8:4-25)

[4]Those who had been scattered preached the word wherever they went. [5]Philip went down to a city in Samaria and proclaimed the Christ there. [6]When the crowds heard Philip and saw the miraculous signs he did, they all paid close attention to what he said. [7]With shrieks, evil spirits came out of many, and many paralytics and cripples were healed. [8]So there was great joy in that city.

[9]Now for some time a man named Simon had practiced sorcery in the city and amazed all the people of Samaria. He boasted that he was someone great, [10]and all the people, both high and low, gave him their attention and exclaimed, "This man is the divine power known as the Great Power." [11]They followed him because he had amazed them for a long time with his magic. [12]But when they believed Philip as he preached the good news of the kingdom of God and the name of Jesus Christ, they were baptized, both men and women. [13]Simon himself believed and was baptized. And he followed Philip everywhere, astonished by the great signs and miracles he saw.

[14]When the apostles in Jerusalem heard that Samaria had accepted the word of God, they sent Peter and John to them. [15]When they arrived, they prayed for them that they might receive the Holy Spirit, [16]because the Holy Spirit had not yet come upon any of them; they had simply been baptized into the name of the Lord Jesus. [17]Then Peter and John placed their hands on them, and they received the Holy Spirit.

[18]When Simon saw that the Spirit was given at the laying on of the apostles' hands, he offered them money [19]and said, "Give me also this ability so that everyone on whom I lay my hands may receive the Holy Spirit."

[20]Peter answered: "May your money perish with you, because you thought you could buy the gift of God with money! [21]You have no part or share in this ministry, because your heart is not right before God. [22]Repent of this wickedness and pray to the Lord. Perhaps he will forgive you for having such a thought in your heart. [23]For I see that you are full of bitterness and captive to sin."

[24]Then Simon answered, "Pray to the Lord for me so that nothing you have said may happen to me."

[25]When they had testified and proclaimed the word of the Lord, Peter and John returned to Jerusalem, preaching the gospel in many Samaritan villages.

The witness to the Samaritans falls into two natural divisions. There is the initial ministry of Philip (vv. 4-8). This is followed by the participation of Peter and John in the Samaritan mission (vv. 14-17). The two passages are linked together by the shadowy figure of Simon the magician (vv. 9-13,18-24).

PHILIP'S WITNESS TO THE SAMARITANS (8:4-8). **8:4** The persecution did not hamper the witness of the Hellenists. If anything, it increased it as they came forth from Jerusalem, preaching the gospel wherever they went (v. 4). Among them was Philip, one of the seven Hellenists who had been set aside for overseeing the daily distribution to the Greek-speaking widows (6:5). He went north of Jerusalem to Samaria and proclaimed Christ in one of their cities. The majority of late manuscripts have Philip going to "the city of Samaria," but that was most unlikely. "The city of Samaria" would designate Sebaste, the capital of Samaria, which had been rebuilt by Herod the Great in Hellenistic style and named for Caesar Augustus.[100] That is not likely where Philip witnessed because its population was predominantly Gentile pagan.

Philip is pictured as witnessing to "Samaritans" proper, those of Samaritan descent and religious persuasion.[101] Their holy city was ancient Shechem, at the foot of Mt. Gerazim. This may have been the Samaritan city in which Philip preached. In preaching to them, Philip was taking a major new step in the fulfillment of Christ's commission. To this point the church's witness had been exclusively to Jews (though Jesus himself had ministered in this area; cf. John 4).

From a Jewish perspective the Samaritans were a sort of *tertium quid*, neither Jew nor Gentile. They were descended from the northern tribes of Israel, the old kingdom of "Israel" that had fallen to the Assyrians in 722 B.C. Those who were not taken captive to Assyria but remained in the land intermarried extensively with the native Canaanite population and the peoples whom the Assyrians resettled in the conquered territory. These Samaritan descendants of the old northern tribes considered themselves still to be the people of God. They had their own form of the Pentateuch for their holy Scriptures, circumcised their sons, and built a temple on Mt. Gerazim to rival the one in Jerusalem (cf. John 4:20). The Hasmonean king John Hyrcanus (135-104 B.C.) destroyed their temple and made them subservient to the Jews. Later liberated by the Romans from Jewish domination, they continued to worship God in their own independent manner and to look for the *taheb*, a prophetlike messiah who would restore the true worship on Gerazim, a messianic expectation based on Deut 18:15 (cf. John 4:25). The Jewish prejudice against the Samaritans is well-known. To the Jews the Samaritans were half-breeds and heretics.[102] Philip's venture into a Samaritan mission was a radical

---

[100]Greek *Sebastos* translates Latin *Augustus*.

[101]R. J. Coggins, "The Samaritans and Acts." *NTS* 28 (1982): 423-34.

[102]Along with the Gospel of John, Luke showed a special concern for the Samaritans. Only in his Gospel is found the tradition of Jesus traveling among the Samaritan villages on his journey to Jerusalem (9:51-56). Luke alone related the story of the grateful Samaritan leper (17:11-19) and the parable of the good Samaritan (10:29-37).

step toward Stephen's vision of a gospel free of nationalistic prejudices.

8:5-8 Philip is described as preaching to them "the Christ" (v. 5). The Samaritans had their own messianic viewpoint involving the *Taheb*. Philip undoubtedly had to lead them to a fuller understanding of the true Messiah just as Jesus had to do with the Samaritan woman (John 4:25f.) and just as Peter had to do in setting forth the unheard-of concept of a suffering Messiah to the Jewish crowds in Jerusalem (Acts 3:18). Philip's preaching, like that of the Jerusalem apostles, was undergirded by "signs," miracles that pointed beyond themselves to the power and life to be found in the one he proclaimed (v. 6). Demons were exorcised. Paralytics and lame persons were healed (v. 7). Ultimately, it was the gospel they responded to, not the miracles (v. 12). Miracles can assist faith but never can be a substitute for it. When the miraculous assumes priority, it can actually become a hindrance to faith. (Nowhere is that more clearly evident than in the story of Simon that follows.)[103] The paragraph on Philip's witness ends on a note of joy. Compare the similar note on the Ethiopian's joy at his baptism (v. 39). The gospel is the great equalizer. In the gospel there are no "half-breeds," no physical rejects, no place for any human prejudices. There is acceptance for all, joy for all, "great joy for all the people" (Luke 2:10).

PHILIP AND SIMON (8:9-13). **8:9-10** Now a shadowy figure appears on the scene. There was a man named Simon, who had been practicing magic among the Samaritans and for a long time had astounded them with his tricks. Like Theudas (5:36) he had been somewhat pretentious, boasting "that he was someone great." That his personal claims were considerably beyond the ordinary is indicated by the acclamation of the people that he was that divine power called "the Great Power" (v. 10). Whatever else might be said of Simon, he seems to have made some claim to at least embody the very power of God.

Luke clearly depicted Simon as a worker of magic, a charlatan who made money from his bag of tricks.[104] Had we only the account in Acts, there would never have been any question about whether he ever was anything more. The early church fathers, however, tell of a heretical Gnostic sect of Simonians in the second and third centuries who traced their beliefs back to the Simon of Acts. The earliest account is that of Justin

---

[103] A point well developed by G. Krodel, *Acts, Proc* (Philadelphia: Fortress, 1981), 162-63.

[104] The term "magician" (μάγος) is not used of Simon in the Acts narrative. Instead he is said to have "practiced magic" (μαγεύω) and to have performed "magic acts" (μαγεία). The terminology of μάγος/μαγεία is ambiguous in Hellenistic Greek. Originally meaning a Persian priest, it could be used in a quite positive sense, as it is of the magi-astrologers of Matt 2. It was also used in a pejorative sense of a mere trickster, as seems to be the case with Simon and Elymas (13:6) in Acts. See *Beginnings* 5:164-88; G. Delling, μάγος, μαγεία, μαγεύω, *TDNT* 4:356-59.

Martyr from the middle of the second century.[105] Justin was himself a Samaritan and wrote that Simon, a Samaritan from the village of Gitto, was worshiped by "almost all" of the Samaritans of his day as "the first god." Dating his rise to acclaim in the reign of Claudius, he spoke of Simon's journey to Rome, where he was worshiped as a god and had a statue erected to him with the inscription "to the holy god Simon." Justin also noted that he was accompanied by a female named Helen, who had been a former prostitute, whom his followers claimed to be "the first idea generated by him." Writing toward the end of the second century, Irenaeus attributed a much more elaborate system to the Simonians.[106] It is quite possible that the Simon of Acts had virtually no connection with Justin's Simonians but was "co-opted" by the later Gnostic group to give a New Testament rootage for their movement.[107]

8:11–13 Simon may have held the attention of the Samaritans for a long time with his dazzling tricks (v. 11). That completely changed with the preaching of Philip (v. 12). The content of the preaching is variously described in this passage. In v. 4 it is "the word"; in v. 5, "the

---

[105] Justin, I *Apology* 26:3. The statue was dredged from the Tiber in the sixteenth century and is inscribed *"Semoni deo sancto"* ("to the holy god Semon"). Semon was a native Sabine divinity. The Simonians (or Justin) evidently mistook "Semoni" for "Simoni" and attributed the statue of the Italian god to Simon.

[106] Irenaeus, *Against Heresies*, 1.23.1-3. Helen becomes Ennoia or wisdom, an emanation from the godhead who is imprisoned by jealous earthly powers in successive female embodiments, including Helen of Troy, and finally as Helen, a prostitute of Tyre, who is rescued by Simon. Simon is himself the great god in person, the originator of all things. He only appeared to be human but was fully divine. His rescue of Helen represents the liberation of all human spirits from their bondage to the earthly powers. Irenaeus describes the Simonians as thoroughly libertine and sees their licentious behavior as evidence of being liberated from the confining earthly powers. Obviously, the Simonian system developed considerably during the fifty or so years between Justin and Irenaeus. The major question is how it developed from the Simon of Acts to the Simon of Justin Martyr. Later sources which speak of Simon include Hippolytus, Epiphanius, and the Clementines. For a full treatment see *Beginnings* 5:151-63.

[107] The whole Simon question has become a major subject for debate among current NT scholars. Some would see the Simon of Acts as being a genuine pre-Christian teacher of Gnosticism: e.g., E. Haenchen, "Gab es eine vorchristliche Gnosis?" *ZTK* 49 (1952): 316-49; G. Ludemann, "The Acts of the Apostles and the Beginnings of Simonian Gnosis," *NTS* 33 (1987): 420-26. For those who deny that the Simon of Acts was Gnostic and who question whether there is even a connection with the later Simonians, see W. A. Meeks, "Simon Magus in Recent Research," *RelSRev* 3 (1977): 137-42; R. Bergmeier, "Die Gestalt des Simon Magus in Act 8 und in der Simonianischen Gnosis," *ZNW* 77 (1986): 267-75; K. Beyschlag, "Zur Simon-Magus-Frage," *ZTK* 68 (1971): 395-426. For a mediating view that sees the Simon of Acts as representative of Samaritan heterodoxy and perhaps a Gnostic precursor, see R. McL. Wilson, "Simon, Dositheus and the Dead Sea Scrolls," *ZRGG* 9 (1957): 21-30; L. Cerfaux, "La Gnose Simonienne," *RSR* 15 (1925): 489-511. A useful research-summary for the whole debate is found in K. Rudolph, "Simon-Magus oder Gnosticus? Zum Stand der Debatte," *TRu* 42 (1977): 279-359.

Christ"; and in v. 12, "the kingdom of God" and "the name of Jesus Christ." All refer to the same reality, the salvation that is in no other name (4:12). It has sometimes been argued that there was something incomplete about the Samaritans' experience, that they only believed Philip and the rational content of his message without the sort of commitment that constitutes true faith.[108] There is really nothing in the text, however, to indicate any deficiency on their part; and if Luke had wished to communicate this, he would have certainly made it more explicit. The Samaritans entrusted themselves to the gospel and were baptized en masse, men and women. Simon also "believed" and was baptized (v. 13). Luke gave us more reason to question his commitment. There is no object given for his believing—no "kingdom of God," no "name of Jesus Christ." In fact, the only response connected with his baptism was his following Philip everywhere, totally entranced by his miraculous signs. Could this have been Luke's way of indicating that Simon's commitment was lacking, more based on Philip's miracles than his preaching, more oriented toward the tricks of his own trade?[109]

PETER AND JOHN AND THE SAMARITANS (8:14-17). **8:14-17** The focus shifted from Philip and even Simon, for the moment, and centered on Peter and John, who had been sent by the Jerusalem apostles upon hearing of the Samaritan reception of the gospel (v. 14). This action could be interpreted as somewhat presumptuous, the mother church checking out this upstart mission. The drift of the text, however, indicates quite the opposite. Peter and John came more as participants, offering the endorsement and support of the apostles in this new missionary enterprise. That the Samaritans had not yet received the Holy Spirit (v. 16) is certainly not the usual pattern of Acts. Normally the receipt of the Spirit was closely joined to baptism as part of the normative experience of conversion and commitment to Christ (cf. 2:38). This is certainly the case with Paul's conversion, where healing, receipt of the Spirit, and baptism are closely joined together (9:17-18). This was the case also with Cornelius and his fellow Gentiles who received the Spirit first and then were immediately baptized (10:44-48).

The closest parallel to the experience of the Samaritans is that of the disciples of John in Ephesus, who were first baptized and then received the Spirit when Paul laid his hands upon them (19:5-6). Obviously Acts presents no set pattern. The Spirit is connected with becoming a Christian.

---

[108]This is argued by J. D. G. Dunn in an attempt to deal with the problem of separation of the Samaritans' baptism from their receiving the Spirit: *Baptism in the Holy Spirit*, 65. For an effective rebuttal, see E. A. Russell, "'They believed Philip preaching' (Acts 8.12)," *IBS* 1 (1978): 169-76.

[109]Stagg concludes that Simon was not converted—everything about him in vv. 12,18-24 indicates only total depravity (*Book of Acts*, 104).

Sometimes the Spirit is connected with the laying on of hands, sometimes not. Sometimes coming of the Spirit precedes baptism. Sometimes it follows. The Spirit "blows where it wills" (John 3:8); the Spirit cannot be tied down to any manipulative human schema.

The current passage is the most difficult case of them all. Why was the receipt of the Spirit so disconnected from the Samaritans' baptism? Luke indicated that such a separation was not normal by the little word "simply" in v. 16. They had "simply been baptized"—one would usually have expected them to have received the Spirit as well. Many interpreters point to the significance of the experience being one of an outward demonstration of the Spirit in some visible sign that Simon could "see" (v. 18). Therefore this does not rule out the Spirit's having worked inwardly in them at the point of their initial conviction and commitment.[110] Interpreters also have noted that it was not an individual as much as a community experience when the Spirit fell on them in an outward demonstration of power, much as it had at Pentecost (2:3-4) and much as it would later with Cornelius and his fellow Gentiles (10:44). It is not without justification that many refer to this as the "Samaritan Pentecost."[111] It is a major stage of salvation history. The Spirit as it were indicated in a visible manifestation the divine approval of this new missionary step beyond Judaism.

There is further significance to the Samaritan experience occurring in two stages. Through Peter and John's participation, the Samaritan mission was given the stamp of approval of the mother church in Jerusalem. It was not just the undertaking of a maverick Hellenist missionary. It was endorsed, received, and enthusiastically participated in by the whole church. But is there any significance in the fact that the Spirit was received through the apostles laying their hands on the Samaritans? Some would see this as an indication of a rite of "confirmation" separate from and subsequent to baptism.[112] Again the evidence of Acts will not bear this reading of the practice of a later age back into the New Testament text.[113] Peter and John's laying on of their hands is best seen as a gesture of the apostolic solidarity and fellowship with the Samaritans.[114] The receipt of the Spirit is above all God's answer to their prayer (v. 15).

---

[110]J. D. Williams, *Acts*, GNC (San Francisco: Harper & Row, 1985), 142.

[111]Rackham, *Acts*, 117-18. See also M. Gourgues, "Espirit des Commencements et Espirit des Prolongements dans les Actes. Note sur la 'Pentecote des Samaritains' (Act.VIII, 5-25)," *RB* 93 (1986): 376-85.

[112]So Rackham, *Acts*, 117-18. For a full exposition of the "confirmation" view, see N. Adler, *Taufe und Handauflegung* (Münster: Aschendorffsche, 1951).

[113]If anything, a case can be made for hand-laying accompanying baptism (not confirmation) in Acts (cf. 9:17; 19:6), but even this is not a consistent picture. In the following scene with the Ethiopian, neither hand-laying nor receipt of the Spirit is mentioned—only baptism.

[114]Bruce, *Acts*: NIC, 183.

PETER AND SIMON (8:18-24). **8:18-19**   Just as Philip's miracles caught
Simon's attention, so the visible outpouring of the Spirit was absolutely
irresistible to the magician. Just what he "saw," the text does not say
(v. 18). Luke was not interested in the concrete mode of the Spirit's
appearance, only in the fact that the Spirit came to the Samaritans in an
objective, verifiable fashion.[115] Whether Simon himself received the
Spirit is also not related. One would assume he did not from the drift of
the text. He appears as more the onlooker than the participant, and his
behavior scarcely betrays any spiritual enlightenment on his part. As a
professional Simon was impressed with the commercial possibilities of
the phenomenon he had just witnessed. He therefore offered Peter and
John money for the trade secret of how to dispense the Spirit through the
laying on of one's hands. Though a complete misunderstanding of the
Holy Spirit, Simon's behavior was completely in character for a professional magician.[116] Tricks of the trade were often exchanged among them
in financial transactions. They were viewed almost as commercial com-
modities (cf. the enormous "market value" of the magical scrolls Paul
persuaded the Ephesians to burn—Acts 19:19).

8:20   In his characteristic role as spokesman, Peter responded for
himself and John: "May your money perish with you" (v. 20). Peter's
words could be viewed as a prediction as much as a condemnation.
Simon's greed was leading him down the path toward eternal destruction.[117] Throughout Acts human greed is always depicted as a most
destructive force. It certainly was so for Judas (1:18) and for Ananias and
Sapphira (5:1-11). It would continue to be so in many subsequent episodes in Acts. Simon was in severe danger that his avarice would destroy
him as well. Simon was explicitly depicted as wanting the right to dispense the Spirit, but he probably desired the ability to manipulate the
Spirit at his own will, to be able to work miracles and the like (cf.
v. 13).[118] But one can never manipulate the Spirit; he is always God's
"gift" (v. 20) and never subject to the human will.[119] Even in this
instance, the Spirit came as God's response to the apostles' prayer. Simon

---

[115]Many would see the visible phenomenon as glossolalia, but Luke's stress was more on
its visibility than its audibility. See O. C. Edwards, Jr., "The Exegesis of Acts 8:4-25 and Its
Implications for Confirmation and Glossalalia," *ATRSup* 2 (1973): 100-12.

[116]For a picture of Simon as a professional Near Eastern exorcist, see J. D. M. Derrett,
"Simon Magus (Acts 8:9-24)," *ZNW* 73 (1982): 52-68.

[117]The phrase εἰς ἀπώλειαν could be rendered in the sense of "leading to destruction."

[118]H. Conzelmann, *The Acts of the Apostles*, trans. J. Limburg, A. Kraabel, and D. Juel,
Her (Philadelphia: Fortress, 1987), 66.

[119]That Simon wanted to purchase the Spirit for himself and not just the right to dispense
the Spirit may be implied from Peter's reference to his wanting to procure the "gift" of the
Spirit. See D. A. Koch, "Geistbesitz, Geistverleihung und Wundermacht: Erwägungen zur
Tradition und zur lukanischen Redaktion in Act 8:5-25," *ZNW* 77 (1986): 64-82.

completely misunderstood when he saw the Spirit as coming through the human gesture of the apostles' laying their hands on the Samaritans. He was viewing the whole matter through a magician's eyes. But Christianity has nothing to do with magic, and God's Spirit is not subject to a charlatan's manipulation—not in Simon's day or for any profit-making Christian charlatan of our own day. The term "simony" has come into our vocabulary from this incident; however, it is too restrictive, referring primarily to the attempt to secure ecclesiastical office or privilege through monetary means. Were the term fully based on Simon's behavior, it would be extended to cover any attempt to manipulate God for personal gain.

8:21-23 Peter's confrontation with Simon was particularly harsh (v. 21). In the Old Testament "part or share" refers to the privileges of belonging to God's people and sharing the inheritance he has granted.[120] To be denied this share is a virtual formula of excommunication, exclusion from God's people. In Simon's instance the words may imply more a statement of nonmembership. His behavior betrayed that he had no real portion in God's people. Luke spoke of Simon's not having a share "in this ministry." The word translated "ministry" is *logos*, a word used throughout Acts for the gospel (cf. 8:4).[121] Simon had not responded to the gospel; he had responded to greed. He lacked the contrition and inner conviction that accompany a true response to the gospel. His heart was "not right before God." Peter did not merely pronounce a curse on Simon. He offered him the chance to repent (v. 22). God can forgive even such a thought as Simon's greedy desire to manipulate the divine Spirit.[122] Apart from his repentance, Simon's state would remain one filled with the "gall of bitterness"[123] and captivity to the "bonds of sin" (v. 23).[124]

8:24 The question is whether Simon did in fact repent. His response (v. 24) may express a degree of remorse but scarcely the sort of complete turnabout of will and mind that marks true repentance. In fact, Simon expressed no repentance. Instead, he asked the apostles to intercede for him. There was no prayer of contrition from Simon, just the fear that Peter's predicted judgment might come down upon him.[125]

---

[120] Cf. Deut 12:12; 14:27.

[121] C. K. Barrett, "Light on the Holy Spirit from Simon Magus," *Les Actes*, 294.

[122] Ludemann argues that the term ἐπίνοια ("thought") is the same word used by Justin for Simon's consort Helen and therefore is a veiled allusion to the developed Simonian Gnostic system ("Simonian Gnosis," 420-26). This, however, is to place undue weight on a common Greek noun.

[123] Cf. Deut 29:18, where the phrase "gall of bitterness" ("bitter poison," NIV) refers to idolatry as a root that bears the bitter fruit of apostasy.

[124] Cf. Isa 58:6.

[125] Of course, the matter would be settled if one could trust the judgment of Justin and

Luke gave no further information on Simon the magician. He remains a shadowy figure. Luke, however, made his point. Christianity has nothing to do with magic; magic is powerless before the genuine power of the Holy Spirit. God's Spirit can neither be manipulated nor bought. Simon illustrated that. A proper response to God's gift of salvation is much more than simply a "what-is-in-it-for-us?" approach. It involves genuine commitment in response to the work of God's Spirit.

CONCLUSION TO THE SAMARITAN NARRATIVE (8:25). **8:25** Verse 25 is a transitional verse. The reference to the apostles "preaching the gospel" forms an "inclusion" with the identical words in v. 4, thus rounding off the narrative (the inclusion is not readily apparent in the NIV as it is in the Greek text). The reference to the apostles evangelizing the Samaritan villages is significant. Not only did they endorse the Samaritan mission, but they also enthusiastically participated in it. A new stage in the Christian mission had been reached—the witness to Samaria.[126] Begun by the Hellenist Philip, it was embraced by the entire church. The "they" of v. 25 is ambiguous. It certainly refers to Peter and John but may include Philip as well.[127] If so, Philip would have been returning to Jerusalem and would have been set for his call still further south to encounter the Ethiopian eunuch.

(2) The Witness to the Ethiopian Treasurer (8:26-40)

[26]Now an angel of the Lord said to Philip, "Go south to the road—the desert road—that goes down from Jerusalem to Gaza." [27]So he started out, and on his way he met an Ethiopian eunuch, an important official in charge of all the treasury of Candace, queen of the Ethiopians. This man had gone to Jerusalem to worship, [28]and on his way home was sitting in his chariot reading the book of Isaiah the prophet. [29]The Spirit told Philip, "Go to that chariot and stay near it."
[30]Then Philip ran up to the chariot and heard the man reading Isaiah the prophet. "Do you understand what you are reading?" Philip asked.
[31]"How can I," he said, "unless someone explains it to me?" So he invited Philip to come up and sit with him.
[32]The eunuch was reading this passage of Scripture:
"He was led like a sheep to the slaughter,
    and as a lamb before the shearer is silent,
    so he did not open his mouth.

Irenaeus about Simon. For Irenaeus the Simon of Acts 8 was the father of all Christian heresy. But Irenaeus wrote 150 years after the events of Acts 8, and his view of Simon may have been based more on the claims of his Simonian Gnostic contemporaries than the actual historical Simon.

[126]There is some limited archaeological evidence for Samaritan Christianity thriving in the fourth to sixth centuries. See the cautious treatment of R. Pummer, "New Evidence for Samaritan Christianity?" *CBQ* 4 (1979): 98-117.

[127]*Beginnings* 4:95.

[33]In his humiliation he was deprived of justice.
    Who can speak of his descendants?
    For his life was taken from the earth."
[34]The eunuch asked Philip, "Tell me, please, who is the prophet talking about, himself or someone else?" [35]Then Philip began with that very passage of Scripture and told him the good news about Jesus.
    [36]As they traveled along the road, they came to some water and the eunuch said, "Look, here is water. Why shouldn't I be baptized?" [38]And he gave orders to stop the chariot. Then both Philip and the eunuch went down into the water and Philip baptized him. [39]When they came up out of the water, the Spirit of the Lord suddenly took Philip away, and the eunuch did not see him again, but went on his way rejoicing. Philip, however, appeared at Azotus and traveled about, preaching the gospel in all the towns until he reached Caesarea.

Having established the mission to the Samaritans, Philip then became involved in an even more far-reaching missionary breakthrough, as he was led to witness to an Ethiopian. Indeed, Philip's witness to the eunuch may be considered the first conversion of a Gentile and in many ways parallels the story of Cornelius in chap. 10. Ethiopia was considered "the end of the earth" by the Greeks and Romans, and Philip's witness to the Samaritans and the Ethiopian comprises a "foretaste" of the completion of Christ's commission (1:8) by the whole church in the subsequent chapters of Acts.

A pronounced emphasis is on the activity of the Spirit in this passage. In fact, chaps. 8–10 witness an ever-increasing degree of the Spirit's involvement.[128] It has already been seen in the "Samaritan Pentecost" (8:17). It is more pronounced still in Philip's conversion of the eunuch. Paul's conversion is depicted as totally due to God's activity apart from human agency (9:1-30). Finally, the conversion of Cornelius and his fellow Gentiles caps the picture and emphasizes God's activity more thoroughly than any of the preceding narratives. All of these conversion stories mark major advances in the Christian mission, and the heightened emphasis on the Spirit underlines that all the initiative lies ultimately with God, even through a variety of means. The story of Philip and the eunuch falls into three natural parts: the preparation (vv. 26-29), the witness (vv. 30-35), and the commitment (vv. 36-40).

THE PREPARATION (8:26-29). God's initiative in this story is unquestionable. An angel of the Lord came to Philip in a vision and called him to witness in a most unlikely place. The angel was God's mouthpiece and was the functional equivalent to the Spirit, who continued to lead Philip throughout the story (vv. 29,39).

---

[128]See R. F. O'Toole, "Philip and the Ethiopian Eunuch (Acts viii, 25-40)," *JSNT* 17 (1983): 25-34.

8:26 The place of witness was the road to the south of Jerusalem that leads to Gaza, the last watering place before the desert on the route to Egypt.[129] Obeying the divine directive, Philip started out and on his way encountered an unusual prospect for witness. He was an Ethiopian, a eunuch, an official in charge of the queen's treasury (v. 27). The Ethiopia referred to is in all probability the ancient kingdom of Meroe, the ancient Nubian empire that lay south of Aswan between the first and sixth cataracts of the Nile.[130] It is not to be confused with modern Ethiopia, or Abyssinia, which is in the hill country to the east of the upper Nile. The ancient kingdom of Meroe was a flourishing culture from the eighth century B.C. until the fourth century A.D. Referred to in the Old Testament as the Kingdom of Cush, its population consisted of blacks.[131] This remote, advanced culture was an object of endless curiosity for the Greeks and Romans and represented for them the extreme limits of the civilized world.[132] Their kings were viewed as incarnations of the sun god and held a primarily ceremonial role. The real administration of the kingdom was in the hands of powerful queen mothers who had the title of "the Candace."[133]

8:27 In modern terminology the Ethiopian whom Philip encountered would perhaps be called the Minister of Finance. Whether he was an actual physical eunuch is not certain. In the ancient world slaves were often castrated as boys in order to be used as keepers of the harem and the treasury. Eunuchs were found to be particularly trustworthy and loyal to their rulers.[134] So widespread was the practice of placing them over the treasury that in time the term "eunuch" became a synonym for "treasurer" and did not necessarily imply that the one bearing the title

---

[129]The term μεσημβρίαν in v. 26 is generally translated "south." Its basic meaning is *noon*, and it acquired the additional idea of *south* since the sun lies directly south at noon. If it is translated "noon" here, the unlikeliness of the angel's call is further enhanced, sending Philip into the desert in the hottest part of the day. There is some question about whether the term "desert" should be connected with the road (as in the NIV), which really only becomes strictly a desert road after leaving Gaza for Egypt, or with Gaza itself. The road was not heavily traveled, and this seems to have been Luke's meaning.

[130]For an excellent treatment of this passage, see P. de Meester, "'Philippe et l'eunuque ethiopien' ou 'Le baptême d'un pelerin de Nubie'?" *NRT* 103 (1981): 360-74.

[131]Ps 68:31; Zeph 3:10. Many scholars see Isa 18:7 as a reference to the "tall and smooth-skinned" Ethiopians.

[132]The earliest reference is found in Homer (*Odyssey* 1.23), who referred to Ethiopia as "the ends of the earth." The Romans undertook a military expedition there in 23 B.C. and visited it again in A.D. 61–62 in a quest for the source of the Nile. The Nubian Empire is the subject of discussion in many classical writers, such as Herodotus, Pliny, Strabo, and Seneca. For full references see Meester, "'Philippe et l'eunuque'" and F. F. Bruce, "Philip and the Ethiopian," *JSS* 34 (1989): 377-86.

[133]Pliny, *Natural History* 6.186.

[134]H. J. Cadbury, *The Book of Acts in History* (New York: Harper & Bros., 1955), 17.

was castrated. In the present passage it is likely that Philip's Ethiopian was an actual physical eunuch, however, since the terms "eunuch" and "official over the treasury" are both given. His physical status was then highly significant for the story. He had been on a pilgrimage to Jerusalem and was in all probability, like Cornelius, one of those "God-fearing" Gentiles who believed in the God of Israel but had not become a proselyte, a full convert, to Judaism. In his case, as a eunuch, full membership in the congregation of Israel was not even possible because of his physical blemish (cf. Deut 23:1). He could visit the temple in Jerusalem, as he had done; but he could never enter it.

8:28-29 Probably not by accident, the eunuch was reading from a scroll of the prophet Isaiah as his carriage lumbered slowly homeward (v. 28). In all the Old Testament, Isaiah holds forth the greatest hope for the eunuch in his picture of God's ideal future, a future that promises them a monument in God's house, a name better than sons and daughters, an "everlasting name which will not be cut off" (Isa 56:3-8). Little did the eunuch know that he was about to experience the fulfillment of those promises. And little did Philip know his own role in their fulfillment. He probably was still wondering why in the world God had sent him to this lonely place, and perhaps he was a bit bemused by the strange spectacle of the carriage plodding in front of him with its exotic passenger and retinue of servants.[135] Philip had to be prodded by the Spirit: "Go to that chariot and stay near it" (v. 29). Philip had no idea what he should do. The Spirit assumed the lead all the way.

THE WITNESS (8:30-35). **8:30-31a** Complying with the Spirit's directions, Philip ran up to the slow-moving wagon and began to trot alongside it. He heard the Ethiopian as he read aloud from the text of Isaiah (v. 30). There was nothing unusual about this. The letters on ancient manuscripts were often crowded and difficult to decipher, and reading aloud was the customary manner in that day. Philip's question to the eunuch contains a play on words that is not reproducible in English: "Do you understand [ginōskeis] what you are reading [anaginōskeis]?" "How can I . . . unless someone explains it to me?" replied the eunuch (v. 31). His response enunciates a basic principle that runs throughout Luke-Acts concerning the interpretation of the Old Testament prophetic texts—the need for a Christian interpreter. The disciples themselves had needed such guidance, and Christ had "opened . . . the Scriptures" for them (Luke 24:45). They in turn sought to explain the Scripture in light of Christ to the Jews in

---

[135]In keeping with ancient practices, most interpreters picture an ox-drawn covered wagon with the eunuch seated beside the driver and a retinue of the high-ranking officials' servants following the wagon on foot. See I. H. Marshall, *The Acts of the Apostles*, TNTC (Leicester: Inter-Varsity, 1980), 162.

Jerusalem. How indeed would this Gentile pilgrim from a distant land understand the real meaning of Isaiah's servant psalms without a guide?

8:31b-33 Responding to the eunuch's invitation, Philip mounted the wagon and sat down beside him. Luke produced the text from which he had been reading, the Septuagintal translation of Isa 53:7-8. The passage is one of the most difficult texts to interpret of all the servant psalms and even more obscure in the Greek than the Hebrew. In general, however, it depicts the basic pattern of the suffering, humiliation, and exaltation of Christ.[136] The picture of the slaughtered lamb evokes the image of Jesus' crucifixion, the lamb before his shearers, that of Jesus' silence before his accusers. The deprivation of justice reminds one of the false accusations of blasphemy leveled at Christ and the equivocation of Pilate. But what does "who can speak of his descendants?" mean—that his life was cut off short or perhaps the opposite, that the tragedy of his death had been followed by a whole host of disciples who had come to believe and trust in him? In addition to the silent suffering and humiliation, the question concerning descendants likely was a point of identification that attracted the eunuch to this text. There is no question what the final phrase would mean to a Christian like Philip. When Christ's life was taken from the earth, it was taken up in the glory of the resurrection, exalted to the right hand of God.

8:34-35 Isaiah 53:7-8 was not the whole story, just the starting place for Philip as he "opened the Scriptures" about Christ to his Ethiopian inquirer. The Ethiopian's question was extremely intelligent and not a little informed: "Who is the prophet talking about, himself or someone else?" (v. 34). Contemporary Jews debated about whether the prophet was speaking of his own suffering or of that of the nation as a whole or of the Messiah. One cannot doubt how Philip answered him. What we would like to know is what other texts Philip shared with him. Perhaps we have them already, in the many scriptural proofs in Peter's speeches earlier in Acts. Most striking of all, of course, is that the eunuch was reading from the servant psalms of Isaiah, the Old Testament texts that point most clearly to the suffering death of Christ. What a perfect introduction for Philip to share the gospel! This was surely no mere coincidence. It is further evidence of the Spirit's activity in the whole incident.

THE COMMITMENT (8:36-40). **8:36** Philip had shared the gospel with the Ethiopian treasurer and had surely ended on a note of invitation and commitment. The wagon passed a pool of water, and the Ethiopian was ready. "Is there anything to prevent my being baptized *right now?*" (author's paraphrase). Many have sought to determine the exact site of the

---

[136]J. B. Tyson, "The Gentile Mission and the Authority of Scripture in Acts," *NTS* 33 (1987): 622-23.

spring in question,[137] but surely the more significant consideration is that at precisely the critical time they came to water, there along the arid route they were traveling (cf. v. 26). The coincidences are too numerous to be coincidences. The Spirit was in *all* of this. Significance has often been seen in the verb "hinder/prevent" which the eunuch employed when asking if there was any reason why he should not be baptized (*kōlyō*, v. 36). Some see this as part of an early Christian baptismal formula uttered before the baptism of new candidates: "Is there anything to hinder their being baptized?"[138] Surely F. Stagg's view is more on target. The verb indicates that barriers have been removed, hindrances to the spread of the gospel to all people.[139] In this case a double barrier of both physical and racial prejudice had fallen. A eunuch, a Gentile, a black, was baptized and received into full membership in the people of Jesus Christ.

[8:37] Verse 37 is omitted from the NIV text of Acts, and for good reasons. It is not found in the early manuscripts of Acts and seems to be a later scribal addition. It is given in a footnote of the NIV and consists of a profession of faith on the part of the eunuch. Evidently a scribe felt this was lacking and so provided the missing confession of faith. He did not need to do so. Luke had summarized Philip's sharing the gospel with the eunuch in v. 35, and one can assume it included an appeal for the eunuch to respond. The eunuch's desire for baptism would indicate a favorable response to Philip's appeal. The added verse, however, has considerable value. It seems to embody a very early Christian baptismal confession where the one baptizing asked the candidate if he believed in Christ with all his heart, to which the candidate would respond by confessing Jesus Christ as the Son of God. This old confession is of real significance to the history of early Christian confessions and would be appropriate to the baptismal ceremony today. To that extent we can be grateful to the pious scribe who ascribed to the eunuch the baptismal confession of his own day.

8:38-39 Verse 38 relates the baptism of the Ethiopian treasurer. Since the verb employed is *baptizō*, which always carried the idea of total submersion, there is no reason to assume that the eunuch was baptized in any other way than the consistent New Testament pattern of immersion.

---

[137]The two most popular suggestions are (1) the "traditional site" known as the "spring of Philip" at Ain Dirweh near Beth Sur, north of Hebron and (2) the Wadi el Hasi just north of Gaza. See Schneider, *Apostelgeschichte* 1:506.

[138]So O. Cullmann, who notes that the verb κωλύω is also used in 10:47 and 11:17 in connection with baptism: *Baptism in the New Testament* (London: SCM, 1950), 71-80. This argument is carried even further by those who would use the occurrence of the same verb in Luke 18:16 as a basis for infant baptism: e.g., Krodel, *Acts*, 170. For a refutation see A. W. Argyle, "O. Cullmann's Theory Concerning Kōluein," *ExpTim* 67 (1955-56): 17.

[139]Stagg, *Book of Acts*, 108.

When the two emerged from the water, they departed in opposite directions. Philip disappeared, being snatched up by the Spirit, much like the prophet Elijah (1 Kgs 18:12; 2 Kgs 2:16). The Spirit had led him to this encounter. Now, the witness completed, the Spirit closed the scene and transported Philip to further witness in the coastal cities to the north. The eunuch continued southward on his long journey home. Somehow it did not now seem so arduous. He was filled with joy, a genuine manifestation of the Spirit's work in his life.

Summary. Many interpreters have seen parallels in this story to various Old Testament traditions. Many of the same places occur in Zeph 2— Ethiopia, which is identical with Cush (Zeph 2:12; 3:10) and the Philistine cities of Gaza and Ashdod, which is identical with Azotus (2:4). The strong picture of Philip's control by the Spirit reminds one of Elijah.[140] The most interesting correspondences, however, are to be found in the Emmaus story of Luke 24:13-32—the presence of travelers, the sudden appearances of Jesus and Philip, the opening of the Scriptures to a new understanding of Christ (Luke 24:27; Acts 8:35), and the disappearance of Jesus in the breaking of bread and of Philip on completion of the baptism.[141] The differences are too great to argue that Luke based either story on the other, but perhaps he saw a pattern of common witness to strangers in the stories, with Philip very much following the example of his master in witness through the interpretation of Scripture. Whatever one makes of such parallels, they do not comprise the main point of the story. The main point is the remarkable missionary advance taken in the conversion of the Ethiopian. Even were he a "God-fearer," the witness was still to a *Gentile* and in this instance a Gentile who was not eligible for full proselyte status within Judaism because of his physical status as a eunuch. It was a radical step for a Jew, even for a Hellenist Jew like Philip. Still, Philip was not the radical. The *Spirit* was the radical. Philip's openness to the Spirit's leading enabled this major progress toward fulfilling Christ's commission for a worldwide gospel.

What became of the Ethiopian eunuch? Later church fathers relate that he became a missionary to Ethiopia.[142] Such traditions are often legendary and should not be accepted uncritically. More certain evidence dates the evangelization of the Nubian area as beginning in the fourth century.

---

[140]T. L. Brodie has recently argued for the influence of the Naaman story of 2 Kgs 5 on Acts 8:9-40—the foreign official, the washing in water, the greed of Simon Magus and Gehazi: "Towards Unraveling the Rhetorical Imitation of Sources in Acts: 2 Kings 5 as one Component of Acts 8:9-40," *Bib* 67 (1986): 41-67.

[141]J. Dupont, "Le Repas d'Emmaus," *Lumen Vitae* 31 (1957): 90; J. A. Grassi, "Emmaus Revisited (Luke 24, 13-35 and Acts 8, 26-40)," *CBQ* 26 (1964): 463-67.

[142]Irenaeus, *Heresies* 3.12.8. Epiphanius had him evangelizing Arabia and the Red Sea coastal area as well. See *Beginnings* 4:98.

Archaeology has uncovered a flourishing Christian community there between the fifth and tenth centuries. One is tempted to see the converted treasurer as at least planting the seed. It is in any event of interest to note that the first converted Christian "foreigner" in Acts was an African, and one could say that the mission began there, long before Paul ever took it to European soil.[143]

8:40 Verse 40 concludes the story of Philip's missionary activity. He appeared in Azotus, Old Testament Ashdod, and traveled about, preaching in the coastal cities.[144] Finally arriving at Caesarea,[145] he seems to have settled there. In Caesarea he appeared in Acts on the occasion of Paul's visit with him (Acts 21:8) some twenty years or so after the events of chap. 8. We are told that at the time he had four unmarried daughters who all prophesied (21:9). Like their father, evidently they were open to the Spirit. All in all, Philip's accomplishments had been considerable. He had pioneered the Samaritan mission. He had paved the way for the Gentile mission. Peter would later follow him in this with the conversion of Cornelius—interestingly in Caesarea—just as Peter followed him in Samaria. Peter was instrumental in securing community endorsement of the new missionary efforts, but Philip stood in the background as the Hellenist who first caught the vision.

---

[143]E. Dinkler, "Philippus und der Anēr Aithiops," *Jesus und Paulus*, Kümmel Festschrift (Göttingen: Vandenhoeck & Ruprecht, 1957), 85-95.

[144]Azotus/Ashdod was an ancient Philistine city twenty miles north of Gaza and thirty-five miles west of Jerusalem. Like Gaza, it had been rebuilt by the Romans and was a Hellenistic-style city.

[145]Caesarea was also a Hellenistic city. Originally known as Strato's Tower, it was rebuilt by Herod the Great in lavish Hellenistic style and was particularly renowned for its harbor. Renamed for Caesar Augustus, it was the seat of the Roman prefect beginning in A.D. 6. It is appropriate that Philip the Hellenist worked primarily in Hellenistic cities that shared his Greek language and cultural background.

―――― **IV. PETER JOINS THE WIDER WITNESS (9:1–12:25)** ――――

Chapters 9–12 continue the story of the Christian breakthrough to a wider missionary outreach that began in chaps. 6–8 with the Hellenists Stephen and Philip. Chapters 9–12 are transitional, as can be seen in the roles played by the major characters of Acts: Peter and Paul. Paul was introduced briefly in connection with the martyrdom of Stephen (7:58; 8:1,3). With the story of his conversion, the spotlight turned on him (9:1-30). Peter, on the other hand, was the primary figure in the first five chapters of Acts. The focus was once again placed on him as he witnessed in the coastal towns of Judea and served as God's instrument in the conversion of the Gentile Cornelius (9:32–11:18). Peter's escape from prison comprises the main subject of the last chapter in this portion of Acts (12:6-19) and is the last narrative in Acts that has Peter as its main character. From then on, Paul occupies center stage.

In content the major subject of these chapters is the Gentile mission. The conversion of Paul introduced at this point prepares for the major part he would play in taking the gospel to the Gentiles in chaps. 13–28. His conversion is closely linked to Peter's conversion of the Gentile Cornelius in chap. 10. Peter was the first to witness to Gentiles, but Paul was the major figure who would carry out that witness. It is true that Philip had already witnessed to a God-fearing Gentile in the person of the Ethiopian eunuch. That, however, was an isolated incident and had no further repercussions for the church as a whole.

Such was not the case with the conversion of Cornelius and his household. That event attracted the attention of the Christians in Jerusalem and necessitated Peter's defending it before them (11:1-8). Peter's defense and the resulting endorsement of the Gentile mission by the Jerusalem church is absolutely programmatic for Acts and for the mission of Paul. It provided the church's authorization and acceptance of the apostles' Gentile mission. Paul, of course, was not alone in his outreach to Gentiles. The Hellenists who settled in Antioch began a major mission among them (11:20f.). Their concern for the Gentile mission must have had a profound influence on Paul, who worked among them for some time (11:25f.) and who was ultimately commissioned by them for missionary service (13:1-3).

Jerusalem's role in these transitional chapters is instructive. It served primarily as the place where the apostles resided who guaranteed the authentic linkage of the church to the life and ministry of Christ. In these chapters the Jerusalem church primarily endorsed and authenticated the ever-widening Christian witness. This began with their acceptance of the Samaritan mission of Philip (8:14-25). It moved to their acceptance of Paul, who would become the primary missionary to the Gentiles (9:26-28). The Jerusalem church, even if somewhat reluctantly, finally conceded its approval to the Gentile witness begun by Peter with Cornelius (11:18). Finally, through its representative Barnabas, the Jerusalem church supported the mission of the Antioch Christians among the Gentile "Greeks" (11:22f.). Not all the problems had been resolved at this point, and a final settlement would be reached only in the Jerusalem Conference of chap. 15. The major principle of the mission to the Gentiles, however, had been accepted by the Jerusalem church; and this provided the authorization for Paul's Gentile witness that began in chap. 13.

1. Paul's New Witness to Christ (9:1-31)

It would be hard to overestimate the significance of Paul's conversion, not only for the subsequent narrative of Acts but for the history of Christianity as a whole. He was, in his own words, called to be a missionary to the Gentiles (cf. Gal 1:16), and Acts certainly confirms that picture. For Luke and for Paul (cf. 1 Cor 15:9f.) there was no more certain evidence of God's power and grace than in his transformation of the church's persecutor into its greatest witness. Paul's was a radical conversion experience, a total turnabout accomplished by Christ himself. Its importance for Luke is evidenced by the fact that he told the story in some detail three times in Acts—here in 9:1-30, then in Paul's speech before a Jewish crowd in the temple area (22:3-21), and finally in Paul's defense before the Jewish King Agrippa (26:2-23).[1]

Acts 9:1-30 emphasizes the complete transformation of Paul from the persecutor of the church to the one who was persecuted for his witness to Christ. Scholars have often pointed to various stories that at certain points offer analogies to Paul's experience, such as that of Heliodorus's vision and resulting blindness as related in 2 Macc 3[2] or the radical repentance and conversion of Asenath in the story of Joseph and Asenath.[3] The closest affinities of Paul's conversion account, however, are to be found in the many Old Testament allusions and strong flavor of Old Testament language that permeates the narrative. The closest "parallel" is to be found in the emphasis on visions and the divine leading in the story of Cornelius's

---

[1] In an earlier phase of biblical criticism, scholars argued that Luke depended on separate sources for his three accounts. Exemplary of these was E. Hirsch, who argued that 26:9-18 is based on Paul's personal account; 9:1-19, on the tradition of the Damascus church; and 22:4-16, on Luke's mixing of the two other accounts ("Die drei Berichte der Apostelgeschichte über die Bekehrung des Paulus," *ZNW* 28 [1929]: 305-12). Most contemporary scholars attribute the differences between the three accounts to Luke's own adaptation of a single tradition to the three separate contexts. See D. M. Stanley, "Paul's Conversion in Acts: Why the Three Accounts?" *CBQ* 15 (1953): 315-38; C. W. Hedrick, "Paul's Conversion/Call: A Comparative Analysis of the Three Reports in Acts," *JBL* 100 (1981): 415-32.

[2] For a full treatment of the parallels in the Heliodorous story, see K. Loening, *Die Saulustradition in der Apostelgeschichte* (Muenster: Aschendorff, 1973).

[3] For the parallels in Joseph and Asenath, see C. Burchard, *Die dreizehnte Zeuge* (Göttingen: Vandenhoeck und Ruprecht, 1970). Further parallel material is found in H. Windisch, "Die Christusepiphanie vor Damaskus (Act 9, 22 und 26) und ihre religionsgeschichtliche Parallelen," *ZNW* 31 (1932): 1-23 and A. Wikenhauser, "Die Wirkung der Christophanie vor Damaskus auf Paulus und seine Begleiter nach den Berichten der Apostelgeschichte," *Bib* 33 (1952): 313-23.

conversion in the next chapters of Acts.[4] Both incidents are essential to the Gentile mission, and both are wholly due to God's direct intervention. Paul's conversion account falls into two main parts: vv. 1-22 relate the story of his transformation from persecutor of the church to witness for Christ, and vv. 23-31 show how the former persecutor became the one persecuted for bearing the name of Christ.

(1) Paul the Converted (9:1-22)

[1]Meanwhile, Saul was still breathing out murderous threats against the Lord's disciples. He went to the high priest [2]and asked him for letters to the synagogues in Damascus, so that if he found any there who belonged to the Way, whether men or women, he might take them as prisoners to Jerusalem. [3]As he neared Damascus on his journey, suddenly a light from heaven flashed around him. [4]He fell to the ground and heard a voice say to him, "Saul, Saul, why do you persecute me?"

[5]"Who are you, Lord?" Saul asked.

"I am Jesus, whom you are persecuting," he replied. [6]"Now get up and go into the city, and you will be told what you must do."

[7]The men traveling with Saul stood there speechless; they heard the sound but did not see anyone. [8]Saul got up from the ground, but when he opened his eyes he could see nothing. So they led him by the hand into Damascus. [9]For three days he was blind, and did not eat or drink anything.

[10]In Damascus there was a disciple named Ananias. The Lord called to him in a vision, "Ananias!"

"Yes, Lord," he answered.

[11]The Lord told him, "Go to the house of Judas on Straight Street and ask for a man from Tarsus named Saul, for he is praying. [12]In a vision he has seen a man named Ananias come and place his hands on him to restore his sight.

[13]"Lord," Ananias answered, "I have heard many reports about this man and all the harm he has done to your saints in Jerusalem. [14]And he has come here with authority from the chief priests to arrest all who call on your name."

[15]But the Lord said to Ananias, "Go! This man is my chosen instrument to carry my name before the Gentiles and their kings and before the people of Israel. [16]I will show him how much he must suffer for my name."

[17]Then Ananias went to the house and entered it. Placing his hands on Saul, he said, "Brother Saul, the Lord—Jesus, who appeared to you on the road as you were coming here—has sent me so that you may see again and be filled with the Holy Spirit." [18]Immediately, something like scales fell from Saul's eyes, and he could see again. He got up and was baptized, [19]and after taking some food, he regained his strength.

Saul spent several days with the disciples in Damascus. [20]At once he began to preach in the synagogues that Jesus is the Son of God. [21]All those who heard him were astonished and asked, "Isn't he the man who raised havoc in Jerusalem among those who call on this name? And hasn't he come here to take them as

---

[4]R. Pesch, *Die Apostelgeschichte*, Teilband 1: *Apg. 1-12* (Zurich: Benziger, 1986), 301.

prisoners to the chief priests?" [22]**Yet Saul grew more and more powerful and baffled the Jews living in Damascus by proving that Jesus is the Christ.**

The first half of Paul's conversion account[5] divides into three main sections: the appearance on the Damascus road (vv. 1-9), the ministry of Ananias to Paul (vv. 10-18a), and the final confirmation of Paul's conversion through his bold witness in the Jewish synagogues of Damascus (vv. 18b-22).

CHRIST'S APPEARANCE TO PAUL (9:1-9). **9:1-2** The first two verses provide the chronological and geographical setting. More significantly, they picture the preconversion Paul, which contrasts radically with the picture of Paul after the encounter on the Damascus road. Verse 1 picks up the picture in 8:3. Paul was still the church's number one enemy, still raging against it, "breathing out murderous threats."[6] Paul's role was not one of executioner but of arresting officer. His intent was to stamp out the new movement; and when it did come to a question of execution of Christians, he did not hesitate to vote for the death penalty (cf. 26:10). Originally, Paul's activity had primarily been directed at the Christians in and around Jerusalem (8:3; 26:10). Evidently, some had fled the city and taken refuge in Damascus. Paul approached the high priest, who probably was still Caiaphas at this time. He requested not official extradition papers but more likely introductory letters from the Sanhedrin to the synagogues of Damascus in order to secure their support in his efforts to apprehend the Christian fugitives and return them to Jerusalem for trial.[7]

Much debate centers on whether the Sanhedrin would have jurisdiction in such cases, but there is some evidence the high priest was given the right of extradition in an earlier time.[8] The possibility remains open that the Romans still granted him similar rights. How much autonomy the Jewish synagogues enjoyed during the Roman period with regard to discipline of their members for religious offenses is unclear. Paul himself spoke of his receiving scourgings from the synagogues on five occasions (2 Cor 11:24). His very desire to go to Damascus betrays his searing rage against the Christians, especially if one remembers that Damascus was a

---

[5]Most commentators close the first section with 18a and see 18b as beginning a new section centering on Paul's witness in Damascus. The outline followed here is that of Pesch (*Apostelgeschichte* 1:298f.), which connects vv. 18b-22 with the preceding as the witness of Paul that confirms his conversion and sees vv. 28-31 as a unit around the theme of Paul's suffering for Christ.

[6]The expression "breathing out threat and slaughter" (ἐμπνέων ἀπειλῆς καὶ φόνου) is capable of several renderings, but the most likely is "full of threatening and slaughter." See P. W. van der Horst, "Drohung und Mord Schnaubend (Act ix.1)" *NovT* 12 (1970): 257-69.

[7]That these were Jerusalem refugees is perhaps indicated in 26:11 with the reference to Paul's "pursuing" (διώκω) them even "to foreign cities."

[8]See 1 Macc 15:15-21; cf. Josephus, *Ant.* 14.192-95.

good six-day foot journey from Jerusalem.[9] The detail that the Christians were referred to as those who belonged to "the way" (v. 2) perhaps reflects an early self-designation of the Jewish Christian community in which they saw themselves as the "true way" within the larger Jewish community.[10]

9:3-6 As Paul approached the gates of Damascus, suddenly a great light from heaven flashed around him. The light must have been intense, for the time of the occurrence was "around midday" (cf. 22:6; 26:13). The light represents the heavenly epiphany, the divine glory that enveloped the little caravan.[11] At the sight the awe-struck Paul fell to the ground, a reaction found in the Old Testament from those who experienced a similar divine visitation. Then a voice came from heaven, "Saul, Saul, why do you persecute me?"[12] Paul answered, "Who are you, Lord?" Some note that at this point Paul did not recognize Jesus as the one speaking to him and that his reference to "Lord" need not mean more than a polite "sir," a meaning the Greek word *kyrie* often has. But Paul did recognize the voice of a heavenly messenger and probably intended "Lord" in that sense (cf. Exod 3:13). In any event, he quickly learned who the "Lord" was: "I am Jesus, whom you are persecuting." It would be hard to imagine how these words must have struck Paul. They were a complete refutation of all he had been. He had persecuted Christians for their "blasphemous lie" that Jesus was risen, that he was the Lord reigning in glory. Now Paul himself beheld that same Jesus and the undeniable proof that he both lived and reigned in glory.

From this point on, Paul said nothing. He was completely broken. How could he respond? He had not persecuted a band of miscreant messianists. In persecuting the church, he had persecuted the risen Lord himself. It is unlikely that the concept of the body of Christ is behind the expression

---

[9]F. A. Schilling suggests that Damascus's being associated with earlier refugees belonging to the Zadokite movement may have given it a reputation of being a "hotbed of heresy," which fueled Paul's intent to go there ("Why did Paul go to Damascus?" *ATR* 16 [1934]: 199-205).

[10]The term occurs six times in Acts (9:2; 19:9,23; 22:4; 24:14,22). The Qumran community also referred to itself as "the way" (J. A. Fitzmyer, "Jewish Christianity in Acts in Light of the Qumran Scrolls," *Studies in Luke-Acts*, ed. L. Keck and J. L. Martyn [Nashville: Abingdon, 1966], 240-41). The designation could easily have developed in Christian circles from the usage of ὁδός in the teachings of Jesus (cf. Matt 7:13f.; John 14:6). Similar concepts are found in other religions, such as the *halakah* ("walk, way") of the rabbis and the *tao* ("way") of Taoism. See S. V. McCasland, "The Way," *JBL* 77 (1958): 222-30.

[11]For light accompanying a heavenly epiphany, see Luke 2:9; 9:29; Acts 12:7; 22:6. One wonders whether Paul's references to such radiance in 2 Cor 3:18; 4:6 are reminiscent of his conversion experience.

[12]The doubling of the name is a common OT form of address (cf. 1 Sam 3:10) and is found also in Luke's Gospel (Luke 8:24; 10:41; 22:31).

here, but surely the germ of Paul's later theology of the church is. Christ is identified with his disciples. When they suffer, he suffers (cf. Luke 10:16). Jesus' final words to Paul were not a commission but a directive.[13] He was to go into the city and await further instruction. There was no elaboration of Paul's vision. All the emphasis was on the fact that Paul saw the Lord—nothing more. This is very much in keeping with Paul's own testimony about his conversion, which concentrated on one fact—that he *saw* the Lord (cf. 1 Cor 9:1; 15:8; Gal 1:16).[14] And that was enough. The certainty of the resurrection turned Paul from Jesus' most zealous persecutor to his most ardent witness.

9:7-9 Paul's traveling companions served as authenticators that what happened to Paul was an objective event, not merely a rumbling of his inner psyche. They heard a sound, but they did not see the vision of Jesus. Acts 22:9 says that they saw the light but did not hear the voice of the one who spoke with Paul.[15] The two accounts are not contradictory but underline the same event. Paul's companions heard a sound and saw a light. They could verify that an objective heavenly manifestation took place. They did not participate in the heavenly communication, however, neither seeing the vision of Jesus nor hearing the words spoken to Paul. The revelation was solely to Paul. So powerful was that revelation that Paul was totally blind when he rose to his feet and opened his eyes. The miracle was not a punitive one, as with Elymas the magician (Acts 13:11). Rather, the picture is of Paul in his brokenness and helplessness.[16] The radiance of his vision had blinded him. Reduced to total powerlessness, he had to be led by others into the city. That he neither ate nor drank for three days could be an expression of penitence on Paul's part[17] but is

---

[13]There is an interesting parallel structure between the conversion of Paul and the commissioning narratives of the OT, such as that of Moses (Exod 3:4-10), Jacob (Gen 46:2-4), and Abraham (Gen 22:1f.). See G. Lohfink, "Eine alttestamentliche Darstellungsform für Gotteserscheinungen in den Damaskus Berichten (Apg. 9; 22; 26)," *BZ* 9 (1965): 246-57.

[14]J. Munck, "La vocation de l'Apôtre Paul," *ST* (1947): 131-45.

[15]It is well recognized that one cannot reconcile the seeming contradiction between "hearing" in Acts 9:7 and "not hearing" in 22:9 on the basis of the old classical distinction between hearing and understanding (with genitive case) and hearing without understanding (accusative), a distinction that will not hold for Luke-Acts. See R. Bratcher, "Akouō in Acts ix.7 and xxii.9," *ExpTim* 71 (1959-60): 243-45. The distinction is perhaps to be seen in the qualifying participial phrase of 22:9, hearing a "voice" (φωνή) *which was speaking*, whereas 9:7 need mean no more than hearing a "sound." They heard a noise but did not comprehend the conversation.

[16]Pesch (*Apostelgeschichte* 1:305) notes that such total brokenness of self-will and pride is a necessary stage of all genuine conversions.

[17]It is unlikely that Paul's fast should be seen here as an example of the practice of fasting in preparation for baptism as practiced by the later church (cf. *Did.* 7:4; Justin, *Apology* 1.61.2; Tertullian, *Bapt.* 20).

more likely the result of his shock, confusion, and utter brokenness of will. The raging persecutor had been reduced to a shambles.

THE CALL TO BE PERSECUTED (9:10-18a). **9:10a** The second scene in Paul's conversion story took place in Damascus and revolved around a disciple named Ananias. Damascus was an ancient city, dating back at least into the second millennium B.C. It was an oasis city on the border of the Arabian desert and along the main trade route linking Egypt and Mesopotamia. From 64 B.C. it had been under Roman influence and belonged to the association of ten Hellenistic cities known as the Decapolis. It had a large Jewish population, as is attested by the many Jews Josephus reported were killed there during the Jewish war with Rome.[18]

How Christians first reached Damascus is unknown. Ananias seems to have been a disciple in Damascus before the current stream of refugees from Paul's persecution arrived. Luke gave a selective, not a complete, picture of the geographical spread of Christianity. The evidence of Acts itself would indicate the early spread of the Christian witness to places like Damascus and Rome, perhaps through normal social routes such as trade, military service, and the like.

9:10b-12 The "Lord" appeared to Ananias in a vision. That it was Jesus and not God who was so designated is clear from vv. 14-16. Ananias responded with, "Here am I, Lord" ("Yes, Lord," NIV), words reminiscent of the response of Old Testament characters to a vision of God, such as Abraham (Gen 22:1f.; 11) and the boy Samuel (1 Sam 3:4-14). Jesus instructed Ananias to seek out Paul. His instructions were precise, giving the exact location Paul was to be found. He was staying with a man named Judas who lived on "Straight Street." This street can still be seen today, though somewhat farther to the north from the ancient street, and is now known as the Darb-el-Mostakim. It runs in an east-west direction, and in Paul's day it had colonnades on both sides and large gates at both ends.[19] One is intrigued by Jesus' informing Ananias of Paul's vision—a vision within a vision! The information was necessary for Ananias to know that Paul was prepared for him. Further, it emphasized the centrality of the divine leading in the entire episode.[20]

This was the third vision in the story of Paul's conversion. The Lord was behind every detail in the story. Ananias learned of his own role

---

[18]Josephus, *War* 2.561; 7.368 gives the figures of 10,500 and 18,000, respectively, both of which seem grossly exaggerated but still allow for an extensive population even when exaggeration is taken into consideration.

[19]For a discussion of the traditional sites in Damascus (such as the houses of Judas and Ananias) and of Paul's escape and conversion, see O. F. Meinardus, "The Site of the Apostle Paul's Conversion at Kaukab," *BA* 44 (1981): 57-59.

[20]Double visions are found frequently in Greco-Roman and early Christian literature. See A. Wikenhauser, "Doppeltraume," *Bib* 29 (1948): 100-11.

through the vision of Paul. He was to enter Judas's house and lay his hands upon Paul so that Paul might recover his sight (v. 12). Ananias in no way established the legitimacy of Paul. There was no "succession" through the laying on of his hands. He was merely a pious, but otherwise unknown, Jewish Christian of Damascus whom Jesus commissioned as his agent in the healing and baptism of Paul.[21]

9:13-14 Ananias at first protested the commission. He was all too aware of who Paul was. Perhaps he had learned of Paul's reputation as a persecutor from some of the Christians who had fled Jerusalem and taken refuge in Damascus. Word was even out that he had papers from the Sanhedrin authorizing him to arrest any and every Christian. Surely Jesus did not want him to go to *this* man. Ananias's reaction is understandable and should not be seen as his refusing the Lord. Much more it underlines once again the sheer miracle of Paul's radical turnabout from his former role as persecutor.

9:15-16 Verses 15-16 comprise the heart of Ananias's vision, as the Lord outlined Paul's future role. He was the Lord's "chosen instrument." The expression is an unusual one and finds its closest New Testament parallels in Paul's own writings.[22] The emphasis on Paul's being "chosen" recalls his own strong sense of the divine call, which set him apart from birth (Gal 1:15). His call was described here in terms of his bearing Jesus' name before Gentiles, kings, and the sons of Israel. His mission "to the ends of the earth" immediately comes to mind, but the reference probably is to Paul's appearance in trial before these entities. The expression of bearing one's witness "before" is the language of giving one's testimony in a legal setting and is a fulfillment of Jesus' words in Luke 12:11f. and Luke 21:12.[23] It is thus a picture of Paul on trial before Gentile rulers like Felix and Festus (chaps. 24–25), before kings like Agrippa (chap. 26), before local Jewish synagogues and even the Sanhedrin (chap. 23). Verse 15 is thus closely linked to v. 16. Paul would *suffer* for the name of Christ. The one who once was the church's most vehement persecutor would now be the one who would willingly accept persecution for the sake of the name (cf. 5:41). This is the core point of the Pauline conversion narrative. It reappears at its conclusion as Paul is shown persecuted by the Jews both in Damascus (9:23) and in Jerusalem (9:29). In nothing is his conversion more clearly illustrated than in his transformation from persecutor to persecuted.

---

[21]S. Lundgren, "Ananias and the Calling of Paul in Acts," *ST* 25 (1971): 117-22.

[22]For σκεῦος ἐκλογῆς cf. Rom 9:22f., where in a context that speaks of election, Paul spoke of God's chosen vessels of wrath and of mercy. Even more striking is 2 Cor 4:7, where Paul spoke of earthenware vessels that bear the treasure of the gospel. Paul was speaking of the weakness and suffering that accompanied his ministry. Note the parallel emphasis on Paul's suffering in Acts 9:16.

[23]See G. Lohfink, "'Meinen Namen zu Tragen . . . ' (Apg. 9.15)," *BZ* 10 (1966): 108-15.

9:17-19a Ananias fulfilled his commission, going to Paul and laying his hands upon him as he had been instructed. Ananias's greeting is striking: "Brother Saul." He could have said this as a fellow Jew, but it was surely as a brother in Christ that Ananias greeted Paul. Something of a "conversion" had taken place in his own heart through *his* vision of the Lord, so that now he could receive as a fellow disciple the one whom he so shortly before had feared and distrusted. Ananias told Paul that the Lord had sent him with a dual purpose, the recovery of his sight and his receipt of the Spirit. The first occurs immediately as Ananias performed the healing gesture of laying his hands upon Paul.[24] Something "like flakes" fell from his eyes.[25] Paul's receipt of the Spirit is not narrated. It did not seem to have come with Ananias's laying his hands on Paul. Recovery of his sight followed that. Perhaps it accompanied his baptism, since the two generally are closely connected in Acts.[26] Certainly Paul did receive the Spirit, as his boldness in witness indicates in the following narrative. Paul's bold witness, like the Ethiopian's joy, expands the picture of the evidence of the Holy Spirit in believers' lives. All believers should give evidence of the Spirit's presence in their lives, but there is no normative evidence of that presence. The scene in Judas's house concluded with Paul's receiving nourishment and recovering his strength. Paul's recovery was now complete. More than that, his conversion was now complete.

THE FORMER PERSECUTOR'S WITNESS TO CHRIST (9:19b-22). **9:19b-22** This section of Acts illustrates the authenticity of Paul's conversion experience. It begins with the brief notice that Paul spent several days with the disciples in Damascus after his baptism. This probably refers to their instructing him in Christ. Even though Paul was steeped in the Old Testament and would have had some familiarity with Christian views from his experience as persecutor, he was still a new convert and needed further introduction to the teachings about Christ before he would be ready to strike out on his own witness. Evidently he was soon ready because we find him "at once" preaching in the Jewish synagogues that Jesus is the Son of God.

It is noteworthy that Luke described Paul as preaching Christ as "Son of God." This is the only occurrence of the title in all of Acts, and yet for

---

[24]For hand-laying in healing, cf. Luke 4:40; 13:13; Acts 28:8.

[25]Λεπίδες can refer to any small, flaky substance, like thinly sliced vegetables or the scales of a fish. It is used in the book of Tobit as in Acts to describe healing from blindness (Tob 3:17; 11:12f.).

[26]Somewhere the question was raised whether Paul ever referred to his baptism in his epistles. He certainly seems to have included himself among the baptized in Rom 6:3. See R. H. Fuller, "Was Paul Baptized?" in *Les Actes*, ed. J. Kremer, 505-08; E. Fascher, "Zur Taufe des Paulus," *TLZ* 80 (1955): 643-48.

Paul it was a central concept. In fact, Paul connected the term "Son of God" with his call as an apostle in Gal 1:16 and in Rom 1:1-4.[27] Luke's close connection of this term with Paul's conversion and call would seem to be a rather accurate reminiscence of Paul's distinctive views. The astonishment of his Jewish listeners in the synagogue furnishes a sort of "choral response" to the completeness of Paul's conversion. As Ananias before them (vv. 13-14), they simply could not believe that the former persecutor had made such a radical about-face. Paul simply preached all the more forcefully. One could even say that his zeal as a Christian was even stronger than his former zeal as persecutor.[28] Luke described him as "proving" (*symbibazō*) that Jesus is the Christ. The Greek word means to *join* or *put together* and seems to picture his assembling Old Testament texts to demonstrate how Christ fulfilled them. No wonder the Damascene Jews were astounded and totally unable to respond to the skillful interpretations of the former student of Gamaliel.

Paul gave another picture of his experience following his conversion in Damascus. He stated in Gal 1:15-17 that he did not consult anyone or go to the apostles in Jerusalem, but rather he went off for a period in Arabia before returning to Damascus. "Consult any man" does not rule out Paul's interaction with the Damascene Christians or the Jewish synagogue. The "consulting" to which Paul alluded was the idea that he received his apostleship and his apostolic credentials from the apostles in Jerusalem. No, said Paul, he did not go to Jerusalem to confer with the apostles there and receive instructions from them. In Galatians, Paul took pains to emphasize in the face of his Judaizing opponents that his apostleship to the Gentiles was a direct call from God and in no way was dependent on or subservient to the Jerusalem apostolate. Acts would certainly verify that picture. Luke did not mention the Arabian period, it is true. Perhaps he was unaware of it. Perhaps he chose not to deal with it in order to concentrate on the Jewish opposition to Paul and the persecution that resulted.

Summary. Many attempts have been made to "explain" Paul's conversion, often in the form of rationalistic explanations, such as a thunderstorm outside Damascus, or an epileptic seizure, or psychogenic blindness as the result of repressed guilt.[29] Others see Paul's conversion as a total rational experience, a coming to awareness of the correctness of the Christian views.[30] Others have sought for the factors that prepared

---

[27] I. H. Marshall, *The Acts of the Apostles*, TNTC (Leicester: Inter-Varsity, 1980), 174.

[28] G. Schneider, *Die Apostelgeschichte*, HTKNT (Freiburg: Herder, 1980), 2:36.

[29] For a nonsympathetic survey of the various rationalistic and psychological theories, see J. L. Lilly, "The Conversion of St. Paul," *CBQ* 6 (1944): 180-204.

[30] For a totally "nonmiraculous" reconstruction, see W. Prentice, "St. Paul's Journey to Damascus," *ZNW* 46 (1955): 250-55.

him for his conversion—his coming to the end of his rope with the utter hopelessness of Pharisaic legal righteousness[31] or his being steeped in Pharisaic apocalypticism.[32] All such attempts to get into the mind of Paul are at best speculative, for Paul never provided us with such an analysis of his conversion, nor did Luke. Surely experiences with the Christians must have impressed Paul. Surely the Stephen incident made its impression. But Luke never drew such connections, nor did Paul. What both picture is a *radical conversion* experience. Paul the persecutor was stopped dead in his tracks on the Damascus road. The risen Jesus showed himself to Paul; and with this confirmation that the Christian claims were indeed true, Paul was completely turned from persecutor to witness. Only one category describes Paul's experience, a category not uncommon in Acts. It was a *miracle*, the result of direct divine action. When all is said and done, both Acts and Paul give strikingly similar pictures of his conversion. Both speak of Paul's former life as persecutor of the church (1 Cor 15:9), even use the same vocabulary to describe how he "ravaged it" (Gal 1:13).[33] Both speak of his intense zeal (Phil 3:6). Both place the conversion in Damascus (Gal 1:17). Both describe the experience as a vision of the risen Lord, a Christophany (1 Cor 15:8; 9:1; cf. 2 Cor 4:6). Both speak of his testifying to Christ as "God's Son" immediately after his conversion (Gal 1:16; Acts 9:20). For both it was a radical turning (Phil 3:6-7).[34] For Paul and for Luke, a totally different man emerged from that vision of the risen Lord; and that is conversion.[35]

(2) Paul the Persecuted (9:23-31)

23After many days had gone by, the Jews conspired to kill him, 24but Saul learned of their plan. Day and night they kept close watch on the city gates in

---

[31]There can be no question that Paul's conversion caused considerable rethinking on his part and that this is reflected in his later rejection of a righteousness based on law. See J. Dupont, "The Conversion of Paul and Its Influence on His Understanding of Salvation by Faith" in *Apostolic History and the Gospel*, ed. W. Gasque and J. Martyn (Grand Rapids: Eerdmans, 1970), 176-94.

[32]U. Wilckens argues that Paul was an *apocalyptic* Pharisee, and his encounter with the risen Lord convinced him that not the law but Christ was the center of God's saving activity ("Die Bekehrung des Paulus als religionsgeschichtliches Problem," *ZTK* 56 [1959]: 273-93).

[33]C. Masson argues that the use of similar vocabulary such as the verb πορθέω ("to ravage") in Gal 1:13 and Acts 9:21 shows that Luke made use of Galatians ("A Propos de Act 9:19b-25," *TZ* 18 [1962]: 161-66). His "parallels" are too scant to be persuasive.

[34]Pesch, *Apostelgeschichte* 1:301-02.

[35]K. Stendahl argues that the term "call" is more descriptive of Paul's experience than "conversion" ("The Apostle Paul and the Introspective Conscience of the West," *HTR* 56 [1963]: 199-215). Certainly Paul's call to be an apostle to the Gentiles accompanied his conversion (cf. 22:15; and esp. 26:16-18). But the picture in Acts is above all a conversion, if conversion is understood as a radical turn-about and new commitment.

order to kill him. [25]But his followers took him by night and lowered him in a basket through an opening in the wall.

[26]When he came to Jerusalem, he tried to join the disciples, but they were all afraid of him, not believing that he really was a disciple. [27]But Barnabas took him and brought him to the apostles. He told them how Saul on his journey had seen the Lord and that the Lord had spoken to him, and how in Damascus he had preached fearlessly in the name of Jesus. [28]So Saul stayed with them and moved about freely in Jerusalem, speaking boldly in the name of the Lord. [29]He talked and debated with the Grecian Jews, but they tried to kill him. [30]When the brothers learned of this, they took him down to Caesarea and sent him off to Tarsus.

[31]Then the church throughout Judea, Galilee and Samaria enjoyed a time of peace. It was strengthened; and encouraged by the Holy Spirit, it grew in numbers, living in the fear of the Lord.

The remainder of the Pauline conversion narrative illustrates the fulfillment of 9:16. Paul the persecuted became Paul the sufferer, first in Damascus (vv. 23-25) and then in Jerusalem (vv. 26-30). The Jerusalem section also legitimizes the ministry of Paul because he was then accepted by the circle of apostles. A summary statement (v. 31) caps off the whole of 9:1-30.

PERSECUTED IN DAMASCUS (9:23-25). **9:23-25** Unable to refute Paul (cf. 6:10), the exasperated Damascene Jews finally "conspired to kill him."[36] With customary chronological imprecision, Luke described this as occurring "after many days." Paul gave more definite data. In the third year after his conversion, Paul departed from Damascus for Jerusalem (Gal 1:17-18). When Paul and his disciples learned of the plot, plans were made for assuring his escape from the Jews. That Paul had "disciples" at this point (v. 25) is somewhat surprising. Perhaps they were converts from the synagogues who had responded to his preaching and scriptural argumentation (vv. 20,22).[37] Since the Jewish plotters were carefully watching the city gates for Paul, another route was selected for his escape. He was lowered in a basket through the window of a house built along the city wall.[38]

Paul also referred to this event in 2 Cor 11:32-33. Although there are differences between the two accounts, the correspondences are remarkable: the setting in Damascus, the plot against Paul, the watching of the gates, the window in the wall, the lowering in a basket. The most significant difference is that in 2 Corinthians the Nabatean *ethnarch* ("governor") is described as watching the gates for Paul, while in Acts it

---

[36]The Greek verb for "kill" here (ἀνειλεῖν) literally means *to do away with*.

[37]Schneider, *Apostelgeschichte* 2:37.

[38]Acts 9:25 describes the basket as a σπύρις, a large wicker basket. The term used in 2 Cor 11:33 is σαργάνη, a larger mesh or woven bag used for bales of wool and the like.

was the Jews who did so. Paul's account raises problems itself. Why, for instance, were the Nabateans after Paul?[39] Possibly Paul had carried on a mission among them during his Arabian period (Gal 1:17) and had incurred the resistance of the authorities. In that event Acts pictures a coalition against the common enemy, the Jews watching the gates from within and the Nabateans from without. The Nabateans perhaps held some jurisdiction over Damascus at this time, in which case the Jews would have enlisted the authorities in their attempt to apprehend Paul.[40] In any case, Paul saw the incident as particularly humiliating, listing it as the crowning event of his trials as an apostle (2 Cor 11:23-33). Acts pictures the same—Paul under trial, Paul the persecuted.

PERSECUTED IN JERUSALEM (9:26-31).   According to Paul's account, in the third year after his conversion he went to Jerusalem.[41] Paul's version of this first postconversion visit to Jerusalem differs considerably from that in Acts.[42] Paul and Luke referred to the occasion in order to make totally different points. In Gal 1:18-23 Paul contended with Judaizing opponents who argued that Paul was not a "real" apostle but totally subordinate and inferior to the Jerusalem apostles. Paul's account of his first Jerusalem visit thus reveals a definite "tendency." In order to maintain the independence of his call to be an apostle to the Gentiles, he stressed the minimal contact with the apostles in order to show that he was in no way subordinate to them. Luke's emphases were totally different. He too did not show Paul's subordination to the apostles, but he emphasized Paul's acceptance by them, which was essential in his unfolding picture of the church's mission to the ends of the earth. Paul was not a maverick missionary, nor were his Gentile converts maverick Christians. The apostles provided an unbroken continuity with the risen Lord and with his commission. Paul's acceptance by the apostles assures this continuity and the legitimacy of the mission to the Gentiles.[43] Luke had another

---

[39]Nabatea was the prosperous and well-populated kingdom of Arabia located just east of Damascus in the desert area and stretching south to the Arabian Gulf. At this time it was ruled by King Aretas IV (9 B.C.–A.D. 40), whom Paul mentioned in 2 Cor 11:32.

[40]In an earlier period the Nabateans had jurisdiction over Damascus, but it is open to question whether this still applied under first-century Roman rule. An "ethnarch" was a subordinate official appointed by the king. Possibly Aretas's "ethnarch" held jurisdiction over the Arabian community in Damascus. More likely his authority was among the Arabian communities outside the city. See H. J. Cadbury, The Book of Acts in History (New York: Harper, 1955), 19-21.

[41]In Gal 1:18 Paul said "after three years." In biblical reckoning any part of a year was considered a year. "Three years" would thus refer to two full years and any portion of the third, from its beginning to its end, or even one full year and any portion of two others.

[42]For the unlikely view that Acts 9:26-30 parallels the Jerusalem visit of Gal 2:1-10 rather than 1:18-23, see D. R. de Lacey, "Paul in Jerusalem," NTS 20 (1973): 82-86.

[43]J. Cambier, "Le Voyage de S. Paul à Jerusalem en Act. ix, 26ss. et le Schema Missionaire

point to make—the further persecution of Paul at the hands of the Hellenist Jews in Jerusalem, additional evidence that the former persecutor was now the persecuted. No fact more fully illustrated the reality of his conversion.

9:26-28 The emphasis on Paul as the converted persecutor is first struck in v. 26. On arriving in Jerusalem, Paul attempted to join up with the Christian community there but was at first spurned. Like Ananias, they knew his reputation as persecutor and were not convinced that so vehement an enemy could now be a Christian brother. Barnabas then entered the picture as mediator, his characteristic role in Acts.[44] He took Paul to the apostles and testified to his conversion.[45] Through Barnabas's words the reader is once again reminded of the absolute centrality of this event and the divine action that brought it about. Why Barnabas did not share the fear of the other Jerusalem Christians is not specified. Perhaps he had learned of Paul's conversion through some of his fellow Greek-speaking Christians who had come from Damascus. In any event, Barnabas fulfilled his mediating role, securing Paul's acceptance in the apostolic circle. Paul was now "with them" (v. 28). The Greek text says literally that he was "going in and out among them" in Jerusalem. The expression is familiar from Acts 1:21, where it refers to the circle of apostles. That meaning may well be intended here. Paul was fully accepted into the apostolic circle. He too was a "witness" for Christ.[46]

9:29-30 In vv. 29-30 the pattern begun in Damascus again repeats itself.[47] Paul witnessed in the synagogues and was resisted. This time Paul debated with his fellow Greek-speaking Jews. One is reminded of Stephen, and it may have been in the same synagogue that Paul gave his testimony for Christ (cf. 6:9-10). Earlier they had succeeded in having Stephen killed. Now they determined to do the same to Paul. Again the Christians learned of the plot and hastened Paul off to the port of Caesarea and thence, presumably by boat, to his hometown of Tarsus.[48] Paul

---

Theologique de S. Luc," *NTS* 8 (1961-62): 249-57. He notes that the Acts picture of Paul's mission beginning in Jerusalem accords well with Paul's own treatment in Rom 15:19-29.

[44] See D. France, "Barnabas-Son of Encouragement," *Themelios* 4 (1978): 3-6.

[45] The Greek is ambiguous. The subject of "he told" is unclear and could be Paul rather than Barnabas. The name "Saul" (NIV) does not occur in the reference to the testimony. The Greek has simply "how he on his journey had seen" and so could be Paul's own testimony.

[46] Luke reserved the term "apostle" for the Twelve, in contradistinction from Paul, who characteristically called himself an apostle. (The term is only applied to Paul in Acts 14:4, 14.) Paul's inferiority or subordination to the apostles is not at issue. Acts 9:28 indicates his full acceptance and equality within the apostolic circle.

[47] Material in 9:26-30 corresponds to the whole of 9:13-25. See D. Gill, "The Structure of Acts 9," *Bib* (1974): 546-48.

[48] An ancient city, dating as far back as the second millennium B.C., Tarsus was located some thirty miles south of the Cilician gates and on the major trade route between Asia

gave the same itinerary in Gal 1:21: from Jerusalem he went to "Syria and Cilicia." Tarsus was located in Cilicia and came under the Roman provincial administration of Syria.[49]

During this residence in his home territory, Paul presumably continued his witness for Christ. There we leave him until Barnabas brought him back to Antioch (Acts 11:25f.). The time span between Paul's sailing to Tarsus and Barnabas's bringing him to Antioch covered some ten years or so. Since neither the Pauline Epistles nor Acts covers his activity during this period in Syria-Cilicia, these are often referred to as Paul's "silent years."[50]

9:31 Verse 31 concludes the Pauline conversion narrative and completes the entire "persecution" story that began in 8:1b. The persecution was now over with the conversion of its most ardent advocate into a witness for Christ. The "church" was at peace. Luke's use of the singular "church" could be taken in the "universal sense" as the whole body of Christians in all their local assemblies. That meaning does seem to be found in Paul's speech at Miletus (Acts 20:28), but everywhere else in Acts "church" refers to a local body of believers. Perhaps the church that Luke focused on here is the Jerusalem church pictured in its witness, which extended throughout all these regions.[51] This is the only mention of Galilean Christians in Acts. Galilee is probably to be included within the reference to "all Judea" in Acts 1:8. Here Luke mentioned it separately to emphasize how the commission to "all Judea" was being fulfilled. Already the witness had reached Galilee. The following passage will show its extension to the coastal towns of Judea. The "peace" of the church is described in terms of the encouragement of the Spirit, the growth of the church, and its reverence and worship ("the fear of the Lord"), terms reminiscent of the earlier summaries in Acts (cf. 2:43-47). It is a familiar pattern. The Lord brings his people through a time of crisis. Through his

---

Minor and Syria. Strabo, *Geog.* 15.5, 13, rates it as the third-ranking center of learning in the Greco-Roman world, next to Athens and Alexandria. Paul's familiarity with such things as the Stoic style of argumentation, so apparent in his letters, probably derived from his background in Tarsus. For further information on Tarsus, see F. F. Bruce, *Commentary on the Book of Acts*, NIC (Grand Rapids: Eerdmans, 1977), 207-08.

[49] E. M. B. Green, "Syria and Cilicia—A Note," *ExpTim* 71 (1959-60): 52-53.

[50] In Gal 1:22 Paul said that he was "personally unknown" (literally "unknown by face") to the churches in Judea. Acts does not necessarily conflict with this. Paul may have been known more by reputation than by face, and his persecution efforts probably concentrated more on Jerusalem than the rest of Judea. See H. E. Dana, "Where Did Paul Persecute the Church?" *ATR* 20 (1938): 16-26. Gal 1:23, on the other hand, is strikingly in agreement with the entire picture of Acts 9:1-30: "The man who formerly persecuted us is now preaching the faith he once tried to destroy."

[51] K. N. Giles, "Luke's Use of the Term 'Ekklesia' with Special Reference to Acts 20.28 and 9.31," *NTS* 31 (1985): 135-42.

deliverance the church finds peace and continues to flourish (cf. 5:42). In this case the respite would last until a fresh outbreak of persecution occurred under Herod in chap. 12.

2. Peter's Witness in the Coastal Towns (9:32-43)

With Paul home in Tarsus, the narrative focuses once more on Peter. He last appeared in connection with the Samaritan mission (8:14-25). Now he participated in the greater Judean mission, evangelizing the coastal cities. Finally, he would witness to a Gentile, a key incident in establishing the mission "to the ends of the earth" (10:1–11:18). This small section on Peter's witness to the coastal towns consists of two miracle stories: the healing of Aeneas (vv. 32-35) and the raising of Dorcas (vv. 36-43).

(1) The Healing of Aeneas (9:32-35)

[32]As Peter traveled about the country, he went to visit the saints in Lydda. [33]There he found a man named Aeneas, a paralytic who had been bedridden for eight years. [34]"Aeneas," Peter said to him, "Jesus Christ heals you. Get up and take care of your mat." Immediately Aeneas got up. [35]All those who lived in Lydda and Sharon saw him and turned to the Lord.

9:32-35 Peter is described as "traveling about," evidently indicating a preaching tour.[52] He stopped in Lydda to visit the "saints" there.[53] Just how the Christian community began there we are not told. Perhaps it was the product of Philip's ministry, since he would have passed through Lydda on his journey northward from Azotus to Caesarea (8:40). At Lydda, presumably in the Christian community,[54] Peter found a paralytic by the name of Aeneas, who had been bedridden for eight years.[55] Peter took the initiative to heal Aeneas without any request, much as Jesus did on occasion (cf. Luke 7:13-15; 13:12). The healing was accomplished by a healing word, calling on the name of Jesus.[56] Peter then told Aeneas to

---

[52]Basing his view on Acts 12:17, with its reference to Peter's going to "another place," F. W. Beare argues that the ministry of Peter in the coastal cities should come chronologically at that point, i.e., after his escape from prison in chap. 12 ("The Sequence of Events in Acts 9-15 and the Career of Peter," *JBL* 62 [1943]: 295-306).

[53]Lydda is the OT town of Lod (cf. 1 Chr 8:12). Located some thirty miles northwest of Jerusalem on the old road to Joppa, it was a center of the purple dye trade and later a center of rabbinic learning. See K. Lake and H. J. Cadbury, *The Beginnings of Christianity*, Part 1: *The Acts of the Apostles*, vol. 4: *English Translation and Commentary* (London: Macmillan, 1933), 108.

[54]It is often argued that Aeneas was not a Christian. If, however, the "there" of v. 33 is taken as referring to the "saints in Lydda," rather than merely "Lydda," he is associated with the Christians. See Pesch, *Apostelgeschichte* 1:318.

[55]The Greek could also be rendered "bedridden from the age of eight."

[56]The verb ἰᾶται is generally taken as a present: "Jesus *heals* you." It could possibly be

rise and "prepare [his] couch" ("take care of your mat," NIV). The expression is thoroughly ambiguous. It could be taken in the sense of his folding up his mat, just as Jesus commanded another paralytic to rise and take up his (Mark 2:11; Luke 5:24). The same wording, however, is used for preparing a couch for dining, the Jewish custom being to dine while reclining on a couch. If Peter's directions are taken in this sense, the reference would be to the man's thorough recovery and taking of sustenance for further strength (cf. Luke 8:55; Acts 9:19). In either case, Aeneas's ability to rise to his feet and prepare the mat is certain evidence that his paralysis had been cured.

Lydda was located in the fertile coastal plain of Sharon, which extends north from Joppa to Mt. Carmel. Luke said the people of the region turned to the Lord as a result of Aeneas's healing. One recalls how the news of Jesus' miracles also spread to the surrounding neighborhood and attracted crowds to him. As we have seen before, the miracles in Acts are signs of the power of Jesus and often serve as the initial basis that leads to ultimate commitment. They are never, however, a substitute for faith (cf. 3:9f. with 3:19f.).

An interesting linkage exists between the two healing stories in 9:32-43. For one, the person healed is designated by name, which was usually not the case in early miracle stories and perhaps reflects vivid community reminiscence. Second, the Christians are referred to as "saints" in both accounts (vv. 34,41), a point the NIV obscures by using "believers" in v. 41. "Saints" is a rather rare designation for believers in Acts. Finally, the command to "rise" (*anastēthi*) is central to both healings, Aeneas from his paralysis (v. 34), Dorcas from death (v. 40). These close relationships could indicate that these two stories of Peter's healing in the Plain of Sharon were bound inseparably in the tradition Luke followed.[57]

(2) The Raising of Dorcas (9:36-43)

[36]In Joppa there was a disciple named Tabitha (which, when translated, is Dorcas), who was always doing good and helping the poor. [37]About that time she became sick and died, and her body was washed and placed in an upstairs room. [38]Lydda was near Joppa; so when the disciples heard that Peter was in Lydda, they sent two men to him and urged him, "Please come at once!"

[39]Peter went with them, and when he arrived he was taken upstairs to the room. All the widows stood around him, crying and showing him the robes and other clothing that Dorcas had made while she was still with them.

[40]Peter sent them all out of the room; then he got down on his knees and prayed. Turning toward the dead woman, he said, "Tabitha, get up." She opened

---

a perfect: "Jesus has healed you." See H. J. Cadbury, "A Possible Perfect in Acts ix.34," *JTS* 49 (1948): 57-58.

[57] Schneider, *Apostelgeschichte* 2:47.

her eyes, and seeing Peter she sat up. [41]He took her by the hand and helped her to her feet. Then he called the believers and the widows and presented her to them alive. [42]This became known all over Joppa, and many people believed in the Lord. [43]Peter stayed in Joppa for some time with a tanner named Simon.

The story of Dorcas is reminiscent of earlier raisings of the dead, such as Elijah's raising the son of the widow of Zarephath (1 Kgs 17:17-24) and the raising of the Shunammite woman's son by Elisha (2 Kgs 4:32-37), both of which are in turn echoed in the story of the widow's son, who was raised by Jesus (Luke 7:11-17). The closest correspondence of all, however, is to be found in Jesus' raising of Jairus's daughter (Luke 8:49-56; Mark 5:35-43).

9:36 The story takes place in Joppa, the main port city of Judea, located on the Philistine coast some ten or eleven miles northwest of Lydda. In Joppa was a "female disciple" named Tabitha.[58] Luke provided the translation "Dorcas" for his Greek readers. Both terms mean *gazelle* in English. She is described as "always doing good and helping the poor," which enhances the pathos of her death.

9:37-38 While Peter was still in Lydda, Tabitha became sick and died. According to custom, her body was washed for burial. It was then placed in an upper room, which was not particularly the custom. Perhaps this was the most available room. It could also be that the Christians of Joppa were performing, as it were, a symbolic act, indicating their faith that she would rise.[59] In any event, knowing that Peter was close by—a distance of three hours journey by foot—they sent two men to Lydda to urge Peter to hasten to Joppa without delay.[60]

9:39 When Peter arrived at Joppa, he was taken to the upper room and there greeted by a group of widows who were in mourning. Acts 6:1-6 already evidenced numerous Jewish Christian widows. In the later Pauline churches a special order of "senior" widows looked after the other widows in the congregations (1 Tim 5:9f.). Though such a degree of organization probably had not developed in the churches of Dorcas's day, her charity to the widows would qualify her as a genuine precursor of those women who helped widows so that the church would not be burdened (1 Tim 5:16). The helplessness of these widows further heightens the pathos of the story. Their neediness is exemplified in their showing Peter the tunics and robes Dorcas had made, which they probably were wearing.[61]

---

[58]"Female disciple" (μαθήτρια) occurs only here in the NT, although it is not uncommon in Greek literature.

[59]Marshall, *Acts*, 178.

[60]Note how frequently messengers occur in pairs in Luke-Acts: Luke 7:18f.; 10:1; 19:29; 22:8; Acts 8:14; 10:17; 15:35.

[61]Cf. Bruce (*Acts:* NIC, 212), who points to the middle voice for the verb "show"— "showing on themselves."

9:40 Peter requested that they leave him alone in the room with the body, just as Jesus had sent everyone from the room except the girl's parents and his three most trusted disciples when he raised Jairus's daughter (Mark 5:40). Falling to his knees before the body, Peter prayed, turned to the body, and said, "Tabitha, arise." Naturally Peter addressed her by the Aramaic form of her name, and Luke was careful to preserve the distinction. He had used the Greek form Dorcas in his narrative (v. 39). But Luke was perhaps aware of more than a linguistic nicety. Jesus' words to Jairus's daughter were, "Little girl, arise," which Mark preserved in the original Aramaic form, "*Talitha koum*" (Mark 5:41). In Aramaic, Peter's words would have been almost identical, "*Tabitha koum*"—only a single consonant's difference. In the Aramaic churches who cherished the story of Tabitha, the similarity would not be missed. In the footsteps of his Master, and through the power of his Master (the *prayer* shows that), Peter worked the same miracle of "resurrection." As with Jairus's daughter, the widow's son at Nain, Lazarus, and Dorcas, it was not a matter of resurrection but of resuscitation, of temporary restoration of life. But all the miracles of raising from the dead are in a real sense "signs," pointers to the one who has power even over death and is himself the resurrection and the life for all who believe and trust in him.

9:41-42 The story concludes with Peter presenting Dorcas alive to "the believers and the widows." That the widows are separated from the believers does not indicate the widows were not Christians but serves to single them out as the group who served to benefit most from her restoration to life. The description that Peter "presented" her to them reminds one of the similar expression of how Elijah "gave" her son back to the widow of Zarephath (1 Kgs 17:23) and how Jesus "gave" her son back to the widow of Nain (Luke 7:15). In these two instances the restoration of an only son to a destitute widow was indeed a gift, and Peter's presentation of Dorcas alive was no less a gift to the widows of Joppa. As with the healing of Aeneas, so with the raising of Dorcas, the news spread quickly in Sharon's Plain; and many believed in the Lord, in the *risen* Lord.

9:43 Peter remained in Joppa, residing with a tanner who shared with him the name of Simon. Luke often mentioned the names of hosts or the particular trade of persons.[62] He had an eye for human-interest detail. This particular tanner lived by the sea. This location may be due to the fact that tanners used sea water in their trade, but the ultimate significance of the "address" would be to help Cornelius's messengers find

---

[62]For hosts see 9:11; 21:8,16; 28:7; for occupations see 8:9,26; 10:1; 13:6-7; 14:13; 16:14,16; 18:3; 19:24.

Peter in the story that follows.[63] In a real sense, Peter had been moved by God ever closer to Caesarea, where the greatest demonstration of God's leading would take place when Peter was urged to witness there to the Gentile Cornelius.

3. Peter's Witness to a Gentile God-fearer (10:1–11:18)

Chapter 10 marks a high point in the church's expanding mission. God led Peter to witness to the Gentile Cornelius. Through that experience Peter became fully convinced of God's purposes to reach all peoples and hence became one of the greatest advocates of the mission to the Gentiles. The Hellenists had been the leaders in this outreach, Philip having evangelized Samaria and having baptized the Ethiopian eunuch. The latter incident in many ways parallels that of Peter and Cornelius. Like Cornelius, the eunuch seems to have been both a "God-fearer" and a Gentile. The significant new development in chap. 10 is that Peter became committed to the Gentile mission. His testimony would be instrumental in leading the mother church in Jerusalem to endorse the Gentile mission and thus lend it legitimacy and continuity with the ministry of the apostles (11:1-18; 15:7-11).

The Gentile mission was not an easy step for the Jewish Christians to take. It involved two major issues. One was the question of whether Gentiles had to become Jews in order to become Christians, i.e., should they undergo Jewish proselyte procedure when they were converted to Christianity? This would have required the circumcision of male converts and the adoption for all converts of such Jewish legal distinctives as the kosher food laws. Because God granted the gift of the Spirit to the Gentiles in Cornelius's home without their subscribing to proselyte procedure, Peter became convinced that such Jewish conversion procedures were not necessary for the Christian mission to the Gentiles (cf. 15:7-11). The second major issue involved the question of table fellowship between Jewish and Gentile Christians. Since Gentiles did not follow kosher practices, Jewish Christians like Peter were exposed to a real situation of compromise when they associated with them. It is not by chance that Peter's vision at Joppa involved the question of clean and unclean foods. His association with the Gentiles in Cornelius's home raised that question acutely. Both questions were answered for Peter in the experience with Cornelius because he was convinced that God accepted Gentiles without circumcision and that he could himself in good

---

[63]The sea breeze certainly did not hurt either; it removed the odor of the hides. For the view that Simon was a tanner of fishnets, see J. McConnachie, "Simon a Tanner (Burseus) (Acts ix.43, x.6, 32)," *ExpTim* 36 (1924-25): 90. The linguistic evidence, however, would indicate that the word βυρσεύς in Greek is generally restricted to the tanning of hides.

faith enjoy table fellowship with his Gentile-Christian brothers and sisters. The issues were not, however, fully settled for the Jewish Christians as a whole. Both issues resurfaced at the Jerusalem Conference (chap. 15) after Paul and Barnabas's successful mission to the Gentiles, and a compromise solution was agreed upon at that time.

Acts 10:1–11:18 is the longest single narrative in all of Acts. This in itself witnesses to the great importance Luke placed on the incident. It usually is organized into seven separate "scenes."[64] The narrative begins with the vision of Cornelius (10:1-8) and immediately follows with a corresponding vision of Peter (10:9-16). The two visions link together and result in Peter's journey to Cornelius's home (10:17-23). Three scenes take place at Cornelius's house. Peter's initial encounter with Cornelius involved their sharing their visions with each other (10:24-33). This was followed by Peter's sermon to Cornelius and his associates (10:34-43). The sermon was broken off by God's intervention when he sent the Holy Spirit upon the Gentiles (10:44-48). The final scene takes place in Jerusalem, where Peter defended his conduct with Cornelius before the Christians there and convinced them of God's intention to reach the Gentiles for Christ (11:1-18). There is considerable duplication between the scenes. Cornelius's vision is told four times (10:3-6,22,30-32; 11:13-14). Peter's vision is given in detail twice (10:9-16; 11:4-10). In fact, all of 11:3-17 is basically a summary of chap. 10.

This device of repetition serves a twofold function.[65] First, it makes for a vivid narrative; it is related in dialogue, which gives the reader a sense of "being there." Second, and more significantly, it underlines the importance of the event. It will be repeated yet a final time in Peter's testimony at the Jerusalem Conference (15:7-11).[66]

---

[64]Among modern commentators following the seven-part outline are Schneider and Haenchen. It is an ancient division of the text, found in the earliest church fathers. See F. Bovon, *De Vocatione Gentium* (Tübingen: Mohr-Siebeck, 1967), 25.

[65]For a structural analysis that views the repetition as conveying "the limitlessness" of God's grace, see R. Barthes, "L'Analyse Structurale du Recit—A Propos d'Actes x-xi," *RSR* 58 (1970): 17-37.

[66]In an influential essay, M. Dibelius argued that the original nucleus of Acts 10 was the story of Gentile conversion which Luke elevated to the rank of a central event by adding the motifs of Peter's speech, his vision, and the clean/unclean question ("The Conversion of Cornelius," *Studies in the Acts of the Apostles*, ed. H. Greeven and trans. M. Ling [London: SCM, 1956], 109-22). For a development of this view, which sees Luke working with three originally separate traditions (the two visions and Peter's speech), see F. Bovon, "Tradition et redaction en Actes 10, 1-11, 18," *TZ* 26 (1970): 22-45. For an opposing view that sees the two visions as being part of a unitary tradition from the beginning, see K. Löning, "Die Korneliustradition," *BZ* 18 (1974): 1-19 and Marshall, *Acts*, 182-83.

(1) The Vision of Cornelius (10:1-8)

[1]At Caesarea there was a man named Cornelius, a centurion in what was known as the Italian Regiment. [2]He and all his family were devout and God-fearing; he gave generously to those in need and prayed to God regularly. [3]One day at about three in the afternoon he had a vision. He distinctly saw an angel of God, who came to him and said, "Cornelius!"

[4]Cornelius stared at him in fear. "What is it, Lord?" he asked.

The angel answered, "Your prayers and gifts to the poor have come up as a memorial offering before God. [5]Now send men to Joppa to bring back a man named Simon who is called Peter. [6]He is staying with Simon the tanner, whose house is by the sea."

[7]When the angel who spoke to him had gone, Cornelius called two of his servants and a devout soldier who was one of his attendants. [8]He told them everything that had happened and sent them to Joppa.

10:1 The narrative begins by introducing the first main character. His name was Cornelius, a centurion of the Italian regiment who resided in Caesarea. Each of these details is significant. That he was mentioned by name is perhaps indicative that he was well known in the early Christian communities for whom Luke wrote.[67] He was a military man with the rank of centurion, which placed him in command of 100 soldiers.[68]

One is immediately reminded of Jesus' encounter with a centurion at Capernaum who was described as well respected by the Jewish community, much like Cornelius (Luke 7:1-10). Centurions generally are depicted in a favorable light throughout the Gospels and Acts, and this may well be evidence of the success of the early Christian mission among the military. Cornelius's division is described as the "Italian regiment," a group that is documented as occupying Palestine after A.D. 69.[69] The place of his residence is of some importance, since Caesarea

---

[67]"Cornelius" represents the second of three names Romans generally bore and was fairly common among the military, largely because in 82 B.C., P. Cornelius Sulla freed 10,000 slaves. Many of these freedmen served in the military and took the name of their benefactor. See Cadbury, *The Book of Acts in History*, 76.

[68]The main division in a Roman army was the *legion*, consisting of 6,000 men. These were divided into ten cohorts of 600 soldiers each. These in turn were subdivided into groups of 100 under a centurion, which groups were considered the backbone of the army. The Roman historian Polybius described centurions as "not seekers of adventure but men who can command, steady in action, reliable." Cf. F. J. Foakes-Jackson, *The Acts of the Apostles*, MNTC (New York: Harper, 1931), 88.

[69]An inscription found in Austria indicates the Italian cohort was an auxiliary division. (Auxiliary forces usually consisted of soldiers drawn from the territory where they were located rather than consisting of Roman citizens, as was the case with the regular legions.) See *Beginnings* 5:427-45. Whether a Roman division would have been located in Caesarea in the period of Herod Agrippa's rule over Palestine (A.D. 41–44) is debated. Quite possibly some Roman auxiliary forces were under his command, and one corps is known to have been

was from A.D. 6 the provincial capital and place of residence of the Roman governor. Unlike Lydda and Joppa, which were mainly inhabited by Jews, Caesarea was a Hellenistic-style city with a dominant population of Gentiles. Originally a small town named Strato's Tower, it was rebuilt on a grand style by Herod the Great, complete with a man-made harbor, a theater, an amphitheater, a hippodrome, and a temple dedicated to Caesar. There was a substantial Jewish minority there and considerable friction between the Jews and the larger Gentile community.[70] It was fitting that it should be the place where Peter came to terms with his own prejudices and realized that human barriers have no place with the God who "does not show favoritism."

10:2 Cornelius already had some preparation for the gospel he was soon to hear. Luke described him as "devout" (*eusebēs*) and "God-fearing" (*phoboumenos ton theon*). There is some question about whether the term "God-fearer" should be seen as a technical term designating a special class of Gentile adherents to the Jewish synagogue who had not taken the full step of becoming proselytes to Judaism.[71] Cornelius, however, was clearly a Gentile who worshiped God and supported the Jewish religious community. In fact, he was described as performing two of the three main acts of Jewish piety—prayer and almsgiving. (Only fasting is not mentioned.) In short, his devotion to God put him well on the way, preparing him for receiving the gospel and for the full inclusion in God's people that he could not have found in the synagogue.

10:3 In the course of the practice of Cornelius's piety, God spoke to him. Cornelius was keeping one of the three traditional Jewish times of

---

located in Caesarea. See Bruce, *Acts:* NIC, 214-15. That Cornelius was retired from service and settled in Caesarea is also possible, as the presence of his rather large household might indicate.

[70] J. D. Williams, *Acts*, GNC (San Francisco: Harper & Row, 1985), 171.

[71] The view that the terms σεβούμενος and φοβούμενος refer to a special class of Gentile synagogue worshipers has been generally assumed by scholars. For example, see G. F. Moore, *Judaism in the First Centuries of the Christian Era* (Cambridge: Harvard University Press, 1927), 1:323-26. One of the first to challenge whether they are technical terms was Lake in *Beginnings* 5:74-96. More recently A. T. Kraabel has questioned, largely on the archaeological evidence, whether there was a significant group of Gentiles attached to the Diaspora synagogues at all ("The Disappearance of the God-fearers," *Numen* 28 [1981]: 113-26). See also M. Wilcox, "The 'God-fearers' in Acts—A Reconsideration," *JSNT* 13 (1981): 102-22. There is, however, considerable literary evidence for such a group of non-proselyte Gentile adherents to the synagogues of the NT period. See T. M. Finn, "The God-fearers Reconsidered," *CBQ* 47 (1985): 75-84. It probably is best not to consider σεβούμενος and φοβούμενος as technical terms invariably referring to such Gentile adherents but to give attention to each separate context in which the word occurs. In the case of Cornelius, the context clarifies that he was indeed a Gentile worshiper of God and seemingly not a proselyte to Judaism.

prayer, the afternoon hour of 3 p.m., which coincided with the *Tamid* sacrifice in the temple. God's agent was an angel who appeared to him in a vision. Frequently in Luke-Acts God used prayer time as the opportunity for leading to new avenues of ministry.[72] Prayer is a time for opening oneself up to God, thus enabling his leading. Visions occur frequently in Acts as a vehicle of divine leading, which illustrates that the major advances in the Christian witness are all under divine direction.[73] In no case is that clearer than in the present instance. Cornelius and Peter took no initiative in what transpired. Their mutual visions illustrate that all was totally under God's direction.

10:4 Cornelius's response to the heavenly epiphany is understandable. It was a response of awe and reverence (*emphobos*), not of cowering fear (v. 4). Much like Paul, Cornelius addressed his heavenly visitant with a respectful "Lord." The angel responded by noting that God was aware of his piety.[74] His prayer and his acts of charity had gone up as a "memorial offering" in the presence of God. The term "memorial" (literally, "remembrance," *mnemosynon*) is Old Testament sacrificial language.[75] Cornelius's prayers and works of charity had risen like the sweet savor of a sincerely offered sacrifice, well-pleasing to God (cf. Phil 4:18). The importance of Cornelius's piety is reiterated throughout the narrative (vv. 2,4,22,35).

10:5-8 One would like to know the content of Cornelius's prayer. Could it possibly have requested his full acceptance by God, his full inclusion in God's people?[76] At this point the angel revealed nothing to Cornelius about his ultimate purpose for him, simply that he was to send to Joppa for a certain Simon named Peter. The additional note that Peter was staying with the tanner Simon serves to link the narrative with the previous (9:43) and was essential in providing the needed directions for locating him. Still very much in the dark about what God had in store for him, Cornelius neither questioned the angel further nor hesitated in complying with directions. He called forth two of his servants[77] and a "devout" soldier, who probably was a worshiper of God like himself. The Greek text adds that all three "continually waited on him," which is a classical expression for "orderlies," for those who are most tried and true. Cornelius was thus careful to choose his most trustworthy attendants to go to Joppa and seek Peter.

---

[72]Luke 3:21f.; 6:12-16; 9:18-22,28-31; 22:39-46; Acts 1:14; 13:1-3.

[73]Cf. 9:10,12; 10:3,17,19; 11:5; 16:9-10; 18:9; 27:23,25.

[74]Angels were often viewed as intercessors in prayer (cf. Tob 12:12).

[75]Lev 2:2,9,16; cf. Phil 4:18; Heb 13:15f.

[76]Suggested by Pesch, 1:337.

[77]The word for servant (οἰκέτης) refers to household servants who were considered part of the family, as opposed to mere slaves (δοῦλοι). Cf. Luke 16:13; Rom 14:4; 1 Pet 2:18.

(2) The Vision of Peter (10:9-16)

⁹**About noon the following day as they were on their journey and approaching the city, Peter went up on the roof to pray. ¹⁰He became hungry and wanted something to eat, and while the meal was being prepared, he fell into a trance. ¹¹He saw heaven opened and something like a large sheet being let down to earth by its four corners. ¹²It contained all kinds of four-footed animals, as well as reptiles of the earth and birds of the air. ¹³Then a voice told him, "Get up, Peter. Kill and eat."**

¹⁴**"Surely not, Lord!" Peter replied. "I have never eaten anything impure or unclean."**

¹⁵**The voice spoke to him a second time, "Do not call anything impure that God has made clean."**

¹⁶**This happened three times, and immediately the sheet was taken back to heaven.**

10:9 Joppa was about thirty miles to the south of Caesarea. Having set out the same day as Cornelius's vision or early the next morning, the attendants approached Joppa about noon the next day. Peter in the meantime had gone up to the flat roof of Simon's house in order to pray.[78] Hungry and waiting for a meal to be prepared, he fell into a trance.

10:10-16 Noon was not a usual weekday meal time. The custom was to have a light midmorning meal and a more substantial repast in the late afternoon. If Peter had missed his midmorning breakfast, it would explain his drowsiness all the more.[79] Roofs were often covered with awnings. Perhaps that or the glimpse of a distant sail at sea provided the vehicle for the vision Peter had. He saw a large vessel or container like a large sheet descending from heaven, held by its four corners. Some interpreters suggest a symbolic meaning here, the four corners representing the ends of the earth in a vision, the ultimate meaning of which points to the worldwide mission.[80] The sheet contained representatives of all the animals of the earth—four-footed animals, reptiles of the land, and birds of the air.[81] It thus symbolized the entire animal world and included

---

[78]Roofs were a common place of prayer and worship. Cf. 2 Kgs 23:12; Neh 8:16; Jer 19:13; 32:29; Zeph 1:5. Noon was not a set hour of prayer for Jews, but prayer was not confined to the prescribed times.

[79]The word πρόσπεινος, used here for Peter's hunger, is only found elsewhere in first-century literature in an account about an eye doctor named Demosthenes from Laodicea. See F. W. Dillistone, "Prospeinos (Acts x.10)," *ExpTim* 46 (1934-35): 380. This observation is often cited in support of the medical theory for Lukan authorship, as is the occurrence of ἀρχαῖς ("corners") in v. 11, a term that is used in medical writings for the ends of bandages.

[80]So Pesch, *Apostelgeschichte* 1:338.

[81]This is the same threefold division of the animal world as found in the Noah account of Gen 6:20 and the creation account of Gen 1:30. Cf. Rom 1:23.

clean as well as unclean animals.[82] A voice from heaven commanded Peter to rise, kill from among the animals, and satisfy his hunger. Peter was perplexed by the vision and protested vigorously. What the voice requested was strictly against the law.[83] Never had he eaten anything defiled and unclean.[84] The voice ignored his protest, reissuing the command and adding, "Do not call anything impure that God has made clean." The command came three times; each time Peter objected and fell into further confusion.[85]

Some scholars feel that Peter's vision dealt more with food laws than with interaction with Gentiles. This is to overlook the fact that the two are inextricably related. In Lev 20:24b-26 the laws of clean and unclean are linked precisely to Israel's separation from the rest of the nations. The Jewish food laws presented a real problem for Jewish Christians in the outreach to the Gentiles. One simply could not dine in a Gentile's home without inevitably transgressing those laws either by the consumption of unclean flesh or of flesh that had not been prepared in a kosher, i.e., ritually proper, fashion (cf. Acts 15:20). Jesus dealt with the problem of clean and unclean, insisting that external things like foods did not defile a person but the internals of heart and speech and thought render one truly unclean (Mark 7:14-23). In Mark 7:19b Mark added the parenthetical comment that Jesus' saying ultimately declared all foods clean. This was precisely the point of Peter's vision: God declared the unclean to be clean.[86] In Mark 7

---

[82]In general, unclean animals were those which showed some anomaly with reference to their species as a whole. Thus sea creatures without the usual fish scales were unclean. Four-footed beasts were considered normal if they had cloven hooves and chewed the cud. Pigs do not chew the cud and are thus unclean. See Lev 11. See also G. J. Wenham, "The Theology of Unclean Food," *EvQ* 53 (1981): 6-15.

[83]Cf. Lev 11:2-47; Deut 14:3-21. Although no evidence suggests that clean animals were defiled by mere contact with unclean animals, one would assume Peter's reaction was provoked by his sheer disgust at so many unclean animals making any further discrimination impossible. Possibly *only* unclean animals were in the sheet.

[84]C. House argues that the two terms (κοινός and ἀκάθαρτος) in v. 14 should be distinguished, κοινός referring to something defiled by association and ἀκάθαρτος being something inherently unclean, thus making the application to the Gentile mission more precise— unclean Gentiles and Jewish Christians defiled by association with them ("Defilement by Association: Some Insights from the Usage of Koinos/Koinoō in Acts 10 and 11," *AUSS* 21 [1983]: 143-53). This might hold for 11:8, where a disjunctive ἤ ("or") occurs, but not for 10:14, where the two terms are linked by the conjunctive καί ("and").

[85]Pesch (*Apostelgeschichte* 1:339) cites an ancient source, according to which one could only be certain that a vision was truly from God rather than from demonic influences if it occurred three times. Whether or not this ancient mode of "testing the spirits" is at play here, surely the importance of its message for Peter was the primary reason for the repetition.

[86]E. Haulotte sees a "new creation" theme in Peter's vision. The animals represented all those of God's original creation. God declared them all clean, thus establishing a new community in Christ in which all people are acceptable ("Foundation d'une communauté de

Jesus' teaching on clean/unclean was immediately followed by his ministry to a Gentile woman (7:24-30), just as Peter's vision regarding clean and unclean foods was followed by *his* witness to a Gentile. It is simply not possible to fully accept someone with whom you are unwilling to share in the intimacy of table fellowship. The early church had to solve the problem of kosher food laws in order to launch a mission to the Gentiles. Purity distinctions and human discrimination are of a single piece.

(3) Peter's Visit to Cornelius (10:17-23)

[17]While Peter was wondering about the meaning of the vision, the men sent by Cornelius found out where Simon's house was and stopped at the gate. [18]They called out, asking if Simon who was known as Peter was staying there.

[19]While Peter was still thinking about the vision, the Spirit said to him, "Simon, three men are looking for you. [20]So get up and go downstairs. Do not hesitate to go with them, for I have sent them."

[21]Peter went down and said to the men, "I'm the one you're looking for. Why have you come?"

[22]The men replied, "We have come from Cornelius the centurion. He is a righteous and God-fearing man, who is respected by all the Jewish people. A holy angel told him to have you come to his house so that he could hear what you have to say." [23]Then Peter invited the men into the house to be his guests.

The next day Peter started out with them, and some of the brothers from Joppa went along.

10:17-23 At this point Peter was still in the dark about the meaning of his vision. What possible point could this implied nullification of the food laws have? At that very moment the answer to his puzzle was beginning to come forth, as Cornelius's messengers arrived at Simon the tanner's. Now the Spirit spoke to him directly. With Cornelius it had been an angel; with Peter's vision, a voice from heaven. Now it was the Holy Spirit. All three represent the same reality—the direction of God. Nothing was left to chance. All was coordinated by the divine leading. The Spirit directed Peter to the three messengers standing at the gate and identified them as men he had sent (v. 19f.).[87] In accordance with the Spirit's direction, Peter descended the outside staircase that led from the roof to the courtyard below, identified himself, and eagerly inquired why they were seeking him. By now he had a good notion that they were a key piece in the puzzle of his vision. The men replied with the information Peter

---

Type Universal: Actes 10, 1-11, 18," *RSR* 58 [1970]: 63-100). The most fascinating interpretation was that of Augustine, who applied the vision of Peter directly to the mission of the church. The church is to "kill and eat," to kill the sins of the godless and digest them into the life of the church (Bovon, *De Vocatione Gentium*, 177-80).

[87]B reads "two men" at v. 19, and many scholars feel this may be the original reading. If so, the soldier would not be considered a messenger but one who functioned as a guard.

needed, which is all material the reader has already encountered. Luke could have summarized by simply noting that they told him of Cornelius's vision. Instead, by employing dialogue, he repeated and thus underlined the important points of the vision.

Two things in particular are emphasized—the devoutness of Cornelius and the leading of God.[88] There is a slight advance over the original account of the vision in vv. 4-6. The messengers informed Peter that Cornelius was to "hear what you have to say" (v. 22). Peter began to see the ramifications of his vision. He was to witness to this centurion whom God had directed to him. That Peter was beginning to understand is exemplified by his inviting them to spend the evening as guests. Already he was beginning to have fellowship with Gentiles he formerly considered unclean.[89]

(4) Shared Visions (10:24-33)

[24]The following day he arrived in Caesarea. Cornelius was expecting them and had called together his relatives and close friends. [25]As Peter entered the house, Cornelius met him and fell at his feet in reverence. [26]But Peter made him get up. "Stand up," he said, "I am only a man myself."

[27]Talking with him, Peter went inside and found a large gathering of people. [28]He said to them: "You are well aware that it is against our law for a Jew to associate with a Gentile or visit him. But God has shown me that I should not call any man impure or unclean. [29]So when I was sent for, I came without raising any objection. May I ask why you sent for me?"

[30]Cornelius answered: "Four days ago I was in my house praying at this hour, at three in the afternoon. Suddenly a man in shining clothes stood before me [31]and said, 'Cornelius, God has heard your prayer and remembered your gifts to the poor. [32]Send to Joppa for Simon who is called Peter. He is a guest in the home of Simon the tanner, who lives by the sea.' [33]So I sent for you immediately, and it was good of you to come. Now we are all here in the presence of God to listen to everything the Lord has commanded you to tell us."

10:24-26 Peter and the three messengers set out the next morning accompanied by several of the Jewish Christians from Joppa. According to Peter's report in Jerusalem, there were six of the latter (11:12). After spending the night en route, they arrived at Caesarea on the fourth day

---

[88]The reference to the angel "telling him" in v. 22 employs the word χρηματίζω, which in this context has the meaning of a divine communication by revelation. The word seems to have originally meant *to do business*, then *to consult an oracle*, then *to be divinely directed* (as here), and finally *to receive a name* (from one's activity or business). The latter meaning occurs in Acts 11:26. See A. T. Robertson, *WP* 3:139.

[89]To be sure, the problem of table fellowship was less acute when a Jew entertained a Gentile than in the reverse situation, as would be the case when Peter dined at Cornelius's (v. 48b). Still, scrupulous Jews avoided any association with Gentiles (G. Krodel, *Acts*, ACNT [Minneapolis: Augsburg, 1986], 192, citing *Jub.* 22:16 and Joseph and Asenath 7:1).

from Cornelius's original vision (cf. v. 30). Cornelius had invited a number of relatives and close[90] friends to hear Peter, and they were all gathered at his home when the party from Joppa arrived. This would prove to be of considerable importance to subsequent events. The movement of the Spirit in Cornelius's home would not be an isolated conversion but would involve a considerable number of Gentiles, what Luke called "household" salvation (11:14). As Peter entered the house,[91] Cornelius fell at his feet in a gesture of reverence and respect.[92] Peter protested vigorously—even more in the Western text, which adds, "What are you doing?" to the Alexandrian reading, "I am only a man myself." Compare the similar protest of Paul and Barnabas when the Gentiles at Lystra attempted to sacrifice to them as gods (Acts 14:14f.).[93]

10:27-29 After a polite introductory conversation with Cornelius, Peter related the unusual circumstances of his coming. He did not tell of his vision but rather of the conclusion he had drawn from the experience. Everyone present needed to realize how unacceptable it was for a Jew to associate closely or even visit in the home of a person of another race.[94] God, however, had shown Peter that he should not call another person common or unclean (v. 28). Actually, Peter's vision had only related to unclean foods, but he had understood fully the symbolism of the creatures in the sheet. All were God's creatures; all were declared clean. God had led him to Cornelius, and God had declared Cornelius clean. The old purity laws could no longer separate Jew from Gentile. Since God had shown himself no respecter of persons, neither could Peter be one anymore. Still, Peter had not realized the full implication of God's sending

---

[90] Ἀναγκαίους—"intimate, familiar, close."

[91] The Greek text has simply "as Peter entered" and does not specify "the house." Assuming Peter was entering the outskirts of the city, the Western text adds that Cornelius sent a slave out as a scout, who returned to announce Peter's arrival. For a similar practice among present-day Arabs, see E. F. F. Bishop, "Acts x.25," *ExpTim* 61 (1949-50): 31.

[92] Such behavior would not have been unusual for a Gentile like Cornelius. Prostrating oneself at the feet of another was a common Near Eastern gesture of respect, and Cornelius surely identified Peter with his angelic vision and may well have seen him as more than an ordinary man. Bowing as an act of reverence is particularly frequent in Matthew: cf. 8:2; 9:18; 15:25; 18:26; 20:20; cf. Luke 8:41; Acts 9:4; 22:7.

[93] Even the angel of Rev 19:10; 22:9 refused such gestures of worship. Such strict monotheism was absolutely essential in a Gentile culture where humans were often revered as being related to divinities. Herod Agrippa offers a contrast with Peter's refusal to be revered (Acts 12:22f.).

[94] No specific law forbade Jews to associate with Gentiles, but the purity regulations rendered close social interaction virtually impossible. Robertson (*WP* 3:141) cites Juvenal's *Satire* 14.104f. and Tacitus's *Hist.* 5.5 as evidence from Gentile writers that such Jewish refusal to associate with Gentiles was in fact the practice. According to S. Wilson, this passage is the closest in Acts to actually abrogating the Jewish laws (*Luke and the Law* [Cambridge: University Press, 1983], 63-73).

him to Cornelius. He did not yet understand that God intended him to accept Cornelius as a *Christian brother*. So he asked Cornelius why he had sent for him. Cornelius responded by reiterating his vision (vv. 30-32).

10:30-32 This is now the *third* time the reader has encountered this experience. It is virtually a summary of vv. 3-8 with slight variations, such as the notice that it was now four days since the vision occurred[95] and the fact that he spoke of a "man in shining clothes" rather than an angel. A man in shining clothes is, of course, an angel; so it is merely a variation in expression.[96] Even Peter's location in Joppa is repeated in detail. The emphasis and the reason for the repetition is to underscore the importance of the divine direction that led to this scene. Peter was not yet fully certain *why* he was at Cornelius's house.

10:33 Everyone there, however, *including* Peter, was certain of one thing: *God* had brought them together. Cornelius also knew that God brought Peter to him to share something important. That is why he assembled family and friends. All were now waiting to hear the Lord's message from Peter (v. 33).[97] God had led him to Cornelius's house. But Peter had a message, *the* message, the word of life. It was now clear to him why God had led him there. He was to bear his witness to the gospel before this gathering of Gentiles.

(5) Peter's Witness (10:34-43)

34"Then Peter began to speak: "I now realize how true it is that God does not show favoritism 35but accepts men from every nation who fear him and do what is right. 36You know the message God sent to the people of Israel, telling the good news of peace through Jesus Christ, who is Lord of all. 37You know what has happened throughout Judea, beginning in Galilee after the baptism that John preached—38how God anointed Jesus of Nazareth with the Holy Spirit and power, and how he went around doing good and healing all who were under the power of the devil, because God was with him.

39"We are witnesses of everything he did in the country of the Jews and in Jerusalem. They killed him by hanging him on a tree, 40but God raised him from the dead on the third day and caused him to be seen. 41He was not seen by all the people, but by witnesses whom God had already chosen—by us who ate and drank with him after he rose from the dead. 42He commanded us to preach to the people and to testify that he is the one whom God appointed as judge of the living

---

[95]The Greek could be construed in v. 30 as "four days ago until this hour, I was praying," thus indicating Cornelius's continual prayer for four days. The NIV is surely correct in translating "at this hour."

[96]For dazzling garments representing heavenly beings, cf. Luke 9:29f.; 24:4; Acts 1:10.

[97]Cornelius's reference to being gathered together "in the presence of God" is very much the language of being assembled for *worship*, which is not inappropriate to this context. Cf. 1 Cor 5:4; Marshall, *Acts*, 189. The group gathered in Cornelius's home recalls the group gathered in Acts 1:13-14 awaiting Pentecost.

and the dead. [43]All the prophets testify about him that everyone who believes in him receives forgiveness of sins through his name."

10:34-35 Peter's sermon is somewhat unique among the speeches in Acts. Since it was addressed to Gentiles, one would expect it to differ somewhat from the other sermons of Peter, all of which were addressed to Jews. Still, it is quite different from Paul's sermons addressed to the Gentiles of Lystra (14:15-18) and Athens (17:22-31).

Cornelius and his family already were worshipers of God and thus had some prior preparation for the gospel. Peter could have assumed such knowledge on their part and not have to start by first introducing the basic monotheistic message of faith in God as he did when preaching to pagan Gentiles. Peter's sermon at Cornelius's basically followed the pattern of his prior sermons to the Jews but with several significant differences. One is found at the very outset, where he stressed that God shows no favoritism, accepts people from every nation, and that Jesus is "Lord of all." This emphasis on the universal gospel is particularly suited to a message to Gentiles. Peter's vision had led him to this basic insight that God does not discriminate between persons, that there are no divisions between "clean" and "unclean" people from the divine perspective. The Greek word used for favoritism (v. 34) is constructed on a Hebrew idiom meaning *to lift a face*.[98] Peter saw that God does not discriminate on the basis of race or ethnic background, looking up to some and down on others. But God does discriminate between those whose behavior is acceptable and those whose attitude is not acceptable. Those who reverence God and practice what is right are acceptable to him (v. 35; cf. Luke 8:21).

Peter was basing this statement specifically on Cornelius. Throughout the narrative his piety had been stressed—his constant prayers, his deeds of charity. This raises the problem of faith and works. Was God responding to Cornelius's works, "rewarding" him, so to speak, by bringing Peter with the saving gospel and granting him his gift of the Spirit? One must be careful not to introduce Paul's theology into a context that is not dealing with the same issues, but one should also note that even Paul was capable of describing the impartial justice of God as being based on one's good or evil works (Rom 2:9-11).[99] The early church fathers struggled with the question of faith and works in Cornelius, and perhaps Augustine's view

---

[98]For God's judgment on the basis of one's conduct, see also Gen 4:7; Rom 2:6; Rev 20:12f. For God's impartiality cf. Eph 6:9; Col 3:25; Jas 2:1,9; 1 Pet 1:17; 22:12. The idiom "lifting a face" pictures God as an oriental monarch lifting the face of a petitioner. To lift the petitioner's face is to receive him or her with favor (cf. Esth 4:11; 5:32, where the custom is different but the import is the same).

[99]For a helpful contrast between Rom 2 and Acts 10, see J. M. Bassler, "Luke and Paul on Impartiality," *Bib* 4 (1985): 546-52.

offers as good an answer as any. Cornelius, like Abraham, had shown himself to be a man of faith and trust in God. God was already working his grace in him, and it manifested itself in his good deeds.[100] Now God would show him his greatest grace in the gospel of Jesus Christ and the gift of the Spirit. The stress on both Cornelius's devoutness *and* his works is perhaps, then, a good corrective to an abused doctrine of grace with no implications for behavior and a reminder of James's dictum that at base, faith and works are inseparable.

10:36 As with Peter's other addresses in Acts, considerable stress is placed on God's act in Jesus Christ. This theme is introduced in v. 36, where Peter stressed the good news of peace through Jesus Christ.[101] There is an interesting interplay in the verse between the limited nature of the gospel's beginnings and its unlimited scope. God sent the gospel message to his people, "the people of Israel." But its *content* was peace, the peace Christ brings, who is "Lord of all." If he is truly Lord of *all*, then the gospel *and* Christ's peace are for all peoples, not just the people of Israel. Verse 36 echoes Isa 52:7; 57:19. In Eph 2:17 Paul employed the latter passage to argue the universal gospel and the reconciliation of Jew and Gentile in Christ. Peter also had come to see that it is a natural corollary that there can be no barriers between those who profess Christ as "Lord of all." He could not allow such nonessentials as particularistic Jewish food laws to separate him from Gentiles like Cornelius who were, like him, those for whom Christ died. Where Christ is Lord of all, a worldwide witness and a worldwide fellowship of believers free of all cultural prejudice are absolutely imperative.

10:37-38 Verse 37 begins the explicit treatment of Jesus' life, which continues through v. 42. This section is unique among the speeches of Acts in the amount of attention it gives to the ministry of Jesus. The other speeches of Peter emphasize the death and resurrection, as does this speech (vv. 39-40). Only the sermon in Cornelius's house, however, provides an outline of Jesus' earthly ministry (vv. 37-38). In fact, these verses are almost a summary of the outline of Jesus' life as presented in Mark's Gospel: the baptism of John, the Galilean period with its extensive

---

[100]Bovon, *De Vocatione Gentium*, 315.

[101]The Greek syntax of vv. 36-38 is notorious, consisting of several dangling clauses whose relationships to the main sentence are unclear. In general, translators take three main approaches: (1) to transpose "you know" from v. 37 to v. 36 and see "the word" (v. 36) as its object (RSV); (2) to drop the relative pronoun after "word" in v. 36 and make two separate sentences for vv. 36-37 (NEB, NIV); (3) to see v. 36 as in apposition to the phrase "God is no respecter of persons" of v. 34 (first suggested by H. Riesenfeld). See Marshall, *Acts*, 191. The NIV (option 2) provides the best solution from a grammatical perspective. Theologically, option 3 is extremely attractive, making God's impartiality the underlying assumption of the entire gospel message.

healing ministry, the death and resurrection.[102] That Peter began the summary of Jesus' career with "you know" (v. 37) is interesting. He could perhaps have assumed that Cornelius, residing in Caesarea, would have heard some prior report of John's baptizing and Jesus' reputation for miracles. Paul later made a similar assumption that these events could not have escaped king Agrippa's knowledge because they "did not happen in a corner" (26:26). His reference to Jesus' being anointed with the Spirit (v. 38) most likely refers to the descent of the Spirit on Jesus at his baptism (Luke 3:22). In turn, the anointing with the Spirit is closely tied with Jesus' miracles in Luke's Gospel, as it is here (Luke 4:18f., citing Isa 61:1f.).[103]

10:39-42 In v. 39 Peter turned to his role as apostolic witness to the entire ministry of Jesus (cf. 1:22) and above all to his death and resurrection. As in 5:30, Jesus' crucifixion is described as "hanging him on a tree." As always in Peter's speeches, the crucifixion is attributed to the inhabitants of Jerusalem. In v. 40 the familiar kerygmatic formula occurs: *they* killed him, but *God* raised him up on the third day.[104] Particularly striking and unique to this sermon is Peter's stress on Jesus' appearance to the apostles after his resurrection, even his eating and drinking with them.[105] This emphasis would have been particularly important in preaching to Gentiles like Cornelius for whom the idea of a bodily resurrection was a new concept (cf. 17:18). Peter concluded his treatment of the apostolic witness by referring to Jesus' command for them to preach the word (Acts 1:8) and especially to testify that Jesus is the one appointed by God as eschatological judge (v. 42).[106] The role is that of the Danielic Son of

---

[102]C. H. Dodd in *The Apostolic Preaching and Its Developments* (London: Hodder & Stoughton, 1936) argued that Mark wrote his Gospel on the basis of the sort of kerygmatic summary found in Acts 10:37-42. This line has recently been take up by P. Stuhlmacher, "Zum Thema: Das Evangelium und die Evangelien," and R. Guelich, "The Gospel Genre," in *Das Evangelium und die Evangelien*, ed. P. Stuhlmacher (Tübingen: Mohr, 1983), 1-26; 183-219. For an opposing view, which would trace Acts 10:37-43 to Luke rather than kerygmatic tradition, see A. Weiser, "Tradition und lukanische Komposition in Apg. 10, 36-43," in *A Cause de l'Evangile*, ed. F. Refoulé (Paris: Cerf, 1985); cf. U. Wilckens, "Kerygma und Evangelium bei Lukas (Beobachtungen zu Acta 10, 34-43)," *ZNW* 49 (1958): 227-30.

[103]Jesus' miracle-working is described as εὐεργετῶν in v. 38, a term that would have been meaningful to a Gentile—"one who works good deeds." It was a term often applied to Hellenistic kings (cf. Ptolemy Euergetes). The true disciple, however, eschews such honorific titles and is instead a servant (cf. Luke 22:25f.). Only God is the true "benefactor."

[104]"On the third day" occurs only here and in Paul's resurrection tradition in 1 Cor 15:3. By Jewish inclusive reckoning, which would have considered Friday the "first day," Jesus rose on the third day.

[105]Cf. Luke 24:30, 41-43; Acts 1:4.

[106]For Jesus' being "appointed" by God, see 2:23; 3:20; and especially 17:31, where the reference is to his appointment as eschatological judge, as it is here. For the phrase "the living and the dead," cf. 2 Tim 4:1; 1 Pet 4:5.

Man, and Peter perhaps was interpreting the title in terms that would have been comprehensible to a Gentile.[107]

One characteristic element of other sermons by Peter has to this point been lacking in this one—the proofs from the Old Testament Scriptures.[108] Peter seems to have been moving in this direction when he referred to the witness of the prophets to Jesus (v. 43), and he connected this closely with repentance and forgiveness of sins. Perhaps Peter's line of thought was related to Jesus' words to the disciples after the resurrection, where the Scriptures that predict Christ's suffering and resurrection are also closely tied to repentance and forgiveness in his name (Luke 24:46-48). In any event, Peter seems to have been moving toward his appeal with the references to the coming judgment and to repentance and forgiveness through Jesus' name. He was, however, cut short. The miracle of repentance and forgiveness occurred before he could even extend the invitation, and the Spirit sealed the event.

(6) The Impartiality of the Spirit (10:44-48)

[44]While Peter was still speaking these words, the Holy Spirit came on all who heard the message. [45]The circumcised believers who had come with Peter were astonished that the gift of the Holy Spirit had been poured out even on the Gentiles. [46]For they heard them speaking in tongues and praising God.

Then Peter said, [47]"Can anyone keep these people from being baptized with water? They have received the Holy Spirit just as we have." [48]So he ordered that they be baptized in the name of Jesus Christ. Then they asked Peter to stay with them for a few days.

10:44-48 As they listened to Peter's words about forgiveness for everyone who believes in Christ, the Holy Spirit suddenly descended upon all the Gentiles assembled in Cornelius's house (v. 44). They began to speak in tongues and to praise God (v. 46).[109] It was an audible, visible, *objective* demonstration of the Spirit's coming upon them. Peter and

---

[107]For the Son of Man as eschatological judge, see Dan 7:13f. and John 5:22,27.

[108]Parallels to Acts 10 and the story of Jonah include: the mention of Joppa (Jonah 1:3; Acts 10:8), the importance of the number 3 (Jonah 3:2; Acts 10:20), the repentance of the Gentiles (Jonah 3:5; Acts 10:43), the hostile response to their repentance (Jonah 4:1; Acts 11:2), and God's rebuttal of this response (Jonah 4:2-11; Acts 11:17-18). See R. W. Wall, "Peter, 'Son of Jonah': The Conversion of Cornelius in the Context of the Canon," *JSNT* 29 (1987): 70-90.

[109]The NIV footnote gives the alternative "other languages"; that reflects the Western text, which adds ἑτέραις. This makes the event in Acts 10 parallel to Pentecost. "Speaking in tongues" (λαλούντων γλώσσαις) is the better-attested reading and refers most likely to the phenomenon of tongue-speaking, which Paul sought to regulate in 1 Cor 12-14. In Peter's report in Jerusalem, the mode of the Spirit's expression is never mentioned. Peter was interested not in the manner of the Spirit's expression but that the Spirit had been granted to the Gentiles. See J. Dupont, *Nouvelles Etudes sur les Actes des Apôtres* (Paris: Cerf, 1984), 102.

the Jewish Christian brothers from Joppa witnessed the event and were astounded that God had so given the gift of the Spirit to the Gentiles (v. 44). It has often been described as the "Gentile Pentecost," and that designation is appropriate. In v. 47 Peter practically gave it that designation when he described the Gentiles as having received the Holy Spirit "just as we have." Like the Pentecost of Acts, it was a unique, unrepeatable event. It was scarcely programmatic. The sequence, for one, was most unusual, with the Spirit coming before their baptism. The pattern of a group demonstration of the Spirit invariably accompanies a new breakthrough in mission in Acts. We see it in the initial empowering of Pentecost, the establishment of the Samaritan mission (8:17-18), the reaching of former disciples of John the Baptist (19:6), and the foundation of the Gentile mission and its legitimation for the Jerusalem church.

Always the demonstration of the Spirit serves a single purpose—to show that the advance in witness comes directly from God, is totally due to divine leading. This was especially important in this instance. Peter had already shown his own hesitancy to reach out to Gentiles. More conservative elements in Jerusalem would be even more reticent. Only an undeniable demonstration of divine power could overrule all objections, and God provided precisely that in Cornelius's house. Surely the Spirit had already moved among the Gentiles gathered there in a more inward experience of repentance and faith. Luke hinted at this. The very last words in the Greek text of Peter's sermon before the Spirit descended are "everyone who believes in him." The faith of the Gentiles is even more explicit in Peter's report to Jerusalem, where he compared his own experience of belief in Christ and receipt of the Spirit with the experience of Cornelius and his fellow Gentiles (11:17).

Peter called for the baptism of the Gentiles (v. 47) in language that is highly reminiscent of the Ethiopian eunuch's request for baptism (8:36). As with the eunuch, there was now no barrier, no way anyone could hinder (*kōlyō*) the baptism of these Gentiles and their full inclusion into the Christian community. The NIV obscures the similarity in the questions "Why shouldn't I be baptized?" and "Can anyone keep these people from being baptized?" Both questions involve the verb "to hinder.

Another obstacle had been overcome in the ever-widening scope of Christian mission, the barrier of national and racial particularism and separatism, the barrier of prejudice that looks down on others as "unclean."[110] It is interesting that Peter gave orders for them to be baptized. Evidently he did not baptize them himself but committed the task to some of those who had accompanied him from Joppa. This is further evidence

---

[110]See F. Stagg, *The Book of Acts: The Early Struggle for an Unhindered Gospel* (Nashville: Broadman, 1955), 120.

that the early Christian leaders put no premium on *who* administered the rite.[111]

The narrative concludes with the note that Peter spent several days with his new Christian brothers and sisters in Caesarea (v. 48b). This inevitably involved table fellowship, but that now presented no problem for Peter.[112] It would, however, constitute a major difficulty for more conservative Jewish-Christians in Jerusalem.

(7) Endorsement of the Witness to the Gentiles (11:1-18)

[1]The apostles and the brothers throughout Judea heard that the Gentiles also had received the word of God. [2]So when Peter went up to Jerusalem, the circumcised believers criticized him [3]and said, "You went into the house of uncircumcised men and ate with them."

[4]Peter began and explained everything to them precisely as it had happened: [5]"I was in the city of Joppa praying, and in a trance I saw a vision. I saw something like a large sheet being let down from heaven by its four corners, and it came down to where I was. [6]I looked into it and saw four-footed animals of the earth, wild beasts, reptiles, and birds of the air. [7]Then I heard a voice telling me, 'Get up, Peter. Kill and eat.'

[8]"I replied, 'Surely not, Lord! Nothing impure or unclean has ever entered my mouth.'

[9]"The voice spoke from heaven a second time, 'Do not call anything impure that God has made clean.' [10]This happened three times, and then it was all pulled up to heaven again.

[11]"Right then three men who had been sent to me from Caesarea stopped at the house where I was staying. [12]The Spirit told me to have no hesitation about going with them. These six brothers also went with me, and we entered the man's house. [13]He told us how he had seen an angel appear in his house and say, 'Send to Joppa for Simon who is called Peter. [14]He will bring you a message through which you and all your household will be saved.'

[15]"As I began to speak, the Holy Spirit came on them as he had come on us at the beginning. [16]Then I remembered what the Lord had said: 'John baptized with water, but you will be baptized with the Holy Spirit.' [17]So if God gave them the same gift as he gave us, who believed in the Lord Jesus Christ, who was I to think that I could oppose God?"

[18]When they heard this, they had no further objections and praised God, saying, "So then, God has granted even the Gentiles repentance unto life."

11:1-2 Peter had himself been convinced of God's inclusion of the Gentiles. Now his fellow Jewish-Christians in Jerusalem needed convincing.

---

[111]Cf. Paul's disclaimer in 1 Cor 1:14-17 and Jesus' refusal to administer the rite in John 4:2.

[112]It would later become a problem for Peter when the same conservative elements pressured him to withdraw from table fellowship with Gentiles in Antioch (Gal 2:11-13), a reminder that enough social pressure can thwart even the strongest convictions.

The strongest reservations seem to have been entertained by a group of especially conservative Jewish Christians whom Luke called "those of the circumcision" (v. 2, NKJV; "circumcised believers," NIV).[113] These seem to be distinguished from the apostles and wider group of Judean brethren mentioned in v. 1.[114] Evidently they represented a strongly Jewish perspective and felt that any Gentile who became a Christian would have to do so by converting to Judaism and undergoing full Jewish proselyte procedure, which included circumcision. Hence they were known as the circumcision group, since they would require it of all Gentile converts. They may well have been the same group as those believers mentioned in 15:5 who belonged to the Pharisees and required Gentiles to be circumcised and to live by the Mosaic law. Their perspective is understandable, given that at this point Christianity was still seen as a movement within Judaism. It followed that if Gentiles became Christians they also became Jews by so doing and should thus undergo the normal procedure for converts to Judaism. Needless to say, if this line had been adopted, there never would have been an effective Gentile mission. Most Gentiles had real problems with some of the more "external" aspects of the Jewish law, such as circumcision and the food laws. Such factors doubtless had kept many Gentiles like Cornelius, who believed in the God of the Jews, from becoming full proselytes.

11:3-12 It is interesting that the circumcision group raised a question about Peter's table fellowship with the Gentiles rather than about their being baptized. As has already been shown in the discussion of 10:9-16, the issues of table fellowship and acceptance of the Gentiles were closely related.[115] Peter's eating with the Gentiles showed his acceptance of them as fellow Christians, and they were still *uncircumcised* (v. 3). In any event, Peter's response quickly led them to the *real* issue—God's acceptance of the Gentiles. Luke basically summarized chap. 10, again using the device of repetition to underscore the significance of the event. The account contains only slight differences from the earlier one. It is considerably condensed, and Peter occasionally added a previously unmentioned detail. Naturally, Peter began with his own vision in 11:5-10, which is a detailed retelling of 10:9-16.[116] In fact, that is the most exten-

---

[113]This is exactly the phrase (οἱ ἐκ περιτομῆς) used of the Jewish Christians from Joppa in 10:45, but there it simply means *circumcised* (i.e., Jewish) Christians. In 11:2 the group was distinguished from the Jewish Christians as a whole, and it seems to refer to a limited group within them.

[114]The Western text provides a much lengthier version of v. 2, which has Peter carrying on an extensive preaching tour on the way back to Jerusalem after the conversion of Cornelius. See Bruce, *Acts:* NIC, 232, n. 2.

[115]See also K. Haacker, "Dibelius und Cornelius: Ein Beispiel formgeschichtlicher Überlieferungskritik," *BZ* 24 (1980): 240.

[116]The most significant difference in 11:5-10 is the mention of a fourfold division of the

sive repetition in Peter's report to Jerusalem. For Peter it was the heart of the matter. There are no unclean people. God accepts the Gentiles. Verses 11-12 summarize the narrative of 10:17-25, relating the arrival of the three messengers from Cornelius and Peter's accompanying them to Caesarea. The most significant difference from the earlier account is the additional detail that there were six Christians from Joppa who accompanied Peter to Caesarea (v. 12). More than that—it was "these" six whom Peter brought to Jerusalem as witnesses to what transpired in Cornelius's home (cf. 10:45).[117]

11:13-16 Verses 13-14 summarize the vision of Cornelius, how the angel instructed him to send to Joppa for Peter. Verse 14 is more specific than any of the accounts of Cornelius's vision in chap. 10. Peter was to bring a message to Cornelius "through which [he] and all [his] household [would] be saved." This expansion elucidates the reference to Peter's words in v. 22 and above all explains Cornelius's eager anticipation of Peter's message in 10:33. There was no need for Peter to summarize his sermon before the Jerusalem Christians, so he quickly moved to the coming of the Spirit on the Gentiles at Cornelius's house (v. 15). Peter noted how the event interrupted his sermon. He added that the Spirit came upon them just "as he had come upon us at the beginning." The comparison is to Pentecost. Peter made explicit here what was implicit in 10:46. He continued to draw the comparison in v. 16, which harks back to Acts 1:5 and Jesus' prediction of a baptism with the Holy Spirit. Jesus' prediction was fulfilled for the apostles at Pentecost; for Cornelius and his fellow Gentiles it was fulfilled with the coming of the Spirit at Cornelius's house. Certainly for Peter it was a Gentile Pentecost. He could hardly make more explicit comparisons!

11:17-18 Peter concluded his report in Jerusalem by reminding his hearers once again that God gave the gift of the Spirit to the Gentiles and added, "Who was *I* to think that *I* could oppose God?" Once again he used the verb *kōlyō* in expressing the idea of opposition to God, just as he employed the same verb in 10:47 to question whether anyone could oppose the baptism of the Gentiles. Opposition to the Gentiles' baptism *would* be opposition to God, for God's leading of Peter and of Cornelius proved beyond doubt his intention to include them in his people. There really was not much the "circumcision group" could say now. God was clearly in it. Who could object? Silence quickly gave way to praise of

---

animal world (θηρία), which follows Ps 148:10, rather than the threefold vision that appears in 10:12. Also in v. 10 the more colorful verb ἀνεσπάσθη is used for the "drawing up" of the sheet back into heaven rather than ἀνελήμφθη ("taken up") of 10:16.

[117]Cadbury and Lake see a possible significance in there being six witnesses. Peter made the seventh. Seven seals were often attached to official Roman documents such as wills. Cf. Rev 5:1. See *Beginnings* 4:126.

God in his triumphant advance of the gospel. God had granted "repentance unto life" to the Gentiles.

Not all the problems were solved, however. Not all the Jewish Christians were satisfied with taking in Gentiles without circumcision. As yet there had been no mass influx of Gentiles, and the problems were not altogether evident. Things would change, particularly with the great success of Paul and Barnabas's mission among the Gentiles. Once again the issue would be raised by the more staunchly Jewish faction—"Shouldn't Gentiles be circumcised when they become Christians?" "Can we really have table fellowship with uncircumcised Gentiles who do not abide by the food laws?" (author's paraphrase). These issues would surface once more for a final showdown in the Jerusalem Conference of chap. 15.

4. Antioch's Witness to Gentiles (11:19-30)

Chapter 11 as a whole is devoted to the foundational events in the Gentile mission of the church. Two different churches play the primary roles. The Jerusalem church, led by the apostles and comprised mainly of Aramaic-speaking Jewish Christians, recognized the divine leading in Peter's witness to Cornelius and concluded that God intended to lead the Gentiles to repentance and life (11:1-18). The Antioch church, established by Hellenists, those Greek-speaking Jewish Christians who had to flee Jerusalem after the martyrdom of Stephen, began to put this principle into practice and to reach out to the Gentile population (11:19-30).

Antioch was a natural setting for the Gentile mission to begin in earnest. It was the third largest city in the Roman Empire, its population of some 500,000 to 800,000 only being exceeded by Rome and Alexandria.[118] Founded in 300 B.C. by the first Seleucid ruler, Seleucus Nicator, it was from the first a "hellenistic city," promoting Greek culture.[119] Seleucus named the city Antioch for his father, Antiochus, and made it the capital of his empire. It was a planned city, carefully laid out in a grid pattern with streets positioned to assure maximum exposure to the cool afternoon breezes. Noted for its beauty, it was located in the large fertile plain of the Orontes River. In fact, the Orontes from the point it flowed into the Mediterranean was navigable some fifteen miles upstream where

---

[118]For a thorough treatment of Antioch, see G. Downey, *A History of Antioch in Syria* (Princeton, N.J.: University Press, 1961) and his abridged version, *Ancient Antioch* (Princeton, N.J.: University Press, 1963). For treatments more focused on the early Christian community in Antioch, see W. Meeks and R. Wilcken, *Jews and Christians in Antioch* (Missoula, Mont.: Scholars, 1978); R. E. Brown and J. P. Meier, *Antioch and Rome* (New York: Paulist, 1982), esp. 28-44.

[119]The Seleucid (or Syrian) Empire, along with the Ptolemaic Empire in Egypt, was established by the Greek generals of Alexander the Great and dominated the Near East for two hundred years until both came under Roman dominion in the first century B.C.

Antioch was located.[120] At the mouth of the Orontes stood Antioch's major port, the town of Seleucus, and at Antioch itself there was a significant harbor. From 64 B.C., Antioch came under Roman jurisdiction, being granted by the Roman general Pompey the status of "free city," which allowed it a measure of self-jurisdiction and exemption from the provincial taxes. In 23 B.C. the areas of Syria, Cilicia, and Palestine were organized into the Roman "province of Syria" with Antioch as the seat of the imperial legate (governor).

Religiously, Antioch was an amalgam. Five miles from the city was a major cult center for the Greek goddess Daphne and her consort Apollo. The Antioch version of the cult seems to have been but a weak Hellenization of the worship of the ancient Assyrian goddess Astarte, in which sacred prostitution played a major role. This practice evidently continued because Antioch was notorious throughout the Roman Empire for its immorality. A typical statement is that of the satirist Juvenal who, in complaining about Rome's degenerating morality, remarked that the "filth of the Orontes" had flowed into the Tiber (*Satire* 3.62). There was an extensive Jewish community in Antioch, its population in the first century A.D. being variously estimated from 25,000 to 50,000. Though some of the more Hellenized Jews may have participated in the larger government of the city, the Jewish community seems to have been accorded a separate identity within the city with a major degree of self-government.[121]

Obviously, Antioch was a natural location for Christian witness. An extensive Jewish community was there, and the witness evidently began with them. The witness quickly spread to the Gentile majority, perhaps beginning naturally with Gentiles like Cornelius, who had already been attracted to the Jewish worship of God. Cosmopolitan center and port center that it was, it is not surprising that the Christians there caught the vision of an empire-wide mission. Paul would be the one who most carried it out, and Antioch was his sponsoring church.

The beginnings of all this are traced in 11:19-26. Verses 19-21 depict the establishment of the church at Antioch and the beginnings of its Gentile outreach. Verses 22-24 deal with the endorsement of the Antioch witness by the Jerusalem church through the bridge-figure of Barnabas. Verses 25-26 show the increase of the mission among the Gentiles through the efforts of Paul. Finally, vv. 27-30 illustrate the unity of the entire Christian community through all this as exemplified in Antioch's offering for Jerusalem in a time of famine.

---

[120]One of Herod the Great's major building projects was the lavish decorating of the main street that led through town to the harbor. He paved it with marble and erected colonnades on both sides.

[121]See C. H. Kraeling, "The Jewish Community at Antioch," *JBL* 51 (1932): 130-60; S. E. Johnson, "Antioch, the Base of Operations," *LTQ* 18 (1983): 64-73.

(1) Establishing a Church in Antioch (11:19-26)

[19]Now those who had been scattered by the persecution in connection with Stephen traveled as far as Phoenicia, Cyprus and Antioch, telling the message only to Jews. [20]Some of them, however, men from Cyprus and Cyrene, went to Antioch and began to speak to Greeks also, telling them the good news about the Lord Jesus. [21]The Lord's hand was with them, and a great number of people believed and turned to the Lord.

[22]News of this reached the ears of the church at Jerusalem, and they sent Barnabas to Antioch. [23]When he arrived and saw the evidence of the grace of God, he was glad and encouraged them all to remain true to the Lord with all their hearts. [24]He was a good man, full of the Holy Spirit and faith, and a great number of people were brought to the Lord.

[25]Then Barnabas went to Tarsus to look for Saul, [26]and when he found him, he brought him to Antioch. So for a whole year Barnabas and Saul met with the church and taught great numbers of people. The disciples were called Christians first at Antioch.

THE HELLENISTS IN ANTIOCH (11:19-21). **11:19-21** Verse 19 refers to the "Hellenists" and looks back to 8:1, repeating the verb "scattered" and reminding the reader of these Greek-speaking Jewish Christian associates of Stephen who had to flee Jerusalem as a result of his martyrdom. One of those who was "scattered" was Philip (8:4), and he witnessed to the Samaritans, an Ethiopian, and to the seacoast communities as far north as Caesarea (8:5-40). Another group of Hellenist refugees is described as evangelizing the seacoast towns further to the north, in the Phoenician plain, which extended some seventy-five miles along the coast of middle Syria from Mt. Carmel north to the river Eleutheros. Its principal cities were Ptolemais, Tyre, Sidon, and Zarephath.[122] Others began work on the island of Cyprus, the easternmost island of the Mediterranean and some 100 miles off the Syrian coast. Paul and Barnabas would later continue the witness on Cyprus (13:4-12).

Those who traveled farthest north arrived in Antioch. These coastal towns were all heavily Hellenized, and the Greek language would have been dominant. It was thus an appropriate area for witness by these Greek-speaking Hellenist Christians. Quite naturally, they witnessed at first to Jews only, probably to fellow Greek-speaking Jews, as Stephen had done in the Diaspora synagogues of Jerusalem (6:9). But at Antioch they took a bolder step and began preaching to Gentiles as well.[123] This

---

[122]For the later Christian communities in Tyre, Ptolemais, and Sidon, see Acts 21:3-7; 27:3.

[123]"Greeks" is virtually equivalent to Gentiles. Cf. Paul's frequent contrast of "Jew and Greek" (Gal 3:28). Several important manuscripts (B, D [the uncorrected D lacks the variant, though D corrected maintains this reading], E) have "Hellenists" instead of "Greeks," but the context calls for Greeks/Gentiles whichever reading is followed. The Jews the Hellenists

step was taken by those who were themselves Diaspora Jews from Cyrene
and Cyprus. Perhaps the Lucius of Cyrene, who is described as one of the
"prophets and teachers" at Antioch in 13:1, was one of these. Barnabas,
who himself was a native of Cyprus, would later become active in this
witness (cf. 4:36). Paul was a Diaspora Jew from Cilicia (cf. 22:3). It was
only natural that a concern for evangelization of the Gentiles should be
especially felt by the Jewish Christians of the dispersion who had grown
up in a Gentile environment and had a more worldwide perspective than
the more provincial Palestinian Christians. Their message also betrayed
their sensitivity to Gentile concerns. They did not preach Jesus as the
Messiah (Christ) but rather as Lord, a title far more familiar to Gentiles
than Jewish messianic ideas.[124] Their witness bore great results; a large
number of the Gentiles believed and turned to the Lord (v. 21) because
"the hand" of the Lord, that is, his power and Spirit, was with them, just
as it had been so dramatically in the conversion of Cornelius.[125]

BARNABAS SENT BY JERUSALEM (11:22-24). **11:22** Jerusalem was the
"mother church" for all Christians in those days. It was the church of the
apostles, the link to Jesus. It was only natural for the Jerusalem church to
show an interest in the total Christian witness wherever it was carried.
This concern had already expressed itself in their sending Peter and John
to Philip's mission in Samaria (8:14-17) and their inquiring of Peter about
his witness to Cornelius (11:1-18). It would reappear when Paul and Barnabas reported to Jerusalem on their successful Gentile mission (15:1-35).
Although this could certainly be seen as a sort of "supervision" by Jerusalem, in each instance the Christians of Jerusalem enthusiastically
endorsed the new work and gave it their stamp of approval. In this
instance, when Jerusalem heard of the Gentile mission in Antioch, the
church did not send apostles, as it did when Philip preached to Samaritans. Instead, they sent a nonapostolic delegate but a wise choice
indeed—Barnabas, "the son of encouragement" (4:36).

---

witnessed to (v. 19) were most likely fellow Greek-speakers. The contrast set up by the word
δε in v. 20 calls for an advance beyond this, and that could only be Gentiles. Also the concern
expressed in Jerusalem (v. 22) would imply a more radical witness than one to Greek-
speaking Jews. For a contrary opinion, see P. Parker, "Three Variant Readings in Luke-
Acts," *JBL* 83 (1964): 165-70; D. R. Fotheringham, "Acts xi.20," *ExpTim* 45 (1933-34): 430.

[124] In its origin the title Lord was most likely applied to Jesus first in *Jewish* Christian
circles, using the OT title for God (*Adonai/Maran*). But Messiah was a particularly meaningful title to Jews, and the frequency of its use (χρίστος) in the sermons to Jews in Acts testifies to this. "Lord" was a title used by Gentiles for rulers and cult gods and was more
understandable to them. Note its frequent use in Gentile contexts in Acts. It was also Paul's
favorite title for Jesus in his Epistles, where "Christ" is more a proper name than a title. See
Beginnings 5:357-62.

[125] For God's "hand" expressing his power, cf. Exod 9:3; 1 Sam 5:6; 6:9; Isa 59:1; 66:14;
Ezek 1:3; Luke 1:66; Acts 4:30; 13:11.

11:23-24 Barnabas had a natural relationship with the Hellenists. As a native of Cyprus, he most likely was fluent in Greek. On the other hand, he did not seem to have originally belonged to their group but rather to have had ties from the beginning with the non-Hellenist church in Jerusalem and particularly with the apostles. He participated in exemplary fashion in the church's practice of sharing (4:36f.). He introduced Paul into the circle of apostles (9:27). He was chosen as their delegate to Antioch. Barnabas was a "bridge-builder," one who was able to see the positive aspects in both sides of an issue and to mediate between perspectives. That was the sort of person needed now to investigate the new mission of the more adventurous Hellenists of Antioch and allay the concerns of the more conservative "circumcision" group in Jerusalem (cf. 11:2). Luke emphasized these positive qualities in Barnabas. "He was a good man" (v. 24), a phrase Luke used elsewhere only of Joseph of Arimathea (Luke 23:50). He was "full of the Holy Spirit and faith," just like Stephen (Acts 6:5). When Barnabas arrived in Antioch, far from criticizing the new undertaking, he was able to see the grace of God at work in all the Gentile conversions, and he rejoiced (v. 23).[126] More than that, he encouraged them in the ministry, thus living up to his nickname of being the "Son of Encouragement" (4:36). This quality of encouragement, of looking for the best in others, would reappear when Barnabas interceded on Mark's behalf (15:36-40).

People like Barnabas are always needed by the church. They are the peacemakers, the go-betweens who seek no glory for themselves but only seek to bring out the best in others. But "would-be" Barnabases of today need to heed a further lesson from this outstanding biblical figure. Barnabases want everyone to be happy, but sometimes it simply is not possible to please everyone without serious compromise of one's basic convictions. Barnabas found that out later at Antioch when, in order to placate the conservative Jewish Christians "from James" (Jerusalem), he withdrew from table fellowship with those very Gentile-Christian converts we see him here witnessing to so enthusiastically (Gal 2:11-13).

Paul and Barnabas in Antioch (11:25-26). **11:25-26** With the growing missionary success in Antioch, Barnabas needed help; and Paul immediately came to mind. Paul was in the area of his native Cilicia (cf. Acts 9:30; Gal 1:21), to which he had departed after his first visit to Jerusalem following his conversion. The text of Acts is compressed and selective, but the most likely reconstruction of Pauline chronology from Gal 1–2 would indicate that some ten years or so had elapsed from the time he first departed from Cilicia to when Barnabas set out to find him. The

---

[126]There is a Greek wordplay in the words "grace" (χάρις) and "joy" (χαρά). Coming from the same root, the relationship is obvious: one who experiences *grace* is filled with *joy*.

verb Luke employed (*anazēteō*) means *to seek out* and implies he had some difficulty in finding him. Quite likely Paul was off somewhere busily engaged in missionary activity. When Barnabas finally located Paul, he brought him back to Antioch where the two were heavily occupied in preaching and teaching to "great numbers" (v. 26). Likely they particularly continued the witness to Gentiles. This would prepare them for their first mission together in Cyprus and southern Turkey (13:4–14:26).

Luke appended the interesting note to v. 26 that the term "Christian" was first applied to disciples in Antioch. This may be of more significance than might appear on first sight. The term only occurs in two other places in the New Testament (Acts 26:28; 1 Pet 4:16). In all three instances it is a term used by outsiders to designate Christians. Evidently the term was not originally used by Christians of themselves. They preferred terms like "believers, disciples, brothers." The first extensive usage by a Christian writer to designate fellow believers was by Ignatius, bishop of Antioch, around the turn of the second century. The term (*Christianoi*) consists of the Greek word for Christ/Messiah (*Christos*) with the *Latin* ending *ianus*, meaning *belonging to, identified by*. Examples of similar formations are *Herodianoi*, partisans of Herod, and *Augustianoi*, the zealotic followers of Nero.[127] The term was often used by Roman writers to designate followers of Christ.[128] The early usage in Antioch is perhaps indicative of two things. For one, it is the sort of term Gentiles would have used and perhaps reflects the success of Antioch's Gentile mission. Gentiles were dubbing their fellow Gentiles who became followers of Christ "Christians." Second, it reflects that Christianity was beginning to have an identity of its own and no longer was viewed as a totally Jewish entity. Again, the success among Gentiles would have hastened this process in Antioch.

How is one to relate the two "Gentile missions" of Acts 10–11, that is, Peter's and that of the Antioch church? In all likelihood the two overlapped in time, with the Antioch witness covering several years. On all appearances the Antioch mission involved much greater numbers (cf. v. 21). And certainly it was the Antioch church that was the great "Gentile mission" church in sponsoring Paul's missionary activity. Peter did not follow up his conversion of Cornelius by a personal mission to the

---

[127]Most commentators are in agreement that the term was first applied to Christians by outsiders. For an opposing view, which sees it as first used by Christians as a self-designation, see H. B. Mattingly, "The Origin of the Name Christiani," *JTS* 9 (1958): 26-37; E. J. Bickerman, "The Name of Christians," *HTR* 42 (1949): 109-24; C. Spicq, "Ce que signifie le titre de Chretien," *ST* 15 (1961): 68-78.

[128]Cf. Josephus, *Antiquities* 18.64; Tacitus, *Annals* 15.44; Pliny, *Epistles* 10.96-97; Lucian, *Alexander* 25.38.

Gentiles. All indications are that he continued primarily to witness to the Jews (cf. Gal 2:7). Still, the experience with Cornelius was essential. It convinced the leading apostle of the legitimacy of the Gentile mission, and he in turn became its prime advocate with the other apostles and the Jerusalem church (cf. 11:1-18; 15:7-11). In a real sense it paved the way with the church as a whole for Paul's mission to the Gentiles.

(2) Sending Famine Relief to Jerusalem (11:27-30)

[27]During this time some prophets came down from Jerusalem to Antioch. [28]One of them, named Agabus, stood up and through the Spirit predicted that a severe famine would spread over the entire Roman world. (This happened during the reign of Claudius.) [29]The disciples, each according to his ability, decided to provide help for the brothers living in Judea. [30]This they did, sending their gift to the elders by Barnabas and Saul.

11:27-30 Verses 27-30 conclude the Antioch narrative with the tradition of a relief offering sent by the Antioch church to Jerusalem during a time of severe famine. Here we are first introduced to the prophet Agabus. He had the gift of foretelling,[129] and the gift was again manifested in 21:10-11, when he prophesied in a graphic way Paul's impending arrest in Jerusalem. He is said to have been among a group of prophets who came from Jerusalem to Antioch. There is ample evidence for such early Christian prophets, and they seem to have largely been itinerant, as the present passage would indicate.[130] In Antioch Agabus predicted that there would be a worldwide famine.[131] Luke added the "aside" that this famine did indeed occur during the time of Claudius, who was Roman emperor from A.D. 41–54.[132]

---

[129]Christian prophets are mentioned also in Acts 13:1; 15:32. Cf. Philip's prophesying daughters (21:9). Paul ranked prophets second only to apostles in his list of those gifted by the Spirit (1 Cor 12:28). The gift of prophecy is treated throughout 1 Cor 14 and is primarily valued for its role in edification and encouragement. The Jews believed that prophecy had ceased during the time of the exile but would return with the coming of the Messiah. Peter's quote of Joel at Pentecost reflected his conviction that the gift had been poured out on the Christian community (cf. 2:17-18) and was indeed a sign of the Messiah's coming. In the NT prophecy is primarily viewed as a word spoken under the inspiration of the Holy Spirit intended for the direction or edification of the Christian community. Inspiration was normative to the experience but not necessarily the ability to predict future events. In this sense Agabus's gift was unusual.

[130]Itinerant prophets existed as late as the second-century church (cf. Didache 11:7-12).

[131]NIV has "entire Roman world" for the Greek οἰκουμένη, meaning inhabited, civilized world, which in that day was virtually the "Roman world."

[132]Luke's concern for world history is illustrated by the fact that he was the only NT writer to mention a Roman emperor by name. Claudius was the only one Luke mentioned more than once (here and in 18:2). See F. F. Bruce, "Christianity under Claudius," BJRL 44 (1962): 309-26.

The reign of Claudius was in fact marked by a long series of crop failures in various parts of the empire—in Judea, in Rome, in Egypt, and in Greece. The Judean famine seems to have taken place during the procuratorship of Tiberius Alexander (A.D. 46–48), and Egyptian documents reveal a major famine there in A.D. 45–46 due to flooding.[133] The most likely time for the Judean famine would thus seem to have been around A.D. 46.[134] In any event, the Antioch church decided to gather a collection to relieve their fellow Christians in Judea, each setting something aside according to his or her ability.[135] Eventually, when the famine struck, the collection was delivered to the elders in Jerusalem by Paul and Barnabas.[136] Actually, v. 30 does not mention Jerusalem, but 12:25 does in speaking of Paul and Barnabas's return from this visit.

The subtle transition in the leadership of the Jerusalem church throughout these chapters is noteworthy. In the early days of the Jerusalem church, the apostles had taken responsibility for matters of charity (cf. 4:34–5:11). A transition seems to have begun with the selection of

---

[133]K. S. Gapp argued that failures in Egypt and Judea would put severe supply-and-demand pressures through large parts of the empire, creating higher prices and a "famine" in a real sense for the poorer classes ("The Universal Famine under Claudius," *HTR* 28 [1935]: 258-65).

[134]F. F. Bruce, "Chronological Questions in the Acts of the Apostles," *BJRL* 68 (1986): 278-79.

[135]Note how much Paul's own collection for the Jerusalem church fit the Antioch pattern. The same Greek term for "ministry," "help," or "service" is used in Acts 11:29 and in 2 Cor 8–9. Each is to set something aside regularly (cf. 1 Cor 16:1-4) and to give according to his or her means (cf. 2 Cor 8:11-12).

[136]How is one to reconcile the visits of Paul after his conversion as recorded in Acts and in Galatians? If one equates Gal 2:1-10 with the "circumcision" conference of Acts 15, which content suggests as the most natural course, then the "collection visit" of Acts 11:27-30 becomes a "third" visit, whereas Galatians only mentions two. Innumerable "solutions" to the problem have been offered. Bruce (*Acts:* NIC, 244) suggests that Acts 11:27-30 and Gal 2:1-10 refer to the same ("second") visit and that Galatians was written prior to the Acts 15 conference; so also Marshall, *Acts*, 200 and D. R. de Lacey, "Paul in Jerusalem," *NTS* 20 (1973): 82-86, and (in somewhat modified form that allows for Galatians coming after the Acts 15 conference) C. Talbert, "Again: Paul's Visits to Jerusalem," *NovT* 9 (1967): 26-40. A number of scholars see Acts 11:27-30 as a doublet of Acts 15 (P. Benoit, "La deuxième visite de Saint Paul à Jerusalem," *Bib* 40 [1959]: 778-92; Pesch, *Apostelgeschichte* 1:356). Jeremias also took the doublet approach but with the added nuance that he saw the famine as aggravated by A.D. 47–48's being a sabbatical year and thus extending into the spring of A.D. 49, when he believed the Acts 15 conference took place ("Sabbathjahr und neutestamentliche Chronologie," *ZNW* 27 [1928]: 98-103). A number of recent scholars argue that Acts 11:27ff. is wholly due to Lukan redaction: e.g., G. Strecker, "Die sogenannte zweite Jerusalemreise des Paulus (Act. 11:27-30)," *ZNW* 53 (1962): 67-77. An often overlooked solution recognizes the polemical nature of Galatians, where Paul was listing only those times when he had contact with the apostles in Jerusalem. Since this was not evidently the case with the collection from Antioch, he simply overlooked that "visit." See J. Polhill, "Galatia Revisited, the Life-Setting of the Epistle," *RevExp* 69 (1972): 443-47.

the seven Hellenists (6:1-6). Paul and Barnabas laid the gift from Antioch at the feet of "the elders." Evidently the apostles were giving themselves more and more to the word, like Peter on his mission tours in Samaria and along the coast. More and more responsibility would be assumed by these lay elders, based almost surely on the pattern of the elders in the Jewish synagogue. Paul would organize his own churches along the same pattern (cf. 14:23; 20:17).[137]

5. Persecution Again in Jerusalem (12:1-25)

After the glimpse at the Antioch church, attention focused once more on Jerusalem in chap. 12. If the apostles had remained largely untouched by the persecution that followed Stephen's death, the situation radically changed when Herod Agrippa assumed rule over Judea. The apostles then became the specific target of the king's efforts to suppress the Christians. James was beheaded, and Peter was put in prison in anticipation of the same fate. But not even the king was able to stem the tide when God was behind it. Indeed, the king found himself fighting against God and suffered the consequences (cf. 5:39; 11:17).

The whole story is told in one of the most delightful and engaging narratives in all of Acts. The villainy of Herod is established in vv. 1-5 with his execution of James and arrest of Peter. His designs were thwarted in the latter instance, however, when God delivered Peter in a miraculous manner (vv. 6-19). Peter's escape is told in two scenes, both related with consummate artistry. The first scene pictures the angel delivering Peter from jail (vv. 6-11). It has a vivid, almost comic touch; the angel had to prompt the groggy Peter every step of the way. One can almost hear Peter telling the story: "I tell you, I was completely out of it. It was all God's doing. I thought I was having a particularly pleasant dream." The second scene is no less entertaining, as Peter hastened to the house of John Mark's mother (vv. 12-19a). There is again a comic touch (with Rhoda leaving him knocking at the gate) and also a decidedly dramatic effect. Would he get inside before Herod's men discovered his escape and came after him? The story was still not over. There was a final deliverance of the apostles, as God dealt with their persecutor, Herod, in a definitive manner (vv. 19b-23). Once more at peace, the witness of the church prospered (vv. 24-25). The whole story of the deliverance of the apostles from

---

[137]In v. 28 the Western text adds at the beginning "when *we* were gathered together." It is most unlikely that this variant is authentic. Some scholars, however, find it "irresistible" since it would allow for Luke's own presence in Antioch and lend still further support to the ancient tradition that Luke came from that city and is perhaps even the same as the Lucius of Cyrene of Acts 13:1. See E. Delebecque, "Saul et Luc avant le premier voyage missionaire," *RSPT* 66 (1982): 551-59.

Herod's clutches is bracketed by references to Paul and Barnabas's delivery of the Antioch relief offering (11:30; 12:25). It is the last narrative in Acts that deals exclusively with the apostles and the Jerusalem church. From this point on, whenever Jerusalem was involved, it would be in connection with Paul's ministry. Peter and his fellow apostles faded into the background, and Paul took center stage.

(1) Herod Agrippa's Persecution of the Apostles (12:1-5)

[1]It was about this time that King Herod arrested some who belonged to the church, intending to persecute them. [2]He had James, the brother of John, put to death with the sword. [3]When he saw that this pleased the Jews, he proceeded to seize Peter also. This happened during the Feast of Unleavened Bread. [4]After arresting him, he put him in prison, handing him over to be guarded by four squads of four soldiers each. Herod intended to bring him out for public trial after the Passover.

[5]So Peter was kept in prison, but the church was earnestly praying to God for him.

12:1 The story begins with a vague time reference. It was "about this time." Evidently Luke meant about the time the Antioch church was preparing its relief offering for the Jerusalem church (11:27-30). Considering the history of Herod Agrippa I, the Herod of this story, the time most likely would have been the spring of A.D. 42 or 43.[138] The Greek of v. 1 is quite vivid: Herod "laid violent hands" on some of the Christians. To understand why he would do this, it is necessary to understand something of Herod Agrippa I and his relationship to the Jews. Agrippa was the grandson of Herod the Great. His father, Aristobulus, had been executed in 7 B.C. by his grandfather for fear that he might usurp his throne. After his father's death, while still a child, Agrippa was sent to Rome with his mother, where he was reared and educated along with the children of the Roman aristocracy. These childhood friendships eventually led to his ruling over a Jewish kingdom nearly the extent of that of his grandfather. In A.D. 37 the emperor Caligula gave him the title of king and made him ruler over the territories formerly ruled by his uncle Philip, lands in the Transjordan and the Ten Cities (Decapolis) north of Galilee. In A.D. 39 Caligula extended Agrippa's rule by giving him Galilee and Perea, the territory of his uncle Antipas, who had been sent into exile. Finally, when his former schoolmate Claudius became emperor in A.D. 41, he was given rule of Judea and Samaria, which had been under Roman procurators for thirty-five years. He was truly "king of the Jews" now, ruling over all of Judea, Samaria, Galilee, the Transjordan, and the Decapolis.

---

[138]Bruce, "Chronological Questions," 276-78.

Though king, Agrippa was hardly secure. Much of his good fortune was due to his friendship with Caligula, and Caligula had not been a popular emperor with the Romans. In fact, Agrippa could not count on always being in the good graces of Rome. It became all the more important for him to win the loyalty of his Jewish subjects in order to give him at least a firm footing at home. Everything Josephus said about Agrippa[139] would indicate that he made every attempt to please the Jews, particularly currying the favor of the influential Pharisees. His "Jewishness," however, seems to have been largely a face he put on when at home. When away, he lived in a thoroughly Roman fashion.[140] Why persecution of the Christians was particularly pleasing to them at this time is not stated. Perhaps the acceptance of uncircumcised Gentiles as related in chap. 11 had something to do with their disfavor.[141]

12:2 Agrippa began his persecution of the Christians by having James killed "with a sword." This James is described as "brother of John" and thus was the apostle, the son of Zebedee. Some interpreters have suggested that his brother John was also executed at this time, interpreting Mark 10:39 as a prediction that both would be martyred. John 21:23, however, seems to predict the opposite; and early church tradition has John living to an old age and dying a natural death.[142] If Herod executed James in the Roman fashion "with the sword," he was beheaded. If he used the Jewish mode of execution, which forbade beheading as a desecration to the body, he had "the edge of the sword" thrust through his body.[143] The martyrdom of James is told with the utmost brevity.[144] Luke

---

[139]For Agrippa sections see Josephus, *Ant.* 18.126, 131-34, 143-69, 179-204, 228-301; 19.236-44, 265, 274-77, 288, 292-354. See Bruce, *Acts:* NIC, 246-47.

[140]For Agrippa's Roman life-style, see P. Gaechter, "Hatred of the House of Annas," *TS* 8 (1947): 23-29.

[141]For the suggestion that the incident over Caligula's statue in A.D. 40 may have produced increased Jewish zealotism, which was behind the persecution of the Christians, see J. W. Swain, "Gamaliel's Speech and Caligula's Statue," *HTR* 37 (1944): 341-49.

[142]Cf. Irenaeus, *Haer*, 2.22.5. Evidence for John's martyrdom is sparse and quite late— the ninth-century George the Sinner and fifth-century Philip of Side. See *Beginnings* 4:133-34.

[143]Cf. Deut 13:15; 1 Sam 22:18f.; 2 Sam 1:13,15 (implied, but not explicitly mentioned); Jer 26:23. See J. Blinzler, "Rechtgeschtliches zur Hinrichtung des Zebedaiden Jakobus (Apg. xii.2), *NovT* 5 (1962): 191-206. Blinzler also argues that the Jewish king never had the right of capital punishment in religious matters and that Agrippa must have been carrying out the order of the Sanhedrin. Apparently the OT practice was to behead after execution (1 Sam 17:46,51; 31:9; 2 Kgs 10:6-8). This was clearly desecration of a body. Whether it was forbidden in OT times is another question.

[144]A later tradition, which should be taken with considerable reservation, tells of how the officer who led James to trial was converted by James's testimony, professed his faith, and was himself condemned and executed together with James (Eusebius, *Eccl.Hist.* 2.9.2f., quoting Clement of Alexandria). For the view that James's zealotic nature ("son of thunder,"

did not want to dwell on it but used the incident to set the stage for his main emphasis—God's deliverance of Peter.

12:3-5 Having won points with the Jews by the execution of James, Agrippa then moved against the chief of the apostles, Peter, arresting him and placing him in prison. Luke noted that it was the Feast of the Unleavened Bread. Herod would not risk his favor with the Jews by executing Peter during this time, since that would be considered a desecration. The Passover was eaten on the eve of Nisan 14 and was followed by seven days of eating unleavened bread, ending on Nisan 21. Luke used the term "Passover" for the entire period. It would have been after the holy days had ended that Agrippa would have brought Peter forth for public trial and surely also for execution (v. 4).[145] Peter was placed under heavy security, being guarded by four squads of four soldiers each. This was the usual Roman practice, changing guards every three hours throughout the twelve night hours to assure maximum alertness.[146] Why the heavy guard? Perhaps the Sanhedrin had informed Agrippa of their own experience in jailing the apostles on a previous occasion (5:19). While Peter waited in prison, the Christians used their most effective means of assistance. They prayed continually for him (v. 5).

(2) Peter's Miraculous Deliverance from Prison (12:6-19a)

⁶The night before Herod was to bring him to trial, Peter was sleeping between two soldiers, bound with two chains, and sentries stood guard at the entrance. ⁷Suddenly an angel of the Lord appeared and a light shone in the cell. He struck Peter on the side and woke him up. "Quick, get up!" he said, and the chains fell off Peter's wrists.

⁸Then the angel said to him, "Put on your clothes and sandals." And Peter did so. "Wrap your cloak around you and follow me," the angel told him. ⁹Peter followed him out of the prison, but he had no idea that what the angel was doing was really happening; he thought he was seeing a vision. ¹⁰They passed the first and second guards and came to the iron gate leading to the city. It opened for them by itself, and they went through it. When they had walked the length of one street, suddenly the angel left him.

---

cf. Luke 9:54f.) made him a political threat to Agrippa, see O. Cullmann, "Courants Multiples dans la Communauté Primitive: A Propos du Martyre de Jacques fils de Zébédée," *RSR* 60 (1972): 55-68.

[145] A number of scholars see a "Passover deliverance" motif in the story of Peter's escape from prison. There are Jewish traditions that God particularly used Passover eve as the time to deliver his people. Certain phrases in Acts 12 are seen to echo the Passover narrative of Exodus: cf. "the night before" (12:6; Exod 12:12), "quick, get up" (12:7; Exod 12:11), "put on your . . . sandals" (12:8; Exod 12:11), "the Lord has rescued" (Acts 12:11; Exod 18:4,8-10). For a full development see J. Dupont, *Nouvelles Etudes*, 338-41; A. Strobel, "Passa Symbolik und Passa-wunder in Act. xii.3ff., *NTS* 4 (1958): 210-15.

[146] H. Conzelmann, *Acts of the Apostles*, trans. J. Limburg, A. Kraabel, and D. Juel, *Her* (Philadelphia: Fortress, 1987), 93.

¹¹Then Peter came to himself and said, "Now I know without a doubt that the Lord sent his angel and rescued me from Herod's clutches and from everything the Jewish people were anticipating."

¹²When this had dawned on him, he went to the house of Mary the mother of John, also called Mark, where many people had gathered and were praying. ¹³Peter knocked at the outer entrance, and a servant girl named Rhoda came to answer the door. ¹⁴When she recognized Peter's voice, she was so overjoyed she ran back without opening it and exclaimed, "Peter is at the door!"

¹⁵"You're out of your mind," they told her. When she kept insisting that it was so, they said, "It must be his angel."

¹⁶But Peter kept on knocking, and when they opened the door and saw him, they were astonished. ¹⁷Peter motioned with his hand for them to be quiet and described how the Lord had brought him out of prison. "Tell James and the brothers about this," he said, and then he left for another place.

¹⁸In the morning, there was no small commotion among the soldiers as to what had become of Peter. ¹⁹After Herod had a thorough search made for him and did not find him, he cross-examined the guards and ordered that they be executed.

12:6-8a The story of Peter's deliverance begins with the notice that it was the night before Peter's trial. This heightens its dramatic impact. It was the last minute before the sealing of the apostle's doom. Peter is described as sleeping, bound with two chains, each fastened to a guard, one on his right and one on his left.[147] The other two guards of the squadron of four stood watch at the doors of the prison. Perhaps one stood at each of the two inner gates of the prison (cf. v. 10).[148] That Peter could sleep so soundly the night before his trial is perhaps indicative of his calm assurance that he was in God's hands. It may also reflect that the guards were asleep on either side of him. Suddenly, an angel of the Lord appeared,[149] and a flash of heavenly light filled the cell.[150] Peter was still fast asleep, and the angel had to arouse him, perhaps with a kick in the ribs. Still not fully alert, Peter really had no idea what was happening. The angel had to direct every single movement of the apostle: "get up"; "put your coat on"; "tie your sandals"; "follow me." Obviously, this was

---

[147]For the Roman practice of chaining prisoners to their guards, cf. Seneca, *Epistles* 5.7. See also Schneider, *Apostlegeschichte* 2:104. Agrippa himself had earlier been a prisoner in Rome and was at that time chained to a guard (Josephus, *Ant.* 18.196).

[148]*Beginnings* 4:135.

[149]There is a close parallel to the angel's sudden appearance to the shepherds in the Western and Byzantine traditions of Luke 2:9 (cf. KJV): καὶ ἰδού ἄγγελος κυρίου ἐπέστη.

[150]A number of interpreters see "angel" in its general sense of "messenger" and argue that a human deliverer worked an "inside job" in freeing Peter. Such details as the flash of light and "automatic" opening of the iron gate (v. 10) tell strongly against this. A heavenly messenger also delivered the apostles in 5:17-23, and a miraculous deliverance of Paul and Silas is told in 16:25f.

not Peter's *escape*. It was rather his *deliverance*. Peter was totally passive throughout the entire incident.

12:8b-11 Peter dutifully followed the angel's direction. Still half-asleep, he imagined that he was having some sort of vision (v. 9). With a pronounced dramatic tone, each step of their progress was noted. They safely passed the first sentry guarding the inner gate to the cell. Perhaps a "deep sleep from the Lord" had fallen upon the guards (cf. 1 Sam 26:12). Suspense mounted: Would they make it past the rest of the guard? They passed the second gate safely and then came to the outer gate that led into the city, a forbidding iron barrier.

Most likely the place of Peter's confinement was the Tower of Antonia, where the Roman troops were barracked. Located at the northeastern corner of the temple complex, its eastern entrance led into the streets of the city. Even this formidable iron barrier proved no hindrance to Peter and the angel, opening of its own accord and allowing their safe passage.[151] The angel led Peter down the length of the first street from the prison. Perhaps coming to a corner and allowing Peter to turn into a side street and out of sight of the prison and having delivered the apostle to safety, the angel disappeared. Only then did Peter come to full alertness and realize that God had indeed delivered him from Herod's clutches and his anticipated death (v. 11).[152]

12:12 The scene shifts to the Christian community who had been praying fervently for Peter (vv. 12-17). One group had gathered at the home of John Mark's mother, and Peter headed there.[153] It is unusual that Mary was identified through Mark; usually the child was identified by the parent. The reason possibly is that Mark was the better known of the two in Christian circles, or it may be that there were several prominent women named Mary in the early church. They were perhaps distinguished by their children. John Mark would soon play a significant role

---

[151]The automatic opening of gates is found elsewhere in Greco-Roman literature. Josephus, *War* 6.293 described the miraculous opening of the massive iron eastern gate of the temple on one occasion at midnight. For similar "automatic openings, cf. Euripides' *Bacchae* 443-48, Ovid's *Metamorphoses* 3.695f., and Homer's *Iliad* 5.749. See Talbert, *Acts*, 52-53.

[152]Peter's description of the Lord's deliverance uses the same language employed throughout the OT for God's deliverance of Israel in the exodus from Egypt (particularly the verb ἐξαιρέω). See W. Radl, "Befreiung aus dem Gefängnis," *BZ* 27 (1983): 89.

[153]The specific mention of Mark and his mother Mary indicates they were well-known to the larger Christian community. The text contains no warrant for the speculative assumption that Mary's home was the scene of the last supper and/or the upper room where the disciples gathered before Pentecost. That Mary retained her home, and a sizable one at that with its outer courtyard and servants, is a further example that the Jerusalem church's practice of sharing was voluntary and not communal ownership. That the community gathered there and made free use of it, however, is testimony that "no one claimed any of his possessions were his own" (4:32); they shared freely.

in the first missionary journey of Paul and Barnabas (12:25; 13:5,13; 15:37,39).[154]

12:13-14 The scene at Mary's house is played out in a delightful fashion with the servant-girl Rhoda as the main character. Rhoda was a common Greek name, often borne by servants and meaning *rose*. When Peter arrived, he stood at the outer gate that entered into the courtyard. Rhoda probably was responsible for keeping the gate, a task often delegated to female servants (cf. John 18:16f.). Responding to Peter's knocking, she hurried out to the gate and discovered who was there. For all her joy, she ran back into the house to announce the good news, forgetting altogether that Peter would really like to have come in. This heightened the suspense all the more. Peter did not need to be standing outside in the street, exposed to possible recapture. "Peter is at the door!" Rhoda announced excitedly, interrupting the prayers of the Christians who had gathered there. "No, it can't be," they replied; "it must be his angel."

12:15-16 This response reflects the Jewish belief that each person has a guardian angel as his or her spiritual counterpart.[155] It was believed that one's angel often appeared immediately after the person's death, and that idea may lurk behind the response to Rhoda. "You've seen his ghost," we would say. Such a reply is remarkable coming from a group that had been totally occupied in prayer for Peter's deliverance. They found it easier to believe that Peter had died and gone to heaven than that their prayers had been answered. In any event, who could trust a hysterical servant girl? "You're crazy," they said. Some things are just too good to be true (cf. Luke 24:11). But it was true, and Peter's persistent knocking finally got a response (v. 16).

12:17 Verse 17 is a key verse. Basically, it gives three pieces of information: (1) Peter's report of his miraculous delivery, (2) his instruction to tell the news to James, and (3) his departure to "another place" where he would find refuge from the wrath of Agrippa. The first item is exactly what one would expect under the circumstances. That Peter had to

---

[154]Though Paul eventually quarreled with Mark (15:37,39), he was evidently later reconciled to him and mentioned him as a trusted coworker in his later epistles (Col 4:10; 2 Tim 4:11; Phlm 24). In 1 Pet 5:13, Mark was with Peter in Rome (Babylon) and was affectionately called "son" by the apostle. Early tradition ascribed the Gospel of Mark to him, noting that it was based on the reminiscences of Peter. It has sometimes been suggested that he was the "young man" who fled Gethsemane in Mark 14:51f. and that this was his "signature" to his Gospel, but this is not provable. For the early traditions on Mark, see Eusebius, *Church History* 2.151.1-16; 3.39.14-16; 5.8.3; 6.14.6.

[155]The popular idea of a guardian angel is found in extrabiblical literature such as Tobit 5:4-16. The biblical evidence for such an idea, however, is scant. Passages that are cited for the idea generally deal with a protecting group of angels, not one's "personal" guardian (cf. Ps 91:11; Luke 16:22; Matt 18:10; Heb 1:14). See E. F. Harrison, *Interpreting Acts* (Grand Rapids: Zondervan, 1986), 204.

motion them to silence[156] in order to share his story is indicative of the excited hubbub created by his totally unexpected presence. The second item, though seemingly incidental, is actually a keynote for the subsequent text of Acts. The James who was to be informed of Peter's deliverance was James the oldest of Jesus' brothers, who from this point on assumed the leadership of the church in Jerusalem (cf. 15:13-21; 21:18).[157] It is interesting that "the brothers" are to be informed along with James. Perhaps this refers to the elders, who were assuming an increasing role in the governance of the Jerusalem church (cf. 11:30). The other apostles are not mentioned. At this time they may have been absent from Jerusalem, having taken refuge from Agrippa's persecution. The third piece of information in v. 17 has perhaps provoked more scholarly attention than it deserves, largely due to the tradition that the "other place" to which Peter went was Rome.[158] Luke evidently did not consider the place all that important and did not specify where it was. The point is simply that he had to go elsewhere to find safety from Agrippa. Later, after Herod's death, he was back in Jerusalem (15:7). That Peter went to Rome at this early date is most unlikely, and Paul's Epistle to the Romans seems to speak against it (15:20).

12:18-19a The final scene in the story of Peter's escape returns to the prison (vv. 18-19a). When the guards awoke in the morning, they found no one attached to their chains and likely no evidence of an escape other than the obvious fact that Peter was not there. After interrogating the guards and failing to locate Peter, Agrippa had the guards executed. This was in accordance with Roman law, which specified that a guard who allowed the escape of a prisoner was to bear the same penalty the escapee would have suffered.[159] Agrippa had every intention of subjecting Peter to the same fate as James.

---

[156]For this gesture of motioning a crowd to silence in order to address them, cf. 13:16; 21:40; 26:1.

[157]For James's relationship to Jesus, see Chap. I, n. 47. James is listed among Jesus' brothers in Mark 6:3. Paul attested to the prominence of James in the Jerusalem church (Gal 1:19), listing him along with Peter and John as one of its "pillars" (Gal 2:9) and showing the strong influence he had even over Peter and Barnabas (Gal 2:12f.). Paul listed him among those to whom the risen Jesus appeared (1 Cor 15:7), and he is the traditional author of the Epistle of James. For a characterization of his leadership and the tradition of his martyrdom, see the commentary on 21:17-26.

[158]For Rome as the "other place," see J. Wenham, "Did Peter Go to Rome in A.D. 42?" *TB* 23 (1972): 94-102. Antioch has often been suggested as well as the Mesopotamian Diaspora (R. E. Osborne, "Where Did Peter Go?" *CJT* 14 [1968]: 274-77). For the unlikely view that Peter was actually martyred at this time and that the "other place" means *beyond this earth*, see D. F. Robinson, "Where and When Did Peter Die?" *JBL* 64 (1945): 255-67 and W. M. Smaltz, "Did Peter Die in Jerusalem?" *JBL* 71 (1952): 211-16.

[159]The Roman Code of Justinian 9.4.4. The Greek literally says that Agrippa commanded that the guards be "led away," ἀνάγω, but that verb is often used euphemistically for execution.

(3) Herod's Self-destructive Arrogance (12:19b-23)

Then Herod went from Judea to Caesarea and stayed there a while. [20]He had been quarreling with the people of Tyre and Sidon; they now joined together and sought an audience with him. Having secured the support of Blastus, a trusted personal servant of the king, they asked for peace, because they depended on the king's country for their food supply.

[21]On the appointed day Herod, wearing his royal robes, sat on his throne and delivered a public address to the people. [22]They shouted, "This is the voice of a god, not of a man." [23]Immediately, because Herod did not give praise to God, an angel of the Lord struck him down, and he was eaten by worms and died.

12:19b-20 There are two climaxes to the account of Agrippa's persecution. One is Peter's escape from his clutches. The other is Agrippa's own grisly fate. Chronologically, his death came anywhere from several months to a year after Peter's escape, but the Christians viewed it very much as a divine retribution for what they had suffered under the king.[160] Josephus also gave an account of Agrippa's death (*Ant.* 19.343-52) which, though going into greater detail, is very much in agreement with the narrative in Acts. Josephus and Acts both set the event in Caesarea (Acts 12:19b). Josephus did not mention the quarrel with the Phoenician coastal cities of Tyre and Sidon. Evidently it was some sort of economic war in which Agrippa had the upper hand, since these coastal towns were indeed totally dependent for their food on the inland territories Agrippa ruled (v. 20).[161] We know nothing more of Blastus. He is described as being the king's "chamberlain," or "personal servant." As a trusted servant, he was evidently able to gain the king's ear on the matter and negotiate for a settlement suitable to the Tyrians and Sidonians. Blastus was likely given some "financial consideration" by them in exchange for his role as mediator.

12:21-23 Verse 21 describes Agrippa as appearing before the people "on the appointed day." Josephus specified that it was the day of a festival in honor of Caesar. Evidently the king chose this as the occasion for formally concluding the agreement with Tyre and Sidon. Josephus also

---

[160]The chronological question turns on the particular occasion when Agrippa made his oration in Caesarea (v. 21). If it was at the games held in Caesarea every five years, it would have been in March A.D. 44 when Agrippa was struck dead. Since the Passover came later than that in A.D. 44, Peter's escape would have been Passover of A.D. 43. The occasion could have been the celebration of the emperor's birthday in August. In that event Peter would have been arrested in the spring (Passover) of A.D. 44 with Herod dying the summer of the same year. See *Beginnings* 5:446-52.

[161]The OT attests to this dependency. Cf. 1 Kgs 5:11; Ezek 27:17. M. Strom notes the parallel between the judgment that was spoken against the pride of the king of Tyre in Ezek 28 and the fate that befell Agrippa ("An Old Testament Background to Acts 12, 20-23," *NTS* 32 [1986]: 289-92).

went into greater detail on the "royal robes" worn by Agrippa. The garment was made of silver and glistened radiantly in the morning sun. As Herod, in all his glory, turned and addressed the people, they shouted, "This is the voice of a god, not of a man" (v. 22). Josephus recorded a like response from the people, who hailed Herod as a god and "more than mortal." Josephus at this point added significant detail, noting that Herod neither affirmed nor denied the people's ascription of divinity to him. Then, looking up, he saw an owl. On an earlier occasion, when imprisoned in Rome, he had seen a vision of an owl; and a fellow prisoner told him it was the harbinger of good fortune for him. That had indeed proved true, for he was released and eventually became king of the Jews. The same prisoner, however, had warned him that if he ever again saw an owl, he would have but five days to live (*Ant.* 18.200). Josephus added that he was immediately stricken with pain and carried to his bed chamber, and he died exactly five days later. Luke's account also speaks of an immediate death, making explicit what is implicit in Josephus—he was struck down by "an angel of the Lord."

Once again we see a motif already familiar in Acts. There is both mercy and judgment with the Lord. The Spirit blessed the faithful Christians with miraculous works and great growth (5:12-16). The same Spirit brought judgment to Ananias and Sapphira (5:1-11). The Lord's angel delivered Peter from mortal danger (12:6-17). The Lord's angel struck Agrippa dead for all his arrogance (12:20-23). He did not "give praise to God"—neither in his acceptance of the people's blasphemous acclamation nor in his persecution of God's people. Josephus spoke of acute pain in Agrippa's abdomen. Luke said that he was "eaten by worms."[162]

(4) Peace for the Church (12:24-25)

[24]But the word of God continued to increase and spread.
[25]When Barnabas and Saul had finished their mission, they returned from Jerusalem, taking with them John, also called Mark.

12:24 With Agrippa's sudden removal, the persecution of the church ended, and once more the word of God flourished. The Greek says literally that it "grew and multiplied," just as the seed that fell on good ground in Jesus' parable of the sower. This is the last summary of the

---

[162]The same word is used of worm-eaten crops. Neither Josephus nor Acts provides sufficient detail to make a proper medical diagnosis. Many suggestions have been offered—a ruptured appendix, arsenic poisoning, or tapeworms (see E. M. Merrins, "The Deaths of Antiochus IV, Herod the Great, and Herod Agrippa I," *BibSac* 61 [1904]: 561f). As his title suggests, those former villains of Jewish history, Antiochus Epiphanes and Herod the Great, also died in a "worm-eaten" state according to Josephus.

Jerusalem church in Acts. It ends on a positive note. God continued to bless the witness of the Jerusalem community.

12:25 Verse 25 moves the narrative forward, mentioning the return of Paul and Barnabas to Antioch on completion of their mission of delivering the famine relief offering (11:30). Viewed chronologically, it would have most likely been around this time, around A.D. 46 and thus a couple of years after the death of Agrippa, that the famine struck Judea and Antioch sent its offering.[163] The best manuscripts read "to," not "from," Jerusalem, but that would scarcely make sense. Clearly, the two were returning from Jerusalem to Antioch and were set for the following narrative, which took place in Antioch (13:1-3). The NIV has chosen, as most translations do, to follow the more poorly attested reading "from Jerusalem," since the context seems to demand it. Another solution, however, is to put the phrase "to Jerusalem" with "ministry," a construction found elsewhere in Luke-Acts. The translation would then read, "Barnabas and Saul returned, having finished their ministry to Jerusalem."[164] In any event, they took a companion along with them—John Mark (cf. 12:12). The church at Antioch would soon send the three of them on a mission (13:1-3) that would result in tremendous success among the Gentiles. The witness to Judea and Samaria had now been well-established. The way to the Gentiles had already been paved by Philip, by Peter, and by the church at Antioch. From this point it would be Paul who above all would take up the Gentile witness and move the gospel to "the ends of the earth.

---

[163]See Bruce, *Acts:* NIC, 257; also Harrison, *Acts*, 208f.

[164]This is argued convincingly by J. Dupont, "La Mission de Paul à Jerusalem' (Actes 12, 25)," *NovT* 1 (1956): 275-303.

———————————— *SECTION OUTLINE* ————————————

———— **V. PAUL TURNS TO THE GENTILES (13:1–15:35)** ————

Chapters 13–15 begin the story of the mission to the "ends of the earth." The Gentile mission started in earnest with Paul and Barnabas's work on Cyprus and in the Roman province of Galatia (chaps. 13–14). Their successes provoked a reaction from the more conservative Jewish Christians of Judea, which led to a major conference on the Gentile question in Jerusalem (chap. 15). The conference worked out a solution agreeable to all; the legitimacy of the Gentile mission was recognized, and Paul was given the go-ahead for continuing his outreach to the larger Greco-Roman world.

The mission to the Gentiles is not new to this section of Acts. The "breakthrough" had already occurred in chaps. 8–11, with Philip's witness to the solitary Ethiopian, the conversion of Cornelius and his household through Peter's testimony, and the extensive evangelization of the Gentiles in their community by the Antioch church. Indeed, Paul and Barnabas had played a major role in Antioch's witness to the Gentiles (11:26). What is new to these chapters is that for the first time a local Christian church was led to see the need for a witness beyond them to the larger world and commissioned missionaries to carry out that task. Prior to this, witness had been restricted more or less to their own locale or the larger environs of Judea and Samaria. At this point the witness to the "ends of the earth" began (cf. 1:8).

Even in these chapters there is a gradual development toward the mission to the Gentiles. From his experience in witnessing to the Diaspora Jewish synagogues, Paul came more and more to be committed to the Gentile witness to which he had been called (cf. 9:15). Especially in Antioch of Pisidia, he first became impressed with the receptivity of the Gentiles (13:46-48). In this sense, these chapters can be considered as "capping off" Paul's commitment to his Gentile mission.

Traditionally, the mission depicted in chaps. 13–14 has been referred to as the first of Paul's "missionary journeys." The designation perhaps best fits this period of his witness, as one is given the impression throughout that he and Barnabas are constantly on the move, witnessing first in one town and then moving to another. For his second (15:36–18:22) and third (18:23–21:14) periods of missionary activity, however, the designation "journey" can be somewhat misleading if the conception is that of Paul being constantly on the move. The lion's share of the second period was spent in the city of Corinth and in Ephesus on his third mission. Although Paul engaged in extensive travel at the beginning and end of each of these periods, his pattern was to establish work in the major metropolitan centers with the witness radiating out into the surrounding regions, largely through the assistance of associates like Timothy, Titus, and Epaphras.

1. Paul and Barnabas Commissioned (13:1-3)

[1]In the church at Antioch there were prophets and teachers: Barnabas, Simeon called Niger, Lucius of Cyrene, Manaen (who had been brought up with Herod the tetrarch) and Saul. [2]While they were worshiping the Lord and fasting, the Holy Spirit said, "Set apart for me Barnabas and Saul for the work to which I have called them." [3]So after they had fasted and prayed, they placed their hands on them and sent them off.

13:1 The Antioch church was the first Christian congregation to witness to the Gentiles in its own city (11:19f.). It then became the first to send missionaries forth into the larger world. Judging from Acts, Antioch was the first church to catch the vision of "foreign missions." The leadership is described in unique terms as comprised of "prophets and teachers" (v. 1), and five names are listed. Although it is possible grammatically to construe the first three as being prophets and the last two as teachers, it probably is best to see all five as comprising the congregational leadership as prophet-teachers. Paul and Barnabas already had been described as "teaching" the congregation (11:26), and the additional designation of "prophet" would emphasize the inspired, Spirit-led dimension to their teaching.

In Paul's epistles the role of "prophet" is regularly depicted as a gift of the Spirit (cf. Rom 12:6; 1 Cor 12:10,28; 14:1-5,24-25,31; Eph 4:11). The gift of prophecy can be that of foretelling future events, as with Agabus (Acts 11:27). More often it is that of speaking an inspired word from God for the edification and direction of the community.[1] In this latter sense the gift is exemplified in the present passage, as these "prophetic teachers" were inspired by the Spirit to set Paul and Barnabas apart for a special mission (v. 2).

One is intrigued by the list of five names. Those of Barnabas and Paul are quite familiar, and they become even more so in the following narrative. Of the other three, nothing else is known for certain. "Simeon called Niger" perhaps indicates that he was a black, since *niger* is the Latin word for black. Some have suggested that he might have come from Cyrene, like Lucius, or from elsewhere in North Africa. From the time of the early church fathers, some have equated "Lucius of Cyrene" with Luke and seen this solitary reference as Luke's "signature" to his book. Little evidence, however, substantiates this; and the Greek "Luke" and Latin "Lucius" are different names.[2] Manaen is described as having been brought up with Herod the Tetrarch. The Herod referred to would be Antipas (cf. Luke 3:1; Acts 4:27). The term used to describe Manaen's relationship to Herod is *syntrophos*, which literally referred to someone suckled by the same nurse as a baby. Later it came to mean someone "reared together" with someone. Manaen was thus of considerable social standing, a courtier and childhood companion of the king.[3] Manaen was

---

[1] See F. V. Filson, "The Christian Teacher in the First Century," *JBL* 60 (1941): 317-28; H. Greeven, "Propheten, Lehrer, Vorsteher bei Paulus," *ZNW* 44 (1952-53): 1-43; O. Knoch, "'In der Gemeinde von Antiochia gab es Propheten und Lehrer' (Apg. 13, 1)," *Liturgisches Jahrbuch* 32 (1982): 133-50.

[2] Some have gone further and connected Luke/Lucius with the Lucius of Rom 16:21. For the view that Lucius was a Cypriot and that "Cyrene" is a scribal error for an original text that read Kyrenia (a town in Cyprus), see F. F. Bishop, "Simon and Lucius: Where did they come from? A Plea for Cyprus," *ExpTim* 51 (1939-40): 148-53.

[3] Josephus (*Ant.* 15.373-78) tells of an Essene of similar name who rose to favor in the

possibly the source of Luke's rather extensive treatment of Antipas (cf. Luke 8:3; 13:31f.; 23:7-12).

13:2 In v. 2 "they" likely refers to the entire Antioch congregation gathered for worship,[4] but the directive of the Holy Spirit may well have been mediated through the inspiration of the prophet-teachers. That they were fasting indicates the church was in a mood of particular expectancy and openness to the Lord's leading. Although evidence suggests the Jewish practice of fasting was regularly observed in some early Christian circles, the association of fasting with worship suggests a time of intense devotion when normal human activities like eating were suspended. This is still a valid form of fasting for Christians today.[5] The Spirit directed the community "to set apart" Barnabas and Saul. The Spirit led the church in its mission. As throughout Acts, *God* took the initiative in every new development of the Christian witness; however, the church did its part. It fasted and prayed, seeking the divine leading in a mode of expectant devotion. The Spirit was not specific at this point, referring only to "the work to which I have called them." The little word "work" (*ergon*) refers to Paul and Barnabas's mission. It forms an "inclusion" for the whole mission, occurring here at its inception and again at its conclusion (14:26).

13:3 The congregation responded in faith. It is not clear who laid hands on Paul and Barnabas, whether the other prophet-teachers, the elders of the church (who can only be assumed from the structure of the other churches in Acts), or the whole congregation. The gesture almost certainly was *not* an ordination. No one in Antioch had any rank exceeding that of Paul and Barnabas. The gesture was more a symbol of the congregation's endorsing the work of the two. They separated them for a task in which they would perform a witness on behalf of the whole church.[6] In modern terms it was a commissioning service for the two missionaries.

---

court of Herod the Great for predicting Herod's rise to kingship. Some would see this as possibly the grandfather of the Manaen of Acts 13:1, but this is strictly speculative. Unlikely is the view that Luke confused Barnabas's nickname with that of Manaen since the Hebrew form of Manaen (Menachem) means *comforter* (cf. 4:36).

[4] The word for "worship" is λειτουργέω, which in secular Greek referred to a public service rendered without pay. In the NT it is employed widely for any ministry rendered in the name of the Lord. In the OT it was used of the service of the priests and Levites in the temple worship, a similar context to that of Acts 13:2.

[5] For the linking of fasting with prayer and worship, cf. Luke 2:37; Acts 14:23.

[6] E. Best, "Acts xiii:1-3," *JTS* 11 (1960): 344-48. For the unlikely view that it was an ordination to the apostolate, see R. B. Rackham, *The Acts of the Apostles: An Exposition* (London: Methuen, 1901), 191-93; S. Dockx, "L'ordination de Barnabé et de Saul d'après Actes 13, 1-3," *NRT* 98 (1976): 238-50.

2. Sergius Paulus Converted on Cyprus (13:4-12)

[4]The two of them, sent on their way by the Holy Spirit, went down to Seleucia and sailed from there to Cyprus. [5]When they arrived at Salamis, they proclaimed the word of God in the Jewish synagogues. John was with them as their helper.

[6]They traveled through the whole island until they came to Paphos. There they met a Jewish sorcerer and false prophet named Bar-Jesus, [7]who was an attendant of the proconsul, Sergius Paulus. The proconsul, an intelligent man, sent for Barnabas and Saul because he wanted to hear the word of God. [8]But Elymas the sorcerer (for that is what his name means) opposed them and tried to turn the proconsul from the faith. [9]Then Saul, who was also called Paul, filled with the Holy Spirit, looked straight at Elymas and said, [10]"You are a child of the devil and an enemy of everything that is right! You are full of all kinds of deceit and trickery. Will you never stop perverting the right ways of the Lord? [11]Now the hand of the Lord is against you. You are going to be blind, and for a time you will be unable to see the light of the sun."

Immediately mist and darkness came over him, and he groped about, seeking someone to lead him by the hand. [12]When the proconsul saw what had happened, he believed, for he was amazed at the teaching about the Lord.

13:4 Paul and Barnabas set out on their mission, departing from Seleucia, the main port for Antioch, lying about sixteen miles downstream and five miles from where the Orontes flowed into the Mediterranean. Their destination was Cyprus, some sixty miles distant. Barnabas was himself a Cypriot by birth (4:36), the Hellenists had already begun some witness on the island (11:19), and other natives of Cyprus belonged to the Antioch church (11:20).

The island had been settled from ancient times; it was occupied as early as the eighteenth century B.C. and was colonized successively by Egyptians, Phoenicians, Greeks, Assyrians, Persians, and the Egyptian Ptolemies. Since the mid-first century B.C. it had been under Roman jurisdiction and from 22 B.C. had been organized as a senatorial province administered by a proconsul. It is a testimony to Luke's accuracy in details that he designated Sergius Paulus (v. 7) the Roman proconsul (*anthypatos*), the correct term for the administrator of a senatorial province.[7]

13:5 Barnabas and Paul landed at Salamis, the closest Cypriot port to Seleucia. Here they began a pattern that Paul would perpetuate throughout his missionary career. Where there were local synagogues, he began his ministry by preaching first in them. There was an extensive Jewish

---

[7]There were two types of Roman provinces. Imperial provinces were under the emperor, had legions stationed in them, and were administered by legates (governors). Senatorial provinces were under the Roman senate, had no legions, and were administered by proconsuls. Antioch was in the *imperial* province of Syria. For further information on Cyprus, see M. F. Unger, "Archaeology and Paul's Tour of Cyprus," *BibSac* 117 (1960): 229-33.

292

community at Salamis, and evidently several synagogues were there.[8]
Only at this point do we learn that John Mark was part of the entourage.
He is described as their "helper" (*hypēretēs*). This term is used in Luke
1:2 for "servants of the word" and in Luke 4:20 for the worship leader in
the synagogue. Some have seen Mark's role as that of catechist, or keeper
of written documents on Jesus' life, or even the administrator of baptism.[9]
Keeping the more general meaning of the term, which is that of a servant
or helper, probably would be wisest. Mark assisted Barnabas and Paul in
whatever way they needed him.

13:6-7 From Salamis the three traversed the width of the island,
arriving at Paphos some ninety miles to the west. It may well be that they
evangelized the villages along the way,[10] but Luke did not dwell on this.
He rather focused on the high point of the Cyprus experience—the conversion of the proconsul and the defeat of a false prophet's attempt to
thwart their witness to him. Paphos was a fairly new city and the seat of
Roman government on the island.[11] The proconsul at this time was named
Sergius Paulus. Although there is no certain archaeological verification of
his proconsulship on Cyprus at this time, several inscriptions might point
in that direction.[12] Further, the family of the Pauli was an influential
Roman patrician family, producing many officials throughout the empire
over a long period, which in itself lends credence to a Paulus as proconsul
of Cyprus.

13:8 Paul's efforts to witness to the proconsul did not go unopposed,
however. In the official's entourage was a certain Jewish "false prophet"
named "Bar-Jesus." Luke described him as a "magos," a term that could
be used favorably, as it is of the Persian astrologer-magi of Matt 2. It was
often used in the sense of a charlatan, a trickster, a claimant to false pow-

---

[8]For Jews on Cyprus see Philo, *Embassy to Gaius* 282 and Josephus, *Antiquities* 13.284-87.

[9]For catechist see R. O. P. Taylor, "The Ministry of Mark," *ExpTim* 54 (1942-43): 136-
38. For keeper of written documents, see B. T. Holmes, "Luke's Description of John Mark,"
JBL 54 (1935): 63-72.

[10]The verb used for traversing in v. 6 is often used in Acts with the connotation of witnessing along the way.

[11]The old settlement of Paphos was originally established by the Phoenicians and lay
some seven miles to the southeast of the new city of that name. This original settlement had
been destroyed by earthquake in 15 B.C. The new city had thus been built during the Roman
period in Roman style.

[12]There are problems with all the inscriptions that are relevant, either about date or the
incompleteness of the inscription due to damage. Two inscriptions have been found in Pisidian Antioch, one to an L. Sergius Paullus and another to a female Sergia Paulla. At Soli on
the northern coast of Cyprus was found an inscription to a Paulus, but his office was not
specified; and he seems to date too late for the Paulus of Acts. A Lucius Sergius Paullus is
given on a Roman list as a curator of the Tiber, but there is no evidence to link him with service on Cyprus. On the whole question see F. F. Bruce, "Chronological Questions in Acts,"
BJRL 68 (1986): 279-80.

ers; and it is in this derogatory sense that Luke referred to Bar-Jesus. One should not be altogether surprised that a Roman official could be hoodwinked by such a figure. Romans put great stock in powers of divination and even had their own sacred oracles. Charlatans like Bar-Jesus were usually smooth and highly knowledgeable, practicing a sort of pseudoscience. His Jewish credentials did not hurt him either. The Jews had a reputation among the Romans for their antiquity and depth of religious knowledge. Josephus mentioned a number of such Jewish sorcerers who had great successes among the Gentiles.[13] Bar-Jesus probably offered his services to Paulus in terms of divining future events for him. In any event, just as with Simon-Magus (8:9-13,18f.), the setup was a lucrative one; and Bar-Jesus saw the Christian missionaries as a potential threat. In v. 8 Luke added that the magician also had the name of Elymas and that "is what his name means." The etymology is anything but clear, but the connection seems to be between "magician" and Elymas, not with "Bar-Jesus.

13:8-10 Any number of suggestions have been made to show the possible etymological relationship between the two terms. Of these the most likely are that Elymas comes from the Arabic root *alim*, which means *sage*, or that it comes from the Aramaic *haloma*, which means *interpreter of dreams.*[14] Either of these derivations would point to the same fact— Elymas claimed to predict the future. For Luke such claims were unfounded. Elymas was a "false prophet" (v. 6). Threatened, Elymas sought to thwart the Christian missionaries by turning "the proconsul from the faith" (v. 8). At this point Sergius Paulus was not a believer. Elymas sought to hinder the missionaries from their witness to the faith, to divert Paulus's attention from the proclamation. This was a serious mistake, poor judgment on his part. Like Peter with Simon Magus (8:20-23), Paul turned on Elymas with a vengeance. Luke clarified that it was ultimately not Paul but the Spirit of God whom Elymas had taken on. Paul was "filled with the Holy Spirit." Looking at him with a withering gaze, Paul began to denounce Elymas, "You are a child of the devil." No one familiar with Aramaic (as Elymas probably would have been) could

---

[13]His most intriguing reference is in *Antiquities* 20.236-37, where he spoke of a Cyprian Jewish sorcerer who aided Felix in seducing Drusilla away from her husband Azizus, the king of Emesa. Some interpreters would see this as none other than Elymas/Bar-Jesus. (Josephus's event was some five to ten years later than Paul's encounter with Elymas.) Such an identification is at best speculative.

[14]A number of interpreters point to the variant found in several Western witnesses, where ἕτοιμος occurs in place of Elymas. He would thus claim to be "son of readiness." For the derivation from Aramaic *haloma*, see L. Yaure, "Elymas, Nehelamite, Pethor," *JBL* 79 (1960): 297-314; C. Daniel, "Un Essenien mentionné dans les Actes des Apôtres: Barjesu," *Museon* 84 (1971): 455-76. F. C. Burkitt follows the Western reading ἕτοιμος and emends it to ὁ λοίμος—"pestilent fellow" ("The Interpretation of Bar-Jesus," *JTS* 4 [1903]: 127-29).

have missed the pun. His name, Bar-Jesus (in Aramaic Bar-Jeshua), meant etymologically *son of the Savior*. He was no son of the Savior; quite the opposite, he was son of the devil.

Paul's language is filled with Old Testament phrases. "Enemy of everything that is right" surely could refer to his general moral opposition to all that was good and just. The phrase is literally, however, "enemy of all righteousness"; and "righteousness" is a primary attribute of God throughout the Bible. Paul could have implied that Elymas had set himself up as an enemy of God. He was filled with "deceit" (*dolos*) and "trickery" (*rhadiourgia*). *Dolos* originally meant *bait* by which something or someone was lured into a trap. This was what Elymas had been doing all along with Sergius Paulus, deceiving him with all his false claims. Now he was adding to his evil ways—not only tricking the proconsul but perverting the straight paths of the Lord himself in attempting to divert the official from the gospel.

13:11 One might have been able to take advantage of a proconsul, but one could not withstand the ways of the Lord with impunity. Sometimes in Acts the inevitable punishment came swiftly, as it did for Ananias and Sapphira (5:1-11). It descended with equal immediacy on Elymas. Paul predicted it: "You are going to be blind, and for a time you will be unable to see the light of the sun" (v. 11). Paul himself had experienced blindness, not, however, as punishment but as a sign of the Lord's presence in his conversion.[15] One would like to agree with Chrysostom, who argued that Paul inflicted his own blindness on Elymas in the hope that it would lead to his conversion, just as it had been a sign of his own. More likely, however, the blindness was symbolic of Elymas's own spiritual state of being (cf. John 3:19-20; 9:39).

Paul's prediction was immediately fulfilled. "Mist and darkness" overcame Elymas, and he began to grope around and seek for someone to lead him about. There was some clemency in his judgment. The blindness would be limited, "for a time." Luke did not say how long. The significant witness was given by the miracle—to Elymas of the judgment that had come from opposing God, to Sergius Paulus of the power of the God Paul proclaimed. For the Christian reader a further important point has been made: Christianity has nothing to do with the magic and superstition of this world; its power, the power of the Word and Spirit, overcomes them all. This theme will return in Acts 19.

13:12 Verse 12 describes the effect of the miracle on the proconsul: he believed. He was not only impressed by the miracle but also by the

---

[15]In the OT the phrase "not see the light" referred to *death* (cf. Job 3:16; Num 12:12), but later it came to mean *blindness* (E. Richard, "The Old Testament in Acts," *CBQ* 42 [1980]: 330-41).

teaching about the Lord. This familiar pattern already has been illustrated in Acts. The miracles wrought by the Spirit often provide an opening for faith. It is much as with the lame beggar of chap. 3. The crowds were attracted to the apostles by the healing (3:11). They believed in the Lord as the result of Peter's preaching the gospel (4:4). So here Paulus was impressed by what had happened to Elymas. He believed as a result of the teaching about the Lord. There is no reason to doubt the reality of his conversion.[16] This has been the main point of the whole Cyprus narrative. No other conversions have been mentioned, though there were surely others as a result of the missionaries' preaching. Luke left us with one major result of the mission—the conversion of a prominent Roman official.

Before leaving the Cyprus narrative, one small but significant note must be treated. In v. 9 Luke identified Saul by his Roman name, "who was also called Paul." From this point on in Acts, the name Paul appears, whereas before it had been "Saul." The only exceptions hereafter are Paul's recounting his conversion experience when he repeated the call of Jesus to him, "Saul, Saul, why do you persecute me?" Why did Luke change the designation at this point? Some have argued that he did so because of the presence of Sergius Paulus in the narrative, a man of the same name. That may well have something to do with it but only in an indirect way. Paul was now entering Greco-Roman territory as he worked on Cyprus, no longer working primarily among Palestinian Jews. He almost certainly had both names. Paul was his Roman cognomen, and every Roman citizen had such a name.[17] It would be the name natural to every Greek and Roman who crossed his path—like Sergius Paulus. Paul also had a Hebrew name, called a signum, an additional name used within his own community. It was Saul, the same name as the ancient Jewish king who was also a Benjamite. This signum "Saul" was surely that used of him in Jewish circles. Luke's switch at this point is thus natural and quite observant of the situation. Moving into Greco-Roman territory, Paul would be the name primarily used to address him. There is a further subtle dimension. With the change in name, there also came a shift in status. Heretofore, Barnabas had always been mentioned before Paul. It was "Barnabas and Saul" (cf. 13:1, 7; 11:30; 12:25). From here on it was "Paul and Barnabas" (cf. 13:42, 46).[18] Even more significantly, it was "Paul and his companions" (13:13).

---

[16]See J. Foster, "Was Sergius Paulus Converted? (Acts xiii.12)," *ExpTim* 60 (1948): 354-55.

[17]Romans had three names: a praenomen, a nomen, and a cognomen, as in Gaius Julius Caesar. "Paul" seems to have been a cognomen. We simply do not know his first two Roman names. The practice of having an "ethnic" signum was common in the East. See G. A. Harrer, "Saul who also is called Paul," *HTR* 33 (1940): 19-33.

[18]The only exceptions are 14:12,14 and 15:12,25, where Barnabas actually did have priority in the view of the Lystrans (Zeus) and the church in Jerusalem (their former delegate to Antioch).

Paul was more and more on his own ground as he moved into Greco-Roman territory. He assumed leadership.

3. Paul's Address to the Synagogue at Pisidian Antioch (13:13-52)

The remainder of chap. 13 is set primarily in Pisidian Antioch. It consists of three main parts: (1) the journey to Antioch and the setting of the stage for Paul's speech in the synagogue (vv. 13-16a), (2) Paul's address to the synagogue (vv. 16b-41), and (3) the final response of the Jews and Gentiles on the occasion of a second visit to the synagogue in Antioch (vv. 42-52).

(1) The Setting (13:13-16a)

[13]From Paphos, Paul and his companions sailed to Perga in Pamphylia, where John left them to return to Jerusalem. [14]From Perga they went on to Pisidian Antioch. On the Sabbath they entered the synagogue and sat down. [15]After the reading from the Law and the Prophets, the synagogue rulers sent word to them, saying, "Brothers, if you have a message of encouragement for the people, please speak."
[16]Standing up, Paul motioned with his hand and said:

Leaving Cyprus, Paul and his party sailed from Paphos northwest to the coast of present-day Turkey. Their stopping place was Perga, some twelve miles inland. Perga was located in Pamphylia, the land that lay between the Taurus mountains and the Mediterranean Sea. The area of Lycia lay to the west and Cilicia to the east. Pamphylia was under Roman jurisdiction, having been a separate province from 25 B.C. to A.D. 43 and then being merged with Lycia into the province of Pamphylia-Lycia from A.D. 43–68. Perga could be reached by traveling seven miles up the Cestrus River from the Mediterranean port of Attalia and then going about five miles west by foot to Perga. The Cestrus is not navigable in this area today, and it may not have been in Paul's day. If not, the missionaries would have landed at Attalia and traveled by foot to Perga.[19] At this point Perga seems to have been only a stopping place on their journey. On their return trip they would preach there (14:25).

At Perga, John Mark decided to leave them, and he returned home to Jerusalem. Just why he did so has long been a fruitful subject for speculation.[20] Was he intimidated by the prospect of the arduous and dangerous

---

[19]F. J. Foakes-Jackson and K. Lake, eds., *The Beginnings of Christianity* (London: Macmillan, 1922), 4:147; 5:224.

[20]For the view that it was youthful rebellion at a change of Paul's plans, see T. J. Pennell, "Acts xiii, 13," *ExpTim* 44 (1932-33): 476; R. Hughes, "Acts xiii, 13," *ExpTim* 45 (1933-34): 44f. W. Ramsay argued that Paul contracted malaria at Perga and that he changed an original plan to go to Ephesus in order to reach the highlands of Antioch for relief (*St. Paul the Traveller and Roman Citizen* [London: Hodder & Stoughton, 1897], 89-97).

task of crossing the Taurus mountains to reach Antioch? Was he angered that Paul was assuming more and more authority and forcing his cousin Barnabas to a lesser role? Did he contract malaria in the Pamphylian low-lands? Did he disagree with Paul's concept of a law-free mission to the Gentiles? All of these have been suggested; none can be substantiated. Luke was simply silent on the reason. He did clarify that it was a serious matter for Paul, serious enough to create a falling out with Barnabas on a subsequent occasion (cf. 15:37f.).

Luke's note that they went from Perga to Pisidian Antioch is extremely terse, and one is apt to miss the difficulty of the trek. Antioch lay some 100 miles to the north across the Taurus mountain range. The route was barren, often flooded by swollen mountain streams, and notorious for its bandits, which even the Romans had difficulty bringing under control.[21] Antioch itself was in the highlands, some 3,600 feet above sea level. It was one of the sixteen cities named Antioch that had been established around 300 B.C. by Seleucus Nikator in honor of his father Antiochus. Although referred to as "Pisidian Antioch" to distinguish it from the others, it was actually in Phrygia but just across the border from Pisidia. In Paul's day it belonged to the Roman province of Galatia and was the leading city of the southern part of the province, having the status of a "colony city" with its privileges of local autonomy and exemption from imperial taxes. The Seleucid rulers had moved many Jews to the city, and there was a large Jewish population there.[22]

13:14-16 As was their custom, Paul and Barnabas went first to the synagogue in the city. The Diaspora synagogue was more than a house of worship. It was the hub of the Jewish community—house of worship, center of education, judicial center, social gathering place, general "civic center" for the Jewish community. If one wished to make contact with the Jewish community in a town, the synagogue was the natural place to begin. It was also the natural place to begin if one wished to share the Christian message. Jesus was the expected Jewish Messiah, and it was natural to share him with "the Jews first." There had perhaps been an arrangement already for Paul to speak that day, as the invitation from the rulers of the synagogue would suggest (v. 15b). Usually a synagogue had only one ruling elder, but evidence suggests that the title was retained by those who formerly served as well as sometimes being conferred strictly as an honor, which explains why it occurs sometimes in the plural, as here.[23] The ruling elder was responsible for worship, appointing lay

---

[21]Foakes-Jackson, *Acts*, 114.

[22]On Antioch see W. Ramsay, *The Cities of St. Paul* (London: Hodder & Stoughton, 1907), 247-96.

[23]*Beginnings* 4:149.

members to lead in prayer and read the Scripture lessons. He also would invite suitable persons to deliver the homily on the day's Scripture when such were available. The form of the service as depicted in v. 15 is exactly that known from rabbinic sources, the sermon following the readings from the Law and the Prophets.[24] There seem to have been a number of styles of homilies, but one that linked the Torah and prophetic texts together was considered ideal. One is tempted to try to derive the texts on which Paul expounded in Pisidian Antioch. Deuteronomy 1:1–3:22 for the Torah (*seder*) and Isa 1:1-22 for the prophetic text (*haphtarah*) were suggested by Ramsay.[25] More recently J. Bowker has suggested Deut 4:25-46 as the *seder* and 2 Sam 7:6-16 as the *haftarah*, with 1 Sam 13:14 as the "*proem* text," that is, the text that links the two together.[26]

(2) The Sermon (13:16b-41)

"Men of Israel and you Gentiles who worship God, listen to me! [17]The God of the people of Israel chose our fathers; he made the people prosper during their stay in Egypt, with mighty power he led them out of that country, [18]he endured their conduct for about forty years in the desert, [19]he overthrew seven nations in Canaan and gave their land to his people as their inheritance. [20]All this took about 450 years.

"After this, God gave them judges until the time of Samuel the prophet. [21]Then the people asked for a king, and he gave them Saul son of Kish, of the tribe of Benjamin, who ruled forty years. [22]After removing Saul, he made David their king. He testified concerning him: 'I have found David son of Jesse a man after my own heart; he will do everything I want him to do.'

[23]"From this man's descendants God has brought to Israel the Savior Jesus, as he promised. [24]Before the coming of Jesus, John preached repentance and baptism to all the people of Israel. [25]As John was completing his work, he said: 'Who do you think I am? I am not that one. No, but he is coming after me, whose sandals I am not worthy to untie.'

---

[24]There was a set cycle of readings for 154 Sabbaths used in Palestine and the Western Diaspora. The service consisted of six basic parts. First was the recitation of the basic confession, the Shema, based on Deut 6:4-9; 11:13-21; Num 15:37-41. Then followed prayers, including the Shemoneh'esreh, or "eighteen benedictions." Third came the Torah-reading from the books of the Law, usually divided into portions and read by several laypersons. Fourth was a reading from the Prophets. In Palestine this was usually followed by a paraphrase of the readings from an Aramaic Targum. Fifth was a homily on the day's readings, which was optional, depending on the availability of a suitable speaker. Finally came the priestly blessing based on Num 6:22-26, or, in the absence of a priest, a benediction pronounced by the ruler of the synagogue. E. Schürer, *The History of the Jewish People in the Age of Jesus Christ*, trans. S. Taylor and P. Christie, 5 vols. (Edinburgh: T & T Clark, 1892) 2:447-54.

[25]Ramsay, *St. Paul the Traveller*, 100.

[26]J. W. Bowker, "Speeches in Acts: A Study in Proem and Yelammedenu Form," *NTS* 14 (1967-68): 96-111.

²⁶"Brothers, children of Abraham, and you God-fearing Gentiles, it is to us that this message of salvation has been sent. ²⁷The people of Jerusalem and their rulers did not recognize Jesus, yet in condemning him they fulfilled the words of the prophets that are read every Sabbath. ²⁸Though they found no proper ground for a death sentence, they asked Pilate to have him executed. ²⁹When they had carried out all that was written about him, they took him down from the tree and laid him in a tomb. ³⁰But God raised him from the dead, ³¹and for many days he was seen by those who had traveled with him from Galilee to Jerusalem. They are now his witnesses to our people.

³²"We tell you the good news: What God promised our fathers ³³he has fulfilled for us, their children, by raising up Jesus. As it is written in the second Psalm:

"'You are my Son;
    today I have become your Father.'

³⁴The fact that God raised him from the dead, never to decay, is stated in these words:

"'I will give you the holy and sure blessings promised to David.'

³⁵So it is stated elsewhere:

"'You will not let your Holy One see decay.'

³⁶"For when David had served God's purpose in his own generation, he fell asleep; he was buried with his fathers and his body decayed. ³⁷But the one whom God raised from the dead did not see decay.

³⁸"Therefore, my brothers, I want you to know that through Jesus the forgiveness of sins is proclaimed to you. ³⁹Through him everyone who believes is justified from everything you could not be justified from by the law of Moses. ⁴⁰Take care that what the prophets have said does not happen to you:

⁴¹"'Look, you scoffers,
    wonder and perish,
for I am going to do something in your days
    that you would never believe,
    even if someone told you.'"

It is instructive to compare Paul's sermon in Pisidian Antioch with the other speeches in Acts. It has much in common with Peter's speeches—the emphasis on the Jerusalem Jews' responsibility for Jesus' death, the contrast between the death on the cross and the triumph of the resurrection, the apostolic witness, the proofs from Scripture (even some of the same texts), and the call to repentance. One would expect many of the same emphases. This, as with most of Peter's sermons, was a speech to Jews. Paul's sermons to Gentiles (chaps. 14; 17) would be radically different. This sermon has a feature in common also with Stephen's speech—namely, the long introductory sketch of Jewish history. There is a radically different function for the historical sketches in the two speeches, however. Stephen used Old Testament history to depict the rebelliousness of the Jews toward their divinely appointed leaders. Paul used it to show God's faithfulness to his promises for Israel, promises that were ultimately fulfilled in Christ.

The speech falls into three main parts. Verses 16b-25 provide a sketch of Old Testament history that emphasizes God's providence and promise to Israel. Verses 26-37 demonstrate by means of apostolic witness and scriptural proof how those promises are fulfilled in Christ. Finally, vv. 38-41 issue an invitation to accept the promises and a warning against rejecting God's marvelous deed in Christ.

THE PROMISE TO ISRAEL (13:16b-25). **13:16b-21** Paul was aware of two groups in his congregation and addressed them both—"men of Israel" and "Gentiles who worship God" (vv. 16b,26).[27] It was to the first group that the primary content of the sermon was addressed. It was from the second group that he would receive the most positive response. The keynote of Paul's sketch of Old Testament history was God's mercy to Israel, his acts of lovingkindness. This is particularly to be seen in the verbs he used to depict each stage of history. God "chose" the patriarchs (*eklegomai*, "elected," v. 17). He "made the people prosper" in Egypt (*hypsoō*, "exalted," v. 17). He "led them out" (*exagō*, v. 17) of Egypt. He "endured their conduct," or "cared for them in the wilderness" (v. 18).[28] He "gave the land of Canaan to them as an inheritance" (*kataklēronomeō*, v. 19). He "gave" them judges (v. 20).[29] Upon their request he "gave" them Saul as king (v. 21).[30] Finally, he "made" (literally "raised up," *egeiren*) David as king (v. 22). No point is dwelt upon until we get to David. All the stress is on God's mercy—his election of Israel, his exaltation of his people, his gift of an inheritance in the promised land, his gift of rulers and kings.

13:22-23 The pace slows with David because this is the point Paul wanted to stress. God "raised up" David, a common Old Testament expression for God bringing forth a prophet or ruler to serve his people but also an expression for Jesus' resurrection. The parallelism may not be accidental, for in a real sense David and the promises to him foreshadow

---

[27]Despite Kraabel's objections, the terms φοβούμενοι and σεβόμενοι do often seem to designate pious Gentiles who worship God, especially in such contexts as v. 50, where σεβομένας are set over against "Jews." See A. T. Kraabel, "Greeks, Jews, and Lutherans in the Middle Half of Acts," *HTR* 79 (1986): 147-57.

[28]There are variants in the LXX as well as Acts between the verbs προποφορέω ("put up with") and προφοφορέω ("treat gently like a nurse"). The Hebrew of Deut 1:31 (אָשָׂא) has the same ambiguity. See R. P. Gordon, "Targumic Parallels to Acts xiii, 18 and Didache xiv, 3" *NovT* 16 (1974): 285-89.

[29]The reference to 450 years seems to cover the period of the Egyptian sojourn to the time of the judges, allowing 400 years in Egypt, forty in the wilderness, and ten for the conquest. The Western text reads, "There were judges for 450 years," but this conflicts with the OT. See *Beginnings* 4:150-51.

[30]The tradition that Saul was king for forty years is not given in the OT but does not conflict with the OT evidence and is found in Josephus, *Ant.* 6.378 (eighteen years during Samuel's lifetime and twenty-two more after his death).

the promise fulfilled in Christ. David was a special expression of God's mercy, a man who fulfilled all God's will for him, a man after God's own heart.[31] David also received a special promise from God, a promise of a descendant who would be God's own Son and with whom he would establish a kingdom that would last forever. This promise was embodied in Nathan's prophecy to David (2 Sam 7:12-16). It lies behind v. 23 with its reference to God's promise. The promised descendant of David was Jesus the Savior. This promise to David had been the goal of Paul's entire historical sketch. It would continue to be the main subject of Paul's sermon as he showed how Christ fulfilled the promise.

13:24-25 The verses dealing with John the Baptist are difficult to place on an outline of Paul's sermon (vv. 24-25). Should they go with the opening sketch of Israel's history (vv. 16-23) or with the section on God's sending Jesus (vv. 26-37)? Does John belong with the period of Israel or the period of Christ? The very fact that John was placed between these two major sections of the speech emphasizes his transitional role. John was the eschatological messenger, the last in the line of Old Testament prophets, who heralded the coming of the Messiah. He was the link-figure, joining together the period of Israel and the period of God's new community in Christ. The outline followed here places John with the section on Israel's history because the structure of Paul's speech seems to do so. The key is Paul's address to his hearers ("brothers," etc.). The speech contains three direct addresses (vv. 16,26,38), and each seems to mark a transition to a major division in the sermon.

The references to Jesus' being the "coming" one in vv. 24-25 may reflect the prophecy of Mal 3:1, which looks to the sending of God's messenger as a herald to the coming of the Lord. Contemporary Judaism interpreted Mal 3:1 messianically, and throughout the New Testament John is depicted in this role of the herald, the forerunner of the Messiah Jesus. John's message and his baptizing were both aimed at the repentance of the people in preparation for the coming Messiah (cf. Mark 1:4). John's denial that he was the Messiah and his statement that he was unworthy to perform even the slave's task of untying the "coming" one's sandals (v. 25) is found in all four Gospels (cf. Matt 3:11; Mark 1:7; Luke 3:15f.; John 1:27). Here in Paul's speech it appears in wording that is closest to that of John's Gospel (cf. John 1:20f.,27).[32] Quite possibly Paul's listeners in the synagogue of Pisidian Antioch had heard about

---

[31]The quote in v. 22 is a mixed quote based on three passages: "I have found David" (Ps 89:20), "a man after my own heart" (1 Sam 13:14), "who will do everything I want him to do" (Isa 44:28). For "son of Jesse," cf. 1 Sam 16:1.

[32]See C. H. Dodd, *Historical Tradition in the Fourth Gospel* (Cambridge: University Press, 1963), 253-56.

John the Baptist. A few years later Paul encountered a group of the Baptist's disciples even further to the west in Ephesus (Acts 19:1-7). Paul wanted his hearers to see John's role in its proper perspective. John was in every way subordinate to the one whose coming he proclaimed. But he was a first bold *witness* to the coming of the Messiah.

THE PROMISE FULFILLED IN CHRIST (13:26-37). **13:26** There may be a distant echo of Ps 107:20 in v. 26. In any event, it is a key verse, linked directly with the reference to God's sending the promised "Savior" Jesus in v. 23. That had been the whole point of the opening section of Paul's sermon—God's mercy to Israel from the patriarchs to David, especially as epitomized in the promise to David that he would send a descendant whose kingdom would have no end.[33] Now that promise had been fulfilled in the Savior Jesus; now that message of salvation had been sent. Jesus *was* the Son of David; it was above all to David's own people, the people chosen in Abraham (v. 17), the Jews, that God had sent the Messiah and the message of salvation in him. Paul addressed a synagogue consisting of Jewish listeners and devout God-worshiping Gentiles who identified closely with the Jewish faith and looked to the promises given to Israel. The tragedy of this speech would be that the Jews, the very ones to whom the Messiah had first been sent, would ultimately reject this message of salvation (13:45f.).

13:27-28 Verses 27-31 tell the story of Jesus' rejection, death, and resurrection in the basic kerygmatic form already familiar from Peter's speeches earlier in Acts. The people of Jerusalem, and especially their rulers, did not recognize Jesus as their God-sent Messiah. What they did to him was done in ignorance (cf. 3:17). And yet, in condemning him to death, they unknowingly fulfilled the prophecies that the Messiah must suffer and die (cf. Luke 24:46; Acts 3:18). The irony of it all was that they were the very ones who should have understood who Jesus was, who read those very prophecies in their synagogues every sabbath (v. 27b). Paul highly compressed his summary. His reference to their finding no real legal basis for the death penalty (v. 28a) recalls Pilate's protest of Jesus' innocence (cf. Luke 23:4; Acts 3:13).

13:29-30 Verses 29-30 complete the gospel summary, noting that the Jews of Jerusalem fulfilled all that the prophets had written concerning his suffering and death.[34] Like Peter, Paul referred to Christ's crucifixion as hanging on "a tree" (5:30; 10:39; Gal 3:13). His compression of the story is particularly evident in his referring to "their" taking him down

---

[33]See G. W. McRae, "Whom Heaven Must Receive Until the Time," *Int* 27 (1973): 151-65.

[34]The servant psalms, especially Isa 52:13–53:12, would be especially in mind. Cf. Luke 18:31; 22:37; 24:44-46; Acts 8:32.

from the cross and laying him in the tomb, which could be taken to refer to the Jews of Jerusalem. The reference is, of course, to Joseph of Arimathea (Luke 23:53) and Nicodemus (John 19:38-42). The removal of the body and its placement in the tomb underlines the full reality of the death of Christ. He was dead and buried (cf. 1 Cor 15:4). This heightens the contrast with the next statement: God raised him from the dead.[35] The emphasis on the burial also prepares for the explanation of Ps 16:10 in vv. 34-37. It is the contrast between the seeming defeat of the cross and the victory of the resurrection so familiar in Peter's speeches: "*You* killed him but *God* raised him" (cf. 2:24; 3:15; 4:10; 5:30; 10:39f.).

13:31 The kerygmatic portion of Paul's speech ends with the familiar reference to the apostolic witness (cf. 1:8; 2:32; 3:15). It is striking that Paul did not include himself among these witnesses. But here it was not just the resurrection he wished to emphasize but the entire Christ event, embracing the journey from Galilee and the witness to his crucifixion (cf. Luke 23:49,55; Acts 1:13f.) as well as the whole forty-day period of his resurrection appearances (Acts 1:3). Above all the Twelve could attest to these events (cf. Acts 1:21f.). But another "witness" to these things was the testimony of the Scriptures. To these Scripture proofs Paul now turned.

13:32-33a Just as Peter's sermons to the Jews relied heavily on Old Testament texts that were shown to have their fulfillment in Jesus, so now in vv. 32-37 Paul turned to the Scriptures to demonstrate that Jesus is the Messiah who fulfilled the promise to David. In that generation ("to us their children," said Paul) God accomplished his promise to David. This he did by "raising up" Jesus. The expression "raising up" could be connected with God's bringing Jesus onto the stage of history. It is the same verb (*egeiren*) used in v. 22 for God's "raising up" David as king ("made . . . king"). In the immediate context, however, the emphasis is on the resurrection of Jesus. By the *resurrection* of Jesus, God demonstrated that he had truly accomplished his promise by bringing forth the Son who abides forever.

13:33b-34 Paul quoted three Old Testament texts that establish Jesus as the one who fulfills the promise. The first is Ps 2:7, a psalm that already in contemporary Judaism was applied to the Messiah and was itself based on the Nathan prophecy of 2 Sam 7.[36] God said to the Messiah: "You are

---

[35]That Jesus rose "from the dead" (ἐκ νεκρῶν) is a familiar confessional formula found throughout the NT: with ἐγείρω in Luke 9:7; Acts 3:15; 4:10; 13:30; Rom 4:24; 6:4; 7:4; 8:1; 1 Cor 15:4; Gal 1:1; Eph 1:20; Col 2:12; 1 Thess 1:10; 2 Tim 2:8; Heb 11:19; 1 Pet 1:21; with ἀνίστημι in Acts 13:34; 17:31.

[36]Psalm 2:7 is also applied to Jesus' resurrection in Heb 1:5; 5:5. See R. O'Toole, "Christ's Resurrection in Acts 13, 13-52," *Bib* 60 (1979): 361-72. The promise of 2 Sam 7 lies behind the entire argument here; see D. Goldsmith, "Acts 13, 33-37: A Pesher on 2 Samuel 7," *JBL* 87 (1968): 321-24. See also E. Lovestam, *A Study of Acts 13:32-37* (Lund: Gleerup, 1961), 37-48.

my Son; today I have become your Father" (Acts 13:33). To what does "today" refer? In the context Paul seems to have been implying the day of Jesus' resurrection. Jesus was indeed the Son of God from all eternity and recognized as such throughout his earthly life (Luke 1:35; 3:22; 9:35). But it was through the resurrection that he was exalted to God's right hand, enthroned as Son of God, and recognized as such by believing humans. It was through the resurrection that he was declared Son of God *with power* (Rom 1:4). Paul's second Old Testament text, Isa 55:3, also relates to the Nathan prophecy of 2 Sam 7:4-17: "I will give to you the holy and sure blessings promised to David." It is somewhat more difficult to determine the exact purpose of this quotation in the total argument, but Paul gave a key in introducing the verse by saying that it established that God raised Jesus from the dead, never to decay. The "holy and sure" blessings to David are God's promise that he would establish in his descendant an eternal throne, a kingdom that would last forever (cf. 2 Sam 7:13,16).[37] But God's promise was not fulfilled in David, who did not himself enjoy an eternal reign.

13:35-37 The final Old Testament text, Ps 16:10, is quoted in v. 35 to establish this.[38] The text of the psalm refers to God's Holy One who will not suffer decay. Peter also cited this same text in his Pentecost sermon (Acts 2:25-28). Paul applied it in much the same fashion. David could not have been speaking about himself in the psalm because he died, was buried, and his body decayed (v. 36; cf. 2:29-31). Only the one whom God raised from the dead escaped death and decay. Paul's argument had come full circle. Only by virtue of the resurrection of Jesus were the promises to David fulfilled. Jesus is God's Holy One who saw no decay. He is the one who received the sure and holy promises to David. He is the Son of God whose throne is forever. Paul's witness was now complete. Apostles and Scripture attested to the resurrection of Jesus in fulfillment of the promises to David. It now only remained for his hearers to accept him as the promised Savior (v. 23).

APPEAL TO ACCEPT THE PROMISE (13:38-41). **13:38-39** With the third address to his Jewish "brothers" in the synagogue, Paul turned to the final and most important part of his sermon—the call to repentance. Through-

---

[37]See J. Pillai, *Apostolic Interpretation of History: A Commentary on Acts 13:16-41* (Hicksville, N.Y.: Exposition, 1980), 83-87; E. Schweizer, "The Concept of the Davidic Son of God," *Studies in Luke-Acts*, 186-93. Dupont stresses the phrase "to you" in v. 34 and sees Paul's point as being that God will give "to you [believers]" the holy promises to David— forgiveness, justification, and service: "Ta Hosia David ta Pista (Acts 13, 34=Isaie 55:3)," *Etudes sur les Actes des Apôtres* (Paris: Cerf, 1967), 337-59.

[38]In the Greek text of verses 34-35 there is a word linkage in the words "give" (δώσω, δώσεις) and "holy" (ὅσια, ὅσιον), suggesting that the two texts may have already been linked in a collection of OT Christological testimonies.

out the sermon he had appealed to God's constant acts of mercy. Now he offered God's greatest act of mercy, the forgiveness of sins through Jesus.[39] The next statement, which is a fuller explication of the forgiveness of sins, could hardly be more Pauline: "Through him everyone who believes is justified from everything you could not be justified from by the law of Moses" (v. 39). "Through him" recalls Paul's favorite phrase, "in Christ." "Everyone who believes" is reminiscent of Paul's constant emphasis on the sole necessity of faith in Christ. Justification was his favorite term for describing the saving work of Christ. It is a law-court term and carries the idea of being acceptable to God. Through faith in Christ, one is "put right with God" and becomes acceptable to him. The idea is that the law of Moses could never serve as a basis for acceptability to God.[40] Only in Christ is one truly "justified," forgiven of sin, and acceptable to God.

13:40-41 Having begun his appeal with an invitation, Paul concluded with a warning. His warning took the form of a quote from Hab 1:5, which originally had warned Israel of King Nebuchadnezzar's rise to power and the threat of an invasion from Babylon if the nation failed to repent. In the present context the threat seems to be that God would once again have to bring judgment upon his people if they failed to accept the mercy and forgiveness now offered to them in Jesus. If they continued in their rejection, they would be rejected. It is remarkable how quickly Paul's warning came to bear. In the ensuing narrative, Habakkuk's prophecy was once again fulfilled—among the Jews of Pisidian Antioch, as they rejected the words of salvation. God did something they would never have dreamed of—he turned to the Gentiles.[41]

(3) The Sermon's Aftermath (13:42-52)

[42]As Paul and Barnabas were leaving the synagogue, the people invited them to speak further about these things on the next Sabbath. [43]When the congregation was dismissed, many of the Jews and devout converts to Judaism followed

---

[39]Throughout Luke-Acts, the work of Christ is described in terms of the forgiveness of sins: Luke 1:77; 3:3; 24:47; Acts 2:38; 5:31; 10:43; 26:18. It is often argued that this concept is not found in Paul. It is, however, very much involved in his whole idea of justification. Cf. also such explicit references as Rom 4:7; Col 1:14; Eph 1:7.

[40]Some interpreters take v. 39 to mean that the law could atone for some sins, but not for all, and that Christ justifies us in those areas where the law fails. This idea is totally alien to Paul's thought and is found nowhere else in Luke-Acts. The more "absolute" meaning seems to apply best: the law can never set us right with God; only Christ can. See F. F. Bruce, "Justification by Faith in the Non-Pauline Writings of the New Testament," *EvQ* 24 (1952): 69-71.

[41]See D. Moessner, "Paul in Acts: Preacher of Eschatological Repentance to Israel," *NTS* 34 (1988): 101.

Paul and Barnabas, who talked with them and urged them to continue in the grace of God.

[44]On the next Sabbath almost the whole city gathered to hear the word of the Lord. [45]When the Jews saw the crowds, they were filled with jealousy and talked abusively against what Paul was saying.

[46]Then Paul and Barnabas answered them boldly: "We had to speak the word of God to you first. Since you reject it and do not consider yourselves worthy of eternal life, we now turn to the Gentiles. [47]For this is what the Lord has commanded us:

" 'I have made you a light for the Gentiles,
     that you may bring salvation to the ends of the earth.' "

[48]When the Gentiles heard this, they were glad and honored the word of the Lord; and all who were appointed for eternal life believed.

[49]The word of the Lord spread through the whole region. [50]But the Jews incited the God-fearing women of high standing and the leading men of the city. They stirred up persecution against Paul and Barnabas, and expelled them from their region. [51]So they shook the dust from their feet in protest against them and went to Iconium. [52]And the disciples were filled with joy and with the Holy Spirit.

13:42-43 Paul's synagogue audience was at first favorably impressed by what he had to say. On first sight vv. 42-43 seem almost to be doublets, but they probably are best viewed as sequential. At the conclusion of the service, as they were all exiting, the congregation urged Paul and Barnabas to return for a further exposition on "these things" the next Sabbath (v. 42). At this point they expressed a somewhat detached interest. When next Sabbath arrived, they would become anything but detached. Others in the congregation showed a genuine interest in the witness of Paul and Barnabas, following them and talking with them as they left the synagogue (v. 43). Among these were both Jews and "devout converts."[42] The latter were undoubtedly proselytes, Gentiles who had become full converts to Judaism. Other Gentiles in the congregation had believed in and worshiped God but had not yet undergone the rites like circumcision, which would qualify them as converts (cf. vv. 16,26). Some of these also may have been among this group who showed a keener interest in Paul and Barnabas's testimony. The two missionaries urged them to continue along the path they had started and to remain open to the grace of God (v. 43b).

13:44-45 When next Sabbath arrived and Paul and Barnabas returned to the synagogue in accordance with the Jews' invitation, the situation rapidly deteriorated. "Almost the whole city" had gathered to hear the

---

[42]Luke spoke of σεβομένων προσηλύτων, which Foakes-Jackson suggests may indicate that καί has dropped out, the original reading referring to two distinct groups of God-fearers and proselytes (*Acts*, 120).

Christian missionaries (v. 44). Because Pisidian Antioch was predominantly Gentile, this would indicate that the Jews were considerably eclipsed by the large numbers of Gentiles who came to hear Paul's witness. Evidently the "God-fearing Gentiles" who had heard Paul's sermon the previous Sabbath had understood that the salvation he proclaimed in Christ included *them*. The word had spread like wildfire through the Gentile populace, and they were there en masse. The Jews were filled with jealousy and began to speak abusively against the things Paul was saying, perhaps even blaspheming the gospel itself (v. 45).[43] The reason for their sudden change in receptivity was evident: their "jealousy" was over the presence of all these Gentiles. It was one thing to proclaim the coming of the Messiah to the Jews. It was quite another to maintain that in the Messiah God accepted the Gentiles on an equal basis. To them this was little short of blasphemy, and Paul's witness to them was over.

13:46-48 Paul and Barnabas responded "boldly" (v. 46). The reference to "bold witness" generally appears in contexts that emphasize the inspiration of the Spirit behind the testimony, and that is most likely implied here.[44] Paul was led to a decisive turning point. The Jews had rejected the gospel that embraces all people without distinction. Paul had to focus his attention on those who were receptive—the Gentiles. Since Jesus was the Messiah who fulfilled God's promise to the Jews, it was essential to proclaim the gospel to the Jews *first* (cf. vv. 26,32f.).[45] But the Jews in Antioch had rejected the eternal life that is to be found in Jesus, and Paul had to turn to those who were "worthy" (v. 46).[46] Paul backed his decision to turn to the Gentiles by quoting Isa 49:6, an Old Testament text that was "programmatic" for the Christian mission in Acts (Acts 1:8; 26:23; cf. Luke 24:47). The text of Isaiah, a "servant" passage, originally envisaged Israel's destiny as being that of a witness to God to all the nations of the world. As Servant-Messiah, Jesus fulfilled this divine destiny. He was to be "a light to the nations."[47] Now, the messengers of the Messiah are likewise commanded to be "a light for the

---

[43]The Greek reads literally "blaspheming, they spoke against the things said by Paul." Although the word "blaspheme" is used in some NT contexts for slander against persons (cf. Acts 18:6), it is usually used of blasphemy against God or Jesus, and that may be the implication here (cf. Luke 22:65; 23:39; Acts 26:11).

[44]Cf. 4:8 ("filled with the Holy Spirit") with the bold witness in 4:13,19,31. Cf. 9:17 with 9:27,29. Behind this concept of bold witness is the promise of Jesus (Luke 21:13-15).

[45]Cf. the similar concept of "to the Jew first" in Paul's Epistle to the Romans (1:16; 2:9f.; 3:1-4).

[46]Behind the expression "eternal life" (ζωῆ αἰώνιος) lies the OT concept of sharing in the life of the age to come, God's eschatological kingdom. It is essentially the same as "salvation" (cf. v. 26). Cf. Acts 11:18; Luke 10:25; 18:18, 30.

[47]See J. Dupont, "Je t'ai établi lumière des nations (Ac. 13, 14; 43-52)," *Nouvelles Etudes*, 347-49. Cf. P. Grelot, "Note sur Actes xiii, 47," *RB* (1981): 368-72.

Gentiles" (v. 47). The Jews of Pisidian Antioch could not accept a Messiah who embraced the Gentiles. In rejecting Paul's witness to the Gentiles, they thus rejected their Messiah as well.

Verses 46-48 are programmatic for Paul's mission in Acts, establishing a pattern that would appear again and again. One could view the present statement as definitive: Paul would no longer turn to the Jews; he would now witness only to Gentiles. Such was not the case. In the very next city on his missionary itinerary he would again begin his witness in the synagogue (14:1).[48] Again and again he experienced the rejection of the Jews and turned to the Gentiles of that town. But he never gave up on his fellow Jews. It was very much the problem he wrestled with in Rom 9-11. In spite of the overwhelming rejection of the gospel by his own people, Paul could not bring himself to believe that the rejection was final and that God had deserted them. His great successes in witness were indeed among the Gentiles, but he never abandoned his witness to Jews. The ambiguity of the witness to the Jews persists to the very end of Acts and is never definitively settled (cf. 28:17-28). The contemporary church can learn from Paul's persistence. His actions caution against a mission policy that only targets those who are most receptive to the gospel message.

13:48 The *Gentiles* of Pisidian Antioch were those who accepted Paul's message, honoring (glorifying) the word of the Lord (v. 48). Perhaps it was the specific "word" of Isa 49:6 they praised, with its good news that the light of Christ and his salvation extended to Gentiles such as they. Many of them believed, accepting Christ as Savior. They were those who were "appointed for eternal life." In this phrase we encounter the same balance between human volition and divine providence that is found throughout Acts. On their part these Gentiles took an active role in believing, in committing themselves to Christ; but it was in response to God's Spirit moving in them, convicting them, appointing them for life. All salvation is ultimately only by the grace of God.

13:49-52 The Antioch mission ended on a mixed note of both opposition and success. On the one hand, the gospel was well received by the Gentiles and spread throughout the whole region.[49] On the other hand, the rejection by the Jews became even stronger and broke out in outright persecution of Paul and Barnabas. Evidently the opposition was spearheaded by some of the Gentile women who attended the synagogue. Both Josephus and Strabo attested to the fact that many Gentile women were attracted to the Jewish religion in the Diaspora, attending the synagogues

---

[48]See also 16:13; 17:1,10,17; 18:4,19; 19:8.

[49]Ramsay (*Traveller*, 104) argued that χώρα is used here in a technical sense of the whole district officially under the jurisdiction of Antioch. Χώρα, however, does not bear this meaning in other places in Acts (cf. 16:6; 18:23).

and even becoming proselytes.[50] Just who the "leading men" were whom they incited is not clear. Evidently they were Gentiles who had sufficient social standing or political power to force the departure of Paul and Barnabas.[51] In any event, Paul and Barnabas followed the directions given by Jesus for dealing with an unreceptive town: they shook the dust of the city off their feet as they departed.[52] The gesture had a certain irony about it. The rabbis attested to the Jewish practice of shaking the dust off their feet when they returned from a sojourn in Gentile territory, symbolizing their leaving their defilement behind as they stepped on the "holy land" once again. Paul and Barnabas's dust-shaking symbolized their ridding themselves of all responsibility for the unreceptive Jews. The gesture, however, did not apply to everyone in Antioch. Not all had been unreceptive, and the story ends on a positive note. There were many Gentile converts in Antioch, and these new disciples rejoiced in their experience in the Holy Spirit and their newfound acceptance in Christ.

4. Acceptance and Rejection at Iconium (14:1-7)

[1]At Iconium Paul and Barnabas went as usual into the Jewish synagogue. There they spoke so effectively that a great number of Jews and Gentiles believed. [2]But the Jews who refused to believe stirred up the Gentiles and poisoned their minds against the brothers. [3]So Paul and Barnabas spent considerable time there, speaking boldly for the Lord, who confirmed the message of his grace by enabling them to do miraculous signs and wonders. [4]The people of the city were divided; some sided with the Jews, others with the apostles. [5]There was a plot afoot among the Gentiles and Jews, together with their leaders, to mistreat them and stone them. [6]But they found out about it and fled to the Lycaonian cities of Lystra and Derbe and to the surrounding country, [7]where they continued to preach the good news.

14:1 The pattern of a mixed response set in Pisidian Antioch again greeted the missionaries at their next place of witness, Iconium.[53] It was

---

[50]Josephus (*War* 2.561) said that a majority of the women in Damascus had become Jewish converts. In his sixth satire (542), Juvenal complained of the addiction of the Roman women to the Jewish religion. See Robertson, *WP* 3:201.

[51]Ramsay (*The Cities of St. Paul*, 313) suggested that the leading men were the magistrates of the city.

[52]Cf. Luke 10:11. For a full discussion of this gesture, see *Beginnings* 5:266-77.

[53]Streams from the mountains irrigated the level plains to the east of the city, making it a flourishing agricultural area in an otherwise arid region. Particularly noted for its orchards and woolen industry, it was an important commercial center, since several major trade routes conjoined with the via Sebaste at Iconium. Located in the ancient region of Phrygia, it had been incorporated by the Romans into the province of Galatia in 25 B.C. The ancient literary sources are somewhat divided about whether Iconium was in Pisidia or Lycaonia. It seems to have been located on the border of the two areas but inside Phrygian territory, as has been shown by Ramsay (*Cities of St. Paul*, 317-70). For a description of Iconium, see also M. F.

no easy journey. Iconium was some ninety miles southeast of Antioch by the Sebastian way, the main route that connected Ephesus with Syria and Mesopotamia. Iconium was located on a plateau 3,370 feet in elevation. In many ways the city was strongly Hellenized because it had been under Seleucid rule during the second and third centuries before Christ. In Paul's day the Roman influence was particularly in evidence, as is indicated by the name Claudiconium, which was granted to it in A.D. 41 by the emperor Claudius. It was considered a particular honor for a city to be given the right to bear the emperor's name. In short, at Iconium Paul and Barnabas encountered a cultural amalgam—native Phrygians whose ancestors had occupied the area from ancient times, Greeks and Jews who dated back to the Seleucid period (312–65 B.C.), and Roman colonists whose presence dated from more recent times. Geographically it was the most ideal place for human settlement in an otherwise desolate area, and there is evidence for a town there from ancient times right down to the present.[54]

14:1-3 In setting up their witness in the major city of the area, the two missionaries followed a pattern Paul would continue to follow—establishing his work in the major population centers. Paul and Barnabas began their work in the usual manner.[55] They went first to the Jewish synagogue. Even though Paul's words in Pisidian Antioch had a somewhat definitive ring to them about turning to the Gentiles (13:46), they evidently only applied to that city. Throughout Acts, Paul's usual method would be to go first to the synagogues. There was wisdom to this. For one, Paul never gave up on the Jews. There would be some who would hear gladly the message of Messiah's coming. Also there would be present in the synagogues Gentile proselytes and other Gentiles who believed in God and would be particularly open to the inclusive Christian message. Indeed, v. 1 attests to Paul and Barnabas having success among both these groups, Jews as well as Gentiles. Verse 2, however, points to a reaction from the nonbelieving Jews. Not only did they resist the missionaries' witness themselves, but they also poisoned the minds of the Gentile populace against the Christian witnesses.[56] Verse 3 creates something of a problem.

Unger, "Archaeology and Paul's Visit to Iconium, Lystra, and Derbe," *BibSac* 118 (1961): 107-12.

[54]The modern Konya is located on the site of ancient Iconium.

[55]The Greek (κατὰ τὸ αὐτὸ) could be construed like ἐπὶ τὸ αὐτὸ and translated "Paul and Barnabas *together* entered the synagogue." The NIV rendering "as usual" is preferable. Luke was pointing to their general pattern of going first to the Jews.

[56]Behind "poison their minds" is the verb κακόω, which usually has the meaning *to ill-treat* but which can also have the meaning *to embitter someone against someone else.* Cf. Ps 106 (LXX 105): 32. This picture of the Gentile opposition to the Christians in Iconium is greatly elaborated in "The Acts of Paul and Thecla," a second-century piece of Christian

One wonders why Luke said "so" Paul and Barnabas spent a long time in Iconium after such opposition had erupted against them. Verse 4 would seem to follow more naturally on v. 2 with its note of the city being divided against the apostles, and some scholars have concluded that v. 3 is a later scribal addition and not part of the original text of Acts.[57] It is not necessary to do so. Verse 3 is in deliberate tension with the preceding and emphasizes the power of the Christian witness and the divine enabling behind it. Even though there was strong resistance to the Christians (v. 2), still they were able to maintain their witness. The two apostles were not about to back down. They had the power of the Holy Spirit to speak "boldly" for the Lord (cf. 4:29-31). Far from being intimidated, they were inspired to even bolder witness.

14:4 As the apostles continued their witness, the city became more and more polarized into those who supported them and those who opposed them (v. 4). It is noteworthy that Luke used the term "apostle" here to refer to Paul and Barnabas. Here and 14:14 are the only places where he applied the term to anyone other than the Twelve disciples. The word means literally *one who is sent* and is used of official delegates or emissaries. Paul used the term regularly to refer to his own commission as an emissary of Christ. He applied the term to others as well: James, the Lord's brother (Gal 1:19; 1 Cor 15:7), Andronicus and Junias (Rom 16:7), and an unnamed group whom he distinguished from the Twelve (1 Cor 15:7; cf. 15:5). In Acts, Luke used the term in a restricted sense, which denotes only the Twelve who were eyewitnesses to Jesus' entire ministry.[58] Acts 14:4,14 are the exceptions to the rule. Perhaps Luke indicated here that Paul and Barnabas were delegates of the Antioch church, commissioned by them for their mission. Perhaps it indicates Luke's awareness of the wider application of the word and that he here slipped into the more customary and less specialized usage.

14:5-7 The opposition to the two grew to such a point that a plot was hatched to stone them (v. 5). It does not seem to have been a question of official synagogue stoning since the Gentile populace was equally

fiction with a pronounced ascetic tendency. The deacon who wrote the work was removed from office for producing it, and it is probably wise not to use it for elucidating Paul's ministry in Iconium, as some commentators are tempted to do (cf. Rackham, *Acts*, 226-27).

[57] So conservative a scholar as Ramsay argued this (*St. Paul the Traveller*, 107-09). Moffatt solved the problem by transposing vv. 2-3 in his translation. The Western scribes of Codex Bezae made explicit what is already implicit in v. 3, adding "the Lord gave them peace." One scholar even suggests moving v. 3 to the middle of v. 48 in chap. 13 (J. H. Michael, "The Original Position of Acts xiv, 3," *ExpTim* 40 [1929-30]: 514-16). For the view that μὲν οὖν should be translated not as "therefore" but as "rather," see D. S. Sharp, "The Meaning of μὲν οὖν in Acts xiv, 3," *ExpTim* 44 (1932-33): 528.

[58] For bibliography and further discussion, see chap. I, n. 61.

involved with the Jews. The whole picture seems to have been one of mob violence rather than expulsion by the city officials, as was the case in Pisidian Antioch (13:50).[59] In any event, Paul and Barnabas learned of the plot and fled to the nearby towns of Lystra and Derbe in Lycaonia. The region of Lycaonia lay east of Iconium and was also in the Roman province of Galatia.[60] Lystra lay some twenty miles to the south of Iconium, and Derbe was another sixty miles or so southeast of Lystra. Verses 6-7 are best seen as an introductory paragraph for the Lycaonian ministry. The ministry in Lystra will be depicted in vv. 8-20a. The work in Derbe is summarized in vv. 20b-21a. There were no other significant towns in the region, but the reference to the "surrounding country" in v. 6 might indicate that they evangelized the smaller towns and countryside of Lycaonia as well.

5. Preaching to Pagans at Lystra (14:8-21a)

The major episode of chap. 14 takes place in Lystra. It began with Paul healing a cripple there (vv. 8-10). This precipitated a remarkable reaction from the native Lystrans, who attempted to honor the apostles as gods (vv. 11-13). The attempted homage of the populace prompted a strong protest from Paul and Barnabas, which was mainly expressed in a brief sermon (vv. 14-18). Ironically, the Lystran ministry was concluded when the same crowd who tried to worship Paul and Barnabas turned against Paul and attempted to stone him to death (vv. 19-20a). The section ends with a brief note of the work established in Derbe (vv. 20b-21a).

(1) A Lame Man Healed (14:8-10)

8In Lystra there sat a man crippled in his feet, who was lame from birth and had never walked. 9He listened to Paul as he was speaking. Paul looked directly at him, saw that he had faith to be healed 10and called out, "Stand up on your feet!" At that, the man jumped up and began to walk.

14:8-10 The site of Lystra was identified only in 1885, lying near the modern village of Khatyn Serai. Located in the hill country and surrounded by mountains, it was a small country town in Paul's day. Its main significance was as a Roman military post, and for that reason it had been given the status of a colony in 6 B.C. A Roman military road connected it with the other colony city in the region, Pisidian Antioch, 100 miles or so to the northwest. A statue has been found at Antioch which Lystra pre-

---

[59]Ramsay (*Cities*, 371-73) interprets the "leaders" of v. 5 as the city magistrates.

[60]In A.D. 41 Lycaonia was divided into two areas, Lycaonia Galatica (within the Roman province of Galatia) and Lycaonia Antiochiana (to the east and under the Roman client-king Antiochus). See *Beginnings* 4:162 and Ramsay, *Traveller*, 110-13.

sented to that city in the second or third century and commemorating a concordat between the two cities. Perhaps this interaction between the two towns explains why Jews would have come so far in pursuit of Paul (v. 19).[61]

The healing of the lame man in vv. 8-10 has many features in common with Peter's healing of Aeneas (9:32-35) and particularly with his healing the lame man at the temple gate (3:2-10). Like the latter, this man had been lame from his birth. Also like the man at the Beautiful Gate, this man leaped up and walked about when healed.[62] There are differences in the two narratives. In this instance the lame man showed a glimmer of faith (v. 9).[63] Perhaps it was in response to Paul's speaking; he may well have been bearing testimony to the gospel. In any event, the healing is told with the utmost brevity. Paul directed him to stand, and the man immediately jumped to his feet and began to walk about. There is no mention of the name of Jesus or the power of God, but the reader of Acts has had sufficient examples by now to know that it is indeed through the divine power that the miracle was worked (cf. 3:16; 4:30; 9:34). The people at Lystra did not know that, and this ignorance led them to the wrong reaction.

(2) Paul and Barnabas Paid Homage (14:11-13)

[11]When the crowd saw what Paul had done, they shouted in the Lycaonian language, "The gods have come down to us in human form!" [12]Barnabas they called Zeus, and Paul they called Hermes because he was the chief speaker. [13]The priest of Zeus, whose temple was just outside the city, brought bulls and wreaths to the city gates because he and the crowd wanted to offer sacrifices to them.

14:11-13 There was evidently no Jewish synagogue in Lystra. There was at least one family of Jewish extraction there, since Lystra was the home of Timothy and his Jewish mother (16:1). By and large, however, Lystra seems to have consisted primarily of Gentile pagans; and their reaction to the lame man's healing reflects that background. "The gods have come down to us in human form!" they exclaimed (v. 11). At this point Paul and Barnabas had no inkling of what was transpiring because

---

[61]Ramsay, *Cities*, 407-18.

[62]The Acts narratives contain a remarkable number of parallels between Peter and Paul. It may well be that Luke selected these particular incidents from the traditions available to him in order to highlight how God worked in the same manner through the apostle to the Gentiles as he had the apostle to the Jews.

[63]Faith is often connected to healings in the miracles of Jesus, usually noted by Jesus after the healing with the words "your faith has made you whole" (cf. Luke 7:50; 8:48; 17:19; 18:42). With the lame man at the temple gate, there is no mention of faith in the healing story, but Peter did seem to refer to it in his subsequent sermon (Acts 3:16).

the crowd's exclamation was in their own native Lycaonian dialect.[64] The
people even delineated *which* gods had come to visit them. They probably
started with Paul. Since he was doing most of the speaking, he must be
Hermes, the Greek god of oratory and the inventor of speech. Barnabas
was dubbed Zeus, the head of the Greek pantheon. Just why Barnabas
received this honor Luke did not specify. Perhaps it was because of an
ancient legend found in their region that Zeus and Hermes had once
descended to earth in human guise.[65]

Paul and Barnabas did begin to sense that something was afoot when
the priest of Zeus arrived on the scene with bulls for sacrifice (v. 13). The
temple evidently stood just outside the city gates, and it is unclear
whether the intended sacrifice was to take place at the city gates or before
the gates of the temple.[66] The latter would be the more normal procedure.
The sacrifice was to be anything but perfunctory, since the victims were
garlanded with festive woolen wreaths.[67] Only the best for visiting gods!

(3) Paul and Barnabas Dismayed (14:14-18)

[14]But when the apostles Barnabas and Paul heard of this, they tore their
clothes and rushed out into the crowd, shouting: [15]"Men, why are you doing
this? We too are only men, human like you. We are bringing you good news, telling you to turn from these worthless things to the living God, who made heaven
and earth and sea and everything in them. [16]In the past, he let all nations go their

---

[64]Lycaonian was an isolated hill-country dialect, and there are few literary remains of it.
Centuries of Hellenistic influence in their area would have given them knowledge of Greek,
and they would have had no difficulty in understanding Paul's koine. As residents of a
Roman colony, they may have had some familiarity with Latin as well. See H. J. Cadbury,
Book of Acts in History (London: Black, 1955), 21-22.

[65]Seeking hospitality, these gods were rejected by everyone except for an impoverished
elderly couple by the name of Philemon and Baucis. The couple not only took them in but
forfeited their own meager repast in order to give it to the strangers. The gods rewarded the
generous couple by transforming their cottage into a magnificent temple with a gilded roof.
The inhospitable neighbors were punished by being inundated by a severe flood. The populace at Lystra may well have wanted to avoid the same mistake with regard to the miracle-
working pair that now had come to visit them. The story is told in Ovid's *Metamorphoses*
viii, 626ff., where it is traced to Phrygia-Lycaonia. It is sometimes argued that the Lycaonians would not have had Greek gods, but there is ample evidence that by the first century
the ancient gods had been thoroughly Hellenized. In the 1920s two inscriptions were found close
to Lystra, both of which are dedicated to Zeus and Hermes, attesting to the presence of this
particular pair in the mythology of the area. See "Acts 14, 12," *ExpTim* 37 (1925-26): 528.

[66]Likely the temple was designated "the Zeus before the city," with the prepositional
phrase functioning almost adjectivally (equivalent to the adjective πρόπολις often found in
inscriptions).

[67]G. D. Kilpatrick argues for the text of Codex Bezae being the correct reading in v. 13.
Instead of θύειν, it has ἐπιθύειν for "sacrifice," a term used in the LXX and Josephus for an
improper, *pagan* sacrifice ("*Epithuein* and *epikrinein* in the Greek Bible," *ZNW* 74 [1983]:
151-53).

own way. [17]Yet he has not left himself without testimony: He has shown kindness
by giving you rain from heaven and crops in their seasons; he provides you with
plenty of food and fills your hearts with joy." [18]Even with these words, they had
difficulty keeping the crowd from sacrificing to them.

14:14-18 By now the two apostles were fully aware of what was taking place. They rushed into the crowd, rending their garments. The tearing of one's clothes is a gesture found elsewhere in the Bible. It could
dramatize a state of mourning (cf. Gen 37:29, 34), express extreme distress (Josh 7:6), or protest a perceived blasphemy (Mark 14:63). Here the
gesture expressed ardent protest and was designed to put a stop to the
intended sacrifice. "We too are only men, human like you," they shouted
(v. 15). They were not about to be a party to such a blasphemous act.
Herod Antipas had himself been given homage as a god, and he fared
none too well for failing to deny it (12:22-23). It seems to be human
nature to want gods that can be seen and touched, gods in the likeness of
men. "Holy men" in every age succumb to the temptation to be venerated. Ministers should follow the example of the apostles and take warning from Herod.

Once they had gotten the crowd's attention, they explained their protest
in the form of a minisermon (vv. 15-18). It is the first sermon in Acts to a
purely pagan group, which believed in many gods and had no knowledge
whatever of the God of the Jews and Christians. The apostles had to start
at the very beginning, not with the coming of Christ but with the basic
theological assumption of monotheism—that God is one (Deut 6:4). As
such the sermon has its parallel in Paul's address to the Areopagus
(17:22-31), and in many ways the address to the Athenians is the best
commentary on the sermon at Lystra. The text reads almost as if the sermon was delivered by both apostles, but it is probably a fair assumption
that Paul was the spokesman on this occasion as well (cf. 14:12).

Paul's introduction had to do with the vanity of their worship. Any
religion is pretty empty that would venerate men as gods. The pagan
polytheism was vanity, emptiness, worthlessness, idolatrous worship of
gods who were nongods (cf. Jer 2:5; Rom 1:21-23). Paul exhorted them to
abandon this vain worship and turn to the one true and *living* God, the
source of all that truly lives. This was the main theme of the sermon—*the
living God.*[68] Three things are said about God.

First, he is *Creator* of all life, all that dwells on earth and in the seas
and in the skies. Paul was perhaps quoting from Ps 146:6, but it is in any
event the threefold division of creation familiar from the Old Testament
(cf. Exod 20:11; Acts 4:24; 17:24). Paul's second point deals with God's

---

[68]For a similar treatment of turning from idolatry to the living God, cf. 1 Thess 1:9. For
God as the source of all true life, cf. 1 Cor 8:6.

forbearance and mercy. In former generations God allowed the Gentiles to go their own way (v. 16). The implication is that then their deeds were done in ignorance and to that extent they were not held accountable for them (cf. 17:30a). But then implies now. Then they had had no revelation; now they did. Then they had not known the true God. Now Paul was revealing him to them. Then they had not been held accountable; now they were accountable (cf. 17:30b). Yet even in the past God had not left himself without a witness. He had revealed himself in his works of natural *providence*. This was Paul's final point (v. 17). God had been sending rain from heaven and causing the crops to flourish. Fruitful harvests had brought plenty of food to nourish the body and cheer the soul.[69] Such ideas of divine providence would not have been strange to the ears of the Lystrans. They were often expressed by pagan writers in speaking of the benevolence of the gods.[70] What was new to them was Paul's message of the *one* God—that all the benevolence of nature came from the one and only God who was himself the source of all creation.

It has often been argued that Paul drew opposite conclusions from the argument from natural providence in the Lystran sermon as compared to Rom 1:18-25. That is true, but it is equally true that the two are in no way contradictory. The basic premise is identical in both: God has revealed himself in his works, in creation. The contexts and hence the application of the premise are radically different in the two instances. In the speech at Lystra as well as the speech on the Areopagus (cf. 17:24-28), Paul used the argument from creation to build bridges, to establish a point of identification with his pagan hearers. While they may never have heard of his God before, they had *seen* him—in his providential works of nature. In Rom 1:18-25 Paul was seeking to establish humanity's responsibility before a just God. The Gentiles could not claim that they had no responsibility before God on the grounds that they had received no revelation. They had received revelation in God's providential works of creation and had perverted that revelation by worshiping nature itself, exchanging the Creator for the creation. The Gentiles were thus without excuse (Rom 1:20). We simply do not know how Paul would have moved to establish the Lystrans' need to repent had he moved on to discuss repentance and judgment. His sermon was not completed at Lystra. The Areopagus speech gives an idea of how he would have proceeded. There the call to

---

[69]The Greek is somewhat obscure in v. 17, literally reading "filling your hearts with food and rejoicing." The NIV preserves the intended sense well. See O. Lagercrantz, "Act 14, 17," *ZNW* (1932): 86-87.

[70]See F. G. Downing, "Common Ground with Paganism in Luke and in Josephus," *NTS* 28 (1982): 546-52. For an argument that the basic source of this emphasis on providence is Jesus' teaching on the mercy of God, see E. Lerle, "Die Predigt in Lystra (Acta xiv, 15-18)," *NTS* 7 (1960-61): 46-55.

repentance is very closely linked to the Gentile idolatry (Acts 17:29f.), which is precisely the argument of Rom 1:18-25.

Evidently Paul and Barnabas were cut short in their witness. It is anything but a complete exposition of the gospel. Paul never got beyond the basic monotheistic message of one God. There is no reference to Christ at all. Luke was well aware of its incompleteness. Verse 18 indicates that the sermon was cut off. The crowd was still intent on sacrificing to the apostles, so impressed had they been by the healing of the lame man. Even with his brief sermon on God, Paul could scarcely restrain them. The time in Lystra, however, was not over. There would be occasion in the future to introduce them to Christ. Just how he would have moved on to speak of Christ to a pagan Gentile group we will see in the Areopagus sermon of chap. 17.

(4) Paul and Barnabas Rejected (14:19-20a)

[19]Then some Jews came from Antioch and Iconium and won the crowd over. They stoned Paul and dragged him outside the city, thinking he was dead. [20]But after the disciples had gathered around him, he got up and went back into the city.

14:19-20a The apostles evidently worked for a while in Lystra as is indicated by the presence of disciples there (v. 20a).[71] One would have thought that Lystra would be particularly receptive, given its mainly Gentile population and the fact that they had even taken the apostles for gods. But crowds are fickle, especially when their expectations are not fulfilled. Perhaps their regard for the apostles soured when they discovered that they were not bringing them the material blessings of the gods. In any event, they were turned against Paul and Barnabas by a group of Paul's former Jewish opponents who had come from Iconium and even the 100 miles from Pisidian Antioch. In an act of mob violence, they stoned Paul and dragged him out of the city, taking him for dead. Just why Barnabas was spared is not indicated. He was evidently not present on the occasion when Paul was attacked. Some of the disciples from Lystra came out of town and encircled Paul's body, perhaps indicating that they had some question about his death and desired to protect him from further harm. Suddenly Paul rose in their midst and was able to accompany them back into the city. The question has often been raised whether Paul actually was restored from death. Luke's reference to their "thinking he was dead" (v. 19) would indicate that this was not the case. A miracle did occur, however. God's deliverance of his own from a dire threat like this is a

---

[71]The Western text adds the note in v. 19 that the apostles "spent some time [in Lystra] and taught," thus making explicit what is implicit in the mention of the Lystran "disciples" in v. 20.

special testimony to his protective providence, and that is always a miracle. In his catalogue of his trials, Paul mentioned in 2 Cor 11:25 the one time when he had been stoned, probably referring to this incident at Lystra (cf. 2 Tim 3:11).

(5) The Ministry at Derbe (14:20b-21a)

The next day he and Barnabas left for Derbe.
²¹They preached the good news in that city and won a large number of disciples.

14:20b-21a Paul and Barnabas did not linger in Lystra. It was no longer safe to remain there. The very next morning they set out for Derbe (v. 20b). Since Derbe was some sixty miles southeast of Lystra, the journey would have taken several days on foot.[72] Luke related no specific anecdote about the ministry in Derbe but only gave the essential details that a successful witness was carried on there and many disciples were won to the Lord. Derbe was the easternmost church established on the mission of Paul and Barnabas. Had the two chosen to do so, they could have continued southeast from Derbe on through the Cilician gates the 150 miles or so to Paul's hometown of Tarsus and from there back to Syrian Antioch. It would have been the easiest route home by far. They chose, however, to retrace their footsteps and revisit all the congregations that had been established in the course of the mission. In so doing they gave an important lesson on the necessity of follow-up and nurture for any evangelistic effort. Paul would again visit these same congregations on his next mission (16:1-6).

6. The Missionaries' Return to Antioch (14:21b-28)

Then they returned to Lystra, Iconium and Antioch, ²²strengthening the disciples and encouraging them to remain true to the faith. "We must go through many hardships to enter the kingdom of God," they said. ²³Paul and Barnabas appointed elders for them in each church and, with prayer and fasting, committed them to the Lord, in whom they had put their trust. ²⁴After going through Pisidia, they came into Pamphylia, ²⁵and when they had preached the word in Perga, they went down to Attalia.
²⁶From Attalia they sailed back to Antioch, where they had been committed to the grace of God for the work they had now completed. ²⁷On arriving there,

---

[72]Recent epigraphic evidence indicates that Derbe was located further south and east of the site formerly maintained. The new site is at Kerti Huyok, thirteen miles northeast of modern Karaman. If this is correct, Derbe would have been located on the frontier as a Roman military post between the province of Galatia and the client-kingdom of Antiochus. See B. van Elderen, "Some Archaeological Observations," *Apostolic History and the Gospel*, 156-61; G. Ogg, "Derbe," *NTS* 9 (1962-63): 367-70. Because this new site is as yet unexcavated, the location of Derbe remains somewhat uncertain.

they gathered the church together and reported all that God had done through them and how he had opened the door of faith to the Gentiles. **²⁸And they stayed there a long time with the disciples.**

14:21b-23 The two apostles returned the way they had come, revisiting the newly established churches along the route—first Lystra, then Iconium, and finally Pisidian Antioch. In each congregation they performed three essential ministries. First, they strengthened the disciples (v. 22a). This probably refers to their further instructing the Christians in their new faith. Second, they encouraged them "to remain true to the faith" and pointed out the "many hardships" they might encounter for bearing the name of Jesus (v. 22b).[73] Paul and Barnabas had themselves experienced persecution on this trip in almost every city where they witnessed. They reminded the Christians that this was not just the lot of missionaries but could be expected of all who carry Christ's name. The theme is one Paul often sounded in his epistles—we must be willing to suffer with Christ if we expect to share in his glory (Rom 8:17; cf. 2 Thess 1:4; 2 Tim 2:12); the path to resurrection is by way of the cross.

The final ministry of the apostles was to establish leadership in the new congregations. For these early churches there was no professional clergy to assume their leadership. Consequently, the pattern of the Jewish synagogues seems to have been followed by appointing a group of lay elders to shepherd the flock. There is some question in this particular instance about who appointed the elders—the apostles or the congregation. The NIV text follows the most natural rendering of the Greek construction: Paul and Barnabas appointed the elders (v. 23).[74] This seems to be an exception to the more common practice of the congregation appointing its leadership (cf. Acts 6:1-6).[75] Perhaps in these early congregations the wisdom of the apostles was needed in establishing solid leadership over those so recently converted from paganism. Perhaps even in these instances the selections of the apostles were confirmed by vote of the congregations.

14:24-25 Verses 24-25 complete the mission of Paul and Barnabas, giving the final leg of the return trip. Again they traversed the rugged

---

[73]The occurrence of "we" in v. 22 belongs to the apostles' address to the churches and is in no way evidence for a "we source" or Luke's presence on this occasion. See H. J. Cadbury, "Lexical Notes on Luke-Acts," *JBL* 48 (1929): 417.

[74]The NIV footnotes indicate the alternative—that the congregation may have elected the elders, with Paul and Barnabas confirming this by laying their hands on them. The evidence for *this translation* is that the verb χειροτονέω often has the meaning *to elect by vote* as well as *to appoint.*

[75]In the letters of Ignatius around the turn of the first/second century and in *Didache* 15:1, it is clear that the congregations elected their leadership. See J. M. Ross, "The Appointment of Presbyters in Acts xiv.23," *ExpTim* 63 (1951): 288-89.

mountain paths of Pisidia into the lowlands of Pamphylia and arrived at Perga, where they had started (cf. 13:13-14a). No mention was made earlier of any witness in Perga, but now they devoted some time to preaching the gospel there. Then they descended to Attalia (modern Adalia), the main port town of that region.

14:26-28 The first missionary journey was completed with the return of the apostles to Syrian Antioch. Verse 26 forms an *inclusio*, or bracket, with 13:2f. It was the Antioch church that had commissioned the apostles, committing them to the Lord by prayer and fasting and identifying with their mission ("work") by the laying on of hands. The work was now complete, and the two missionaries gave their report to the sponsoring congregation. Verse 27b marks a transition. The subject of opening "the door of faith to the Gentiles" would be the main topic of the Jerusalem Conference in the next chapter.[76] It summarizes the primary significance of the mission in chaps. 13-14. Evidently the report of this mission did not immediately reach Jerusalem, and Paul and Barnabas remained in Antioch for "a long time" (v. 28). Word would eventually spread to Jerusalem and provoke the major debate that is the subject of chap. 15.

7. Debate in Jerusalem over Acceptance of the Gentiles (15:1-35)

Acts 15:1-35 stands at the very center of the book. Not only is this true of its position halfway through the text, but it is also central in the development of the total plot of the book. The first half of Acts has focused on the Jewish Christian community, particularly on the influential Jerusalem church. The Christian witness had begun there (chaps. 1-5). Through the Hellenists especially it had spread to Samaria and all of the land of the Jews (chaps. 6-9). Through the witness of Peter to Cornelius, the outreach of the Antioch church, and especially through the first major mission completed by Paul and Barnabas, the gospel had broken through to the Gentiles (chaps. 10-14). All the preliminary steps had been taken for a major effort to reach the Gentile world. The precedents had been established; the first major successes among the Gentiles had been witnessed.[77] The stage was set for Paul's mission to the heart of the Greco-Roman world as *the* missionary to the Gentiles.

There remained only one final hurdle, and that was the agreement of the whole church on the Gentile mission. There were still those among the Jewish Christians who had serious reservations about the way the outreach to Gentiles had been conducted. These reservations and the final

---

[76] The metaphor of an "open door" as an opportunity for witness is a favorite expression of Paul. Cf. 1 Cor 16:9; 2 Cor 2:12; Col 4:3.

[77] For the centrality of 15:1-35 in the total outline of Acts, see J. C. O'Neill, *The Theology of Acts in Its Historical Setting* (London: SPCK, 1970), 66.

solution to them worked out in a major conference in Jerusalem are the subject of 15:1-35. There the whole church agreed on the Gentile mission. The way was now open for the mission of Paul, and that will be the subject of the rest of Acts. Hereafter the Jerusalem church fades into the background. When it does reappear, as in chap. 21, it will be wholly in connection with Paul's Gentile ministry. The focus is entirely on him.

The debate in Jerusalem revolved around the issue of *how* Gentiles were to be accepted into the Christian fellowship. The more conservative Jewish Christians felt that they should be received on the same basis that Jews had always accepted Gentiles into the covenant community— through proselyte initiation. This involved circumcision of the males and all proselytes taking upon themselves the total provisions of the Mosaic law. For all intents and purposes, a Gentile proselyte to Judaism *became a Jew*, not only in religious conviction but in life-style as well. That was the question the conservative group of Jewish Christians raised: Should not Gentiles be required to become Jews in order to share in the Christian community? It was a natural question. The first Christians were all Jews. Jesus was a Jew and the Jewish Messiah. God had only one covenant people—the Jews. Christianity was a messianic movement within Judaism. Jews had always demanded of all Gentile converts the requirements of circumcision and rituals of the Torah. Why should that change?

Evidently the requirements *had* changed. There was no indication that Peter had laid such requirements on Cornelius, or the Antioch church on the Gentiles who became a part of their fellowship, or Paul and Barnabas on the Gentiles converted in their mission. This was a cause for serious concern from the more conservative elements. Not only was it a departure from normal proselyte procedure; it also raised serious problems of fellowship. How could law-abiding Jewish Christians who seriously observed all the ritual laws have interaction with Gentile Christians who did not observe those laws? The Jewish Christians would run the risk of defilement from the Gentiles. These were the two issues that were faced and resolved in Jerusalem: (1) whether Gentile converts should submit to Jewish proselyte requirements, especially to circumcision and (2) how fellowship could be maintained between Jewish and Gentile Christians.

In Gal 2 Paul told of a conference in Jerusalem that had many similarities to Acts 15:1-35. Although the two accounts contain significant differences, the similarities seem to outweigh these, and it is probable that they relate to the same event.[78] Both dealt with the issue of circumcision,

[78]One of the major reasons scholars are hesitant to equate Gal 2 and Acts 15 is that of fitting together the visits of Paul related in Galatians and Acts. This problem is given disproportionate significance, and many follow Ramsay's suggestion that Gal 2:1-10 refers to the visit of Acts 11:30–12:25. This is to ignore totally the question of content, the really

Paul and Barnabas defended their views against the more conservative
Jewish Christians in both accounts, and the final agreement was reached
in both that the Gentiles would not be required to submit to Jewish proselyte circumcision. In Gal 2:1-10 Paul did not go into the question of
table fellowship between Jewish and Gentile Christians (though Gal 2:11-
14 clearly concerns table fellowship between Gentile and Jewish Christians), but that issue was a natural outgrowth of the decision not to
require Gentiles to live by the Torah. That it comprised part of the agenda
at the Jerusalem Conference is highly plausible.[79] In any event, it will be
assumed in the commentary that follows that Paul and Luke were referring to the same conference, and where appropriate Paul's account will be
cited to supplement that of Acts.

Acts 15:1-35 falls into four natural parts. The first comprises an *introduction* and relates how the debate arose in Antioch and led to the conference in Jerusalem to attempt some resolution (vv. 1-5). The second part
focuses on the *debate* in Jerusalem (vv. 6-21) and primarily centers on the
witness of Peter (vv. 6-11) and of James (vv. 12-21). The third part deals
with the final *solution*, which takes the form of an official letter sent to
Antioch (vv. 22-29). The narrative *concludes* where it began—in Antioch—with the delivering of the letter by two delegates of the Jerusalem
church (vv. 30-35).

(1) The Criticism from the Circumcision Party (15:1-5)

**¹Some men came down from Judea to Antioch and were teaching the broth-
ers: "Unless you are circumcised, according to the custom taught by Moses, you
cannot be saved." ²This brought Paul and Barnabas into sharp dispute and
debate with them. So Paul and Barnabas were appointed, along with some other
believers, to go up to Jerusalem to see the apostles and elders about this question.
³The church sent them on their way, and as they traveled through Phoenicia and**

---

important consideration. Acts 11:30–12:25 deals only with an offering for famine relief.
Acts 15 deals with the requirement of circumcision for Gentile converts, as does Gal 2. The
problem of the visits can be treated with less drastic surgery, such as assuming that Paul
failed to mention the brief famine visit because he had no contact with any apostles on that
occasion. This was the solution proposed by Zahn and followed in the commentaries of
Rackham (239), Stagg (157), and Robertson (*WP* 3:221-22). See also the discussion in chap.
IV, n. 136. For additional arguments for equating Gal 2:1-10 with Acts 15, see R. Stein,
"The Relationship of Gal 2:1-10 and Acts 15:1-35: Two Neglected Arguments," *JETS*
(1974): 239-42.

[79]A number of German scholars would divide Acts 15:1-35 into two separate occasions:
(1) the original Jerusalem Conference when only the issue of requirements for Gentile converts was debated and (2) a letter from Jerusalem ("the decrees" of 15:22-29), which was
sent later, after the dispute over table fellowship arose in Antioch (to which Paul referred in
Gal 2:11-14). See Schneider, 2:189-91; A. Weiser, "Das 'Apostelkonzil' (Apg. 15:1-35),"
BZ 28 (1984): 145-67.

Samaria, they told how the Gentiles had been converted. This news made all the brothers very glad. ⁴When they came to Jerusalem, they were welcomed by the church and the apostles and elders, to whom they reported everything God had done through them.

⁵Then some of the believers who belonged to the party of the Pharisees stood up and said, "The Gentiles must be circumcised and required to obey the law of Moses."

15:1-2 There were many Gentiles in the church at Antioch (cf. 11:20f.). There is no indication that they had been circumcised when they joined the Christian fellowship. This was disturbing to some Jewish Christians who came from Judea and insisted that circumcision in strict obedience to the Jewish law was necessary for salvation (v. 1).[80] Evidently they shared the views and perhaps were even some of the same persons as the "circumcision party," who are identified in the Western text as belonging to the sect of the Pharisees and who challenged Peter for having table fellowship with Cornelius (11:2). The group evidently represented the strict Jewish viewpoint that there was no salvation apart from belonging to the covenant community, the people of Israel. To be a part of that community a Gentile must take on the physical sign of the covenant, the mark of circumcision, and live by all the precepts of the law of Moses, ritual as well as moral. In the sharp debate that this demand provoked, Paul and Barnabas were the main opponents to this Judaizing perspective (v. 2). They had laid no such requirements on the Gentiles converted in their recent mission. It is altogether likely that the large number of such converts in their successful mission had attracted the attention of this Judaizing group in the first place.

The group soon realized that such a basic issue could not be settled in Antioch. It needed the attention of the whole church, since all Christians, Jew and Gentile, would be affected by its resolution. An "ecumenical conference" was arranged in Jerusalem. Jerusalem was the "mother church." The apostles were there. It was the suitable site to debate such an important issue. It is unclear who appointed Paul and Barnabas and "some other believers" to represent Antioch in Jerusalem. The Western text has the Judaizing group summoning Paul and Barnabas to Jerusalem "to be judged."[81] More likely the Antioch church appointed them as its official delegates to the meeting. Paul mentioned that Titus accompanied him and Barnabas to Jerusalem (Gal 2:1), so he may well have been one of the "others" of Acts 15:2.

---

[80]The Western text has the group make two demands: circumcision *and* conduct according to the law of Moses. This is perhaps a harmonization with v. 5.

[81]I. M. Ellis, "Codex Bezae at Acts 15," *IBS* 2 (1980): 134-40.

15:3-4 The distance between Antioch and Jerusalem was in excess of 250 miles, and the apostles may well have spent a month or so on their journey. They used the opportunity to visit congregations along the way. It could almost be described as a "campaign trip," since most of these congregations would likely be sympathetic with their viewpoint that Gentiles should not be burdened with circumcision and the Torah.[82] This would be especially true of the Christians of Phoenicia whose congregations were likely established by the same Hellenists who reached out to the Gentiles in Antioch (11:19-20). The congregations along their route rejoiced at the news of Paul and Barnabas's success among the Gentiles. Evidently they did not share the misgivings of the Judaizing Christians. When the Antioch delegation arrived in Jerusalem, they were well received by the "apostles and elders" (v. 4). These would be the central groups in the deliberation. Peter would be the spokesperson for the apostles, and James would represent the elders. Just as Paul and Barnabas had reported the success of their mission to the sponsoring church at Antioch (14:27) and to the congregations on their way (15:3), so now they shared with the leaders in Jerusalem what *God* had done through them. The emphasis on God's blessing was essential. That God's *leading* was so evident in accepting the Gentiles apart from the law would determine the final outcome of the conference.

15:5 The reception was somewhat cooler from a group of believers "who belonged to the party of the Pharisees" (v. 5). It was perhaps some of their group who had first stirred up the controversy in Antioch. They at least shared the same viewpoint: Gentiles who become Christians must undergo Jewish proselyte procedure. They must be circumcised. They must live by the entire Jewish law. It was not the moral aspects of the law that presented the problem but its ritual provisions. The moral law, such as embodied in the Ten Commandments, was never in question. Paul, for instance, constantly reminded his churches of God's moral standards in his letters. The ritual aspects of the law presented a problem. These were the provisions that marked Jews off from other people—circumcision, the food laws, scrupulous ritual purity. They were what made the Jews Jews and seemed strange and arbitrary to most Gentiles. To have required these of Gentiles would in essence have made them into Jews and cut them off from the rest of the Gentiles. It would have severely restricted, perhaps even killed, any effective Gentile mission. The stakes were high in the Jerusalem Conference.

It should come as no surprise that some of the Pharisees had become Christians. Pharisees believed in resurrection, life after death, and the coming Messiah. They shared the basic convictions of the Christians.

---

[82]P. Gaechter, "Geschichtliches zum Apostelkonzil," *ZTK* 85 (1963): 339-54.

Because of this they are sometimes in Acts found defending the Christians against the Sadducees, who had much less in common with Christian views (cf. 5:17; 23:8f.). A major barrier between Christians and Pharisees was the extensive use of oral tradition by the Pharisees, which Jesus and Paul both rejected as human tradition. It is not surprising that some Pharisees came to embrace Christ as the Messiah in whom they had hoped. For all their emphasis on law, it is also not surprising that they would be reticent to receive anyone into the fellowship in a manner not in accordance with tradition. That tradition was well-established for proselytes—circumcision and the whole yoke of the law.

(2) The Debate in Jerusalem (15:6-21)

[6]The apostles and elders met to consider this question. [7]After much discussion, Peter got up and addressed them: "Brothers, you know that some time ago God made a choice among you that the Gentiles might hear from my lips the message of the gospel and believe. [8]God, who knows the heart, showed that he accepted them by giving the Holy Spirit to them, just as he did to us. [9]He made no distinction between us and them, for he purified their hearts by faith. [10]Now then, why do you try to test God by putting on the necks of the disciples a yoke that neither we nor our fathers have been able to bear? [11]No! We believe it is through the grace of our Lord Jesus that we are saved, just as they are."
[12]The whole assembly became silent as they listened to Barnabas and Paul telling about the miraculous signs and wonders God had done among the Gentiles through them. [13]When they finished, James spoke up: "Brothers, listen to me. [14]Simon has described to us how God at first showed his concern by taking from the Gentiles a people for himself. [15]The words of the prophets are in agreement with this, as it is written:
[16]"'After this I will return
    and rebuild David's fallen tent.
Its ruins I will rebuild,
    and I will restore it,
[17]that the remnant of men may seek the Lord,
    and all the Gentiles who bear my name,
    says the Lord, who does these things'
[18]that have been known for ages.
[19]"It is my judgment, therefore, that we should not make it difficult for the Gentiles who are turning to God. [20]Instead we should write to them, telling them to abstain from food polluted by idols, from sexual immorality, from the meat of strangled animals and from blood. [21]For Moses has been preached in every city from the earliest times and is read in the synagogues on every Sabbath.

The central section of Acts 15:1-35 relates the debate in Jerusalem over the circumcision issue. There were two major witnesses, both in defense of the view that the Gentiles should not be burdened by circumcision and the law. Peter spoke first (vv. 7-11), followed by James (vv. 13-21). Both speeches are preceded by brief summary notices that set the larger context of the conference (vv. 6, 12).

PETER'S WITNESS (15:6-11). **15:6** Verse 6 relates the gathering for the conference. Since it mentions only the apostles and elders, many interpreters see this as a reference to the private conference Paul mentioned in Gal 2:2 with "those who seemed to be leaders." These interpreters would see the full church being first gathered together for the "discussion" in v. 7 or even later—with the mention of the whole assembly in v. 12. If Luke mentioned Paul's private conference at all, it would more likely be the initial meeting with the apostles and elders in v. 4. Verses 6-29 are a continuous narrative, and one would assume the whole group was gathered together for the discussion—the apostles and elders, other members of the Jerusalem church (including the Pharisaic Christians), Paul and Barnabas, and the other members of the Antioch delegation. The apostles and elders were singled out as the leaders of the assembly. They initiated the formal inquiry.[83]

15:7-9 The meeting began with a lively discussion (v. 7). After the various viewpoints had been aired, Peter rose to speak. He began by reminding the assembly of his own experience in the household of Cornelius (v. 7b). Even though it was "some time ago," possibly as much as ten years before, the experience had made an indelible impression on Peter. God had chosen him to witness to the Gentiles (cf. 10:5,20,32). Peter could expect the Jerusalem Christians, including the circumcisers, to remember this because he had given them a full report following the incident (cf. 11:1-18). What he had learned on that occasion was that God looks on the heart, not on external matters. God is no respecter of persons (10:34). Perhaps Peter had in mind the distinction made by the prophets that God does not look to the external circumcision of the flesh but the internal circumcision of the heart (Jer 4:4; 9:26; cf. Rom 2:29). God had convicted Cornelius, looked to the inner circumcision of his heart, and accepted him on that basis. God had proved his acceptance of Cornelius and the Gentiles at his home by granting them the gift of his Spirit. God only grants his Spirit to those he has accepted (cf. 10:44,47; 11:17). The fact that they had received the Spirit just as Peter and the Jewish Christians had was proof that God had accepted Cornelius and his fellow Gentiles on an equal footing (v. 9). He "purified their hearts" by faith. Peter undoubtedly was thinking of his vision: "Do not call anything impure that God has made clean" (10:15). For the Jew circumcision was a mark of sanctity and purity, of belonging to God's people and being acceptable to

---

[83]For the view that ἰδεῖν περί is a Latinism based on *videre de* and indicating a former investigation, see J. L. North, "Is *idein peri* (Acts 15, 6, cf. 18, 5) a Latinism?" *NTS* 29 (1983): 264-66.

him. But in Cornelius God had shown Peter that true purity comes not by an external mark but by faith. In the account of Cornelius in chap. 10, his faith is never explicitly mentioned but is certainly evidenced in his following without question every direction God gave him. Here Peter made explicit what was implicit there: Cornelius had been accepted by God on the basis of his faith.

15:10-11 In v. 10 Peter gave his conclusion drawn from the experience with Cornelius. It was an emphatic no to the question of Gentile circumcision and the "yoke" of the law. God had accepted the Gentiles at Cornelius's house without either of these. How could Jewish Christians demand anything more than the faith already shown? To demand more would be to put God to the test, to act against God's declared will, to see if God really meant what he had already shown in accepting Gentiles apart from the law.[84] Peter's statement in v. 10 is strong but should not be misconstrued. By speaking of the "yoke" of the law, he did not mean that the law was an intolerable burden that Jewish Christians should abandon. Peter was using a common Jewish metaphor for the law that had the same positive meaning Jesus had given it (Matt 11:29f.).[85] Peter did not urge *Jewish Christians* to abandon the law, nor did they cease to live by it. Peter's meaning was that the law was something the Jews had not been able to fulfill. It had proven an inadequate basis of salvation for them. Neither they nor their fathers had been able to fully keep the law and so win acceptance with God (cf. Rom 2:17-24). For the Jewish Christians the law would remain a mark of God's covenant with them, a cherished heritage. It could not save them. Only one thing could—faith, believing in the saving grace of the Lord Jesus (v. 11).

Faith alone, grace alone—one could hardly sound more like Paul. Paul had said much the same thing at Pisidian Antioch (13:38f.). It is something of an irony that Paul had to remind Peter of this same truth just a short time later in Antioch when his actions went counter to his convictions (Gal 2:14-17). It is interesting to observe Peter's progression throughout his speech. He began by pointing out how God had accepted the Gentiles "just like he accepted us" (v. 8). Now the shoe was on the other foot. The Gentiles had become the example for the Jews—"we are saved, just as they are" (v. 11). God's acceptance of the Gentiles had drawn a basic lesson for the Jews as well. There is only *one* way of salvation—"through the grace of our Lord Jesus." The emphasis on grace in 15:11 fits well with the emphasis on God's sovereign activity in the salvation of the Gentiles.

---

[84]For the concept of "tempting/testing" God, cf. Deut 6:16; Exod 17:2; Ps 78:18; Matt 4:7.

[85]For the law as a "yoke" see *m. Abot* 3:5. The rabbis saw the Torah not as an instrument of enslavement but as a yoke that bound them to God's will. It was a gift of his mercy. See E. P. Sanders, *Paul and Palestinian Judaism* (Philadelphia: Fortress, 1977); J. Nolland, "A Fresh Look at Acts 15:10," *NTS* 27 (1980): 105-15.

Peter's ultimate point was that God is free to save whomever and however he pleases.

JAMES'S TESTIMONY (15:12-21). **15:12** At the end of Peter's speech the entire assembly sat in silence. The hubbub with which the conference began (v. 7) now ceased. Paul and Barnabas had already shared their missionary experience with the leaders (v. 4).[86] Now they gave their testimony before the entire congregation (v. 12). Their emphasis was again on *God's* initiative in the mission, his work through them, the signs and wonders that had attested to his presence and affirmation of their ministry.[87] This missionary report was the entire role that Paul and Barnabas had in the conference. The main arguments were offered by Peter and James, the leaders of the apostles and elders. Paul and Barnabas evidently offered no defense of their position on the Gentile question other than the implicit argument that God had endorsed it. This was wise procedure. Often those who are most involved in an issue cannot be heard objectively by their opponents. A third party can address the issue with less passion and more authority. This was the role filled by Peter and James, who were in essence the spokespersons for the two missionaries.

15:13 When Paul and Barnabas had completed their testimony, James rose to speak (v. 13). It was James the brother of Jesus. Paul also mentioned James's role at the Jerusalem Conference (Gal 2:9; cf. 1:19) and called him one of the "pillars" of the church, along with Peter and John. James had evidently become the leading elder of the Jerusalem congregation. His leadership of the church has already been indicated in 12:17. Upon Paul's final visit to Jerusalem he appears to have been the sole leader of the congregation, and the apostles no longer seem to have been present in the city (21:18-25). Here James continued the defense of Peter's position that the Gentiles should not be required to be circumcised or embrace the Jewish law. Peter's argument had been based primarily on his personal experience, which had shown that God had accepted the Gentiles by sending his Spirit on them solely on the basis of their faith. James furthered Peter's position by giving it scriptural grounding (vv. 14-18). Then, realizing that such a solution would create real problems for Jewish Christians in their fellowship with Gentile Christians, he offered a suggestion for alleviating that situation (vv. 19-21).[88]

---

[86]Luke usually had "Paul and Barnabas," but the order of names is reversed in v. 12. This may reflect Luke's awareness that because of his long personal association with the Jerusalem church Barnabas held a certain priority there.

[87]The Western text offers a significant variant in v. 12, adding at the beginning, "And when the elders had agreed to the words spoken by Peter, the whole assembly became silent." The silence is thus interpreted as the Judaizers having been silenced.

[88]In James's speech of Acts 15:13-21 there are a number of verbal coincidences with the Epistle of James, as has been noted by J. B. Mayor, *The Epistle of James* (London: Macmillan, 1897), 3-4.

15:14-18 James began by referring to Peter's just-completed witness to God's acceptance of the Gentiles at Cornelius's home and described it as God's "taking from the Gentiles a people for himself" (v. 14).[89] James used the word *laos* to describe the Gentiles, a term usually applied to Israel. In Zech 2:11 (LXX 2:15), the Septuagint also applies the term *laos* to the Gentiles who will in the final days come to dwell in the renewed Zion and be a part of God's people.[90] Something like this seems to be the meaning here. In Christ God brings Jew and Gentile together into a single *laos*, a single people "for his name."[91]

James now showed how the coming of the Gentiles into the people of God was grounded in the Old Testament prophets. Basically he quoted from the Septuagint text of Amos 9:11-12, with possible allusions from Jer 12:15 and Isa 45:21.[92] In the Hebrew text of Amos 9:11-12, the prophet spoke of the coming restoration of Israel, which God would bring about. The house of David would be rebuilt and the kingdom restored to its former glory. Edom and all the nations over which David ruled would once again be gathered into Israel. The Greek text differs significantly and speaks of the remnant of humankind and all the nations seeking the Lord.[93] In both traditions there is the concept of "the nations which are called by my name," which links directly with "a people for his name"

---

[89]James referred to Peter as "Simeon," an Aramaizing form used of Peter elsewhere in the NT only in 2 Pet 1:1. Some early church fathers, notably Chrysostom, confused the Simeon of Acts 15:14 with the Simeon of Luke 2:29-32. Others have identified him with Simeon the Black (Acts 13:1). Clearly James was referring to Peter's speech in v. 14. See E. R. Smother, "Chrysostom and Symeon (Acts xv, 14)," *HTR* (1953): 203-15.

[90]See J. Dupont, *"Laos ex ethnon," Etudes*, 361-65; Dupont, "Un Peuple d'entre les nations (Actes 15:14)," *NTS* 31 (1985): 321-35; N. A. Dahl, "A People for His Name (Acts xv. 14)," *NTS* 4 (1957-58): 319-27.

[91]Acts 15:14-18 is a key passage in traditional dispensational theories. The reference to "first" in v. 14 is taken to refer to the coming of the Gentiles; v. 16 is taken as the subsequent restoration of Israel. See W. M. Aldrich, "The Interpretation of Acts 15:13-18," *BibSac* 111 (1954): 317-23. The context of the Jerusalem Conference, however, does not call for prophecy. James was describing what was happening in his day, Jew and Gentile coming together into a single people of God. See W. C. Kaiser, Jr., "The Davidic Promise and the Inclusion of the Gentiles (Amos 9:9-15 and Acts 15:13-18): A Test Passage for Theological Systems," *JETS* (1977): 97-111.

[92]Jeremiah 12:15 seems to be behind the opening words, "After this I will return" (v. 16). Isaiah 45:21 may lie behind the phrase "known for ages" (v. 18), but the phrase may also have been drawn from the reference to the "ages" in Amos 9:11. See G. D. Kilpatrick, "Some quotations in Acts," *Les Actes*, ed. J. Kramer, 84-85.

[93]The problem is, of course, that James's argument is best carried by the Septuagint text. It is not impossible that James knew Greek and quoted the Septuagint text in a conference that had a number of Greek-speaking delegates. Even if Luke was responsible for providing the Septuagint text (for his Greek readers), the key phrase "nations [Gentiles] called by my name" occurs in *both* the Hebrew and Greek texts, and either would have suited James's argument.

("for himself," NIV) in v. 14. This is the main concept James wished to develop. In the Gentiles, God was choosing a people for himself, a new *restored* people of God, Jew and Gentile in Christ, the true Israel. In the total message of Acts it is clear that the rebuilt house of David occurred in the Messiah. Christ was the scion of David who fulfilled the covenant of David and established a kingdom that would last forever (2 Sam 7:12f.; cf. Acts 13:32-34). From the beginning the Jewish Christians had realized that the promises to David were fulfilled in Christ. What they were now beginning to see, and what James saw foretold in Amos, was that these promises included the Gentiles.[94]

15:19-20 Having established from Scripture the inclusion of the Gentiles in the people of God, James drew his conclusion to the question of *requirements* for Gentile membership (v. 19). Gentiles should not be given undue difficulties; no unnecessary obstacles should be placed in their way. Though somewhat more restrained in expression, his conclusion was basically that of Peter (v. 10): Gentiles should not be burdened with the law and circumcision. The leading apostle and the leading elder were in agreement. The issue was all but settled. Resolving it, however, raised another problem. If Gentiles were not being required to observe the Jewish ritual laws, how would Jewish Christians who maintained strict Torah observance be able to fellowship with them without running the risk of being ritually defiled themselves? James saw the question coming and addressed it in his next remark (v. 20). Gentiles should be directed to abstain from four things: from food offered to idols, from sexual immorality (*porneia*), from the meat of strangled animals (*pnikton*), and from blood (*haima*).

When looked at closely, all four of these belong to the ritual sphere. Meat offered to idols was an abomination to Jews, who avoided any and everything associated with idolatry. "Strangled meat" referred to animals that had been slaughtered in a manner that left the blood in it. Blood was considered sacred to the Jews, and all meat was to be drained of blood before consuming it. The prohibition of "blood" came under the same requirement, referring to the consumption of the blood of animals in any form.[95] These three requirements were thus all ritual, dealing with matters of clean and unclean foods. The fourth category seems somewhat less ritual and more moral: sexual immorality (*porneia*). It is possible that this category was also originally intended in a mainly ritual sense, referring to

---

[94]See J. Dupont, "Apologetic Use of the Old Testament," *Salvation of the Gentiles*, 139. See also M. A. Braun, "James' Use of Amos at the Jerusalem Council: Steps Toward a Possible Solution of the Textual and Theological Problems," *JETS* 20 (1977): 113-21.

[95]On "blood" as a sign of paganism, see I. Logan, "The Decree of Acts xv," *ExpTim* 39 (1927-28): 428.

those "defiling" sexual relationships the Old Testament condemns, such as incest, marriage outside the covenant community, marriage with a close relative, bestiality, homosexuality, and the like.[96] It is also possible that a broader meaning was intended including all illicit "natural" relationships as well, such as fornication, concubinage, and adultery. Gentile sexual mores were lax compared to Jewish standards, and it was one of the areas where Jews saw themselves most radically differentiated from Gentiles. The boundary between ritual and ethical law is not always distinct, and sexual morality is one of those areas where it is most blurred. For the Jew sexual misbehavior was both immoral *and* impure. A Jew would find it difficult indeed to consort with a Gentile who did not live by his own standards of sexual morality.[97]

The four requirements suggested by James were thus all basically ritual requirements aimed at making fellowship possible between Jewish and Gentile Christians. Often referred to as "the apostolic decrees," they belonged to a period in the life of the church when there was close contact between Jewish and Gentile Christians, when table fellowship especially was common between them. In a later day, by the end of the first century, Jewish Christianity became isolated into small sects and separated from Gentile Christianity. There no longer existed any real fellowship between them. The original function of the decrees no longer had any force, and they tended to be viewed in wholly moral terms. This tendency is very much reflected in the textual tradition of Acts 15:20,29 and 21:25, particularly in the Western text, which omits "strangled meat," adds the negative form of the golden rule, and reads "idolatry" rather than idol meat. There are thus four moral prohibitions: no idolatry, no sexual immorality, no murder ("blood" now viewed as the shedding—not consuming—of blood), and "do not do to another what you wouldn't wish done to yourself."[98]

15:21 The question might be raised: Why were the original decrees ritual rather than moral in the first place? The answer quite simply is that the moral rules, such as the Ten Commandments, were already assumed. *All* Christians, Jew and Gentile, lived by them. The Gentiles needed no

---

[96]That πορνεία should be seen in a wholly ritual sense is argued by M. Simon, "The Apostolic Decree and Its Setting in the Ancient Church," *BJRL* 52 (1970): 437-60.

[97]For the interesting suggestion that the decrees were designed to give social identity to Gentiles as being Christians alongside Jewish Christians, see C. Perrot, "Les Decisions de l'Assemblée de Jerusalem," *RSR* 69 (1981): 195-208.

[98]For further treatment of the complex textual tradition of the "decrees," see T. Boman, "Das textkritische Problem des sogennanten Aposteldekrets," *NovT* 7 (1964): 26-36; G. Resch, *Das Aposteldecret nach seiner ausserkanonischen Textgestalt* (Leipzig: Hinrichs'sche, 1905); A. F. J. Klijn, "The Pseudo-Clementines and the Apostolic Decree," *NovT* 10 (1968): 305-12.

reminder of such basic marks of Christian behavior. Morality was not the issue at the Jerusalem Conference.[99] Fellowship was, and the decrees were a sort of minimum requirement placed on the Gentile Christians in deference to the scruples of their Jewish brothers and sisters in Christ.[100] They were really not something radically new. The Old Testament lays down similar rules for the resident alien dwelling in Israel and for much the same purpose: to assure the purity of the Jewish community and to allow for social interaction between the Jews and the non-Jews in their midst. In fact, all four of the "apostolic decrees" are found in Lev 17 and 18 as requirements expected of resident aliens: abstinence from pagan sacrifices (17:8), blood (17:10-14), strangled meat (17:13), and illicit sexual relationships (18:6-23). Perhaps this is what James meant in his rather obscure concluding remark (v. 21): the law of Moses is read in every synagogue everywhere; so these requirements should come as no shock to the Gentiles. They are in the Old Testament and have been required of Gentiles associating with Jews from the earliest times. James's remark could also be taken in another sense, which would fit the context well: there are Jews in every city who cherish the Torah. Gentile Christians should be sensitive to their scruples and not give them offense in these ritual matters, for they too may be reached with the gospel.[101]

(3) The Decision in Jerusalem (15:22-29)

[22]**Then the apostles and elders, with the whole church, decided to choose some of their own men and send them to Antioch with Paul and Barnabas. They chose Judas (called Barsabbas) and Silas, two men who were leaders among the brothers.** [23]**With them they sent the following letter:**

The apostles and elders, your brothers,

---

[99]Some scholars would disagree strongly with this and maintain that the decrees were primarily ethical from the beginning; e.g., S. G. Wilson, *Luke and the Law* (Cambridge: University Press, 1983), 73-102. H. Sahlin argues that the Western reading is original and based on the three "cardinal sins" of the rabbis, "Die drei Kardinalsunden und das neue Testament," *ST* 24 (1970): 93-112.

[100]The basis of the decrees in providing a means for fellowship of Jewish and Gentile Christians is also argued by M. A. Seifrid, "Jesus and the Law in Acts," *JSNT* 30 (1987): 39-57. A. Weiser describes it as providing a "modus vivende" between the two: "Das 'Apostelkonzil' (Apg. 15:1-35)," *BZ* 28 (1984): 145-67.

[101]Verse 21 is difficult, and a wide variety of interpretations have been offered. In addition to the two given in the commentary, it has also been viewed as meaning that the Gentiles had already heard the law propounded and hadn't responded; it would thus be futile to impose it on them: D. R. Schwartz, "The Futility of Preaching Moses (Acts 15, 21)," *Bib* 67 (1986): 276-81. J. Bowker sees v. 21 in the context of a formal *taqqaneh* or "alleviation of Torah." Verse 21 serves to reassert the primacy of the Torah even though it has been relaxed with regard to Gentile proselyte procedure: "The Speeches in Acts: A Study in Proem and Yelammedenu Form," *NTS* 14 (1967-68): 96-111.

To the Gentile believers in Antioch, Syria and Cilicia:
Greetings.
[24]We have heard that some went out from us without our authorization
and disturbed you, troubling your minds by what they said. [25]So we all
agreed to choose some men and send them to you with our dear friends
Barnabas and Paul—[26]men who have risked their lives for the name of our
Lord Jesus Christ. [27]Therefore we are sending Judas and Silas to confirm
by word of mouth what we are writing. [28]It seemed good to the Holy Spirit
and to us not to burden you with anything beyond the following requirements: [29]You are to abstain from food sacrificed to idols, from blood, from
the meat of strangled animals and from sexual immorality. You will do well
to avoid these things.
Farewell.

15:22-23a James had provided a suitable solution that jeopardized
neither the Gentile mission nor the fellowship between Jewish and Gentile
Christians. All parties seem to have been satisfied and to have agreed to
James's suggestion (vv. 22-23a). They decided to draft a letter presenting
the solution and to send two delegates from the Jerusalem church to Antioch along with Paul and Barnabas. The two delegates would be able to
give their personal interpretation of the letter's contents and of the conference in Jerusalem. They are described as "leaders" in the church of Jerusalem, a term that is not further defined. In v. 32 they are called
"prophets." Of Judas Barsabbas ("Sabbath-born") we know nothing more.
He may have been related to the Joseph Barsabbas of 1:23, but even that
is uncertain. Silas, who is a major New Testament character, is another
story. He accompanied Paul on his second missionary journey and is mentioned often in that connection (nine times in the Greek text of 15:40–
18:5; fourteen times in the NIV since it often supplies subjects). Silas is a
shortened form of the Greek name Silvanus, and the Greek name has led
some to suggest that he may have been a Hellenist. That would certainly
be likely if he is the same Silvanus who served as Peter's amanuensis
(1 Pet 5:12). He definitely seems to be the Silvanus whom Paul mentioned
as a coworker in several of his epistles (2 Cor 1:19; 1 Thess 1:1; 2 Thess
1:1). The churches of Corinth and Thessalonica were established on Paul's
second missionary journey when Silas accompanied him. It was thus natural for him to include Silas/Silvanus when writing to them. Like Paul,
Silvanus may have been a Roman citizen. Acts 16:37f. seems to indicate
so. It is interesting to note that Paul's mission companions came from
those who represented the Jerusalem church (cf. Barnabas, 11:22). This is
another way in which the close bond between Paul's missionary activity
and the Jerusalem church is exemplified. Not only did the Jerusalem
Christians approve Paul's law-free Gentile mission in principle at the conference, but they ultimately furnished his personnel as well.

Verses 23b-29 give the letter sent from the Jerusalem church to the Christians in Antioch. It was written in a very formal style, beginning with the salutation typical of Greco-Roman letters, listing first the senders, then the recipients. This was followed by the customary greeting (*chairein*). The only other places in the New Testament where this characteristic Greek greeting form was used are in Acts 23:26 and in the Epistle of James 1:1. The letter ends on an equally formal note with "farewell" (*errōsthe*), the Greek equivalent of the Latin *valete*.[102] The formality is most pronounced in the long "periodic" sentence that runs from v. 24 through v. 26, one long complex sentence very tightly woven together. There is only one other periodic sentence in all of Luke-Acts, Luke's prologue to his Gospel (1:1-4). Since the overall style of the letter is so markedly Greco-Roman, one has the impression that the basically Jewish congregation of Jerusalem was making every effort to communicate clearly and in the style of their Greek-speaking brothers and sisters at Antioch.

15:23b-24 The letter was written in the name of the Jerusalem leaders, "the apostles and elders." The recipients were denoted "the Gentile believers in Antioch, Syria and Cilicia." Actually, this could be considered almost as a single address. Syria-Cilicia was administratively a single Roman province, and Antioch was a city within it. It was at Antioch that the debate had arisen (15:1), and so it was to Antioch that the Jerusalem leaders sent their response. Verse 24 provides some additional clarification concerning the Judaizers of 15:1. They may have come from Jerusalem, but they were in no sense official representatives of the church. In fact, the language of the letter expresses some dismay with this group. They are described as "troubling" (literally "plundering" or "tearing down") the minds of the people in Antioch. The word was a military metaphor (*anaskeuazō*), meaning originally *to plunder or loot a town*. The Jerusalem leadership was obviously not happy with the wholly unauthorized Judaizers and their so upsetting the Gentiles of Antioch.

15:25-26 Verses 25-26 basically recapitulate the content of v. 22 with the additional commendation of Barnabas and Paul as those who had "risked their lives" for the name of Jesus. The verb used here (*paradidōmi*) can mean either *to devote* or *to risk*, and the distinction between the two in this context would be slim. It was in their wholehearted devotion to Christ that the two missionaries had incurred so many dangers. The Jerusalem leaders referred to them as their "dear friends" (*agapētos*, "beloved"). One is reminded of Paul's account of the conference (Gal 2:9), where he spoke of the Jerusalem leaders' giving them the "right hand of fellowship."

---

[102]This form occurs nowhere else in the NT except in a variant reading in Lysias's letter (Acts 23:30).

15:27-28 Verse 27 continues to delineate the circumstances of the letter, noting the role of Judas and Silas. Only at v. 28 does the "meat" of the letter begin. The assembly had decided not to burden the Gentiles— no circumcision, no law, only these "necessary things" (author's translation). The idea was really that there was to be no burden on the Gentiles. Instead of a burden, the Gentiles were to be asked to follow the four proscribed areas of the "apostolic decree"—not as a law, but as a basis for fellowship. The addition of the Holy Spirit in v. 28 is significant. Just as the Spirit had been instrumental in the inclusion of the Gentiles (15:8,12), so now in the conference the Spirit had led the Jerusalem leaders in considering the conditions for their inclusion.

15:29 Verse 29 lists the four provisions of the apostolic decree just as originally proposed by James (v. 20). There is one slight variation. Whereas James had spoken in terms of "food polluted by idols," the letter defined this with the more precise term "food sacrificed to idols" (*eidōlothytōn*). The proscriptions will be referred to one more time in Acts (21:25) and there in the same four terms that appear in 15:29. Evidently these regulations continued to be taken seriously in large segments of the church. Two of them, food sacrificed to idols and sexual immorality, appear in the letters to the churches in Revelation (Rev 2:14,20). Tertullian attests to the churches of North Africa abstaining from blood and illicit marriages. In the fourth century the Syrian church forbade sexual immorality, the consumption of blood, and strangled meat.[103]

It has often been argued that Paul either didn't know of the decrees or flatly rejected them, since he never referred to them in his letters. Some have observed further that in his own account of the Jerusalem Conference, Paul stated that "nothing" was added to his message (Gal 2:6). This does not necessarily conflict with the existence of the decrees. The conference did approve Paul's basic message of a law-free gospel for the Gentiles—no circumcision, no Torah, no "burden." The decrees were a strategy for Jewish-Gentile fellowship, and that was something different. The assumption that Paul showed no knowledge of the decrees in his letters is also questionable. In 1 Cor 5–10 Paul seems to have dealt with two of its provisions: sexual immorality in chaps. 5–7 and food sacrificed to idols in chaps. 8–10. The latter treatment is particularly instructive, where Paul advised the "strong" not to eat idol meat in the presence of the "weak." This reflects the basic "accommodation" principle of the decrees—to enable fellowship between Christians. True, Paul did not accept the decrees as "law"; he did seem to embrace their spirit.[104]

---

[103]Simon, "Decrees," 455-59.

[104]See M. D. Goulder, "Did Luke Know Any of the Pauline Letters?" *PIRS* 13 (1986): 97-112. Goulder argues that the form of the decrees may have been influenced by 1 Corinthians.

(4) The Decision Reported to Antioch (15:30-35)

[30]The men were sent off and went down to Antioch, where they gathered the church together and delivered the letter. [31]The people read it and were glad for its encouraging message. [32]Judas and Silas, who themselves were prophets, said much to encourage and strengthen the brothers. [33]After spending some time there, they were sent off by the brothers with the blessing of peace to return to those who had sent them. [35]But Paul and Barnabas remained in Antioch, where they and many others taught and preached the word of the Lord.

15:30-33 Paul and Barnabas and the other delegates returned to the church of Antioch along with the two representatives of the Jerusalem church, Judas and Silas. Upon their arrival, the church was assembled and the letter read in the presence of all. Everyone found its message "encouraging" (v. 31),[105] undoubtedly because it confirmed their practice of accepting the Gentiles without demanding circumcision and the obligations of the Torah. As prophets (v. 32) Judas and Silas were able to go beyond their role of interpreters of the Jerusalem Conference and to further strengthen and encourage their brothers and sisters at Antioch. In the New Testament prophecy is primarily the gift of inspiration whereby one delivers a word from God that addresses the present needs in the life of the church.[106] The two were well received in Antioch and remained there some time, ministering to the church through their gift of inspiration. When they departed, they were sent off with the ancient blessing of *shalom*, that the peace of God would abide with them.[107]

[15:34] Verse 34 is one of the Western readings that found its way into the *Textus Receptus* and from thence into many of the sixteenth and seventeenth century translations. It is the consensus of textual criticism that it was not in the original text of Acts and is thus omitted in modern translations. It reads: "But Silas decided to remain with them. Only Judas departed." Undoubtedly the scribe responsible for this addition wanted to solve the problem of Silas's being present in Antioch again in v. 40. In so doing, a much more serious conflict was created with v. 33, which clearly states that they (plural) both returned to Jerusalem. There really is no problem with v. 40 anyway, because it takes place some time later (v. 36), allowing plenty of room for Silas to return to Antioch from Jerusalem.

---

[105]The word is παράκλησις, which can mean *comfort* or *exhortation*. Either nuance fits this particular context. The letter both comforted them and encouraged them by the conciliatory spirit of its exhortations.

[106]Codex Bezae adds that they were prophets "full of the Spirit," to emphasize what is already implicit in the term "prophecy" itself.

[107]"Go in peace." Cf. Mark 5:34; Luke 7:50; 8:48; Acts 16:36; and Paul's customary greeting of "grace and peace" (Rom 1:7; 1 Cor 1:3; etc.).

15:35 Verse 35 concludes the narrative of the Jerusalem Conference in summary fashion. Now that the Gentile question had been settled, the church prospered under the teaching and preaching of Paul and Barnabas and "many others." The "many others" are significant. This verse is the final glimpse into the life of the Antioch church. Paul and Barnabas would soon be leaving for mission fields elsewhere. The church was left in good hands. There were "many others" who were competent to carry on its witness.

Summary. The concord reached at the Jerusalem Conference was a most remarkable event and established a major precedent for dealing with controversy within the Christian fellowship. One should realize the sharp differences that existed between the Jewish Christians and the Gentile Christians. Jewish Christians were faithful to all the traditions of their heritage. They observed the provisions of the Torah, circumcised their male children, and kept all the Jewish holy days. They did not cease to be Jews when they became Christians. James was himself a perfect example. In their accounts of his later martyrdom, both Josephus and Eusebius noted the tremendous respect the nonbelieving Jews gave him because of his deep piety and scrupulous observance of the law.[108] Not requiring Gentiles to be circumcised upon entry into the covenant community was a radical departure from the Jewish tradition. That James and his fellow Jewish Christians were willing to bend on such a basic principle is testimony to two things about them. First, they were open to the leading of God. Throughout the account God's leading is stressed—in his sending the Spirit on Cornelius (v. 8), in the "signs and wonders" that God worked through Paul and Barnabas (v. 12). It was this evidence of *God's* acceptance of the Gentiles that determined the decision of the council to accept Gentiles with no further burden. And the Spirit of God was present with them in the conference, leading them in their decision (v. 28). This is a consistent picture in Acts: wherever Christians are open to God's Spirit, there is unity.

Second, the Jewish Christian leadership showed a concern for the world mission of the church that overshadowed their own special interests. They took a step that was absolutely essential if the Gentile mission was to be a success. To have required circumcision and the Torah would have severely limited the appeal to Gentiles, perhaps even killed it. Yet the Jewish Christians only stood to lose by not requiring Jewish proselyte procedure of the Gentile converts. It was bound to create problems with nonbelieving Jews. That it indeed did so is indicated in a later passage in Acts (21:20-22). If the Jerusalem leadership had only been concerned

---

[108]Josephus, *Ant.* 20.200 and Eusebius, *Hist. Eccl.* 2.23. For the tradition of James's martyrdom, see commentary on Acts 21:18.

about the effectiveness of their own witness among the Jews, they would
never have taken such a step. That it did so is testimony of their concern
for the total mission of the church. Their vision stretched beyond their
own bailiwick—indeed, to the ends of the earth.

---------------------------- *SECTION OUTLINE* ----------------------------

VI. PAUL WITNESSES TO THE GREEK WORLD (15:36–18:22)
1. Parting Company with Barnabas (15:36-41)
2. Revisiting Derbe, Lystra, and Iconium (16:1-5)
3. Called to Macedonia (16:6-10)
4. Witnessing in Philippi (16:11-40)
   (1) Founding a Church with Lydia (16:11-15)
   (2) Healing a Possessed Servant Girl (16:16-24)
   (3) Converting a Jailer's Household (16:25-34)
   (4) Humbling the City Magistrates (16:35-40)
5. Establishing Churches in Thessalonica and Berea (17:1-15)
   (1) Acceptance and Rejection in Thessalonica (17:1-9)
   (2) Witness in Berea (17:10-15)
6. Witnessing to the Athenian Intellectuals (17:16-34)
   (1) The Athenians' Curiosity (17:16-21)
   (2) Paul's Testimony before the Areopagus (17:22-31)
      The "Unknown" God (17:22-23)
      The Creator God (17:24-25)
      The Providential God (17:26-27)
      The Worship of God (17:28-29)
      The Judgment of God (17:30-31)
   (3) The Mixed Response (17:32-34)
7. Establishing a Church in Corinth (18:1-17)
   (1) The Mission in Corinth (18:1-11)
      Paul's Arrival in Corinth (18:1-4)
      The Witness in the City (18:5-8)
      The Assuring Vision of Jesus (18:9-11)
   (2) The Accusation before Gallio (18:12-17)
8. Returning to Antioch (18:18-22)

— VI. PAUL WITNESSES TO THE GREEK WORLD (15:36–18:22) —

Paul saw himself above all as Christ's apostle to the Gentiles (e.g., Rom 1:5; 15:18; Gal 2:8). This calling is very much confirmed by the account of his missionary activity in Acts. His witness to the Gentiles was first revealed at his conversion (9:15) and was exemplified by his joining Barnabas in the evangelization of the Gentiles in Antioch (11:26). On the first missionary journey this special calling was confirmed for him—in the conversion of the Roman proconsul on Cyprus (13:12), in the mass response of the Gentiles in Pisidian Antioch (13:48), and in the formation of a group of disciples among the pagans at Lystra (14:20). At Jerusalem, Paul's witness to the Gentiles was confirmed by the apostles and elders of the mother church, and the way was cleared for his further ministry. Paul was now ready for a major outreach to the Gentiles, and this comprises the subject of chaps. 16–20.

He was first led to a major ministry in Macedonia and Achaia (15:36–18:22). After returning for a brief visit to Jerusalem and a "furlough" in Antioch (18:22f.), he set out again for the Greek cities of the Aegean, this time centering around the city of Ephesus (18:24–21:14). Luke's account is selective. His purpose was not to give a complete account of all Paul's missionary activities. One is well aware of this from Paul's epistles. Acts does not cover the establishment of churches at Colosse, Hierapolis, and Laodicea; nor does it go into the complex relationship between Paul and Corinth during the period of his Ephesian ministry. It is even virtually silent about the collection that took up so much of Paul's time before his final return to Jerusalem. Luke simply did not provide a full "history" of Paul's missionary activity. What he did do was to hit the high points, provide a basic framework for Paul's mission, and show how in Paul's ministry the commission to the "ends of the earth" was carried forward.

Acts 15:36–18:22 covers what has customarily been referred to as Paul's second missionary journey. The term is particularly applicable for the first part of the narrative, where Paul was extensively involved in travel from Antioch to Troas (16:1-10). The pace slowed down thereafter with more extensive stays and the establishment of the churches in Philippi (16:11-40), Thessalonica (17:1-9), and Berea (17:10-15). After a seemingly brief visit to Athens with his notable address from the Areopagus (17:16-34), Paul concluded this period of work in Corinth, staying there at least eighteen months, perhaps half the time of the total mission (18:1-17). Most of his time was thus spent in a major urban center, which set the pattern followed in Ephesus on his third mission.

1. Parting Company with Barnabas (15:36-41)

³⁶Some time later Paul said to Barnabas, "Let us go back and visit the brothers in all the towns where we preached the word of the Lord and see how they are doing." ³⁷Barnabas wanted to take John, also called Mark, with them, ³⁸but Paul did not think it wise to take him, because he had deserted them in Pamphylia and had not continued with them in the work. ³⁹They had such a sharp disagreement that they parted company. Barnabas took Mark and sailed for Cyprus, ⁴⁰but Paul chose Silas and left, commended by the brothers to the grace of the Lord. ⁴¹He went through Syria and Cilicia, strengthening the churches.

15:36-41 Paul's second major mission began like the first in the city of Antioch. Paul and Barnabas had been preaching and teaching there after their return from the Jerusalem Conference (15:35). "Some time later" Paul suggested to Barnabas that they revisit "all the towns" where they had established churches on their first mission (15:36). The imprecise time expression is perhaps more significant as Luke's way of marking a major new division in the narrative.[1] A new division indeed does begin at this point—Paul's second major mission. Actually, Paul did not fulfill in person his desire to revisit "all" the churches of their first mission. He did not return to Cyprus. As things turned out, however, all the churches were revisited, with Barnabas going to Cyprus (v. 39).

The reason for their going their separate ways was not a happy one and involved a major disagreement between them (vv. 37-39). John Mark was the center of contention. He was Barnabas's cousin, and Barnabas suggested that he accompany them as he had on their first mission (13:5). Paul did not think this a wise move since Mark had abandoned them on that occasion (13:13).[2] It is possible that there was an additional source of tension between Paul and Barnabas. Galatians 2:11-13 speaks of an incident that took place in Antioch, evidently after the Jerusalem Conference, in which Peter and Barnabas gave in to pressure from "certain men" from James and withdrew from table fellowship with Gentiles. Paul sharply confronted Peter on that occasion for his "hypocrisy" and was none too happy with Barnabas for following Peter's example. Even though Paul had now been sufficiently reconciled to Barnabas to request his companionship on the mission, there may have been lingering wounds and possibly still some differences over Paul's "law-free" Gentile outreach. Mark may himself have represented a more conservative Jewish-Christian outlook. However that may be, Paul did eventually become reconciled to Mark and mentioned him as a coworker in several of his letters (cf. Col 4:10; Phlm 24; 2 Tim 4:11). Standing in the background was Barnabas, always the encourager, showing faith in Mark when others had lost theirs and eventually redeeming him—ironically, *for Paul*.

Barnabas and Mark departed for further work on Cyprus. Though disagreements are regrettable, at least in this instance there was a fortunate outcome. Now there were two missions instead of one. Paul needed a suitable replacement for a traveling companion and chose Silas (v. 40).[3]

---

[1] The expression μετά plus an expression of time in the accusative case was Luke's usual manner of marking major divisions in the second half of Acts. Cf. 18:1; 21:15; 24:1; 25:1; 28:11,17.

[2] The Western text of v. 38 is somewhat harder on Mark, stating that he abandoned them and did not accompany them "in the work to which they had been sent," thus having him abandon his commission. See E. Delebecque, "Silas, Paul et Barnabé à Antioche selon le Texte 'Occidental' d'Actes 15, 34 et 38," *RHPR* 64 (1984): 47-52.

[3] For Silas see the commentary on Acts 15:22. For the rather unique view that Silas did not accompany Paul from Antioch but only joined him later at Corinth, see S. Dockx, "Silas a-t-il été le compagnon de voyage de Paul d'Antioche à Corinthe?" *NRT* 104 (1982): 749-53.

For this journey Paul had pretty much made the decision on his own. Still, as for the first mission, he had the support of the Antioch church and was commended by the brothers and sisters there to the grace of the Lord for his new undertaking. Paul and Silas headed north from Antioch by foot and visited the churches of Syria and Cilicia along the way. Since the "apostolic decrees" were originally addressed to all the churches in Syria and Cilicia (15:23), one would assume that Paul and Silas shared these with them.[4] This is all the more likely since Silas was one of the two originally appointed by the Jerusalem church to deliver the decrees (15:22).

2. Revisiting Derbe, Lystra, and Iconium (16:1-5)

[1]He came to Derbe and then to Lystra, where a disciple named Timothy lived, whose mother was a Jewess and a believer, but whose father was a Greek. [2]The brothers at Lystra and Iconium spoke well of him. [3]Paul wanted to take him along on the journey, so he circumcised him because of the Jews who lived in that area, for they all knew that his father was a Greek. [4]As they traveled from town to town, they delivered the decisions reached by the apostles and elders in Jerusalem for the people to obey. [5]So the churches were strengthened in the faith and grew daily in numbers.

16:1-5 According to plan, Paul proceeded northward, this time on foot, through the Cilician gates to the cities where he and Barnabas had established churches on the first mission tour. This time they went from east to west and so reached the towns in the reverse order from their first visit—Derbe first, then Lystra, and finally Iconium. At Lystra they found a disciple by the name of Timothy. Evidently Timothy's conversion dated back to Paul and Barnabas's first witness in that city (cf. 14:20). Luke added that Timothy was well spoken of by the Christians in Lystra and Iconium. Derbe is not mentioned because it lay some sixty miles southeast of Lystra.[5] Lystra was only twenty miles or so from Iconium, and a close relationship between the Christians of the two cities would have been natural.

Luke's note that Timothy's mother was Jewish and his father Greek (v. 1) is essential to understanding why Paul had Timothy circumcised (v. 3). Many scholars have argued that Paul would never have asked Timothy to be circumcised, since he objected so strenuously to that rite in Galatians (cf. 6:12f.; 5:11). That, however, is to overlook the fact that

---

[4]As so often with the Western text, nothing is left to conjecture. It adds to v. 41 "handing over the commands of [the apostles] and elders." See Y. Tissot, "Les Prescriptions des Presbytres (Actes xv, 41, d)," *RB* 77 (1970): 321-46.

[5]Some of the church fathers, such as Rufinius and Origen, saw Timothy as coming from Derbe. This may have come from a misreading of Acts 20:4, where Timothy is listed immediately after Gaius of Derbe.

Galatians was written to Gentiles and Timothy was considered a Jew.
There was no question of circumcising Gentiles. The Jerusalem Conference agreed on that. Gentiles would not be required to become Jews in
order to be Christians. The converse was also true: Jews would not be
required to abandon their Jewishness in order to become Christians. There
is absolutely no evidence that Paul ever asked Jews to abandon circumcision as their mark of membership in God's covenant people. According to
later rabbinic law, a child born of a Jewish mother and a Greek father was
considered to be Jewish. The marriage of a Jewish woman to a non-Jew
was considered a nonlegal marriage; and in all instances of nonlegal marriages, the lineage of the child was reckoned through the mother.[6]
According to this understanding, Timothy would have been considered a Jew. His father, however, being a Greek, would not have had his
son circumcised; and the local Jews were aware of this (v. 3). Thus Paul
had Timothy circumcised. Paul always worked through the Jewish synagogues where possible. To have had a member of his entourage be of
Jewish lineage and yet uncircumcised would have hampered his effectiveness among the Jews. It was at the very least a matter of missionary
strategy to circumcise Timothy (1 Cor 9:20). It may have been much
more. Paul never abandoned his own Jewish heritage. He may well have
wanted Timothy to be true to *his* (cf. Rom 3:1f.). In any event, Paul had
no missionary companion more thoroughly involved in his subsequent
work than Timothy. Paul considered him a "son" (cf. 1 Cor 4:17; 1 Tim
1:2). Not only did he address two letters to him, but he also listed him as
cosender in six others (2 Cor 1:1; Phil 1:1; Col 1:1; 1 Thess 1:1; 2 Thess
1:1; Phlm 1). He considered him his "fellow worker" (Rom 16:21; cf.
1 Cor 16:10) and, indeed, as much more—"as a son with his father" in
the work of the gospel (Phil 2:22).[7] Now three, the missionary group
continued along the way, visiting the churches "from town to town."
Luke did not specify the towns they visited, but one would assume they
were Iconium and Pisidian Antioch and any other villages where there
may have been a Christian community resulting from the first missionary
tour. They shared the decrees from the Jerusalem Conference. All of
these churches were in the southern part of the Roman province of

---

[6]*Mishna Qiddushin* 3:12. See S. Belkin, "The Problem of Paul's Background," *JBL* 54
(1935): 41-60. For an opposing view, which argues that the Mishnaic law was not in force in
Paul's day and that Timothy would have been considered a Gentile, see S. J. D. Cohen, "Was
Timothy Jewish (Acts 16:1-3)? Patristic Exegesis, Rabbinic Law, and Matrilineal Descent,"
JBL 105 (1986): 251-68. For the view that Timothy's circumcision was actually that of Titus
in Gal 2:3-5, see W. O. Walker, "The Timothy-Titus Problem Reconsidered," *ExpTim* 92
(1981): 231-35.

[7]For the portrait of Timothy in the Pastoral Epistles, see J. P. Alexander, "The Character
of Timothy," *ExpTim* 25 (1913-14): 277-85.

Galatia and not a part of Syro-Cilicia, to which the decrees were addressed. Perhaps they felt that these churches were involved because they were the product of the Antioch mission. Luke did not mention Paul's promulgating them in any other cities after this, and Paul never mentioned them in his letters.[8]

Verse 5 concludes the narrative of Paul's return visit to these churches of his first mission. This summary statement[9] is not perfunctory, however. It underlines the importance of Paul's concern to fortify and nurture the churches of his prior missionary efforts. He was not only concerned with planting the seed but also to see them grow and bear fruit. This led him to undertake the rigorous trip to southern Galatia through rugged terrain and mountain passes. He accomplished what he sought: the churches were strengthened. They flourished. They were more prepared than ever to carry on when he left.

3. Called to Macedonia (16:6-10)

[6]Paul and his companions traveled throughout the region of Phrygia and Galatia, having been kept by the Holy Spirit from preaching the word in the province of Asia. [7]When they came to the border of Mysia, they tried to enter Bithynia, but the Spirit of Jesus would not allow them to. [8]So they passed by Mysia and went down to Troas. [9]During the night Paul had a vision of a man of Macedonia standing and begging him, "Come over to Macedonia and help us." [10]After Paul had seen the vision, we got ready at once to leave for Macedonia, concluding that God had called us to preach the gospel to them.

16:6 Having completed their visit of the churches established on Paul's first mission, the three now headed north, probably from Antioch in Pisidia. Somewhere along the way they determined to go to "Asia." Just what is intended by "Asia" is uncertain. The term was used in various ways. It could refer to the Roman province of Asia, which included Lycia, portions of Phrygia, and Mysia, as well as ancient Asia. It could be used in a much narrower sense as the cities along the Aegean coast, with Philadelphia as the eastern limit. It probably is in this narrower sense that Paul determined to go to Asia, perhaps to the major city of Ephesus, where he eventually did spend the greater part of his third mission. At this point he was stopped from so doing by the Holy Spirit. The medium of the Spirit's revelation is not given. The important point is that he was stopped. God had other plans for him at the time.

---

[8]W. Ramsay (*St. Paul the Traveller and Roman Citizen* [1897; reprint, Grand Rapids: Baker, 1987], 182-84) suggests that the rise of the Judaizing problem may have led Paul to abandon the decrees because of abuse in a legalistic direction by that group.

[9]For other summaries, cf. 2:41,47; 4:4; 5:14; 6:7; 9:31,42.

16:7 The route of the missionaries from this point is anything but clear. They obviously traveled northward because they eventually came to Mysia. The questionable point is how far eastward they traveled. To what does "the region of Phrygia and Galatia" refer?[10] The most natural reading would give a consecutive travel narrative, starting from Antioch, moving into northern Phrygia, and then evidently swinging eastward into portions of northern Galatia before arriving in the northeast corner of Mysia where it bordered Bithynia. A good guess is that it was somewhere around Dorylaeum, where they were stopped in their travel plans a second time. Their intention was to go into Bithynia, probably to witness in the populous cities along the Marmara Sea like Nicomedia, Nicea, and Byzantium. Again they were prevented, this time by "the Spirit of Jesus," possibly a special vision of the risen Jesus but more likely a variant expression of the Holy Spirit.[11] The third expression of the divine leading is indicated in terms of God's calling (v. 10). The geographical scheme is certainly not the dominant motif in this section: the divine leading *is*. Father (v. 10), Son (v. 7), and Spirit (v. 6) together led Paul to the decisive new breakthrough—the mission to Macedonia, the witness on European soil.

16:8 The missionary group must have been thoroughly perplexed as they were led away from the cities of Bithynia through the wild backwoods country of Mysia over to the coast and down to Troas.[12] Troas lay in the region associated with Troy, some thirty miles to the south of the ancient city. It had been founded in the fourth century B.C. by Antigonus and from the start was primarily a port city. An artificial harbor constructed there provided the main sea access to Macedonia and was a significant harbor for sea traffic to and from the Dardanelles.[13] Having

---

[10]W. Ramsay (*St. Paul the Traveller*, 210-12) argued that the two terms should be taken as a single entity, the Phrygio-Galatian region, referring to the area of southern Galatia around Antioch. This, however, creates an overlap with 16:1-5 and allows no progress in the travel narrative. More likely Luke meant by "Galatia" the old kingdom of Galatia in the north and not the southern portions of the Roman province of Galatia which Luke had heretofore designated as Phrygia, Pamphilia, Pisidia, Lycaonia, etc. If so, Paul perhaps established at this time the churches to which he later addressed the Galatian epistle. For a full discussion see J. Polhill, "Galatia Revisited: The Life-Setting of the Epistle," *RevExp* 49 (1972): 437-43. For "Phrygia" used adjectivally in support of Ramsay's view, see C. J. Hemer, "The Adjective 'Phrygia,'" *JTS* 27 (1976): 122-26 and "Phrygia: A Further Note," *JTS* 28 (1977): 99-101.

[11]For the Spirit as the Spirit of Jesus, cf. Rom 8:9; Gal 4:6; Phil 1:19; 1 Pet 1:11.

[12]W. P. Bowers suggests that they already must have had some thought of a Macedonian mission because they took the unlikely route to Troas ("Paul's Route through Mysia: A Note on Acts xvi, 8," *JTS* 30 [1979]: 507-11).

[13]For a thorough treatment of Troas, see C. J. Hemer, "Alexandria Troas," *TB* 26 (1975): 79-112.

been given the status of a colony city by Augustus, Troas had a sizable population and would itself have been a suitable candidate for a major mission.[14]

16:9 But God had other plans and sent a vision to Paul, perhaps in a dream in the middle of the night. A man of Macedonia appeared to him begging him to come and witness to the Macedonians. Scholars have often speculated about whether this person might be defined more closely. Ramsay suggested he may have been Luke himself, that possibly Paul had needed a physician's aid and consulted him in Troas. This is based on the fact that the "we" narrative first occurs in verse 10, indicating Luke's presence.[15] It is an attractive view, but ancient tradition connects Luke with Antioch, not Macedonia, and the Philippian narrative contains not the slightest inkling that he was on home territory. Somewhat more fanciful is the view that the man in the vision was that most famous of all Macedonians, Alexander the Great. Alexander had a vision of "one world"; Paul would make it a reality through the gospel.[16] Luke gave us no basis for such speculations. The identity of the man as a Macedonian was all that counted.

16:10 Paul realized that this vision was God's medium for calling him to a mission in Macedonia (v. 10). Timothy and Silas readily agreed, once Paul had shared the experience with them. Since the text states that "we got ready," the first certain occurrence of the narrative first-person speech in Acts, the most likely assumption is that Luke joined the missionary party at this time.[17] Now four shared the vision of evangelizing Macedonia.[18]

4. Witnessing in Philippi (16:11-40)

The remainder of chap. 16 concerns Paul's work in Philippi. It falls into four separate scenes. Verses 11-15 relate the group's journey to Phi-

---

[14]A church may have been established at Troas as early as this first visit of Paul. Acts 20:5-12 indicates a Christian community existed there. Paul spoke of his witnessing there on a later occasion (2 Cor 2:12; cf. 2 Tim 4:13).

[15]Ramsay, *St. Paul the Traveller*, 200-205.

[16]W. Barclay, *The Acts of the Apostles*, DSB (Philadelphia: Westminster, 1955), 131f.

[17]For the significance of the "we" passages, see the discussion on authorship in the introduction. Recently V. K. Robbins has argued that the "we" is a literary device associated with sea narratives ("By Land and By Sea: The We-Passages and Ancient Sea Voyages," *Luke-Acts: New Perspectives from the SBL Seminar*, ed. C. Talbert [New York: Crossroad, 1984]), 215-42. The difficulty with this is that the "we" extends into the narrative far beyond the voyage (cf. 16:17) and only occurs in three of the ten or twelve voyages in Acts. See G. Krodel, *Acts*, PC (Philadelphia: Fortress, 1981), 303.

[18]O. Glombitza points to the significance of the accusative case in v. 10 as the object of εὐαγγελίσασθαι ("Der Schritt nach Europa: Erwägungen zu Act 16, 9-15," *ZNW* 53 [1962]: 77-82). It is not a matter of *preaching* the good news *to* the Macedonians (dative case) but of "evangelizing them," bringing them into a new existence through the gospel.

lippi and the conversion of a prominent woman named Lydia. Verses 16-24 deal with the healing of a possessed servant girl and its unfortunate result. Verses 25-34 tell of the conversion of the Philippian jailer. Verses 35-40 treat the final encounter of Paul the Roman citizen with the city magistrates.

(1) Founding a Church with Lydia (16:11-15)

[11]From Troas we put out to sea and sailed straight for Samothrace, and the next day on to Neapolis. [12]From there we traveled to Philippi, a Roman colony and the leading city of that district of Macedonia. And we stayed there several days.

[13]On the Sabbath we went outside the city gate to the river, where we expected to find a place of prayer. We sat down and began to speak to the women who had gathered there. [14]One of those listening was a woman named Lydia, a dealer in purple cloth from the city of Thyatira, who was a worshiper of God. The Lord opened her heart to respond to Paul's message. [15]When she and the members of her household were baptized, she invited us to her home. "If you consider me a believer in the Lord," she said, "come and stay at my house." And she persuaded us.

16:11 Verses 11-12 relate the journey from Troas to Philippi. The weather must have been good and the winds favorable because their ship sighted Samothrace the first day. Samothrace was a mountainous island with a peak rising 5,000 feet above sea level. It lay off the Thracian coast on a direct line between Troas and Neapolis, the port of Philippi. The next day they arrived at Neapolis. In Acts 20:6 the voyage from Philippi to Troas took considerably longer—five days in all.

16:12 The group would have taken the Via Egnatia the ten miles or so to Philippi. This route was the main east-west highway through Macedonia, beginning at Dyrrhachium on the Adriatic coast, traveling through Thessalonica, Amphipolis, and Philippi and terminating at Neapolis. Paul often traveled this road.

Philippi was settled from ancient times largely because of the copper and gold deposits in the region. Formerly known as Krenides, it was seized in the fourth century B.C. from the native Thracians by Philip of Macedon, the father of Alexander the Great. Philip renamed the city for himself and enlarged the gold-mining operations. It came under Roman domination in 168 B.C. and was enlarged in 42 B.C. when Antony and Octavian defeated Brutus and Cassius on the plains southwest of the city. In 31 B.C., after defeating Antony at the battle of Actium, Octavian granted the city the status of a colony. Subsequently a number of military veterans were settled there. The Roman influence was particularly strong in Philippi as reflected in Paul's Letter to the Philippians and in the present narrative. When Macedonia had first come under Roman influence, it had been divided into four administrative districts. Although these were later dissolved into a single provincial structure with Thessalonica as capital, the distinction between the four districts seems to have persisted. This is perhaps reflected in Luke's designating the city as "the leading city of that district of Macedonia" (v. 12).[19] Actually, Amphipolis was the larger city and had been capital of the district before the provincial reorganization. Perhaps Luke reflected a local claim that Philippi was Macedonia's "foremost city," a claim not totally unjustified when one considers its illustrious history.

16:13 The four missionaries evidently set themselves up in the city and waited until the next Sabbath before beginning their witness. According to Paul's usual pattern, they sought out the Jewish place of worship first. In this instance there does not seem to have been a Jewish synagogue at Philippi.[20] Instead, they learned of a place of prayer outside the city gates.[21] It was by a river, probably the Gangites, which lies about a mile and a quarter from the city gates. The Romans were sometimes uneasy about foreign cults. Judaism was a recognized religion; but perhaps because there was no formally constituted synagogue, the women had to meet outside the city.[22] If there were no Jews present and all the women were Gentile "God-fearers" like Lydia, this may have made their gathering even more suspect in the city. In any event, the gathering of women was the closest thing to a synagogue at Philippi; and Paul took the usual posture a speaker assumed in a synagogue, sitting down, to address the women. Most likely the event took place in the open air beside the river.

16:14 Among the women gathered there, one stood out. Her name was Lydia, the same as the ancient territory in which her native city of Thyatira was located. She is described as a dealer in goods dyed purple, a likely occupation since Thyatira was indeed a center of the purple dye

---

[19]The problem is somewhat more complicated than the NIV would indicate. The best manuscripts read "the first city of the district of Macedonia." The Western text reads "the capital" (κεφαλή) of Macedonia. Only a couple of Latin minuscules have the reading "a leading city of the first district of Macedonia," but this reading fits the facts best.

[20]At least ten males were required to form a synagogue. Since only women are mentioned in the gathering outside Philippi, there were likely not sufficient Jewish males to constitute a synagogue there.

[21]"Place of prayer" is sometimes used to designate a synagogue, and some interpreters argue that there was an actual synagogue building in this instance. Synagogues were often, but not necessarily, located close to a water supply because of their needs for the rites of purification.

[22]The ruins of an arched gateway stand outside the walls of Philippi. It has been suggested that this gateway is the one mentioned in v. 13 and served as a marker for the area within which no foreign cults could be observed. See W. A. McDonald, "Archaeology and St. Paul's Journeys in Greek Lands," *BA* 3 (1940): 18-24.

trade.[23] Lydia's business is not an incidental detail. It marks her as a person of means. Purple goods were expensive and often associated with royalty; thus the business was a lucrative one.[24] Lydia's invitation to the four missionaries to stay in her home in itself indicates that she had considerable substance, such as guest rooms and servants to accommodate them adequately. Of all Paul's churches, the Philippians' generosity stood out. They continued to send him support in his missionary endeavors elsewhere (Phil 4:15-18; cf. 2 Cor 11:8). One is tempted to see Lydia as a principal contributor. It is surely to go too far with such speculations, however, to argue that Paul married Lydia and that she was the "loyal yokefellow" of Phil 4:3.[25] Women like Lydia were particularly prominent in Paul's missionary efforts in this portion of Acts—the women of Thessalonica (17:4) and of Berea (17:12), Damaris in Athens (17:34), and Priscilla in Corinth (18:2). Priscilla and Lydia took an active role in the ministry of their churches.[26] This was in part due to the more elevated status of women in the contemporary Greek and Roman society. This was particularly true in the first century when women were given a number of legal privileges such as initiating divorce, signing legal documents, even holding honorary public titles. The prominent role of the women in Acts is perhaps due even more to the message Paul brought them: "In Christ Jesus, there is neither male nor female" (Gal 3:28).[27]

Lydia was a "worshiper of God" (16:14), one of those devout Gentiles like Cornelius who believed in God but had not become a full convert to Judaism. There was an extensive Jewish community at Thyatira, and she had perhaps first come to her faith in God there. As he had with Cornelius, God responded to her faith and "opened her heart" to receive the gospel of Jesus Christ which Paul proclaimed. As always with divine grace, it was God's Spirit moving in her heart that led to faith.

16:15 Lydia made the missionaries' acceptance of her hospitality the test of whether they *really believed* she had become a believer, "Come and

---

[23]E. Haenchen (*The Acts of the Apostles: A Commentary* [Philadelphia: Westminster, 1971], 494) mentions a monument excavated at Thessalonica with which the purple dyers of that city honored a fellow tradesman from Thyatira.

[24]There were evidently two methods for producing the expensive purple dyes. One was to extract the color from the glands of the murex shell. This is the known method employed in the extensive dye industry at Sidon. Another method still employed in the region of ancient Thyatira extracted the dye from the juice of the madder root.

[25]Several Victorian exegetes, such as E. Renan and T. Zahn, argued just that (Haenchen, *Acts*, 494). "Yokefellow" is masculine gender in Phil 4:3 and probably should not be understood as the designation for a wife.

[26]For an excellent treatment of Lydia, see R. Ryan, "Lydia, a Dealer in Purple Goods," *TBT* 22 (1984): 285-89.

[27]See W. D. Thomas, "The Place of Women in the Church at Philippi," *ExpTim* 83 (1971-72): 117-20.

see for yourself if the Lord has come to rule in my life" (author's paraphrase). It was an offer they could not refuse. But she did not merely open her home to the missionaries; she allowed it to become the gathering place for the entire Christian community (v. 40). Perhaps the wealthiest member of the Philippian church, Lydia embraced the ideal of the early church, not laying claim to what was hers but freely sharing it with her sisters and brothers in Christ (4:32).

Not only did Lydia share her goods, but she shared her faith as well. As the leader of her household, she led them to join her in commitment and baptism (16:15). This is the first time the baptism of a "household" is *narrated* in Acts. Another will follow shortly (v. 33). There is no evidence whatever that this included infants, and it cannot be used in support of infant baptism. Previous references to Cornelius's household indicate that those who were baptized both heard and believed the message (10:44; 11:4,17). Throughout Acts baptism is based on personal faith and commitment, and there is no reason to see otherwise in the household baptisms.[28]

(2) Healing a Possessed Servant Girl (16:16-24)

[16]Once when we were going to the place of prayer, we were met by a slave girl who had a spirit by which she predicted the future. She earned a great deal of money for her owners by fortune-telling. [17]This girl followed Paul and the rest of us, shouting, "These men are servants of the Most High God, who are telling you the way to be saved." [18]She kept this up for many days. Finally Paul became so troubled that he turned around and said to the spirit, "In the name of Jesus Christ I command you to come out of her!" At that moment the spirit left her.

[19]When the owners of the slave girl realized that their hope of making money was gone, they seized Paul and Silas and dragged them into the marketplace to face the authorities. [20]They brought them before the magistrates and said, "These men are Jews, and are throwing our city into an uproar [21]by advocating customs unlawful for us Romans to accept or practice."

[22]The crowd joined in the attack against Paul and Silas, and the magistrates ordered them to be stripped and beaten. [23]After they had been severely flogged, they were thrown into prison, and the jailer was commanded to guard them carefully. [24]Upon receiving such orders, he put them in the inner cell and fastened their feet in the stocks.

16:16 Verse 16 opens a new scene but connects with the previous one to make a continuous narrative. On one of the occasions when the four missionaries were going outside the city to the place of prayer, they were encountered by a slave girl who had a spirit by which she predicted

---

[28]For the view that household baptisms included infants, see J. Jeremias, *Infant Baptism in the First Four Centuries* (London: SCM, 1960). For the opposing viewpoint, see G. R. Beasley-Murray, *Baptism in the New Testament* (Exeter: Paternoster, 1972), esp. 312-20.

the future. The Greek speaks literally of a "python spirit." The python
was the symbol of the famous Delphic oracle and represented the god
Apollo, who was believed to render predictions of future events. The serpent had thus become a symbol of augury, and anyone who was seen to
possess the gift of foretelling the future was described as led by the
"python." Greeks and Romans put great stock on augury and divination.
No commander would set out on a major military campaign nor would an
emperor make an important decree without first consulting an oracle to
see how things might turn out. A slave girl with a clairvoyant gift was
thus a veritable gold mine for her owners.

16:17-18 Like the demoniacs during Jesus' ministry, the possessed
girl was evidently able to see into the true nature of Paul's preaching, particularly into the reality of the God he proclaimed (cf. Luke 4:34; Mark
1:24). She constantly followed the missionaries about, shouting that they
were servants of the "Most High God" and proclaimers of "a way of
salvation" (author's translation).

None of this would have been very clear to Gentiles. The term "God
most high" was a common Old Testament term for God, but the same term
was equally common in the Gentile world and was particularly applied to
Zeus. Neither would "way of salvation" be immediately clear to a Gentile.
The Greco-Roman world was full of "saviors." Savior/deliverer, salvation/
deliverance were favorite terms. The emperor dubbed himself "savior" of
the people. All of which is to show why Paul finally became irritated with
the girl's constant acclamations.

These acclamations may have been true enough, but they were open to
too much misunderstanding for pagan hearers. The truth could not be so
easily condensed for those from a polytheistic background. Jesus might
be seen as just another savior in the bulging pantheon of Greek gods.[29]
So Paul, in a form reminiscent of Jesus' exorcisms, commanded the spirit
to exit the girl. The spirit did so immediately.

16:19 That was not the only thing to vanish. With the spirit the owners' prospects for further profit also exited. Luke probably intended the
wordplay. He used the same verb (*exēlthen*) for the demon's coming out in
v. 18 as for the money's going in v. 19. The latter created the problem.
Healing a possessed girl was one thing; but when that involved considerable economic loss, that was a wholly different matter. The scene was
reminiscent of the Gerasene pigs incident (Mark 5:16-17). The profit
motive was a frequent obstacle to the gospel in Acts. It was certainly the
downfall of Simon Magus (8:19f.). It would lead Demetrius and his fellow

---

[29]For this view that the girl's acclamation was open to serious misunderstanding by
pagans, see P. R. Trebilco, "Paul and Silas—'Servants of the Most High God' (Acts 16, 16-
18)," *JSNT* 36 (1989): 51-73.

Ephesian silversmiths to violently oppose Paul (19:24-28). Here the greed of the slave girl's owners was in marked contrast to the generosity of Lydia, who shared her house with the missionaries and the Philippian Christians. One's relationship to material goods marks a major distinction between believers and nonbelievers in Acts. (Note how "believer" and "stay at my house" are closely linked in v. 15.)

The first-person narrative stops at v. 17 and does not reappear in Acts until Paul's return to Philippi in 20:6.[30] Some scholars have seen this as an indication that Luke remained behind to minister in Philippi and did not rejoin Paul in his travel until this return visit at the end of his third mission.[31] This is placing a great deal of faith in a basically stylistic matter, assuming that Luke always took pains to distinguish his presence by the use of the first person. What does seem to be indicated in the present context is that Luke and Timothy dropped out of the picture at this point. Only Paul and Silas got the brunt of the owners' ire and were dragged before the magistrates (v. 19). The scene is filled with local color and very much fits what is known from elsewhere about Philippi. The apostles were dragged into the marketplace (agora). In the excavations at Philippi, this agora, or forum, has been uncovered. On its northwest side stood a raised podium with stairs on two sides. This would have been the city tribunal where civil cases were tried. The city prison was located immediately adjacent to the agora. Although these ruins date from the second century A.D., it is likely that they were built on the same sites as the agora and prison where Paul and Silas were tried and incarcerated.[32]

16:20-21 The officials mentioned in vv. 20,35 correspond to the pattern of authority for Roman colonies. The "magistrates" (*stratēgoi*) of v. 20, who probably were the same as the "authorities" of v. 19, would be the two men (known in Latin as the *duuviri*) who tried civil cases and were generally responsible for maintaining law and order. The "officers" mentioned in vv. 35,38 (*rhabdouchoi*) were designated *lictors* in Latin and were responsible to the magistrates. They were the enforcement officers. Their symbol of office was a bundle of rods with an axe protruding from the middle, tied together with a red band called the *fasces*. (This symbol was revived in modern times by Mussolini for his "fascist" movement.) The rods were not mere decorations but were used in scourgings. The lictors in Philippi would have used them in the beating of Paul and Silas (v. 22). In fact, the word used for "beating" (*rhabdizein*) means literally *to beat with rods*, the customary manner of Roman scourgings.

[30]See H. J. Cadbury, "'We' and 'I' Passages in Luke-Acts," *NTS* 3 (1957): 129.
[31]See F. F. Bruce, "St. Paul in Macedonia," *BJRL* 61 (1979): 337-54.
[32]McDonald, "Archaeology and St. Paul's Journeys," 20-21.

The owners of the slave girl were careful in their charges to avoid the real issue of her healing and their resulting loss of profit. Basically their charges were threefold. The first was calculated to awaken latent prejudices in the crowd: "These men are Jews."[33] The second was extremely nebulous but would have evoked the attention of the magistrates who were responsible for "law and order": They "are throwing our city into an uproar." The last charge seems to be the only one with any substance: They are "advocating customs unlawful for us Romans." This is generally interpreted as illegal proselytizing for Judaism,[34] but the evidence is that Jews were not forbidden to proselytize until the time of Hadrian, well into the second century.[35]

16:22-24 None of the charges were valid, but they had their effect. The appeal to anti-Jewish sentiments and to nationalistic Roman pride won over the crowd (v. 22). The insinuation of a threat to civil order evidently won over the magistrates (v. 23). The magistrates had Paul and Silas stripped for scourging,[36] and the lictors applied their rods. This probably was one of the three instances Paul mentioned in 2 Cor 11:25 when he received the Roman punishment of a flogging with rods. Finally, they were thrown into prison and placed under the tightest security. The prison keeper placed them in the innermost cell of the prison, the dungeon, we would say. Their feet were placed in wooden stocks, which were likely fastened to the wall. Often such stocks were used as instruments of torture; they had a number of holes for the legs, which allowed for severe stretching of the torso and thus created excruciating pain. Luke did not indicate that any torture was involved this time. The entire

---

[33]Roman satirists evidenced strong anti-Semitic tendencies in the first century. Diaspora Jews generally lived in their own enclaves; and their customs appeared narrow and superstitious to Gentiles, particularly their rite of circumcision, abstention from eating pork, and scrupulous observance of the Sabbath. See J. Polhill, "Circumcision," *MDB*, 156.

[34]For instance, Haenchen (*Acts*, 496, n. 5) states that it was illegal to proselytize Roman citizens and notes that this would have been particularly true in a city like Philippi with colony status.

[35]See A. N. Sherwin-White, *Roman Society and Roman Law in the New Testament* (Oxford: Clarendon, 1963), 81-82. Awareness that Jewish proselytism was not illegal in Paul's day leads D. R. Schwartz to suggest that the circumstantial participle in v. 20 should be translated as a concessive—"*although* these men are Jews, they are teaching unlawful customs" ("which Jews would *not* do," being implied; "The Accusation and the Accusers at Philippi [Acts 16, 20-21]," *Bib* 65 [1984]: 357-63).

[36]Verse 22 reads literally, "And the magistrates, tearing off their garments, commanded rodding." The "their" is ambiguous and could be seen as the magistrates tearing their own garments in horror at Paul and Silas's "crime." Since prisoners were always stripped for lashing, the present context seems more naturally to call for the stripping of Paul and Silas. See K. Lake and H. J. Cadbury, eds., *The Beginnings of Christianity*, vol. 5: *Additional Notes* (London: Macmillan, 1933), 272-73.

emphasis is on the tight security in which the two were held. This makes the miracle of their subsequent deliverance all the more remarkable.

(3) Converting a Jailer's Household (16:25-34)

[25]About midnight Paul and Silas were praying and singing hymns to God, and the other prisoners were listening to them. [26]Suddenly there was such a violent earthquake that the foundations of the prison were shaken. At once all the prison doors flew open, and everybody's chains came loose. [27]The jailer woke up, and when he saw the prison doors open, he drew his sword and was about to kill himself because he thought the prisoners had escaped. [28]But Paul shouted, "Don't harm yourself! We are all here!"

[29]The jailer called for lights, rushed in and fell trembling before Paul and Silas. [30]He then brought them out and asked, "Sirs, what must I do to be saved?" [31]They replied, "Believe in the Lord Jesus, and you will be saved—you and your household." [32]Then they spoke the word of the Lord to him and to all the others in his house. [33]At that hour of the night the jailer took them and washed their wounds; then immediately he and all his family were baptized. [34]The jailer brought them into his house and set a meal before them; he was filled with joy because he had come to believe in God—he and his whole family.

The reader of Acts is not surprised to find Paul and Silas miraculously delivered from their confinement. It had happened before: to the apostles in 5:19-26 and to Peter in 12:5-19. The present narrative perhaps has more in common with the apostles' deliverance, since in both these instances the primary emphasis is not on the rescue as such but on the divine power manifested in bringing about their freedom, which provides a stronger base for witness. In chap. 5 the apostles did not run away but willingly returned to the Sanhedrin for their scheduled trial. The miracle considerably strengthened their position before the Sanhedrin, however, and paved the way for Gamaliel's counsel (5:38f.). In the present narrative the same holds true. Though freed, Paul and Silas did not attempt to escape. The miracle served not to deliver them but rather to deliver the jailer. It served as the basis for Paul and Silas's witness to him and for his conversion. The story thus falls into two divisions, the first relating Paul and Silas's deliverance (vv. 25-28) and the second the conversion of the jailer and his household (vv. 29-34).

THE DELIVERANCE (16:25-28). **16:25-28** It was the middle of the night. Paul and Silas were singing hymns of praise to God. In Acts, Christians are always full of hope. Peter slept peacefully the night before his trial (12:6); Paul and Silas sang. Their praise and good cheer was in itself a witness to God, and the other prisoners listened intently. The area around Philippi often experiences earthquakes and tremors, but this one happened at just the right time. The prison doors probably were locked by bars; these flew up, and the doors opened. Everyone's chains came loose.

The chains may have been attached to the walls and wrenched loose by the violence of the quake. The jailer was aroused by the earthquake and spotted the open doors. Supposing that the prisoners had already escaped, he drew his sword to kill himself, preferring death by his own hand than by Roman justice. Jailers and guards were personally responsible for their prisoners and in some instances were executed for allowing them to escape (cf. 12:19). The jailer's prisoners had not escaped; and when Paul looked up in the open doorway and saw what he was about to do, he shouted for him to stop, assuring him they were all still in the cell. To this point the reader would have expected the story of Paul and Silas's escape.[37] It was not to be so. The miraculous release did not lead to their escape but to the far more significant event of the jailer's conversion.

THE WITNESS (16:29-34). **16:29-34** Calling for lamps or torches, the jailer rushed in and fell at the feet of Paul and Silas. It may have been a gesture of worship, but Paul did not object, as at Lystra (14:15). It was certainly an expression of subservience.[38] Paul had saved his life, and Paul's God, who had reduced in an instant all his efforts at prison security, was obviously one to be respected. It has often been argued that his question ("What must I do to be saved?") was intended in the secular sense of the word "salvation," that he was asking how his life should be spared. But his life had already been spared. No one had escaped. More likely he asked about his salvation in the full religious sense. Perhaps he had heard the servant girl's proclamation that Paul spoke of the way of salvation (v. 17). Perhaps he had heard Paul's preaching or reports of his preaching but had not fully understood. Perhaps he had fallen asleep to the sound of Paul and Silas's hymns to God. Now he was ready for understanding. The miracle of the earthquake and the prisoners who wouldn't flee arrested his attention and prepared his heart to receive Paul's message. His question is a classic expression that has lived through the centuries and must be asked by everyone who comes to faith. Paul's answer is equally classic. It cannot be put any simpler: "Believe in the Lord Jesus, and you will be saved—you and your whole household" (cf. 11:14).

At some point the jailer's household entered the scene. Luke did not specify when. Perhaps the mention of the household triggered the jailer's awareness that Paul and Silas were about to share something his whole family should hear. In any event, all were present when Paul and Silas

---

[37]There are many interesting parallels between this narrative and other "rescue" stories in the ancient literature. The closest are found in the noncanonical Jewish tradition with regard to Joseph's imprisonment (*T. Jos.* 8:4-5). See W. K. L. Clarke, "St. Luke and the Pseudepigrapha: Two Parallels," *JTS* 15 (1913-14): 598f. There are similar elements, such as loosened bonds and doors flying open in an escape story in Euripides (*Bacchae*, 443-48).

[38]Leaving nothing to the imagination, the Western text adds that the jailer resecured all the other prisoners before leading Paul and Silas out of the cell (v. 30).

shared the words of the Lord. Here Luke made explicit what was implicit in the Lydia story: the whole household heard the gospel proclaimed. There was no "proxy" faith. The whole family came to faith *in God* (v. 34). Coming from a pagan background as they did, their newfound faith had a double dimension—faith in Jesus as Savior and faith in God as the one true God.

The witness to Christ was primary and took precedence over everything else. Now the jailer became aware of the two prisoners' suffering and bathed the wounds from their beating. Perhaps this took place in the courtyard where the household water supply would be located. Throughout Luke's story he focused attention on the various signs evidencing conversion (i.e., speaking in tongues, expressions of joy, and hospitality). Here the evidence of conversion is the jailer's washing of the apostles' wounds. There then took place an even more significant "washing," when the jailer's family was baptized.[39] Then the jailer treated Paul and Silas in a most unusual fashion for prisoners. He took them into his house and fed them at his own table.[40] They were no longer prisoners in his eyes; they were brothers in Christ.

(4) Humbling the City Magistrates (16:35-40)

[35]When it was daylight, the magistrates sent their officers to the jailer with the order: "Release those men." [36]The jailer told Paul, "The magistrates have ordered that you and Silas be released. Now you can leave. Go in peace."

[37]But Paul said to the officers: "They beat us publicly without a trial, even though we are Roman citizens, and threw us into prison. And now do they want to get rid of us quietly? No! Let them come themselves and escort us out."

[38]The officers reported this to the magistrates, and when they heard that Paul and Silas were Roman citizens, they were alarmed. [39]They came to appease them and escorted them from the prison, requesting them to leave the city. [40]After Paul and Silas came out of the prison, they went to Lydia's house, where they met with the brothers and encouraged them. Then they left.

16:35-36 Luke did not tell us why the magistrates changed their minds and decided to release the two prisoners. Perhaps they were more interested in having them outside of the city limits than keeping them in further incarceration.[41] However that may be, they sent the "officers" to instruct the jailer to release them. These officers were the lictors (*rhabdouchoi*), the "rod-bearers," who had earlier given Paul and Silas

---

[39]Surely all those who understood and responded to Paul and Silas's preaching—not the infants. See n. 28.

[40]The text gives no warrant for seeing the "meal" as the Lord's Supper, as is maintained by some commentators.

[41]The Western text provides an answer, greatly expanding on verse 35f., in which the magistrates are said to have changed their minds for fear after the earthquake.

the flogging (v. 23). The jailer was all too glad to inform the two that they had been released and to send them off with the Christian greeting of "peace."[42]

16:37 Paul, however, would not go and insisted that the magistrates come to jail in person and request their departure. He had the upper hand in the matter. He was a Roman citizen; evidently Silas was also (cf. v. 37). The magistrates had had them publicly flogged and thrown in prison, and all that without a trial. It was strictly an illegal procedure. Evidently local magistrates did have the right to mete out minor punishments like flogging of noncitizens, even without a hearing. They seem in Paul's day to have had this authority even for offending Roman citizens— but not without a trial.[43] They had scourged and imprisoned two Roman citizens with no formal condemnation, and that was beyond their authority. In this case the magistrates were unaware that Paul and Silas were Roman citizens.[44] Evidently in the hubbub of the original "hearing," the slave owners did all the talking and the crowd all the shouting; and the two missionaries were unable to communicate the fact.

16:38 The "alarm" of the magistrates was understandable (v. 38). Abuse of the rights of a Roman citizen was a serious offense. Magistrates could be removed from office for such; a municipality could have its rights reduced. For instance, the emperor could deprive Philippi of all the privileges of its colony status for such an offense.

16:39-40 The situation was ironic. Paul and Silas had been treated as criminals but were innocent. The magistrates who condemned them now found themselves genuine lawbreakers. They lost no time in getting to the jail and requesting the departure of the citizens.[45] Evidently they were still concerned about all the commotion Paul and Silas had stirred up among the citizenry and requested that they leave town also. The two missionaries complied, but they were in no rush—nor did they really have to be. The magistrates would give them no trouble now. So before departing they once again visited the Christians of the city. The church

---

[42]It is the customary Jewish greeting (*shalom*). Cf. Judg 18:6; Mark 5:34; Luke 7:50; 8:48; Acts 15:33; Jas 2:16.

[43]See Sherwin-White, *Roman Society and Roman Law*, 71-76.

[44]How did one prove citizenship? We don't know. Public records were kept, usually on small wooden diptychs which were small enough to be carried on one's person. Evidence indicates that this was not usually done, but rather they were deposited with one's valuables. Except for the military and merchants, society was not all that mobile; and transients like Paul and Silas were somewhat rare. One probably did not normally lie about citizenship; it was an offense punishable by death. See H. J. Cadbury, *The Book of Acts in History* (New York: Harper, 1955), 68-78; Sherwin-White, *Roman Law and Roman Society*, 151-52.

[45]The Western text is again quite expansive at v. 39. It has the magistrates request the two to leave in order that *they* might not again make such a horrible mistake and condemn citizens unjustly.

had grown; Lydia, not surprisingly, made her home available as a house church (v. 40). Satisfied that all was in good order, the two missionaries left for the next city.

Paul may have seemed a bit huffy in his demand for a formal apology from the magistrates, but that is not the point. It was essential that the young Christian community have a good reputation among the authorities if its witness was to flourish. Christians broke none of the Roman laws. Luke was at pains to show this. It would continue to be a major emphasis in Acts. In this instance Paul and Silas were totally innocent of any wrongdoing. It was important that the magistrates acknowledge their innocence and set the record straight. This was why Paul made such a major point of it.

5. Establishing Churches in Thessalonica and Berea (17:1-15)

Paul, Silas, and Timothy proceeded from Philippi to the major seaport city of Thessalonica some 100 miles distant (vv. 1-4). Thessalonica was then (as now) the second largest city in Greece, with a population estimated at 200,000.[46] It was founded in 315 B.C. by Cassander on the site of ancient Therme and named for his wife, who was a step-sister of Alexander the Great. When the Romans first took over Macedonia in 167 B.C., it was made capital of one of the four divisions. It became the seat of government for all of Macedonia in 148 B.C. when that region was reorganized into a single province. As a reward for siding with Antony and Octavian in the battle of Philippi, Thessalonica was given the status of a free city in 42 B.C., which meant that it had local autonomy. Its government consequently followed more the Greek than the Roman pattern of administration, as is reflected in the text of Acts. At Thessalonica Paul was perhaps intending to follow the pattern of establishing himself in and working out of the major population centers, a pattern clearly pursued in Corinth and Ephesus later. In this instance his mission was cut short by strong opposition (vv. 5-9).

From Thessalonica the three missionaries went to Berea (vv. 10-15). Their reception was more favorable, but Paul was again forced to leave because of opposition aroused by Jews who had come from Thessalonica. Overall, in the description of Paul's ministry in these two cities, a familiar pattern of initial acceptance and rising opposition repeats itself. At Thessalonica the Jews initiated the resistance to Paul's witness, as was the case at Pisidian Antioch (13:50) and Iconium (14:2) on his first missionary journey. At Berea the opposition was instigated by Jews coming from Thessalonica, just as previously Jews from Antioch and Iconium initiated

---

[46]Since the ancient city lies beneath modern buildings, it remains largely unexcavated. See McDonald, "Archaeology and St. Paul's Journeys," 21-24.

his difficulties at Lystra (14:19). There is also a reminiscence of the experience at Philippi, as the case against Paul was presented before the city magistrates (17:6; cf. 16:20). This would happen again at Corinth (18:12), and perhaps the appearance before the Areopagus is to be seen in this light (17:19), although almost certainly in this instance not as a formal trial. In these appearances before the local officials, the Lord's words at the time of Paul's conversion were very much fulfilled: he was Christ's witness before the Gentiles and their rulers (9:15). In the consistent opposition Paul's ministry encountered, the remainder of the Lord's words were also fulfilled: Paul suffered for the sake of the name of Jesus (9:16).

Paul's ministry in Thessalonica is told with the utmost economy. The basic pattern of initial witness in the synagogue is set forth (vv. 1-4). The pattern continues with the picture of the opposition to Paul (17:5-9), this time filled out by the significant role played by Jason. The summary of the work in Berea is even briefer (17:10-15). From a literary perspective, Luke assumed the preceding Thessalonian narrative and did not repeat. For instance, he did not repeat the *method* of Paul's witness in the synagogue (17:2-4). He could assume the reader would know that the same basic procedure was followed at Berea. What was different at Berea was the response of the Jews there, and this was what he elaborated (17:11).

(1) Acceptance and Rejection in Thessalonica (17:1-9)

¹When they had passed through Amphipolis and Apollonia, they came to Thessalonica, where there was a Jewish synagogue. ²As his custom was, Paul went into the synagogue, and on three Sabbath days he reasoned with them from the Scriptures, ³explaining and proving that the Christ had to suffer and rise from the dead. "This Jesus I am proclaiming to you is the Christ," he said. ⁴Some of the Jews were persuaded and joined Paul and Silas, as did a large number of God-fearing Greeks and not a few prominent women.

⁵But the Jews were jealous; so they rounded up some bad characters from the marketplace, formed a mob and started a riot in the city. They rushed to Jason's house in search of Paul and Silas in order to bring them out to the crowd. ⁶But when they did not find them, they dragged Jason and some other brothers before the city officials, shouting: "These men who have caused trouble all over the world have now come here, ⁷and Jason has welcomed them into his house. They are all defying Caesar's decrees, saying that there is another king, one called Jesus." ⁸When they heard this, the crowd and the city officials were thrown into turmoil. ⁹Then they made Jason and the others post bond and let them go.

17:1-3 The journey from Philippi to Thessalonica followed the Via Egnatia through the cities of Amphipolis and Apollonia. Each of these cities was about a day's journey apart when traveling by horseback. Luke gave no time frame; and if the company traveled by foot, one would have to assume the 100-mile journey took more than three days and that there were other stopping places than the two major towns Luke designated on their itinerary.

Amphipolis was some thirty miles southwest of Philippi. Formerly capital of the first division of Macedonia and a "free city," it was important for its strategic position, controlling access to the Hellespont and the Black Sea.[47] It would have been a significant place for witness, but Luke did not indicate that Paul carried on any mission there or anywhere else along the route to Thessalonica. He simply indicated these as stopping places, Appollonia being the next mentioned, some thirty miles from Amphipolis and thirty-eight miles from the final destination of Thessalonica.

Once arrived in Thessalonica, Paul followed his usual pattern of beginning his witness in the synagogue. This continued on three successive Sabbaths (v. 2).[48] This is the only time reference in the Thessalonian narrative, but one would assume from Paul's Thessalonian correspondence that his initial ministry in Thessalonica was of somewhat longer duration.[49] The pattern of Paul's synagogue preaching as indicated in vv. 2-3 is very much that of the preaching to Jews in the earlier portions of Acts. It consisted primarily of scriptural pointers to Christ from the Old Testament. Luke described this as reasoning with them from the Scriptures.[50] This is further elaborated as "explaining" and "proving" that the Messiah must suffer and rise from the dead.[51]

17:4 "A large number" of the Thessalonian Jews were persuaded by Paul's Old Testament expositions (v. 4), some also of the "God-fearing" Greeks who attended the synagogue. Among the latter group were a number of prominent women. That Luke singled out the influential female con-

---

[47] For a full treatment of Amphipolis, see R. Riesner, "Amphipolis," *BK* 44 (1989): 79-81. For a description of all Paul's Macedonian mission points, see O. F. Meinardus, *St. Paul in Greece* (Athens: Athens Publishing Center, 1972).

[48] The plural form *sabbata* regularly occurs in the NT for a single Sabbath day. This is the only occurrence in the NT where it is unambiguously used of more than one Sabbath. See *Beginnings* 4:202-3.

[49] It was long enough for a church to be established and leadership appointed (1 Thess 5:12). It was of sufficient duration that Paul received financial support from Philippi "time and again" while in Thessalonica (Phil 4:16). Evidently he took up his trade and supported himself as well during this period (1 Thess 2:9). Most of Paul's converts in Thessalonica seem to have come out of paganism, judging from 1 Thess 1:9, which would indicate a more extensive Gentile witness than one might gather from Luke's highly compressed account.

[50] Luke used the terminology of formal rhetoric, the art of persuasion. Paul appealed to the reason of the Jews and persuaded them with scriptural demonstrations. See D. W. Kemmler, *Faith and Human Reason: A Study of Paul's Method of Preaching as Illustrated by 1-2 Thessalonians and Acts 17, 2-4* (Leiden: Brill, 1975).

[51] That the Scriptures point to the suffering of Christ is a common theme in Luke-Acts: Luke 24:26,46; Acts 3:18; 26:22f. Cf. 1 Cor 15:3f.; 1 Pet 1:11. The servant psalms of Isaiah would have comprised a major part of these OT proofs of the passion of Christ.

verts in the Macedonian congregations (cf. 16:14 and 17:12) is very much in keeping with inscriptional evidence that in Macedonia women had considerable social and civic influence.[52] One should also note the prominence of Silas in this section, particularly in connection with the synagogue witness (vv. 4,10). He is usually in the background, with the focus being on Paul. It could be that in mentioning him in these synagogue contexts, Luke wanted to remind us of his connection with the Jerusalem church and the Jewish-Christian endorsement of Paul's mission.[53]

17:5 Verses 5-9 depict the opposition to Paul's ministry in Thessalonica initiated by the Jews. They are described as being "jealous," perhaps at the number of God-fearing Gentiles whom Paul was attracting away from the synagogue and into the Christian community. The Gentiles' presence in the synagogue probably gave the Jewish community a degree of acceptance in the predominantly Gentile city and probably also some financial support. One should not, however, get the impression that it was always the Jews who opposed Paul. In chaps. 16–19 there is an equal balance between opposition initiated by Jews and that begun by Gentiles.[54] Even in this instance, it was ultimately the Gentile populace who opposed Paul. Beginning with the gang of ruffians who hung around the marketplace,[55] the Jews succeeded in rousing the Gentiles into mob action against Paul and Silas.[56]

At this point Jason entered the picture. We know nothing more about him than his role in this scene. Evidently Paul and Silas had been lodging with him. Consequently he probably was a convert and may have been a Jew since Jason was a name often taken by Diaspora Jews.[57] It is also possible that he shared Paul's trade. Later in Corinth Paul stayed with Aquila and Priscilla, who were of the same trade as he (18:3). In any event, the crowd did not find the missionaries at Jason's. Possibly they had learned of the riot and had fled elsewhere.

17:6-7 So Jason served as Paul's proxy and was dragged before the city officials (v. 6). Luke's description is very accurate, using the term "politarchs" for the officials, which is the precise term that occurs for the

---

[52]See E. Harrison, *The Interpretation of Acts* (Grand Rapids: Zondervan, 1986), 280. The Western text habitually makes the women "wives" of prominent men (here and in v. 12) rather than those with significant status in their own right. See B. Witherington, "The Anti-Feminist Tendencies of the 'Western' Text in Acts," *JBL* 103 (1984): 82-84.

[53]See B. N. Kaye, "Acts' Portrait of Silas," *NovT* 21 (1980): 13-26.

[54]Twice by Jews (17:5-7; 18:12-13), twice by Gentiles (16:19-21; 19:24-27) in formal accusations before the authorities. See R. C. Tannehill, *The Narrative Unity of Luke-Acts* (Minneapolis: Fortress, 1990), 2:209.

[55]Greek ἀγοραῖος, the ill-bred, coarse class; loafers who frequent the marketplace.

[56]First Thessalonians 2:14-16 carries this dual picture of the combined Jewish ("who drove us out") and Gentile ("your own countrymen") opposition in Thessalonica.

[57]As the equivalent of Ἰησοῦς (Jesus/Joshua).

local magistrates in inscriptions uncovered in Macedonia.[58] Three
charges were leveled against the Christians. The first was directed against
Paul and Silas: they "caused trouble all over the world." This was a
rather nebulous charge—"troublemakers."[59] The second was directed
against Jason: he was harboring these troublemakers. The third was
directed against Paul and Silas and, by implication, Jason as their host.
They were said to be "defying Caesar's decrees." This was a dangerous
charge. To defy Caesar would be pure sedition. But what decrees were
they defying? Probably the final clause in v. 7 is to be seen as an explanation of the charge. They were claiming that there was another king than
Caesar—Jesus. This was virtually the same charge leveled at Jesus (cf.
Luke 23:2-4; John 19:12,15). Jesus claimed a kingdom not of this world,
and Paul and Silas spoke of the same. But to a Roman, the charge
sounded very much like a breach of the oath of loyalty that every person
in the empire was required to render to Caesar.[60] The magistrates had to
take note of this charge.

17:8-9 The magistrates showed a great deal of discretion in handling
the charges. They evidently did not take the charge of sedition too seriously, but they were quite aware of the commotion and were responsible
for maintaining order. They evidently decided, much like the Philippian
magistrates, to preserve law and order by banning the troublemakers from
the city. Jason was required to post bond, depositing a sum of money that
would be forfeited should there be any sequel to the civil disturbance.
That meant the absence of Paul and Silas. Paul may have been referring
to this ban in 1 Thess 2:18 when he spoke of "Satan's hindrance" to his
returning to the city.

(2) Witness in Berea (17:10-15)

[10]As soon as it was night, the brothers sent Paul and Silas away to Berea. On
arriving there, they went to the Jewish synagogue. [11]Now the Bereans were of
more noble character than the Thessalonians, for they received the message with
great eagerness and examined the Scriptures every day to see if what Paul said
was true. [12]Many of the Jews believed, as did also a number of prominent Greek
women and many Greek men.
[13]When the Jews in Thessalonica learned that Paul was preaching the word of
God at Berea, they went there too, agitating the crowds and stirring them up.

---

[58]See F. F. Bruce, *Commentary on the Book of Acts*, NIC (Grand Rapids: Eerdmans,
1977), 314. There seem to have been five locally elected magistrates in Thessalonica in
Paul's day. They were responsible for law enforcement. Legislature was in the hands of the
local citizens, referred to as the *dēmos*. This term occurs in v. 5, but there it seems to be virtually equivalent to "crowd" and is so translated by the NIV.

[59]The verb for "causing trouble," ἀναστατόω, can mean *to stir up sedition, be a political
agitator*. In light of the third charge, that may be the implication here.

[60]See E. A. Judge, "The Decrees of Caesar at Thessalonica," *RTR* 30 (1971): 1-7.

14The brothers immediately sent Paul to the coast, but Silas and Timothy stayed at Berea. **15**The men who escorted Paul brought him to Athens and then left with instructions for Silas and Timothy to join him as soon as possible.

When the three missionaries left Thessalonica, they also left the Egnatian Way, the route they had been following since they first landed in Macedonia at Neapolis (16:11). This main east-west highway went northwest of Thessalonica to Dyrrachium on the Adriatic. It was the main land route to Rome. At Dyrrachium travelers would take a boat across the Adriatic Sea to Brundisium in southern Italy and from there north to Rome. It has been suggested that Paul might have entertained the idea of taking this route to Rome even as early as this point in his missionary career.[61] In his Letter to the Romans (15:22) he spoke of his having "often" been hindered in coming to them. The hindrance at this time may well have been the news that the emperor Claudius had expelled all the Jews from Rome (18:2). Whatever the case, Paul headed in another direction at this time, going southwest to Berea and well off any main thoroughfare.

17:10 About fifty miles from Thessalonica, Berea lay on the eastern slopes of Mt. Vermion in the Olympian mountain range. In a somewhat remote region, Berea was the most significant city of the area, having been capital of one of the four divisions of Macedonia from 167–148 B.C. It evidently had a sizable population in Paul's day. The journey from Thessalonica began in the nighttime because of the hasty departure. By foot it would have taken about three days.

17:11-12 On arriving in the town, the witness began, as it had in Thessalonica, in the synagogue. The Jews of Berea, however, were of a different breed. Luke described them as being "more noble" than the Thessalonians. He used a word (*eugenesteros*) that originally meant *high born* but came to have a more general connotation of being open, tolerant, generous, having the qualities that go with "good breeding."[62] Nowhere was this more evident than in their willingness to take Paul's scriptural exposition seriously. They did not accept his word uncritically but did their own examination of the Scriptures to see if they really did point to the death and resurrection of the Messiah as Paul claimed (cf. 17:3). This was no cursory investigation either, no weekly Sabbath service, as at Thessalonica. They met daily to search the Scriptures. No wonder so many contemporary Bible study groups name themselves "Bereans." The Berean Jews were a "noble" example.[63] And many of them found out for themselves that Paul's claims were true and so believed (v. 12). Many

---

[61]Bruce, "St. Paul in Macedonia," 351f.

[62]See F. W. Danker, "Menander and the New Testament," *NTS* 10 (1963-64): 368.

[63]See J. Kremer, "Einführung in die Problematik heutiger Acta-Forschung anhand von Apg. 17, 10-13," *Les Actes*, 11-20.

Greeks also believed, not just men but prominent Macedonian women as well, just as in Thessalonica (cf. v. 4). Some of these may have been worshipers of God attached to the synagogue. Some may not have been. One would assume that Paul would not neglect his witness to Gentiles of pagan background even in a situation like Berea, where the synagogue was so unusually open to his message.

17:13-14 This ideal situation did not last forever. It was soon broken by Jews from Thessalonica who heard of Paul's successes in Berea. They stirred up "the crowds" in the city against Paul, evidently not the Jews of the city but the general Gentile populace, just as they had done at Thessalonica. Evidently this time the main attack was on Paul, the primary preacher of the word (v. 13), since Silas and Timothy did not have to leave town with him (v. 14).

That Paul had to flee Berea and finally wound up in Athens is clear. How he got there is another question. If one follows the Western text of Acts, he traveled to Athens by sea.[64] The generally most reliable manuscripts, however, have Paul going "as far as the sea." This is followed by the NIV, which translates "to the coast." A third group of manuscripts (the Byzantine text) reads that Paul was sent "as to the sea." This latter text has been followed by a number of commentators who argue that Paul was using a "diversionary tactic," making *as if* to go by sea but then hurrying down to Athens by the coastal road. Even the "as far as" text could also allow for his not taking a boat but rather following the coastal road to Athens. It is obviously not a serious matter in any event.

17:15 Of more significance is the question of when Timothy and Silas joined Paul in Athens. First Thessalonians 3:1f. indicates that Paul sent Timothy to Thessalonica from Athens. This leads many scholars to argue that Luke must have been in error in seeing Paul as traveling to Athens alone; Timothy was with him and was then sent from Athens back to Thessalonica. Obviously both Luke and Paul may have been right, each giving only part of the picture. Paul may have traveled to Athens alone, summoning Timothy and Silas to join him there as soon as possible (Acts 17:15). They did so, and then Paul dispatched both from Athens, Timothy to Thessalonica (1 Thess 3:1) and Silas to parts unknown. One can never be dogmatic about any such harmonization for which the text itself gives no specific warrant, but the possibility of some such simple solution guards against overhasty conclusions about the unreliability of a text. In any event, Timothy and Silas did finally join Paul in Corinth (Acts 18:5).

---

[64]E. Delebecque, "Paul à Thessalonique et à Béreé selon le Texte occidental des Actes (xvii, 4-15)," *RevThom* 82 (1982): 605-15.

6. Witnessing to the Athenian Intellectuals (17:16-34)

Paul's brief visit to Athens is a centerpiece for the entire book of Acts. The scene revolves around Paul's famous address before the Areopagus (vv. 22-31). This is preceded by an introductory narrative that portrays the "Athenian scene" in vivid local color (vv. 16-21). This narrative is very much keyed to the content of the speech and provides the framework for its major themes. The same is true for the conclusion of the Athenian narrative (vv. 32-34), which is primarily a conclusion to the speech. As a whole, one can scarcely speak of an Athenian "mission." Although there were several converts and a fellowship may well have grown out of Paul's ministry there, Luke did not dwell on this or mention the establishment of a church in Athens. It would be a mistake, however, to see Paul's Athenian experience as a "maverick" episode. The opposite is true. The central item, the speech on the Areopagus, is the prime example in Acts of Paul's preaching to Gentiles. The only other example is the brief sermon at Lystra (14:15-17), which is itself almost a precis of this one. In the following narrative Paul works among Gentiles for eighteen months in Corinth and for nearly three years in Ephesus, but no example of his preaching is given. The reason quite simply is that it has already been given—in Athens, in the very center of Gentile culture and intellect.

(1) The Athenians' Curiosity (17:16-21)

[16]While Paul was waiting for them in Athens, he was greatly distressed to see that the city was full of idols. [17]So he reasoned in the synagogue with the Jews and the God-fearing Greeks, as well as in the marketplace day by day with those who happened to be there. [18]A group of Epicurean and Stoic philosophers began to dispute with him. Some of them asked, "What is this babbler trying to say?" Others remarked, "He seems to be advocating foreign gods." They said this because Paul was preaching the good news about Jesus and the resurrection. [19]Then they took him and brought him to a meeting of the Areopagus, where they said to him, "May we know what this new teaching is that you are presenting? [20]You are bringing some strange ideas to our ears, and we want to know what they mean." [21](All the Athenians and the foreigners who lived there spent their time doing nothing but talking about and listening to the latest ideas.)

In Paul's day Athens was but a shadow of its former glory in its "golden age" in the fourth and fifth centuries B.C. Corinth was now the leading city of Greece commercially and politically. Even Athens' native population had dwindled, estimated at some 5,000 voting citizens. But this was considerably augmented by the nonnative population, particularly the artists, the students, and the tourists. And there were the buildings and the works of art, mute testimony to its former grandeur. This is not to say that Athens was no longer an important city. It was still considered the cultural and intellectual center of the Roman Empire, and it is in this perspective that Luke portrayed it.

17:16 Athens was known the world over for its magnificent art and architecture. The art, however, characteristically portrayed the exploits of the various gods and goddesses of the Greek pantheon, and most of the impressive buildings were temples to the pagan gods. For Paul, Jew that he was with his strong monotheism and distaste for graven images, the scene was most unappealing. The NIV is too gentle in saying that he was "greatly distressed" (v. 16). The Greek word Luke used is much stronger (*paroxynō*). We get our word "paroxysm" from it. Paul was "infuriated" at the sight. Ancient descriptions testify that the marketplace was virtually lined with idols, particularly the "herms," the monuments to Hermes with the head of the god on top.[65] For Paul a thing of beauty was decidedly not a joy forever, particularly when it embodied so distorted a view of divinity.

17:17 Paul evidently stuck to his usual pattern of missionary preaching. On the Sabbath he reasoned with the Jews, evidently following the same method of scriptural proof that Christ was Messiah as he used at Thessalonica (v. 17). But during the week, on a daily basis, he bore his witness in the agora, the famous marketplace and hub of Athenian life. There he got his most pronounced response, especially from some of the philosophers. The Epicureans and Stoics were among the leading schools of the day,[66] and they serve as representatives of the confusion caused by Paul's preaching.

17:18 Epicurians were thoroughgoing materialists, believing that everything came from atoms or particles of matter. There was no life beyond this; all that was human returned to matter at death. Though the Epicureans did not deny the existence of gods, they saw them as totally indifferent to humanity. They did not believe in providence of any sort; and if one truly learned from the gods, that person would try to live the same sort of detached and tranquil life as they, as free from pain and passion and superstitious fears as they.

The Stoics had a more lively view of the gods than the Epicureans, believing very much in the divine providence. They were pantheists, believing that the ultimate divine principle was to be found in all of nature, including human beings. This spark of divinity, which they

---

[65]For very thorough descriptions of the Athenian idols and temples, see O. Broneer, "Athens 'City of Idol Worship,'" *BA* 21 (1958): 2-28 and G. T. Montague, "Paul and Athens," *TBT* 49 (1970): 14-23.

[66]Together with the Cynics, Stoics and Epicureans represented the most popular philosophies of the day. Epicureans received their name from their founder Epicurus, who lived from 341–270 B.C. Stoicism was founded by the Cypriot Zeno (ca. 335–263 B.C.) and was named for the stoa or colonnade in the agora where Zeno had taught.

referred to as the *logos*, was the cohesive rational principle that bound the entire cosmic order together. Humans thus realized their fullest potential when they lived by reason. By reason, i.e., the divine principle within them which linked them with the gods and nature, they could discover ultimate truth for themselves. The Stoics generally had a rather high ethic and put great stock on self-sufficiency. Since they viewed all humans as bound together by common possession of the divine logos, they also had a strong sense of universal brotherhood. The mention of these schools is not incidental. Paul would take up some of their thought in his Areopagus speech, particularly that of the Stoics, and thoroughly redirect it in line with the Creator God of the Old Testament.

It was not particularly complimentary when the philosophers dubbed Paul a "babbler." They used a colorful word (*spermologos*), "seed-speaker," which evoked images of a bird pecking indiscriminately at seeds in a barnyard. It referred to a dilettante, someone who picked up scraps of ideas here and there and passed them off as profundity with no depth of understanding whatever.[67] They could not understand Paul's concept of resurrection at all. Epicureans did not believe in any existence after death, and Stoics believed that only the soul, the divine spark, survived death.[68] So what was this idea of a bodily resurrection (*anastasis*)? "He must be speaking of a new goddess named resurrection ("Anastasia") along with this new god Jesus he keeps talking about" (author's paraphrase).[69] How ironical that they were making Paul into a polytheist like themselves. Before the Areopagus he would eliminate such thinking with his clear monotheistic exposition of God the Creator.

17:19-20 Verse 19 has provoked one of the most lively discussions surrounding Paul's Areopagus address. Was Paul tried before a formal Athenian court named Areopagus, or did he deliver a public address from a hill known as the Areopagus? The NIV has already solved the problem by translating "a meeting of the Areopagus," which is a clear opting for the first possibility. The Greek is not so unambiguous, merely stating that the Athenians took hold of Paul and led him "to the Areopagus." The Areopagus was both a court *and* a hill, due to the fact that the court traditionally met on that hill. The term Areopagus means *hill of Ares*. Ares was the Greek god of war. The Roman equivalent god was Mars, hence the KJV "Mars' hill" (17:22).

---

[67]Robinson fails to convince in his argument that "seed" and "word" are to be derived from Paul's preaching the parable of the sower in the agora (M. A. Robinson, "SPERMO-LOGOS: Did Paul Preach from Jesus' Parables?" *Bib* 56 [1975]: 231-40).

[68]G. D. Kilpatrick, "The Acts of the Apostles, xvii.18," *TZ* 42 (1986): 431f.

[69]P. H. Menoud, "Jésus et Anastasie (Actes xvii, 18)," *RTP* 32 (1944): 141-45.

This hill was located beneath the acropolis and above the agora. From ancient times a court met there that decided on civil and criminal cases and seems to have had some jurisdiction in matters of religion. Since it traditionally met on the Areopagus, it came eventually to be known by the name of the hill, just as for us Wall Street would designate either the street or the stock exchange. So the name will not help in deciding whether Paul gave a public lecture on the hill or made a formal appearance before the court. Although many scholars advocate the public lecture view,[70] several factors tip the scale toward the possibility that Paul appeared before the Athenian court. First, there is quite possibly a conscious parallel between Paul's experience and the trial of Socrates. According to Plato (*Apologia* 24B), Socrates was accused of "introducing [*epispherōn*] other new gods." Paul likewise was described as "introducing" (*eisphereis*, v. 20) "strange ideas," which in v. 18 are described as "foreign gods." If Luke intended the parallel, he likely saw Paul also as appearing before the court.[71] Second, that one of Paul's converts was Dionysius, a member of the Areopagus (v. 34), is all the more likely if Paul appeared before that body. Finally, one should note that throughout Acts Paul appeared before the leading magisterial bodies—the magistrates of Philippi, the proconsul at Corinth, the Roman governors at Caesarea, the Jewish Sanhedrin, the Jewish King Agrippa, and finally, at least in anticipation, the Roman emperor. It would fit the pattern well if he appeared here before the venerable Athenian court.

It is probably erroneous to see it as a trial in any formal sense. Paul was not formally charged. Once finished he made an easy exit—there were no deliberations. Perhaps it was nothing but a more-or-less public hearing of the new teacher to satisfy the curiosity of the philosophers who led him there.[72] It probably was not even on the hill of Ares where Paul spoke. The evidence is that in his day the Areopagus met in the *Stoa Basileios* or Royal Portico in the northwest corner of the agora.[73] This would be all the more natural since the portico frequented by the

---

[70]A. Ehrhardt, *The Acts of the Apostles: Ten Lectures* (Manchester: University Press, 1969), 97f.; Haenchen (*Acts*, 519, n. 1), who likens the hill to "Hyde Park"; W. G. Morrice, "Where did Paul speak in Athens—on Mars' Hill or before the Court of the Areopagus? (Acts 17:19)," *ExpTim* 83 (1972): 377f.

[71]Socrates, however, did not appear before the Areopagus but rather the court of the "King Archon," a special jury. See *Beginnings* 4:212.

[72]Ramsay sees the council acting in its role as regulator of public lecturers (*St. Paul the Traveller*, 245-48). B. Gärtner sees Paul as being taken before the "education commission" of the court (*The Areopagus Speech and Natural Revelation* [Uppsala: Gleerup, 1955], 52-65).

[73]C. J. Hemer, "Paul at Athens: A Topographical Note," *NTS* 20 (1974): 341-50. For the view that the court still met on the hill in Paul's day, see T. D. Barnes, "An Apostle on Trial," *JTS*, n.s. 20 (1969): 407-19.

philosophers, whom Paul had just encountered, was adjacent to the Royal Portico.

17:21 Luke ended his narrative introduction to Paul's speech in an "aside," which refers to the insatiable curiosity of the Athenians (v. 21). Their love for novel ideas was proverbial. Perhaps the most telling quip was that of Demosthenes, who remarked how the Athenians were going about the city asking for the latest news at the very moment when the armies of Philip of Macedon were knocking at their door.[74] Luke's remark is quite ironical. The Athenians had accused Paul of being the dilettante (v. 18), an accusation much more pertinent to themselves. Their curiosity had a beneficial side, however. It set the stage for Paul's witness.

(2) Paul's Testimony before the Areopagus (17:22-31)

[22]Paul then stood up in the meeting of the Areopagus and said: "Men of Athens! I see that in every way you are very religious. [23]For as I walked around and looked carefully at your objects of worship, I even found an altar with this inscription: TO AN UNKNOWN GOD. Now what you worship as something unknown I am going to proclaim to you.

[24]"The God who made the world and everything in it is the Lord of heaven and earth and does not live in temples built by hands. [25]And he is not served by human hands, as if he needed anything, because he himself gives all men life and breath and everything else. [26]From one man he made every nation of men, that they should inhabit the whole earth; and he determined the times set for them and the exact places where they should live. [27]God did this so that men would seek him and perhaps reach out for him and find him, though he is not far from each one of us. [28]'For in him we live and move and have our being.' As some of your own poets have said, 'We are his offspring.'

[29]"Therefore since we are God's offspring, we should not think that the divine being is like gold or silver or stone—an image made by man's design and skill. [30]In the past God overlooked such ignorance, but now he commands all people everywhere to repent. [31]For he has set a day when he will judge the world with justice by the man he has appointed. He has given proof of this to all men by raising him from the dead."

No text in Acts has received more scholarly attention than the ten verses of Paul's speech before the Areopagus. Debate has particularly raged over whether the core thought of the speech is that of the Old Testament or of Greek philosophy.[75] How one answers that question will

---

[74]Cited by Bruce (*Acts:* NIC, 352) with other similar contemporary allusions to the Athenian inquisitiveness.

[75]The work by E. Norden, *Agnostos Theos* (Stuttgart: Teubner, 1923) argued for a thoroughly philosophical background to the speech. This approach has been subsequently modified and developed by such scholars as M. Dibelius, "Paul on the Areopagus," *Studies in the Acts of the Apostles* (London: SCM, 1956); H. Conzelmann, "The Address of Paul on

very much determine how one views the total argument of the speech. For instance, those who maintain the basically philosophical background to the speech often see its main thrust as being the knowledge of God as perceived through nature. The concluding references to the resurrection and judgment are seen as a sort of afterthought that does not coordinate well with the main speech. The gist of the speech is, however, thoroughly rooted in Old Testament thought throughout. The main theme is God as Creator and the proper worship of this Creator God. The language often has the ring of Greek philosophy, for Paul was attempting to build what bridges he could to reach the Athenian intellectuals. The underlying thought remains thoroughly biblical.

The sermon can be divided into five couplets that follow a more-or-less chiastic structure (an A-B-C-B-A pattern). Verses 22-23 introduce the main theme—the ignorance of the pagan worship. Verses 24-25 present the true object of worship, the Creator God, and the folly of idolatrous worship with temples and sacrifices. Verses 26-27 deal with the true relationship of human beings to their Creator, the central theme of the chiasm. Verse 28 provides a transition, capping off the argument of the relationship of persons to God and providing the basis for a renewed attack on idolatry in verse 29. The final two verses return to the original theme. The time of ignorance was now over. With revelation came a call to repent in light of the coming judgment and the resurrection of Christ.

THE "UNKNOWN GOD" (17:22-23). **17:22** Paul's opening remark that he had observed the Athenians in every respect to be "very religious" has often been described as a *capitatio benevolentiae*, an effort to win the favor of his hearers and thus secure their attention.[76] Such introductions were a standard device in Greek rhetoric, and Paul probably did have some such intention. He surely did not wish to alienate his audience at the

---

the Areopagus," *Studies in Luke-Acts* (Nashville: Abingdon, 1966), 217-30; M. Pohlenz, who argued for a Stoic background ("Paulus und die Stoa," *ZNW* 42 [1949]: 69-104); H. Hommel, who defined the Stoic background more narrowly as the thought of Poseidonius ("Neue Forschungen zur Areopagrede Acts 17," *ZNW* 46 [1955]: 145-79); and Hommel, "Platonisches bei Lukas: Zu Act 17:28a (Leben-Bewegen-Sein)," *ZNW* 48 (1957): 193-200. B. Gärtner's Areopagus Speech and Natural Revelation argues that the background to the speech is thoroughly that of the OT. W. Nauck sees the background in the Hellenistic Jewish missionary preaching ("Die Tradition und Komposition der Areopagrede," *ZTK* 53 [1956]: 11-51). F. G. Downing notes the similarities between Acts and Josephus in addressing paganism ("Common Ground with Paganism in Luke and in Josephus," *NTS* 28 [1982]: 546-59). Like Gärtner, A. M. Dubarle argues a thoroughly OT background ("Le Discours à l'Aréopage [Acts 17:22-31] et son Arrière-plan Biblique," *RSPT* 57 [1973]: 576-610).

[76] The piety of the Athenians was often noted by contemporary writers. Cf. Sophocles (*Oedipus Tyranus* 260), "Athens is held of states the most devout," and Pausanias 1.17.1, "The Athenians venerate the gods more than others." See Conzelmann, *Acts*, 140.

very outset. The term he used for "religious" (*deisidaimonesteros*), however, had a definite ambiguity in current usage. It could be used in a positive sense for one who was very devoted to religious matters. It was also used with a negative connotation for those who were overly scrupulous, even superstitious, in their religious observance. The context in which the word is used determines which connotation it has.[77] Perhaps Paul deliberately chose the ambiguous word. For the Athenians his remark would be taken as commending their piety. For Paul, who was already fuming at their idolatry (v. 16), the negative connotation would be uppermost in his mind. By the end of the speech, the Athenians themselves would have little doubt about Paul's real opinion of their religiosity.

17:23a As so often in the speeches of Acts, Paul began his discourse with a point of contact with his audience. In this case it was the altars Paul had already observed in the city (v. 16). One in particular caught his attention. It was dedicated "TO AN UNKNOWN GOD." This gave him the perfect launching pad for his presentation of monotheism to the polytheistic and pantheistic Athenians. Piety had no doubt led the Athenians to erect such an altar for fear they might offend some deity of whom they were unaware and had failed to give the proper worship. Paul would now proclaim a God who was unknown to them. In fact, this God, totally unknown to them, was the only true divinity that exists.

It has often been discussed whether Paul took a certain degree of "homiletical license" in his reference to the inscription "TO AN UNKNOWN GOD." Jerome thought so, arguing in his *Commentary on Titus* (1:12) that there were altars in Athens dedicated to "unknown gods" and that Paul had adapted the plural "gods" to the singular "god" in light of his monotheistic sermon.[78] Pagan writers also attested to the presence of altars "to unknown gods" but always in the plural. For instance, the Traveler Pausanias, writing in the middle of the second century A.D., described the presence of altars to gods of unknown names on the road from Phalerum to Athens and an altar "to unknown gods" at Olympia.[79] Written in the third century, Philostratus's *Life of Apollonius of Tyana* also refers to these Athenian altars "to unknown gods."[80] There is thus ample literary evidence that Paul did

---

[77]H. A. Moellering, "Deisidaimonia, a Footnote to Acts 17:22," *CTM* 34 (1963): 466-71.

[78]For a thorough treatment of the evidence for altars to the unknown gods, see *Beginnings* 5:240-46.

[79]Pausanias 1.1.4 and 5.14.8.

[80]*Life of Apollonius* 6.3.5. By putting this reference to the altars together with another reference from a far-removed context in *Life of Apollonius*, which referred to the philosopher's having preached against idolatry in Athens, Norden argued that the Apollonius tradition provided the base for the Areopagus sermon (*Agnostos Theos*, 35-56). This view has been almost universally rejected by scholars. See P. Corssen, "Der Altar des unbekannten Gottes," *ZNW* 14 (1913): 309-23.

not fabricate his allusion, that there were in fact such altars in Athens. Whether they were invariably inscribed in the plural or whether there was one dedicated to a single "UNKNOWN GOD" remains an open question. Even should Paul have made an adaption, as Jerome alleged, it would have been a small matter. The Athenians would have understood his allusion, and Paul scarcely wanted to expound on gods in the plural. This was precisely what he wanted to deny, as he introduced the Athenians to the one true Creator God.[81]

17:23b Verse 23b sets the tone for the remainder of the speech. There is a play on the concept of ignorance. To worship an unknown (*agnōstō*) god is to admit one's ignorance. If he is unknown to you, you are then in total ignorance of his true nature. Thus Paul said, "What you worship in ignorance [*agnoountes*], this I proclaim to you" (author's translation). Two things should be noted. First, Paul referred to "what" they worshiped, not "who" they worshiped. Their worship was totally wrongheaded. They did not know God; they didn't worship *him* at all. Their worship object was a thing, a "what," and not a personal God at all. Second, there is a strong emphasis on ignorance, on not knowing. For Greeks, as for Stoics, ignorance was a cardinal sin. The greatest virtue was to discover truth through pursuing the divine reason within oneself. Not to live in accordance with reason, to live in ignorance, was the greatest folly imaginable. Paul accused them of precisely this ignorance, this sin.[82] He would return to this theme in v. 30 with his call to repentance. The time had arrived when such ignorance of God was wholly without excuse.

THE CREATOR GOD (17:24-25). **17:24-25** Paul began with the basic premise that runs throughout his speech: God is Creator. He referred to God as the maker of the "world" (*kosmos*), a term that would be familiar to every Greek. The concept of God as absolute Creator, however, would not be so easy for them to grasp. For them divinity was to be found *in* the heavens, *in* nature, *in* humanity. The idea of a single supreme being who stood *over* the world, who created all that exists, was totally foreign to them.[83] This was indeed an "UNKNOWN GOD."

---

[81]Norden's view that the "UNKNOWN GOD" should be seen as the unknowable, inscrutable high god of the Gnostics (*Agnostos Theos*, 56-83) has also been generally rejected. E. des Places argues similarly (though rejecting the Gnostic thesis) that Paul intended his phrase to refer to the "unknowable" God, which would have appealed to Greek piety ("'Au Dieu Inconnu' [Act 17, 23]," *Bib* 43 [1962]: 388-95). Paul, however, was arguing the opposite—God *could* be known, had *made* himself known through *revelation*, not through human reason.

[82]H. Kulling, "Zur Bedeutung des Agnostos Theos: Eine Exegese zu Apostelgeschichte 17, 22-23," *TZ* 36 (1980): 65-83.

[83]See H. P. Owen, "The Scope of Natural Revelation in Rom. I and Acts XVII," *NTS* 5 (1958-59): 133-43.

Once granted the premise that God is Creator, two things follow. First, God "does not live in temples built by hands." This is a thoroughly biblical thought. Compare Solomon's similar remark at the dedication of his temple (1 Kgs 8:27) and Stephen's critique of the Jerusalem temple (Acts 7:48-50). The more philosophically minded Athenians would have had no problem with this, however. Plato advocated a religion based on worship of the heavenly bodies as being superior to that observed in earthly temples, and Zeno and Seneca both scorned temples.[84] The philosophers also would have had no problem with Paul's second critique of human worship, "He is not served by human hands" (v. 25). Paul's qualifier, "as if he needed anything," would particularly have resonated with them. It was a commonplace of Greek philosophy to view divinity as complete within itself, totally self-sufficient, totally without need.[85] And they would have agreed with Paul also that the divinity is the giver of "life and breath and everything else."[86] But there was a world of difference between the philosopher's pantheism and Paul's strict monotheism.

Every statement Paul made was rooted in Old Testament thought. The idea of God's being the granter of life and breath, as indeed the entire point of vv. 24-25, can be found in passages like Isa 42:5 and Ps 50:7-15.[87] It is not the philosophical concept of a divine immanent principle that pervades all nature and humankind. It is the biblical concept of a sovereign Creator God who stands above his creation and to whom humanity as creature is ultimately responsible. Such a God could not be enshrined in human temples or manipulated by human cult. Much of the conceptuality may have struck a responsive chord with the Athenians. Paul probably was struggling to communicate the gospel in terms understandable to them. But on the basic premise there was no compromise. There is but one sovereign God, Creator of all. To know him they must abandon all their other gods. Otherwise he would remain to them the "UNKNOWN GOD."

THE PROVIDENTIAL GOD (17:26-27). These verses form the center of the speech. As such, they should be central to Paul's argument, and they are. They contain two emphases: (1) God's providence over humanity and (2) human responsibility to God. The two verses comprise a single

---

[84]For a thorough treatment of the philosophers' critique of temples, see E. des Places, "'Des temples fait de main d'homme' (Actes des Apôtres 17, 24)," *Bib* 40 (1959): 793-99.

[85]See R. Bultmann, "Anknüpfung und Widerspruch," *TZ* 2 (1946): 410-11. Cf. Euripides, *Hercules* 1345f.: "God, if he be truly God, has need of nothing."

[86]Cf. Seneca, *Epistles* 95.47: "God seeks no servants . . . he himself serves mankind." For other parallels from the philosophers, see E. des Places, "Actes 17, 25," *Bib* 46 (1965): 219-22.

[87]For the view that vv. 24-25 are based on Isa 42:5, see E. Fudge, "Paul's Apostolic Self-Consciousness at Athens," *JETS* 14 (1971): 193-98.

sentence in the Greek text. The sentence consists of a main clause ("From one man he made every nation of men") and two subordinate purpose clauses. The thought thus runs: God made humanity for two purposes: (1) to inhabit the earth (v. 26) and (2) to seek him (v. 27). The dominating thought is thus still that of God as Creator.

17:26a God "made" every human nation. There is the added nuance, however, that he made every nation "from one man." The reference is most likely to Adam, and the emphasis is on the universality of humankind's relationship to God. Although there are many nations, though they are scattered over the face of the earth, they are one in their common ancestry and in their relationship to their Creator. One can see the significance of this in an address before Gentiles. The God whom Paul proclaimed was no local Jewish cult God. He was the one sovereign Lord of all humankind.

17:26b The precise meaning of verse 26b is somewhat problematic. To what do the "times" (*kairoi*) refer? They could either refer to the seasons or to historical epochs. The same ambiguity exists in the term "exact places where they should live." Does this refer to the habitable areas of the planet or to the boundaries between nations? If Paul was talking of seasons and habitable zones, he was pointing to God's providence in nature.[88] If the reference is to historical epochs and national boundaries, the emphasis is on God's lordship over history.[89] In either instance Paul's point would be the same—the care and providence of God in his creation. These statements do seem to contain an underlying thought of "natural revelation." Much as Paul argued in Rom 1:18-20 and in the speech at Lystra (14:17), God made himself known in some sense by the works of his creation.[90] All people, Gentiles included, have experienced this and to that extent are responsible before God. This led to the climactic statement about seeking God in v. 27.

17:27 Verse 27 gives the second purpose of humankind in God's creation—"that men would seek him." The idea of seeking God is common in the Old Testament,[91] but that does not seem to be the background here. For the Old Testament writers, the call to "seek God" was always made to those within the covenant community, to Israel to whom God had

---

[88]This is the position of Dibelius, "Paul on the Areopagus," 30-32. A similar position is taken by W. Eltester with the difference that he sees the "boundaries" not as habitable zones but as the boundaries of the creation account, the "firmament" or boundary between the earth and the watery chaos ("Schöpfungsoffenbarung und natürliche Theologie im frühen Christentum," *NTS* 3 [1957]: 93-114).

[89]See Gärtner, *Areopagus Speech and Natural Revelation*, 146-51.

[90]For a discussion of the relationship between Rom 1 and Acts 17, see the commentary on 14:14-18.

[91]Cf. Isa 55:6; 65:1; Ps 14:2; Prov 8:17; Jer 29:13.

already made himself known. In the present context it is a call for Gentiles for whom the true God is "unknown." The connection is with the preceding verse and its emphasis on God's providence in his creation. God's purpose in all this is stated as his desire that people might seek him and find him. The Stoics would have been in complete agreement. They would have argued that the divine principle was to be found in all of nature and that one should strive to grasp it as fully as possible through cultivating reason, that part of divinity that dwelt in one's own human nature. They firmly believed that through the proper discipline of reason one could come to a knowledge of divinity. Paul would not have agreed. Even a knowledge of God from nature would still not be a human attainment but a *revelation* of God in his works. But Paul was not confident in the human ability to grasp such a natural revelation. Perhaps that is why he used the optative mood in v. 27, a mode of Greek grammar that here expresses strong doubt. God created humans, Paul said, so they might seek him and just possibly grope after him and find him. He had his doubts. People likely would not discover God in this fashion, even "though he is not far" from them. There is no question about God's providence; there *is* about humanity's ability to make the proper response. There is also no question about God's purposes. God *did* create humans "to seek him." This is the proper response of the creature. The responsibility of humanity is the worship of God.[92]

THE WORSHIP OF GOD (17:28-29). **17:28** Verse 28 is transitional, linking up with the theme of God's proximity in v. 27b and providing the basis for the critique of idolatrous worship in v. 29. It also serves the rather unique function of providing the "scriptural base" for the speech. In this instance it isn't a matter of Scripture at all but rather a quote from a pagan philosopher.[93] Scripture would have been meaningless to the Athenians. Paul still continued to address them as much as possible in their own terms. Some argue that two quotes from Greek poets are in v. 28, but more likely the verse contains only one. The phrase "in him we live and move and have our being" seems to have been a more or less traditional Greek triadic formula.[94] Paul surely did not understand this in the

---

[92]R. F. O'Toole, "Paul at Athens and Luke's Notion of Worship," *RB* 89 (1982): 185-97.

[93]J. Calloud notes that the Greeks often viewed their poets as inspired ("Paul devant l'Aréopage d'Athenes: Actes 17, 16-34," *RSR* 69 [1981]: 209-48).

[94]Those who argue that it is a quotation attribute it to Epimenides of Crete, basing this on a reference in the ninth-century Syriac commentary of Ishodad of Merv, who may have been dependent on Theodore of Mopsuestia. The poem of Epimenides consists of a hymn of Minos to his father Zeus. Minos attacks his fellow Cretans as being liars for building a tomb for Zeus, but Zeus is very much alive, and Minos praises him with the words "in thee we live and move and have our being." It is interesting that the tradition of Cretans being liars in Titus 1:12 seems to come from this same poem of Epimenides. Pohlenz ("Paulus und die

Greek sense, which would emphasize the pantheistic view of the divinity residing in human nature. His view was that of v. 25: God is the giver of life and breath and all that is. Through God the Creator people live and move and have existence. The second statement is introduced as the quote from the Greek poets. It is generally agreed that the quote is found in the Stoic poet Aratus of Soli, who lived in the first half of the third century B.C. Aratus may himself have been quoting a hymn to Zeus from the poet Cleanthes, which would perhaps explain Paul's plural reference to "some of your poets." For Aratus "we are his offspring" referred to Zeus and to humanity's sharing in the divine nature. In the context of Paul's speech, it referred to God and to humanity's being his creation.

17:29 In v. 29 Paul returned to his earlier critique of artificial worship with which the speech began (vv. 24-25). Earlier he had critiqued temple and cult. Now he attacked idolatry. The attack was based on the previous statement that humans are God's offspring. The idea is that of people being made in God's image. If humankind is the true image of God, the work of God's hands, it follows that no image made by human hands can render proper homage to God. If humanity is like God, then God is not like gold or silver or any such material representation. Only the creature can express the true worship of the Creator, not the creation of the creature, not something made by human design and skill.

Here Paul spoke very much in the line of the Old Testament critique of idolatry.[95] The Stoics would have agreed. They too saw idolatry as the folly of popular religion. But if they truly understood Paul's teaching of the one true Creator God, they would have realized that they too were idolaters. In their attempt to reach the divine through their own striving, in their view that the divine indwelt their own human nature, they had transgressed the relationship of creature to Creator. If they had genuinely accepted Paul's major premise that God is Creator, they would have had to acknowledge their own self-idolatry, their own need for repentance.

THE JUDGMENT OF GOD (17:30-31). **17:30-31** Paul now directed his attention to the Athenians, returning to the theme of ignorance with which he began. They were guilty of ignorance. All their acts of piety were in vain, for they did not know or worship the one true God. In his forbearance God formerly "overlooked" such ignorance (cf. 14:16; Rom 3:25). The times of forbearance had now ended because their ignorance had now ended. Now they knew the one true God through Paul's proclamation. He was no longer an "unknown God"; and should they continue in their false

---

Stoa," 101-4) gives a rather strong case for questioning the Ishodad tradition. For the argument that the statement is based on Euripides, *Bacchae*, see P. Colaclides, "Acts 17:28A and Bacchae 506," *VC* 27 (1973): 161-64.

[95]Cf. Deut 4:28; Ps 115:4-8; Isa 40:18-20; 44:9-20; Song of Songs 13:10–14:2; 15:7-17.

worship and fail to acknowledge his sole lordship of heaven and earth, their sin would no longer be a sin of ignorance but a high-handed sin.

Only one course was open—repentance, a complete turnabout from their false worship and a turning to God.[96] The concept of repentance must have sounded strange to the Athenians. Even stranger was Paul's warning of God's coming day of judgment (v. 31).[97] Strangest of all was his reference to the resurrection of Christ. Paul's train of thought was clear enough. God is the one true God and should be acknowledged by his creatures. All people must ultimately stand before God and give an account for their relationship to him. God appointed "the man" who would carry out this judgment. (The "man" was Christ, "the Son of Man," in his role as judge; cf. Dan 7:13f.) God clearly demonstrated this truth by the miracle of raising him from the dead. Just as Peter had pointed to the resurrection as proof to the Jews that Jesus is Messiah, so to the Gentiles Paul pointed to the resurrection as proof that he is the coming judge of all humanity. Paul had reached the climax of his testimony and made his appeal. He may have had more to say, but he had said enough to convict at least one Areopagite (v. 34). In any event, with the mention of resurrection the jeering started, and Paul's speech ended (v. 32).

Commentators often have said that the Paul of the epistles would never have preached the Areopagus sermon because its thought would have been alien to him. Such is not the case. The appeal to a "natural revelation" is certainly present in Rom 1:18-32 even though the application differs. More significant are passages like 1 Thess 1:9-10, where Paul summarized his preaching to the Gentiles at Thessalonica. There the elements are strikingly the same as in the Areopagus speech: turning from idols to a living God, the return of the Son from heaven, the resurrection, the wrath to come. This is almost a summary of the appeal in Acts 17:29-31.

What of course is unique in the Areopagus speech is its appeal to Greek philosophical thought. Paul was attempting to build bridges with the intellectuals in Athens in the hope of winning some (cf. 1 Cor 9:19). He used their language, quoted their poets, and sought to reach them in terms they would understand. As such his speech in Athens became a model for the Christian apologists who later attempted to present the faith to the pagan intellectuals of a later day.[98] It should be noted that Paul

---

[96]E. des Places, "Actes 17, 30-31," Bib 52 (1971): 526-34; J. Dupont, "Le discours à l'Aréopage," Nouvelles Etudes, 410-23.

[97]A. J. Mattill, Jr., argues that the occurrence of μέλλω in v. 31 implies an imminent judgment ("Näherwartung, Fernerwartung, and the Purpose of Luke-Acts: Weymouth Reconsidered," CBQ 34 [1972]: 281-83).

[98]H. Gebhardt shows how the second- and third-century Christian apologists developed the same basic arguments as in the Areopagus speech ("Die an die Heiden gerichtete Missionsrede der Apostel und das Johannesevangelium," ZNW 6 [1905]: 236-49).

never compromised the basic Christian principles of God as Creator and Judge and the resurrection of Christ. In the end these were the most difficult concepts for the Athenians to grasp, but there could be no accommodation on these. Bridge building is essential in Christian witness, particularly when addressing different cultures, as missionaries must often do. Paul's Areopagus address provides both a precedent and a pattern for this essential task.[99]

(3) The Mixed Response (17:32-34)

[32]When they heard about the resurrection of the dead, some of them sneered, but others said, "We want to hear you again on this subject." [33]At that, Paul left the Council. [34]A few men became followers of Paul and believed. Among them was Dionysius, a member of the Areopagus, also a woman named Damaris, and a number of others.

17:32-33 Epicureans believed in no human existence after death. Stoics believed that only the immaterial spirit survived death. To Greeks the idea of a body surviving death did not make any sense—even a transformed body. So many in the Areopagus simply scoffed at Paul's reference to the resurrection. As so often with the preaching of the gospel in Acts, however, the response was mixed. Others wanted to "hear [him] again." There is no reason to see this response as anything but genuine. They were not convinced by Paul, but they were still willing to give him further hearing. At this point the scoffers must have had the majority, for Paul did not tarry before the Areopagus but left the assembly (v. 33).

17:34 There was a third response to Paul's witness in Athens, however. A few people responded in faith.[100] At least one of these, Dionysius the Areopagite, seems to have been converted by Paul's address before the council. Another convert is mentioned by name—Damaris. It is significant that of the two believers designated by name, one is male and the other female. One cannot fail to observe the prominence of women in Paul's Greek congregations of Macedonia and Achaia. We have no further reliable tradition on either Dionysius or Damaris. Some later writings under the name of Dionysius the Areopagite exist, but these are the product of a fifth-century Christian monk writing pseudonymously under the name of the New Testament character. Later traditions that Dionysius became the first bishop of Athens have no reliable basis.[101] Neither do we

---

[99]See K. O. Gangel, "Paul's Areopagus Speech," *BibSac* 127 (1970): 308-12.

[100]Verse 34 is rather clear evidence that ἄνδρες is not gender specific in Acts because Damaris is included in the relative clause dependent upon it. The sentence runs literally: "Some *people* joined him and believed, among whom were Dionysius the Areopagite and a woman named Damaris" (the NIV "men" should be translated "people").

[101]For these traditions see Eusebius, *Church History* 3.4.11 and 4.23.3.

know anything more of Damaris. Chrysostom saw her as Dionysius's wife, but this is probably purely conjectural on his part.[102] The "others" who are mentioned as converts in v. 34 may have resulted from Paul's larger witness in the synagogue and agora of Athens rather than from his address before the Areopagus. The same may have been true of Damaris.

The well-worn sermon idea that Paul totally abandoned his efforts to preach to intellectuals after his experience in Athens is a misreading of both Acts and 1 Corinthians. Luke did not present Paul's Areopagus sermon as a failure. The Arepoagus council consisted of about thirty members according to the best evidence. If Dionysius were the only convert from the address, one out of thirty is scarcely negligible, particularly when addressing skeptical intellectuals![103] And the first chapter of 1 Corinthians is not an anti-intellectual manifesto. It is a rather profound exposition of revelation and reason and still challenges the best minds. Paul's determination to preach the crucified Christ was only confirmed by his Areopagus experience. He never did otherwise than major on the center of the gospel, the death and resurrection of Christ. The climax of the Areopagus speech was the resurrection, and it received the predictable response—to the Greeks, folly (cf. v. 32; 1 Cor 1:23).

7. Establishing a Church in Corinth (18:1-17)

That Luke did not intend to present a full-scale history of the Pauline mission is well illustrated by his treatment of Corinth. During the time of the church's founding, Paul spent a year and a half in Corinth, as Luke attests (18:11). And yet the coverage is briefer than that of Paul's work in Philippi, which lasted no longer than several months. It is several verses shorter than the Athenian section, which probably represents only a matter of weeks. We know from Paul's two Epistles to the Corinthians, both of which were written during his third missionary period, that this was a time of severe problems for the church and a stormy relationship between it and Paul. For this period, Luke only mentioned Paul's final three-month visit there, and that in but one sentence (20:2b-3). Luke's method was selective—to depict the establishment of work in the various areas where

---

[102]The name Damaris is otherwise not found in first-century Greek literature. Some old Latin manuscripts read Damalis at v. 34, which was a common name and meant *heifer*. Some commentators want to see Damaris as a courtesan or dancing girl. Evidently this conjecture is based on the assumption that she was converted as a result of Paul's Areopagus address and that no respectable Greek woman would have been present in the agora or in any public gathering unaccompanied. This fails to recognize that v. 34 is a summary of Paul's total ministry in Athens—not just the Areopagus speech. For the interesting suggestion that Damaris may have had an Egyptian background (from Egyptian T'-mr, "beloved one"), see J. G. Griffiths, "Was Damaris an Egyptian? (Acts 17:34)," *BZ* 8 (1964): 293-95.

[103]See J. H. MacLean, "St. Paul at Athens," *ExpTim* 44 (1932-33): 550-53.

Paul worked and to relate individual episodes that were typical of Paul's experiences and edifying for his Christian readers. In the present section vv. 1-11 furnish the history of the church's foundation, and vv. 12-17 furnish the episode—the appearance before the proconsul Gallio.

(1) The Mission to Corinth (18:1-11)

[1]After this, Paul left Athens and went to Corinth. [2]There he met a Jew named Aquila, a native of Pontus, who had recently come from Italy with his wife Priscilla, because Claudius had ordered all the Jews to leave Rome. Paul went to see them, [3]and because he was a tentmaker as they were, he stayed and worked with them. [4]Every Sabbath he reasoned in the synagogue, trying to persuade Jews and Greeks.

[5]When Silas and Timothy came from Macedonia, Paul devoted himself exclusively to preaching, testifying to the Jews that Jesus was the Christ. [6]But when the Jews opposed Paul and became abusive, he shook out his clothes in protest and said to them, "Your blood be on your own heads! I am clear of my responsibility. From now on I will go to the Gentiles."

[7]Then Paul left the synagogue and went next door to the house of Titius Justus, a worshiper of God. [8]Crispus, the synagogue ruler, and his entire household believed in the Lord; and many of the Corinthians who heard him believed and were baptized.

[9]One night the Lord spoke to Paul in a vision: "Do not be afraid; keep on speaking, do not be silent. [10]For I am with you, and no one is going to attack and harm you, because I have many people in this city." [11]So Paul stayed for a year and a half, teaching them the word of God.

Corinth in Paul's day was the largest, most cosmopolitan city of Greece.[104] Located at the southern end of the isthmus that connects the Peloponnesus with the Greek mainland, it was a major center for commerce. It had two ports, Lechaeum on the west, which gave access to the Adriatic Sea, and Cenchrea on the east, opening into the Aegean Sea. The isthmus is only three and a half miles wide at its narrowest point. Nero began a canal there, but this was not completed. The canal presently there was dug in the nineteenth century. In Paul's day ships were often

---

[104]Excavations at Corinth have uncovered settlements on the site that date back to the early Bronze Age (3000 B.C.). During the age of the Greek city-states, Corinth was a major power, being known for its pottery and shipbuilding industries. When Persia attempted to conquer Greece, Corinth was head of the league of city-states that halted its advance (338 B.C.). Later it headed the Achaean league in its attempt to stop Rome. This leadership proved fatal to Corinth. The league was defeated, and Roman vengeance was vented on the city. In 146 B.C. it was razed. Such a strategic site could not remain unutilized for long; and in 44 B.C. Julius Caesar established a Roman colony there, primarily for the purpose of providing territory for the Roman proletariat. The new city was renamed *Colonia Laus Julia Corinthiensis.* In A.D. 27, when Achaia was organized as a separate senatorial province, it became the capital city and seat of the Roman proconsul.

unloaded at one of the ports and the load carried overland the short distance and reloaded on another ship at the other port. Small boats were placed on carts called *diolkoi* and transferred from one port to the other by means of a roadway specially designed for that purpose. Either method was generally preferable to hazarding the treacherous waters around the Peloponnesus. All of this made Corinth *the* Greek center for east-west trade. With it came some of the undesirable elements that often plague a maritime center. Among the Greeks the word translated "to live like a Corinthian" (*korinthiazesthai*) meant *to live immorally.*

In Paul's day Corinth was a new city. No major building was more than 100 years old. It was also the most Roman city of Greece, with its extensive group of resettled *coloni* as the core of its citizenry. As in Athens, the religion of the Corinthians seems to have been primarily that of the traditional Greek gods. The temple of Aphrodite, goddess of love, commanded the city from its perch on the Acrocorinth, the 1,900-foot hill that dominated the city from its perimeter.[105] Inside the city walls, close to the agora, stood the temple of the sun god Apollo, the patron god of the city. Just inside the city wall excavations have uncovered a temple to Asklepius, the Greek god of healing. Elaborate canals and reservoirs connected with the temple provided water for the various healing rites. A number of clay replicas of human body parts have been found on the site. Evidently these were brought as offerings to the god and as petitions for healing, representing the part of the body in which the suppliant was afflicted.

Worship of God, however, was present in the city before Paul's time. There was a Jewish settlement in Corinth, and it was with them that Paul began his mission (18:4). A large stone lintel from a doorway was excavated at the base of the steps that led into the agora and was inscribed as the synagogue of the Jews. Although it dates from the second century, it may mark the site of an earlier synagogue where Paul debated with the Jews of Corinth.[106]

Luke's brief account of Paul's establishment of the work in Corinth provides an invaluable supplement to Paul's letter to that congregation. The two Corinthian letters date from a later period—that of Paul's third mission. The Acts account deals with Paul's foundation of the church during his second missionary period. Though they thus deal with different epochs in Paul's relationship with the Corinthians, there are a number of

---

[105]Conzelmann, however, questions whether there was actually temple prostitution at the temple of Aphrodite, as Strabo maintained (*Acts*, 151). That there was widespread prostitution in Corinth is beyond dispute (cf. 1 Cor 6:12-20).

[106]Excavation in Corinth was carried out by the American School of Classical Studies. See W. A. McDonald, "Archaeology and St. Paul's Journeys in Greek Lands: Part III— Corinth," *BA* 5 (1942): 36-48.

remarkable agreements in detail between Luke's account and the apostle's two epistles as well as between all three and the archaeological evidence. These will be noted as they appear in the text. The following exposition is divided into three parts: (1) vv. 1-4: Paul's arrival in Corinth; (2) vv. 5-8: the witness in the city; and (3) vv. 9-11: the assuring vision of Jesus.

PAUL'S ARRIVAL IN CORINTH (18:1-4).   **18:1-2** Corinth was approximately fifty miles from Athens and almost due west. When Paul arrived in the city, he quickly met a Jewish couple by the name of Aquila and Priscilla. The couple is also mentioned in Paul's letters (Rom 16:3; 1 Cor 16:19; 2 Tim 4:19). Paul *and* Luke always mentioned them together, never separately. Paul referred to the wife as Prisca, which was her formal name. Luke's "Priscilla" was a diminutive, less formal designation, the form that would be used among acquaintances. Luke often used the more "familiar" form of a name. Compare his "Silas" with Silvanus. "Aquila" is a Latin name and derives from the word for "eagle."

Some have surmised from Luke's giving the detail that he came from Pontus, the Roman province along the Black Sea, that he may have been a Roman citizen; but that is not sufficient evidence. Others have wanted to see Priscilla as the Roman citizen, basing this on the fact that there was a Roman patrician family by the name of Prisca *and* on the fact that Priscilla is generally named first (cf. 18:18,24; Rom 16:3; 2 Tim 4:19). That she is usually mentioned before her husband is indeed remarkable for first-century usage but probably is less due to her social status than to her prominence in Christian circles. Not to detract from Aquila's ministry, but Priscilla seems to have been one of those women like Lydia whose service in the Christian community stood out.[107]

Luke only mentioned as an incidental detail that the couple had recently come from Rome because the emperor Claudius had expelled the Jews from the city. The detail is very important for Pauline chronology. Luke probably referred to the same incident the Roman historian Suetonius mentioned in his *Life of Claudius* (25.4). According to Suetonius, Claudius expelled all the Jews because of a tumult instigated by "Chrestus." The later church historian Orosius dated this event during the ninth year of Claudius, i.e., between Jan. 25, 49 and Jan. 24, 50. If Orosius's date can be trusted, this sets a certain date for Paul's arrival in Corinth.[108] Since Aquila and Priscilla preceded him there, it is not likely

---

[107]One perhaps would not want to go so far as Harnack, who saw Priscilla and Aquila as coauthors of the Epistle to the Hebrews.

[108]Dio Cassius referred to an edict of Claudius in which the emperor did not expel the Jews but only limited their right of assembly. He dated this around A.D. 41. Some scholars see this as the same as Suetonius's reference and opt for the earlier date. They seem, however, to be two separate edicts. See *Beginnings* 5:459-60; F. F. Bruce, "Christianity under Claudius," *BJRL* 44 (1962): 315-18.

Paul would have arrived in Corinth before the middle of A.D. 49.

The reference in Suetonius is significant for other reasons as well. Likely, his attributing the tumult among the Jews to "Chrestus" resulted from his confusion over the name "Christus," the Latin for Christ. This is evidence that Christianity had already reached Rome by A.D. 50. How would it have done so? Here is the perfect example before us—by Christians like Priscilla and Aquila traveling the routes of trade and commerce and carrying their faith wherever they went. Priscilla and Aquila likely were Christians already when they left Rome. The Jewish Christians would have been seen as ringleaders in the Jewish unrest over "Chrestus" and would have received the brunt of Claudius's edict.[109] Luke said nothing about Paul's witnessing to the couple, and one would assume Paul readily took up with them because they were not only fellow Jews and fellow tentmakers but, most important of all, fellow Christians.

18:3 Paul mentioned working to support himself in his letters (1 Cor 4:12; 1 Thess 2:9; cf. 2 Cor 11:7). In Acts 20:34 he reminded the Ephesian elders that while in Ephesus he had supported himself and his coworkers with the labor of his own hands. Only in Acts 18:3 are we told the trade by which he supported himself—that of "tentmaker." Exactly what this involved is often discussed. A number of the early church fathers rendered the term used here by a more general word, "leather worker." This is quite plausible. Tents were often made of leather, and tentmakers probably used their skills on other types of leather products as well. Some interpreters have suggested, however, that Paul may not have worked in leather at all but rather in *cilicium,* a cloth of woven goat's hair that was often used as a material for tents. Since cilicium originated in and was named for Paul's native province of Cilicia, he may well have learned the trade there. The later rabbinic writings required students of the law to adopt a trade in order to keep the mind from becoming idle and so as to never depend on profit from the teaching of the Torah.[110] Paul may well have been influenced by this ideal. First Corinthians 9 (cf. v. 12) particularly reveals such an attitude, where Paul spoke of foregoing any support from the Corinthians in order to avoid any obstacle to the gospel.[111]

---

[109]Because there were perhaps 50,000 Jews in Rome, Claudius may have had difficulty enforcing his edict; and it may have been confined to the leaders. In any event, there was a Jewish community in Rome eight years or so later when Paul arrived there (Acts 28:17-28).

[110]See *m.Abot* 2.2 and 4.7.

[111]R. Hock notes that Paul's references to his work by such terms as "enslaved" (see 1 Cor 9:19) and "demeaning myself " (see 2 Cor 11:7) and being "a spectacle to the world" (see 1 Cor 4:9,12) reflect a decidedly upper-class attitude toward work and may, along with his Roman citizenship, indicate his coming from a higher social level ("Paul's Tentmaking and the Problem of his Social Class," *JBL* 97 [1978]: 555-64).

The obstacle in the case of the Corinthians may well have been the distrust they had for those who went about making profit from their message. The originator of the Cynic school of philosophy, Diogenes, was a Corinthian native. By Paul's day the Cynic movement was widespread. Cynic philosophers were peripatetic, traveling from town to town, often preaching to crowds on street corners and in marketplaces. Their ideal was a life-style free from want, totally nonmaterialistic. They depended on contributions for their basic needs. In actual fact, some seem to have fallen somewhat short of the ideal and had a reputation for fleecing the gullible crowds. Paul may have been particularly careful in places like Corinth to avoid any associations with these street preachers. In fact, Paul may have actually used his work as an opportunity for witness. According to available evidence, a number of Greek philosophers, beginning with Socrates, followed a pattern of witness in the shops and the workplace; and Paul may well have utilized such an opportunity in exercising his own trade.[112]

18:4 Whether he did so while at work during the week or on the Sabbath, Paul followed his customary pattern in Corinth. He went to the synagogue and sought to persuade both the Jews and God-fearers there that Christ is the Messiah (v. 4; cf. 17:2-4).

THE WITNESS IN THE CITY (18:5-8). **18:5-6** One gets the impression that when Silas and Timothy arrived in Corinth from Macedonia they brought a contribution for Paul's ministry. Second Corinthians 11:8f. speaks of the support of other churches while Paul ministered in Corinth, and Phil 4:15f. speaks of the generous support of that congregation in his continuing mission endeavor. Now Paul was freed to witness more continually, not just on Sabbaths.

The seemingly inevitable results followed, however, and Jewish opposition arose. Paul turned from the synagogue and turned to the Gentiles (v. 6). The pattern was the same as in the synagogue of Pisidian Antioch (13:44-47), and it would be repeated again, right up to the end of Acts (28:23-28; cf. 19:8-9). Why did Paul keep returning to the Jews after he seemingly had turned decisively to the Gentiles, and especially when he knew the almost certain resistance that would arise? Perhaps he gave us a clue in his statement that the Corinthian Jews' blood would be on their own heads, not on his hands. We find the same language in Ezekiel's picture of the prophet as a watchman over Israel (33:1-7; cf. 3:18).[113] So

---

[112]See Hock, "The Workshop as a Social Setting for Paul's Missionary Preaching," *CBQ* 41 (1979): 438-50.

[113]If the watchman blew the warning trumpet, anyone who failed to heed would be responsible for the consequences that came. If the watchman didn't blow the trumpet, then the watchman would be responsible. Paul was a watchman to Israel, proclaiming the coming

Paul always fulfilled his role of witness to his fellow Jews. When it was no longer possible to bear that witness, he moved to the Gentiles. But in the next city he would be back to the synagogue, blowing his warning trumpet.

18:7-8 When Paul left the synagogue, he moved his place of witness to the house of a Gentile God-fearer named Titius Justus, who probably was one of those mentioned in v. 4 as present in the Corinthian synagogue. He probably continued to live with Aquila and Priscilla. Going just next door might appear as somewhat noningratiating toward the Jews, but it could also be indicative that he had not completely given up on them. Indeed, the ruler of the synagogue became a believer. He likely was the same Crispus mentioned in 1 Cor 1:14 as one of the few in Corinth upon whom Paul himself administered baptism.

Some have wanted to see Titius Justus as the Gaius who is also mentioned as having been baptized by Paul in 1 Cor 1:14. Their reasoning is that Titius and Justus would constitute the last two of the customary three Roman names and that Gaius could well have been his praenomen, or first name. This same Gaius is mentioned as Paul's Corinthian host in Rom 16:23, and these interpreters would see v. 7 as referring to Paul's changing his place of lodging from Aquila and Priscilla's to Titius's.[114] This view is attractive but unfortunately too conjectural. In any event, the witness among the Gentiles was a success; many of the Corinthians believed and were baptized.

We know from Paul's Corinthian correspondence that the church there was sizable, sufficiently so to develop church factions (cf. 1 Cor 1:10-17). Seemingly the majority were ordinary working people, not the "first families" of Corinth (cf. 1 Cor 1:26). Still, some were from the upper social classes. Social cleavage seems to have been the major problem at their gathering for the agape feast in connection with the Lord's Supper (1 Cor 11:17-22). Particularly of note in Paul's Letter to the Romans (cf. 16:23), which was written in Corinth, is the mention of Erastus, the "director of public works" in Corinth.

An inscription has been excavated in a plaza adjacent to the theater at Corinth. It mentions Erastus as the treasurer (*aedile*) of the city who provided the funds for the plaza. This quite possibly is the same Erastus associated with the Corinthian congregation in Rom 16:23.

---

of the Messiah and the coming judgment. When he had borne his witness, he had fulfilled his responsibility.

[114]See E. J. Goodspeed, "Gaius Titius Justus," *JBL* 69 (1950): 382f. Neither is Titius to be confused with Titus as in some of the manuscripts (א) and church fathers. Titus was present with Paul at the Jerusalem Conference (Gal 2:1-3), which almost surely took place before Paul's visit to Corinth.

THE ASSURING VISION OF JESUS (18:9-11). **18:9-11**   Verses 9-11 are a
sort of interlude in the narrative. They seem to interrupt the account of
the increasing Jewish opposition to Paul, which became full-blown when
he was brought before Gallio (vv. 12-17). They are, however, an essential
part of the story and are closely related to the trial scene. Their form is
that of a divine commissioning narrative in which God or his angel
appears to a human agent, gives a task to be performed, and gives an
assurance of his presence.[115] The form already is familiar from previous
incidents in Acts (5:17-21; 9:10-18; 16:6-10), and Paul would have similar visions on subsequent occasions (23:11; 27:23-24). All of these have
elements familiar from the Old Testament texts that treat the call of the
prophets—Moses (Exod 3:2-12), Joshua (Josh 1:1-9), Jeremiah (Jer 1:5-
10), and the servant of the Lord (Isa 41:10-14). Even the same wording
binds all these together: "Fear not; do not be silent; I am with you; no one
will harm you" (author's translation).

In the present instance Paul's vision fortified him for the extensive witness in Corinth. Corinth was the first city where Paul settled for an *extensive* period of missionary activity. The pattern heretofore had been for
such strong opposition to arise against Paul and his companions in cities
where they witnessed as to force their departure. He had no reason to
expect otherwise in Corinth. In 1 Cor 2:3 he even stated the fear and misgivings he had on first coming to the city. How would these Greeks and
Roman colonials receive him? Already the familiar pattern of strong Jewish opposition was rearing its head. How long could his Corinthian ministry continue? The vision from the Lord provided an answer. Paul was to
remain in Corinth and continue his witness there. The Lord was with him.
No harm would befall him, no opposition withstand him. This assurance
fortified Paul for the eighteen-month ministry in Corinth (v. 11). The successful outcome of his appearance before Gallio further assured him the
Lord had indeed kept his promise.

(2) The Accusation before Gallio (18:12-17)

**[12]While Gallio was proconsul of Achaia, the Jews made a united attack on
Paul and brought him into court. [13]"This man," they charged, "is persuading the
people to worship God in ways contrary to the law."**

**[14]Just as Paul was about to speak, Gallio said to the Jews, "If you Jews were
making a complaint about some misdemeanor or serious crime, it would be reasonable for me to listen to you. [15]But since it involves questions about words and
names and your own law—settle the matter yourselves. I will not be a judge of**

---

[115]For a full discussion of this commissioning form, see B. J. Hubbard, "The Role of
Commissioning Accounts in Acts," *Perspectives on Luke-Acts*, 187-98.

such things." [16]So he had them ejected from the court. [17]Then they all turned on Sosthenes the synagogue ruler and beat him in front of the court. But Gallio showed no concern whatever.

The appearance of Paul before Gallio is of particular importance in two respects. First, it established a precedent for the manner in which the Roman leaders should consider charges against Christians brought before them. Second, the mention of Gallio is an important reference point for determining the date of Paul's work in Corinth and for establishing the entire Pauline chronology.

18:12 To begin with the second, a great deal is known of Gallio both from literary sources (Seneca and Tacitus) and from inscriptions.[116] His service in Corinth occurred during the proconsular period of his career.[117] Achaia at this time was a province of second rank, and these were administered by proconsuls. Generally in this region proconsuls served a one-year term, two at the most; and tenure seems to have begun in the early summer. An inscription discovered at Delphi, which relates to the dedication of an aqueduct, mentions Gallio as being proconsul of Achaia and dates this during the period of Claudius's twenty-sixth acclamation as emperor. Such "acclamations" were made by the Roman senate at irregular intervals as affirmations of an emperor's rule. On the basis of other inscriptions, Claudius's twenty-sixth acclamation can be dated as covering the first seven months or so of A.D. 52. On this basis he is assumed as having begun his office in the summer of either A.D. 51 or A.D. 52.[118] If one assumes that Gallio served the maximum two-year term, his tenure would have ended in summer of A.D. 54 at the latest. Putting this together with the date of Claudius's edict,[119] Paul's eighteen months in Corinth would have occurred sometime between winter of A.D. 49/50 and summer of A.D. 54. Most interpreters are inclined to see Gallio as having the more usual one-year tenure and Paul as having appeared before him

---

[116]Born in Spain, he was taken to Rome by his father during the reign of Tiberius and educated for a diplomat's career. He was the elder brother of Seneca, the famous philosopher-statesman, who described him as being of an unusually amiable disposition. Gallio's career took him through the usual steps of serving as a praetor, then a proconsul, and finally rising to the rank of consul.

[117]Shortly after his Corinthian tenure, Gallio seems to have contracted a rather serious illness that plagued him for the rest of his life. He was executed in the latter half of the 60s, a victim of Nero's paranoia. For further treatment of his life, see R. Pesch, *Die Apostelgeschichte*, Teilband 2: *Apg. 13-28* (Zurich: Benziger, 1986), 150.

[118]For full discussions of the chronology of Gallio's tenure and the relevant inscriptional evidence, see *Beginnings* 5:460-61 and A. Deissmann, *Paul* (New York: Doran, 1926), 261-86.

[119]See commentary on 18:2.

during the early days of his term of office. This would place Paul's Corinthian ministry roughly between early 50 and late 52.[120]

18:13-16 Returning to the first point, the Gallio episode is almost paradigmatic for Paul's appearances before Roman officials in Acts. None of them found him guilty of having broken any Roman law. This becomes very explicit with Gallio's judgment regarding the Jewish charge against Paul. Their charge was that Paul was "persuading the people to worship God in ways contrary to the law." The charge as it stands is ambiguous. What law? Roman law or Jewish law? There were Roman laws against proselytizing of Roman citizens by foreign cults,[121] but Gallio obviously did not take the charge in this sense. He saw it for what it was—an internal dispute within the Jewish community—their interpretations of "words" (the Scriptures?), of "names" (Jesus as Messiah?), of "law" (the Torah).[122] In v. 15 Gallio seems to have used a technical term for taking up a case (*anechomai*) when he refused to judge ("listen to," NIV) the Jews' complaint against Paul. It was within his right as a proconsul to make such a refusal. In instances where it was not a clear-cut case of infraction of an established Roman law, it was left to the discretion of the judge whether or not to formally hear the case.[123] In this instance Gallio did not see the charges as deserving his time. He didn't even give Paul a chance to make a defense (v. 14). The Jews could settle the matter themselves. He drove them all from the court (v. 16). One should not see Gallio as taking Paul's side, however. Paul would have been ejected along with the Jews. Gallio saw the entire matter as an internal Jewish affair and would have nothing to do with it.

18:17 The incident must have taken place in the open, as would be indicated by the mob scene that occurred in the presence of the proconsul

---

[120]Luke's arrangement of material could be construed that the Gallio incident took place toward the end of Paul's Corinthian ministry, but this is not certain; nor can one assume that Paul appeared before him in the early days of his tenure. Verse 12 is quite indefinite ("while Gallio was proconsul") as is v. 18 ("Paul stayed on in Corinth for some time"). The only definite chronological statement in Acts 18 is the eighteen months that constituted the entire period of his Corinthian ministry (v. 11). See K. Haacker, "Die Gallio-Episode und die paulinische Chronologie," *BZ* 16 (1972): 252-55.

[121]See the discussion in Sherwin-White, *Roman Society and Roman Law*, 101-4.

[122]Appeal to the concept of *religio licita* is somewhat precarious, the view that the Romans kept a list of accepted foreign religions and that the Jews were attempting to divorce themselves from Christians, thus making the latter an officially unrecognized religion. No first-century evidence exists that the Romans kept such a list (see Conzelmann, *Acts*, 153). The Jews were given privileges by Claudius assuring them of freedom of worship and protection from official harassment. Because of their identity with Judaism, the early Christians would have perhaps enjoyed some benefit from this.

[123]The technical term for such cases was *cognitio extra ordinem*. See Sherwin-White, *Roman Society and Roman Law*, 99-100.

(v. 17). This has been verified by the excavations at Corinth. A raised platform of blue marble has been uncovered on the south side of the agora that served as the *bēma* (v. 12), or judgment seat of the Roman officials. The unruly beating of Sosthenes is anything but clear. Who are "all" who beat him in front of the proconsul—the Jews or the Gentiles who had come from elsewhere in the agora to see the goings-on before the *bēma?* The question is complicated by the fact that Paul mentioned a Sosthenes in 1 Cor 1:1 as a close Christian companion who joined him in writing the Corinthians. Sosthenes is not an uncommon name, and the two may be different persons. If they are the same, then clearly the ruler of the synagogue subsequently became a Christian, just like his predecessor Crispus. In this instance the Jews may have beat Sosthenes, who may already have been indicating his Christian sympathies. On the other hand, the Gentiles may have been the culprits. Gallio's ejection of the Jews may have unleashed their latent anti-Semitic tendencies. This would have rendered a sort of "poetic justice." The one who as synagogue ruler probably was the chief speaker against Paul now received himself the punishment he had wished on the apostle. Such an interpretation does not rule out the possibility that this is the same Sosthenes as 1 Cor 1:1, in which instance his conversion would be subsequent to this event.

Through it all Gallio remained wholly indifferent. He turned a blind eye on the whole incident (v. 17). This was not so much callousness on his part as his firm refusal to have anything to do with the matter. It was wholly an internal Jewish affair. The incident set an important precedent. Proconsular decisions over such unusual cases were often followed by Roman officials in other provinces. Had Gallio decided against Paul, it would have been a dangerous precedent that not only would have ended his effectiveness in Achaia but hindered his witness elsewhere.

8. Returning to Antioch (18:18-22)

[18]Paul stayed on in Corinth for some time. Then he left the brothers and sailed for Syria, accompanied by Priscilla and Aquila. Before he sailed, he had his hair cut off at Cenchrea because of a vow he had taken. [19]They arrived at Ephesus, where Paul left Priscilla and Aquila. He himself went into the synagogue and reasoned with the Jews. [20]When they asked him to spend more time with them, he declined. [21]But as he left, he promised, "I will come back if it is God's will." Then he set sail from Ephesus. [22]When he landed at Caesarea, he went up and greeted the church and then went down to Antioch.

Acts 18:18-22 provides a transition between Paul's second and third missions. On the one hand, it concludes the second, with Paul returning to Antioch where his journey began (15:35-41). On the other hand, Paul's brief visit to Ephesus looks toward the third missionary period, which would be spent primarily in that city.

18:18 The note that Paul remained "for some time" in Corinth after the appearance before Gallio confirms the importance of the latter's refusal to hear the case. Paul was able to stay in Corinth afterwards and continue his witness without hindrance. Just why Paul decided to end his initial ministry in Corinth and sail to "Syria" is not specified.[124] It may have had something to do with his vow. At Cenchrea, their port of departure and the Aegean harbor of Corinth, Paul is said to have shaved his hair in connection with a vow he had made. This seems to have been a Nazirite vow, the type of vow discussed in Num 6:1-21.[125] Just why Paul had made a vow is not clear. It was perhaps in connection with his vision (Acts 18:9-10), a means of expressing thanksgiving and seeking the continued blessing of the Lord in his Corinthian mission. The reference to his having cut his hair at this point presents some difficulty. Generally one cut the hair at the end of the vow and made a sacrifice at the temple in Jerusalem, throwing the shorn hair into the burnt offering as a part of the sacrifice. Some interpreters suggest that at Cenchrea Paul was beginning a vow that he would later complete in Jerusalem, but the past tense of the Greek verb indicates Paul had already taken the vow. There also is no evidence for cutting the hair at the initiation of a vow—only at its completion. A passage in Josephus seems to indicate the practice of cutting the hair elsewhere before going to Jerusalem to make the sacrifices.[126] Perhaps this is what Paul was doing. In any event, the significance of the vow is that it shows Paul to have been a loyal, practicing Jew. In his mission to the Gentiles, he did not abandon his own Jewishness. He was still a "Jew to the Jews" and still continued his witness in the synagogues. Interestingly, on Paul's final visit to Jerusalem, when James wanted him to demonstrate his Jewish loyalty before the more legally zealous Jewish Christians, participation in a similar vow was chosen as the means to accomplish this (21:20-24).

18:19-22 Aquila and Priscilla accompanied Paul to Ephesus. They remained there and undoubtedly continued the Christian witness in the city after Paul's departure (cf. 18:26). At this point Paul made an appear-

---

[124]Syria may be intended in the provincial sense of all Syro-Cilicia, which included Palestine, since Caesarea is the actual final port of disembarkation (v. 22). On the other hand, Syria may indicate Antioch as Paul's final destination and end of his journey.

[125]Samson and John the Baptist are famous exemplars of such a vow. For them it was a lifelong vow, but there were provisions for vows of shorter term, thirty days seeming to be the minimum period. During the course of a Nazirite vow, one was forbidden to cut one's hair, to consume wine or strong drink, and to come into contact with a corpse. Vows could be taken for various reasons—to seek divine blessing in an undertaking, to express thanksgiving, or to seek deliverance from an illness.

[126]Josephus, *War* 2.3.13. The Greek text could be construed as having Aquila cut his hair, but such a detail would be meaningless and would serve no point in the narrative.

ance in the Ephesian synagogue (18:19). It was nothing more. Ephesus
was not a major point on his itinerary for the second journey.[127] It was
often a port of call for ships traveling from Corinth to the Syrian coast,
and that probably was the case in this instance. Paul was in a hurry to
catch his boat to Syria and refused the invitation of the Ephesian Jews to
stay with them longer (v. 20). He promised to return, "If it is God's
will."[128] The stage was set for Paul's third mission (cf. 19:1–21:16). In
the meantime Aquila and Priscilla would carry on the witness in Ephesus
until his return. Paul caught his ship. Why the rush to get to Palestine?
The Western text provides an answer, adding to v. 21 the note that Paul
was hurrying to Jerusalem for the upcoming festival.[129] Although that is
almost surely not the original text, it may be an accurate conjecture. Possibly Paul was hurrying to Jerusalem to complete his vow. Whatever his
purposes, his ship landed at Caesarea, the port for Jerusalem. He then
"went up" and greeted "the church," then "down" to Antioch (v. 22).
"The church" referred to is almost certainly Jerusalem. It was traditional
language to speak of going "up" to the holy city, which sat high on
Mt. Zion. Paul's second mission finally ended with his return to the congregation that had sent him forth (15:35-41), the great missionary church
of Antioch.[130]

---

[127]For a description of Ephesus, see the introduction to Chap. VII.

[128]The expression "God willing" was a Greek expression that was taken over by Hellenistic Judaism. Cf. Epictetus, *Dissertations* 1.1.17; Josephus, *Antiquities* 7.373; Heb 6:3;
Jas 4:15.

[129]Probably the Western editor had Passover in mind.

[130]One should note the recurrent pattern of Paul's three missionary journeys. Each began
in Antioch. Each ended in Jerusalem. Each had a major speech: in Pisidian Antioch (first
journey) Paul preached to Jews; in Athens (second journey) he preached to Gentiles; at
Miletus (third journey) he preached to Christian elders.

——————————— *SECTION OUTLINE* ———————————

VII. PAUL'S WITNESS OVERCOMES OPPOSITION IN EPHESUS
  (18:23–21:16)
  1. Apollos in Ephesus (18:23-28)
  2. Paul's Witness to the Disciples of John (19:1-7)
  3. Paul's Preaching in Ephesus (19:8-12)
  4. Paul's Encounter with False Religion in Ephesus (19:13-20)
      (1) Jewish Exorcists (19:13-16)
      (2) Overcoming Magic (19:17-20)
  5. Paul's Determination to Go to Jerusalem (19:21-22)
  6. Opposition to Paul by the Craftsmen of Ephesus (19:23-41)
      (1) Instigation of a Riot by Demetrius (19:23-27)
      (2) Uproar in the Theater (19:28-34)
      (3) Pacification by the City Clerk (19:35-41)
  7. Paul's Journey to Jerusalem (20:1–21:16)
      (1) Final Ministry in Macedonia and Achaia (20:1-6)
      (2) Restoration of Eutychus (20:7-12)
      (3) Voyage to Miletus (20:13-16)
      (4) Farewell Address to the Ephesian Elders (20:17-35)
           Paul's Past Example (20:18-21)
           Paul's Future Prospects (20:22-27)
           Paul's Warning of Future Heresies (20:28-31)
           Paul's Blessing and Final Admonition (20:32-35)
      (5) Final Leave-taking (20:36-38)
      (6) Voyage to Jerusalem (21:1-16)
           Warning at Tyre (21:1-6)
           Warning of Agabus (21:7-14)
           Arrival in Jerusalem (21:15-16)

——— **VII. PAUL'S WITNESS OVERCOMES OPPOSITION** ———
IN EPHESUS (18:23–21:16)

Acts 18:23–21:16 covers the third and culminating period of Paul's
mission in the east. The narrative revolves primarily around the city of
Ephesus, beginning with Priscilla and Aquilla's ministry to Apollos there
(18:24-28). All of chap. 19 is devoted to Paul's three-year ministry in
Ephesus, and the major portion of chap. 20 treats his farewell address to
the leaders of the Ephesian church.

As was the case with Paul's first two missionary periods, the narrative
begins and ends with a travel motif. This is extremely brief for the

beginning of the third mission, covering but two verses (18:23; 19:1). The conclusion of the Ephesian period, however, is marked by extensive travel and constitutes a major journey-to-Jerusalem emphasis. This begins with Paul's decision while still in Ephesus to visit Jerusalem and to go from there to Rome (19:21). The determination to visit Rome marks a major turning point in the story of Paul's witness. From then on, Rome becomes the major focal point in the narrative. The road to Rome, however, leads Paul first by way of Jerusalem; and his journey to Jerusalem is a major theme of 20:1–21:16. Much as Jesus' own journey to Jerusalem was marked by his awareness that he would suffer in that city, Paul's journey was marked by his premonition of trials that awaited him there (20:22f.) and constant warnings from fellow Christians about the danger of his going to the holy city (21:4,11-14).

Paul's three-year ministry in Ephesus followed the pattern already established at Corinth of setting up his mission in the major metropolitan center of a region and working outward from there. In Paul's day Ephesus was the most populous city of Asia Minor and the commercial and political hub of the entire province. An ancient city, there was a settlement on the site well back into the second millennium before Christ. From these earliest times the area seems to have been a cult center for the worship of the Anatolian mother goddess. In 1044 B.C. the region was conquered by the Ionian Greeks, who took over the ancient cult and renamed it for the corresponding Greek goddess Artemis. In subsequent centuries the city came under the dominion of various foreign powers—under Croesus of Lydia (560 B.C.), the Persians (546 B.C.), the Macedonians under Alexander (334 B.C.), and the Seleucid kings (281 B.C.). Roman influence was first felt in 190 B.C. under the client-kings of Pergamum, and in 133 B.C. the last king of Pergamum ceded the city to Rome in his will. In Paul's day the city was the seat of the Roman proconsul.

Through all these political changes the ancient shrine to the mother goddess persisted, and Ephesus was renowned throughout the Roman Empire as the temple keeper of Artemis. Excavations were first begun on the site of ancient Ephesus in 1813. Among the most famous of the findings were the ruins of this temple to Artemis, considered one of the seven architectural wonders of the ancient world. Also unearthed was a stadium rebuilt by Nero in Paul's day and the theater, which had a capacity of 24,000. Particularly spectacular must have been the major street that led from the theater to the city harbor. It was thirty-five feet wide and had on both sides colonnades that ran fifteen feet deep with shops behind them.

Located on the main highway connecting the Aegean with the rich trade routes in the east, Ephesus was the main commercial center of Asia. It had a natural harbor with access to the Aegean by way of the Cayster

River. According to Pliny, the original city was built on the sea; but because of silting from the Cayster, the city lay several miles inland up the river in the first century. The ruins of the city are some five miles inland today. To the north of Ephesus lay the city of Smyrna at the mouth of the Hermus River, and to the south was Miletus at the mouth of the Maeander River. The coastal plain connected Ephesus with both these cities and the commerce that traveled through them.[1] In fact, no better site could have been picked for the evangelization of all of Asia Minor than Ephesus. The seven churches of Rev 2–3 may well have owed their origin to Paul's Ephesian ministry.

1. Apollos in Ephesus (18:23-28)

[23]After spending some time in Antioch, Paul set out from there and traveled from place to place throughout the region of Galatia and Phrygia, strengthening all the disciples.
[24]Meanwhile a Jew named Apollos, a native of Alexandria, came to Ephesus. He was a learned man, with a thorough knowledge of the Scriptures. [25]He had been instructed in the way of the Lord, and he spoke with great fervor and taught about Jesus accurately, though he knew only the baptism of John. [26]He began to speak boldly in the synagogue. When Priscilla and Aquila heard him, they invited him to their home and explained to him the way of God more adequately.
[27]When Apollos wanted to go to Achaia, the brothers encouraged him and wrote to the disciples there to welcome him. On arriving, he was a great help to those who by grace had believed. [28]For he vigorously refuted the Jews in public debate, proving from the Scriptures that Jesus was the Christ.

18:23 Paul's third missionary period led him first from Syrian Antioch to "the region of Galatia and Phrygia," where he was "strengthening the disciples" (v. 23; cf. 14:22; 15:41). His route most likely led through the Cilician gates to the cities where he had established churches on his first journey—Derbe, Lystra, Iconium, and Pisidian Antioch. The reference to the Galatian religion and Phrygia might indicate the area further north and be evidence that Paul established churches in the northern portion of the Roman province of Galatia on his second missionary journey.[2] In any event, Paul's final destination was Ephesus (cf. 19:1). He had been prevented from working there on an earlier occasion (16:6). He had had to cut his first visit there short (18:20) and was eager to begin his mission in the city. Still, his desire for the new ministry did not lead him to neglect the old. He returned to his former fields and further ministered to

---

[1]For a further treatment of ancient Ephesus, see M. M. Parvis, "Archaeology and St. Paul's Journeys in Greek Lands, Part IV: Ephesus," *BA* 8 (1945): 62-73; F. V. Filson, "Ephesus and the New Testament," *BA* 8 (1945): 73-80.

[2]Cf. Acts 16:6 and see the comments on that text.

the churches there. A journey to Ephesus by sea would have been much easier. The foot journey from Antioch to Ephesus was well in excess of 1,000 miles. Paul set a notable example of the importance of continued nurture of new converts.

18:24 While Paul was en route, revisiting his former mission fields, Apollos arrived in Ephesus (18:24). Luke described him as a Jew and an Alexandrian native. Apollos was indeed a common name in Egypt, being a shortened form of Apollonius.[3] He is further described as "learned" (*logios*) and "powerful [*dynatos*] in the Scriptures," which the NIV accurately interprets as his having a thorough knowledge of them.[4]

18:25 At v. 25 the description of Apollos becomes more ambiguous. He is pictured as having been instructed in "the way of the Lord." Does this mean he was thoroughly acquainted with the gospel, the way of those who belong to the Lord? Or does it refer to the teaching of the earthly Jesus, the way that *he* taught? And what does the next phrase mean? The Greek reads literally "fervent in the spirit" (*zeōn tō pneumati*). The presence of the article before *spirit* would most naturally seem to indicate the Holy Spirit, and Paul used exactly the same phrase to refer to being "aglow with the Spirit" (Rom 12:11).[5] Still, many translators and interpreters see this as a reference to Apollos's own spirit, to his having a zealous temperament. (Compare NIV, "He spoke with great fervor.") Their reticence to see this as a reference to the Holy Spirit is the last phrase used to describe Apollos, "He knew only the baptism of John." In the Gospels and Acts, it is precisely the Holy Spirit who distinguishes the baptism of John from that of Jesus (cf. Mark 1:8; Acts 1:5). How one could have known only the baptism of John and yet have received the Holy Spirit is hard to understand. Equally confusing is the reference to Apollos's teaching about Jesus *accurately*. Obviously the teaching was not complete, or he would have known Christian baptism as well. Still, Luke depicted Apollos as a Christian. Apollos knew the way of the Lord, taught accurately about Jesus, and *may* have experienced the Spirit. Still he was deficient. He knew only John's baptism, and he had to be further instructed by Aquilla and Priscilla.

What exactly was the deficiency? Scholars have had a field day trying to define it more precisely. Apollos has been depicted as a disciple of

---

[3]ℵ, a few minuscules, and several ancient versions have "Apelles" instead of Apollos; and G. D. Kilpatrick argues for Apelles as the original reading ("Apollos-Apelles," *JBL* 89 [1970]: 77).

[4]Alexandria was the home of the allegorical-scriptural method associated with Philo and later with Christian scholars such as Clement and Origen. It is tempting to see Apollos as being steeped in such methods, but this is not explicit in Luke's description.

[5]For a persuasive argument that Apollos should be seen as fervent in the Holy Spirit, see J. D. G. Dunn, *Baptism in the Spirit* (Philadelphia: Westminster, 1970), 88f.

John the Baptist,[6] a heterodox Alexandrian Christian,[7] a charismatic Christian,[8] even a Jewish missionary and not a Christian at all.[9] The trouble with all such views is that they concentrate on only one part of Luke's description and do not sufficiently account for his total picture. Perhaps it is best to leave the matter with Luke's description and not try to go beyond it. The one matter of deficiency given is that Apollos knew only the baptism of John. His understanding of Christian baptism was inadequate.[10] Evidently it was not such that he needed further baptism. Luke did not relate his being rebaptized as were the disciples of John (19:5), only of his being further instructed by Priscilla and Aquilla.

18:26 Priscilla and Aquilla had remained in Ephesus to carry on the work there until Paul's return (18:18f.). Evidently the ministry in Ephesus had not yet extended beyond the synagogue; and when Apollos began his Christian witness there, his deficiency quickly caught the couple's attention. They took him aside, probably in the privacy of their home (so NIV), and expounded the way of Christ more fully to him (v. 26). The further instruction may well have included Paul's teaching concerning the Gentile mission. It is noteworthy that Priscilla took an equal role with her husband in further instructing Apollos.

18:27a Apollos then decided to go "to Achaia," i.e., to Corinth, where Paul had already established work. Apollos's work in that city is well documented by 1 Cor 1:12; 3:4-6,22; 4:6. Why he decided to go there is not specified. The Western text provides an explanation, greatly expanding v. 27 by saying that some Corinthian Christians who were sojourning in Ephesus invited him to minister in their native town. Aquilla and Priscilla more likely aroused his interest in Corinth, however, for they surely shared with him their ministry with Paul in that city.

The mention of the Ephesian brothers who provided a letter of recommendation for Apollos is significant because it is the first clear evidence that a church had by now been established in Ephesus. Such letters of recommendation were a common practice in the early church. Paul provided one for Phoebe of Cenchrea (Rom 16:1). He realized, however, that such

---

[6]J. Munck, *The Acts of the Apostles*, rev. W. F. Albright and C. S. Mann, AB (Garden City, N.Y.: Doubleday, 1967), 183.

[7]E. Käsemann, "The Disciples of John the Baptist in Ephesus," *Essays on New Testament Themes* (London: SCM, 1964), 136-48.

[8]M. Walter, "Apollos und die ephesinischen Johannesjünger (Act 18, 24-19, 7)," *ZNW* 78 (1987): 49-73; H. Preisker, "Apollos und die Johannesjünger in Act 18, 24-19, 6," *ZNW* 30 (1931): 301-4.

[9]E. Schweizer, "Die Bekehrung des Apollos, Apg. 18. 24-26," *EvT* 6 (1955): 247-54.

[10]B. T. D. Smith, "Apollos and the Twelve Disciples at Ephesus," *JTS* 76 (1915): 241-46; J. H. E. Hull, *The Holy Spirit in the Acts of the Apostles* (New York: World, 1968), 180-84.

commendatory documents could assume undue importance and could not take precedence over personal acquaintance (2 Cor 3:1-3).

18:27b-28 Apollos was well received in Corinth and was himself a great help to the congregation. Luke's description of the Corinthians as "those who by grace had believed" is particularly appropriate. As a Pauline congregation the gospel they responded to was surely his appeal to salvation solely by God's grace through faith.

Apollos's power in scriptural interpretation (cf. v. 24) suited him for debate with the Jews of Corinth. Much like Peter with the Jews of Jerusalem, he would have used the Old Testament to demonstrate that the Messiah must suffer and rise and that consequently Jesus was the promised Messiah. Evidently Apollos returned to Ephesus. When Paul wrote 1 Corinthians, probably in the latter part of his Ephesian ministry, Apollos was with him in Ephesus (1 Cor 16:12).[11]

2. Paul's Witness to the Disciples of John (19:1-7)

¹While Apollos was at Corinth, Paul took the road through the interior and arrived at Ephesus. There he found some disciples ²and asked them, "Did you receive the Holy Spirit when you believed?"

They answered, "No, we have not even heard that there is a Holy Spirit."

³So Paul asked, "Then what baptism did you receive?"

"John's baptism," they replied.

⁴Paul said, "John's baptism was a baptism of repentance. He told the people to believe in the one coming after him, that is, in Jesus." ⁵On hearing this, they were baptized into the name of the Lord Jesus. ⁶When Paul placed his hands on them, the Holy Spirit came on them, and they spoke in tongues and prophesied. ⁷There were about twelve men in all.

19:1 Verse 1 completes the travel narrative begun in 18:23. From Phrygia the most natural route to Ephesus would have led Paul through the Lycus Valley. Here Pauline churches were later established at Colosse, Laodicea, and Hierapolis. At this point Paul did not seem to have stopped for any witness. Judging from Col 1:7, the churches were established by Paul's coworker Epaphras, probably during the course of Paul's Ephesian ministry. When Paul arrived at Ephesus, he encountered "some disciples." We learn from v. 7 that there were "about twelve" of them. Evidently they were not at this point strictly Christian disciples but

---

[11] Apollos is an intriguing figure. He has often been seen as a ring leader in Paul's opposition at Corinth, but Paul doesn't seem to have depicted him as such. The Corinthians were guilty of pitting the two ministers against each other, but Paul did not indicate any personal antagonism between them. Apollos's Alexandrian associations have made him a prime candidate for the authorship of Hebrews, a suggestion first made by Luther; but that remains wholly speculative. Titus 3:13 would indicate that Apollos remained associated with Paul as a coworker in his later ministry.

rather disciples of John the Baptist. Elsewhere Luke used the term "disciples" for followers of John the Baptist (cf. Luke 5:33; 7:18f.).[12] He might have found a fine distinction between Baptist and Christian disciples strained. For him a true disciple of John, a *completed* disciple of John, *was* a Christian. That is the whole point of the present narrative.

19:2 Paul's interrogation of the disciples revealed that at no point had they advanced beyond John the Baptist's initial preaching of repentance in preparation for the coming Messiah. The NIV translation of their reply to Paul's question "Did you receive the Holy Spirit?" (v. 2) is literal, "We have not even heard that there is a Holy Spirit." John's disciples would surely have been acquainted with the Spirit and especially with his teaching that with the coming of the Messiah the Spirit would be poured out (cf. Luke 3:16). What they would not be aware of, if they had not heard of Jesus' death and resurrection and of the event at Pentecost, was that this proclamation of John had been fulfilled in Christ. Evidently that was the case with this group.[13] They had not heard that the Spirit had been poured out. They were unaware of Pentecost.

19:3 Their reply to Paul's second question only confirms the impression that their understanding had not progressed beyond John's ministry. The only baptism they were aware of was John's baptism. They knew nothing of baptism in the name of Jesus.

19:4 Paul's statement in v. 4 is the critical point. John's baptism was a baptism of repentance, preparatory to the coming of the Messiah. John's entire role as forerunner was to prepare the people for the Messiah's coming. The Messiah had indeed come, and he is Jesus. Thus, to be a true disciple of John was to confess Jesus, for he is the one whom John had heralded. The real deficiency of these twelve or so was not their baptism. It was much more serious. They failed to recognize Jesus as the one whom John had proclaimed, as the promised Messiah.[14]

19:5-6 Unlike Apollos, who had already been instructed in "the way" and who accurately taught about Jesus, this group was totally unacquainted with the gospel. They knew only John's preparatory message. But John had prepared them well, and they immediately responded to Paul's good news that Christ the Messiah had come; they were baptized in

---

[12]Dunn (*Baptism in the Holy Spirit*, 83-88) notes that this is the only time in Acts that the word "disciples" occurs without a definite article and argues that this is Luke's way of distinguishing them from Christians.

[13]There is evidence for groups well into the fourth century who claimed John the Baptist as their founder. See C. H. H. Scobie, *John the Baptist* (Philadelphia: Fortress, 1964), 187-202; H. Lichtenberger, "Taufergemeinden und frühchristliche Tauferpolemik im letzen Drittel des 1. Jahrhunderts," *ZTK* 84 (1987): 36-57.

[14]J. K. Parratt, "The Rebaptism of the Ephesian Disciples," *ExpTim* 79 (1967-68): 182f.

his name (v. 5). Paul then laid his hands on them, and they received the Spirit.

Some argue on the basis of this text that the gesture of hand-laying accompanied early Christian baptism. This, however, is the only instance in Acts where hand-laying directly follows baptism; and there is no evidence it was associated with baptism as a regular practice before A.D. 200.[15] In this instance the gesture is closely associated with the disciples' receiving the Spirit, much as with the case of the Samaritan disciples in 8:15-17. In both instances the reality of their experience was demonstrated in an ecstatic manifestation, with this group speaking in tongues and prophesying. As throughout Acts, there is no set pattern. The Spirit came at various times and in various ways. What is consistent is that the Spirit is always a vital part of one's initial commitment to Christ and a mark of every believer.

19:7 Luke ended the narrative with the note that there were "about twelve" of these disciples (v. 7). One could be tempted to see a symbolism here, such as that they were the apostolic nucleus of the Ephesian church. It is unlikely that any special sense should be attached to their number. Luke certainly made nothing of it.

3. Paul's Preaching in Ephesus (19:8-12)

[8]Paul entered the synagogue and spoke boldly there for three months, arguing persuasively about the kingdom of God. [9]But some of them became obstinate; they refused to believe and publicly maligned the Way. So Paul left them. He took the disciples with him and had discussions daily in the lecture hall of Tyrannus. [10]This went on for two years, so that all the Jews and Greeks who lived in the province of Asia heard the word of the Lord.

[11]God did extraordinary miracles through Paul, [12]so that even handkerchiefs and aprons that had touched him were taken to the sick, and their illnesses were cured and the evil spirits left them.

This section gives a brief summary of Paul's long period of ministry in Ephesus, covering both his testimony to Christ (vv. 8-10) and the miracles accomplished through him (vv. 11-12).

19:8 According to his customary pattern, his witness began in the synagogue. He had already made a preliminary appearance in the Ephesian synagogue and had been asked to stay (cf. 18:19f.). Now he fulfilled the invitation, returning for a longer presentation of Christ, speaking "boldly" there as Apollos had before him (cf. 18:26). The Ephesian Jews seem to have been open to his witness because he was able to debate with them about the kingdom of God for a period of three months before opposition arose.

---

[15]See R. P. C. Hanson, *The Acts*, NCB (Oxford: Clarendon, 1967), 190f.

19:9 Not all the Jews resisted Paul but only a group within the synagogue who became hardened in their disbelief, maligning the message of Jesus the Messiah as the true "Way" for God's people. Some of the Jews had become Christian believers, and Paul took them with him and moved to another location for presenting his testimony. The new site was the lecture hall of Tyrannus. We know nothing of Tyrannus, whether he was the owner of the building or a teacher who taught there. If the latter, one wonders if his students saw him as living up to his name, "the Tyrant." The Western text adds to v. 9 that Paul taught there between the fifth and the tenth hour, i.e., between eleven a.m. and four p.m. This is altogether plausible since these hours would constitute the heat of the day when most Asians took an extensive siesta. The hall would likely have been vacant at such a time, and Paul would have taken a break from his own trade during this period (cf. 20:34).

19:10 Since it was a public setting, the new site offered the opportunity to reach Greeks as well as Jews, thus affording all the inhabitants of Asia the chance to hear the gospel. Luke said that the witness in the hall of Tyrannus continued for a period of two years. When this is added to the initial three months in the synagogue plus the "little longer" of v. 22, one arrives at the three years or so Paul later gave as the length of his Ephesian ministry (20:31).

That Paul made no definitive statement to the Ephesian synagogue about turning exclusively to the Gentiles is noteworthy. A number of the Ephesian Jews did become disciples, and Paul seems to have continued his witness to the Jews there after moving from the synagogue (v. 10; cf. 20:21). The Jews of Ephesus were evidently seriously divided over Christ. On the one hand, there were those who became believers. On the other, there were those who strongly opposed Paul. It would indeed be some of these "Asian Jews" who would provoke mob action against Paul in Jerusalem (cf. 21:27f.).[16]

19:11-12 The other aspect of Paul's ministry in Ephesus involved the miracles God worked through him. Luke described these as being "extraordinary," which is something of an understatement. The people would take cloths Paul had touched and carry them to the sick for healing. The words used for the cloths are both Latin loan-words, and their meaning is not absolutely clear. One is *soudaria*, which could refer either to handkerchiefs (as the NIV) or to "sweat bands" tied around the head. The other, *simikinthia*, are variously seen as aprons tied around the waist or towels used for wiping off perspiration. Whichever translation is followed, the basic idea is the same. The people believed that even the

---

[16]See R. C. Tannehill, *The Narrative Unity of Luke-Acts* (Minneapolis: Fortress, 1990), 2:234f.

cloths that had touched the apostle's body had healing efficacy, and Luke indicated that such was indeed the case.

This practice often strikes the modern mind as too close to the relic worship that plagued the medieval church. It is, however, present in other New Testament miracle traditions—the healing hem of Jesus' garment (Mark 5:27-34; 6:56) and the healing shadow of Peter (Acts 5:15). Perhaps it is to be viewed as God's accommodation to the mind-set of the people of that age. In any event, the miracles wrought by the apostles are never presented as ends in themselves but always as opportunities, assistance to faith and commitment. That is true in the present instance. The power of God manifest in Paul's miracles ultimately led to the Ephesians' overcoming their magic and superstition (cf. 19:17-20).

There was a final aspect to Paul's Ephesian ministry which Luke did not elaborate but which can be gleaned from Paul's letters. It was a period of extensive interaction with his churches elsewhere. This is particularly true of Corinth. First Corinthians was written from Ephesus, and during this period Paul seems to have made a brief, unpleasant visit to Corinth to deal with the troubles in that congregation (2 Cor 2:1). A number of scholars would date Paul's Prison Epistles from his Ephesian ministry, but this is predicated upon Paul's having been imprisoned in Ephesus, a matter that is open to serious question.[17] Many scholars would see Galatians as being written during the course of Paul's Ephesian ministry. This was also the period during which Paul began to organize his collection for Jerusalem (cf. 1 Cor 16:1-4).[18] In all it was a period of extensive activity, not just in the city of Ephesus itself but throughout Paul's mission in the Greek world.

4. Paul's Encounter with False Religion in Ephesus (19:13-20)

The example of Paul's genuine miracle-working is followed by two episodes that involve false attempts to accomplish the miraculous. The first relates the unsuccessful attempt of a group of Jewish exorcists to use the name of Jesus in their practice (vv. 13-16). The second shows the triumph of the gospel over magic and the occult (vv. 17-20).

---

[17]See G. S. Duncan, "Were Paul's Imprisonment Epistles Written from Ephesus?" *ExpTim* 67 (1955-56): 163-66. Certain references in Paul's letters indicate the possibility of an Ephesian imprisonment: the "wild beasts" he fought with in Ephesus (1 Cor 15:32), the "deadly peril" he faced in Ephesus (2 Cor 1:8-10), and the "far more imprisonments" (RSV) of 2 Cor 11:23. T. W. Manson does not agree with the hypothesis of an Ephesian imprisonment but sees Philippians as written in the course of Paul's Ephesian ministry. He argues that Philippians was not written from prison ("St. Paul in Ephesus: The Date of the Epistle to the Philippians," *BJRL* 23 [1939]: 182-200).

[18]See comments on 20:3-4 for a discussion of Paul's collection and Luke's strange silence on the matter.

(1) Jewish Exorcists (19:13-16)

[13]Some Jews who went around driving out evil spirits tried to invoke the name of the Lord Jesus over those who were demon-possessed. They would say, "In the name of Jesus, whom Paul preaches, I command you to come out." [14]Seven sons of Sceva, a Jewish chief priest, were doing this. [15][One day] the evil spirit answered them, "Jesus I know, and I know about Paul, but who are you?" [16]Then the man who had the evil spirit jumped on them and overpowered them all. He gave them such a beating that they ran out of the house naked and bleeding.

19:13 Paul's miracles had an impact on the wrong element as well as those genuinely seeking his help. Much as Simon Magus had been enamored with Philip's miracle-working, a group of itinerant Jewish exorcists had observed how Paul drove out evil spirits by invoking the name of Jesus and undertook to do the same themselves. In the Greco-Roman world, Jewish exorcists were held in high esteem for the venerability of their religion and the strangeness of their Hebrew incantations. Magicians and charlatans were omnipresent in the culture, offering various cures and blessings by their spells and incantations, all for a financial consideration. The more exotic the incantation, the more effective it was deemed to be.

A number of magical papyri from the ancient world have been discovered. These consist of various spells that often invoke the names of foreign gods and employ various kinds of gibberish. In the Paris collection of magical papyri, various Old Testament terms are found, such as Iao (for Yahweh), Abraham, and Sabaoth, terms which would have sounded exotic to Greeks and Romans. One spell reads, "I abjure thee by Jesus, the God of the Hebrews." Another from the same papyrus reads, "Hail, God of Abraham, hail, God of Isaac, hail, God of Jacob, Jesus Chrestus, Holy Spirit, Son of the Father."[19] Ancient magicians were syncretists and would borrow terms from any religion that sounded sufficiently strange to be deemed effective. These Jewish exorcists of Ephesus were only plying their trade. Paul's "spell" in Jesus' name seemed effective for him, so they gave it a try.

19:14 The attempt backfired. The group that made it were seven in number and are described as the sons of a Jewish high priest named Sceva (v. 14). The reference to Sceva's high priesthood creates a problem. Josephus lists all the names of the Jewish high priests up to the fall of the temple, and none is named Sceva. Evidently the scribes of the Western text were the first to note this, for they altered the text to simply read

---

[19]Both from the Paris papyrus 574, cited in K. Lake and H. J. Cadbury, eds., *The Beginnings of Christianity*, Part 1: *The Acts of the Apostles*, vol. 4: *English Translation and Commentary* (London: Macmillan, 1933), 241.

"priest," not "high priest."[20] More recent scholars have taken other routes to solve the problem, such as arguing that Sceva was not a Jewish but a pagan high priest.[21] Now it is true that the same term, "high priest" (*archiereus*), was often used in pagan cults, indeed in the imperial cult at Ephesus; but Luke plainly described *this* high priest as *Jewish*. Perhaps the key is that Sceva belonged to one of the priestly families from whom the high priests were drawn, i.e., he belonged to the high priestly "circle."[22] Perhaps Sceva or those who claimed to be his sons made a false claim to a high priestly lineage in order to enhance their reputation. As high priest, the only one who could enter the holy of holies, he would have been deemed to have extraordinary powers among those who practiced the magical arts.

19:15-16 Whoever these would-be exorcists were, their attempt to invoke Jesus' name failed. It is interesting that the targeted demon, not Paul, was responsible for their undoing. Luke must have enjoyed writing this episode. It is filled with humor. Upon their abjuration, the demon responded: "Jesus I *know* [*ginōskō*], and Paul I *respect* [*epistamai*], but who are you?" (author's translation). As so often with the exorcisms performed by Jesus, the demon *confessed* Jesus and even acknowledged that the power of Jesus worked through Paul. He was, however, not about to yield any turf to these seven. They had no power over him whatever. He turned on them with a vengeance, overpowered them, and sent them running naked from the house.[23] With the extreme sense of modesty characteristic of Judaism, the nakedness of the Jewish exorcists was almost symbolic of their total humiliation in the incident.

Two lessons emerge from the story. For one, Christianity has nothing to do with magic. The name of Jesus is no magical incantation. The power of Jesus drives out the demonic, and his Spirit only works through those who, like Paul, confess him and are committed to him. Second, the demon did confess the power of Jesus over him, "Jesus I know." Compare Jas 2:19, "Even the demons believe and shudder." The people of

---

[20]See E. Delebecque, "La Mésaventure des fils de Scévas selon ses deux Versions (Actes 19, 13-20)," *RSPT* 66 (1982): 225-32. W. A. Strange even argues for the Western text as having the original reading at this point ("The Sons of Sceva and the Text of Acts 19:14," *JTS* 38 [1987]: 97-106).

[21]See B. E. Taylor, "Acts xix.14," *ExpTim* 57 (1945-46): 222.

[22]See B. A. Mastin, "Scaeva the Chief Priest," *JTS* 27 (1976): 405-12.

[23]In v. 16 the Greek text literally has the demon overpowering them "both" (ἀμφοτέρων). This has led to various attempted solutions: that only two sons did the exorcism—G. M. Lee, "The Seven Sons of Sceva (Acts 19:13-16)," *Bib* 51 (1970): 237—or that "both" refers to the names of Jesus and Paul—C. Lattey, "A Suggestion on Acts xix.16," *ExpTim* 36 (1924-25): 381f. The simplest solution is the observation that in koine Greek, ἀμφοτέρων is often used with the meaning *all*—not just two (H. G. Meechan, "Acts xix.16," *ExpTim* 36 [1924-25]: 477f.).

Ephesus recognized this and extolled the powerful name of Jesus as a result (v. 17). What was true for them is still true. In the name of Jesus is all the power needed to drive out the demonic forces in every age.

(2) Overcoming Magic (19:17-20)

[17]When this became known to the Jews and Greeks living in Ephesus, they were all seized with fear, and the name of the Lord Jesus was held in high honor. [18]Many of those who believed now came and openly confessed their evil deeds. [19]A number who had practiced sorcery brought their scrolls together and burned them publicly. When they calculated the value of the scrolls, the total came to fifty thousand drachmas. [20]In this way the word of the Lord spread widely and grew in power.

19:17-18 The demon's acknowledgment of Jesus and the reversal of power on the unauthorized exorcists had its effect on the Ephesians. Obviously the name of Jesus was powerful and not to be toyed with. A reverent fear seized them, and they magnified the name of the Lord Jesus. For some it taught an even more profound lesson. These were Christians who had delved in the magical arts before their conversion who now came and openly confessed their former deeds (v. 18).[24] On their part this was more than a confession of former ways. It was a commitment to forsake such practices altogether.

Ephesus was reputed as a center for magic. The famous statue of Artemis, the centerpiece of her temple, was noted for the mysterious terms engraved on the crown, girdle, and feet of the image. Referred to as the "Ephesian scripts," this magical gibberish was considered to have great power.[25] It was not by accident that Paul's encounter with magic took place in Ephesus, nor is it a surprise that his converts there had been involved in such practices. Magic was part of Ephesian culture. Nor should one question the integrity of these Ephesian Christians who only now openly forsook such ways. Salvation involves a process of growth, of increasing sanctification. And after all, the Ephesian spells were not that remote from the horoscopes and board games that supposedly communicate telepathic messages with which many Christians dabble in our own day.

19:19 The Ephesian abandonment of magic was not without some personal sacrifice. Their magical books must have been much like the

---

[24]Those concerned in v. 18 were evidently already confessing Christians, as the perfect tense πεπιστευκότων would indicate. That the "evil deeds" (πράξεις) were magical arts is indicated both by the context (cf. v. 19) and by the fact that πράξεις was a technical term for magic spells. Likewise, in v. 19, περίεργα was a technical term for magic arts/sorcery. See A. Deissmann, *Bible Studies* (Edinburgh: T & T Clark, 1901), 323, n. 5.

[25]See B. M. Metzger, "St. Paul and the Magicians," *Princeton Seminary Bulletin* 38 (1944): 27-30.

papyrus collections that have been unearthed and are now on display in museums in Paris, Berlin, Rome, and London. All ancient books were expensive, but magical collections brought a considerable premium. Luke estimated the value of those burned in Ephesus at 50,000 pieces of silver. If the piece of silver concerned is the drachma, the most common Greek silver coin, that would come to about $35,000 in current silver value.[26] Translated into terms of living standards, however, the sum was greater still, since the drachma was an average day's wage.

19:20 Verse 20 provides a summary of Paul's Ephesian ministry, much like the summaries at 6:7 and 12:24, which also refer to the growth of the word.[27] The word bore fruit as more and more people responded in faith to the preaching of Paul and to the witness of the Ephesian Christians through such examples as their personal sacrifice in the public burning of their magical books. As a summary v. 20 provides a closure to Luke's treatment of Paul's Ephesian witness. Now, toward the end of his Ephesian period, two matters remain to be related: a major decision regarding Paul's future (vv. 21-22) and a final tumultuous episode involving the temple of Artemis (vv. 23-41).

5. Paul's Determination to Go to Jerusalem (19:21-22)

²¹After all this had happened, Paul decided to go to Jerusalem, passing through Macedonia and Achaia. "After I have been there," he said, "I must visit Rome also." ²²He sent two of his helpers, Timothy and Erastus, to Macedonia, while he stayed in the province of Asia a little longer.

19:21 While in Ephesus, toward the end of his ministry there, Paul made a major decision. He determined to conclude his mission in the east and to move farther westward to Rome. The best commentary on this passage is Paul's own discussion of his plans in Rom 15, which was written from Corinth probably within a year or so of this point in the Ephesian ministry. There Paul spoke of his desire to carry on a mission in Spain and the western portion of the empire, probably hoping that Rome would sponsor him in the undertaking (Rom 15:24,28). As in Acts 19:21, he explained that his route must first take him to Jerusalem. Acts is silent about the reason for going first to Jerusalem, but Paul explained to the Romans that a collection for the Jerusalem Christians necessitated his going there before proceeding to Rome (Rom 15:25-31).[28] This also

---

[26]The Attic drachma contained 67.5 grains of silver, or approximately 14 percent of a troy ounce. With silver at $5 a troy ounce, the drachma would contain about 70 cents in silver value.

[27]It might also be noted that the recurrence of the phrase "word of the Lord" in vv. 10, 20 form a bracket, with vv. 10-20 exemplifying this two-year portion of his Ephesian ministry.

[28]The collection is discussed in the commentary on 20:4.

explains the reference to his visiting Macedonia and Achaia in Acts 19:21. Paul made it a point to revisit and strengthen his congregations, but in this particular instance his epistles reveal that he was particularly preoccupied with the collection on this final visit to Macedonia and Achaia.

Paul's decision to go to Rome marks a major transition in the story line of Acts. From this point on, the narrative will continually drive toward Rome as Paul's final destination. For the more immediate context of Acts, his determination to go to Jerusalem begins an additional emphasis, his journey to Jerusalem, which occupies Acts 20:1–21:16. In many ways it parallels Jesus, "who resolutely set out for Jerusalem" (Luke 9:51). Throughout Acts 20:1–21:16 is an ominous note concerning what awaited Paul in Jerusalem, just as there was for Jesus in the city that "kills the prophets" (Luke 13:33f.).

19:22 Paul sent two of his coworkers ahead into Macedonia to prepare for his own coming. Timothy was last mentioned in 18:5, where he had joined Paul at Corinth. It is quite possible that he accompanied Paul with Priscilla and Aquilla to Ephesus (18:18) and remained there. Erastus was a Corinthian and is mentioned in Paul's greetings in both Rom 16:23 and 2 Tim 4:20. Whether or not this is the same Erastus referred to on a paving stone excavated at Corinth is open to question.[29] The primary mission of these two in Macedonia likely was in connection with Paul's collection for Jerusalem.[30]

6. Opposition to Paul by the Craftsmen of Ephesus (19:23-41)

In direct opposition to the Ephesian Christians, who were willing to make a monetary sacrifice for their faith, were the pagan craftsmen of Ephesus, who found Paul's witness to be damaging their financial interests. They succeeded in provoking a considerable public demonstration against Paul. The remainder of chap. 19 is devoted to this incident, which consists of three scenes: the instigation of the riot by Demetrius (vv. 23-27), the uproar in the theater (vv. 28-34), and the pacification of the crowd by the city clerk (vv. 35-41).[31]

---

[29] See commentary on Acts 18:5-8. See also H. J. Cadbury, "Erastus of Corinth," *JBL* 50 (1931): 42-58; W. Miller, "Who Was Erastus?" *BibSac* 88 (1931): 342-46.

[30] For the view that Paul was imprisoned in Ephesus about this time, see W. Michaelis, "The Trial of St. Paul at Ephesus," *JTS* 29 (1928): 368-75; G. S. Duncan, "Paul's Ministry in Asia—the Last Phase," *NTS* 3 (1957): 211-18.

[31] For a slightly different outline, which sees the phrase "Great is Artemis" as the literary dividing mark, see E. S. Fiorenza, "Miracles, Mission, and Apologetics: An Introduction," in *Aspects of Religious Propaganda in Judaism and Early Christianity* (Notre Dame, Ind.: Notre Dame Press, 1976), 16f.

(1) Instigation of a Riot by Demetrius (19:23-27)

[23]About that time there arose a great disturbance about the Way. [24]A silver-smith named Demetrius, who made silver shrines of Artemis, brought in no little business for the craftsmen. [25]He called them together, along with the workmen in related trades, and said: "Men, you know we receive a good income from this business. [26]And you see and hear how this fellow Paul has convinced and led astray large numbers of people here in Ephesus and in practically the whole province of Asia. He says that man-made gods are no gods at all. [27]There is dan-ger not only that our trade will lose its good name, but also that the temple of the great goddess Artemis will be discredited, and the goddess herself, who is wor-shiped throughout the province of Asia and the world, will be robbed of her divine majesty."

19:23-24 Throughout the Ephesian narrative, Luke referred to Chris-tianity as "the Way." In 18:26 Priscilla and Aquilla explained "the Way" more fully to the somewhat deficient Christian Apollos (cf. v. 25). In 19:9 some of the Jews in the Ephesian synagogue opposed Paul's message as being a valid "way" for them. Here in v. 23 a new resistance to the Way arises, this time from the pagan worshipers of Artemis. The whole inci-dent was instigated by one of the silversmiths of Ephesus named Dem-etrius. His own trade consisted of fabricating silver shrines of Artemis, i.e., silver replicas of the temple of Artemis for which Ephesus was renowned. The manufacture of such shrines was a common practice. Pil-grims would purchase them for use in their own home altars or as a votive offering to be presented to the temple. Replicas of the Ephesian temple of Artemis have been unearthed; they usually were made of terra cotta.[32] None has yet been found in silver, though silver images of the goddess Artemis have been discovered as well as numerous silver coins bearing an image of the temple.[33] That no silver shrines have been located is likely because their considerable metallic value would have made them a prime target for the melting pots of looters through the centuries.

The temple of Artemis was indeed a hub of Ephesian economic life. It was an impressive building, some 165 feet by 345 feet in dimension and built on a platform 240 by 420 feet. The entire edifice was elaborately

---

[32]E. C. Hicks argued that Demetrius was not a craftsman but a "vestryman" of the temple, the term νεωποίος (vestryman) being confused in the tradition for ναοὺς ποιῶν (temple-maker) ("Demetrius the Silversmith: An Ephesian Study," *The Expositor* 41 [1890]: 401-22).

[33]For an example of a bronze image of the mother goddess from the second or first cen-tury B.C., see E. D. Reeder, "The Mother of the Gods and a Hellenistic Bronze Matrix," *American Journal of Archaeology* 91 (1987): 423-40. For the image of the Artemis temple on coins, see L. J. Kreitzer, "A Numismatic Clue to Acts 19:23-41. The Ephesian Cistophori of Claudius and Agrippina," *JSNT* 30 (1987): 59-70.

adorned in brilliant colors and gold leaf. The altar area was 20 feet square and contained a massive image of the goddess with a veiled head, with animals and birds decorating her head and lower body and numerous breasts from her waist to her neck.[34] The animals and breasts were symbolic of her status as the ancient Asian Mother Goddess, the goddess of nature who was believed to protect and preserve the fecundity of all living things.

In Ephesus the worship of the goddess centered around the Artemision, a week in the spring dedicated to the goddess. The highlight of the festivities was a solemn processional in which the image of the goddess was carried through the streets between the theater and the temple. Throughout the week there were numerous events, including ritual plays and dances. In former times the primary attendants of the goddess were self-emasculated priests, but there is some question whether the Romans allowed such practices in the cult of Paul's day.[35] Artemis worship was not confined to Ephesus. There was a sanctuary in Rome also and a similar festival there every April. All told there were at least thirty-three shrines to the mother goddess throughout the Roman Empire, and it was perhaps the most popular cult of all. Ephesus was considered to be *the* center of the cult, and pilgrims flocked from all over the empire to worship at its famous temple, especially during the spring Artemision. Economics and religion were closely bound. The temple received lavish votive offerings from the devotees of the mother goddess. In fact, so wealthy was it that it became the principal financial institution of Asia, receiving deposits and making loans.[36]

19:25 It was not by accident then that Demetrius mixed economics and religion in his appeal to his fellow craftsmen. In Ephesus the two were closely linked. Luke left no doubt that Demetrius's real concern was the damage Paul's preaching was doing to his economic interests. Still, as a skilled demagogue Demetrius was quick to bring religion and patriotism into the picture, which were much more prone to get the public attention. Note that he began by assembling all his fellow craftsmen and the workers who assisted them. To them he laid out the real issue: "We receive a good income from this business" (v. 25).[37]

---

[34]For a full discussion of the archaeology of the temple, see *Beginnings*, vol. 5: *Additional Notes* (London: Macmillan, 1933), 251-56; R. Tonneau, "Ephèse au Temps de Saint Paul," *RB* 38 (1929): 5-34.

[35]For a full discussion of the Artemis cult, see Tonneau, "Ephèse," 321-59.

[36]For the economic dimensions of the Artemis cult see S. E. Johnson, "The Apostle Paul and the Riot in Ephesus," *LThQ* 14 (1979): 79-88.

[37]The Western text has Demetrius address the group as "my fellow craftsmen," adding an additional nuance of group mentality (E. Delebecque, "La Revolte des Orfèvres à Ephèse et ses deux Versions [Actes des Apôtres xix, 24-40]," *RevThom* 83 [1983]: 419-29.

19:26-27 He then presented the threat. "It is this fellow Paul," probably said with a sneer, "who is causing all the trouble" (author's paraphrase). Paul was said to be leading astray (literally, "seducing") all the people in Ephesus and throughout Asia, denying that idols were real gods. One only needs to refer to Paul's Areopagus speech (cf. 17:29) to realize that this was indeed the case. If the people took Paul's message seriously, Demetrius's sales would plummet. Knowing that this rational appeal probably would not suffice, Demetrius then appealed to their emotions. Paul was said to be endangering religion, discrediting the reputation of Artemis, robbing her of her greatness. In his reference to her cult being spread throughout the whole world there was an implicit appeal to civic pride: "The great temple of Artemis is here in Ephesus. Its reputation through all the world is based on the fame of this temple. To attack Artemis is to attack Ephesus" (author's paraphrase).[38]

In all fairness to Demetrius, his argument was not without solid foundation. Paul did preach forcefully against idolatry and was indeed a threat to anyone who made a living from idols. He was likewise a genuine threat to the Artemis cult. He considered not only her images but the goddess herself as "no god at all." But one should not miss the real point of Demetrius's opposition. It was not his piety that was offended but his pocketbook. For Paul to hold his sessions in the hall of Tyrannus was one thing. People could listen to his teachings all they wanted. But when those teachings began to have ramifications for the town economy, that was quite another matter. It may well have been around the time of the spring Artemision that Paul's attack on idolatry became most vehement.[39] If so, the craftsmen's ire is understandable. It would be equivalent to someone's standing at the entrance of Churchill Downs in my own hometown during Derby week and preaching against horse racing. The gospel is always at its most controversial when it comes into conflict with economic interests.

(2) Uproar in the Theater (19:28-34)

[28]When they heard this, they were furious and began shouting: "Great is Artemis of the Ephesians!" [29]Soon the whole city was in an uproar. The people seized Gaius and Aristarchus, Paul's traveling companions from Macedonia, and rushed as one man into the theater. [30]Paul wanted to appear before the crowd,

---

[38]That Ephesus did not take threats to the Artemis cult lightly is evidenced by an inscription found there, dating from several centuries B.C., which pronounces death on forty-five people from Sardis who maltreated an Ephesian embassy from the temple of Artemis. See F. Sokolowski, "A New Testimony on the Cult of Artemis of Ephesus," *HTR* 58 (1965): 427-31.

[39]This is likely on the basis of the mention of Paul's sending Timothy in v. 22. If that is the sending referred to in 1 Cor 16:10, then the time is the spring, as Paul's reference to Pentecost in 1 Cor 16:8 would indicate.

but the disciples would not let him. [31]Even some of the officials of the province, friends of Paul, sent him a message begging him not to venture into the theater.

[32]The assembly was in confusion: Some were shouting one thing, some another. Most of the people did not even know why they were there. [33]The Jews pushed Alexander to the front, and some of the crowd shouted instructions to him. He motioned for silence in order to make a defense before the people. [34]But when they realized he was a Jew, they all shouted in unison for about two hours: "Great is Artemis of the Ephesians!"

19:28-31 Demetrius's appeal had the desired effect, with all the craftsmen running forth and shouting, "Great is Artemis of the Ephesians!" Note that it was his appeal to religious and civic pride that was picked up. They were not shouting "our business is in danger," even if that was the real issue. A crowd quickly formed and joined in the chant. Two of Paul's traveling companions from Macedonia were seized. One was Aristarchus, from Thessalonica according to Acts 20:4. Gaius, a common name, is likely not the one mentioned in Acts 20:4, who is said to have come from Derbe, which was not in Macedonia.[40] The two probably were seized in lieu of Paul, who was not present. Although he would have liked to have addressed the crowd, his fellow Christians realized the extreme danger and held him back. Likewise, the Asiarchs sent Paul an urgent message not to venture into the mob (v. 31). The exact role of the Asiarchs is not entirely clear, but their existence is well documented on numerous inscriptions found throughout Asia. Their primary role seems to have been connected with the maintenance of the imperial cult in Asia.[41] Significantly, they are described as Paul's "friends," indicating that Paul was well-respected by his fellow Roman citizens in high places. Their gesture in this instance was entirely friendly because they were concerned for Paul's personal safety.

The mob rushed into the theater, the largest public building in Ephesus (v. 29). It was an open-air amphitheater, 495 feet in diameter, built onto the western slope of Mt. Pion. Its seating capacity has been estimated at 24,500. Town meetings were held there, and since the technical term for town meeting (*dēmos*) occurs in vv. 30,33, it could be that this was considered a sort of emergency meeting of the popular assembly. The term *dēmos* is often used, however, in the general sense of "the populace"; and since this occasion was so unruly, the NIV probably is correct in translating it "crowd." The same applies to the term *assembly* (*ekklēsia*), which

---

[40]The scribes evidently sought to make these the same, some ancient manuscripts having "Macedonia" in 19:29 in the singular, thus making only Aristarchus a Macedonian. Others alter Derbe in 20:4 to Doub(e)rios, a town in Macedonia.

[41]Asiarchs were evidently elected for one-year terms, there being one for each city where there was an imperial shrine, which would make for three or four in Paul's day. See *Beginnings* 5:256-62.

occurs in v. 32.[42] Although this is the usual term for a gathering of the
populace, a town meeting, the picture here is of an unruly gathering, not
a formally constituted assembly.

19:32-34 The scene was one of utter confusion, some shouting one
thing, some another. The majority had merely succumbed to mob mentality and did not know what was going on (v. 32). The scene with Alexander the Jew only added to the confusion. What was his role, and why
did the Jews push him forward to address the crowd?[43] Very likely it was
to disassociate the Jews from the Christians. The Jews wanted the crowd
to know that *they* had done nothing to impugn Artemis, that they were no
threat to the Ephesian cult. Whatever his purpose in getting before the
crowd, Alexander had no opportunity to speak. His voice was drowned
out by the din of the incessant chant "Great is Artemis of the Ephesians."
This went on for two hours. Only the city clerk prevented the rally from
developing into a full riot.

(3) Pacification by the City Clerk (19:35-41)

[35]The city clerk quieted the crowd and said: "Men of Ephesus, doesn't all the
world know that the city of Ephesus is the guardian of the temple of the great
Artemis and of her image, which fell from heaven? [36]Therefore, since these facts
are undeniable, you ought to be quiet and not do anything rash. [37]You have
brought these men here, though they have neither robbed temples nor blasphemed our goddess. [38]If, then, Demetrius and his fellow craftsmen have a grievance against anybody, the courts are open and there are proconsuls. They can
press charges. [39]If there is anything further you want to bring up, it must be settled in a legal assembly. [40]As it is, we are in danger of being charged with rioting
because of today's events. In that case we would not be able to account for this
commotion, since there is no reason for it." [41]After he had said this, he dismissed
the assembly.

19:35-36 Alexander may not have been able to seize the crowd's
attention. The town clerk, however, had no difficulty quieting the commotion. He was the chief administrative officer of the city. He presided over
both the council of city magistrates and the public assembly and was the
liaison officer between the city and the Roman provincial administra-

---

[42]Ἐκκλησία is the term used throughout the NT for the Christian assembly, the church.
Behind the NT usage, however, stands not the Greek town meeting but the LXX rendering of
the Hebrew term *qahal* (the "called out" people of God) by the Greek ἐκκλησία.

[43]The Western text has the crowd "pull down" Alexander in place of "prompting" him in
v. 33. It is probably best not to attempt an identification of this Alexander with the copper-
smith of the Pastorals (1 Tim 1:20; 2 Tim 4:14). Alexander was a common name. For the
view that the Demetrius episode has as its purpose to identify with Judaism and its privileges
within the Roman rule, see R. F. Stoops, Jr., "The Social Context of Acts 19:23-41," *JBL*
108 (1989): 73-91.

tion.[44] His main concern was that the disturbance would make an adverse impression on the Roman officials, possibly leading to restrictions on their self-governing privileges. In order to pacify the crowd, he began by assuring them that Artemis was under no real threat (v. 35). "Doesn't all the world know that the city of Ephesus is the guardian of the temple of the great Artemis and of her image, which fell from heaven?"[45] What earthly power could threaten her? The clerk's reference to an "image . . . from heaven" probably meant a meteorite. Meteorites were often associated with the worship of the Mother Goddess. The most famous of these was the sacred stone taken from Pessinus to Rome in 204 B.C. A meteorite also seems to have been associated with the cult of the Taurian Artemis.[46] Although there is no evidence beyond this text for such a sacred stone being connected with the Ephesian cult, it is altogether likely that one existed, given this common association of the mother goddess with a "stone from heaven."

19:37 Having assured the Ephesians that their cult was in no real danger, the clerk then dealt with the legal ramifications of the riot. He first pointed out that the two Christians whom they had seized were not guilty of any crime. They had not blasphemed the goddess or robbed the temple (v. 37). Probably by the latter was meant that they had not robbed the temple of the respect due it. If there was any illegality involved, it was not on the part of the Christians but rather of the Ephesians. They were running the risk of being charged with unlawful assembly.

19:38-39 The clerk then outlined the two primary legal avenues Demetrius and his fellow craftsmen could follow if they had any grievances against the Christians. There was the provincial court conducted by the Roman proconsul on set days (v. 38). There was also the regular town assembly (*ekklēsia*, v. 39). This mob might represent more than the usual turnout for a regular meeting of the *dēmos* in the theater, but this was not a regular day for the town meeting and was certainly not being conducted in an orderly fashion.[47]

---

[44]See A. N. Sherwin-White, *Roman Society and Roman Law in the New Testament* (Oxford: Clarendon, 1963), 86f.

[45]The term "guardian of the temple" (νεωκόρος) was a term often used for a city renowned for its temple. Josephus, for instance, spoke of Israel as God's temple keeper (*War* 5.378). See F. Filson, "Ephesus and the New Testament," *BA* 8 (1945): 80. The terminology of θεός/θεά used in Acts 19:27,37 for Artemis fits the known usage for the Ephesian cult. See S. M. Baugh, "Phraseology and the Reliability of Acts," *NTS* 36 (1990): 290-94.

[46]See F. F. Bruce, *Commentary on the Book of Acts*, NIC (Grand Rapids: Eerdmans, 1977), 397f.

[47]According to Chrysostom (*Hom.* 42:2), the Ephesian ἐκκλησία met three times a month.

19:40-41 The clerk then clinched his argument. The Ephesians were running the danger of being charged with insurrection, since they really had no legally valid basis for their unruly behavior (v. 40). A subtlety occurs in the text at this point. A rather rare word occurs in vv. 27,40, the verb meaning *to be in danger, to be running a risk (kindyneuō)*. In v. 27 Demetrius argued that Paul was a danger to Ephesus. In v. 40 the clerk clarified where the real danger lay—not from Paul but from the unruly Ephesians. The clerk's counsel carried the day. He dismissed the gathering, and the crowd dispersed.

One finds in this episode a theme that will continue to recur in the subsequent narrative of Acts—the innocence of the Christians with respect to the civil law. Paul was never found guilty by any Roman official. On the contrary, even if only implicitly, they pled his case, as with the friendly Asiarchs and the town clerk in this instance.

7. Paul's Journey to Jerusalem (20:1–21:16)

A major portion of the "Ephesian section" of Acts is dominated by a journey motif. Paul concluded his ministry in the churches of Asia, Macedonia, and Achaia (20:1-6). He set out on his final trip to Jerusalem. Awaiting ship at Troas, he restored a youth to life after a fall from an upper-level window (20:7-12). He traveled by sea to Miletus (20:13-16) and sent for the elders of the Ephesian church, to whom he delivered a major farewell address (20:17-38). Resuming his voyage, the last leg of his trip was marked by strong forebodings from Christians along the way of the dangers that awaited him in Jerusalem (21:1-16).

(1) Final Ministry in Macedonia and Achaia (20:1-6)

¹**When the uproar had ended, Paul sent for the disciples and, after encouraging them, said good-by and set out for Macedonia. ²He traveled through that area, speaking many words of encouragement to the people, and finally arrived in Greece, ³where he stayed three months. Because the Jews made a plot against him just as he was about to sail for Syria, he decided to go back through Macedonia. ⁴He was accompanied by Sopater son of Pyrrhus from Berea, Aristarchus and Secundus from Thessalonica, Gaius from Derbe, Timothy also, and Tychicus and Trophimus from the province of Asia. ⁵These men went on ahead and waited for us at Troas. ⁶But we sailed from Philippi after the Feast of Unleavened Bread, and five days later joined the others at Troas, where we stayed seven days.**

20:1-3a Acts 20:1-2 treats Paul's leave-taking in Ephesus and his journey through Macedonia to Corinth in the most summary fashion. The account can be supplemented considerably from 2 Cor 1–7, where Paul discussed the events of the same period. There had been considerable tension with the Corinthian church during the final portion of Paul's Ephesian ministry. Paul seems to have written a rather confrontive letter to that congregation during that period. He described the letter as "painful" and written "with many tears" (2 Cor 2:3f.).[48] Strong opposition to Paul had arisen in the church, and there were attacks on his status as their apostle. In the letter Paul seems to have confronted the opposition directly and severely. The letter was sent by way of Titus, and Paul evidently wanted to hear Titus's report back to him about "how it went" before proceeding himself to Corinth.

At this point the events treated in 2 Cor 1–7 overlap with Acts 20:1-2. Paul took his leave of Ephesus and set out for Macedonia (Acts 20:1). Along the way he hoped that Titus would meet him on his return trip from Corinth with a report on how things went with the letter. He stopped first at Troas and had an opportunity for witness there. His mind was, however, on Corinth. Titus did not join him at Troas, so he moved on to Macedonia—most likely Philippi—in the hopes of intercepting Titus there (2 Cor 2:12f.). There he finally met up with Titus returning from Corinth. Titus brought Paul the joyous news that the letter had had its effect, the offenders had been disciplined, and the church had become reconciled to Paul (2 Cor 2:5-11; 7:5-13). Evidently Paul wrote 2 Corinthians at this point and sent it on ahead of his own coming. Finally he went to Corinth himself. This was the visit referred to in Acts 20:2-3 as his three-month stay in "Greece." It was his final visit to Corinth and probably took place in the winter of A.D. 55–56. During this time he wrote the Roman Epistle.

A major concern of Paul during this period was his collection for the Jerusalem Christians. All of his epistles written during the course of this third missionary period mention this project.[49] Evidently the concept was first put in Paul's mind at the Jerusalem Conference when he was asked to "remember the poor" (Gal 2:10). "The poor" is likely a reference to the Jerusalem Christians (cf. Rom 15:26). Paul already had participated in a relief offering to the mother congregation from the Antioch church (Acts 11:27-30). Now, toward the end of his ministry in Asia, Macedonia, and Greece, Paul determined to put together a major offering from his Gentile churches for the church in Jerusalem. Not only was it to meet a genuine need, but it also was a graphic way of demonstrating the unity in Christ between his Gentile converts and their Jewish Christian brothers and sisters in Jerusalem. The importance the collection held for the apostle is best illustrated in Rom 15:25-29, where he indicated that he was putting

---

[48]This "epistle of tears" is most likely no longer extant, although many scholars feel that 2 Cor 10–13 is a portion of it.

[49]The main texts are Gal 2:10; 1 Cor 16:1-4; 2 Cor 8–9; Rom 15:25-32.

off his visit to Rome and his cherished mission to Spain in order first to deliver the collection to Jerusalem. He was doing this with full awareness that the undertaking involved considerable personal risk from unbelievers and possible rejection from the Jerusalem Christians (Rom 15:31).

20:3b-4 Acts 20:3b-4 should be viewed in light of this collection for Jerusalem. This applies to both Paul's change in travel plans (v. 3b) and the list of his traveling companions (v. 4). He had already experienced opposition from the Corinthian Jews (18:6,12-16), but the danger on the open sea is even better explained if Paul had a considerable amount of money with him.[50] Likewise, the long list of traveling companions given in v. 4 is best seen as the names of the delegates from the Gentile churches who joined Paul both for protection and as official representatives of the churches. In his epistles Paul mentioned his intention to be accompanied to Jerusalem by such representatives of the churches (1 Cor 16:3; 2 Cor 8:18f.). The list in v. 4 would indicate that there was representation from each of the major areas where Paul had established churches. Sopater,[51] Aristarchus,[52] and Secundus came from the Macedonian churches. Gaius[53] and Timothy represented the churches of southern Galatia. Tychicus[54] and Trophimus[55] were the delegates from the churches of Asia.

20:5-6 It is not at all clear from v. 5 whether this whole company of delegates traveled on to Troas ahead of Paul. "These men" possibly refers only to the Asians Tychicus and Trophimus, who went ahead to their native province to seek a ship for the company to travel to Palestine. In any event, Paul traveled to Philippi and spent the Passover there. At this point the "we" narrative resumes. The first-person narration last occurred in the account of Paul's Philippian ministry (16:17), and this may indicate that Luke had stayed behind in Philippi and remained minis-

---

[50]The Western text adds to v. 3 that "the Spirit" bade Paul to return through Macedonia. See E. Delebecque, "Les deux versions du voyage de Saint Paul de Corinthe à Troas (Ac 20, 3-6)," *Bib* 64 (1983): 556-64.

[51]Possibly the Sosipater of Rom 16:21. If so, Sopater may well have represented the church of Corinth since he is listed in the personalia of Romans, which was written from Corinth. (Berea is connected with his father, Pyrrhus.)

[52]For Aristarchus cf. Acts 19:29; 27:2; Col 4:10.

[53]The Western text harmonizes the Gaius of 20:4 with the Macedonian Gaius of 19:29 by changing Derbe to Doub(e)rios, a Macedonian town twenty-five miles from Philippi. Derbe is almost certainly the correct reading, especially since Gaius is paired with Timothy. Both were Lycaonians.

[54]Tychicus was a coworker of Paul mentioned in his later epistles: Col 4:7f.; Eph 6:21f.; 2 Tim 4:12; Titus 3:12.

[55]For Trophimus see Acts 21:29 and 2 Tim 4:20. In v. 4 the Western text has the rather curious reading Eutychus (cf. 20:9) in place of Tychicus and designates the Asians more specifically as "Ephesians."

tering there until this point.[56] After the completion of the Passover, Paul and his companions departed Philippi, sailing from its port of Neapolis. This time the voyage to Troas took five days.[57]

Paul was primarily occupied with his Jerusalem collection during the period covered by Acts 20:1-6. The mystery is why Luke did not mention it. He was certainly aware that Paul took a collection to Jerusalem, for it is mentioned explicitly in Paul's later speech before Felix (24:17). The group that accompanied Paul was almost certainly the collection delegation from the churches. Yet Luke did not mention this, nor did he mention the collection at all in connection with the journey to Jerusalem, which Rom 15:25-28 clearly indicates was undertaken to deliver the gift. Why is Acts silent on the subject?[58] Was there ultimately some problem with the collection?[59] Did Luke deliberately not make much of it because it might have proved an embarrassment for the Jewish Christians in their relations with the Jewish community or for Christian relations with the Roman authorities?[60] Or perhaps were Paul's fears well-founded (Rom 15:31) and the collection not well-received by the Jerusalem Christians?[61] These are unanswerable questions, and any solution would at best be an argument from silence. It is clear, however, what Luke did want to emphasize. He wanted to show how Paul's journey to Jerusalem was as foreboding as that of his master before him, how it ended in chains, but how even in the seeming defeat of his arrest in Jerusalem God turned the events to the

---

[56]Some commentators locate Luke in Corinth on the basis of the "us" in v. 5 and argue that Luke had been sent to Corinth in connection with the collection as "the brother who is praised by all the churches for his service to the gospel" (2 Cor 8:18).

[57]Compare the unusually brief voyage of two days in 16:11f.

[58]Some scholars argue that Acts is not silent on the subject and that the collection of 11:27-30 is Luke's account of Paul's Jerusalem offering. This, however, requires radical revision of the Acts chronology. See C. H. Buck, Jr., "The Collection for the Saints," *HTR* 43 (1950): 1-29; P. S. Minear, "The Jerusalem Fund and Pauline Chronology," *ATR* 25 (1943): 389-96. Equally unlikely is the view that Luke did not know of the collection or that he did not fully understand it (C. R. Bowen, "Paul's Collection and the Book of Acts," *JBL* 42 [1923]: 49-59.

[59]E. B. Allo suggests it may have been seized by brigands or confiscated by the authorities ("La Portée de la Collecte pour Jerusalem dans les Plans de Saint Paul," *RB* 45 [1936]: 529-37.

[60]K. F. Nickle argues that Paul's collection was based on the analogy of the temple tax that was collected from the Jews of the Diaspora. The collection of this tax was carefully regulated by the Romans, and Nickle suggests they might have considered Paul's collection an illegal and unauthorized assessment. Luke would not have wanted to raise this specter, given his apologetic emphasis. See *The Collection* (London: SCM, 1966), 148-51.

[61]Acts 21:20f. reflects James's concern that Paul's association with the Gentiles might be considered an abandonment of the law by the more zealous Jewish Christians. A collection from the Gentile churches might have indeed been coolly received under such circumstances. See D. Georgi, *Die Geschichte der Kollekte des Paulus für Jerusalem* (Hamburg: Evangelischer, 1965), 87-90.

triumph of the gospel, leading Paul to the capital of the empire, the end of
the earth, to bear his witness openly and unhinderedly.

(2) Restoration of Eutychus (20:7-12)

**[7]On the first day of the week we came together to break bread. Paul spoke to
the people and, because he intended to leave the next day, kept on talking until
midnight. [8]There were many lamps in the upstairs room where we were meeting.
[9]Seated in a window was a young man named Eutychus, who was sinking into a
deep sleep as Paul talked on and on. When he was sound asleep, he fell to the
ground from the third story and was picked up dead. [10]Paul went down, threw
himself on the young man and put his arms around him. "Don't be alarmed," he
said. "He's alive!" [11]Then he went upstairs again and broke bread and ate. After
talking until daylight, he left. [12]The people took the young man home alive and
were greatly comforted.**

20:7 Paul and his traveling companions spent a week in Troas (20:6),
evidently awaiting the departure of their ship. On their last day there,
which happened to be a Sunday, Paul met with the Christians for worship.
This is one of the earliest references to Christians meeting for worship on
Sunday, the first day of the week. Christians may have continued to
observe the Jewish Sabbath as well, but eventually the Lord's resurrection
day became the sole day of worship for Christians.

At Troas, aware of his intended departure the next day, Paul hung on
to every minute with the Christians there and spoke well into the night,
even until midnight. There is some question whether this was Saturday
night or Sunday night. If Luke's reckoning was the normal Jewish
method, it would have been Saturday night, since the days were reckoned
as beginning at sunset and running until the following sunset. If Luke was
following Roman reckoning, and this seems to have been the case, days
were reckoned from midnight to midnight, as is our own procedure. It
thus would have been Sunday night, and Paul's projected departure was
Monday morning.[62] In any event, at Troas we are given a glimpse into the
main elements of an early Christian worship service. It was observed on
the first day of the week and consisted of the breaking of bread (the
Lord's Supper) and preaching. That the Lord's Supper was accompanied
by a larger fellowship meal may be indicated by the reference to their
"eating" in v. 11 (cf. 1 Cor 11:20f.).

20:8-9 The story of Eutychus is one of those delightful anecdotes
with which Acts is filled. That Luke intended a gentle touch of humor is

---

[62]For the argument that Luke followed the Jewish method (Saturday night), see W. E. P.
Cotter, "St. Paul's Eucharist," *ExpTim* 39 (1927-28): 235, and R. Staats, "Die Sonntagnachtgottesdienste der Christlichen Frühzeit," *ZNW* 66 (1975): 242-63. For the Roman method
(Sunday) see W. Rordorf, "Sonntagnachtgottesdienste der Christlichen Frühzeit?" *ZNW* 68
(1977): 138-41.

altogether possible. One can sympathize with the lad.[63] A warm spring
evening, a room filled with torches burning up the oxygen supply, a long-
winded preacher going into the wee hours of the morning and probably
long past the lad's normal bedtime—all these factors conspired against
the youth. He probably had taken refuge in the window to catch a breath
of fresh air, fighting his drowsiness. That effort, however, brought disastrous results. He fell asleep, lost his perch, and tumbled from the third
story to the ground below. This, of course, was not a laughing matter. The
fall evidently killed him. It could only be viewed with humor retrospec-
tively in light of its happy ending because through the apostle, God
turned tragedy into joy.

20:10 The story belongs to the category of resurrection miracles,
such as Jesus' raising of the widow's son at Nain (Luke 7:11-15), of Jairus's daughter (Luke 8:49-56), and of Lazarus (John 11:38-44), and of the
restoration of Dorcas through Peter (Acts 9:36-41).[64] There is even a
striking correspondence to the raising of lads by Elijah and Elisha (1 Kgs
17:21; 2 Kgs 4:34f.) when Paul threw himself over the boy's body (v. 10),
just as the prophets had done. In the New Testament, miracles of raising
from the dead present an implicit symbolism of the resurrection. In the
case of Lazarus it is quite explicit. Indeed, in the present case there are
some rather strong linkages with the resurrection. It was Easter time. The
Passover had just ended, the season of Jesus' death and resurrection (v.
6). It was the first day of the week, the day of Jesus' resurrection (v. 7);
and, given the season, Paul may well have been expounding on that event.
The restoration of Eutychus's life was a vivid reminder to the Christians
of Troas that the Jesus whom Paul had been preaching was indeed the resurrection and the life.[65]

20:11-12 We could draw two conclusions to the Eutychus incident.
One focuses on Paul, the other on the lad. The first serves to connect the
incident to the larger narrative of Paul's journey (v. 11). Assured of the

---

[63]Reference to Eutychus as a "young man" is perhaps misleading. The term νεανίας used
in v. 9 can indeed refer to a young man, but in v. 12 he is called a παῖς. Citing Hippocrates,
Philo (*Opif. Mundi* 105) notes that the term παῖς designates a youth between nine and fourteen years of age.

[64]Many interpreters argue that no miracle was intended by this story but that Paul's
remark in v. 10 indicates the lad's life was still in him. The significance of the story is seen
in Paul's "resourcefulness and commonsense" in the face of the crowd's hysteria. See J. E.
Roberts, *The Story of Eutychus*, The Expositor Series 3, 26 (1923): 376-82. Paul's remark in
v. 10, however, is almost surely an indication that the lad's life had returned, and v. 9 states
flatly that he was "picked up dead," not picked up "as if" dead.

[65]In a provocative article B. Tremel argues that the whole of Acts 20:7-12 is penetrated
by a rich symbolism around the brightness of the room and the preaching of Paul, contrasted
by the sleepiness of the lad and his resultant "fall" into darkness and death ("A propos
d'Actes 20, 7-12: Puissance du Thaumaturge ou du Témoin?" *RTP* 112 [1980]: 359-69).

youth's recovery, Paul returned to the upper room, partook of the Lord's Supper with the other Christians, and evidently shared a larger meal with them.[66] He then continued his discourse with them until daybreak. Afterwards he departed, since he would soon need to hasten to Assos to catch his ship (v. 13f.). The second conclusion focuses on Eutychus (v. 12). He was taken home fully recovered. Everyone was immeasurably comforted. It was more than comfort. They were encouraged and strengthened in their faith by what they had witnessed that night.[67]

(3) Voyage to Miletus (20:13-16)

[13]We went on ahead to the ship and sailed for Assos, where we were going to take Paul aboard. He had made this arrangement because he was going there on foot. [14]When he met us at Assos, we took him aboard and went on to Mitylene. [15]The next day we set sail from there and arrived off Kios. The day after that we crossed over to Samos, and on the following day arrived at Miletus. [16]Paul had decided to sail past Ephesus to avoid spending time in the province of Asia, for he was in a hurry to reach Jerusalem, if possible, by the day of Pentecost.

20:13-16 Paul's journey resumed with the collection delegation, including Luke as narrator, setting sail from Troas to Assos (v. 13).[68] Perhaps they took a smaller vessel that ran close to the coast, intending to look for a seagoing ship to Palestine at Miletus. Paul did not at first accompany them but chose to go by foot to Assos, an easy journey of around twenty miles. The boat would have had to round Cape Lectum in order to reach Assos, a longer and more difficult route than the land route. This likely made it possible for Paul to catch up with the boat there. Just why Paul did not depart with the boat at Troas is not specified. He may not have relished the difficult voyage around the Cape, or he may have wished to spend the last possible moment at Troas, or perhaps the incident with Eutychus had delayed him.

The journey from Troas to Miletus is given with exceptional detail. It seems to have taken about five days' sailing time, with each port given representing a day's journey. They evidently put into port each night. The winds usually died during the night, and the rocky coastal area was more

---

[66]Verse 11 seems to reflect two meals, the Lord's Supper (the "breaking of bread") and a further meal, which he "ate" (γεύομαι, "tasted").

[67]The word translated "comforted" in the NIV of v. 12 is παρακαλέω, an important NT word that often means *to encourage, to strengthen*. It is the same verb used in 20:1 for Paul's "encouraging" the disciples at Ephesus and in 20:2 for his speaking words of encouragement to the Macedonians. Paul's encouraging and strengthening of the Christians at Troas was especially through the miracle involving Eutychus.

[68]Like Troas, Assos was located in Mysia. It was south of Troas and somewhat east at the mouth of the gulf of Adramytium.

favorable to daytime sailing.[69] From Assos their voyage took them to Mitylene, the chief city of the island of Lesbos, located on the eastern shore of the island. The next day's voyage took them just offshore of the island of Kios, which was famed as the birthplace of the poet Homer. The following day they passed by the island of Samos, the birthplace of the "founder of mathematics," Pythagoras.[70] On the final day they sailed to Miletus, a major Asian city in Paul's day which lay on the south shore of the Latonian gulf at the mouth of the river Maeander.[71]

Verse 16 presents something of a puzzle, explaining that Paul had decided to avoid stopping at Ephesus in his haste to reach Jerusalem by Pentecost.[72] The next verse then tells how he sent for the elders at Ephesus to come to him at Miletus. Miletus was some thirty miles or so from Ephesus, and the main coastal road was somewhat longer. It has been estimated that the time involved in sending a messenger and for the elders to come would have taken perhaps five days. Saving time would not likely have been the primary factor in Paul's avoiding Ephesus. It may be that it was not safe for him to go to Ephesus at this time (cf. 2 Cor 1:8-11). It also may be that he was tied to his ship's schedule, with Miletus, not Ephesus, as the port of call. Or it may be that Paul simply thought that if he visited Ephesus there would be no way to tear himself away quickly from the Christians there. It would be more expeditious to have the leaders come to him.

(4) Farewell Address to the Ephesian Elders (20:17-35)

[17]From Miletus, Paul sent to Ephesus for the elders of the church. [18]When they arrived, he said to them: "You know how I lived the whole time I was with you, from the first day I came into the province of Asia. [19]I served the Lord with great humility and with tears, although I was severely tested by the plots of the Jews. [20]You know that I have not hesitated to preach anything that would be helpful to you but have taught you publicly and from house to house. [21]I have declared to both Jews and Greeks that they must turn to God in repentance and have faith in our Lord Jesus.

---

[69]See W. Ramsay, *St. Paul the Traveller and Roman Citizen* (1897; reprint, Grand Rapids: Baker, 1987), 293.

[70]Παρεβάλομεν in v. 15 is not altogether clear. It may indicate that they "stopped at" Samos, but more likely it means they "passed by" the island. The Western text adds after "Samos" the words "staying at Trogyllium." This is possibly the original reading. The Trogyllium was a promontory from the mainland adjacent to the southeast side of Samos, forming a narrow passage between the mainland and the island, which was scarcely a mile wide.

[71]See D. Boyd, "Miletus," IDBSup, 597f.

[72]Chronologically, the reference to Pentecost is quite appropriate. Allowing for the seven days of unleavened bread spent in Philippi, the five days to Troas, the week in Troas, and the five days to Miletus, Paul would have arrived in Miletus about halfway between Passover and Pentecost. When Paul arrived in Jerusalem, however, there was no further mention of it being the time of Pentecost.

[22]"And now, compelled by the Spirit, I am going to Jerusalem, not knowing what will happen to me there. [23]I only know that in every city the Holy Spirit warns me that prison and hardships are facing me. [24]However, I consider my life worth nothing to me, if only I may finish the race and complete the task the Lord Jesus has given me—the task of testifying to the gospel of God's grace.

[25]"Now I know that none of you among whom I have gone about preaching the kingdom will ever see me again. [26]Therefore, I declare to you today that I am innocent of the blood of all men. [27]For I have not hesitated to proclaim to you the whole will of God. [28]Keep watch over yourselves and all the flock of which the Holy Spirit has made you overseers. Be shepherds of the church of God, which he bought with his own blood. [29]I know that after I leave, savage wolves will come in among you and will not spare the flock. [30]Even from your own number men will arise and distort the truth in order to draw away disciples after them. [31]So be on your guard! Remember that for three years I never stopped warning each of you night and day with tears.

[32]"Now I commit you to God and to the word of his grace, which can build you up and give you an inheritance among all those who are sanctified. [33]I have not coveted anyone's silver or gold or clothing. [34]You yourselves know that these hands of mine have supplied my own needs and the needs of my companions. [35]In everything I did, I showed you that by this kind of hard work we must help the weak, remembering the words the Lord Jesus himself said: 'It is more blessed to give than to receive.' "

Paul's address to the Ephesian elders is the third and final example in Acts of his speeches during the course of his missionary work. The first, delivered in the synagogue of Pisidian Antioch (13:16-41), was given during the course of his first mission and was to a Jewish audience. The second, delivered before the Athenian Areopagus (17:22-31), was given during his second mission and was to a Gentile audience. The Miletus address was delivered in the course of his third mission and was given before a Christian gathering.[73]

Of all Paul's speeches in Acts, the Miletus address has the most in common with Paul's epistles. There are many parallels both in wording and in general thought. This striking similarity may be due to the fact that this address is not a missionary sermon or a legal defense as with his other addresses in Acts. It is delivered to Christians and thus has more affinity to the epistles, which were also addressed to Christians. In form the address can be characterized as a "farewell address." It is delivered as a conscious final legacy of the apostle to the leaders of the Asian church.

---

[73]For extensive treatments of the Miletus address, see J. Dupont, *Le Discours de Milet: Testament pastoral de Saint Paul (Actes 20:18-36)*, Lectio divina 32 (Paris: Cerf, 1962); H. J. Michel, *Die Abschiedsrede des Paulus an die Kirche, Apg. 20, 17-38* (München: Kösel, 1973); H. Schürmann, "Das Testament des Paulus für die Kirche, Apg. 20, 18-35," in *Unio Christianorum: Festschrift für L. Jager*, ed. O. Schilling and H. Zimmermann (Paderborn: Ferdinand Schöningh, 1962), 108-46.

Paul did not expect to return. As a farewell speech it has much in common with similar speeches in both the Old and New Testaments. Examples are Jacob's legacy to his sons in Gen 49, Joshua's farewell address to Israel in Josh 23–24, and Samuel's farewell to the nation in 1 Sam 12.[74] New Testament examples include Jesus' words to his disciples at the last supper (Luke 22:14-38; John 13–17). The most striking parallels to the Miletus speech are Paul's words to Timothy in 1 Tim 4:1-16 and 2 Tim 3:1–4:8.[75] Certain common features characterize these addresses: the assembling of the family or followers, the note that the speaker will soon depart or die, sometimes an appeal to the personal example of the speaker, exhortations to desired behavior on the part of the hearers, and often a prediction of coming times of trial and difficulty.[76] All of these features are present in Paul's Miletus address. Although delivered specifically to the Ephesian elders, it is a suitable legacy from the apostle for *all* his churches as he left his field of mission and challenged the church leaders to continue in his footsteps.[77]

The Miletus address is not easy to outline. Basically the speech falls into two main portions: Paul's relationship with the Ephesians—his ministry among them, his present plans, and his future prospects (vv. 18-27)—and his exhortation to them for their role as church leaders (vv. 28-35). The following discussion follows a fourfold division: (1) Paul's review of his past example in ministering to them (vv. 18-21), (2) Paul's consideration of his future prospects (vv. 22-27), (3) his warning to the elders to be on guard against future false teachings (vv. 28-31), and (4) a commitment of their ministry to God and final admonition to follow his example (vv. 32-35). Verse 17 provides an introduction to the speech, noting the assembling of the elders in response to Paul's invitation.[78] Paul's speech follows directly.

---

[74]The form is particularly common in the late Jewish literature. Examples are *The Assumption of Moses* and *The Testaments of the Twelve Patriarchs.*

[75]L. R. Donelson argues that the parallels between the Miletus address and the Letters to Timothy reflect an Ephesian tradition of a legacy left to them by Paul ("Cult Histories and the Sources of Acts," *Bib* 68 [1987]: 1-21.

[76]For a full treatment of the farewell discourse form, see J. Munck, "Discours d'adieu dans le Nouveau Testament et dans la littérature biblique," *Aux Sources de la Tradition Chrétienne: Mélanges Maurice Goguel*, ed. O. Cullmann and P. Menoud (Neuchatel: Delachaux et Niestlé, 1950), 155-70.

[77]That the Miletus address marks the culminating point of the entire Pauline mission and is intended as a legacy for the whole postapostolic church is argued by J. Lambrecht, "Paul's Farewell Address at Miletus (Acts 20, 17-38)," in *Les Actes des Apôtres: Traditions, rédaction, theologie*, ed. J. Kremer (Gembloux: Duculot, 1979), 308-37. For a similar view, see O. Knoch, *Die 'Testamente' des Petrus und Paulus* (Stuttgart: KBW, 1973), 32-43; P. R. Tragan, "Les 'Destinataires' du Discours de Milet," *A Cause de l'Evangile* (Paris: Cerf, 1985), 779-98.

[78]Acts is extremely scanty with its information on church organization. At this early stage, how were the Ephesian elders appointed? Perhaps much as in 14:23, with Paul appointing them and the church approving the appointment in a formal commitment service.

PAUL'S PAST EXAMPLE (20:18-21). **20:18-19** The opening section of
Paul's address reminded the elders how Paul had conducted himself during the whole time of his ministry with them (v. 18). He pointed to three
basic characteristics of his ministry. First was the humility that had
marked his service for the Lord (v. 19). Paul's language here is reminiscent of his epistles. He often spoke of "serving" (*douleuō*) the Lord (cf.
1 Thess 1:9; Col 3:24) and described himself as a servant or "bond-slave"
(*doulos*) of Christ (cf. Rom 1:1; Gal 1:10; Phil 1:1). The proper demeanor
of a servant is "humility" (*tapeinophrosynē*), and Paul frequently pointed
to that quality as a major hallmark of the Christian life (Phil 2:3; Col
3:12; Eph 4:2). It is striking that Paul reminded the Ephesian elders of his
trials through the plots of the Jews. The narrative of his Ephesian ministry in Acts does not relate any specific Jewish plot against him, although
such plots occur frequently in the overall story of Paul's mission—at
Pisidian Antioch, Iconium, Lystra, Thessalonica, Berea, and Corinth. The
most recent plot was ultimately responsible for his presence at Miletus at
this time, causing him to change his original plan to sail directly to Syria
from Corinth (20:3).

20:20 A second characteristic of Paul's ministry was the openness of
his proclamation (v. 20). He kept no secrets, held nothing back. Whatever
was true to the gospel and helpful to the faithful, he preached both publicly and from house to house. Mention of public proclamation recalls
Paul's days in the synagogue of Ephesus and the lecture hall of Tyrannus
(19:8f.). The reference to houses most likely is to the house-church meetings of the Ephesian Christians. In contrast, some were not so open in
their witness, i.e., false teachers who advocated hidden and secret doctrines. Paul warned the Ephesian leaders later in his speech that such
would arise to plague their own church (v. 29f.). He reminded them of the
honesty and openness of his own preaching. When one was faithful to the
truth, there was nothing to hide.

20:21 The final characteristic of Paul's ministry was the inclusiveness of his witness. He had preached to everyone, both Jews and Greeks
(v. 21). No one had been left out. This had indeed been the case in Ephesus (19:10). Paul saw his own special calling as being the apostle to the
Gentiles, but he never abandoned the synagogue. Perhaps more clearly
than anyone else in the church of his day, Paul saw the full implications
of his monotheism. God is the God of all. In Christ he reaches out for the
salvation of all who will trust in him. There is no distinction (cf. Rom
3:29f.). There is no room for exclusivism in the gospel in the sense that
the gospel is for Gentiles and Jews, slaves and free, and men and women.
The gospel itself is, however, exclusive in its claims, "for there is no
other name under heaven . . . by which we must be saved" (Acts 4:12).
Salvation is available only in the name of Jesus.

The description of the gospel could hardly be more "Pauline" than as stated in 20:21. It is to repent, to turn from one's former life to God and to "believe," to place one's trust in Jesus.

Commentators sometimes remark that Paul appears to have been on the defensive in his Miletus address. Such was not the case. Paul was not defending his ministry. He was presenting it as an example for the Ephesian leaders to emulate. It is a worthy example for every servant of the Lord: a ministry marked by humility, openness, and inclusiveness and rooted in the gospel.

PAUL'S FUTURE PROSPECTS (20:22-27). **20:22-23** Having reminded the Ephesian leaders of his example during his presence with them, Paul now prepared them for his absence. Paul was leaving them and was on his way to Jerusalem, not knowing what would happen to him there (v. 22). He evidently had first decided to take this course while still in Ephesus (cf. 19:21). He was going to Jerusalem with the collection, and he did indeed have serious misgivings about how it would be received there and was fully aware that the enterprise involved some personal risk (cf. Rom 15:31). Under the compulsion of the Spirit, Paul was going to Jerusalem. On the other hand, the Spirit was warning him that "in every city" hardships, even imprisonment, awaited him (v. 23). Some of these warnings were given through other Christians and are related in the subsequent narrative (cf. 21:4,11). The activity of the Spirit could be seen as contradictory here. On the one hand, Paul was driven on to Jerusalem. On the other hand, he was warned of the extreme risk in going there. These messages of the Spirit were not at odds. Paul was indeed being led to Jerusalem. God had a purpose for his going there. The warnings prepared him for what awaited him in Jerusalem and assured him that whatever happened, God was in it. Paul would undergo severe trials in Jerusalem, but through them he would ultimately bear his witness in Rome, which was his own heart's desire (cf. 19:21; Rom 1:9f.).

20:24 In v. 24 Paul stated the reason he was willing to face the dangers in Jerusalem. He was ready to surrender his life for the gospel. In his epistles Paul often stated his readiness to suffer, even to die, for Christ.[79] The description of his ministry as running a footrace is also common in his letters.[80] The most striking parallel is with 2 Tim 4:7, where the phrase "finished the race" also appears. The race that Paul was running was the ministry he had received from Jesus. That ministry is described as his testimony to the "gospel of God's grace." Oddly, that exact phrase never occurs in the epistles of Paul. One could scarcely summarize the heart of Paul's message better than the "good news of God's grace."

---

[79]Cf. 2 Cor 4:7-12; 6:4-10; 12:9f.; Phil 1:20f.; 2:17; 3:8; Col 1:24.
[80]Cf. 1 Cor 9:24-27; Gal 2:2; Phil 2:16; 3:13f.

20:25-27 Paul now gave his farewell to the Ephesian elders. They would never see his face again (v. 25).[81] Paul was on his way to Jerusalem. Danger awaited him there. Even apart from the danger, Paul had completed his work in the east and now turned to a new mission in the west (cf. Rom 15:23f.). He concluded this portion of the speech with the statement that he was innocent of the blood of all because he had proclaimed the full will of God (v. 26f.). Here he seems to draw from the "watchman" analogy of Ezek 33:1-6.[82] The watchman fulfills his task when he blows the warning trumpet in the face of danger. Once he has sounded his warning, he is no longer responsible for the lives of those he is appointed to warn. Paul had preached the full gospel, the whole will of God. He had called people to repentance. Now the responsibility rested with them. Again this remark is not to be seen so much as Paul's defense of himself as an example to the Ephesian leaders. They were to do what Paul had done before them, herald the gospel and call to repentance. This is the task of a Christian witness, to proclaim the full will of God. Witnesses can do no more. The response is not theirs but the hearer's responsibility.

PAUL'S WARNING OF FUTURE HERESIES (20:28-31). **20:28-31** The third section of Paul's address exhorts the Ephesian leaders to be vigilant shepherds over the flock of God, warning of savage wolves who would arise in the future to prey upon it. The clear function of v. 28 in this appeal is to give a basic charge to the elders to be watchful overseers of their charge. It is important to notice, however, that Paul's first exhortation to the elders called for them to "guard themselves."

A number of details in v. 28 make it perhaps the most discussed part of the entire speech. The first of these has to do with the role of the Holy Spirit, who is described as having "made" or "placed" them as leaders over the flock. The question arises about the manner of appointment. As noted previously (n. 78), Paul may have appointed the first elders himself; but this responsibility soon would have gone over to the congregation if this was indeed not the case from the first. How would the Holy Spirit's activity fit into such a pattern? Most likely the reference here indicates that church office was viewed more functionally than formally. Those

---

[81]The question of whether the Pastoral Epistles indicate that Paul did eventually return to Ephesus is separate from the present text. At this point Paul did not seem to have anticipated further work in the east. Many interpreters (e.g., G. Krodel, *Acts*, ACNT [Minneapolis: Augsburg, 1986], 387) see v. 25 as a reflection of Paul's martyrdom, written after the fact. Others would argue the opposite, noting the evidence of the Pastorals that Paul did eventually return to Ephesus and concluding that Luke's inclusion of this statement reflects his accuracy in preserving Paul's words to the Ephesian elders even though his plans later changed.

[82]See comments on 18:6.

who were recognized by the congregation as having been gifted by the Spirit for a particular role were selected for that responsibility (cf. Eph 4:11f.; also Acts 11:22-26;13:2-3).

A second major issue in v. 28 is the meaning of the word *episkopos*, which is translated "overseer" in the NIV but which has often been translated "bishop." A monarchial bishop ruling over a number of congregations is clearly not in view. Such an organization does not seem to have developed until the second century. In the New Testament, where the term *episkopos* is used of a church office, it seems to be virtually interchangeable with the term "elder" (*presbyteros*).[83] That would seem to be the case here, since the Ephesian leaders are denoted "elders" in v. 17. In this instance, however, the term may not be used to denote an office at all but rather a function—that of overseeing the flock. This would seem to be indicated by the juxtaposition of the term "shepherd" to "overseer" in v. 28 and by the fact that the Septuagint sometimes used the term *episkopos* for shepherds.[84] Thus, the Ephesian leaders were not designated as bishops but rather as elders who functioned to "watch over the flock of God." This image of the leaders as shepherds of God's flock permeates all of vv. 28-30 and is a common biblical theme.[85]

A final major problem in v. 28 is both text-critical and interpretive. It involves the final clause: "Be shepherds of the church of God, which he bought with his own blood." The problem is the very striking statement that *God* purchased the church with his own blood. The reference is surely to the atoning blood of Jesus shed on the cross.[86] It is quite possible to denote this as "God's blood" from the perspective of sound Trinitarian doctrine, but such an expression is really quite unlike anything else in the New Testament.[87] A number of significant manuscripts read "church of

---

[83]This seems to be the case in Phil 1:1 and in the Pastorals (cf. 1 Tim 3:2; Titus 1:7). See J. B. Lightfoot, *St. Paul's Epistle to the Philippians* (London: Macmillan, 1873), 93-97, 189-96. See also P. Livingstone, "The Word *episkopos* in Pre-Christian Usage," *ATR* 21 (1939): 103-12.

[84]The cognate verb *episkeptomai* is used of a shepherd in the LXX of Ezek 34:11f. In fact, Paul may have been drawing from Ezek 33–34 throughout this portion of his speech. As already noted, the watchman motif of Ezek 33:1-6 seems to lie behind v. 26. The theme of negligent shepherds and ravaging beasts runs throughout Ezek 34 and is found in vv. 29-30. See E. Lovestam, "Paul's Address at Miletus," *ST* 41 (1987): 1-10.

[85]Cf. Ezek 34:12-16; Jer 23:2; Zech 10:3; 11:4-17; John 10:1-18; 21:15-17; 1 Pet 2:25; 5:2.

[86]This is the only clear instance in Acts where a redemptive, atoning sense is given to the work of Christ. See C. F. D. Moule, "The Christology of Acts," *Studies in Luke-Acts* (Nashville: Abingdon, 1966), 171; K. N. Giles, "Luke's Use of the Term 'Ekklesia,'" *NTS* 31 (1985): 135-42.

[87]Catholic scholars seem to have less trouble than Protestant scholars with the concept of Christ's blood as "God's blood." See C. F. Devine, "The 'Blood of God' in Acts 20:28," *CBQ* 9 (1947): 381-408.

the Lord," which removes the difficulty; but the reading "church of God" seems to be the more likely original reading.[88] It is possible to argue that "God" is not the intended antecedent but rather Christ, "implicitly," but that is not likely. Another possibility, favored by many recent translations and commentaries, is to translate the final phrase "with the blood of his own," "his own" referring to Christ, God's own beloved Son. This is grammatically arguable and perhaps the best solution for those who find the reference to "God's own blood" unlikely for Paul or for Acts.

20:29-31 The shepherd imagery is continued in vv. 29-30 with Paul warning the Ephesian elders of a time to come when religious predators would ravage the flock of God. They would arise both from outside and inside the church. The term "savage wolves" describes the false teachers from without (v. 29). The term "wolves" often appears in the Jewish apocalyptic literature and in early Christian writings to describe false teachers and prophets.[89] The early Christian writings appear to be influenced by Jesus' warning against false prophets who come in sheep's clothing (Matt 7:15). That false teachers did soon arise to prey upon the Asian churches is well attested by Eph 5:6-14 and Col 2:8 as well as by the Letter to Ephesus in Rev 2:2. The Letters to Timothy, which related to the Ephesian church, confirm Paul's prediction that some from the church's own ranks would succumb to such false doctrines and draw other Christians with them (v. 30).[90] By the second century Asia was a virtual seedbed for Christian heresy. Paul's warning was thus timely and essential. It is not by chance that this section both opens and closes with an exhortation to vigilance (vv. 28,31), and Paul's reference to his three-year ministry with the Ephesians[91] was not just a reminder of his warnings but also an appeal to be faithful to the sound teachings he had brought them (cf. 20:20f.).

PAUL'S BLESSING AND FINAL ADMONITION (20:32-35). **20:32** The conclusion to Paul's Miletus address includes both a benediction upon the elders (v. 32) and a final exhortation to follow his exemplary conduct (vv. 33-35). In his benediction Paul committed the leaders to "the word of [God's] grace," i.e., to the truth of the gospel that has God's saving grace

---

[88]There is perhaps a slight balance of external witnesses in favor of "church of God," with ℵ and B having that reading. Internal probability is the primary consideration. One could picture a scribe altering "church of God" to the easier "church of the Lord," but not the reverse.

[89]Cf. 4 Ezra 5:18; 1 Enoch 89:13ff.; *Didache* 16:3; Ignatius, *To the Philadelphians* 2:2, *2 Clement* 5:2-5; Justin, *Dialogue* 35:3; and *Apology* 1:16:13. See G. W. H. Lampe, "'Grievous Wolves' (Acts 20:29)," *Christ and the Spirit in the New Testament*, ed. B. Lindars and S. Smalley (Cambridge: University Press, 1973), 253-68.

[90]Cf. 1 Tim 1:19f.; 4:1-3; 2 Tim 1:15; 2:17f.; 3:1-9.

[91]For the three-year chronology, see commentary on 19:10.

at its center (cf. v. 24). The language is again strongly reminiscent of Paul's epistles. The reference to "those who are sanctified" (*hēgias-menois*) reflects Paul's favorite designation of Christians as "the saints" (*hoi hagioi*), those who have been "sanctified," i.e., "set apart" as God's people in Christ. He likewise often spoke of the future life of the Christian in terms of sharing in an inheritance (*klēronomian*).[92] In v. 32 Paul passed on the banner to the Ephesian elders to continue to lead the church after his departure, urging them above all to be faithful to his gospel in the light of the coming threats.

20:33-35 There was, however, one matter of personal conduct of prime importance he had not yet treated; and he ended on this note (vv. 33-35). In a real sense he ended as he had begun (vv. 18-21), pointing to his own deportment in ministry as an example for them to emulate. The matter in question was the leaders' relationship to material goods. Paul's detachment from material gain is well-documented in his epistles. He never used his ministry as a "mask to cover up greed" (2 Thess 2:5).[93] At Corinth he supported himself with his own hands (Acts 18:2f.; cf. 1 Cor 4:12; 9:12,15; 2 Cor 11:7; 12:13). The same was true at Thessalonica (1 Thess 2:9; 2 Thess 3:7-8). Verse 34 would indicate that he followed the same pattern of self-support at Ephesus. In his epistles Paul exhorted his Christian readers to follow his example and work with their own hands, not being dependent on others (1 Thess 4:11; 2 Thess 3:9). In the Miletus speech Paul gave the additional incentive that such hard work put one in the position to help the weak. In his epistles he showed a similar concern that Christians help the weak and needy, that they share in one another's burdens (cf. Rom 15:1; 1 Thess 5:14; Eph 4:28; Gal 6:2). Greed is a universal human problem, and church leaders are not exempt (cf. the exhortation in v. 28 for church leaders to "watch yourselves"). That avarice among church leaders was a real problem in Asia Minor seems to be attested by the Pastoral Epistles, in which Paul insisted that a major qualification for church leaders should be their detachment from the love of money (1 Tim 3:3,8; Titus 1:7,11). It may well be that the false teachers were particularly marked by their greed (cf. 1 Tim 6:3-10).

The saying of Jesus with which Paul concluded his address should be seen in light of this context: "It is more blessed to give than to receive."[94] Paul applied this rule to the specific problem of avarice

---

[92]E.g., Rom 8:17; Col 1:12; Eph 1:14,18; 5:5; cf. Acts 26:18.

[93]There were three main forms of wealth in the ancient world: precious metals, foodstuffs, and clothing. Two of these are mentioned in v. 33 (cf. 2 Kgs 5:22f.; 1 Macc 11:24). All three seem to be included in Jas 5:2f. (foodstuffs "rot").

[94]It is striking that this logion is not included among Jesus' sayings in the four Gospels. It has rather extensive parallels in Greek literature (cf. Plutarch, *Moralia* 2.173d, 778c; Thucydides, 2.97.4; Seneca, *Epistles* 81.17). The thought is also found in the Jewish tradition

among church leaders. The minister is to be a servant, a giver and not a taker.[95] Acquisitiveness has been the downfall for many a servant of God. This word of the Lord as applied by Paul is sound ministerial advice. The one who leads the flock of God should focus on the needs of others, be more concerned with giving than with acquiring. Paul had begun his address by listing the qualities of his own ministry as an example for the Ephesian leaders to follow. He concluded with a final quality he had sought to model. Perhaps he held it off to the end because he saw it as the most essential of all for a legitimate ministry.

(5) Final Leave-taking (20:36-38)

[36]When he had said this, he knelt down with all of them and prayed. [37]They all wept as they embraced him and kissed him. [38]What grieved them most was his statement that they would never see his face again. Then they accompanied him to the ship.

20:36-38 Paul's address concluded, the apostle and the elders joined in prayer together. The prayer surely included a commitment of the elders to the Lord in their leadership of the church in Paul's absence and for Paul's safe journey and deliverance in Jerusalem. Then there was a lengthy and emotional farewell, the elders embracing and kissing the apostle. Their embracing is described literally as "falling upon his neck" in language reminiscent of the patriarchal narratives.[96] All the Greek tenses are imperfect, which would indicate that their parting was lengthy. Their sorrow was greatest over Paul's statement that they would not see him again (v. 38; cf. v. 25). Then they "sent him forth" (*proepempon*) to the ship. *Propempō* is used of accompanying or escorting people to their point of departure and often has the additional nuance of giving them food and provisions for their journey. That may well have been the case in this instance.

This section provides a transition between the Miletus speech and Paul's journey to Jerusalem. On the one hand, it concludes Paul's Ephesian ministry with its final farewell to the leaders of the church. For that

---

(cf. Sirach 4:31). It seems to be a question of a proverbial statement. Similar thought is found in the gospel tradition, and the emphasis on giving is found frequently in the sayings of Jesus (cf. Luke 6:30,38; 11:41; 12:33; 18:22). See R. Balgarnie, "Acts xx.35," *ExpTim* 19 (1907-08): 522f.

[95] "Receiving" can be a gracious act, and to refuse the well-intentioned gift of another can be an insult or even a rejection of that person. The saying should not be seen as a judgment against gracious receiving but rather against acquisitiveness, against actively "taking" for oneself, a common meaning for λαμβάνω. The emphasis in any event is on giving. See R. Roberts, "The Beatitude of Giving and Receiving," *ExpTim* 48 (1936-37): 438-41.

[96]Cf. Gen 33:4; 45:14; 46:29.

matter it is the conclusion to his entire ministry in the east. From now on the focus would be on Rome. This section also links up with the narrative of Paul's journey to Jerusalem that follows immediately (21:1-16). The ominous tone set by the elders' concern over not seeing the apostle again would continue and even be heightened in the course of that journey.

(6) Voyage to Jerusalem (21:1-16)

[1]After we had torn ourselves away from them, we put out to sea and sailed straight to Cos. The next day we went to Rhodes and from there to Patara. [2]We found a ship crossing over to Phoenicia, went on board and set sail. [3]After sighting Cyprus and passing to the south of it, we sailed on to Syria. We landed at Tyre, where our ship was to unload its cargo. [4]Finding the disciples there, we stayed with them seven days. Through the Spirit they urged Paul not to go on to Jerusalem. [5]But when our time was up, we left and continued on our way. All the disciples and their wives and children accompanied us out of the city, and there on the beach we knelt to pray. [6]After saying good-by to each other, we went aboard the ship, and they returned home.

[7]We continued our voyage from Tyre and landed at Ptolemais, where we greeted the brothers and stayed with them for a day. [8]Leaving the next day, we reached Caesarea and stayed at the house of Philip the evangelist, one of the Seven. [9]He had four unmarried daughters who prophesied.

[10]After we had been there a number of days, a prophet named Agabus came down from Judea. [11]Coming over to us, he took Paul's belt, tied his own hands and feet with it and said, "The Holy Spirit says, 'In this way the Jews of Jerusalem will bind the owner of this belt and will hand him over to the Gentiles.'"

[12]When we heard this, we and the people there pleaded with Paul not to go up to Jerusalem. [13]Then Paul answered, "Why are you weeping and breaking my heart? I am ready not only to be bound, but also to die in Jerusalem for the name of the Lord Jesus." [14]When he would not be dissuaded, we gave up and said, "The Lord's will be done."

[15]After this, we got ready and went up to Jerusalem. [16]Some of the disciples from Caesarea accompanied us and brought us to the home of Mnason, where we were to stay. He was a man from Cyprus and one of the early disciples.

After the parting scene at Miletus, Paul resumed his final voyage to Jerusalem. At this point the journey motif is quite pronounced with a detailed listing of the ports and stopping points along the way. The most striking characteristic of this section is the warning from Paul's fellow Christians of the dangers that awaited him in Jerusalem. This is a continuation of the emphasis that began in 20:22f., where Paul told the Ephesian elders how the Spirit was leading him to Jerusalem and of the possible dangers that awaited him there. This "journey motif" is strongly reminiscent of Jesus' final journey to Jerusalem in the Synoptic Gospels. The same forebodings marked Jesus' journey—the same strong resolve on

Jesus' part, the same misgivings on the part of his disciples. In the Gospels Jesus' predictions of his coming passion provide the ominous tone. For Paul's journey the warnings of the Christians along his way serve this function. In Luke's Gospel, Jesus' journey is particularly marked by sayings regarding Jerusalem as the place of rejection for God's messengers.[97] In Jerusalem Jesus was arrested and executed. In Jerusalem Paul also was arrested and his life put in extreme jeopardy.

WARNING AT TYRE (21:1-6). **21:1-3**   Luke described the journey from Miletus to Tyre in considerable detail, naming each point along their route.[98] Evidently they took a coasting vessel from Miletus. Their first stopping place was Cos, an island off the Asian mainland about forty miles south of Miletus.[99] Cos was also the name of the capital city of the island, and they probably put in for the night there. The next day they traveled to the island of Rhodes and put in at its main city, which was also named Rhodes, located at the northeastern extremity of the island closest to the mainland.[100] The coasting vessel took them the next day to Patara on the Lycian mainland, which was the main port city and capital of the province. Since coasting vessels were not large enough for travel on the open sea, they evidently changed at Patara to a seagoing vessel in order to make the direct journey to Phoenicia.[101] The journey from Patara to Tyre was approximately 400 miles by a straight course and generally took five days or so under favorable winds. Luke mentioned their sighting the island of Cyprus, which would have been the only land one would view on the open-sea voyage from the Lycian coast to Phoenicia (v. 3).[102]

---

[97]Cf. Luke 13:33f.; 18:31f.; 21:20-24.; 23:28-31. See J. Kelsey, "The Function of the Jerusalem Oracles in the Gospel of Luke," Ph.D. diss., The Southern Baptist Theological Seminary, Louisville, Kentucky, 1990.

[98]Note the "we" narrative throughout Paul's journey to Jerusalem. It begins at 20:5, breaks off at 20:15 for Paul's Miletus address, and then runs throughout 21:1-18, ending with Paul's arrival in Jerusalem.

[99]Cos was an ancient town, first settled by Dorian Greeks and famous for its medical school, established by Hippocrates in the fifth century B.C.

[100]The city of Rhodes was established in 408 B.C. as the consolidation of three earlier towns. A major center of trade, Rhodes was given the status of a free city by the Romans.

[101]The Western text adds the words "and Myra" after "Patara" in v. 1. Myra lay a day's journey farther east on the Lycian coast. Since it was the main port of departure for voyages to Phoenicia, many interpreters are inclined to see the Western text as the more original reading on this point. See Ramsay, *St. Paul the Traveller*, 297-300.

[102]Verse 3 switches from the term "Phoenicia" to "Syria" as their destination. The terms were interchangeable. Phoenicia is the more specific designation, referring to the coastal strip that ran from the river Eleutherus in the north to Mt. Carmel in the south, roughly between the cities of Tyre and Ptolemais. The area had been annexed by the Romans in 64 B.C. and later consolidated into the province of Syria. The administrative area was designated as the province of "Syria and Phoenicia," a term often found in inscriptions (Latin, *Syrie et Phoenice*).

Tyre was the main port for merchant traffic between Asia and Palestine, and it was thus quite natural that Paul's ship put in there to unload its cargo.[103]

21:4 At Tyre, Paul and his traveling companions found the Christian community. The Greek term used (*aneuriskō*) would indicate that they were previously unacquainted with them and had to "seek them out." Most likely the Christian community in Tyre had been established by the Hellenist mission to Phoenicia mentioned in Acts 11:19. Evidently the direct open-sea voyage had saved Paul sufficient time for him to spend a week with the Christians at Tyre and still fulfill his desire to reach Jerusalem by Pentecost (cf. 20:16). During this visit, the Tyrian Christians "through the Spirit" urged Paul not to go to Jerusalem (v. 4). This note has already been struck in Paul's Miletus address, where he indicated to the Ephesian leaders that the Spirit had alerted him to the fact that imprisonment and hardships awaited him in Jerusalem (20:23). Still, the same Spirit was driving him to the city (20:22).

The seeming conflict in the Spirit's directions is even more pronounced here with the note that the Tyrians *under the influence of the Spirit* urged Paul not to go. Obviously the Spirit would not be giving Paul two contradictory messages at the same time. The most likely solution is to see Paul's resolution to go to Jerusalem as the primary emphasis. Paul was absolutely convinced that God was leading him to the city. On the other hand, the warnings along the way prepared Paul for the imprisonment and hardship that did indeed befall him there, fortified him for the experience, and convinced him that God was in it all. This was not at all difficult for Paul to accept. Paul certainly never sought out difficulty. He had no martyr complex. On the other hand, he accepted suffering as a part of his witness and often alluded to this in his letters.[104] The words of the Tyrians are best understood as part of Paul's preparation for the difficult events in Jerusalem. The Spirit's role is best seen as informing them of those coming hardships for the apostle. Their very natural reaction was to urge him not to go. Their failure to deter him only heightens the emphasis on Paul's firm conviction that God was leading him to Jerusalem and had a purpose for him there.[105]

---

[103]Under the Romans, Tyre had the status of a free city. A major commercial center, it was particularly known for its purple-dye industry.

[104]Among the many passages that could be cited are Rom 8:17; 2 Cor 4:7-12; 6:4-10; 11:23-29; 12:10; Col 1:24f.

[105]The subsequent narrative reveals the divine purpose behind Paul's journey to Jerusalem. His arrest there provided him a unique opportunity for witness—before a Jewish crowd, the Jewish Sanhedrin, Roman governors, the Jewish king, and implicitly before the Roman emperor himself. Note how in Phil 1:12-18 Paul expressed how his imprisonment had led to an effective door for witness.

21:5-6 Paul's leave-taking at Tyre is given in considerable detail (vv. 5-6) and recalls his parting with the Ephesian elders (21:36-38). The scene is filled with emotion. *All* the disciples accompanied Paul to the boat; and kneeling in the soft sand of the beach,[106] they prayed. In one of the few references to children in Acts, Luke noted that all the members of the Christian families of Tyre joined Paul for his farewell. The reference to prayer is not incidental. Everyone was fully aware of the difficulties facing Paul at Jerusalem. They were also aware that prayer was the disciple's best fortification in a time of suffering and trial. The good-byes were prolonged. The Tyrian Christians did not want to part with the apostle in the face of his ominous future. They did not want to lose him. Still, they accepted Paul's conviction that he must continue his journey. The inevitable parting time came. Paul's party boarded ship,[107] and the Tyrian Christians returned home.

WARNING OF AGABUS (21:7-14). **21:7** The next stopping point was Ptolemais, some twenty-five miles south of Tyre, the most southerly of the Phoenician ports. An ancient city, it is referred to as Acco in Judg 1:31, was a famous crusader site known as Acre, and today goes by its ancient name of Acco. It was known as Ptolemais in Roman times, after Ptolemy II Philadelphus (285–246 B.C.). Paul spent only a day with the Christians of that city, perhaps again being tied to his ship's schedule.[108]

21:8-9 Paul was already familiar with the Christian community of Caesarea (cf. 9:30; 18:22). He perhaps had previously met there Philip the evangelist, who had settled in that city (cf. 8:40). Philip became his host on this occasion (v. 8), and we are given the rather interesting information that he had four unmarried daughters who prophesied. Nothing is made of their gift in the narrative. Later tradition placed them in Asia Minor with their father and saw them as important witnesses and preserv-

---

[106]The harbor of Tyre consists of a sandy beach. The city was originally built on a small island just off the mainland. In his siege of the city, Alexander the Great built a causeway connecting the island to the mainland. Eventually sand built up on either side of the causeway, and the harbor was located along this beach.

[107]It is uncertain whether Paul continued on the same ship that had brought him to Tyre, especially since that ship is said to have unloaded its cargo at Tyre. On the other hand, the definite article's presence in v. 6 ("the ship") would most naturally be taken to mean the ship previously mentioned, i.e., the same ship. In either case, whether the same or a new ship, it may have been sailing schedules that ultimately determined Paul's spending a full week in Tyre.

[108]Paul possibly traveled by foot from Ptolemais to Caesarea. The verb translated "continued" (NIV) in v. 7 (διανύω) more often means *to finish* and may indicate that the voyage ended at Ptolemais. On the other hand, nautical texts evidence that the verb means *to continue a voyage*. Also the land trip from Ptolemais to Caesarea, though only twenty-seven miles, involved high and difficult terrain around the foot of Mt. Carmel. See *Beginnings* 4:267.

ers of traditions from the apostolic period.[109] Perhaps the most significant observation in the present narrative is the testimony that there were women in the early church who were recognized as having the gift of prophecy. In his Gospel, Luke mentioned Anna, who was also a prophetess who foretold the future redemptive role of the infant Jesus (2:36-38).[110] Peter, in his Pentecost sermon, pointed to the prophesying of "daughters" as a sign of the gift of the Spirit in these last days (Acts 2:17).

21:10-11 In this instance the prophecy was delivered by Agabus (vv. 10-11). Agabus has appeared previously in Acts, prophesying the coming of famine to Judea and prompting the collection from the Antioch church (11:27-30).[111] In a symbolic act much like the acted-out prophecies of the Old Testament prophets, Agabus predicted Paul's coming arrest in Jerusalem.[112] He took Paul's girdle, the long cloth that was wound several times around his waist, and bound with it his hands and feet. Then, just like an Old Testament prophet, he gave the interpretation of the act, introduced by the usual, "Thus says the Lord," here expressed in terms of revelation through the Holy Spirit. Paul would be bound by the Jews of Jerusalem and handed over to the Gentiles. The parallel to the fate of Jesus could hardly be more explicit (cf. Matt 20:18f.; Luke 18:32). This was not so much a warning on Agabus's part as a prediction. Unlike the Christians of Tyre, he did not urge Paul not to go. Rather, he told him what was in store for him. This was all the more certain when one considers the nature of such prophetic acts in the Old Testament. The act itself set into motion the event it foretold. It established the reality of the event, the certainty that it would occur.[113] Agabus's act prepared Paul for the events to come and assured him of God's presence in those events.

---

[109]There is some contradiction in the patristic evidence. Polycrates of Ephesus spoke of three prophesying daughters, two buried with Philip at Hierapolis and one buried in Ephesus (Eusebius, *Hist. Eccl.*, 3.31.3; 5.24.2). Montanist tradition, which placed great emphasis on prophecy, spoke of four daughters being buried with Philip at Hierapolis. The fathers tended to equate Philip the evangelist with Philip the apostle. See P. Corssen, "Die Töchter des Philippus," *ZNW* 2 (1901): 289-99.

[110]See W. V. Whitney, "Women in Luke: An Application of a Reader-Response Hermeneutic," Ph.D. diss., Southern Baptist Theological Seminary, Louisville, Kentucky, 1990, 151-58.

[111]Agabus is said to have come "from Judea." Caesarea was administratively within Judea and was actually the center of government for the district. Due to its largely Gentile population, it was often viewed separately from "Judea," in this case Judea being seen as the "land of the Jews."

[112]For symbolic prophecies in the OT, see 1 Kgs 11:29-31; Isa 8:1-4; 20:1-4; Jer 13:1-11; 19:1-13; 27:1-22; Hos 1:2. This is the only complete example in the NT of the form, which includes the symbolic act, the formula "thus says," and the interpretation of the symbolism.

[113]See H. Patsch, "Die Prophetie des Agabus," *TZ* 28 (1972): 228-32.

21:12-13 Much like the Christians of Tyre, Paul's traveling companions and the Caesarean Christians concluded from this dire prediction that Paul should not go to Jerusalem (v. 12). Luke even included himself by using the narrative "we" as among those who begged the apostle to abandon his plans.[114] They had no more success than the Tyrians. Paul's response contains a picturesque image, "Why are you pounding away at my heart?" (author's translation). The verb (synthryptō) was often used of washing clothes and referred to pounding them with stones in order to whiten them.[115] The well-meant pleas of his Christian friends only heightened the conflict for him. They could not deter him from his firm conviction that the journey was in God's will. He was indeed willing even to die for his Lord if need be (v. 13).[116]

21:14 Paul's resolve finally dissuaded the other Christians, and they ceased in their attempt to stop his journey. They did not want to lose their leader, but they respected his firm conviction that the journey was within God's will for him.[117] If this was God's will for Paul, then they prayed "the Lord's will be done." It was much like Jesus' prayer in Gethsemane. He too did not relish facing the human agony of the cross but nonetheless committed himself wholly to God's purpose for him—"not my will, but yours be done" (Luke 22:42). It is not without reason that many refer to this scene as "Paul's Gethsemane."

ARRIVAL IN JERUSALEM (21:15-16). **21:15-16** Paul's journey was now nearly complete. There remained only the final sixty-four miles between Caesarea and Jerusalem. For this final leg they may have used pack animals.[118] This is all the more likely when one recalls that they were carrying the sizable collection from Paul's Gentile churches. It would have been a considerable group making the trip, including Paul and Luke, those dele-

---

[114]The use of the present infinitive in v. 12 has the nuance of "to cease going up to Jerusalem," to "put a stop" to his plans.

[115]Some interpreters grasp the "bleaching" aspect of the metaphor and see Paul as imploring the Christians not to tempt him to cowardice, not to "make him yellow." The emphasis of the verb, however, is on the pounding; and that is the most natural meaning—"breaking my heart." Paul's conflict was not over whether or not to go. The prospect of separation from his fellow Christians broke his heart.

[116]Compare this with Peter's similar statement in Luke 22:33. Peter did not carry through on his resolve. Paul did. If, however, the early Christian traditions about the martyrdom of the two apostles is correct, both of them did ultimately fulfill these words.

[117]Ultimately individuals are left to themselves to determine God's purposes for them. On the other hand, the understanding of others is significant input in seeking to determine those purposes for oneself. The present incident provides an excellent example of that sort of interchange within the Christian community between conflicting understandings of God's will. See F. Bovon, "Le Saint-Espirit, l'Eglise et les relations humaines selon Actes 20, 36-21, 16," Les Actes, ed. J. Kremer, 339-58.

[118]The verb for "getting ready" (ἐπισκευάζω) is often used in classical Greek for saddling horses or equipping pack animals. See Ramsay, St. Paul the Traveller, 302.

gated by the churches to bear the collection (20:4), and some of the Caesarean Christians (v. 16). Once in Jerusalem, the Caesareans led them to the home of a disciple named Mnason with whom arrangements had been made for their lodging.[119] Showing his characteristic interest in hosts,[120] Luke further described Mnason as a Cypriot and a long-time disciple.[121]

Paul's third missionary journey was complete, having begun after a visit to "the church" in the holy city (18:22) and now ending there. His Greek mission was also complete. He would not return. Luke had prepared his readers well for this reality. Paul had made the fact clear in his address to the Ephesian elders (20:25). Paul's own forebodings (20:22f.) and those of the Christians at Tyre and Caesarea have prepared us for the events that are about to unfold in Jerusalem. Paul would no longer bear his witness as a free man in the subsequent narrative of Acts. He would be in chains, but the chains would be unable to bind his witness. His witness would indeed become bolder still.

---

[119]The Western text has at the beginning of v. 17 "and departing from there, we arrived at Jerusalem." This would put Mnason's home en route between Caesarea and Jerusalem. Some interpreters accept this as the original reading and argue for a two-day journey, with Mnason located halfway between Caesarea and Jerusalem. See E. Delebecque, "La dernière étape du Troisième voyage missionaire de Saint Paul selon les deux versions des Actes des Apôtres (21, 16-17)," *RTL* 14 (1983): 446-55.

[120]Cf. 9:11,43; 16:15; 17:5; 18:3,7; 21:8.

[121]His Cypriot origin most likely links him with the Greek-speaking "Hellenist" group within the Jerusalem Christian community (cf. 4:36; 11:20). Mnason is a variant of the name Jason, a name often taken by Hellenistic Jews. Some manuscripts have Jason in v. 16.

―――――――――― *SECTION OUTLINE* ――――――――――

―――― **VIII. PAUL WITNESSES BEFORE GENTILES, KINGS,** ――――
AND THE PEOPLE OF ISRAEL (21:17–26:32)

This long section of Acts could be considered the most tedious portion
of the whole book. It consists of seemingly endless legal scenes and has

more than its share of speeches. That Luke considered this material of vital importance, however, is indicated by the fact that these chapters constitute the fulfillment of the divine promise given to Paul at the time of his conversion that he would bear the Lord's name before Gentiles, kings, and the people of Israel (9:15). The three major speeches that comprise the framework of this section illustrate the accomplishment of that promise. At the beginning is Paul's witness before a mob in the Jewish temple square (22:1-21). It is in every sense a testimony before the people of Israel. The testimony before Gentiles is seen in the constant conversation between Paul and the Roman officials and particularly in the defense before Felix, which stands at this section's midpoint (24:10-21). Finally, there is the climactic speech before the Jewish titular *King* Agrippa II (26:2-29). Considerable overlap occurs in the content of the speeches. This repetition should be a clue in itself that Luke considered the material to be of vital importance. Indeed, it is in this portion of Acts where the major themes of the entire book come together. In this sense these chapters comprise the climax to Acts.

A useful manner of delineating these themes is to consider the main characters who appear in these chapters. Basically, there are three—Paul, the Roman officials, and the Jews. As for Paul, one could consider this period as the nadir of his career. At the beginning he was nearly killed by an angry mob, was placed in chains by the Roman cohort, and thereafter was shunted from one official to another, one place of confinement to another. He was constantly under accusation, continually placed on the defense.

If one looks carefully at Paul's "defense," however, it always appears as more of a witness, a positive testimony to his Christian faith. This is in keeping with the words of 9:15. Paul is not to be seen as having to give his legal defense so much as to bear his witness to the name of the Lord. With this section 23:11 is a key verse. Whomever Paul stood before— whether the Jews, the Roman procurator, or Caesar himself—it was above all to testify for his Lord. In so doing, he fulfilled the commission of Jesus (cf. Luke 21:12-19). The role Paul shared with the Twelve was that of witness. This was perhaps Paul's time of greatest witness. Far from a low point, it was in many respects the high point of Paul's career. His witness had no social or political bounds. He would ultimately testify to Christ before Caesar himself.

As for the Romans, the picture is less consistent. On the one hand, throughout these chapters they are shown as Paul's constant protectors. The Roman tribune Lysias, for instance, rescued him from death at the hands of a Jewish mob (21:33; 23:27), from being torn to shreds in the Sanhedrin (23:10), and from the ambush attempt of forty Jewish Zealots (23:30). The procurator Felix refused to give in to Jewish demands that

Paul be turned over to them, which would have meant almost certain condemnation (24:22). He gave Paul a great deal of freedom in his confinement and showed an interest in Paul's message (24:23f.). His successor Festus likewise, though perhaps unwittingly, refused to turn Paul over to Jewish jurisdiction and thereby rescued him from another ambush plot (25:1-5). Ultimately the emperor himself became Paul's protector. When Festus seemed to be inclining more toward the Jewish demands for jurisdiction over Paul, it was the process of appeal to Caesar that assured that this would not happen (25:10-12).

Not only did the Romans protect Paul, but they also constantly testified to his innocence. In sending his report to the procurator, the tribune Lysias stated quite emphatically that he had found "no charge against him that deserved death or imprisonment" (23:29). Felix was more indecisive and less committal, but there was in his refusal to hand Paul over to the Jews the implicit acknowledgment that the charges against him were without foundation (24:22f.). Festus gave the most emphatic testimony of them all to Paul's innocence, stating that the Jews could not substantiate any of their charges and that he was at a total loss about how to investigate the matter (25:18,20); indeed, so far as he could ascertain, Paul had done nothing deserving of death (25:25).

The picture of the Romans has another side as well. Paul received some rather rough treatment from Lysias at first, being seized and bound with two chains (21:33). Lysias had no qualms about examining him by the harsh method of Roman scourging—none, that is, until he learned of Paul's Roman citizenship (22:24). His distorting of the facts in his letter to Felix does nothing to alter the picture for the reader (23:27) and only serves to cast his "Roman honor" in a somewhat less favorable light. Felix appears to have been even worse. There was the whole messy question of his marriage to Drusilla, and Luke did nothing to hide it. In fact, he introduced her when it really was quite unnecessary to the narrative and delighted at Felix's squirming when Paul spoke of self-control and the coming judgment (24:25). Then there was Felix's looking for a bribe from Paul (24:26), a thing frowned upon, even condemned by Roman law. Worst of all was the fact that he kept Paul in prison for two years when he had found no grounds for condemning him. The reason given is that he "wanted to grant a favor to the Jews" (24:27). Lysias probably had the right to release Paul when he had found no grounds for imprisonment (23:29); but at least his action could be justified as a sort of protective custody, given the extreme danger to Paul in Jerusalem. Not so Felix and Festus. Festus, who rather strongly asserted Paul's innocence (25:25), actually contemplated taking Paul back to Jerusalem—into enemy territory—for trial. The reason again was "to do the Jews a favor" (25:9). What sort of justification for a miscarriage of justice is favoritism? One is reminded of Pilate's similar equivocation (or cowardice) in giving in to the demands of the mob. The Romans prided themselves in their standards of justice. None of these officials was a worthy example.

Thus the common argument that Luke was offering an apologetic to Romans in Acts needs considerable modification. If he were trying to ingratiate the Romans, it is unlikely he would have portrayed them with quite so many flaws. His picture is realistic enough. It ties in perfectly with Josephus's description of the procurators and with the testimony of the Roman historians about their officials. It was more likely intended for Luke's Christian readers than for pagan Romans. They too might experience both the good points and the bad points of Roman officialdom. Like Paul, they too were to make full use of their legal rights wherever possible and respect the government when it served in its rightful role for justice and peace (cf. Rom 13:1-7). If they, like Paul, did find themselves before the Tribunal, it was not to be for any breach of law but solely for bearing the name of Christ (cf. 1 Pet 4:15). Finally, and above all, if they appeared in court for their Christian faith, they were to bear witness to their Lord with pride and with courage, just as Paul did.

The picture of the Jews in these chapters is, like that of the Romans, somewhat multifaceted. They are depicted consistently as Paul's enemies. It was the temple mob that got him in trouble in the first place. They wanted him dead (21:31,36). They continued to want him dead (22:22). They plotted to kill him in ambush (23:12-15). A similar plot was hatched on a subsequent occasion (25:3). They brought serious accusations against Paul before the Roman procurators (24:5f.). If they could not get jurisdiction over him and condemn him themselves, they sought a Roman conviction on grounds of sedition.

The Jewish portrait, however, had another side. Not all Jews were Paul's enemies. Some Jews had become Christians. Being a Jew and being a Christian were not mutually exclusive. This was what Paul was attempting to demonstrate by his participation in the Nazirite vow in the temple when the mob rose against him (21:23-27). His demonstration was primarily for the Jewish Christians, to make a further point—that Paul's law-free Gentile mission was not incompatible with a Jewish Christianity "zealous for the law" (21:20). In Paul's speeches there is a strong emphasis on his Jewishness—his speaking in Aramaic (22:2), his thorough upbringing in Judaism (22:3; 26:4f.). The picture of Ananias is that of a devout, law-abiding Jew respected by the entire Jewish community (22:12). Twice Paul related his conversion experience, and each time there was a strong emphasis on his zeal for the faith of the fathers (22:4f.; 26:9-11). More significantly, there is no indication that his conviction made him any less zealous for his ancestral faith. A key concept that runs throughout this section is that of "the Way" (cf. 22:4; 24:14,22; 25:3). It is a sectarian type of term that describes Christianity not as a separate entity but as a group, a "way," in fact, Paul would say, the only *true* way within Judaism. In their own manner the Roman officials attested to this concept, maintaining that the whole dispute between Paul and the Jews was a theological difference within their own religion (25:19; 23:29).

The major theological difference centered around the resurrection, and the resurrection was perhaps the major motif in the picture of the Jews in Acts 22–26. Luke's treatment begins with Paul's announcement in the Sanhedrin that he was on trial because of his hope in the resurrection of the dead (23:6). This has often been seen as a clever ploy to divert attention from himself because it provoked a sharp division between the Sadducees and the Pharisees in the Sanhedrin. Actually it was no ploy, since the resurrection was indeed the central matter that separated Paul from the Jews. In the Sanhedrin scene the stage was set. The Pharisees sided with Paul because they shared his hope in the resurrection. Theologically the Pharisees were at one with him. Where they differed was their failure to acknowledge the resurrection of Jesus. They had no Damascus road vision of the risen Christ. Twice in the trial before Felix, Paul spoke of the resurrection. In fact, his concluding remark was almost identical to that in the Sanhedrin, stating that the resurrection was the real agenda for his trial (24:21).

The climactic treatment of the theme occurs in the final "trial" scene, Paul's hearing before Agrippa. Again there are two references to the resurrection in Paul's speech. The first is part of a complex that involves the hope of the Jews, the promises to the fathers, and God's raising of the dead (26:6-8). The second unites the Old Testament proofs of the Messiah's death and resurrection with the mission to the Gentiles and to Israel (26:22f.). One is reminded of the argument in Peter's sermons in Acts 2–3: the Old Testament points to the suffering and resurrection of the Messiah; the fact that Christ had risen proved that he was the promised Messiah. It was the message to the Jews. It would have little meaning for Gentiles. Festus proved that. When Paul mentioned the resurrection, Festus accused him of having left his senses (26:24). Earlier he had expressed similar perplexity over "a dead man named Jesus who Paul claimed was alive" (25:19). But the Pharisees understood (23:8f.). They too believed that resurrection was a part of God's promises, and they were the dominant religious viewpoint among the Jews of the day. Paul was one Jew who believed that the firstfruits of the resurrection had begun with Jesus. Christ was the culmination of the promises, the fulfillment of the hope of Israel and the promises to the fathers. Christianity was "the Way" for the Jews.

This strong treatment in Paul's speeches of the close relationship between Judaism and Christianity has led many scholars to argue that this motif seeks to establish Christianity as a movement within Judaism and thus subject to the recognition granted Judaism under Roman rule. The Latin phrase *religio licita* usually designates this concept. Apart from the problems with the concept itself,[1] this does not seem to be the primary function of the emphasis within Paul's speeches. It is much more a concern for the evangelization of the Jews. Paul never gave up on his hope that his fellow Israelites would trust in Christ (cf. Rom 9–11). In preserving this strong emphasis in Paul's speeches, Luke showed that he had not either.

Two subordinate themes run through these chapters, both of which are closely related to the first theme discussed earlier, Paul's witness. The first involves the rather striking parallels to Jesus' own passion, a phenomenon already noted in the "journey to Jerusalem" motif discussed in the previous chapter. The mob action in the temple square recalls the crowd screaming for Jesus' death. Even the words are the same—"away with him" (Acts 21:36; cf. Luke 23:18). The trials are reminiscent of Jesus' trial—before the Roman procurator, even before the Jewish king, something which only Luke included among the Gospel writers (Luke 23:7-12). Already noted has been the Roman officials' tendency to avoid responsibility and give in to Jewish pressure. There are numerous other minor similarities between Jesus' and Paul's experience, and these will be noted in the commentary. Perhaps Luke included these to remind his readers that the path of discipleship sometimes leads to a sharing in the Lord's suffering, an idea often expressed by Paul (cf. Rom 8:17f.).

Finally there is the concept that is best summarized in Paul's address before Agrippa: "It was not done in a corner" (26:26). There is certainly nothing obscure about the Christian witness in this section since Paul bore his testimony before the leaders of both the Jewish and Gentile communities, before governors and kings. He would ultimately appear before the emperor himself in the capital city of the empire (23:11). The theme is not new. It has appeared before in the apostles before the Sanhedrin, Paul before Sergius Paulus and Gallio, and in Paul's friendship with the Asiarchs in Ephesus. Christianity was no upstart, ephemeral sect. It was empowered by God's Spirit. It was for all the world (cf. 1:8), and that included even those social and political structures the world considered most significant. The world should take note and respond to the gospel.

---

[1]There is no question that Judaism was granted certain privileges by various emperors, such as the banning of the military standards from Jerusalem and exemption from paying homage to the emperor. But the concept that there was an imperial list of officially recognized religions, which the *religio licita* concept maintains, has never been adequately documented.

1. Witness before the Jews (21:17–23:35)

In a sense all of 21:17–26:32 could be described as Paul's testimony before Jews, since even in the Caesarea trial scenes of chaps. 24–26 Paul appeared before a Jewish legal deputation and the Jewish king. But the Roman officials have a more conspicuous presence in chaps. 24–26, and the scene is set on their turf. In 21:17–23:35 Paul was in Jerusalem and in Jewish territory. First he appeared with the elders of the Jerusalem church. There he experienced something of a minitrial even before them, as they urged him to demonstrate his faithfulness to the law for the benefit of the more zealous Jewish Christians in Jerusalem (21:17-26). To comply with their wishes, he participated in a Nazirite vow, which took him to the temple. There Paul was falsely accused by some Asian Jews of having violated the sacred precincts, and a riot ensued (21:27-36).

Rescued from certain death at the hands of the mob, Paul requested from the arresting Roman commander permission to address the crowd (21:37-40). Permission granted, he delivered a major address before the Jewish crowd (22:1-21). The crowd listened attentively as Paul spoke of his thoroughly orthodox Jewish background and of his experience on the Damascus road. Only when he mentioned the Lord's commission for his witness to the Gentiles did they become agitated again, and Paul had to be spirited away by the Romans. In an attempt to find out more about the causes of the riot, the tribune instead learned of Paul's Roman citizenship (22:22-29). The tribune then led Paul to the Sanhedrin in his attempt to ascertain the Jewish complaint against him. With Paul's mention of the resurrection, the Sanhedrin session ended in utter chaos, with Sadducee set against Pharisee (22:30–23:11). Paul's nephew learned of a plot by forty Jews to ambush Paul and warned the tribune of it (23:12-22). The tribune then sent Paul off to the governor in Caesarea under cover of night and heavy guard (23:23-35). The narrative is long and given in considerable detail. That Luke considered this material especially significant is indicated by the slowness of the time of the narrative. Less than twelve days are involved in 21:17–23:35 (cf. 24:11). In contrast, the events of the next three chapters cover two years (cf. 24:27).

(1) The Concern of the Jerusalem Elders (21:17-26)

[17]When we arrived at Jerusalem, the brothers received us warmly. [18]The next day Paul and the rest of us went to see James, and all the elders were present. [19]Paul greeted them and reported in detail what God had done among the Gentiles through his ministry.

[20]When they heard this, they praised God. Then they said to Paul: "You see, brother, how many thousands of Jews have believed, and all of them are zealous for the law. [21]They have been informed that you teach all the Jews who live among the Gentiles to turn away from Moses, telling them not to circumcise their

children or live according to our customs. [22]What shall we do? They will certainly hear that you have come, [23]so do what we tell you. There are four men with us who have made a vow. [24]Take these men, join in their purification rites and pay their expenses, so that they can have their heads shaved. Then everybody will know there is no truth in these reports about you, but that you yourself are living in obedience to the law. [25]As for the Gentile believers, we have written to them our decision that they should abstain from food sacrificed to idols, from blood, from the meat of strangled animals and from sexual immorality."

[26]The next day Paul took the men and purified himself along with them. Then he went to the temple to give notice of the date when the days of purification would end and the offering would be made for each of them.

21:17-20a When Paul arrived in Jerusalem, he received a somewhat mixed reception. On the one hand, he was received "warmly" by the brethren there (v. 17). Just who formed the reception committee is not at all clear. Perhaps it referred only to the associates of Mnason with whom Paul lodged (v. 16). It is more likely that Luke intended v. 17 as a general introduction to Paul's arrival in Jerusalem and that "the brothers" represent his favorable reception by the Jerusalem Christian community as a whole.[2] There were reservations, however, and these quickly unfolded the next day when Paul and his traveling companions reported to the elders of the Jerusalem church (v. 18).[3] The apostles seem no longer to have been present in Jerusalem, and leadership of the congregation was now in the hands of a group of elders, with James, the brother of Jesus, as the presiding elder.[4]

On an earlier occasion—at the Jerusalem Conference—when Paul gave a report of his successful Gentile mission, it was met with stony silence (15:12f.). Now his report was received with greater enthusiasm. The elders "praised God" for the fruits of Paul's work among the Gentiles (v. 20). At the Jerusalem Conference they had endorsed Paul's ministry to the Gentiles, and so they naturally received the report of his missionary success with some elation. But Paul's success had created some problems for them, and they now related those to him. Probably James spoke for the group. The new situation was their own success in the Jewish Christian mission and the many thousands of new converts who had been made. They were all "zealous for the law."

---

[2]Some scholars interpret the "warm" reception as an allusion to Paul's collection for the Jerusalem church; but Luke had been silent about the collection all along, and there is no real basis in the text for seeing even a veiled allusion to it here.

[3]Note that the "we" narrative is discontinued at v. 18 and does not reappear until 27:1, which begins the journey to Rome. For the intervening events, Paul alone was involved.

[4]The Jerusalem Conference of Acts 15:6-29 seems to provide the transition to the new organizational structure. There both apostles and elders assumed the leadership (vv. 6,22,24). Even there, however, James provided the main leadership in the decision-making process.

21:20b Faithfulness to the Torah was nothing new for the Jewish Christians. Basically, that was what the agreement at the Jerusalem Conference was all about. The Jewish Christians would remain faithful to the Jewish law, but Gentile converts would not be subjected to it except for the special provisions of the apostolic decree (cf. v. 25). What was new to the present situation is hidden in the word "zealous." Paul's arrival in Jerusalem probably was in spring of A.D. 56 or 57 during the procuratorship of Felix. Josephus described this period of the mid-50s as a time of intense Jewish nationalism and political unrest. One insurrection after another rose to challenge the Roman overlords, and Felix brutally suppressed them all.[5] This only increased the Jewish hatred for Rome and inflamed anti-Gentile sentiments. It was a time when pro-Jewish sentiment was at its height, and friendliness with outsiders was viewed askance. Considering public relations, Paul's mission to the Gentiles would not have been well received. The Jerusalem elders were in somewhat of a bind. On the one hand, they had supported Paul's witness to the Gentiles at the Jerusalem Conference. Now they found Paul a persona non grata and his mission discredited not only among the Jewish populace, which they were seeking to reach, but also among their more recent converts. They did not want to reject Paul. Indeed, they praised God for his successes. Still they had their own mission to the Jews to consider, and for that Paul was a distinct liability.

21:21 Jews from the Diaspora likely were the ones who spread the reports among the Jerusalem Christians that Paul was inciting Jews to abandon their ancestral customs (v. 21b). The rumor was that he was encouraging Diaspora Jews who lived in his Gentile mission fields to forsake the law of Moses and to abandon the practice of circumcising their children. These were serious charges, for these matters struck at the very heart of the Jews' self-identity as the people of God. The Torah, particularly in its ceremonial aspects, set them apart from all other people. Circumcision in particular was a sort of badge, a physical mark set in the flesh of every Jewish male on the eighth day after birth to denote his membership in God's covenant people.[6] Would Paul have urged Jews to abandon this "sign of the covenant"? There is certainly no question that he argued strongly against seeing circumcision as a guarantee of salvation. It

---

[5]See E. Schürer, *The History of the Jewish People in the Age of Jesus Christ*, ed. G. Vermes, F. Millar, and M. Black (Edinburgh: T & T Clark, 1974), 1:462-45; B. Reicke, "Der geschichtliche Hintergrund des Apostelkonzils and der Antiochia-Episode, Gal 2:1-14," *Studia Paulina* (Haarlem: Bohn, 1953), 172-87.

[6]That by its physical nature circumcision as "the mark of the covenant" was restricted to males shows the strong male orientation of first-century Jewish religion. Females derived their covenantal status indirectly through their relation to their fathers or husbands. They had no independent religious standing. See J. Polhill, "Circumcision," MDB, 156-57.

could be no substitute for faith in Christ, for becoming a new creation in the Spirit (cf. Gal 5:6; 6:15). Consequently, he adamantly opposed circumcision of his Gentile converts. But there is no evidence that he ever encouraged Jewish Christians to abandon the practice and considerable indication to the contrary (cf. Acts 16:3; 1 Cor 7:18f.).

The same can be said for Paul's attitude toward the Torah in general. He rejected flatly the supposition that the law could be a means of salvation. He saw faith in Christ, not law, as the sole basis for one's acceptability to God. He adamantly opposed anyone who sought to impose the Torah on his Gentile converts, and this was very much within the spirit of the Jerusalem Conference (cf. 15:10f.,19,28). But there is no evidence that he urged Jewish Christians to abandon their ancestral law, and Acts would indicate that he himself remained true to the Torah in his own dealings with Jews (cf. 18:18; 20:6; 23:5). In short, Paul saw one's status in Christ as transcending the distinction between Jew and Gentile (Gal 3:28). Being in Christ neither required that the Gentile become a Jew nor that the Jew cease to be a Jew (cf. 1 Cor 9:19f.). Still, there may have been a grain of truth in the rumor that Paul was encouraging Jews of the Diaspora to abandon the Torah. It would not have been Paul's having actually urged the Jews to do so but rather the social situation of Paul's Diaspora churches. In the Diaspora, Jews who became Christians would almost inevitably have transferred from the synagogue to the predominantly Gentile churches. Acts 19:9 would indicate that this had been the case in Ephesus. Having left the base of support for their Jewish identity in the synagogue, there would be the natural inclination to adapt to the ways of the Gentile majority in the Christian churches.[7] Whether or not this was the case, Paul himself had not urged Jewish Christians to abandon the Torah, and there is no evidence that the elders themselves lent any credence to the allegations. Still, they had to deal with them. Paul's presence would soon be known throughout the Jewish Christian community (v. 22). Something had to be done to offset the rumors.

21:22-24 The elders had evidently worked out a possible solution among themselves of a means whereby Paul could by example demonstrate that he was still true to the Jewish law. This they now set before him (vv. 22-24). There were four Jewish Christians who had taken upon themselves a Nazirite vow, a rather extreme expression of Jewish piety.[8] The four were nearing the end of the period of their vow and soon would be completing it with the customary ceremony in the temple. This involved cutting their hair and burning it as an offering. In addition a

---

[7]See R. C. Tannehill, *The Narrative Unity of Luke-Acts* (Minneapolis: Fortress, 1990), 2:269.

[8]For the provisions of the Nazirite vow, see commentary on 18:18.

number of costly sacrifices were required—a male and a female lamb, a ram, and cereal and drink offerings (Num 6:14f.).

Paul was asked to join the four and bear the expenses of these rites. Aside from paying their expenses, Paul's role in the matter is not altogether clear. He obviously did not join in the vow because the minimum period for a Nazirite was thirty days, and only seven were involved here (v. 27). Also it could not have been a matter of a Nazirite "purification" ceremony in which he participated. There was such a purification ceremony in connection with Nazirite vows, but it was not a regular part of the Nazirite commitment; rather, it was a special provision in case the one under the vow came into contact with a corpse or became otherwise defiled (Num 6:9-12). That could not be the situation here because the Nazirite who underwent the purification rite had to begin the minimum thirty-day period of the vow all over again (Num 6:12). The most likely solution is that Paul was the one who underwent purification. Often a Jew on returning to the Holy Land after a sojourn in Gentile territory would undergo ritual purification. The period involved was seven days (cf. Num 19:12), which fits the present picture (v. 27). Paul thus underwent ritual purification to qualify for participation in the completion ceremony of the four Nazirites which took place within the sacred precincts of the temple. This would be a thorough demonstration of his full loyalty to the Torah, not only in his bearing the heavy expenses of the vow but also in his undergoing the necessary purification himself.[9]

21:25 James concluded his proposal to Paul with a reminder of the apostolic decrees. The words in v. 25 are to be seen as an assurance to Paul that the basic decision of the Jerusalem Conference had not been changed. Gentiles still were not being asked to live by the Jewish Torah—only to observe those basic ritual matters that made table fellowship and social interaction possible between Jewish and Gentile Christians.[10] The elders' proposal (vv. 22-24) was strictly for Paul, that he as a Jewish Christian demonstrate his fidelity to the law to offset the rumors in the Jewish Christian community. It was a sort of compromise solution

---

[9]Some interpreters see Paul using a portion of the collection to pay for the expenses of the vow, but this is wholly speculative since Acts is totally silent on the collection except for the single allusion in 24:17. Evidently, paying the expenses of Nazirites was considered a particularly exemplary act of piety. Josephus indicated that paying such expenses was one of the ways Agrippa I sought to win the favor of the Jews upon his return to Palestine (*Ant.* 19.294).

[10]For the meaning of the decrees, see commentary on 15:20. The four provisions of the decree in 21:25 correspond exactly to those in 15:20,29. The Western reading in 21:25, however, differs from the Western reading in 15:20,29. In 21:25 only idols, blood, and unchastity are listed. The negative golden rule is omitted. See H. W. Bartsch, "Traditions-geschichtliches zur 'goldenen Regel' und zum Aposteldekret," *ZNW* 75 (1984): 128-32.

and thoroughly in accord with the picture of James at the Jerusalem Conference. The apostolic decrees were themselves a type of compromise. James wanted both to acknowledge the legitimacy of Paul's law-free Gentile mission and to maintain an effective witness among the Jews, for which faithfulness to the law was absolutely essential. Ultimately the compromise did not work—either in this instance for Paul or in regard to the larger issue of the relationship between Jewish and Gentile Christianity. As Jewish nationalism increased, the Gentile mission became more and more of a liability to Jewish Christianity. In the aftermath of the Jewish War with Rome and the fall of Jerusalem in A.D. 70, Jewish Christianity was declared heretical by official Judaism; and it was no longer possible for a Christian Jew to remain in the Jewish community. James had seen the problem well and sought to present himself as a strict, Torah-abiding Jew, doubtless to strengthen the credibility of his witness to his fellow Jews.[11] Ultimately, he gave his life for his Christian witness, being put to death at the order of the high priest Ananus in A.D. 62.[12]

21:26 Paul was all too ready to be a Jew to the Jews (cf. 1 Cor 9:20). We know from his letters that the collection from the Gentile churches had brought him to Jerusalem, and the major reason for this was to express the unity between Gentile and Jewish Christianity. He knew the risks involved in coming to Jerusalem (cf. Rom 15:31). He was more than willing to participate in this symbolic act of Jewish piety if that would help to justify his Gentile mission in the eyes of the Jewish Christians. He began his purification the next day and announced in the temple the formal date when the Nazirite ceremony would be completed (v. 26). It would take place in seven days, when his own purification was fulfilled.

---

[11]Given the strong Jewish nationalism of the era, it is not necessary to revive the Baur theory and see James as Paul's antagonist as does G. Lüdemann, "Zum Antipaulismus im frühen Christentum," *EvT* 40 (1980): 437-55. Even less plausible is the view of A. J. Mattill, Jr., that the proposal of the Nazirite vow was a "set-up" by the Judaizing Christians designed to get rid of Paul ("The Purpose of Acts: Schneckenburger Reconsidered," *Apostolic History and the Gospel*, ed. W. Gasque and R. Martin [Grand Rapids: Eerdmans, 1970], 116-22).

[12]The martyrdom of James is related in Josephus, *Antiquities* 20.197-203. Evidently, Ananus used the interim between the death of Festus and the arrival of the new procurator Albinus as an opportunity to execute James. Josephus attested to the high reputation of James among the Jews when he noted that the more law-abiding Jews sent a formal protest to Agrippa against Ananus's action toward James. For a later and more legendary account of James's death, see the Tradition of Hegesippus quoted in Eusebius, *Hist. Eccl.,* 2.23, in which James was thrown from the pinnacle of the temple, stoned, and finally beaten to death with a fuller's club.

(2) The Riot in the Temple Area (21:27-36)

[27]When the seven days were nearly over, some Jews from the province of Asia saw Paul at the temple. They stirred up the whole crowd and seized him, [28]shouting, "Men of Israel, help us! This is the man who teaches all men everywhere against our people and our law and this place. And besides, he has brought Greeks into the temple area and defiled this holy place." [29](They had previously seen Trophimus the Ephesian in the city with Paul and assumed that Paul had brought him into the temple area.)

[30]The whole city was aroused, and the people came running from all directions. Seizing Paul, they dragged him from the temple, and immediately the gates were shut. [31]While they were trying to kill him, news reached the commander of the Roman troops that the whole city of Jerusalem was in an uproar. [32]He at once took some officers and soldiers and ran down to the crowd. When the rioters saw the commander and his soldiers, they stopped beating Paul.

[33]The commander came up and arrested him and ordered him to be bound with two chains. Then he asked who he was and what he had done. [34]Some in the crowd shouted one thing and some another, and since the commander could not get at the truth because of the uproar, he ordered that Paul be taken into the barracks. [35]When Paul reached the steps, the violence of the mob was so great he had to be carried by the soldiers. [36]The crowd that followed kept shouting, "Away with him!"

21:27 The purification process required a cleansing on the third and on the seventh days (Num 19:2). Likely it was on the prescribed seventh day that Paul returned to the temple to complete the ritual (v. 27). He was spotted there by some Asian Jews, who immediately began to stir up a crowd against him. Not surprisingly the opposition to Paul came from Asian Jews, probably some from Ephesus. Paul had spent three years in Ephesus and part of the time in their synagogue (19:8). They knew him well. In his Miletus address Paul alluded to plots the Ephesian Jews had already directed against him. Often Diaspora Jews were exceedingly strict in their observance of the Jewish ritual (cf. 6:9), and it may have been some of these same Asian Jews who had spread the rumors about Paul throughout Jerusalem (cf. v. 21).

21:28 The accusations they began to make against Paul were very serious. Two were the same charges leveled against Stephen (cf. 6:13): He speaks against "our law and this place"; i.e., against Torah and temple.[13]

---

[13]There are some rather striking parallels in this section with the Stephen narrative, as noted by R. C. Tannehill, *Narrative Unity*, 2:273. Not only were the charges the same, but both Paul and Stephen experienced mob violence. Both delivered speeches before their accusers, and both speeches began with the same address, "Brothers and fathers" (7:2; 22:1). Both speeches provoked a violent response (7:54-58; 22:22-23). Both Paul and Stephen were accused by Diaspora Jews (6:9-12a; 21:27). And in Paul's speech there is a linking reference to Stephen's death (22:20).

The third charge was less specific but perhaps the most valid—that Paul taught "against our people." In a sense Paul did. His leveling gospel of oneness of all in Jesus Christ, Greek as well as Jew, could ultimately do nothing other than reduce the significance of the Jews as God's chosen people. In this instance they charged him with temple violation. They accused Paul of having violated the temple by taking a Gentile beyond the court of the Gentiles into the sacred precincts that were open to Jews only; i.e., into the area of the temple proper. The large outer courtyard, known as the court of the Gentiles, was open to all. The temple proper was not. In fact, there was a stone barrier that separated the court of the Gentiles from the first courtyard of the temple proper, the court of the women.[14] According to Josephus, there were warning stones set at regular intervals along this barrier, some in Greek and some in Latin, forbidding non-Jews access beyond this point.[15] Two of these have been excavated, both with a Greek text and both with a message to the effect that any foreigner proceeding beyond the barrier did so on pain of death.[16]

There is some question whether the warnings are of a common ancient taboo type, i.e., a warning that the divinity will strike down any violator. From the testimony of Josephus, it seems more likely that the Jews actually did themselves enforce the prohibition. A speech attributed to Titus indicates that the Romans allowed the Jews to execute violators, even if the violators were Roman citizens (*War* 6.124f.). There is no evidence in the extant literature of anyone ever being executed for this offense. Whether Josephus's testimony on this matter can be trusted and whether the warnings were actually enforced, the stones have been found and are a vivid testimony to the exclusiveness of first-century Jewish religion: "No Gentile to defile our temple on pain of death." This barrier with its warning stones is likely the "wall" between Jew and Greek to which Paul alluded in Eph 2:14. Paul certainly was familiar with it. He had experienced it firsthand.

---

[14]The temple proper consisted of four courts that proceeded from greatest access to most restricted access. The first court, the court of the women, was open to all Israelites. From there one proceeded to the court of the men, open only to Israelite males. Further in was the court of the priests, open only to the Israelite priesthood. Innermost was the holy of holies, accessible only to the high priest and to him only on one day a year, the Day of Atonement. For a fuller description of the Herodian temple, see J. Polhill, "The Temple in Jesus' Day," *Biblical Illustrator* (Summer 1988): 75-80.

[15]Josephus, *War* 5.194; *Antiquities* 15.417; *Apion* 2.103f.

[16]The first was discovered in 1871 by C. Clermont-Ganneau and is now in the Museum of Ancient Orient in Istanbul. The second was discovered in 1935 outside St. Stephen's gate in Jerusalem on the road to Jericho and now resides in the Palestine Archaeological Museum in Jerusalem. The fullest treatment of the warning stones available is that of V. R. L. Fry, "The Warning Inscriptions from the Herodian Temple," Ph.D. diss., the Southern Baptist Theological Seminary, Louisville, Kentucky, 1974.

21:29 The charge was unfounded. Luke made that clear (v. 29). The Asian Jews had seen Paul in the city with Trophimus, one of the Ephesian representatives in the collection delegation (20:4). They were looking for something against Paul, and they quickly jumped to the conclusion that Paul had taken the Gentile into the inner area of the temple beyond the warning stones. Paul had in fact been there himself. He would have gone there in connection with his purification. He had not taken Trophimus there. On an occasion when he was trying to establish his Jewishness, it was the last thing he would have done! It was an instance of sheer irony. In the temple for his own purification, Paul was accused of having defiled it.

21:30 Luke could be accused of exaggerating in saying that "the whole city" was aroused (v. 30). But one must recall that the temple area was very much the "town square." The court of the Gentiles was a large area, and great crowds would gather there. When all the hubbub started, people came running from every direction. Paul was dragged out of the temple proper into the court of the Gentiles. The gates to the sacred precincts were slammed shut, perhaps to protect the area from any "further" defilement from the unseemly mob action taking place outside. Some interpreters see a certain symbolism in the shutting of the gates. This is the last scene at the temple in Acts. The gates were closed. Is this symbolic that with this final refusal of God's messenger the temple was forever closed to God's purposes?[17]

21:31 Along the northwest corner of the wall that surrounded the whole temple complex stood the Tower of Antonia, a fortress built by Herod the Great for defense of the temple. The Roman troops were garrisoned there. Antonia had several high towers, one which is said to have been 100 feet high, allowing a full view of the entire temple area. Perhaps it was a sentry posted there who first caught sight of the gathering mob and sent word to his commander, the Roman tribune in charge of the Jerusalem cohort (v. 31). This tribune, whose name is later disclosed as Claudius Lysias (23:26), would play a major role in the following two chapters. As a tribune he was a high-ranking Roman military officer in charge of a cohort, which consisted of 1,000 soldiers (760 infantry and 240 cavalry). Since the procurator resided in Caesarea and only made periodic visits to Jerusalem, Lysias had the prime responsibility for the Roman administration and peace-keeping within the city. Not accidentally the barracks were located in Antonia adjacent to the temple. Stairs led from Antonia directly into the court of the Gentiles. The Romans were well aware that should any unrest arise in the city, it would most likely begin in the temple area.

---

[17]An idea first suggested by T. D. Bernard, as cited by F. F. Bruce, "The Church of Jerusalem in the Acts of the Apostles," *BJRL* 67 (1985): 659.

21:32-33 Lysias lost no time in dealing with this riot. He evidently took a considerable contingent of soldiers with him. Verse 32 indicates that he took along "centurions" ("officers," NIV). Since a centurion commanded a hundred soldiers, and since more than one centurion is indicated, Lysias's force on this occasion consisted of at least two hundred. It must have been a significant show of force, for the crowd immediately stopped beating Paul (v. 32). Since Paul was the obvious object of the crowd's ire, Lysias immediately arrested him, binding him with two chains (v. 33). The significance of the "two" chains is not altogether clear. Paul may have been handcuffed on both arms and chained to a soldier on each side, or he could have been bound hand and foot, as Agabus had predicted he would be (cf. 21:11). In any event, from this point on Paul was "in chains," if not always literally so, at least in the sense that he was a prisoner to the very last word of Acts.

21:34-36 Lysias was totally unable to ascertain any substantive accusation against Paul because of the disorder of the crowd (v. 34). As with most mobs, many of the participants probably did not know what the commotion was all about (cf. 19:32). So Lysias ordered that Paul be taken to the barracks. When they reached the steps to Antonia, the soldiers had to lift Paul up and carry him to protect him from the violence of the mob (v. 35). Why this was necessary is not immediately clear. Paul may have been somewhat incapacitated from the severity of his beating. If he was bound at the feet, this would certainly explain why the soldiers found it more expedient to carry him. As they hastened up the steps, the crowd milled below, shouting, "Away with him!"—the same words the mob had screamed against Jesus (cf. Luke 23:18; John 19:15).

(3) Paul's Request to Address the Crowd (21:37-40)

[37]As the soldiers were about to take Paul into the barracks, he asked the commander, "May I say something to you?"

"Do you speak Greek?" he replied. [38]"Aren't you the Egyptian who started a revolt and led four thousand terrorists out into the desert some time ago?"

[39]Paul answered, "I am a Jew, from Tarsus in Cilicia, a citizen of no ordinary city. Please let me speak to the people."

[40]Having received the commander's permission, Paul stood on the steps and motioned to the crowd. When they were all silent, he said to them in Aramaic:

21:37-38 As they reached the top of the stairs and were about to enter the barracks, Paul asked the tribune for permission to make a request (v. 37). His language was in polite, polished Greek, and the tribune was amazed that he would speak Greek in the first place.[18] Lysias

---

[18]Ἑλληνιστὶ γινώσκεις is an ellipsis for Ἑλληνιστὶ γινώσκεις λαλεῖν. Εἰ ἔξεστίν μοι is very polite language.

then disclosed that he had suspected Paul of being a revolutionary, perhaps the Egyptian who had stirred up a considerable following some time before (v. 38). Josephus also spoke of this Egyptian.[19] According to him, the Egyptian was a false prophet who stirred up a following of some 30,000 "dupes" (ēpatēmenōn), led them into the wilderness and from there to the Mount of Olives, where he promised that the walls of Jerusalem would fall at his command and allow them easy subjugation of the Roman force. Instead of Jerusalem's walls falling, Felix arrived on the scene with heavy troops, killed four hundred of them, took another two hundred captive, and put the Egyptian and the rest to flight. This was just one of the many incidents of unrest and political foment Josephus related as having occurred during the tenure of Felix. The difference between Luke's 4,000 and Josephus's 30,000 is most likely evidence of Josephus's tendency to give exaggerated figures.[20]

In Acts the followers of the Egyptian are described as *sicarii* ("terrorists," NIV). Josephus also spoke of this terrorist group among the more zealous Jewish freedom fighters (*War* 2.254-57). Arising in the time of Felix, they derived their name from the Latin word *sica*, meaning *dagger*. Their practice was to mingle in large crowds on special occasions, plunge the daggers into their pro-Roman political enemies, and then quickly disappear into the crowd.[21] It is easy to see how Lysias might have confused Paul with these movements. He had witnessed many of them rise and fall. He naturally associated them with crowds and riots like the one surrounding Paul. In this instance perhaps he thought the Egyptian had returned and some of his former "dupes" were now repaying him.

21:39-40 Paul was no terrorist. He was not even an Egyptian. He was rather a Jew and a citizen of the proud Hellenistic city of Tarsus, "no ordinary city" as he described it (v. 39).[22] The reference at this point is to his Tarsian citizenship, not his Roman citizenship, which is not divulged to Lysias until later (22:25-29). Originally it was impossible for a Roman

---

[19]There are some discrepancies between Josephus's accounts. *War* (2.261-63) gives the figure of 30,000, but not the number killed and captured. *Antiquities* (20.168-72) mentions the collapsing walls, whereas *War* seems to indicate a more natural seizure of the city by surprise attack.

[20]An ingenious reconciliation of the two figures has been suggested, involving a scribe possibly confusing an original Δ in Josephus (the symbol for the number 4) with a Λ (the number 30). The capital forms of these two letters are obviously quite similar.

[21]For their relation to the larger Zealot movement, see M. Hengel, "Zeloten und Sikarier," *Die Zeloten*, zweite Auflage (Leiden: Brill, 1976), 387-412.

[22]The expression "no ordinary city" (οὐκ ἀσήμου) was a common Greek litotes and is found in many Greek writers. Cf. Strabo 8.6.15. The expression is too common to link it with any one specific writing as does R. Harris, who wants to trace it to Euripides' *Ion* ("Did St. Paul Quote Euripides?" *ExpTim* 31 [1919-20]: 36f.).

citizen to hold dual citizenship, but by the time of the emperors this evidently became quite common.[23] Paul's exchange with Lysias was relevant to his request to address the Jews. That he was a Jew obviously gave him some grounds for addressing his fellow Jews. That he was obviously cultured assured Lysias that he was not one of the rabble and merited the honor of his request. Permission granted, Paul stood at the top of the steps, brought a hush over the crowd with a wave of his hand, and addressed them in their own native tongue (v. 40).[24] The crowd had accused him of teaching against the Jewish people, the law, and the temple. The speech that follows was his defense against these charges.

(4) Paul's Speech before the Temple Mob (22:1-21)

[1]"Brothers and fathers, listen now to my defense."

[2]When they heard him speak to them in Aramaic, they became very quiet.

Then Paul said: [3]"I am a Jew, born in Tarsus of Cilicia, but brought up in this city. Under Gamaliel I was thoroughly trained in the law of our fathers and was just as zealous for God as any of you are today. [4]I persecuted the followers of this Way to their death, arresting both men and women and throwing them into prison, [5]as also the high priest and all the Council can testify. I even obtained letters from them to their brothers in Damascus, and went there to bring these people as prisoners to Jerusalem to be punished.

[6]"About noon as I came near Damascus, suddenly a bright light from heaven flashed around me. [7]I fell to the ground and heard a voice say to me, 'Saul! Saul! Why do you persecute me?'

[8]"'Who are you, Lord?' I asked.

"'I am Jesus of Nazareth, whom you are persecuting,' he replied. [9]My companions saw the light, but they did not understand the voice of him who was speaking to me.

[10]"'What shall I do, Lord?' I asked.

"'Get up,' the Lord said, 'and go into Damascus. There you will be told all that you have been assigned to do.' [11]My companions led me by the hand into Damascus, because the brilliance of the light had blinded me.

[12]"A man named Ananias came to see me. He was a devout observer of the law and highly respected by all the Jews living there. [13]He stood beside me and said, 'Brother Saul, receive your sight!' And at that very moment I was able to see him.

[14]"Then he said: 'The God of our fathers has chosen you to know his will and to see the Righteous One and to hear words from his mouth. [15]You will be his

---

[23]See A. N. Sherwin-White, *The Roman Citizenship*, 2nd ed. (Oxford: Clarendon, 1973), 245-50. For a dissenting view, see J. Schwartz, "A propos du stutut personnel de l'Apôtre Paul," *RHPR* 37 (1957): 91-96.

[24]It is generally agreed that the language of Jerusalem in the first century was Western Aramaic, the common speech of non-Greeks in Western Asia. For a dissenting view that argues for Hebrew as the language of Judea, see J. M. Grintz, "Hebrew as the Spoken and Written Language in the Last Days of the Second Temple," *JBL* 79 (1960): 32-47.

witness to all men of what you have seen and heard. [16]And now what are you
waiting for? Get up, be baptized and wash your sins away, calling on his name.'

[17]"When I returned to Jerusalem and was praying at the temple, I fell into a
trance [18]and saw the Lord speaking. 'Quick!' he said to me. 'Leave Jerusalem
immediately, because they will not accept your testimony about me.'

[19]" 'Lord,' I replied, 'these men know that I went from one synagogue to
another to imprison and beat those who believe in you. [20]And when the blood of
your martyr Stephen was shed, I stood there giving my approval and guarding
the clothes of those who were killing him.'

[21]"Then the Lord said to me, 'Go; I will send you far away to the Gentiles.' "

Paul's speech before the temple crowd was primarily aimed at establishing his full commitment to Judaism. What he evidently could not
accomplish through his participation in the Nazirite vow he now sought
to establish by this address. Basically, the speech was his own first-person
narration of the events Luke related in chap. 9: his former zeal for Judaism (vv. 1-5), his encounter with the risen Christ on the Damascus road
(vv. 6-11), and the visit of Ananias (vv. 12-16). The final portion of his
speech is new to the Acts narrative but evidently occurred on Paul's first
visit to Jerusalem after his conversion, the visit covered by 9:26-30. It
relates a vision Paul had in the temple, where the risen Lord commissioned him for his mission to the Gentiles (vv. 17-21). Up to this point
the crowd had listened attentively to Paul's words. With his reference to
the Gentile witness, Paul was in trouble with them again (v. 22).

HIS FORMER ZEAL (22:1-5). **22:1** In his opening words Paul
addressed the crowd with the formal introduction Stephen used before the
Sanhedrin, "Brothers and fathers" (v. 1; cf. 7:2). Both were making a
defense and were concerned to establish their loyalty to Judaism; hence
this deferential Jewish address. Paul described his address in formal language as a "defense" (*apologia*). His speech did not, however, address
the charge that started the riot—that he had desecrated the temple. It did
address the larger issue—Paul's faithfulness to Judaism. This defense
continues to unfold in the speeches that follow—before Felix and the
Jews in chap. 24 and before Agrippa in chap. 26. In a sense all the
remainder of Acts is Paul's defense before the Jews. Paul is shown to be
a faithful Jew, particularly when one agrees with him that faith in the
risen Christ is the true culmination of Judaism.

22:2-3 As in 21:40, Paul's use of their native tongue underlined his
Jewishness and brought a hush over the crowd (v. 2).[25] Paul then showed
how his early life was in every respect that of a strict, practicing Jew. He
was born in Tarsus, reared in Jerusalem, and educated under Gamaliel

---

[25]Bruce (*Acts:* NIC, 439) describes the effect as like that of an Englishman addressing
Irish nationalists in Gaelic.

(v. 3). "Born, reared, educated" was a fixed biographical formula common in Greek writings. The significance to this is that when Paul referred to his being "brought up" in Jerusalem, the most natural meaning is that he was reared from childhood in Jerusalem, not in Tarsus, as is commonly supposed.[26] His family must have moved to Jerusalem when he was still quite young. This ties in with the later reference to his nephew's being in Jerusalem (23:16). It underscores the point Paul wanted to make to the Jerusalem crowd: he was no Diaspora maverick but was nurtured from childhood in the holy city itself. Acts 22:3 is the sole New Testament reference to Paul's education under Gamaliel,[27] and this tradition has often been challenged by scholars on the grounds that his letters do not reflect formal rabbinic training.[28] More recent scholarship, however, has indicated many points at which Paul reflected thoroughly rabbinic thought,[29] and in his letters Paul himself referred to his thorough training in and zeal for the law (cf. Gal 1:14; Phil 3:4-7). Again, this is the very point Paul wanted to underscore with the Jerusalem Jews: far from being a lawbreaker, as they were now accusing him (21:21,28), Paul's former life had been marked by a zeal for the law that matched or exceeded their own.

22:4-5 Paul then described his former days as a persecutor of the Christian movement. Here his own account parallels Luke's earlier description of Paul's days as persecutor of the Christians (8:3; 9:1f.; cf. 26:9-11), and these other texts supplement the present passage. As in 9:2 Paul referred to Christianity as "the Way," a designation that will recur throughout his defense speeches. It not only serves to link Christianity closely with Judaism[30] but also with Christ. It was "the Way" Christ

---

[26]The common view has been that Paul was reared in Tarsus and only came to Jerusalem at age twelve or thirteen for his study under Gamaliel. Cf. E. F. Synge, "St. Paul's Boyhood and Conversion and His Attitude Toward Race," *ExpTim* 94 (1983): 260-63. The set formula "born, reared, educated" (γεγεννημένος, ἀνατεθραμμένος, πεπαιδευμένος) speaks against this assumption. In the Greek writings ἀνατεθραμμένος refers to childhood upbringing, much like our term "reared." See W. C. Van Unnik, "Tarsus or Jerusalem: The City of Paul's Youth," trans. G. Ogg, *Sparsa Collecta*, Part 1 (Leiden: Brill, 1973), 259-320; and "Once Again: Tarsus or Jerusalem," ibid., 321-27.

[27]Gamaliel the Elder was the leading rabbinic scholar of his day, representing the school of Hillel. See the commentary and notes on 5:34.

[28]E.g., M. S. Enslin, "Paul and Gamaliel," *JR* 7 (1927): 360-75. For a response that shows evidence for the viewpoints of Hillel in Paul's writings, see J. Jeremias, "Paulus als Hillelit," *Neotestamentica et Semitica*, ed. E. E. Ellis and M. Wilcox (Edinburgh: T & T Clark, 1969), 88-94. See also E. F. Harrison, "Acts 22:3—A Test Case for Luke's Reliability," *New Dimensions in New Testament Study*, ed. R. N. Longenecker and M. C. Tenney (Grand Rapids: Zondervan, 1974), 251-60.

[29]E.g., W. D. Davies, *Paul and Rabbinic Judaism* (London: SPCK, 1958).

[30]See the earlier discussion of "the Way" in the introduction to this chapter.

established; to persecute the Way was to persecute Christ himself (9:5; 22:8).[31]

THE ENCOUNTER ON THE DAMASCUS ROAD (22:6-11). At this point Paul related his vision of Christ on the Damascus road. This is one of three detailed accounts of Paul's conversion given in Acts. The first, contained in 9:1-30, is Luke's third-person narrative of Paul's experience. The present account and that of 26:4-23 are Paul's own testimony to the event, delivered in the course of his defense speeches. The three accounts are parallel in their essentials but differ in small details. The most striking differences are to be seen in a comparison between the two accounts given in Paul's defense speeches. These are very much adapted to the audience to whom they were addressed. For instance, in the present speech before the Jewish mob, Paul gave close attention to Ananias and his devout Jewishness. In the speech of chap. 26 before Agrippa and the Roman officials, Ananias is not even mentioned. Paul considered the role of this pious Jewish Christian not as important for the predominantly Gentile audience.[32] The significant matter is that Luke included a detailed treatment of Paul's conversion three times, this device of repetition underscoring the event and testifying to its importance.

22:6-9 Verses 6-11 are essentially parallel to 9:3-8, the only differences being in small details and the first-person narration. Only 22:6 gives the specific detail that it was "about noon" when the vision came upon Paul.[33] This heightened the emphasis on the brightness of the vision. This was no nighttime experience but occurred in broad daylight, at noon when the sun was at its brightest. Verse 7 is closely parallel to 9:4, relating how Paul fell to the ground and heard the heavenly voice addressing him by his Hebrew name, "Saul, Saul, why do you persecute me?" As in 9:5, Paul responded by asking the heavenly visitant to identify himself— "Who are you, Lord?" Of all three conversion accounts, only in 22:8 do the words "of Nazareth" occur. The full designation "Jesus of Nazareth" was appropriate to the Jewish audience before whom Paul was relating his experience. The most significant difference between Paul's account and the earlier conversion narrative occurs in 22:9, where it is said that Paul's traveling companions saw the light but did not understand the voice speaking to Paul. In 9:7 the companions are said to have heard the sound but not to have seen anyone. Paul's account emphasizes their seeing; the earlier account, their hearing. Both accounts make the same point. The companions were witnesses to the experience and could verify

---

[31]S. Lyonnet, "La 'Voie' dans les Actes des Apôtres," *RSR* 69 (1981): 149-64.

[32]For a further treatment of the three conversion accounts and bibliography, see the introductory comments to 9:1-31 and nn. 1-3 of chap. IV.

[33]The same term (μεσημβρία) occurs in 8:26, where it seems to have the meaning *south*.

that something objective took place. It was not merely an inner experience of Paul's psyche. On the other hand, the companions were not participants in the experience: they heard a sound but did not receive the message, saw a light but not the risen Lord. The vision itself was solely Paul's experience.[34]

22:10 Verse 10 parallels 9:6 with the difference that in Paul's account he referred to Jesus as "the Lord" when relating the command to rise and go into Damascus. Paul made his confession known before his Jewish audience. At the outset of his vision he may not have known whom he was addressing as Lord (v. 8). Now he knew that it was Jesus, the risen Lord. Up to this point in his speech, Paul had identified closely with his Jewish listeners. In every way he had shown himself to be as Jewish as they were. Now he began to draw the line that differentiated himself from them. On the Damascus road he had seen the risen Jesus. Now he confessed Jesus as Lord. He surely wished the same for them. It was not inappropriate for a faithful Jew to confess Jesus as Lord. He was himself a living witness to that.

22:11 Verse 11 concludes the opening scene of Paul's conversion account. It closely parallels 9:8, relating Paul's blindness and how his companions had to lead him by hand into Damascus.[35] The most significant difference from the earlier account is the reference to "the brilliance of the light" in Paul's account. Indeed, the emphasis on light is striking when one compares chap. 9 with chap. 22.[36] The light was so great it overwhelmed the noonday sun (v. 6). Paul's companions "saw the light" (v. 9). Paul was blinded by "the brilliance of the light" (v. 11). None of these details occur in chap. 9. Perhaps this was Paul's way of highlighting the significance of his conversion. In his experience on the Damascus road, he came to a confession of the risen Lord. He had "seen the light." He wished the same for his fellow Jews in the temple square.

THE ROLE OF ANANIAS (22:12-16). The account of Ananias's visit to Paul parallels 9:10-17. Although the substance of the two accounts is basically the same, there is not the close verbal agreement that one finds in the two accounts of the vision on the Damascus road. The primary difference is due to the fact that this is Paul's account of his own experience. Thus he did not relate the vision that came to Ananias (9:10-16) but rather Ananias's visit to him. The substance of Ananias's vision is transferred to his visit with Paul as Ananias related that experience to him.

---

[34]For a further treatment of the differences between 9:7 and 22:9, see n. 15 of chap. IV. See also M. W. Meyer, "The Light and Voice on the Damascus Road," *Forum* 2 (1986): 27-35.

[35]In place of οὐκ ἐνέβλεπον B has οὐδὲν ἔβλεπον, which is closer to 9:8 and, on the basis of a scribal error of sight, has some possibility of being the original reading.

[36]See D. M. Stanley, "Paul's Conversion in Acts: Why the Three Accounts?" *CBQ* 15 (1953): 315-38.

22:12 Paul introduced Ananias as a pious Jew, a strict observer of the Torah, and a person held in high esteem by the Jewish community in Damascus. This is in striking contrast to 9:10, where Luke introduced Ananias as a Christian disciple. The difference is due to the different settings of the two accounts. In Luke's account in chap. 9 Ananias was the essential link-up between the newly converted Paul and the Christian community. In Paul's account before the Jerusalem Jews, Ananias's devotion to Judaism was stressed. Paul wished to make the same point about Ananias he had been making about himself—that his Christian faith in no way detracted from his loyalty to Judaism. This emphasis continues throughout Paul's account of Ananias, where he is consistently portrayed as very Jewish.

22:13-15 Verse 13 parallels 9:17-18 with considerably less detail, relating how Paul recovered his sight through the intercession of Ananias.[37] Verse 14 is not really paralleled in chap. 9, although the idea of Paul's being "chosen" is related in Ananias's vision at 9:15. Ananias's words to Paul have a strong Jewish flavor. "God of our fathers" is strong Old Testament language. The "Righteous One" is a Jewish messianic title, found earlier in the speeches of Peter and of Stephen to Jews (3:14; 7:52). Ananias delivered Christ's commission to Paul. He was to be a witness to all people (v. 15; cf. 9:15). The commission was rather general at this point. Obviously the Jewish crowd did not catch on that all people included the Gentiles. This became much more specific in Paul's account of his temple vision (v. 21). At that point the Jewish crowd got the message all too clearly (cf. v. 22).

22:16 The scene with Ananias concludes with v. 16, which relates Paul's baptism (cf. 9:18b). The phrase translated "what are you waiting for?" is a common Greek idiom and implies that it was time Paul acted on this commission from the Lord.[38] The first step obviously was to be baptized into the community of believers. "Be baptized and wash your sins away" could be taken as a proof text for baptismal regeneration. The overarching term, however, is "calling upon the name of the Lord," the profession of faith in Christ that is the basis for the act of baptism.[39]

---

[37]The verb translated "I was able to see him" in NIV is ἀνάβλεψον, which is perhaps an intended double entendre—"I looked up [at him]"; "I saw again."

[38]Τί μέλλεις is found with some frequency in Greek literature and generally with the meaning *What are you waiting for?* It is possible that here it may have the meaning *What are you going to do about it?* (so I. H. Marshall, *The Acts of the Apostles*, TNTC [Grand Rapids: Eerdmans, 1980], 357).

[39]Since βάπτισαι is in the middle voice, it could possibly be taken as a strict reflexive ("baptize yourself") and thus be evidence for self-baptism. It is more likely that it is causative—"have yourself baptized." One would assume from the sole presence of Ananias in the context (9:18; 22:16) that Ananias administered the rite. On baptism see B. S. Easton, "Self-baptism," *AJT* 24 (1920): 513-18.

THE COMMISSION IN THE TEMPLE (22:17-21). **22:17** Paul concluded his conversion account by telling of a vision he had in the temple which occurred on his "return" to Jerusalem (v. 17). This would indicate that it took place on his first visit to Jerusalem following his conversion (Acts 9:26-30). The account of Acts 9 does not relate this incident. Perhaps the reason Paul referred to it is that it indirectly answers the mob's charge that he had defiled the temple. A person who goes to the temple for prayer is not likely to desecrate it.[40] In the temple Paul fell into a trance[41] and had a vision of the Lord. In many ways Paul's vision in the temple parallels the call of Isaiah (Isa 6:1-13). Just as with Isaiah, Paul had a vision of the Lord (for Isaiah the Lord was Yahweh). Both experienced a call, a commission. Both were told that the people would resist their message. In Isaiah's case the prophet was told to remain in the city in the face of the resistance. Paul was told to leave. The content of Paul's commission in the temple is also paralleled by Paul's own references to the experience in his letters. Paul expressed his call to the apostolate in terms of a vision of the Lord (1 Cor 9:1; 15:8). As here, Paul connected his call directly with his conversion and transformation from persecutor to witness for Christ (Gal 1:13-16; 1 Cor 15:9-11). Finally, Paul interpreted his call specifically as a call to the Gentiles (v. 21; Gal 1:16).[42]

22:18-21 Paul's command to leave Jerusalem (v. 18) was perhaps connected with the conflict he encountered in the synagogue of the Hellenistic Jews (9:29). They certainly would not accept Paul's testimony. Still, Paul protested against the order to leave (vv. 19-20). Such protests are a common feature of biblical commissioning narratives.[43] Isaiah protested his unworthiness (Isa 6:5). Paul's protest was that he had a convincing testimony to bear. All Jerusalem knew his former reputation as a persecutor of the Christians, even to the point of participation in Stephen's martyrdom (cf. 7:58b; 8:1a).[44] They would know that something dramatic must have happened to reverse his direction. Still the Lord insisted that Paul go from Jerusalem (v. 21). He had another task for him—to witness to the Gentiles. Paul's Gentile mission was thus con-

---

[40]J. D. Williams, *Acts*, GNC (San Francisco: Harper & Row, 1985), 376.

[41]Cf. Peter's similar trance in 10:10; 11:5, where the same word (ἔκστασις) is used.

[42]The parallels to both Isaiah and to Paul's epistles have been noted by O. Betz, "Die Vision des Paulus in Temple von Jerusalem," *Verborum Veritas*, Festschrift für Gustav Stahlin (Wuppertal: Rolf Brockhaus, 1970), 113-23.

[43]For the "protest" in commission narratives see B. Hubbard, "Commissioning Accounts," *Perspectives on Luke-Acts*, ed. C. H. Talbert (Edinburgh: T & T Clark, 1978), 197f.

[44]In v. 20 Stephen is described as a μάρτυς. This is the earliest NT evidence for the word moving beyond its general sense of "witness" to the more specific nuance of a martyr, a witness unto death. Cf. the latter meaning in Rev 1:5; 2:13; 3:14.

nected closely to the refusal of the Jews to accept his witness to Christ. One recalls Jesus' parable of the great banquet that makes this same point (Luke 14:16-24). It also was the problem Paul wrestled with in Rom 9–11. His answer there was that the obduracy of Israel was perhaps a temporary hardening to allow for the gospel to be taken to the Gentiles. In any event, the reference to the Gentiles led to an immediate fulfillment of Jesus' warning that the people would not accept his testimony. This was certainly true of the temple crowd listening to Paul. With the mention of the Gentiles, the silence ceased, the mob mentality resumed, and Paul was cut off (v. 22).

(5) The Attempted Examination by the Tribune (22:22-29)

22The crowd listened to Paul until he said this. Then they raised their voices and shouted, "Rid the earth of him! He's not fit to live!"
23As they were shouting and throwing off their cloaks and flinging dust into the air, **24**the commander ordered Paul to be taken into the barracks. He directed that he be flogged and questioned in order to find out why the people were shouting at him like this. **25**As they stretched him out to flog him, Paul said to the centurion standing there, "Is it legal for you to flog a Roman citizen who hasn't even been found guilty?"
26When the centurion heard this, he went to the commander and reported it. "What are you going to do?" he asked. "This man is a Roman citizen."
27The commander went to Paul and asked, "Tell me, are you a Roman citizen?"
"Yes, I am," he answered.
28Then the commander said, "I had to pay a big price for my citizenship."
"But I was born a citizen," Paul replied.
29Those who were about to question him withdrew immediately. The commander himself was alarmed when he realized that he had put Paul, a Roman citizen, in chains.

The narrative following Paul's address is extremely dramatic and filled with suspense. At first it looked once more as though Paul might be torn to shreds by the Jewish mob (v. 22), but he was again rescued by the Roman tribune and taken safely into the barracks. But then the tide turned against Paul again as the tribune decided to examine him by the cruel Roman method of scourging (v. 24). Again Paul was rescued—this time by an appeal to his Roman citizenship (vv. 25-29).

22:22-23 Paul should have known better than to refer to his Gentile witness. It was ultimately Paul's openness to Gentiles that got him in trouble with the crowd (21:29). In those days of rising Jewish nationalism, Paul's law-free Gentile mission seemed to be disloyal to all that was Jewish (cf. 21:21). It was no surprise that the crowed resumed its cry of "away with him" (v. 22; cf. 21:36). This time they escalated their outcry, adding that such a scoundrel had no right even to exist. Their clamor was accompanied by wild gestures of outrage. No one is quite sure what they did with their cloaks. They either tore them as a gesture of horror at blasphemy (14:14), or they threw them off their bodies as if ready to stone Paul (cf. 7:58), or they shook them out as if trying to rid themselves of the contamination of his blasphemy, or they waved them wildly in the air to express their collective outrage.[45] Neither is the symbolism of casting dust in the air altogether clear. It may have been a gesture of horror at perceived blasphemy, or it may have been that they hurled dust at Paul for lack of something more solid from the temple courtyard.

22:24 In any event, it was not a safe setting for Paul, and Lysias quickly ordered him to be taken into the barracks. The tribune still did not have any idea of what the crowd had against Paul (cf. 21:34). Paul's address had clarified nothing for him, particularly since it was in Aramaic. Therefore he decided to use the standard Roman method for "getting the truth" out of a slave or a common provincial, the form of examination under torture known by the Latin name *flagellum*. This was a particularly cruel manner of scourging that consisted of a beating across the raw flesh with leather thongs in which were inserted rough pieces of bone or metal. The thongs were set in a stout wooden handle.[46] This was a much more severe manner of beating than that of the rods which Paul and Silas underwent at Philippi (16:22f.,37; cf. 2 Cor 11:25). It was not uncommon for the victim to die as a result of the flagellum.

22:25-26 Paul was not about to undergo such torture unnecessarily; and as they stretched him out for the flogging,[47] he wisely inquired: "Is it legal for you to flog a Roman citizen who hasn't even been found guilty?"[48] The seemingly innocent question immediately caught the attention of the centurion in charge of the scourging. It definitely was not legal to examine a Roman citizen by scourging. The Valerian and Porcian laws clearly established the illegality of such an act, and any Roman officer who transgressed this exemption would himself be guilty of a serious breach of law. The centurion immediately halted the process and

---

[45]The problem is with the meaning of the verb ῥιπτέω. The earliest commentator on this passage, Chrysostom, interpreted it as "shaking out" (*Hom.* 48:2). See K. Lake and H. J. Cadbury, eds., *The Beginnings of Christianity* (London: Macmillan, 1933), 5:275-77.

[46]See Bruce, *Acts:* NIC, 445.

[47]Προέτειναν αὐτὸν τοῖς ἱμᾶσιν (v. 25) could either be "they stretched him out with the thongs" or "they stretched him out for the thongs" (for receiving the beating). The NIV follows the latter.

[48]Ἀκατάκριτον could either be "without condemnation" or "without a charge." Although Paul had neither been charged nor condemned, Roman citizens were evidently subject to scourging only when actually convicted of a crime. Cicero's famous quote would indicate that in his day flogging a Roman citizen was simply not conceivable: "To bind a Roman citizen is a crime, to flog him is an abomination, to slay him is almost an act of murder" (*Verrine Orations* 2.5.66).

lost no time in reporting the new development to his commanding officer (v. 26).

22:27-28 By now Lysias must have been thoroughly perplexed about Paul. At first he mistook him for an Egyptian revolutionary. Then he learned that he was a Jew and a citizen of the important city of Tarsus, a man of some culture who spoke polished Greek. Now he learned that Paul was a Roman citizen. The surprises were not over. Soon he learned that Paul was no Johnny-come-lately to citizenship status like himself but one who was *born* a citizen (v. 28).[49] Lysias's comment that he had purchased his citizenship would have been most unlikely in the earlier empire. Citizenship was often conferred for performance of some service to the state or for military duty. Slaves of a citizen who were freed on the basis of service to their owner were granted citizenship. With the granting of colony status whole towns were given citizenship.[50] But individual purchase of the rights of citizenship would have been looked on askance. There is evidence, however, that under Claudius there was increasing abuse of the privilege; and purchase of citizenship became common.[51] That Lysias purchased his citizenship during this time is highly likely given his name, Claudius Lysias (23:26). One generally took the name of the patron through whom citizenship was obtained.[52] It is possible that Lysias was being a bit sarcastic when he referred to paying a "big price" for his citizenship, the implication being perhaps that "now it seems that just anyone can afford it."[53] If that was so, Paul's response would have been a shocker: no, he did not pay a big price but was *born* into it.

There has been much speculation about how Paul's family received the citizenship. One theory is that they were part of a large resettlement of Jewish freedmen by Pompey in Cilicia in 63 B.C. This is based on a misunderstanding of Pompey's action as well as on a misapplication of a tradition from Jerome that Paul's family migrated to Tarsus from Gischala in Galilee.[54] Another view suggests that the tentmaking trade of Paul's family may have proved useful to the Roman military and been rewarded

---

[49]For a discussion of how one proved citizenship status and the abuse of citizen rights, see A. N. Sherwin-White, *Roman Society and Roman Law in the New Testament* (Oxford: Clarendon, 1963), 151f., and commentary on 16:37.

[50]See H. J. Cadbury, *The Book of Acts in History* (New York: Harper, 1955), 74-77.

[51]See Sherwin-White, *The Roman Citizenship*, 237-50.

[52]Lysias may have worked his way up through the military ranks and bought his citizenship to qualify him as a tribune. Tribunes had to be citizens with equestrian rank. See Sherwin-White, *Roman Society and Roman Law*, 155f.

[53]The Roman historian Dio Cassius (60.17.5f.) seems to bear this out, noting that Claudius's wife Messalina and the members of her court would sell citizenship rights for their own personal gain. He adds that at first the price was high but gradually degenerated to the point where citizenship could be had for a few scraps of glass.

[54]Sherwin-White, *Roman Society and Roman Law*, 151f.

with citizenship. Such suggestions are wholly speculative. We simply do not know how his family came into citizenship status. Luke made his point well, however. Paul was a Roman citizen and one of considerable status. His citizenship would hereafter play a large role in the narrative of Acts as Paul interacted with Roman officials.

22:29 Verse 29 closes the examination scene. On learning of Paul's citizenship, the whole procedure was stopped immediately. Lysias was himself quite alarmed (*ephobēthē*), realizing that he had placed Paul in chains. The picture here is not wholly clear, and our knowledge of Roman law is limited. Evidently the Julian and Porcian laws protected Roman citizens from summary arrest, from being placed in chains without a preliminary hearing. Paul's situation was complicated by the fact that his detention could be considered protective custody rather than arrest.[55] However that may be, from this point on Lysias treated Paul with great respect. He still did not know the charges against him. Examination by scourging had been ruled out. He now turned to another avenue for answering his questions—the Jewish Sanhedrin.

(6) Paul before the Sanhedrin (22:30–23:11)

[30]The next day, since the commander wanted to find out exactly why Paul was being accused by the Jews, he released him and ordered the chief priests and all the Sanhedrin to assemble. Then he brought Paul and had him stand before them.

[1]Paul looked straight at the Sanhedrin and said, "My brothers, I have fulfilled my duty to God in all good conscience to this day." [2]At this the high priest Ananias ordered those standing near Paul to strike him on the mouth. [3]Then Paul said to him, "God will strike you, you whitewashed wall! You sit there to judge me according to the law, yet you yourself violate the law by commanding that I be struck!"

[4]Those who were standing near Paul said, "You dare to insult God's high priest?"

[5]Paul replied, "Brothers, I did not realize that he was the high priest; for it is written: 'Do not speak evil about the ruler of your people.'"

[6]Then Paul, knowing that some of them were Sadducees and the others Pharisees, called out in the Sanhedrin, "My brothers, I am a Pharisee, the son of a Pharisee. I stand on trial because of my hope in the resurrection of the dead." [7]When he said this, a dispute broke out between the Pharisees and the Sadducees, and the assembly was divided. [8](The Sadducees say that there is no resurrection, and that there are neither angels nor spirits, but the Pharisees acknowledge them all.)

[9]There was a great uproar, and some of the teachers of the law who were Pharisees stood up and argued vigorously. "We find nothing wrong with this man," they said. "What if a spirit or an angel has spoken to him?" [10]The dispute

---

[55]E. Haenchen, *The Acts of the Apostles* (Philadelphia: Westminster, 1971), 634, n. 4.

became so violent that the commander was afraid Paul would be torn to pieces by them. He ordered the troops to go down and take him away from them by force and bring him into the barracks.

[11]The following night the Lord stood near Paul and said, "Take courage! As you have testified about me in Jerusalem, so you must also testify in Rome."

22:30 Unable to ascertain the Jewish charges against Paul,[56] Lysias decided to turn to the Sanhedrin in his attempt to establish a substantive accusation.[57] It is unlikely that Roman officials had the authority to summon a Sanhedrin.[58] Many interpreters thus assume that Lysias did not request a formal meeting of the Sanhedrin but only convened its members for an informal hearing.[59] Some even suggest that the meeting was held in the Tower of Antonia rather than the council chamber of the Sanhedrin.[60] In any event, Paul was released from confinement in order to appear before the Jewish high court.[61] Lysias's decision to consult this body was a logical one. They would surely have heard about the riot against Paul, and it would be the Jews who understood most clearly the legal ramifications of the incident.

23:1-2 Placed before the Sanhedrin, Paul seized the first word: "Brothers, I have lived as a citizen before God with all good conscience to this very day" (23:1, author's translation).[62] The implication is that he had nothing on his own mind to condemn him, that he had been faithful in

---

[56]The inability of the Roman officials to formulate charges against Paul is a constant motif throughout these chapters: cf. 22:30; 23:28f.; 24:22; 25:20,26f.

[57]Formal legal language occurs throughout chaps. 22–26, such as κατηγορέω in 22:30. See A. A. Trites, "The Importance of Legal Scenes and Language in the Book of Acts," *NovT* 16 (1974): 278-84.

[58]Josephus seems to reflect the opposite in *Antiquities* 20.20f., where the procurator Albinus informed the high priest Ananus that he had no authority to convene a Sanhedrin without his consent. In that particular instance, however, the Sanhedrin had condemned and executed James the brother of Jesus, and the illegality involved was the Sanhedrin's assumption of capital jurisdiction. See Sherwin-White, *Roman Society and Roman Law*, 54.

[59]Cf. Marshall, *Acts*, 361; R. Pesch, *Die Apostelgeschichte*, Teilband II: *Apg. 13-28* (Zurich: Benziger, 1986), 240-42.

[60]This would explain how Lysias so quickly secured troops (23:10). See A. T. Robertson, *WP* (Nashville: Southern Baptist Sunday School Board, 1930), 3:196.

[61]The reference to Paul's "release" (ἔλυσεν) in v. 30 is ambiguous. It could refer either to his having his chains removed or to his being released from confinement in order to appear before the Sanhedrin. The latter seems the more likely, since the removal of his chains is implied in 23:29.

[62]The word translated "fulfilled my duty" by the NIV is πολιτεύομαι, which is literally "to live as a citizen." Citizenship was a big issue for Paul throughout chaps. 21–26— Tarsian, Roman, Jewish. Here Paul stressed that his ultimate citizenship was lived under God's rule. The word only occurs elsewhere in the NT in Phil 1:27 and there also with the "citizenship" nuance. See R. R. Brewer, "The Meaning of *Polituesthe* in Philippians 1:27," *JBL* 73 (1954): 76-83. Cf. the close proximity of πολιτεία in 22:28.

his conduct toward God in every respect.[63] Such a remark was itself
something of a provocation. If Paul's life as a Christian left him in complete innocence before God, then the Sanhedrin members who did not
share his commitment to Christ were the guilty parties. It is small wonder
that the high priest Ananias immediately ordered him to be struck on the
mouth for blasphemy (v. 2). His action was completely in character. Josephus depicted him as one of the very worst of the high priests, known for
his pro-Roman sentiments, his extreme cruelty, and his greed.[64]

23:3 Given Ananias's character, Paul's angry response is altogether
understandable: "God will strike you, you whitewashed wall" (v. 3). His
words were prophetic. Less than ten years later, Ananias came to an
untimely end at the hand of Jewish freedom fighters.[65] The image of the
whitewashed wall was particularly appropriate, expressing the sheer
hypocrisy of this one who stood there in his fine high-priestly vestments,
symbolic of his role as intercessor between the people and God. His character and his actions belied the outward appearance. Jesus used the same
image to depict hypocrisy, referring to the practice of whitewashing
tombs as a warning to people that the defilement of dead bones lay within
(Matt 23:27). Paul may also have had in mind Ezekiel's image of a crum-
bling wall covered with whitewash to conceal its decay, ready to fall with
the first rainstorm (Ezek 13:10f.). Paul saw Ananias's action in having
him struck as in itself a demonstration of the high priest's hypocrisy.
There he sat in his role of judge, and yet he was himself in need of judgment because his striking Paul was clearly against the law (v. 3b). No
verdict had been reached, no deliberations even begun, and yet the action
of the high priest had already pronounced judgment. This was scarcely
Israelite justice (cf. Lev 19:15).[66]

---

[63]Here the concept of "conscience" seems to be used with its normal secular Greek
meaning of the condemning or guilty self-awareness. In Paul's letters he extended this meaning to include the conscience as a moral guide for future action and for the judgment of the
actions of others. See M. E. Thrall, "The Pauline Use of *Suneidesis*," *NTS* 14 (1967-68):
118-25.

[64]Identified as the son of Nedebaeus, he was appointed high priest by Herod of Chalcis
(brother of Agrippa I) in A.D. 47 and seems to have held the office for eleven or twelve years
(*Antiquities* 20.103). He was noted for his bribery and allowed his servants to plunder the
tithes designated for the common priests (*Antiquities* 20.205-10, 13). He was summoned to
Rome for his part in a Jewish ambush of a number of Samaritan pilgrims (*Antiquities*
20.131).

[65]Because of his pro-Roman sentiments, Ananias was killed by Jewish Zealots at the outbreak of the war with Rome (*War* 2.441f.).

[66]Clearly Paul's anger was not in the spirit of Jesus' words about turning the other cheek
(Matt 5:39) or even within his own ideal of blessing when reviled (1 Cor 4:12); but surely
the apostle can be granted a little humanity, and "righteous indignation" is often expressed
in his epistles. See Marshall, *Acts*, 363.

23:4-5 It was then pointed out to Paul that it was God's high priest he had just reviled (v. 4).[67] The emphasis on his being the representative of God shifts the focus from the man to the role, and in that respect Paul's demeanor underwent a radical change as well. It has often been questioned whether Paul really did not recognize the high priest.[68] His reply would seem to indicate: "I did not realize that he was the high priest" (v. 5a). Paul may have said this with a mild tone of irony: "He didn't act like a high priest should; how could I recognize him as such when he was so totally out of character?" Now that the focus was on the role, Paul made clear that he respected the office. He even quoted Exod 22:28 to underscore that he did respect God's representatives in accordance with the Torah. He was a law-abiding Jew in every respect.

23:6 At v. 6 the whole proceeding takes a radical turn. Still holding the floor, Paul stated what he saw as the real reason for his trial—his "hope in the resurrection of the dead."[69] This is often seen as a clever ruse on Paul's part to divide the assembly and divert attention from himself. Luke seems to prepare for such an understanding by noting that both Pharisees and Sadducees were present in the Sanhedrin. Paul without doubt sought to align himself with the former group by affirming that he was himself a Pharisee and a son of Pharisees.[70] Neither his mention of his Pharisaic affiliation nor of the resurrection is without relevance to the situation. The resurrection was the issue that separated Paul from the rest of the Jews. It was the real issue behind his trials, and in his subsequent defense speeches Paul constantly insisted on that fact.[71] The Pharisees in fact believed in the *concept* of the resurrection. A resurrection of the dead constituted a major part of their hope in God's final deliverance of his

---

[67]Cf. the similar rebuke addressed to Jesus in John 18:22.

[68]All sorts of suggestions have been made—that there was a recent change of high priests, that Paul's weak vision was responsible, that Paul may not have been aware who gave the order, or that in this informal hearing the high priest was not wearing his vestments. Perhaps the suggestion of F. Stagg (*The Book of Acts: The Early Struggle for an Unhindered Gospel* [Nashville: Broadman, 1955], 232) is most on target: that v. 5a be translated, "I spoke without taking note of [i.e., taking into consideration] the fact that he is high priest."

[69]Most interpreters take the phrase περὶ ελπίδος καὶ αναστάσεως νεκρῶν as a hendiadys, "concerning [my] hope in the resurrection of the dead." See O. Lagercrantz, "Act 14, 17," *ZNW* 31 (1932): 86f. It is grammatically possible, however, to argue for two separate items, the hope (of Israel) and the resurrection of the dead (which comprised a part of that hope).

[70]Cf. Phil 3:5. In Philippians Paul said that he counted all that as loss for the sake of Christ. In addressing the Jews in Acts, however, he never abandoned his Pharisaic identity. Cf. 26:5.

[71]For further development of this central theme, see R. J. Kepple, "The Hope of Israel, the Resurrection of the Dead, and Jesus: A Study of their Relationship in Acts with Particular Regard to the Understanding of Paul's Trial Defense," *JETS* 20 (1977): 231-41; K. Haacker, "Das Bekenntnis des Paulus zur Hoffnung Israels nach der Apostelgeschichte des Lukas," *NTS* 31 (1985): 437-51.

people. They were thus theologically "ripe" for the Christian gospel that Christ had risen from the dead and that this proved him to be the hoped-for Messiah. The Pharisee Paul had come to see this. Other of the Pharisees had become Christians (cf. 15:5). Even in the Sanhedrin it was the Pharisaic segment that had on an earlier occasion come to the defense of the Christians (5:34-40). In short, for Paul and for Luke, the natural fulfillment of the Pharisaic hope was in Christ. It was no accident and certainly no ruse that he made his appeal to the Pharisees in the Sanhedrin.[72]

23:7-8 With Paul's mention of the resurrection, a violent discussion erupted in the Sanhedrin (vv. 7-8). This body largely consisted of the high priestly aristocracy and the ruling elders, who were primarily Sadducees. The Pharisees were in the minority and were represented among the scribes who sat in the Sanhedrin.[73] Luke explained in a narrative aside that Sadducees rejected the concepts of resurrection, angels, and spirits, while the Pharisees believed in them all. The Sadducees' rejection of resurrection is well attested. The Sadducees only accepted the books of the Law as Scripture, and they saw no reference to resurrection in these. Angels and spirits, however, are found in the Pentateuch; and the Sadducees' denial of them is not attested anywhere other than in Acts 23:8. It is most unlikely that the Sadducees rejected the existence of angels and spirits as such. To what, then, was Luke referring? He may have meant that the Sadducees rejected the eschatology of the Pharisees, which involved an elaborate hierarchy of good and evil angels.[74] Or perhaps it was the idea that an angel or a spirit can speak through a human being as an agent of revelation that Luke depicted the Sadducees as rejecting (cf. v. 9).[75] A final possibility is that the reference was a further elaboration of their rejection of the resurrection—they rejected an afterlife in an angelic or spiritual state.[76]

---

[72]The contrasting portrait of the Pharisees in Luke's two volumes is interesting. In his Gospel they were Jesus' enemies. In Acts they are generally portrayed in a favorable light. Surely behind this difference is the fact that for the early church it was the Pharisees who were most amenable to Christianity. See D. B. Gowler, "A Socio-Narratological Character Analysis of the Pharisees in Luke-Acts," Ph.D. diss., the Southern Baptist Theological Seminary, 1989.

[73]For a discussion of the Sadducees, see commentary on 4:1; for the Pharisees, see the commentary on 5:34.

[74]T. W. Manson, "Sadducee and Pharisee—the Origin and Significance of the Names," *BJRL* 22 (1938): 144-59.

[75]B. J. Bamberger, "The Sadducees and the Belief in Angels," *JBL* 82 (1963): 433-35. A related view sees the Sadducees refusing to accept angels as a substitute for the OT anthropomorphism (i.e., as mediators for God); see G. G. Stroumsa, "Le Couple de l'Ange et de l'Espirit: Traditions Juives et Chrétiennes," *RB* 88 (1981): 42-61.

[76]Marshall, *Acts*, 365. This would be much in keeping with Luke 20:36, where Jesus described the resurrection existence as "equal to the angels."

23:9-10 Whatever was intended, it soon became clear that the Pharisees were Paul's defenders. Not only did they not find the resurrection a ridiculous idea, they were even willing to grant that God may have spoken to Paul through a spirit or an angel (v. 9).[77] It is possible that they were trying to give some explanation for Paul's Damascus road experience. The dispute at this point became so violent that Lysias had to send a messenger to bring down troops in order to prevent Paul from being torn to shreds between the two opposing groups (v. 10). Whereas Lysias's original seizing of Paul could be seen as an arrest (21:33), this time there is no doubt the tribune served as his protector.

23:11 Alone, under detention, the following night Paul had a reassuring vision (v. 11).[78] The Lord had certainly prepared him well for the events that had just transpired in Jerusalem (20:23; 21:10f.). Still they had been particularly trying—the mob in the temple square, the arrest, the attempted scourging, the violence of the Sanhedrin. To what was it all leading? The Lord's words assured him that there was a divine purpose in all that had happened to him. As he had borne his witness in Jerusalem, so would he bear it in Rome.[79] Paul had already expressed his own desire to visit Rome (19:21). Now the visit received the Lord's endorsement. The key word is, of course, "testify." All Paul's troubles the past two days had ultimately derived from his testifying to Christ before the Jews. Now his trip to Rome and all of the legal hassle in between also would be a testimony. With v. 11 the final portion of Acts is mapped out.

(7) The Plot to Ambush Paul (23:12-22)

[12]The next morning the Jews formed a conspiracy and bound themselves with an oath not to eat or drink until they had killed Paul. [13]More than forty men were involved in this plot. [14]They went to the chief priests and elders and said, "We have taken a solemn oath not to eat anything until we have killed Paul. [15]Now then, you and the Sanhedrin petition the commander to bring him before you on the pretext of wanting more accurate information about his case. We are ready to kill him before he gets here."

[16]But when the son of Paul's sister heard of this plot, he went into the barracks and told Paul.

[17]Then Paul called one of the centurions and said, "Take this young man to the commander; he has something to tell him." [18]So he took him to the commander.

---

[77]Verse 9 is an ellipsis—"but if an angel or a spirit has spoken to him." The Western text completes the statement by drawing from Acts 5:39, reading, "If it is true that an angel or spirit has spoken to him, let us not contend with God." See E. Delebecque, "Paul entre les Juifs et Romains selon les deux Versions de Act.xxiii," *RevThom* 84 (1984): 83-91.

[78]Paul had experienced such visions before, particularly at critical junctures in his career. Cf. 18:9f.; 16:9; 22:17f.; 27:23f

[79]It is interesting that the words "take courage" (θάρσει, θάρσειτε) are only spoken by Jesus in the NT: Matt 9:2,22; 14:27; Mark 6:50; 10:49; John 16:33; Acts 23:11.

The centurion said, "Paul, the prisoner, sent for me and asked me to bring this young man to you because he has something to tell you."

[19]The commander took the young man by the hand, drew him aside and asked, "What is it you want to tell me?"

[20]He said: "The Jews have agreed to ask you to bring Paul before the Sanhedrin tomorrow on the pretext of wanting more accurate information about him. [21]Don't give in to them, because more than forty of them are waiting in ambush for him. They have taken an oath not to eat or drink until they have killed him. They are ready now, waiting for your consent to their request."

[22]The commander dismissed the young man and cautioned him, "Don't tell anyone that you have reported this to me."

23:12-15 The Lord's assuring vision to Paul was timely, for his troubles were far from over. The threat came from a group of forty zealous Jews who placed themselves under a vow to neither eat nor drink until they had killed Paul (vv. 12-13).[80] The Greek word used to express their oath is particularly strong (*anathematizō*). They placed themselves under an anathema, a curse, probably in some such form as "May I be cursed/ eternally damned if . . . " One wonders if they died of hunger or thirst, for their vow was surely not fulfilled. Actually, the Jewish law provided for the release from a vow that was unfulfillable because of some unforeseen circumstance (Mishna, *Nedarim* 3.3). Paul's removal under heavy Roman guard would have qualified. The forty conspirators hatched a plot to fulfill their vow, which involved the cooperation of the Sanhedrin. The Sanhedrin was to call a session and have the tribune deliver Paul to them under the pretense of giving him a further hearing (vv. 14-15). On the way between Antonia and the council chamber,[81] they would ambush and kill Paul.[82] It is perhaps significant that it was the high priestly aristocracy and the elders whom they approached, the Sadducees on the Sanhedrin. The scribes (Pharisees), with their greater openness to Paul (cf. 23:9), are not mentioned.

23:16-22 Little is known of Paul's family. The present passage is the sole mention of his sister and of her son. Likewise, how Paul's nephew learned of the plot is anybody's guess. He seems to have been a young man, perhaps in his late teens.[83] His accessibility to Paul was not

---

[80]The text has "the Jews" but obviously means only the forty of v. 13. Some Western and Byzantine texts have the easier reading "some of the Jews."

[81]The exact location of the council chamber in Paul's day is not certain. See commentary on 4:5-7. Josephus located it just outside the temple precincts, which would make for a more likely ambush spot than if the chamber were located within the temple precincts, as the rabbinic sources have it.

[82]The Western text has the men say (end of v. 15) that they would kill Paul "even if we ourselves should die for it."

[83]He is called a νεανίας in v. 17, which could indicate anywhere from twenty to forty years of age. The diminutive form (νεανίσκος) is used in vv. 18,22.

unusual. Prisoners of high rank, such as Paul with his Roman citizenship, were often given a great deal of liberty for visits from family and friends. In fact, Paul's considerable standing with the Romans is indicated by the ease with which he called the centurion over to himself and by the unquestioning compliance the latter gave to his request (vv. 17-18). He did not even tell the centurion of the plot. Lysias sensed that it was a matter of extreme importance and took the young man aside to receive the report in confidence (v. 19). Paul's nephew gave the report in detail. Verses 20-21 repeat the content of vv. 12-15. From the perspective of information, they contribute nothing new. The repetition, however, increases the dramatic effect considerably. With each new reference to the plot, the threat to Paul's life becomes more ominous.[84] The dramatic effect is continued in v. 22 as Lysias continued the note of strict confidence. It was of utmost importance that the whole matter be kept strictly secret. No one was to know the tribune was aware of the plot.

(8) Paul Sent to Caesarea (23:23-35)

[23]Then he called two of his centurions and ordered them, "Get ready a detachment of two hundred soldiers, seventy horsemen and two hundred spearmen to go to Caesarea at nine tonight. [24]Provide mounts for Paul so that he may be taken safely to Governor Felix."

[25]He wrote a letter as follows:

[26] Claudius Lysias,

To His Excellency, Governor Felix:

Greetings.

[27]This man was seized by the Jews and they were about to kill him, but I came with my troops and rescued him, for I had learned that he is a Roman citizen. [28]I wanted to know why they were accusing him, so I brought him to their Sanhedrin. [29]I found that the accusation had to do with questions about their law, but there was no charge against him that deserved death or imprisonment. [30]When I was informed of a plot to be carried out against the man, I sent him to you at once. I also ordered his accusers to present to you their case against him.

[31]So the soldiers, carrying out their orders, took Paul with them during the night and brought him as far as Antipatris. [32]The next day they let the cavalry go on with him, while they returned to the barracks. [33]When the cavalry arrived in Caesarea, they delivered the letter to the governor and handed Paul over to him. [34]The governor read the letter and asked what province he was from. Learning that he was from Cilicia, [35]he said, "I will hear your case when your accusers get here." Then he ordered that Paul be kept under guard in Herod's palace.

---

[84]The textual variants in v. 20 attest to the obscurity of the participle. Who was "about to" inquire is anything but clear. It could be the Jews (μέλλοντες) or Lysias (μέλλων) or the Sanhedrin (μέλλον).

Lysias decided to send Paul to Caesarea, the seat of the provincial government and residence of the procurator. The immediate occasion was the imminent threat from the forty conspirators. He probably would have made this transfer sooner or later under any circumstances. The Jews were charging Paul with a capital crime, and only the procurator had jurisdiction over such cases.[85] Further, Paul was a Roman citizen, and that too placed Paul under the procurator rather than a lesser official such as himself. As commander of the Jerusalem garrison, his primary responsibility was maintaining peace and order. The mobs, the plots, all must have convinced him that Paul's continued presence in Jerusalem was not only a danger to Paul's own life but a threat to the general peace of the city as well.

23:23-25 Lysias lost no time in sending Paul to Caesarea (vv. 23-24). That the military contingent was sent forth at nine o'clock at night testifies both to the urgency and to his desire to accomplish the transfer as covertly as possible in the face of the ambush threat. His concern was also expressed by the sizable troops under whose guard Paul was dispatched—two hundred foot soldiers, seventy cavalry and two hundred spearmen.[86] This was nearly half the one thousand troops in the Jerusalem cohort.[87] Mounts were also provided for Paul.[88] Lysias then drafted an official letter to the governor.[89] Such letters were required when transferring a prisoner from one jurisdiction to another. They generally contained an account of the circumstances of arrest and the charges. The latter was difficult for Lysias.

23:26-30 Lysias's letter begins with the formal threefold salutation of a Greek letter, giving first the sender (Lysias), second the recipient (Felix), and finally the customary word of greeting (*chairein*). Felix is

---

[85]See A. N. Sherwin-White, "The Early Persecutions and Roman Law Again," *JTS* 3 (1952): 199-213.

[86]The term translated "spearmen" (δεξιολάβοι) is a near hapax, only occurring in later Greek literature from the seventh and tenth centuries A.D. Meaning literally *holding with the right hand*, it is translated "spearman" or "lancers" in the early Latin versions. G. D. Kilpatrick cites an ancient scholion in which it is said that the δεξιολάβοι were "police officers." He argues from this that they were local Jerusalem militia and not part of the Roman cohort, thus reducing the drain on the Jerusalem garrison ("Acts xxiii, 23. *Dexiolaboi*," *JTS* 14 [1963]: 393f.).

[87]The Western text, mainly attested by the Harclean Syriac, has a lesser number—100 horsemen, 200 spearmen. (The text of Bezae is missing from 22:29 to the end of Acts.)

[88]κτήνη is a general term used for pack animals as well as horses.

[89]"As follows" (ἔχουσαν τὸν τύπον τοῦτον) could be taken to mean *in this manner* and to indicate that the following is the gist, not an exact reproduction of the contents. C. Hemer, however, argues that the phrase means that an exact copy follows and suggests Luke had access to the letter in the court records (*The Book of Acts in the Setting of Hellenistic History* [Tübingen: Mohr-Siebeck, 1989], 347f.).

designated by the general word "governor" (*hēgemōn*)[90] and given the
deferential title "His Excellency."[91] After the formalities Lysias's letter
got down to the business at hand, explaining the circumstances of Paul's
arrest (v. 27). He stretched the truth a bit to his own advantage. The reader
knows already that Lysias seized Paul in the temple square and put two
chains on him (21:33). It was true that he probably saved Paul from the
mob, but he certainly at that point had no knowledge of Paul's Roman citizenship. Lysias's account of the hearing in the Sanhedrin was less biased
(vv. 28-29). One wonders how he could have understood what was going
on, since the whole proceeding was doubtless conducted in Aramaic. He
probably arranged for an interpreter, which was the usual practice in such
circumstances. He certainly learned enough from the proceeding to realize
that the whole debate involved "questions about their law" and not any
infraction of Roman law. His official report to Felix flatly stated that
"there was no charge against him that deserved death or imprisonment."
The picture would not change. It was the conclusion reached by all the
Roman officials right up to Paul's appeal to Caesar. The final part of
Lysias's letter related the immediate circumstances leading to his transfer
of Paul—the ambush plot (v. 30). The tribune added the further note that
he had ordered Paul's accusers to prepare their case for presentation
before Felix. At the writing of the letter he would not yet have done this
but surely waited until Paul was at a safe distance from Jerusalem.[92]

23:31-33 Verse 31 resumes the narrative, noting that the soldiers carried out Lysias's orders as commanded (v. 23f.). The new information is
that they took Paul to Antipatris on the first leg of the journey. Antipatris
was a military station fortified by Herod the Great and named for his
father Antipater. It marked the border between Judea and Samaria and lay
about thirty-five miles from Jerusalem, or somewhat more than half the
sixty-mile distance from Jerusalem to Caesarea. It was a natural stopping
place for troops making a two-day journey, but it was a rather long march
for foot soldiers to make without a stopover. Some interpreters thus suggest that the reference to the foot soldiers returning to the barracks (v. 32)
should be placed earlier than the arrival of Antipatris. The picture would
then be that the foot soldiers returned to Jerusalem at some point along
the way to Antipatris when they had reached a safe distance from the city.

---

[90]Ἡγεμών was the general term for the top-ranking official in an area. Felix was the
procurator of Judea. In Luke 2:2 the term ἡγεμών is used of the imperial legate of Syria, an
official of higher rank than procurator. In the papyri the word is used of the prefect (ἔπαρχος)
of Egypt, a still higher rank.

[91]Strictly the term was used for those of equestrian rank, which Felix did not hold. Note
its application to Theophilus in the dedication of Luke's Gospel (Luke 1:3).

[92]In v. 30 both "sent" and "ordered" are epistolary aorists, the past tense being viewed
from the perspective of the letter's recipient.

With the return of the four hundred troops, this would also solve the problem of the heavy reduction of the Jerusalem garrison. However that may have been, it was the cavalry that accompanied Paul the next day the twenty-five miles to the governor's headquarters at Caesarea,[93] handing over to Felix both their prisoner and Lysias's official letter (v. 33).

Claudius Felix, procurator of Judea from A.D. 52–59,[94] plays a major role in the following chapter of Acts. A knowledge of his background and of general conditions during his administration throws significant light on the Acts narrative. Felix owed his high position to his brother Pallas, who had considerable influence in the court of the emperor Claudius. Both brothers were freedmen of the imperial family. The high procuratorial office granted Felix was something almost unheard of for a former slave and was doubtless secured through his brother's influence in the imperial court. That it was considered with disdain in some Roman circles is reflected in Tacitus's judgment that Felix "wielded royal power with the instincts of a slave" (*History* 5.9). The reference to "royal power" could be related to either his administration or to his family life. His administration was marked by the rising tide of Jewish nationalism with many insurrections, both political and religious. All were brutally suppressed by the procurator. He tended to be arbitrary in his dispensation of justice and totally lacking in understanding of or sympathy for the Jews. This only heightened the anti-Roman feelings of the Jews and proliferated the freedom movements. Felix's ambitious and pretentious nature was nowhere demonstrated more clearly than in his marriages. He had three wives. All were princesses. The first was the granddaughter of Antony and Cleopatra. The third was Drusilla, the daughter of Agrippa I (see 24:24). Felix's administrative ineptitude was bound to catch up with him sooner or later, and he was finally removed from office for his total mismanagement of a dispute between the Jews and Gentiles of Caesarea (see 24:27).[95]

23:34-35 At this point in the narrative, Luke gave no hint about Felix's shortcomings. Everything is related in formal, official language to emphasize that Paul's transferral to Caesarea was very much a protective

---

[93]For Caesarea, see chap. III, n. 147 and chap. VII, n. 111. See also L. I. Levine, *Caesarea under Roman Rule* (Leiden: Brill, 1975).

[94]According to Tacitus, Felix's praenomen was Antonius. According to Josephus, it was Claudius. Recent inscriptional evidence supports Josephus. See F. F. Bruce, "The Full Name of the Procurator Felix," *JSNT* 1 (1978): 33-36. The terminal point of his procuratorship is also uncertain. There is conflicting evidence in Josephus, Jerome, and Eusebius, which would place the terminus anywhere from 54 to 61. The evidence of Josephus would indicate that Festus assumed office in 59 or 60, thus placing Felix's terminus in that period. See Schürer, *History* 1:465f., n. 42.

[95]For a full discussion of Felix's procuratorship, see Schürer, *History* 1:459-66.

move on the part of the Roman officials (vv. 34-35). Felix's question about Paul's native province was aimed at determining whether he had legal jurisdiction over Paul in his role as Judean procurator. During the reign of Claudius, both Judea and Cilicia were under the single provincial administration of the imperial legate of Syria. As an official within that administrative unit, Felix determined that it was within his own competency to give Paul a formal hearing. In the meantime Paul was confined to the *praetorium*, a former palace built by Herod the Great which now served as the Roman headquarters.

2. Witness before Gentiles and the Jewish King (24:1–26:32)

The theme of Paul's witness continues in Acts 24–26. The setting for his testimony shifted—from Jerusalem to Caesarea, from the Jews to the Roman officials. Still, the primary focus was on the Jewish antagonism toward Paul. The Roman officials became more and more convinced that Paul had broken none of their laws. Still, in the face of the strong Jewish opposition to Paul, they were hesitant to release him. Only an appeal to Caesar removed Paul from the very real prospect that the officials would ultimately give in to pressure and turn him over to the Jews.

Structurally, the section is built around the three major political figures before whom Paul appeared—the procurators Felix (chap. 24) and Festus (25:1-22) and the titular Jewish King Agrippa II (25:23–26:32). In form it consists of two major speeches of Paul—in the context of a formal trial at the beginning of his Caesarean confinement (24:1-23) and in a hearing before Agrippa II and the Roman notables at the end (25:23–26:32). In between comes the pivotal event of Paul's appeal to Caesar (25:6-12). Thematically, the major emphases are much the same as in the previous three chapters—Paul's innocence and his protection by the Roman procurators, combined with their equivocation in failing to release him. The primary emphasis remains that of Paul's witness—this time before the social and political notables of Palestine, the Roman procurators, and the Jewish king. Though the setting was that of Paul's defense before the Jewish charges, the end result was invariably Paul's witness to Christ. For this witness, the resurrection was primary.

(1) The Trial in Caesarea (24:1-23)

[1]Five days later the high priest Ananias went down to Caesarea with some of the elders and a lawyer named Tertullus, and they brought their charges against Paul before the governor. [2]When Paul was called in, Tertullus presented his case before Felix: "We have enjoyed a long period of peace under you, and your foresight has brought about reforms in this nation. [3]Everywhere and in every way, most excellent Felix, we acknowledge this with profound gratitude. [4]But in order not to weary you further, I would request that you be kind enough to hear us

briefly.

⁵"We have found this man to be a troublemaker, stirring up riots among the Jews all over the world. He is a ringleader of the Nazarene sect ⁶and even tried to desecrate the temple; so we seized him. ⁸By examining him yourself you will be able to learn the truth about all these charges we are bringing against him."

⁹The Jews joined in the accusation, asserting that these things were true.

¹⁰When the governor motioned for him to speak, Paul replied: "I know that for a number of years you have been a judge over this nation; so I gladly make my defense. ¹¹You can easily verify that no more than twelve days ago I went up to Jerusalem to worship. ¹²My accusers did not find me arguing with anyone at the temple, or stirring up a crowd in the synagogues or anywhere else in the city. ¹³And they cannot prove to you the charges they are now making against me. ¹⁴However, I admit that I worship the God of our fathers as a follower of the Way, which they call a sect. I believe everything that agrees with the Law and that is written in the Prophets, ¹⁵and I have the same hope in God as these men, that there will be a resurrection of both the righteous and the wicked. ¹⁶So I strive always to keep my conscience clear before God and man.

¹⁷"After an absence of several years, I came to Jerusalem to bring my people gifts for the poor and to present offerings. ¹⁸I was ceremonially clean when they found me in the temple courts doing this. There was no crowd with me, nor was I involved in any disturbance. ¹⁹But there are some Jews from the province of Asia, who ought to be here before you and bring charges if they have anything against me. ²⁰Or these who are here should state what crime they found in me when I stood before the Sanhedrin—²¹unless it was this one thing I shouted as I stood in their presence: 'It is concerning the resurrection of the dead that I am on trial before you today.'"

²²Then Felix, who was well acquainted with the Way, adjourned the proceedings. "When Lysias the commander comes," he said, "I will decide your case." ²³He ordered the centurion to keep Paul under guard but to give him some freedom and permit his friends to take care of his needs.

When Paul first arrived in Caesarea under Lysias's guard, the procurator Felix put off hearing him until the arrival of his Jewish accusers (23:35). With their arrival he called Paul forth for trial. It is the only formal trial scene in this heavily "legal" section of Acts, consisting of accusations by the prosecuting attorney Tertullus (vv. 1-9) and a response to each charge by the defendant Paul (vv. 10-21). Felix failed to reach a decision and formally adjourned the trial (vv. 22f.).

TERTULLUS'S ACCUSATION (24:1-9). **24:1** In his letter to Felix, Lysias had related that he was sending Paul's accusers to Caesarea to present their case before the governor (23:30). Now they arrived, evidently five days after Paul's own arrival in the administrative capital. The accusing party consisted of the high priest Ananias,⁹⁶ some "elders" who probably

---

⁹⁶Ananias was high priest until A.D. 59. The date of this trial was most likely in A.D. 56 or 57.

were members of the Sanhedrin, and a lawyer named Tertullus. Whether Tertullus was a Jew or a Gentile hired by the Jews is uncertain.[97] It was not uncommon for Jews to hire pagan lawyers who would be more familiar with Roman law than they. The evidence of the text is ambiguous. Tertullus seems to identify himself with the Jews by the use of "we" in vv. 3,4,6, but in v. 9 he seems to be differentiated from "the Jews." In any event, Tertullus showed himself fully skilled in Roman legal procedure, and he lived up to Luke's formal designation of him as a "lawyer" (*rhētōr*).

24:2-4 Felix formally convened the trial, perhaps using a "crier" to call forth the defendant (v. 2).[98] Tertullus began with the convention of a *capitatio benevolentiae*, a flattering appeal aimed at securing the goodwill of the governor. This portion of Tertullus's address was particularly long and considerably stretched the truth of the matter. He praised the governor for the peace he had brought the nation. In fact, there was less peace in Judea during Felix's administration than for any procurator until the final years before the outbreak of the war with Rome.[99] But the Romans prided themselves in preserving the peace (the *pax Romana*), and such a comment was sure to win the governor's favor. Equally strained was Tertullus's appeal to Felix's "foresight" (*pronoia*) in bringing many "reforms" (perhaps better, "improvements") to the Jewish nation. Felix had scarcely done this. He had, in fact, made life miserable for the Jews, as was witnessed by the proliferation of rebellious movements during his term in response to his total lack of sympathy for or understanding of them. But again, the Romans liked to be called benefactors; and their "foresight" (Latin *providentia*) was often inscribed on their coins. Tertullus continued his formal flattery, referring to how the Jews "everywhere and in every way" acknowledged (literally "welcomed") his beneficial rule (v. 3). Few Jews would have felt much gratitude for Felix, and Tertullus's bestowal of the title "most excellent" was hardly deserved.[100] Tertullus's comment that he would be brief and not prevail too severely on the good graces of the governor was again quite conventional. Luke most likely only gave a precis of the proceedings. Judging from the length of his introductory

---

[97]The name Tertullus will not decide the issue. It is a common Latin name, a diminutive of Tertius, and a form of Tertullianus. It was sometimes borne by Hellenistic Jews. See *Beginnings* 4:297.

[98]T. Mommsen notes that the trial scene of 24:1-23 is in agreement in all its details with what is known of Roman legal process ("Die Rechtverhältnisse des Apostels Paulus," *ZNW* 2 [1901]: 81-96).

[99]See the discussion of Felix at 23:23-35.

[100]Technically, κράτιστε was reserved for the equestrian order, and the freedman Felix did not have this rank. The term, however, seems to have been used somewhat loosely for persons of rank. Cf. Lysias's application of the title to Felix (23:26).

flattery, one wonders just how much Tertullus stuck to his promise of brevity.

24:5-6 Finally he got down to the business at hand and set forth the Jewish charges against Paul (vv. 5-6). These were three in number. The first was that Paul was a "troublemaker" (literally, a "pest" or "plague"), stirring up riots among the Jews throughout the entire civilized world. At first glance this seems to be a ridiculous charge, a bit of name-calling with nothing specific to back it up. Actually it was a carefully calculated move. Compare the charge with that of the Asian Jews in 21:28. They too had charged Paul with causing trouble "everywhere," but they had correctly seen it as involving the Jewish law and temple. Tertullus attempted to broaden the scope a bit into that of provoking insurrection throughout the Roman world. It was the charge of sedition, a charge the Romans would not take lightly. Roman officials would scarcely concern themselves with matters of Jewish religion. They *would* take seriously any threat to the *pax Romana*. Felix in particular would have become attentive at the hint of such a charge. His entire administration had been marked by having to put down one insurrection in Judea after another. He had done so decisively and cruelly. He maintained the peace at any cost.

Tertullus's second charge was really a variation on the same theme: Paul was "a ringleader of the Nazarene sect."[101] This was certainly true. Paul was a Christian leader. By linking the comment with the charge of provoking insurrection, however, Tertullus implied that the Christians as a whole were a dangerous and seditious sect and that Paul was one of their main collaborators. The ramifications of the Jewish charges now became infinitely clear. Should such a charge be made to stick for Paul, the whole Christian community would be viewed as a dangerous, revolutionary movement. Fortunately, Tertullus could not substantiate the charge, and Felix was already too informed about Christians to take it seriously (v. 22).

Tertullus's third charge was another matter—that Paul had violated the temple. Evidently the Romans did grant the Jews the right to enforce their ban on Gentile access to their sacred precincts.[102] Paul had been charged by the Asian Jews with violating the ban (21:28). Had Tertullus substantiated this charge, it would have obligated Felix to turn Paul over to juris-

---

[101]The term "sect" does not necessarily have a negative connotation. It is used of the Sadducees in 5:17 and the Pharisees in 15:5. The term "Nazarene" most likely derived from Nazareth and was perhaps first applied to Christians pejoratively on the basis of the insignificance of the hometown of their founder (cf. John 1:46). Later Jewish Christian sects were known as "Nazarenes," and the Talmud characteristically refers to Christians by the term (*Nozrim*).

[102]Cf. Josephus, *War* 6.124-28 and see discussion on the warning stones in the commentary on 21:28.

diction of the Sanhedrin and almost certain death. The accusation, however, was totally false and based on an erroneous conclusion by the Asian Jews (cf. 21:29). This probably is why they were not present to substantiate the charge (v. 19).[103]

24:6 There is a major variation in the textual tradition at the end of v. 6, a number of witnesses[104] adding after "so we seized him" the following words: "And would have judged him according to our law. But the Tribune Lysias snatched him from our hands with great force, commanding his accusers to come before you." A number of commentators argue for the originality of this longer reading[105] on the basis that it clarifies the Jewish position—namely, that they objected to the Romans intervening and taking Paul from what they felt rightfully came under their own jurisdiction. If one accepts the longer reading, then v. 8 would refer to Lysias. Tertullus would then have been instructing Felix to consult with Lysias, who would confirm all these accusations against Paul.[106] The manuscript evidence, however, seems to support the shorter text followed by the NIV. Following the shorter reading, v. 8 refers to Paul. Tertullus told Felix to examine Paul carefully himself and he would be able to substantiate these charges: "Just give him enough rope, and he'll hang himself." "Oh, yes," joined in the rest of the Jewish delegation, "all these charges are true" (author's paraphrase).

PAUL'S DEFENSE (24:10-21). **24:10-13** Perhaps indicative of his sense of power, without a word, by a mere nod of the head, Felix gestured for Paul to enter upon his defense. Paul also began with a *capitatio benevolentia*, but his was markedly contrasting to Tertullus's—no fawning, no stretching of the truth, only a reference to Felix's having for some time been judge over the Jewish nation, which should qualify him to handle the matter at hand (v. 10).[107]

Paul then answered the charges. First came the charge of stirring up insurrection. Paul answered this with a threefold response. First, he had no history of inciting the Jews. He had only been in Jerusalem for twelve

---

[103]Note that both Jesus (Mark 14:57f.) and Stephen (Acts 6:13f.) were also charged with violating the temple.

[104]Mainly in Western and Byzantine witnesses. By way of the latter, the longer reading entered the *Textus Receptus* and ultimately the KJV.

[105]E.g., *Beginnings* 4:299f.

[106]It is possible to take Paul as the subject of v. 8 even if one follows the longer reading, as is done by E. Delebecque, "Saint Paul avec ou sans le Tribun Lysias en 58 à Caesarea (Actes xxiv, 6-8)," *RevThom* 81 (1981): 426-34.

[107]Felix had been governor for four or five years at the time of Paul's trial. Paul's reference to a "number of years" may include the additional four years or so when Felix served in Samaria as a subordinate to Cumanus immediately prior to his becoming procurator. See Hemer, *Book of Acts*, 129. The Western text adds to v. 10 that Paul assumed a "godlike state" *(statum divinum)*.

days at the time of his arrest and had been there solely to worship (v. 11).[108] Twelve days was scarcely time enough to organize a rebellion, and pilgrims are not generally rabble-rousers.[109] Paul turned Tertullus's word against him. The latter had said that by examining Paul, Felix would be able to verify the charges against him (v. 8). Paul responded that the opposite was the case; Felix would verify that Paul was worshiping, not inciting sedition.[110] Second, Paul stated that he had not stirred up any crowds—not in the temple area, not in the Jewish synagogues, not anywhere in the city (v. 12). There had been quite a crowd in the temple area, but it was the Asian Jews—not Paul—who incited it (21:27). If the Romans wanted to charge someone with disturbing the peace, they had best look elsewhere, not to Paul. In short, Paul replied with his third response, the Jews simply could not give any proof for their accusations that would stand up in court.[111]

24:14-16 In vv. 14-16 Paul responded to the charges that somehow his treasonous behavior was bound up with his being a ringleader of the "Nazarene sect." He used the opportunity to deliver a sort of minisermon, changing his defensive posture into more of a positive witness. Tertullus may have referred to the Christians as a "sect," a party within Judaism. Paul would not deny his affiliation with the group, but he preferred another term. He preferred to be seen as a follower of "the Way," not a party, not a "Jewish denomination," but the true, the *only* way of the Lord for his people.[112] His was no offshoot tangential faith but right at the center of Jewish religion. He believed the Scriptures—just like the Pharisees—the Prophets as well as the Law. Just like the Pharisees, he shared the hope in

---

[108]The reference to twelve days has caused interpreters no end of problems. It would seem to cover the period from his arrival in Jerusalem up to the moment he was making his defense. One can arrive at the figure simply by adding the seven days of Paul's purification (21:27) to the five days of 24:1, but there are other days involved. The purification did not begin until at least the third day after his arrival in Jerusalem (cf. 21:18,26). The most likely solution is to construe the rather awkward Greek expression in v. 11 as meaning that not more than twelve days were involved in his worship in Jerusalem, thus referring to the time between his arrival in Jerusalem to his arrest. This best fits Paul's response to the charge of sedition; obviously he could not stir up many crowds after his arrest—that period was hardly germane. See G. Krodel, *Acts*, ACNT (Minneapolis: Augsburg, 1986), 438.

[109]Προσκυνέω was commonly used for the act of making a pilgrimage, which involved worship and giving an offering. This seems to be the meaning in Paul's defense (cf. v. 17).

[110]This is somewhat more obvious in the Greek text, where the same phrase occurs in both vv. 8 and 11, "Be able to verify for yourself" (δύνασθαι αὐτὸς/σύ ἐπιγνῶναι). See R. C. Tannehill, *Narrative Unity*, 2:298.

[111]Paul used formal legal and rhetorical language—παραστῆσαι, "provide proof, put evidence alongside one's argument."

[112]For a discussion of the term "the Way" and further bibliography, see. chap. IV, n. 10. See also J. Pathrapankal, "Christianity as a 'Way' according to the Acts of the Apostles," in *Les Actes des Apôtres*, ed. J. Kremer (Gembloux: Duculot, 1979), 533-39.

the coming resurrection, the *total* resurrection of the wicked as well as the righteous.[113] Paul's words had a certain ominous tone. To mention the resurrection of the unjust could only imply one thing—the coming judgment. Paul was not about to miss the opportunity for witness. Even the Gentiles present, who might not comprehend the idea of the resurrection, would have some understanding of judgment (cf. 24:25).[114]

Paul's reference to the resurrection is the high point of his witness in all the speeches of Acts 23–26. This was not by accident. Paul's conviction in the resurrection constituted the real point of contention with the other Jews. In the present passage this was precisely Paul's point. He believed the same Scriptures, worshiped the same God, shared the same hope.[115] But it was precisely at this point that "the Way" parted ways with the rest of the Jews. The Christians believed that the resurrection already had begun in Christ. One should observe how the theme of the resurrection unfolds in Paul's successive speeches. Before the Sanhedrin the theme was set, but there Paul merely enunciated the idea of a resurrection, the belief in and hope for the coming resurrection (23:6). In 24:15 he was more explicit. The resurrection was more precisely defined as including both the just and the unjust, implying thereby a coming judgment. That Paul so understood it is clear from v. 16, where he spoke of his own blameless conscience—blameless, that is, with regard to the judgment that all would eventually face.[116] Paul again made clear in his Caesarean trial what the real issue was between him and his Jewish accusers—it was the resurrection (24:21). The resurrection reached its fullest treatment in the final, climactic scene before Agrippa II. Again it was enunciated twice by Paul (26:8,23), the apostle constantly focusing on what was the real issue. This time it became clear that it was not resurrection in general but specifically the resurrection of Christ that separated him from the Jews and constituted the focal point of his witness

---

[113]The Jews of Paul's day were very much divided over the idea of the resurrection. The Sadducees denied the idea altogether. Some intertestamental Jewish sources speak only of the resurrection of the just, others of a resurrection of all persons. In his epistles Paul never explicitly referred to the resurrection of the unjust but characteristically connected resurrection with believers (cf. 1 Thess 4:13-18; 1 Cor 15:20-23; Phil 3:20f.), although passages that speak of a final judgment could be construed to imply the twofold resurrection (cf. 2 Cor 5:10; 2 Tim 4:1). The resurrection of both just and unjust is elsewhere clearly attested in the NT (cf. John 5:28f.; Matt 25:31f.; Rev 20:11-15).

[114]If one follows Weymouth's argument that μέλλω implies close proximity in time, then Paul's reference to the resurrection in v. 15 is all the more urgent: "*Before long* there will be a resurrection." See A. J. Mattill, Jr., "*Näherwartung, Fernerwartung*, and the Purpose of Luke-Acts: Weymouth Reconsidered," *CBQ* 34 (1972): 276-93.

[115]One wonders how the Sadducees in the Jewish delegation of Caesarea reacted to Paul's words. They shared neither his faith in the prophetic writings nor the resurrection.

[116]For Paul's idea of the conscience, see commentary and footnotes on 23:1.

(26:23). For Paul, for Luke's church, and for contemporary Christians this remains the primary dividing line between Christian and Jew and the basic starting point for any dialogue between the two.

24:17-19 Verses 17-19 constitute Paul's response to Tertullus's third charge—the accusation that he had desecrated the temple. Paul briefly summarized the events covered in Acts 21:27-30—his presence in the temple for purification in connection with the vows of the four Nazirites and the disturbance created by the Asian Jews. The absence of the Asian Jews at his trial comes as no surprise (v. 19). Luke already had explained that their accusation that Paul had violated the temple was based on a totally false conclusion drawn from having seen him earlier in the city with Trophimus (21:29). Paul was obviously quite incensed by the thought of these accusers, as is indicated by his breaking off in midsentence at the end of v. 19. They should have been there and brought charges against him face-to-face. That was good Roman legal procedure (cf. 25:16). Instead, with their total lack of supporting evidence, they were now nowhere to be found. Paul had scored a rather telling legal point, and Felix was bound to have observed it. For Tertullus to have made an accusation against Paul with the total absence of the witnesses for the prosecution was a serious breach of court procedure. There was simply no evidence to counter Paul's own defense. Far from having defiled the temple, he was himself in a state of scrupulous ceremonial cleanness (v. 18). Far from desecrating the temple, he had come there to bring offerings (v. 17).[117]

24:20-21 Having successfully demonstrated that all of Tertullus's accusations were totally without supporting evidence, Paul proceeded to the one genuine charge that could be brought against him. There were even "witnesses for the prosecution" present to support this charge—namely, the high priest and elders who had come with Tertullus who had been present when Paul appeared before the Sanhedrin. They could testify to the one issue that surfaced in that hearing—Paul's belief in the resurrection of the dead (v. 21; cf. 26:8). Paul now had the whole trial scene in his own control. He had the issue where he wanted it, where it really was. He had broken no law—certainly no Roman law, and not even the Jewish religious law. The resurrection was the bone of contention with the Jews. And most Jews shared that conviction in principle. What separated him from his fellow Jews was that he was a follower of

---

[117]Most interpreters see v. 17 as Luke's sole allusion to Paul's collection. It may be, however, that Luke's silence on the subject was total. "My people" (τὸ ἔθνος μου) most likely refers to the whole Jewish nation and not just the Jewish Christians (for whom the collection was destined). Likewise "offerings" most naturally refers to a pilgrim's offerings to the temple, not to a collection for the poor. See R. C. Tannehill, *Narrative Unity*, 2:300. For Luke's silence on the collection, see commentary on 20:1-4.

"the Way," that he believed that the Messiah had come and the resurrection had begun in Christ. The stakes were high. Paul was on trial for nothing less than his Christian faith. It was essential that the Roman courts realize this was a matter of Jewish religious conviction and not a matter involving Roman law.

FELIX'S INDECISION (24:22-23). **24:22-23** The outcome of the trial could only be described in terms of the procurator's indecision, his refusal to give a verdict. In rather technical legal language, Luke stated that Felix "adjourned" (*anebaleto*) the proceedings, meaning that he refused to pass judgment until he had gathered further evidence. Manifestly, he was waiting for Lysias to come and give his report. Lysias had already sent his report and indicated that he saw the whole thing as a matter of Jewish religious law. Lysias had even stated that in his opinion Paul had done nothing deserving of death or imprisonment (23:29). Felix wasn't waiting for Lysias's report. There is no indication that Lysias ever came or that Felix even sent for him. Felix was putting the whole matter off. He didn't *want* to pass a verdict, for the verdict would surely have been one of acquittal. Luke seems to have hinted at this by noting that Felix was "well acquainted" with "the Way." This probably indicates that the procurator knew that the Jewish charges of sedition against Paul were totally without foundation and that "the Nazarene sect" was not a band of revolutionaries. Like Lysias before him and Festus after him, he must have realized that Paul was guilty of no crime by Roman law. Still he ruled over the Jews and had to live with them. And there were powerful Jews in this delegation calling for Paul's condemnation. He didn't want to incur their wrath. It was easier to put off the whole matter, even if it meant that Paul would be jailed for it. Felix's conscience might have bothered him for doing this, so he had Paul placed under the rather liberal sort of detainment known as "military custody" ("under guard," NIV), which gave the prisoner considerable movement and allowed free visitation from family and friends (v. 23). Also his awareness of Paul's Roman citizenship may have contributed to the special courtesy he granted this particular prisoner.

(2) Paul and Felix in Private (24:24-27)

[24]Several days later Felix came with his wife Drusilla, who was a Jewess. He sent for Paul and listened to him as he spoke about faith in Christ Jesus. [25]As Paul discoursed on righteousness, self-control and the judgment to come, Felix was afraid and said, "That's enough for now! You may leave. When I find it convenient, I will send for you." [26]At the same time he was hoping that Paul would offer him a bribe, so he sent for him frequently and talked with him.

[27]When two years had passed, Felix was succeeded by Porcius Festus, but because Felix wanted to grant a favor to the Jews, he left Paul in prison.

24:24-27 The concluding portion of Luke's treatment of Felix provides a glimpse into the procurator's personal life. The reader is first introduced to his Jewish wife Drusilla. Josephus related the unusual circumstances of Felix's marriage to this strikingly beautiful woman, and the topic must have been a major source of gossip in Palestine.[118] Felix's third wife, Drusilla, was born around A.D. 38, the youngest daughter of Agrippa I (the "Herod" of Acts 12). At age fourteen, through an espousal arranged by her brother Agrippa II, she was wed to Azizus, the king of Emesa, a Syrian petty state. Struck by her beauty, Felix determined to have her for himself. Through the mediation of a Cypriot magician named Atomos, Drusilla, who was herself unhappy in her marriage to Azizus, was talked into leaving him for the procurator. Josephus mentioned that Felix promised to make her "happy," doubtless a pun on his name *felix*, the Latin word for "happy." Drusilla was sixteen at the time of her marriage to the Judean procurator. She may have been the source of his information on "the Way" (v. 22) as well as the driving force behind the desire to speak with Paul in private (v. 24).[119]

Whatever the driving force behind the desire of the couple to visit Paul, the apostle used the opportunity to share the gospel with them and "spoke about faith in Christ" (v. 24). For this particular couple, he focused on the prospect of the coming judgment (v. 25). His emphasis on "righteousness" (*dikaiosynē*) was surely intended in its more strictly ethical connotation of measuring up to God's standards, which will ultimately be the basis for the coming judgment.[120] The relevance of "self-control" (*enkrateia*)[121] to this subject and to their own particular situation must have been self-evident for Felix and Drusilla. It surely explains Felix's alarm and abrupt curtailment of the conversation with Paul. Luke added an even more telling comment on the procurator by noting that he sent for Paul frequently in hopes of receiving a bribe.[122] Such bribe-

---

[118]Josephus, *Antiquities* 20.139-44.

[119]The Western text, represented in a marginal note of the Harclean Syriac and a Bohairic manuscript, adds to v. 24 that Drusilla "asked to see Paul and hear him speak" and that Felix consequently summoned Paul "wishing to satisfy her."

[120]Even in Paul's more "forensic" use of the word (δικαιοσύνη) (being "acceptable to" God) the ethical sense is always present. A person becomes acceptable to God, "righteous" before him, through relationship to the only truly righteous one, Jesus Christ.

[121]The word ἐγκρατεία means *self-control* in its broadest sense and would even apply to Felix's bribe-taking proclivities. In the presence of both Drusilla and Felix, however, it is likely that Paul had a more specific focus on their sexual behavior. A later Christian celibate movement was known as the "Enkratites."

[122]It is not necessary to speculate on whether Paul had personal means or whether Felix was aware of the sizable collection he had brought to Jerusalem. Bribes were the common oil for the bureaucratic cogs and would be sought whatever one's financial circumstances might be.

ACTS 24:27

taking was frowned upon officially, even forbidden by law, but was rampant in the Roman administration.[123] Other Judean procurators were known for their propensity to receive bribes, and Felix was not himself above the temptation.[124]

In any event, Felix did nothing to hasten the disposal of Paul's case. He played the delaying game, keeping the apostle in prison for two years, to the very end of his administration (v. 27). His desire for a bribe may have played a part in this long delay, but it is far more likely that the desire "to grant a favor [charita] to the Jews" was his primary motivation. On the one hand, knowing there was no real case against Paul, he was unwilling to turn him over to Jewish jurisdiction. On the other hand, fearful of the power of Paul's Jewish opponents, he would not free the apostle either. So ultimately he took the safe way out and kept Paul in prison. He might have done so indefinitely had he not been removed from office.[125] The corruption and brutality of his administration finally caught up with him. An incidence of civil strife in Caesarea between the Jewish and Gentile communities there, which Felix mismanaged with a decidedly anti-Jewish bias, led to his downfall. This provoked the Jews to send an angry delegation to Rome protesting his actions, which ultimately resulted in his removal.[126]

Luke's portrayal of Felix presents a genuinely tragic plot.[127] There is no reason to doubt the sincerity of his coming to Paul to inquire about faith in Christ (v. 24). Neither was his frequent sending for Paul to converse with him likely to have been based *solely* on greed (v. 26). Felix demonstrated a genuine concern to hear the apostle's testimony. His alarm at Paul's message was real (v. 25). A thorough skeptic would have dismissed Paul's reference to the judgment as sheer fantasy, but not Felix. His fear was genuine. He was at the point of conviction. But he was never willing to go beyond the point and take the leap of faith. In the end his greed, his lust, and his desire to preserve his power carried the day.

With the change of administration, there was renewed hope for Paul. New procurators generally undertook a quick disposal of the cases their

---

[123]The *Lex Iulia derepetundis* prescribed removal from office and exile for an official who accepted bribes.

[124]Josephus often referred to the acceptance of bribes by the Roman procurators, among them Pilate and Felix's predecessor Cumanus. Perhaps most notorious of all was Festus's successor Albinus (cf. *Ant.* 20.215).

[125]The date of Felix's removal and Festus's accession is uncertain due to conflicting accounts in the sources and is dated anywhere from A.D. 56 to 60. A date around A.D. 58 or 59 seems to best fit the evidence. See Hemer, *Book of Acts*, 254; F. F. Bruce, "Chronological Questions," *BJRL* 68 (1986): 284ff.

[126]Josephus, *Antiquities* 20.182; *War* 2.266-70.

[127]See R. C. Tannehill, *Narrative Unity*, 303.

predecessors left behind. Often prisoners were released. With Festus's coming, there was the prospect that Paul's case would soon find a favorable resolution. Such was not to be.

(3) Festus Pressured by the Jews (25:1-5)

¹Three days after arriving in the province, Festus went up from Caesarea to Jerusalem, ²where the chief priests and Jewish leaders appeared before him and presented the charges against Paul. ³They urgently requested Festus, as a favor to them, to have Paul transferred to Jerusalem, for they were preparing an ambush to kill him along the way. ⁴Festus answered, "Paul is being held at Caesarea, and I myself am going there soon. ⁵Let some of your leaders come with me and press charges against the man there, if he has done anything wrong."

Very little is known about the administration of Porcius Festus as Judean procurator. The only sources available are Luke's account in Acts 25–26 and two brief references in Josephus.[128] Evidently his term was quite brief, beginning in A.D. 58/59 and ending abruptly with his death from illness in A.D. 62.[129] Josephus gave him rather high marks, noting that he succeeded in suppressing the brigands and revolutionaries who had so plagued the countryside during Felix's administration. Luke's portrait does not conflict with this, showing Festus as a fair-minded man concerned with preserving Roman justice. Still, Luke's picture is more nuanced. Like Felix, Festus found himself unable to rise above the pressure exerted by the Jewish power structures and ultimately compromised his sense of justice with respect to Paul. In this regard Festus behaved much like Pilate in the trial of Jesus. In fact, many striking parallels occur between Paul's experience in Acts 25–26 and the trial of Jesus in Luke 23:1-25.[130]

25:1-3 The opening scene of Luke's account of Festus's dealings with Paul is set at the beginning of his administration. It was quite natural for the new procurator to want to visit Jerusalem as soon as possible because this was the religious and cultural center of the people now under his jurisdiction. So Festus lost no time, and on the third day after his arrival in the administrative capital of Caesarea, he set out for Jerusalem (v. 1). No sooner had he gotten there than the most influential figures in the Jewish power structure began to pressure him about Paul. They were the members of the high priestly circle and "the foremost of the Jews"

---

[128]Josephus, *War* 2.271; *Antiquities* 20.182-88.

[129]It was during the interim period between Festus's sudden death and the arrival of the new procurator Albinus that the high priest Ananus moved to have James the brother of Jesus put to death (Josephus, *Ant.* 20.200).

[130]For a thorough treatment of the parallels between Acts 25–26 and the trial of Jesus in Luke 23:1-25, see R. F. O'Toole, "Luke's Notion of 'Be Imitators of Me as I am of Christ' in Acts 25-26," *BTB* 8 (1978): 155-61.

("Jewish leaders," NIV), which probably refers to the ruling elders on the Sanhedrin (v. 2). Their request was that Festus transfer Paul to Jerusalem. They may have been requesting his transfer to their own jurisdiction. They were certainly desirous of his physical transfer to Jerusalem, for they planned an ambush to kill him along the way (v. 3). One immediately recalls the former ambush plot from which Lysias rescued Paul. There is a major difference, however. Formerly, the forty zealotic Jews enlisted the Sanhedrin as collaborators (23:15). Now it was the Jewish leaders themselves who plotted his death. The threat to Paul had escalated considerably. The chief power structure was determined to kill Paul.

25:4-5 Festus was totally unaware of the present plot and probably the former one as well. In any event, he had no intention of turning Paul over to Jewish jurisdiction at this point. Paul was under *his* jurisdiction as procurator, and he would be returning to Caesarea soon. Any hearing would thus have to take place there under a Roman tribunal (v. 4f.).[131] Festus's response was made on purely pragmatic grounds—it was simply more convenient for him to give a hearing in Caesarea. Inadvertently, therefore, he became Paul's protector, delivering him once again from a dangerous threat to his life.

(4) Paul's Appeal to Caesar (25:6-12)

⁶After spending eight or ten days with them, he went down to Caesarea, and the next day he convened the court and ordered that Paul be brought before him. ⁷When Paul appeared, the Jews who had come down from Jerusalem stood around him, bringing many serious charges against him, which they could not prove.

⁸Then Paul made his defense: "I have done nothing wrong against the law of the Jews or against the temple or against Caesar."

⁹Festus, wishing to do the Jews a favor, said to Paul, "Are you willing to go up to Jerusalem and stand trial before me there on these charges?"

¹⁰Paul answered: "I am now standing before Caesar's court, where I ought to be tried. I have not done any wrong to the Jews, as you yourself know very well. ¹¹If, however, I am guilty of doing anything deserving death, I do not refuse to die. But if the charges brought against me by these Jews are not true, no one has the right to hand me over to them. I appeal to Caesar!"

¹²After Festus had conferred with his council, he declared: "You have appealed to Caesar. To Caesar you will go!"

25:6-8 In a little over a week, Festus returned to Caesarea. Paul's Jewish accusers evidently accepted his invitation (v. 5) and accompanied him. On the next day Festus convened a court, formally taking his place

---

[131]For a history-of-research on the intricate legal issues arising in vv. 1-12, see U. Holzmeister, "Der hl. Paulus vor dem Richterstuhle des Festus (Ag. 25, 1-12)," *ZTK* 36 (1912): 489-511, 742-83.

on the judgment seat.[132] Paul's accusers assumed a threatening posture, surrounding him both physically and with their accusations. As was the case before Felix, they were unable to prove any of the accusations (v. 7). Luke did not specify their charges, but it is clear from Paul's response (v. 8) that they were the same as those directed at him by the Asian Jews and Tertullus—teaching against the Jewish law (cf. 21:28), defiling the temple (cf. 21:28; 24:6), and plotting treason (cf. 24:5). Paul emphatically denied the charge of sedition; he had done nothing "against Caesar." It was *this* charge that had kept him in Roman hands. The other charges, especially the temple charge, would place him under Jewish jurisdiction; and that was the last thing Paul wanted.

25:9 Festus was otherwise minded, however. He was no more convinced by Paul's accusers than Felix had been. He perhaps entertained the notion that more evidence would be forthcoming at Jerusalem, the "scene" of the alleged crime. He may have been aware that this was not altogether advantageous for Paul, for he virtually asked his permission to take the case to Jerusalem (v. 9). Tactfully, he assured Paul that he would not hand him over to Jewish jurisdiction. It would be a Roman trial, "before me," as he put it. What Festus had in mind is not certain. It may have been something like the hearing before the Sanhedrin arranged by Lysias (23:1-10). Perhaps he envisaged a formal trial with some of the Jewish leaders on his advisory judicial council.[133] It was in any event a dangerous proposal from Paul's perspective, and Festus's motives were not altogether innocent. Luke hinted at this by noting that Festus wanted to grant the Jews a "favor" (v. 9a). It was such favoritism that had kept Paul in prison for two years (cf. 24:27). Earlier Festus had refused the Jews the "favor" of transferring Paul to Jerusalem (v. 3). Now he was bending to their political pressure. Favoritism is never a basis for justice, and Paul knew it. He knew how he had once narrowly escaped an ambush plot in Jerusalem, and he knew that a procurator who once set out on the road of favoritism might well continue down that road and ultimately hand him over to the Jews.

25:10-11 Paul's response was immediate and to a degree defiant. He was obviously rebuking the procurator when he told him that he knew "very well" that he had in no way wronged the Jews (v. 10).[134] He detected the procurator's motive and threw it back in his face: "You want to 'grant a favor' to the Jews by 'granting me' [handing me over] to them"

---

[132]For sitting on the *bēma* representing the assumption of one's official role, cf. 12:21; 18:12,16f.; 25:10,17.

[133]Marshall, *Acts*, 385.

[134]R. J. Cassidy, *Society and Politics in the Acts of the Apostles* (Maryknoll, N.Y.: Orbis, 1988), 109.

(v. 11, author's translation).[135] Paul knew that he would have no hope if surrendered to Jewish jurisdiction. It was only under a Roman tribunal that he could hope for any shred of justice. Now that the procurator appeared to be on the verge of handing him over to the Jews, he resorted to the only avenue left to assure his continuance under Roman jurisdiction—he made use of his citizen-right of appeal to Caesar.

There are many unanswered questions about this process and how it worked in the middle of the first century, Acts itself being one of the main sources for this period. Paul seems to have made use of an ancient right of Roman citizens that goes back to at least the fifth century B.C. Known as *provocatio*, it gave a citizen the right to appeal a magistrate's verdict to a jury of fellow citizens.[136] Under the empire the emperor himself became the court of appeal, replacing the former jury of peers. Although governors seem to have had the right to pass capital sentences and even to deny appeal in instances involving established laws, in cases not involving well-established precedent (*extra ordinem*) such as Paul's, the right of appeal seems to have been absolute; a procurator such as Festus would not have been in the position to deny it.[137] Though appeal was generally made only after a verdict had been reached, Paul's appeal *before* condemnation seems to have been in order.[138] It is unclear whether the process was irrevocable, i.e., whether a magistrate could stop the appeal should the innocence of the appellant be determined before remission to the emperor. Probably in Festus's case it would not have made much difference. He really had no desire to establish Paul's innocence for fear of the repercussions from the Jews. He probably was relieved by Paul's appeal. It took the whole troublesome matter out of his hands.

25:12 A procurator generally had an advisory council that consisted of the higher officials in his administration. Although ultimate decisions were solely in his hands, he could turn to this group for consultation on difficult matters of law. Paul's appeal was certainly no everyday occurrence, and Festus turned to his council before giving formal acknowledgment (v. 12). Then he formally ratified Paul's appeal: "To Caesar you will

---

[135]There is a clear wordplay between χάριν ("favor") in v. 9 and χαρίσασθαι ("hand over") in v. 11. See J. Dupont, "Aequitas Romana: Notes sur Actes 25, 16," *Etudes sur les Actes des Apôtres* (Paris: Cerf, 1967), 530.

[136]*Provocatio* should be distinguished from the process of *appellatio*, an appeal from one magistrate to another in the event of an unfavorable verdict.

[137]See Hemer, *Book of Acts*, 130f.; Sherwin-White, *Roman Society and Roman Law*, 57-70; B. Reese, "The Apostle Paul's Exercise of His Rights as a Roman Citizen as Recorded in the Book of Acts," *EvQ* 47 (1975): 138-45.

[138]For a contrary opinion—that *provocatio* could only be made *after* condemnation and that the procurator always had the right to reject an appeal, see P. Garnsey, "The *Lex Julia* and Appeal under the Empire," *JRS* 56 (1966): 167-89.

go." In this particular instance, the Caesar in question was Nero (A.D. 54–68). Anyone familiar with Nero's later persecution of the Christians in Rome might assume that this did not bode well for Paul. This was in the earlier years of Nero's reign, however, years marked by a general stability. His "dark side" had not yet surfaced. Perhaps more significant was that Paul was going *to Caesar*. He was headed *to Rome* to bear his ultimate witness (cf. 19:21; 23:11).

(5) Festus's Conversation with Agrippa (25:13-22)

[13]A few days later King Agrippa and Bernice arrived at Caesarea to pay their respects to Festus. [14]Since they were spending many days there, Festus discussed Paul's case with the king. He said: "There is a man here whom Felix left as a prisoner. [15]When I went to Jerusalem, the chief priests and elders of the Jews brought charges against him and asked that he be condemned.

[16]"I told them that it is not the Roman custom to hand over any man before he has faced his accusers and has had an opportunity to defend himself against their charges. [17]When they came here with me, I did not delay the case, but convened the court the next day and ordered the man to be brought in. [18]When his accusers got up to speak, they did not charge him with any of the crimes I had expected. [19]Instead, they had some points of dispute with him about their own religion and about a dead man named Jesus who Paul claimed was alive. [20]I was at a loss how to investigate such matters; so I asked if he would be willing to go to Jerusalem and stand trial there on these charges. [21]When Paul made his appeal to be held over for the Emperor's decision, I ordered him held until I could send him to Caesar."

[22]Then Agrippa said to Festus, "I would like to hear this man myself."

He replied, "Tomorrow you will hear him."

25:13 Within days of Paul's appeal to Caesar, Festus received a visit from the Jewish King Agrippa II and his sister Bernice. Likely this was a more-or-less official visit to establish relationships with the new procurator upon his assumption of office. Agrippa II was the son of Herod Agrippa I (cf. 12:1, 19-23) and the great-grandson of Herod the Great and the Hasmonean princess Miriamne. Born in A.D. 27, he was reared in Rome and in A.D. 48 upon the death of an uncle was given the latter's rule over the small kingdom of Chalcis. In A.D. 53 he exchanged this for the former territories of Philip and Lysanias (cf. Luke 3:1), which included Abilene, Batanea, Traconitis, and Gaulinitis. His rule was further extended in A.D. 56, when Nero placed him over several additional villages in the vicinity of the Sea of Galilee, including Caesarea Philippi. The regions over which he ruled were primarily of a Gentile population, and he never reigned over the main Jewish territory of Judea, Samaria, and Galilee as his father had. This remained under the jurisdiction of procurators. The Romans granted him the custody of the ceremonial vestments worn by the high priest on the Day of Atonement. He also held the authority to appoint the high priest. In this respect he could be considered "king of the Jews."[139]

Agrippa's relationship to his sister Bernice was something of a scandal in its day. A year younger than her brother, she could perhaps be described as a "Jewish Cleopatra." She had been married at age thirteen to her uncle, Herod of Chalcis. When her husband/uncle died in A.D. 48 and her brother Herod was granted rule over Chalcis, she moved in with him and remained his constant companion for many years. The rumors were rampant that they were maintaining an incestuous relationship. In A.D. 63 she married King Polemon of Cilicia, perhaps to avert the rumors, but she doesn't seem to have lived with him for long. She accompanied Agrippa to Rome in the early 70s and quickly became the mistress of Titus, the emperor Vespasian's son. The relationship created a major scandal in Roman patrician circles.[140] Titus evidently wanted to marry her, but marriage to a Jewess was not socially acceptable; when he became emperor himself in A.D. 79, he was forced to abandon his liaison with her.[141]

25:14 As king of the Jews, Festus felt that Agrippa was in a unique position to assist him in the matter of Paul's appeal. He needed to formulate an official report of the charges against Paul to be sent with the appeal. All of these were initiated by the Jews and primarily concerned Jewish religious matters. He keenly felt his own incompetence in this area.

25:15-17 His conversation with Agrippa is enlightening—but not for any new information on the situation. Basically vv. 15-21 are Festus's own version of the events covered in 25:1-12. What is interesting are the small differences in his version. Like Lysias, he sought to depict himself in the most favorable light, even at the expense of bending the truth somewhat (cf. 23:27). This tendency already surfaces in v. 15 when Festus stated that the Jews were seeking Paul's condemnation. This is at some variance with the account in v. 3, where only the charges and request for transferal are mentioned. Festus was already presenting himself in the role of Paul's protector. The discrepancy in his version is most blatant in v. 16. According to Festus, the Jews wanted him handed over without a fair trial, and he made it clear to them that this would not be permitted. Paul's accusers would have to confront him face-to-face, and

---

[139]For references in Josephus to Agrippa II, see *War* 2.245-47, 309, 337-407; 3.56-58; *Antiquities* 19.354, 360ff.; 20.104, 135-40, 159, 179-214; *Life* 38f., 46ff., 52, 61, 74, *et passim.* See also Bruce, *Acts:* NIC, 481f.

[140]See the references to Bernice in Juvenal 6.156ff. and in the Roman historians Tacitus (*Hist.* 2.2), Seutonius (*Titus* 7), and Dio Cassius (65.15; 66.18).

[141]For references to Bernice in Josephus, see *War* 2.217-21, 310-14, 333f., 405, 426, 595; *Antiquities* 19.277, 354; 20.104, 143-47.

Paul would be given his due right to answer their charges. This was certainly the Roman standard of justice,[142] and this was perhaps the way Festus saw the situation in retrospect. But this is not the picture conveyed in vv. 1-12. There it was not initially a question of delivering Paul to the Jews without a fair trial—only of where the trial would be held. In fact, Paul's concern about receiving justice and the basis for his appeal was precisely that Festus would yield to the Jewish pressure and compromise his standards of justice (v. 9f.). Festus comes off much better in his own account. He continued to insist on his total efficiency in maintaining Roman jurisprudence. He did not delay the case for a minute but the very next day convened the trial and set Paul's accusers before him (v. 17). From this point on, his own version is perhaps less tendentious and closer to the facts, but it still raises serious questions about Festus's actions.

25:18-20 Festus told Agrippa that the Jews raised none of the charges "which [he] expected" (v. 18). This most likely means that the Jews were not able to charge Paul with treason or any crime by Roman law. His next statement would bear that out: their charges only dealt with matters of their own religion and a "dead man named Jesus who Paul claimed was alive" (v. 19).[143] Festus's reference to the resurrection is intriguing. It shows how incomprehensible to a pagan the whole concept must have been (cf. 26:24). And this was the whole point. Festus was not competent to try the case, as he himself admitted (v. 20a). It was an internal Jewish religious discussion which in no way involved Roman law. Why, then, did Festus wish to continue the case by transferring it to Jerusalem (v. 20b) if he already had determined that no Roman law had been broken? Why did he not throw it out of court like Gallio (18:15)? Luke has given us the answer: he wanted "to do the Jews a favor" (v. 9). Festus was simply not the sterling example of Roman justice he claimed to be (v. 16) and that, at least implicitly, by his own admission. But there it is for everyone to read in Festus's own words—Paul and the Christians were guilty of no crime against the state (v. 18).

25:21-22 Festus concluded his account by apprising Agrippa of Paul's appeal (v. 21). He was now holding Paul until he could arrange his

---

[142]The right of a defendant to stand before the accusers and to respond to their charges is well-attested in the Roman sources. Cf. Ulpian, *Dig.* 48.17.1; Appian, *Civil War* 3.54 and the references in H. Conzelmann, *The Acts of the Apostles, Her* (Philadelphia: Fortress, 1987), 206. Later Christian writers appeal to this basic legal principle: cf. Justin, *Apology* 1.3; Tertullian, *Apology* 1.3; 2.2.

[143]In v. 19 Festus used the word δεισιδαιμονία to refer to the Jewish "religion." As in Paul's Areopagus address (17:22), the word could have the more negative connotation of "superstition." Since Festus was conversing with the *Jewish* king, the positive nuance is more likely.

remittal to Caesar.[144] In very courteous language,[145] Agrippa replied that
he would like to hear Paul himself. Man of action that he was, Festus
again did not delay (cf. v. 17) and promised Agrippa that his request
would be granted "tomorrow" (v. 22).

(6) Paul's Address before Agrippa: The Setting (25:23-27)

**[23]The next day Agrippa and Bernice came with great pomp and entered the
audience room with the high ranking officers and the leading men of the city. At
the command of Festus, Paul was brought in. [24]Festus said: "King Agrippa, and
all who are present with us, you see this man! The whole Jewish community has
petitioned me about him in Jerusalem and here in Caesarea, shouting that he
ought not to live any longer. [25]I found he had done nothing deserving of death,
but because he made his appeal to the Emperor I decided to send him to Rome.
[26]But I have nothing definite to write to His Majesty about him. Therefore I have
brought him before all of you, and especially before you, King Agrippa, so that
as a result of this investigation I may have something to write. [27]For I think it is
unreasonable to send on a prisoner without specifying the charges against him."**

Paul's speech before Agrippa forms the climax to all his defense in
Acts 22–26. It reaches back to all his previous arguments before the Jewish crowd, the Sanhedrin, and the Roman procurators and presents his
final statement on the Christian position in relation to Judaism. It is also
climactic with regard to its setting because Paul bore his witness before
not only the gathered Roman leaders but before the Jewish king. It is not
surprising that Luke went into some detail in describing the setting for
this address.

25:23 The importance of the address is underlined by all the pag-
eantry of the notables parading into the audience chamber.[146] First there
was the king himself accompanied by Bernice. Luke may have intended a
subtle irony by drawing attention to Bernice's presence on this occasion.
The outward show of pomp belied the stark reality of their inward lives.
Following them came the "high ranking officers." They were the tribunes,
the officers over a cohort of a thousand soldiers. There were perhaps five
of them, since there were five auxiliary cohorts stationed in Caesarea.
After them came the "notables" of the city ("leading men," NIV), the

---

[144]The word ἀναπέμπω is technical language for remitting a prisoner to another authority.
See C. Anderson, "Sending Formulae in John's Gospel: A Linguistic Analysis in the Light of
Their Background," Ph.D. diss., The Southern Baptist Theological Seminary, 1989, 93.
Likewise "to hold over for the emperor's decision" (εἰς τὴν τοῦ Σεβαστοῦ διάγνωσιν) is
technical legal language (Latin: *a cognitionibus Augusti*).

[145]Ἐβουλόμην is an imperfect used for courtesy. "I should like to, I would wish." Robertson, *WP* 3:437.

[146]The word φαντασία (cf. our "fantasy") describes great pomp, a showy parade.

leading figures of Caesarea.[147] Finally, when all the show was over and everyone was seated, Paul was brought in, the last in the procession. Festus gave a brief introduction, explaining the circumstances for the hearing.

25:24-25 Festus's remarks provide nothing new to the narrative, involving only matters that have already surfaced in Acts. That Luke took the time and space to repeat them shows the importance he attached to them. Festus's introduction provides a useful summary for understanding Paul's whole experience. For Festus himself it all began with a petition from the Jews seeking Paul's condemnation (cf. 25:2,7,15). Actually, it all started much earlier—with the Jewish crowd in the temple square screaming that such a man "ought not to live" (cf. 22:22). Festus then explained to his important guests in the audience chamber the circumstances of Paul's appeal. Here again one finds him absolving himself of responsibility: "I found he had done nothing deserving death, but . . . he made his appeal to the Emperor." Festus seemed to imply that Paul was himself responsible for the whole situation with the unnecessary appeal, as if he had not himself virtually forced Paul to do so because of his own yielding to Jewish pressure. In any event, Festus at least once again acknowledged Paul's innocence (cf. 18f.).

25:26-27 Now Festus set forth the immediate agenda. He needed something definite to write in his report to the emperor.[148] He was himself at a total loss for any specific charges that could be listed (cf. v. 20). He had assembled this group to hear Paul on the matter in the hope that they would assist him in drawing up the charges. He was particularly desirous of Agrippa's input since he was more conversant in Jewish matters (v. 26). He added that it would be unreasonable ("senseless," *alogos*) to send a prisoner to the emperor without such a report (v. 27). It would be foolish indeed, perhaps fatal, to one's career. Such reports were not optional.[149] There is strong irony in Festus's remark. The whole situation was indeed "senseless." He had no charges against Paul because there were none to be found. Paul's need to make the appeal, his continued

---

[147]Representative of the Western text, the Harclean Syriac widens the scope of the "notables," adding that they "came down from the province" (and thus represented a larger area than only Caesarea).

[148]In v. 26 Festus referred to the emperor as "lord" (κύριος), translated "his majesty" in the NIV. The title was often used for rulers in the East, being applied to Ptolemy XIII in an inscription dating from 62 B.C. It was used of both Herod the Great and Agrippa I. Augustus and Tiberias refused to accept the title. Later emperors, beginning with Caligula, not only accepted the title but used it as a base for emperor worship. Nero, the emperor at this time, is frequently referred to as κύριος in inscriptions. Domitian liked to be addressed as *dominus et deus noster* ("our Lord and God").

[149]See Conzelmann (*Acts*, 207) for references from Roman legal writings that specify the mandatory nature of submitting such documents in the appeal process.

confinement, the entire situation was "unreasonable"; and it was very much the procurator's own doing.

(7) Paul's Address before Agrippa: The Speech (26:1-23)

[1]Then Agrippa said to Paul, "You have permission to speak for yourself."

So Paul motioned with his hand and began his defense: [2]"King Agrippa, I consider myself fortunate to stand before you today as I make my defense against all the accusations of the Jews, [3]and especially so because you are well acquainted with all the Jewish customs and controversies. Therefore, I beg you to listen to me patiently.

[4]"The Jews all know the way I have lived ever since I was a child, from the beginning of my life in my own country, and also in Jerusalem. [5]They have known me for a long time and can testify, if they are willing, that according to the strictest sect of our religion, I lived as a Pharisee. [6]And now it is because of my hope in what God has promised our fathers that I am on trial today. [7]This is the promise our twelve tribes are hoping to see fulfilled as they earnestly serve God day and night. O king, it is because of this hope that the Jews are accusing me. [8]Why should any of you consider it incredible that God raises the dead?

[9]"I too was convinced that I ought to do all that was possible to oppose the name of Jesus of Nazareth. [10]And that is just what I did in Jerusalem. On the authority of the chief priests I put many of the saints in prison, and when they were put to death, I cast my vote against them. [11]Many a time I went from one synagogue to another to have them punished, and I tried to force them to blaspheme. In my obsession against them, I even went to foreign cities to persecute them.

[12]"On one of these journeys I was going to Damascus with the authority and commission of the chief priests. [13]About noon, O king, as I was on the road, I saw a light from heaven, brighter than the sun, blazing around me and my companions. [14]We all fell to the ground, and I heard a voice saying to me in Aramaic, 'Saul, Saul, why do you persecute me? It is hard for you to kick against the goads.'

[15]"Then I asked, 'Who are you, Lord?'

" 'I am Jesus, whom you are persecuting,' the Lord replied. [16]'Now get up and stand on your feet. I have appeared to you to appoint you as a servant and as a witness of what you have seen of me and what I will show you. [17]I will rescue you from your own people and from the Gentiles. I am sending you to them [18]to open their eyes and turn them from darkness to light, and from the power of Satan to God, so that they may receive forgiveness of sins and a place among those who are sanctified by faith in me.'

[19]"So then, King Agrippa, I was not disobedient to the vision from heaven. [20]First to those in Damascus, then to those in Jerusalem and in all Judea, and to the Gentiles also, I preached that they should repent and turn to God and prove their repentance by their deeds. [21]That is why the Jews seized me in the temple courts and tried to kill me. [22]But I have had God's help to this very day, and so I stand here and testify to small and great alike. I am saying nothing beyond what the prophets and Moses said would happen—[23]that the Christ would suffer and,

**as the first to rise from the dead, would proclaim light to his own people and to
the Gentiles."**

Paul's speech before Agrippa is the culmination and climax of Paul's
defense in chaps. 21–26. It brings together and presents in final form all
the themes of the previous five chapters. The charges against Paul that
began with the temple mob in 21:28 were given their final verdict by the
Jewish king himself: Paul was innocent on all counts—he could have
been set free (26:31f.). Paul's own account of his conversion and commission from Christ, which constituted the main subject of his speech before
the crowd in the temple square (22:3-21), was repeated in the speech
before Agrippa and indeed in its fullest form, as Paul shared his fulfillment of the commission—his witness for Christ (26:19-23). The theme of
the resurrection, which began with the divided Sanhedrin (23:6-10) and
continued to remain a major issue in Paul's defense (24:15,21; 25:19) was
now given its most complete exposition (26:6-8,23). Paul wanted all to
know that his commitment to the *risen* Christ was the real reason for his
bonds. The parallels to the passion of Christ which began with Paul's
journey to Jerusalem in chap. 21 likewise reach their high point in chap.
26. Like Jesus, Paul appeared before not only the Roman procurator but
the Jewish king as well (cf. Luke 23:6-12), and as in Jesus' trial both
procurator and king found him innocent (Acts 26:31f.; Luke 23:14f.).

One final emphasis of the chapter should not be overlooked. The testimony before Agrippa was the fulfillment of Jesus' commission to Paul
that he would witness before kings (Acts 9:15) and of his promise to his
disciples that he would give them "words and wisdom" to make that witness a bold one (Luke 21:12-15).

The speech before Agrippa is strikingly parallel to Paul's speech
before the temple mob, as on both occasions Paul gave a testimony of his
personal experience in Christ: his thoroughly Jewish upbringing (vv. 4-8;
cf. 22:3), his persecution of the Christians (vv. 9-11; cf. 22:4-5), his conversion (vv. 12-15; cf. 22:6-11), and his commission from the risen Lord
(vv. 16-18; cf. 22:17-21). In the Agrippa speech there was no mention of
Ananias, whose Jewish piety would have been of less importance for the
basically Gentile audience in the speech before Agrippa. On the other
hand, the anger of the Jewish mob in the temple square cut Paul off
(22:22) and never allowed him to present his gospel and give his appeal.
Paul did present his gospel before Agrippa (vv. 18,23) and did not hesitate to extend the invitation—even to the king himself (v. 26f.).

INTRODUCTION (26:1-3). **26:1** The first three verses comprise a formal introduction to the speech. Continuing the solemnity of the occasion
already set by the ceremonious arrival of the distinguished audience and
Festus's presentation of the case (25:23-27), the king now formally

granted Paul permission to speak. Paul then motioned to the audience to indicate the beginning of his address. It was not the gesture for silence that he had used to quiet the temple mob (21:40) but rather the outstretched hand of a Greek orator. Throughout his speech Paul would remain in this mode before his distinguished hearers. Of all the speeches in Acts, this one is cast in the most elevated, cultured language. Luke described Paul as beginning his defense (*apologeomai*). It was not a defense in the sense of a formal trial. The occasion was not a trial but only a hearing to assist Festus in drawing up his report to Caesar (25:27). Paul was not defending himself before charges but rather offering his *apologia*, his personal testimony for his life as a Christian. It is noteworthy that Luke consistently referred to Agrippa throughout chaps. 25–26 as simply "Agrippa," never by his full title "Herod Agrippa." This Agrippa always appears in a favorable light, not at all like his father, the hated "Herod" of chap. 12.

26:2-3 Verse 2 provides Paul's *capitatio benevolentiae*, his formal appeal to curry the favor of his famous hearer (cf. Tertullus's in 24:2f.). In this case Paul was quite brief, only noting that he felt himself "fortunate"[150] to be appearing before Agrippa. He pointed to what was the essential factor in the whole occasion. As the Jewish king, he would be familiar with Jewish customs and points of dispute.[151] He was also a thoroughly Hellenistic king and lived a Roman life-style. He was thus in the unique position to give his opinion on both the Jewish and Roman legal aspects of Paul's situation. Festus knew that, and that was the reason for his eagerness for the king to hear Paul and give his opinion on the case. As far as the "accusations of the Jews" were concerned, there was really only one left at this point. Tertullus's two charges had long been dismissed (24:5-7). Festus had already found Paul innocent of the charges of sedition and political agitation (25:18). The charge that Paul had defiled the temple had died out for want of any witnesses (24:18f.). There was really only one left—that Paul was teaching against the Jewish law (21:28). Festus knew himself to be incompetent in such matters. Agrippa was in a better position to judge.

PAUL'S FAITHFULNESS TO THE JEWISH HOPE (26:4-8). 26:4-6 As in the speech in the temple square, Paul began his testimony by referring to his upbringing in strict Judaism. He was reared among his own people, even in Jerusalem.[152] He had been a Pharisee and had lived according to the

---

[150]The word is μακάριος, the familiar "blessed" or "happy" of the Beatitudes.

[151]The accusative phrase γνώστην ὄντα σε is grammatically difficult. It surely modifies the σοῦ of v. 2. Robertson suggests it may be a rare accusative absolute (*WP* 3:443).

[152]"In my own country" (ἐν τῷ ἔθνει μου) probably does not refer to Tarsus but to his upbringing in Judea, as in 22:3. The τε has only slight force, linking Jerusalem to "my country"—"and particularly in Jerusalem."

strictest observances of the Jewish religion.[153] Before the Sanhedrin Paul stressed that his Pharisaic background closely linked up with his faith in the resurrection and that this was the real issue behind his trial (23:6). Here in the speech before Agrippa he made the same connection. The references to his being a Pharisee (26:5) and to his being on trial because of his hope in God's promises to the fathers (v. 6) are closely linked. The "hope" was realized in the resurrection (cf. 24:15). Paul had been born a true Jew, reared a true Jew, trained in the strictest Pharisaic viewpoint of Judaism, and still remained a true Jew. It was precisely his faith in the resurrection of Jesus that most pointed to his fidelity to Judaism because in the resurrection Israel's hope in God's promises had been fulfilled.

26:7-8 The Jews believed fervently in this hope. In their worship they prayed for its fulfillment day and night. The hope was shared by all "Twelve Tribes"—all of Israel.[154] What was inconceivable for Paul was that the Jews, who so fervently prayed for God's fulfillment of the promises, would accuse him precisely because of his conviction that they had indeed now been realized in Christ. At first addressing the king (v. 7), he now turned to the whole crowd in the audience chamber and raised the question why any of them would find it unbelievable that God should raise the dead. Was he putting this question to Jews or to the mainly Gentile gathering in the chamber or to all? Perhaps it was to all. Gentiles like Festus could not comprehend the idea of resurrection at all. Except for the Sadducees, the Jews believed in resurrection, fervently hoped in it, but rejected Paul's conviction that it had begun in Christ. Ultimately, it was Christ's resurrection that Paul had in mind, and all of them—Jew and Gentile alike—found it incredible.

PAUL'S PERSECUTION OF CHRIST (26:9-11). **26:9-11** Paul's allusion to the resurrection had been an aside, a promise of things to come in his address. Now he returned to his main outline—his personal testimony of his experience in Christ. Not only had he been a Pharisee and a strict observant Jew, but he also had been a persecutor of the Christians. Like those Jews who were now accusing him, so he too once felt that it was God's will for him to do everything possible to oppose the name of Christ.[155] Paul

---

[153]Verses 4-5 are written in high Greek style. Such expressions as ἀπ' αρχῆς and ἄνωθεν are typical of Greek biography. The superlative form ἀκριβεστάτην and the verbal form ἴσασι are Atticisms.

[154]Anna in Luke 2:37f. is exemplary of this piety, praying as here "day and night" for "the redemption of Israel." The expression δωδεκάφυλον is interesting; it occurs only here in the Bible and is evidence that Israel still in some sense saw itself as composed of twelve tribes. Anna is herself designated as belonging to the tribe of Asher (Luke 2:36).

[155]For the "name" of Christ as representing Christ's presence and power among his people, see 2:38; 3:6,16; 4:10,12; 5:41. That Paul considered his persecuting zeal as within God's will is perhaps implied by his use of δέω (the *divine* "must") in v. 9.

described his former zeal as a persecutor, an activity already familiar in previous portions of Acts (8:1a; 9:1f.; 22:4f.). Here it appears in its most developed form. The official papers from the Sanhedrin are already familiar to the reader, as are his arrest and imprisonment of the Christians.[156] It was a different Paul who was telling the story now. He called them "saints." What he added in this account was that he gave his consenting vote when the Christians were condemned to death.[157] His allusion to his vote is probably metaphorical, meaning that he was fully in agreement with the verdict (cf. 8:1a; 22:20). In the earlier accounts of Paul's persecuting activity, only the death of Stephen has been mentioned; and it may well be that he was making a generalized statement here based on his participation in that incident.

26:11 Paul continued to paint in ever darker hues the picture of his former persecuting zeal. Not only did he use the Sanhedrin to further his activities, but he also had the Christians punished in the local synagogues (v. 11).[158] Paul's reference to his efforts to make the Christians blaspheme the name of Christ is well translated in the NIV—he "tried" to do so: he did not likely succeed.[159] In his letter to the emperor Trajan of the early second century, the Roman governor Pliny told how it was impossible for him to force any "true" Christian to curse the name of Christ.[160] Paul's description of his fervor as persecutor finally reached its peak: he even pursued them in the cities outside of Jerusalem (v. 11b). One immediately recalls Damascus. That city was likely the limit of his persecutions. It was also where they ended.

PAUL'S COMMISSION FROM CHRIST (26:12-18).   On the road to Damascus, everything changed for the former persecutor of "the name." Here for the third time in Acts, Paul's conversion is recounted (cf. 9:1-30; 22:5-21). Of the three accounts the conversion proper is told with the least detail here. Paul's blindness is not related, and the visit of Ananias is not mentioned. All the emphasis is on Paul's *commission* from Christ, which in chap. 9 was connected with Ananias's visit (9:15f.) and in Paul's account before

---

[156]This is the only text in the NT that could be used to support the view that Paul was a member of the Sanhedrin. His youth and the fact that Paul never alluded to his Sanhedrin membership in those passages in his letters where he strained to prove his former Jewish pedigree make it most unlikely he ever held such a seat. See S. Legasse, "Paul Sanhedrite? A Propos d'Ac 26, 10," *A Cause de l'Evangile* (Paris: Cerf, 1985), 799-807.

[157]The word for casting a vote is highly picturesque, meaning literally *to cast a pebble* (ψῆφον) and reflects the ancient practice of voting by casting a white stone (yea) or a black stone (nay). See Robertson, *WP* 3:446.

[158]The Jewish synagogues had their own courts for disciplinary matters, and Paul himself often suffered their punishment (cf. 13:50; 14:19; 2 Cor 11:24).

[159]The imperfect tense (ἠνάγκαζον) could be translated "forced" but more likely is conative, "attempted to force."

[160]Pliny the Younger, *Epistles* 10.96.5.

the temple mob with his vision in the temple (22:17-21). Here Paul greatly telescoped the experience, relating the commission from the risen Christ closely with the appearance on the Damascus road. In this way Paul communicated to Agrippa and the Gentile audience what was the ultimate significance of the Damascus road experience—his call to bring the light of Christ to all people. In this account the emphasis is decidedly less on Paul's personal experience and more on his commission.[161]

26:12-15 The Damascus road experience is related in vv. 12-15. It is basically the same as the two prior accounts in chaps. 9 and 22 but with several significant differences. The first of these is the mention of the heavenly light that came upon Paul and his traveling companions at noon and "outshone the sun." The noon hour and the bright light are also present in Paul's account before the temple crowd (22:6), but there the light is connected with his blindness (22:11); here it is associated with his commission to witness to the light of the gospel (26:18). In this speech Paul was not interested so much in relating to Agrippa and the Gentiles the miracle of the recovery of his sight as he was in bringing to them the light of the gospel he had himself discovered on the Damascus road and been commissioned to carry to the nations.

Only in this account did Paul mention that his traveling companions also fell to the ground at the appearance of the brilliant light. This detail serves the same function as their hearing the sound in 9:7 and their seeing the light in 22:9. It emphasizes the objective reality of the event. In all three accounts, however, Paul alone *experienced* the appearance, was converted and called. Only in this account is it explicitly said that the heavenly voice spoke in the "Hebrew dialect" ("Aramaic," NIV). This, however, is implicit in the address to Paul in the Hebrew form of his name *Saoul* in the other accounts. All three accounts relate the central question put to Paul by the risen Christ: "Why do you persecute *me*?" (v. 14). In persecuting the community of Christ, Paul was persecuting the Lord himself. Only in this final account are the further words of the Lord added: "It is hard for you to kick against the goads." Perhaps Paul included them here because they were a common proverb of the times, particularly prevalent among the Greeks and Romans, and would hit a responsive chord in his Gentile audience on this occasion.[162] Often the Lord's words are interpreted as asking Paul why he was fighting his con-

---

[161]That the Acts 26 conversion account is basically a commissioning narrative is noted by C. W. Hedrick, "Paul's Conversion/Call: A Comparative Analysis of the Three Reports in Acts," *JBL* 100 (1981): 426f.

[162]The closest parallel is found in Euripides, *Bacchae*, 794f. See A. Vogeli, "Lukas und Euripides," *TZ* 9 (1953): 415-38. The proverb is found in many other sources, such as Aeschylus (*Agamemnon* 1624 and Pindar, *Pythian Ode* 2, 173). The only occurrence in extant Jewish literature is in *Pss. Sol.* 16:4.

science, repressing his inner feelings that the Christians might indeed be on the Lord's side and raging against them with ever greater fury.[163] This, however, was not how Paul's Gentile audience would have understood the words. In the many instances where the proverb occurs in Greek literature, it always has the meaning of resisting one's destiny or fighting the will of the gods. That meaning fit Paul's situation. In persecuting Christ, Paul was fighting the will of the One who had set him apart from birth (cf. Gal 1:15). Like a beast of burden kicking against his master's goads, he would only find the blows more severe with each successive kick. He was fighting the will of God (cf. Acts 5:39). It was a futile, senseless task.

26:16-18 The emphasis in this third conversion account is decidedly on the commission given Paul by the risen Jesus in vv. 16-18. Indeed, this commission constitutes the center and climax of Paul's entire speech. It is virtually repeated in Paul's closing words (vv. 22-23).[164] Christ's commission to Paul is given in words reminiscent of God's commissioning of the Old Testament prophets. Like Ezekiel following his vision of the Lord, Paul was directed to rise and stand on his feet (v. 16; cf. Ezek 2:1). The emphasis on the Lord's *sending* him is characteristic of the call of the prophets (cf. Ezek 2:3), as is the promise to rescue him from his enemies (cf. Jer 1:8).[165] Paul's task is described with two words. He was first to be a "steward" (*hypēretēs*). The word emphasizes his relationship to his Lord. He was to be one who *served* his Master and was faithful to his Master's commission. The second word is "witness" (*martys*). A witness bears testimony to the things he has seen and heard. Paul had seen the risen Lord and heard his commission. His whole story in Acts has shown his faithful witness—before Jews and Gentiles, Greeks and Romans, peasants, philosophers, and kings. It is *witness* to Christ that links Paul with the apostles[166] and other faithful Christians like Stephen (cf. 22:20).

Ultimately, the role of witness is the key role for every disciple. All who have encountered the risen Christ are commissioned to be witnesses (Acts 1:8). The content of that witness is summarized in v. 18, in language reminiscent of the servant psalms of Isa 42:6 and 49:6. Christ is the

---

[163]K. Stendahl sees the guilty conscience interpretation as coming more from the modern Western mentality than the biblical account ("The Apostle Paul and the Introspective Conscience of the West," *HTR* 56 [1963]: 199-215).

[164]This is noted by R. O'Toole, who argues that vv. 12-23 are arranged in diptych form, with 12-15 and 19-21 comprising one half and 16-18 and 22-23 the other (*Acts 26: The Christological Climax of Paul's Defense* [Ac. 22:1-26:32] [Rome: Biblical Institute, 1978]).

[165]There is a grammatical problem with ὀφθήσομαι in v. 16. In the passive the verb means *to appear, to become more visible*. In the present context it seems to mean *to make visible, to show*, as translated in the NIV. The original text may have had ὀφθήσεται ("things which will be shown to you"). See M. Dibelius, *Studies in the Acts of the Apostles* (London: SCM, 1956), 92.

[166]Cf. 1:22; 2:32; 3:15; 5:32; 10:39,41.

servant of God who opens the eyes of those in darkness, who brings light
to the nations. To proclaim him is to bring the light of the gospel. It could
hardly be more aptly summarized than Paul did here. The gospel brings
light, opens one's eyes to the truth in Christ. Paul further described this as
a turning from the power of Satan to the power of God. The sharp dualis-
tic language of light and darkness is found throughout the New Testament
and is metaphorical for two divergent ways of living.[167] The one way can
be described in various ways—living according to the world, under
Satan, in darkness, in sin, apart from God, totally self-centered existence.
The alternative is life in Christ, a life marked by righteousness, walking
in the light, directed by God and not by self.

Paul concluded his summary of the gospel by noting the two results
that come to the one who responds by faith in Christ. First is the forgiveness of sin, the removal of the barrier that separates one from God. With
that barrier removed, the way is then clear for the second result—assurance of a place, a portion among the saints in God's eternal kingdom. One
could hardly give a more succinct presentation of the gospel. Paul may
have been describing his commission from Christ. He did more than
relate the commission, however. He used the opportunity to carry it out
on that occasion. He preached the gospel to Agrippa and the Gentiles
gathered there.

PAUL'S WITNESS FOR CHRIST (26:19-23). **26:19-20a** Returning to the
outline of his ministry, Paul now showed how he had carried out the commission of Christ. He had not been disobedient to his vision of Christ
(v. 19); he had not "kick[ed] against the goads." He had carried out not
only the Lord's commission to him to be a servant and a witness (v. 16)
but indeed the Lord's commission to his disciples on the ascension day,
preaching first in Damascus, then in Jerusalem, then in all the land of
Judea, and finally to the Gentiles (v. 20; cf. Acts 1:8). The narrative of
Acts mentions Paul's preaching in Damascus after his conversion (9:20-
25) as well as his subsequent witness in Jerusalem (9:28f.). There is no
mention of a larger witness of Paul "in all Judea." There are grammatical
and textual problems with this reading, and it may well be that the text
originally referred to Paul's preaching "in every region among both Jews
and Gentiles."[168] Paul's reference would then be to his missionary pattern

---

[167]The closest parallel to Paul's summary of the gospel here is found in Col 1:12-14, where
many of the same themes appear—light and darkness, turning from the rule of sin and darkness to the rule of the Son, obtaining a portion among the saints. For other passages using the
light imagery, cf. Eph 5:8; 2 Cor 4:4-6; 1 Pet 2:9 and throughout the Johannine literature.

[168]In the present text the accusative case of πᾶσάν τε τὴν χώραν is unexplainable. The Byzantine text includes the preposition *eis* before *pasan*, which makes the phrase grammatical.
More significant is the reading of $\mathfrak{P}^{74}$, which has "Jews" instead of "Judea." Such variants

of beginning in the synagogue before turning to the Gentiles, a pattern characteristic of his mission throughout Acts 13–19.

26:20b As is true throughout this speech, Paul did not pass up any opportunity to testify to the gospel before the king. Thus, in speaking of his witness to Jews and Gentiles, he included the characteristic appeal he made—to "repent and turn to God" (v. 20). Repenting (*metanoein*) and turning (*epistrephein*) to God are variant expressions of the same act, for true repentance is a complete change of mind, an about-face *from* sin and self *to* God. The manifestation of this complete change of direction, the proof of the genuineness of repentance, is a life characterized by good works. Works can never be the basis of salvation. They are, however, the inevitable result of a genuine experience of turning to God in Christ.[169]

26:21-22a Verses 21-22a complete Paul's testimony to his life as a Christian witness. It did not always go easily. Ultimately, the mob descended on him in the temple because of his testimony to Christ, leading to his arrest (v. 21). But even in that instance, as in many others, the Lord kept his promise to Paul and rescued him (v. 22a; cf. v. 17). Even though in bonds, his witness was unhindered, as even now he testified before the king. But it was not just before kings and governors that the Lord had enabled Paul to witness. It was before "small and great alike." Just as there were no geographical or racial boundaries in Paul's ministry (v. 20), so there were no social barriers. It was the same gospel for all, and Paul bore his witness to all without discrimination, whether to the peasant farmers of Lystra or the Jewish king himself.

26:22b-23 Verses 22b-23 provide Paul's final and climactic reference to the gospel in his speech. He had spoken of turning the eyes from darkness to light, of repentance and the forgiveness of sins, of obtaining a portion with the saints in the eternal kingdom (vv. 18,20). Now he centered on the key to all of this, the means by which enlightenment, forgiveness, and salvation are all realized—the death and resurrection of Christ. It is a familiar pattern to the reader of Acts—the opening of the Old Testament Scriptures and demonstrating from "Moses and the prophets" that the Messiah must suffer and rise from the dead. In the summary of Paul's

---

have led to the conjecture adopted by W. Ramsay (*St. Paul the Traveller and Roman Citizen* [1897; reprint, Grand Rapids: Baker, 1978], 382) that the original text read "in every land to both Jews and Gentiles" (εἰς πᾶσαν χώραν Ἰουδαίοις τε καὶ τοῖς ἔθνεσιν).

[169]The NIV has paraphrased v. 20 with "prove their repentance by their deeds." A literal translation would read "doing works worthy of repentance," which could be misconstrued in the sense that the works would somehow be the basis of an acceptable repentance, a prerequisite to forgiveness. The phrase is to be taken as subsequent to repentance, descriptive of a truly repentant life. Cf. the similar phrase "fruits worthy of repentance" in the preaching of John the Baptist (Luke 3:8) and the emphasis in the Pauline Epistles on works as the proof or demonstration of genuine salvation (Eph 2:10; Titus 2:14; 3:8).

speech before Agrippa, the explicit texts are not cited; but one is already
familiar with them from Peter's sermons at Pentecost (2:24-36) and before
the temple crowd (3:17-26) and from Paul's sermon in the synagogue of
Pisidian Antioch (13:32-39).[170] This tradition began with Jesus' instruction of the disciples in the upper room (Luke 24:44-49; cf. also 24:25-27,
32).[171]

There he provided them with the scriptural base for their understanding of his death and resurrection, and there he first granted them the commission to proclaim their witness to both Jew and Gentile. In the Old
Testament it is the servant psalms which most clearly point to Christ's
sufferings, and that Paul had them in mind is indicated by his speaking of
the proclaiming of "light to his own people and to the Gentiles." That
was the role of the servant (Isa 42:6f.; 49:6; cf. v. 18). Paul was a servant
of the Servant (cf. v. 16). In fulfilling his commission to be a witness to
Christ, he was enabling Christ to fulfill his role as a light to the
nations.[172] He was enabling all who responded in faith to share in the resurrection life.[173]

(8) Paul's Appeal to Agrippa (26:24-29)

**[24]At this point Festus interrupted Paul's defense. "You are out of your mind,
Paul!" he shouted. "Your great learning is driving you insane."**

**[25]"I am not insane, most excellent Festus," Paul replied. "What I am saying is
true and reasonable. [26]The king is familiar with these things, and I can speak
freely to him. I am convinced that none of this has escaped his notice, because it
was not done in a corner. [27]King Agrippa, do you believe the prophets? I know
you do."**

**[28]Then Agrippa said to Paul, "Do you think that in such a short time you can
persuade me to be a Christian?"**

**[29]Paul replied, "Short time or long—I pray God that not only you but all who
are listening to me today may become what I am, except for these chains."**

26:24-25 With the theme of the resurrection, Paul had come to the
high point of his speech. By this time it had become too much for Festus.

---

[170]For a discussion of the texts used and their messianic interpretation, see comments on
2:24-36; 3:17-26; 13:32-39.

[171]Luke 24:44-49 closely parallels Acts 26:19-23. The same themes appear in both: the
opening of the Scriptures ("Moses and the prophets"), the necessity of the Messiah's suffering and resurrection, the "witness" to both Jews and Gentiles. See J. Dupont, *Nouvelles
Etudes*, 446-56.

[172]For the servant emphasis in Paul's speech before Agrippa, see D. M. Stanley, "Paul's
Conversion in Acts: Why the Three Accounts?" *CBQ* 15 (1953): 315-38.

[173]The phrase "first to rise from the dead" ($\pi\rho\tilde{\omega}\tau o\varsigma\ \dot{\epsilon}\xi\ \alpha\nu\alpha\sigma\tau\dot{\alpha}\sigma\epsilon\omega\varsigma\ \nu\epsilon\kappa\rho\tilde{\omega}\nu$) refers to
Christ's resurrection being the initiation of the general resurrection and is equivalent to the
terms "firstborn" and "firstfruits" of the resurrection. Cf. Rom 8:29; Col 1:18; 1 Cor 15:20;
Rev 1:5.

After all the talk about the Jewish Scriptures, the reference to resurrection was the last straw for the Roman procurator. He already had expressed to Agrippa his own total incomprehension concerning Paul's claim that Jesus had risen from the dead (25:19). "You are out of your mind, Paul," he blurted out. "All your learning, all your searching of the Scriptures, has lifted you out of the real world" (author's paraphrase).[174] It was an offhanded compliment. Festus was showing a genuine respect for Paul's learning. Still, he was showing the kind of popular prejudice often directed against scholars: "Too much learning alters the perspective, puts one out of touch with the real world. People don't rise from the dead. Any sensible Greek or Roman knows that" (cf. 1 Cor 1:18-25). Paul would not be put off by the governor's remark. Politely, addressing the governor with full deference as "most excellent Festus," Paul firmly asserted that he was in possession of his faculties.[175]

26:26 On this particular occasion it was not the governor but the king with whom Paul was most concerned. The audience had been called primarily so Agrippa could hear Paul, and Paul had constantly addressed the king directly throughout his speech (vv. 2,7,19). The content of the speech was particularly suited to the Jewish king, as Paul stressed his thoroughly Jewish background and the roots of his gospel in the hope of Israel and the prophetic Scriptures. So Paul turned from the governor and once again addressed Agrippa: "The king is familiar with these things." Agrippa knew the Jewish hope in the resurrection. He knew the Scriptures, understood what Paul was talking about when he referred to the prophets. More than that, he would know something about the Christians and their faith in Christ's resurrection. The events had been too public to escape the notice of any Palestinian Jew. They had not occurred "in a corner" (v. 26).

The phrase "not in a corner" is somewhat ambiguous. It could mean that the Christian movement was not an esoteric group hidden from public view. It could also mean that Christianity was not a small, insignificant movement, a "corner" affair of no real impact on the larger world. The two possibilities are not mutually exclusive. The expression "not in a corner" is often found in Greek philosophical writings, particularly in contexts where philosophers are accused of withdrawing into their "ivory

---

[174]Festus accused Paul of μανία. The term can refer to inspiration as well as madness. Plato, e.g., used it to describe the inspiration of a poet (*Phaedo*, 245A). "Inspiration," however, was not an acceptable basis for judgments in the Roman legal system; and Festus here was referring to Paul's idea of resurrection, which was foolishness, not inspiration, from *his* perspective.

[175]In the classical literature σωφροσύνη ("reasonableness") is sometimes used as the antithesis of μανία, as here. An interesting parallel is in Justin's *Dialogue* 39.4, where Trypho accused Justin of madness and the latter responded (like Paul) that he was in full possession of his senses.

towers" and not confronting the larger society in the markets and streets.[176] This meaning well fits Paul's situation. His witness had been fully public. He had met the Athenians in the marketplace and addressed them on the Areopagus. He had stood before the magistrates of Philippi and before the proconsul Gallio in Corinth. He had preached to the crowd in the temple square and spoken before the Jewish Sanhedrin. His case had been heard by the Roman governors Felix and Festus and now by the Jewish king himself. Paul's activity was certainly no affair done in a secluded corner but open to full public view. But more than that, his witness was worthy of the serious consideration of all the world, of Jew and Greek, of small and great.[177]

26:27-28 Paul was becoming ever bolder in his witness, speaking ever more "freely" to the king (v. 26).[178] Now he turned to the king and began to press for a decision: "Do you believe the prophets?" Paul had in mind the messianic prophecies, the ones he had already referred to (v. 22f.). His direction was clear. If Agrippa believed the prophets and the prophets point to Christ, then why didn't the king believe that Christ is Messiah? Agrippa sensed Paul's direction immediately. It put him in an awkward position. On the one hand, he did not want to answer no and deny the prophets. On the other hand, he was not ready to answer yes and have Paul press him for a commitment to Christ. Just exactly how he did respond is anything but clear. One thing is certain—he evaded Paul's question. It is also virtually certain that the phrase *en holigo* should be translated "briefly, in a short time," rather than with "almost."[179] It seems all the more certain since Paul played on the statement in the next verse. There are other grammatical and textual problems in Agrippa's response,[180] but the NIV rendering probably preserves the correct understanding. Agrippa was not ready to respond to Paul. Did the apostle really

---

[176]A. J. Malherbe, "'Not in a Corner': Early Christian Apologetic in Acts 26:26," *The Second Century* 5 (1985-86): 193-210.

[177]This emphasis was important to Luke. It can be found from the beginning of his Gospel, where he linked the birth of Christ with the world rulers of the time (Luke 2:1f.). It is found throughout Acts, where the apostles and Paul constantly interacted with the major political leaders. In a real sense the whole emphasis climaxes with this statement.

[178]"Speaking freely" (παρρησιαζόμενος) is a key word in Acts, often used of the bold Christian witness and implying the inspiration of the Spirit. Cf. Acts 2:29; 4:13,29,31; 28:31.

[179]J. E. Harry argues that ἐν ὀλίγῳ should be translated "in small measure" rather than "in a short time" ("Almost thou Persuadest me to Become a Christian," *ATR* 12 [1929-30]: 140-44). Id., "Acts xxvi.28," *ATR* 28 (1946): 135f.

[180]The textual problem is between the ποιῆσαι of 𝔓⁷⁴, ℵ, of A and B, or the γενέσθαι of the Byzantine text. If one adopts ποιῆσαι, it is best to take it as an infinitive of purpose: "In a short time you are persuading me [in order] to make me a Christian." See A. T. Robertson, "The Meaning of Acts xxvi.28," *ExpTim* 35 (1923-24): 185f. For the rendering "you regard it as a light matter to make a Christian of me," see E. E. Kellett, "A Note on Acts xxvi.28,"

think he could turn the mind of the king with so few words? Would he so quickly make him into a Christian?[181]

26:29 Paul gave an object lesson in bold witness at this point. Most Christians would have trouble even witnessing to a king, but to persist when once put off is remarkable. Paul failed to be daunted for a minute by the king's reply. He left the invitation open. Playing on Agrippa's words, he indicated that the timing of the decision made little difference to him, whether long or short. His real prayer was that not just Agrippa but everyone in the audience room would become a Christian believer. At this point Paul may have made several gestures, turning and directly addressing all in the room, then glancing down and perhaps lifting his wrists. He wanted them to share his Lord, but not his chains. Paul may well have seen his trial as a sort of "test case" for the Christian community in the hope that his ordeal would provide a precedent for Christian innocence and thereby relieve others from such an experience. It is not certain that he actually wore chains on this occasion. His status seems to have been one of a privileged free custody (24:23), and the term "chains" was often used in a metaphorical sense for imprisonment.

There is every reason to believe that Paul would have continued his witness had he not been cut short by the king's rising to his feet (26:30). Agrippa had heard enough, enough to know that Paul was innocent of any breach of Roman law. He had heard enough of Paul's witness too, enough to know he was not ready to become a Christian (v. 28). In a sense he represented the more exemplary Jews in Acts—not like the mobs who stoned Paul or dragged him before the magistrates or screamed for his hide. He listened to Paul's testimony politely, even with interest; yet he remained unpersuaded. That was the tragedy of the Jews in Acts. They were God's people; the prophets were their prophets; Christ was their Messiah; his resurrection fulfilled their hopes. Still, in large part, they were not persuaded. This tragic story continued to the last chapter of Acts.

(9) Paul's Innocence Declared by Governor and King (26:30-32)

30The king rose, and with him the governor and Bernice and those sitting with them. 31They left the room, and while talking with one another, they said, "This man is not doing anything that deserves death or imprisonment."

ExpTim 34 (1922-23): 563f. A number of commentators suggest taking ποιῆσαι in the sense of "play the role of"—"you would persuade me to play the role of a Christian" (e.g., Bruce, *Acts:* NIC, 496).

[181]The term "Christian" occurs only here and in 11:26 in Acts (only elsewhere in the NT in 1 Pet 4:16). In all three contexts it might be seen as an "outsider's view" of the Christians. In the Apostolic Fathers, the term does not appear except in Ignatius. It does not thus seem to have been in early use among Christians as a self-designation but as a term used by outsiders for them. See *Beginnings* 5:384-86 and comments on 11:26.

[32]Agrippa said to Festus, "This man could have been set free if he had not appealed to Caesar."

26:30-32   Paul had made his appearance before governors and kings, very much in fulfillment of the Lord's words (Luke 21:12). Agrippa rose to his feet, followed by Bernice, and then all the other leading Gentiles who had attended the hearing (cf. 25:23). The latter probably constituted Agrippa's *consilium*, his advisory council on the matter of Paul.[182] If so, their presence heightened the impression of Paul's innocence; for Luke indicated that the whole group as they departed began to declare to one another that they could find nothing in Paul deserving of death or imprisonment (v. 31). This is now the fifth time Paul's innocence had been declared: first by the Pharisees (23:9), then by the Roman tribune Lysias (23:29), then twice by the governor Festus (25:18f.,25). In a private conversation with Festus, Agrippa went even further: If Paul had not made his appeal to Caesar, he could have been released (v. 32). The reader knows what Agrippa did not know—how Festus had wanted to do the Jews a favor and how Paul had felt forced to appeal to save his life (25:9-11).

Then the question rises about why, with this opinion from the Jewish king, Paul was not now set free. The answer seems to be, just as Agrippa's remark indicates, that it would be no easy matter to stop the appeal process. For Festus to do so would have been an affront to the emperor and an implicit admission of his own ineptitude in allowing the process to be set in motion.[183] Nevertheless, Festus now had what he had been seeking from Agrippa, an opinion to write up in his formal report to the emperor. Evidently in this instance it was the opinion that Paul was innocent of any breach of Roman law. The reminder of Jesus' own experience is stark. Governor and king together declared his innocence (Luke 23:14f.), and still he went to the cross. Governor and king declared Paul innocent likewise, and still he was on his way to Rome in chains.[184]

---

[182]The term συγκαθήμενοι is sometimes used as a technical term for an advisory *consilium*. See Haenchen, *Acts*, 690, n. 1.

[183]Sherwin-White (*Roman Society and Roman Law*, 65) argues that in cases outside ordinary law (*extra ordinem*) the appeal would be automatically valid and precarious for a governor to short-circuit.

[184]For a full treatment of the parallels between Paul's trial and that of Jesus, see S. Legasse, "L'Apologetique à l'Egard de Rome dans le Proces de Paul, *RSR* 69 (1981): 249-56.

—————————————— *SECTION OUTLINE* ——————————————

IX. PAUL WITNESSES TO JEWS AND GENTILES WITHOUT
HINDRANCE (27:1–28:31)
1. Paul's Journey to Rome (27:1–28:16)
   (1) The Journey to Fair Havens (27:1-8)
   (2) The Decision to Sail On (27:9-12)
   (3) The "Northeaster" (27:13-20)
   (4) Paul's Word of Assurance (27:21-26)
   (5) The Prospect of Landing (27:27-32)
   (6) Paul's Further Encouragement (27:33-38)
   (7) The Deliverance of All (27:39-44)
   (8) Paul's Deliverance from the Viper (28:1-6)
   (9) The Hospitality of Publius (28:7-10)
   (10) The Final Leg to Rome (28:11-16)
2. Paul's Witness in Rome (28:17-31)
   (1) First Meeting with the Jews (28:17-22)
   (2) Separation from the Jews (28:23-28)
   (3) Bold Witness to All (28:30-31)

——————— **IX. PAUL WITNESSES TO JEWS AND GENTILES** ———————
WITHOUT HINDRANCE (27:1–28:31)

In the final two chapters of Acts, all the major themes of the book
come together. Not least among these is the journey motif. From the time
the church at Antioch first commissioned Paul and Barnabas, the apostle
had constantly been depicted as traveling—to Cyprus, the towns of southern Galatia, to Asia Minor, Macedonia, Greece, Ephesus. Three times he
made the return trip to Jerusalem. Now he departed Palestine, seemingly
for the last time, bound for the capital of the empire and his appearance
before Caesar. He and his companions traveled this time by sea. Paul had
traveled by sea before, and Luke often depicted these voyages in extensive detail, naming ports and landmarks and even time spent in sailing.[1]
This voyage is different. It is told with considerably more detail, occupying three-fourths of the total text of the last two chapters (27:1–28:16).

---

[1]E. Haenchen (*The Acts of the Apostles* [Philadelphia: Westminster, 1971], 702f.) lists
some eleven likely sea journeys of Paul in the Acts narratives, beginning with his trip from
Caesarea to Tarsus (9:30) and ending with the long final voyage from Philippi to Caesarea
(20:6–21:8). Altogether he calculates these voyages as totaling in the vicinity of 3,000 miles.

This time the voyage was not smooth. A violent storm threatened to destroy all aboard, and the subsequent shipwreck delayed the trip for months. Paul's status differed too. No longer was he a free witness to Christ, traveling from mission point to mission point. Now he was a witness in chains. As such there is a strong linkage with the previous chapters (21–26) in which Paul bore his bold witness even as a prisoner. There is continuity also in the kindnesses shown him by his Roman captors, this time in the person of the centurion Julius. This time, however, the favor was returned because it was ultimately Paul's presence and his faith that insured the deliverance of all aboard the ship.

The overarching theme of the shipwreck narrative is the providence of God. The central verse is 27:24: God delivered Paul and all who sailed with him for the ultimate purpose of the apostle's witness before Caesar. Paul's witness in Rome has been a central focus since he first conceived of it in Ephesus (19:21). While imprisoned in Jerusalem, the Lord assured him in a vision that he would surely witness in that city (23:11). Now, in the midst of the howling storm, Paul was given a final assurance that in God's providence the testimony before Caesar would take place. It is perhaps the major theme of Acts—the triumph of the witness to Christ.

Again and again the apostles and Paul are depicted in extreme circumstances—in prison, under sentence of death, stoned by angry mobs. Always they were delivered, never for who they were but always for what they proclaimed. It was not the apostles who triumphed in Acts—it was the gospel that triumphed. Stephen is the prime example. He gave his life for that witness. But out of the tragedy of his death, the gospel triumphed—spread to Samaria, and all Judea, and ultimately to the ends of the earth. There is a triumphalism in Acts, but it is not a human triumphalism. It is a God-triumphalism, a triumph of his word in Christ. Nowhere is this clearer than in the shipwreck narrative. Paul was delivered, but he was delivered to bear witness. He was still a prisoner in chains when he bore his witness in Rome. The book closes with his bold, unrestricted proclamation in the capital city. The gospel had reached its ultimate destination as set forth in Jesus' commission to the apostles (1:8). It had reached the "ends of the earth." *It* had triumphed. But Paul remained under arrest.

Another motif that runs throughout Acts finds its final treatment in the account of Paul's testimony to the Jews in Rome (28:16-28). It is the whole difficult question of Christianity's relationship to Judaism. A familiar pattern recurs in these verses, a pattern that is first encountered on Paul's first missionary journey in Antioch of Pisidia (13:44-47). The pattern involves Paul's arrival in a town, his going first to the synagogue, his rejection there, and his turning to the Gentiles. Always heretofore, Paul has been shown returning to his witness in the synagogue in the next town he visited. Acts concludes with a final presentation of this same pattern of Paul's turning from the Jews to the Gentiles, but this time it occurs at the conclusion of the book; and there is no subsequent narrative showing Paul returning to the synagogue. The reader is left with considerable ambiguity. Just what is the place of the Jews in the divine history of salvation? This is an issue that has run throughout Acts—from the messianic sermons of Peter to the martyrdom of Stephen, from the Jerusalem Conference to Paul's opposition in the Diaspora synagogues. One senses that perhaps this last scene with the Jews of Rome provides a key to the resolution of the whole question.

1. Paul's Journey to Rome (27:1–28:16)

The predominant portion of the concluding two chapters of Acts is devoted to an extensive narrative of Paul's journey by sea from Caesarea to Rome to appear before Caesar. The account has much in common with ancient sea narratives and has provoked a lively discussion among scholars.[2] The route followed, the landmarks passed, and the times lapsed are all given with considerable detail. Likewise there is a heavy use of technical seafaring terminology, and the account is considered a valuable source for ancient sailing technique by scholars of the history of navigation.[3] Still one of the best treatments of this passage is the work first published in 1848 by the Scot J. Smith.[4] A gentleman scholar of the New Testament and an amateur yachtsman, Smith devoted a considerable portion of his life to the study of Paul's voyage, pursuing on-site investigation of the route as well as a thorough examination of the ancient literary sources pertaining to navigation. He concluded that the account of the voyage in Acts 27:1–28:16 is an accurate description of an actual voyage from Caesarea to Puteoli and that it was written by a layman accustomed to sea travel, but not by a professional sailor. All of this fits well the traditional

---

[2]Modern discussion of the literary nature of the passage can be traced to M. Dibelius, who suggested that the writer of Acts utilized a secular sea narrative in Acts 27 and inserted the Pauline sections into it (*Studies in the Acts of the Apostles* [London: SCM, 1956], 204-6). E. Haenchen rejected Dibelius's sea-narrative-source theory and argued that Acts 27 is based on an account of an actual voyage which the author of Acts thoroughly adapted in his own style ("Acts 27," in *Zeit und Geschichte*, [Tübingen: Mohr-Siebeck, 1964], 235-54). For a tongue-in-cheek rebuttal of Dibelius's theory, see R. P. C. Hanson, "The Journey of Paul and the Journey of Nikias," *Studies in Christian Antiquity* (Edinburgh: T & T Clark, 1985), 22-26.

[3]Among the many works on ancient seafaring, see A. Köster, *Die Antike Seewesen* (Berlin: Schoetz, 1923); H. Balmer, *Die Romfahrt des Apostels Paulus und die Seefahrtskunde im romischen Kaiserzeitalter* (Bern: München Buchsee, 1905); L. Casson, *Ships and Seamanship in the Ancient World* (Princeton: University Press, 1971).

[4]J. Smith, *The Voyage and Shipwreck of St. Paul* (1880; reprint, Grand Rapids: Baker, 1978).

assumption of Lukan authorship and the fact that this section comprises the most extensive "we passage" in all of Acts.[5]

From the perspective of Luke's purposes as a historian and a theologian, one is at somewhat of a loss to explain his detailed treatment of this voyage. It does little to advance knowledge of the spread of the gospel. Theological emphases are surely present and will be noted in the commentary. The greater part of the narrative, however, sets forth no particular edifying emphasis but rather concentrates on the voyage itself and relates in delightful detail the threat of the storm and the narrow escape from death at sea.[6] But it is precisely through this extensive presentation of the story itself that the full theological impact is conveyed. Luke was at his literary best in this account, building up suspense in his dramatic portrayal of the violence of the storm, the desperation of the sailors, the abandonment of all hope. But at each point when the situation seemed most desperate, there came a word of encouragement from Paul—his God would not abandon them, take heart, eat, be of good cheer. Then final deliverance came. All were saved. Paul's God had indeed not abandoned them to the anger of the seas. One cannot miss the emphasis on the divine providence, and it is precisely through the detailed telling of the story that the lesson has its greatest impact. It is "narrative theology" at its best.

This extensive travel narrative is one long, continuous story; and any division is somewhat arbitrary. The structure, however, does seem to involve an interplay between a presentation of the voyage itself interspersed with scenes that focus on Paul. The following outline is arranged accordingly.

(1) The Journey to Fair Havens (27:1-8)

[1]When it was decided that we would sail for Italy, Paul and some other prisoners were handed over to a centurion named Julius, who belonged to the

---

[5]Recently V. Robbins has argued that the use of the first-person plural is a standard literary device in Hellenistic sea narratives and in no way reflects the presence of the author of Acts ("By Land and by Sea: The We-Passages and Ancient Sea Voyages," *New Perspectives on Luke-Acts* (Edinburgh: T & T Clark), 215-42. S. Praeder responded by noting that the use of first-person plural cannot be demonstrated as a standard device of ancient sea narratives but was rather characteristic of training in ancient rhetoric ("Acts 27:1–28:16: Sea Voyages in Ancient Literature and the Theology of Luke-Acts," *CBQ* 46 [1984]: 683-706). That the use of "we" was not a literary convention of sea narratives is also argued by C. K. Barrett, "Paul Shipwrecked," in *Scripture: Meaning and Method*, ed. B. P. Thompson (Hull University Press, 1987).

[6]Though perhaps not agreeing with his judgment that Luke was in no sense an ancient historian, one could concur with R. Pervo that Luke delighted in telling an exciting story. See his *Profit with Delight: The Literary Genre of the Acts of the Apostles* (Philadelphia: Fortress, 1987).

Imperial Regiment. [2]We boarded a ship from Adramyttium about to sail for ports along the coast of the province of Asia, and we put out to sea. Aristarchus, a Macedonian from Thessalonica, was with us.

[3]The next day we landed at Sidon; and Julius, in kindness to Paul, allowed him to go to his friends so they might provide for his needs. [4]From there we put out to sea again and passed to the lee of Cyprus because the winds were against us. [5]When we had sailed across the open sea off the coast of Cilicia and Pamphylia, we landed at Myra in Lycia. [6]There the centurion found an Alexandrian ship sailing for Italy and put us on board. [7]We made slow headway for many days and had difficulty arriving off Cnidus. When the wind did not allow us to hold our course, we sailed to the lee of Crete, opposite Salmone. [8]We moved along the coast with difficulty and came to a place called Fair Havens, near the town of Lasea.

27:1 Festus, having decided that Paul's appeal must be carried out (cf. 26:32), took measures to send him to Italy. Custody of Paul and some other prisoners, who are not further specified, was given to a centurion named Julius. It is noted that Julius belonged to the "Imperial Regiment." The term "imperial" was generally used for auxiliary forces drawn largely from the local population, and it is known that an auxiliary cohort was stationed in Caesarea during the time of Agrippa II.[7] Julius may have belonged to it, or he may have been a special officer representing the emperor and detached from any particular legion, as Ramsay suggested.[8] In v. 1 Luke carefully distinguished between the "we" who sailed with Paul and the prisoners who were under Julius's custody.[9] It is probably unnecessary to speculate how Luke and the other Christians could have shared the voyage along with the prisoners.[10] In all likelihood the vessel was privately owned, and passage was available to any who could pay.

27:2 Julius and his prisoners boarded a ship of Adramyttium, which was evidently returning to its home port (v. 2). Adramyttium was a seaport

---

[7]K. Lake and H. J. Cadbury, eds., *The Beginnings of Christianity*, vol. 5: *Additional Notes* (London: Macmillan, 1933), 443f.

[8]W. Ramsay, *St. Paul the Traveller and Roman Citizen* (1897; reprint, Grand Rapids: Baker, 1978), 314f. Ramsay's suggestion that Julius was a *frumentarius*, an officer connected to the imperial grain service, is less likely since there is no evidence that *frumentarii* were ever given police duties before the period of Hadrian. See A. N. Sherwin-White, *Roman Society and Roman Law in the New Testament* (Oxford: Clarendon, 1963), 109.

[9]The Western text omits the "we" in v. 1, reading: "Thus the governor decided to send him to Caesar, and in the morning of the next day he called a centurion named Julius and remitted Paul to him along with the other prisoners." Following this Western reading, J. Rouge argues that Julius's original intention was to go by land to Rome and not by sea ("Acts 27:1-10," *VC* 14 [1960]: 193-203).

[10]Ramsay (*St. Paul the Traveller*, 316) argued that the other Christians were perhaps allowed to accompany the prisoner Paul as personal valets or slaves, but this is based on his assumption that the vessel was owned by the imperial government rather than being privately owned.

of Mysia, southeast of Troas. The vessel was likely a coasting vessel, which would travel close in to shore and put in at the various ports along the way. Since it was unlikely a vessel bound for Rome would be found along the Palestinian coast, Julius probably took the Adramyttian ship with the intention of transferring to one with a Roman destination. The ports of southern Asia offered a good prospect for finding such a vessel. Luke mentioned that Aristarchus, a Macedonian from Thessalonica, joined him on the voyage.[11]

27:3 The Adramyttian coasting vessel sailed the seventy or so nautical miles north to the old Phoenician port of Sidon (v. 3).[12] There it put in, evidently to load or unload cargo. This allowed Paul time to visit the Christians in that town. The establishment of a church in Sidon is not specifically mentioned in Acts, but it probably went back to the early mission of the Hellenists in Phoenicia (Acts 11:19). It was certainly an act of "kindness" (*philanthrōpōs*) for Julius to allow Paul this visit. It testifies both to the high level of trust and esteem afforded the prisoner and to the generous spirit of the centurion. Much like the tribune Lysias in Jerusalem, Julius represented Roman officialdom with its best foot forward. Ultimately, Julius's confidence in Paul would save his own life as well as the apostle's. The "friends" referred to in v. 3 were undoubtedly the Christians of Sidon, and the occurrence of the word here may indicate that it was a term early Christians used to designate themselves.[13] The indication that they provided for Paul's needs probably refers to their furnishing him with food and supplies for the voyage. In ancient sea travel passengers were often expected to provide for themselves.

27:4-6 In v. 4 the sea narrative resumes. The ship sailed "to the lee" of Cyprus, i.e., under the shelter of the island from the winds. The prevailing summer winds in the eastern Mediterranean come from the west and northwest, so it was the eastern coast that provided shelter. The ship then bore north to the coast of Cilicia and Pamphylia. The offshore winds and the westerly current that runs along this shoreline now allowed the ship to make its westerly course. Finally they arrived at Myra, located in

---

[11]Whether more Christians than Luke and Aristarchus are included in the "we" would be impossible to ascertain. If one assumes the traditional view that Paul wrote Colossians from his Roman imprisonment, it is interesting to note that both Luke and Aristarchus are mentioned in the personalia of that letter (Col 4:10,14). The Western text of Acts 27:2 lists Secundus as a third traveler on the voyage, probably due to his linkage with Aristarchus in Acts 20:4.

[12]For the unlikely theory that the present text of Acts 27:1-10 is the result of two separate voyages of Paul being put together through scribal error, see L. Davies, *St. Paul's Voyage to Rome* (London: Headley, 1931).

[13]Cf. Luke 12:4; John 15:14f.; 3 John 15. The term may later have fallen into disuse because of its appropriation by the Gnostics.

Lycia, the southernmost portion of Asia.[14] They likely put in at Andriace, the port for Myra, which lay some three miles west-southwest of the city. Andriace was a chief port for the ships that supplied the empire with Egyptian grain and especially for those ships which plied between Alexandria and Rome. Myra was almost directly north of Alexandria and was a natural port for vessels sailing under a prevailing westerly wind. A common route for grain ships bound for Rome was evidently from Alexandria to Myra and from thence north of Crete to Sicily. This was likely the intended route of the Alexandrian ship on which Julius boarded his prisoners. It was an Egyptian grain ship headed for Italy (v. 6). Such ships seem to have been privately owned and leased by the Roman government. Adequate supply of grain was absolutely essential to the stability of the empire and seems to have been closely regulated by the state. Grain ships were usually quite large, sometimes in excess of a thousand tons and over a hundred feet in length.[15]

27:7 The Alexandrian ship soon found its course for Italy somewhat difficult. The winds were contrary and made progress slow. From Cnidus to Myra was only some 130 nautical miles and should not have taken the "many days" indicated by Luke (v. 7).[16] Cnidus was on a peninsula at the southwest tip of Asia Minor between the islands of Cos and Rhodes. Already the voyage was somewhat off course because the normal route from Myra would have taken the vessel to the south of Rhodes and from there south to Crete and along the northern coast of that island. In their effort to go south to Crete, they were blown even farther off course, not to the sheltered north of the island but past Cape Salmone, the promontory on its northeastern extremity, and from there to the southern coast of Crete. Traveling along the southern coast, they finally put in at a place named "Fair Havens." This site is not now certain, but Luke's description seems to fit a bay known by natives of Crete today by the same name (*Lime[o]nas Kalous*). It is about twelve miles east of Cape Matala, and ruins have been discovered of an ancient town some five miles to the east, which are perhaps those of Lasea, whose site is equally uncertain.[17] In any event the weather-weary mariners put in at Fair Havens for a respite and to take stock of where they should go from there.

---

[14]The Western text gives the length of the voyage from Cyprus to Myra as fifteen days, which is a fair estimate. Lucian *Navigation* 7 gives nine days as the time taken for the voyage of the Isis from Sidon to the Lycian coast.

[15]Casson estimates 114 feet as the keel length of the Isis, a ship described by Lucian, and puts its tonnage at 1,228 (*Ships and Seamanship*, 186-89).

[16]J. Smith, *Voyage and Shipwreck*, 74-76.

[17]Lasea is probably the Cretan town of Lasos, mentioned by Pliny the Elder (*Hist.Nat.* 4.59). See J. Smith, *Voyage and Shipwreck*, 82f.

(2) The Decision to Sail On (27:9-12)

[9]Much time had been lost, and sailing had already become dangerous because by now it was after the Fast. So Paul warned them, [10]"Men, I can see that our voyage is going to be disastrous and bring great loss to ship and cargo, and to our own lives also." [11]But the centurion, instead of listening to what Paul said, followed the advice of the pilot and of the owner of the ship. [12]Since the harbor was unsuitable to winter in, the majority decided that we should sail on, hoping to reach Phoenix and winter there. This was a harbor in Crete, facing both southwest and northwest.

Evidently a consultation took place at Fair Havens. Just who took part in it is not altogether clear. Obviously Paul was allowed to give his opinion (v. 10). The pilot and the shipowner gave their advice (v. 11).[18] But the centurion seems to have made the final decision. This is perhaps the best evidence for Ramsay's view that the ship was connected with the imperial grain service, making the centurion the ranking officer on board. The text is simply not clear. Verse 12 would indicate that the "majority" made the decision. If one assumes the "majority" represented the sailors aboard, one must still conclude from v. 11 that it was finally up to the centurion to decide whether to follow the combined advice of the pilot, the owner, and the majority of the crew or that of Paul.

27:9-10 Subsequent events proved that Paul's advice was sound: they should have remained at Fair Havens. The season for sea travel was coming to a close. "The fast" (v. 9) refers to the Day of Atonement. Calculated by the phases of the moon, the Day of Atonement fell at various times from year to year but always in late September or early October.[19] For ancient travel on the Mediterranean, mid-September to early November was considered a dangerous time for traveling the open sea. After early November such travel ceased altogether and generally was not resumed until the beginning of February at the earliest. Paul's advice was based on this well-known fact. It was well into the dangerous season. Any travel now would be risky business. They had already encountered bad winds. Paul had been in peril at sea before. He knew the danger (cf. 2 Cor 11:25). Whether his advice was truly prophetic or merely based on his opinion is at this point unclear. He warned that there would be loss both

---

[18]The term translated "pilot" by the NIV (κυβερνήτης) probably represents the captain or "skipper" of the ship. The presence of the ship's owner (ναυκλῆρος) would indicate that the ship was privately owned and perhaps leased for the imperial grain service.

[19]W. P. Workman suggests that A.D. 59 was a likely date for Paul's voyage because the Day of Atonement fell late in that year (Oct. 5). Allowing for the two weeks adrift in the storm (v. 27), this would give the party the months of November, December, and January on Malta (28:11), with their trip resuming in early February. See "A New Date Indication in Acts," ExpTim 11 (1899-1900): 316f.

of cargo and of life. As it turned out, the ship and cargo were indeed lost, but there was no loss of life. The important thing is that his apprehensions proved true. When he later gave his opinion, it was taken seriously by Julius (v. 31). At this point it was not, and that proved nearly disastrous.

27:11-12 The professionals on board were of another opinion. They felt that Fair Havens was not a suitable place for wintering. It was open to half the compass and faced eastward. It did not seem to offer adequate protection from the dangerous east and northeasterly winter winds. They knew of another harbor not far westward on Crete named Phoenix. It faced northwest and southwest, better sheltered from the winds. The site of ancient Phoenix is as uncertain as that of Fair Havens, but a consensus seems to be forming that it is to be located at what is today known as Phineka Bay, a bay on the west side of Cape Mouros about thirty-three miles east of the western extremity of southern Crete. It faces northwest and southwest, just as Acts describes Phoenix, and its modern name preserves the old tradition.[20] This harbor would give much better protection from winter "northeaster[s]," and the sailors set out for it. Unpopular as his advice was, Paul had issued the warning; and in any good narrative when such has been raised, one had better look out—stormy weather ahead![21]

(3) The "Northeaster" (27:13-20)

[13]When a gentle south wind began to blow, they thought they had obtained what they wanted; so they weighed anchor and sailed along the shore of Crete. [14]Before very long, a wind of hurricane force, called the "northeaster," swept down from the island. [15]The ship was caught by the storm and could not head into the wind; so we gave way to it and were driven along. [16]As we passed to the lee of a small island called Cauda, we were hardly able to make the lifeboat secure. [17]When the men had hoisted it aboard, they passed ropes under the ship itself to hold it together. Fearing that they would run aground on the sandbars of Syrtis, they lowered the sea anchor and let the ship be driven along. [18]We took such a violent battering from the storm that the next day they began to throw the cargo overboard. [19]On the third day, they threw the ship's tackle overboard with

---

[20]J. Smith saw Phoenix as modern Lutro, located on the *east* side of Cape Mouros (*Voyage and Shipwreck*, 87-92). This caused him to go against the natural meaning of the Greek text because Lutro looks to the south*east* and north*east*. However, he found Phineka totally unsuitable as a harbor. It is now recognized that major geological shifts have taken place on Crete since Paul's day, and Phineka was likely much more suitable as a harbor in the first century. In fact, an inscription has been found at Phineka from the time of Trajan indicating that an Alexandrian ship wintered there. See C. J. Hemer, "First Person Narrative in Acts 27-28," *TB* 36 (1985): 97-98. See also two articles by R. M. Ogilvie which argue for Phineka rather than Lutro ("The Harbour Phoenix," *Scripture* 4 [1949-51]: 144-46); "Phoenix," *JTS* 9 (1958): 308-14.

[21]A point convincingly made by S. M. Praeder, "Sea Voyages," 690f.

their own hands. **²⁰When neither sun nor stars appeared for many days and the storm continued raging, we finally gave up all hope of being saved.**

27:13-14 As a gentle southerly wind began to blow, the sailors determined that conditions were favorable for the voyage to Phoenix. It was not a long trip. Six miles to the west of Fair Havens, a promontory known as Cape Matala jutted southward. Around this cape the shoreline then proceeded rather sharply northward as one sailed west the thirty or so remaining miles to Phoenix. Since they were sailing close in to shore, the trip should not have taken Paul's ship but a few hours with the favorable south wind. Such was not to be. Crete is dotted with mountains, some of them towering 7,000 feet above the sea. Perhaps as the ship rounded Cape Matala a violent wind rushed down from the mountains, striking the ship broadside. Luke described it as being "typhonic" (*typhōnikos*) in force, a word that in Greek as well as in its English cognate refers to a whirling, cyclonic wind formed by the clash of opposing air masses (v. 14; "hurricane force," NIV). More specifically, he designated the storm as the dreaded "northeaster," the deadly winter storm of the Mediterranean known by sailors as the *gregale*.²²

27:15 Ancient ships were not built to head into such a violent wind, and there was no way the Alexandrian ship could hold its course for Phoenix. The sailors "gave way" to the wind, which probably means they shortened sail and tried to make what progress they could against it (v. 15). It was all to no avail. Helpless before the wind, the ship was carried some twenty-five miles southeast to a small island called Cauda. Cauda is often mentioned in ancient sources, sometimes referred to as "Clauda"; the variant spelling is reflected in the textual tradition of v. 16. Today the island is known as Gozzo.

27:16-17 The ship came under the southern, lee side of Cauda, which offered some protection from the violence of the northeast winds. For the first time the sailors were able to take measures to secure the ship. The first operation was to haul in the lifeboat, or dinghy (v. 16). Luke noted that this was only accomplished with difficulty, and his use of "we" may indicate that some of the passengers assisted. The dinghy probably had

---

²²The *Textus Receptus* has εὐρωκλύδων as the name of the storm, which would seemingly refer to a southeast gale, but this is not the dreaded storm of the Mediterranean. The northeasterly storm *is*, and this seems to be the meaning of the word εὐροκύλων found in the best early text witnesses (𝔓⁷⁴, ℵ, B, A). Εὐροκύλων is a rare word, once considered a hapax, but it has since been found in the excavation of a pavement at Thugga in proconsular North Africa which contains a mosaic design depicting the winds in a twelve-point format. The Latin term *euraquilon* occurs in the position thirty degrees north of east, precisely the direction of the winds in the *gregale*. The term seems to be a hybrid formed from the Greek *euros* (east wind) and Latin *aquilo* (north wind). See C. J. Hemer, "Euraquilo and Melita," *JTS* 26 (1975): 110-11.

filled with water in the course of the storm and become excessively heavy. The next step was to "undergird" the ship (v. 17). Precisely what this involved is not altogether clear. Luke said that they used "helps" (*boētheiais*) to "undergird" (*hypozōnnyntes*) the ship. Evidently the "helps" were cables passed under the ship or around it that served to brace it against the waves and prevent it from breaking up.[23] The third measure taken by the sailors is even less clear. Luke said they lowered "the equipment" (*skeuos*, v. 17). This could mean they set the mainsail, and this is the rendering followed by the KJV. This is, however, most unlikely. Depending on how it was set with relation to the wind, this would either have driven them into the shoals they were trying to avoid or would have exposed the sails to the full violence of the wind and ripped them to shreds. It is more likely that they lowered the gear for the topsails and only set the small storm sail, allowing the ship to drift. A third possibility is that they lowered a drift anchor from the stern that would drag in the water and slow their progress. This is the option followed by the NIV. Whatever the specific measure taken, Luke stated that their greatest fear was running aground on the Syrtis. The Syrtis consisted of sandbars and shoals off the North African coast. They were some 400 miles to the south of Cauda, but their menace was so proverbial and the storm so violent that the sailors considered them a very real threat.[24]

27:18-19 There was really little that an ancient ship could do to fight a violent storm. They surely had the mainsail down and allowed the vessel to be borne along at the whim of the storm. By this time the ship may have developed leaks, and it seemed wise to lighten its load. The excess cargo was jettisoned. Luke did not specify what was thrown from the ship. It may well have been some of the load of grain, though it later

---

[23]There are four possible ways the cables may have been fixed around the ship: (1) they could have been passed under the ship two or three turns to hold the hull together. This method, known as "frapping," has been used on rare occasions in more recent times but is not elsewhere attested for ancient ships. (2) The cables could have been run longitudinally around the entire length of the ship. This is known to have been done for Roman warships to prevent breaking up in battle but seems to have been done while the ships were still in port. It would have been a well-nigh impossible operation on the open sea. (3) The cables could have been run vertically from within the ship, through and across the ship's hold. This possibility is perhaps the most theoretical and has not convincingly been established for ancient ships. (4) The cables could have been run transversely across the deck of the ship from bow to stern. This practice is well known for ancient Egyptian ships which had no beams and always carried this cable across the bow to keep the vessel from breaking its back. It has not been documented for Roman ships. Of the possibilities, the first is probably the most likely; and that is the one followed by the NIV. On the whole discussion, see *Beginnings* 5:345-54.

[24]In ancient literature the Syrtis ranks alongside Scylla and Charybdis as a graveyard for vessels. Seneca, Horace, Pliny, Vergil, Ovid, and many others refer to it. For references see S. Praeder, "Sea Voyages," 692.

became clear that not all of that was jettisoned at this time (cf. v. 38). Still the ship was so threatened that it was necessary on the next day, the third day of the storm, to throw even more overboard. Again it is not clear what was ejected.[25] Luke referred to it as the ship's "equipment" (*skeuēn*, v. 19). Smith suggested that it was the ship's mainyard, the long spar used to support the mainsail. This would explain his reference to the sailors doing this "with their own hands." There would be no equipment sufficient for jettisoning such a huge beam. It would have taken the combined manual effort of the crew.[26]

27:20 The ship now lightened, there was nothing left but to roll with the punching of the wind and waves. The storm raged on. Stars and sun were darkened by clouds, and there was no way to locate their position. They had no compass in those days. Despair set in. All hope was abandoned. Other ancient sea narratives speak of giving up all hope in the midst of a storm,[27] but Luke put it in a special way, saying that they gave up hope of "being saved." Obviously the reference is to their salvation from death at sea, but for a Christian reader "saved" is a term with special meaning. One wonders if Luke didn't intend at least a mild symbolic meaning. Ultimately the pagan seafarers would owe their physical salvation to the presence of the apostle Paul on board. Just as surely, there would be only one way they would ever find *true* salvation—through the message to which that apostle bore testimony. Their conversion is not mentioned in the narrative—not even Paul's preaching to them. Still there is the symbolism implicit in the word "saved" and the reminder that the one who saved the seafarers is the one who brings ultimate salvation and life.

The story of Paul's stormy voyage is reminiscent of the voyage of Jonah. The prophet also encountered a violent storm at sea. Jonah's crew also jettisoned the cargo and began to despair of life. And the crew and passengers of Jonah's ship were ultimately delivered. There is, of course, a major difference between the two. It was Jonah's *presence* on the ship that gave rise to the storm, and only in his *absence* were the others saved. It was altogether different for Paul's ship. The apostle's *presence* on the ship led to the deliverance of all aboard. This becomes evident in the next passage.

---

[25]D. Clark suggests that *both* vv. 18 and 19 may refer to the jettisoning of the mainyard, taking ἐποιοῦντο in v. 18 as a conative imperfect. In v. 18 they "attempt to jettison" it (using equipment) and fail. On the next day (v. 19) they succeeded, using their own hands ("What Went Overboard First?" *BT* 26 [1975]: 144-46).

[26]J. Smith, *Voyage and Shipwreck*, 116. The Western text would suggest that the passengers participated in jettisoning the ship's tackle, reading "with *our* own hands."

[27]See Achilles Tatius, *Leucippe and Clitophon* 5.9.2 and Euripides, *Iphigenia Taurica* 1413.

(4) Paul's Word of Assurance (27:21-26)

[21]After the men had gone a long time without food, Paul stood up before them and said: "Men, you should have taken my advice not to sail from Crete; then you would have spared yourselves this damage and loss. [22]But now I urge you to keep up your courage, because not one of you will be lost; only the ship will be destroyed. [23]Last night an angel of the God whose I am and whom I serve stood beside me [24]and said, 'Do not be afraid, Paul. You must stand trial before Caesar; and God has graciously given you the lives of all who sail with you.' [25]So keep up your courage, men, for I have faith in God that it will happen just as he told me. [26]Nevertheless, we must run aground on some island."

27:21-22 The storm was at its height. All sense of direction was lost. Morale was at its lowest ebb. No one had the stomach for food, as the vessel lurched in the waves.[28] At this dramatic point, Paul came and stood in their midst to offer a reassuring word. We cannot be sure of the exact composition of Paul's audience on this occasion. Perhaps it was primarily the crew struggling on the deck to perform whatever operations they could to avert seemingly inevitable disaster. There is nothing implausible about Paul's action. In ancient literature one often encounters the main character of a narrative giving an address at the very peak of a storm.[29] In those accounts the speech usually emphasizes the danger of the situation and increases the impression of impending doom. *Paul's* words serve the opposite function, introducing a message of hope in the midst of despair. He had given them his opinion previously, and there was perhaps a very human "I told you so" in his reminder that they had failed to follow his advice on the former occasion (v. 21b).[30] He had been right *then*, so his words *now* should be taken with more confidence. Then he spoke of coming disaster. Now he spoke of deliverance. Since their failure to hear his words of warning led to the present catastrophe, they must not fail to heed his message of deliverance; they must keep up their courage and not give in to despair (v. 22).

27:23-26 At this point Paul's prediction changed radically from his former warning. Then he spoke of loss both of ship and of life (v. 10). Now he spoke only of the ship's loss and of the deliverance of all aboard. The words of assurance were not Paul's but were a message from an angel of the Lord who had visited him in the night (v. 23). There were two

---

[28]The meaning of ἀσιτία seems primarily to be *loss of appetite* rather than deprivation of food. See J. R. Madan, "The *Asitia* on St. Paul's Voyage. Acts xxvii," *JTS* 4 (1904): 116-21.

[29]E.g., speeches are delivered in the midst of storms by Odysseus (Homer, *Odyssey* 5.299-312), Caesar (Lucian, *Civil War* 5.653-71), Hannibal (Silius, *Punica* 17.260-67), and Aeneas (Vergil, *Aeneid* 1.92-101). See S. Praeder, "Sea Voyages," 696.

[30]There is an interesting oxymoron at the end of v. 21 which literally reads, "You would not have 'gained' [κερδῆσαι] . . . this 'loss' [ζημίαν]."

promises given by the angel. The first was the dominant one—Paul would appear before Caesar. This was God's purpose, and it would not fail. The second promise followed the first: because God would preserve Paul for his Roman witness, all aboard the ship would be delivered.[31] In short, Paul's presence on the ship would be responsible for the preservation of all the voyagers.[32] Luke again employed an unusual vocabulary when he spoke of God "graciously" granting (*charizō*) the lives of all the travelers, perhaps again pointing to an implicit symbolism for God's salvation. Paul's vision is the center of the narrative and provides the key for interpretation. The deliverance from the storm is due to the providence of God and his preservation of the apostle for the witness before Caesar. This also marks the dramatic turning point in the account of the storm. The storm had reached its fullest fury. Despair had turned to hope. The focus was no longer on destruction but on deliverance. Still their rescue was in the future. Paul exhorted them accordingly to be of good courage but warned them there was more to come, and they would have to run aground on some island before final deliverance (v. 26).

(5) The Prospect of Landing (27:27-32)

[27]On the fourteenth night we were still being driven across the Adriatic Sea, when about midnight the sailors sensed they were approaching land. [28]They took soundings and found that the water was a hundred and twenty feet deep. A short time later they took soundings again and found it was ninety feet deep. [29]Fearing that we would be dashed against the rocks, they dropped four anchors from the stern and prayed for daylight. [30]In an attempt to escape from the ship, the sailors let the lifeboat down into the sea, pretending they were going to lower some anchors from the bow. [31]Then Paul said to the centurion and the soldiers, "Unless these men stay with the ship, you cannot be saved." [32]So the soldiers cut the ropes that held the lifeboat and let it fall away.

27:27-29 Paul's prediction of running aground soon began to materialize. The ship had been adrift in the open sea for a full fourteen days since the storm first struck. Luke described the ship as being driven across "the [sea of] Adria" ("Adriatic Sea," NIV). As the NIV note indicates, this is not to be confused with the modern Adriatic Sea between the coasts of Yugoslavia and western Italy. Ancient writers referred to that as the "Gulf of Adria." By "sea of Adria" they designated the Ionian sea

---

[31]That God preserves from peril at sea is a common biblical theme: cf. Gen 8:1-14, Jonah 1-2; Ps 107:23-32; Matt 8:25f.; 14:30-33. The theme of the gods protecting from danger at sea is also found in the Hellenistic literature. See P. Pokorny, "Die Romfahrt des Paulus und die antike Roman," *ZNW* 64 (1973): 233-44.

[32]I. H. Marshall (*The Acts of the Apostles*, TNTC [Grand Rapids: Eerdmans, 1980], 410) compares this to Abraham's intercession for Sodom in Gen 18:23-33 and the idea that the presence of a few righteous can deliver a multitude of the ungodly.

and the north-central Mediterranean between Greece and Italy, extending south to Crete and Malta.[33] It was across this stretch of ocean that Paul's ship was blown the 475 miles from Cauda to Malta.[34] There was a rocky promontory on the northeast extremity of Malta now known as Point Koura. The breakers against Koura are audible for some distance, and it was perhaps this sound that alerted the sailors to the possibility that they were nearing land (v. 27b). They thus began to take soundings. The first came to twenty fathoms, or a depth of 120 feet.[35] The second, perhaps taken half an hour later, gave fifteen fathoms—a depth of ninety feet. With the rapidly decreasing depth and the sound of the breakers, it was decided to put out anchor rather than risk being dashed against the rocks in the darkness (v. 29). Four anchors were dropped from the stern. Ancient ships generally carried multiple anchors,[36] and the advantage of throwing them off the stern was that this would keep the vessel pointed toward the shore and thus give immediate command of the ship for beaching.[37] As in the shipwreck of Odysseus, the pagan sailors now prayed to their gods for daylight to come and for deliverance through the night.[38] Their prayer was ultimately answered—not by *their* gods but by *Paul's* God. They owed their salvation to *Paul*.

27:30-32 The adventure of the night was not over, however. Evidently the sailors did not trust their gods to deliver them and decided to take matters into their own hands. On the pretext of letting out anchors from the bow, they lowered the dinghy into the water, planning to use it to take them to the shore. On all outward appearances, this would have seemed a perfectly natural operation. Anchors from the bow would have given the ship even greater stability, and it would have been necessary to set these out some distance from the bow, which could only have been accomplished by using the dinghy. Paul, however, realized their true

---

[33]Strabo (*Geography* 2.5.20) includes the Ionian Sea in the Sea of Adria; Pausanias locates the straits of Messina in the Sea of Adria (*Periegesis* 5.25.3); Ptolemy (*Geography* 3.4.1; 15.1) traces the Adriatic as far south as Crete and distinguishes it from the "Gulf of Adria" (modern Adriatic Sea).

[34]J. Smith (*Voyage*, 124-27) calculated that an east-northeast wind would drive a ship from Cauda precisely to Malta and that the rate of drift in such a storm would be approximately 1½ miles per hour. He thus concluded it would have taken 13 days for the 476 miles from Cauda to Malta, or the 14 days since the onset of the storm as specified in v. 27.

[35]Luke used the technical term for "sounding" (βολίζω). Ancient sounding leads had a hollow place on the underside that was filled with grease so some of the bottom would adhere. See C. Hemer, *The Book of Acts in the Setting of Hellenistic History* (Tübingen: Mohr/Siebeck, 1989), 147.

[36]Excavations have uncovered a ship from the fourteenth century B.C. with twenty-three stone anchors and a Roman ship of the first century B.C. with five lead anchors. See N. Hirschfield, "The Ship of St. Paul—Part I: Historical Background," *BA* 53 (1990): 25-30.

[37]J. Smith, *Voyage* 136.

[38]Homer, *Odyssey* 9.151.

motive and reported it to the centurion Julius. He pointed out that there was no way the rest of them could be saved if the seamen abandoned ship. The rescue operation required their expertise. The soldiers' hasty response in cutting away the dinghy might be questioned. It would seem that the small boat could have been used to take the passengers to shore in the morning in shifts, perhaps even avoiding the wrecking of the ship.[39] In any event, Paul's advice was sound. The rest of them would have been doomed had the sailors been allowed to abandon ship. Paul's advice did not go unheeded this time as it had at Fair Havens (v. 11). The apostle had gained the respect of the soldiers. Their deliverance depended upon Paul, and above all on Paul's God.

(6) Paul's Further Encouragement (27:33-38)

[33]Just before dawn Paul urged them all to eat. "For the last fourteen days," he said, "you have been in constant suspense and have gone without food—you haven't eaten anything. [34]Now I urge you to take some food. You need it to survive. Not one of you will lose a single hair from his head." [35]After he said this, he took some bread and gave thanks to God in front of them all. Then he broke it and began to eat. [36]They were all encouraged and ate some food themselves. [37]Altogether there were 276 of us on board. [38]When they had eaten as much as they wanted, they lightened the ship by throwing the grain into the sea.

27:33-34 At the height of the storm, when spirits were at their lowest ebb, Paul had spoken words of reassurance (vv. 21-26). With the thwarted attempt of the sailors, a ship badly battered by the storm, and no assurance they could get it safely to shore, Paul again rose to encourage the shaky voyagers. It was just before the break of day, and daylight would bring the rescue attempt. Everyone needed all the physical stamina they could muster. "For fourteen days you haven't had a square meal," he said;[40] "it's time now to take some food in order to survive" (author's paraphrase). A literal translation of the latter phrase would be "this is necessary for your salvation" (*sōtērias*). There may be a veiled symbol-

---

[39]Some interpreters (e.g., Haenchen, *Acts*, 710) accuse Paul of ultimately being responsible for the shipwreck, but it was the soldiers—not Paul—who decided to solve the problem by cutting away the dinghy. There is certainly nothing implausible in the sailors' panic and attempt to flee. The ship may well have been taking on water. We are simply not given the full circumstances in Luke's brief narrative. For the probability of their actions, one might compare the shipwreck in Achilles Tatius, where the sailors actually fight off the passengers with swords for possession of the dinghy (*Leucippe and Clitiphon* 3:3). See also C. Hemer, *Acts in Hellenistic History*, 148.

[40]Verse 33 builds on the mention of their not taking food in v. 21. Paul may have been speaking hyperbolically when he referred to their having eaten nothing for fourteen days, his point being that they had no real meal in that period. See I. H. Marshall, *Acts*, 413 and A. Wikenhauser, *Die Apostelgeschichte und ihr Geschichtswert* (Münster: Aschendorff, 1921), 225.

ism in the use of this word, a reminder to a Christian reader that the same God who delivered the storm-tossed voyagers from physical harm is the God who in Christ brings ultimate salvation and true eternal life.[41] The theme is not developed in Luke's narrative, however, and remains implicit at most. There is in fact no explicit reference to Paul's witnessing in the entire voyage narrative of 27:1–28:16, though one cannot imagine Paul bypassing the opportunity. The emphasis at this point is the physical rescue. Paul underlined this by assuring everyone with the biblical phrase that not a hair would be lost from anyone's head.[42]

27:35 Paul then set the example, taking food and eating it in the presence of all. The wording is striking: he took bread (*labōn arton*), gave thanks (*eucharistēsen*), and broke it (*klasas*). The familiar terminology is associated with the Lord's Supper (cf. Luke 22:19; 1 Cor 11:23f.). This has led many interpreters to view the meal here in the voyage narrative as a eucharist, a celebration of the Lord's Supper.[43] This is most unlikely. The breaking of bread and giving of thanks was the customary Jewish form of blessing a meal, and Jesus was observing that custom in the Lord's Supper. Paul also was observing that custom and in the presence of a predominantly pagan group. It was scarcely a eucharistic celebration. On the other hand, in Luke's Gospel, Jesus is often depicted in meal scenes. One only has to refer to the closing chapter of Luke with Jesus depicted sharing a meal with the two Emmaus travelers and eating the fish in the presence of his disciples. In the first chapter of Acts, the risen Jesus is presented as eating together with the apostles (v. 4). This presence of Jesus with his own in shared meals has quite naturally carried over into the Lord's Supper and become a major emphasis of that celebration. In short, the eucharistic language of the meal on the ship may not be so much an indication that they celebrated the Lord's Supper there as that Paul and the other Christians were reminded of how Jesus broke bread with his disciples and continues to do so, continues to be present in the lives of his people. The meal thus had a meaning for them it could not have had for the pagans—their Lord continued to be present with them. He was present in that time of particular need. For them the meal was more than needed sustenance—it reassured them of their Lord's presence to deliver them.

---

[41]A symbolic meaning may be present in the heavy accumulation of "salvation" terminology in the voyage narrative: σώζω in 27:20,31; διασώζω in 27:43,44; 28:1,4; and σωτηρία in 27:34. See R. C. Tannehill, *The Narrative Unity of Luke-Acts* (Minneapolis: Fortress, 1990), 2:336-38.

[42]Cf. 1 Sam 14:45; 2 Sam 14:11; 1 Kgs 1:52; Matt 10:30; Luke 12:7; 21:18.

[43]Among those who take the eucharistic interpretation, see A. Ehrhardt, *The Acts of the Apostles: 10 Lectures* (Manchester: University Press, 1969), 125f.; C. K. Barrett, "Paul Shipwrecked," 61-63; B. Reicke, "Die Mahlzeit mit Paulus auf den Wellen des Mittelmeers Act. 27, 33-38," *TZ* 4 (1948): 401-10.

27:36-38 Paul's confidence in their survival and his example encouraged the others to take sustenance. Paul's faith continued to be the source of their courage (cf. vv. 22,25).[44] At this point in the account, Luke abruptly returned to first-person narrative, supplying the information that "we" were in all 276 persons aboard ship (v. 37).[45] The notice is not superfluous. It underlines the main theme of the entire voyage narrative and in particular the emphasis on the Lord's providence in the immediate context of the meal and Paul's encouraging words. It was no small affair—a host of people were delivered from the sea, and not one suffered the least harm (cf. v. 34b).[46] It is interesting to compare Paul's voyage with Josephus's account of his own voyage to Rome, which encountered a smaller shipwreck. There were six hundred aboard Josephus's ship, and only eighty survived (*Life*, 15). The difference was that the Lord was present with Paul, preserving him for witness in Rome (cf. v. 24). His deliverance was the key to the rescue of all 276.[47] All were evidently encouraged by Paul and took steps for the beaching operation, jettisoning the remaining cargo to lighten the ship for running as far up on the beach as possible.[48]

(7) The Deliverance of All (27:39-44)

[39]**When daylight came, they did not recognize the land, but they saw a bay with a sandy beach, where they decided to run the ship aground if they could. [40]Cutting loose the anchors, they left them in the sea and at the same time untied the ropes that held the rudders. Then they hoisted the foresail to the wind and**

---

[44]Note the cluster of "courage/good cheer" words in the passages where Paul assured the voyagers: εὐθυμεῖν (v. 22), εὐθυμεῖτε (v. 25), εὔθυμοι (v. 36).

[45]There is no apparent significance to the fact that 276 is a "triangular" number—i.e., the sum of the numbers from one to twenty-three. See F. H. Colson, "Triangular Numbers in the New Testament," *JTS* 16 (1915): 72. H. Conzelmann (*Acts of the Apostles, Her* [Philadelphia: Fortress, 1987], 220) and R. Pesch (*Die Apostelgeschichte* [Zurich: Benzinger, 1986], 2:293) are in error in stating that 276 is the sum of one to twenty-four. There is no evident "mystical" significance to the number. Its presence only emphasizes the miraculous deliverance.

[46]Perhaps the most pronounced exposition of the "symbolic" interpretation is that of P. Pokorny, who argues that all 276 received eternal salvation. As maintained above in the commentary, there may well be a play on the word σωτηρία (salvation/deliverance), but the spiritual salvation of the voyagers is simply not present in the narrative. See "Die Romfahrt des Paulus," 233-44.

[47]Tannehill (*Narrative Unity*, 2:335f.) notes the large concentration of πᾶς ("all") forms in vv. 33-37 and sees an emphasis on unity. The deliverance of one depended on the deliverance of all. To be sure, in the narrative Paul is *the* "one." Without their solidarity with him, there would be no rescue. God was with *him*.

[48]Verse 18 has already mentioned the process of jettisoning. Either at that point only part of the cargo was thrown overboard or something other than the grain was jettisoned. The latter may well have been the case. Verse 18 only speaks of jettisoning (ἐκβολὴν ἐποιοῦντο) and does not specify what. Verse 38 speaks explicitly of the grain cargo (σῖτον).

made for the beach. ⁴¹But the ship struck a sandbar and ran aground. The bow stuck fast and would not move, and the stern was broken to pieces by the pounding of the surf.

⁴²The soldiers planned to kill the prisoners to prevent any of them from swimming away and escaping. ⁴³But the centurion wanted to spare Paul's life and kept them from carrying out their plan. He ordered those who could swim to jump overboard first and get to land. ⁴⁴The rest were to get there on planks or on pieces of the ship. In this way everyone reached land in safety.

27:39-41 With the natives of Malta, the traditional site for Paul's shipwreck is known today as St. Paul's Bay; and Smith maintained that this site probably is the correct location.⁴⁹ The main port of Malta is further to the west, and St. Paul's Bay would not likely have been familiar to ancient seamen. The west side of the bay has two creeks, one of which has a sandy beach; and it was perhaps here that the sailors decided to beach the ship. The four stern anchors were cut free. The rudders of ancient ships consisted of large paddles. In a storm these would be lifted from the water and tied down.⁵⁰ Now, to guide the ship for the beaching, they were untied and let back down into the water. The next preparatory step was to hoist the foresail, the small sail in the bow of the ship that was primarily used for guiding it.⁵¹ The sailors now made for the beach, but the ship ran aground on a sandbar some distance from the shore.⁵² The bow stuck fast and remained intact, but the stern was pounded to pieces in the surf.⁵³ No alternative now remained but to abandon ship.

27:42-44 The concern of the soldiers that the prisoners might escape is understandable (v. 42). Roman law held guards personally responsible for their charges, and those who allowed prisoners to escape could pay with their own lives (cf. 12:19). Julius, however, intervened, thwarting

---

⁴⁹J. Smith, *Voyage*, 140f. N. Heuger, a Maltese, argues that the correct site is the modern Mellieha: "'Paulus auf Malta' im Lichte der Maltesischen Topographie," *BZ* 28 (1984): 86-88.

⁵⁰J. Smith, *Voyage*, 141.

⁵¹Luke referred to the sail as the ἀρτέμων, which is not found previous to this in Greek literature. It is evidently a Latinism and is used in later Italian literature for the foresail. Roman ships usually had two sails, the mainsail and this foresail for guidance, although there is evidence that some ships may have carried a third sail on the stern. See M. Fitzgerald, "The Ship of Saint Paul—Part II: Comparative Archaeology," *BA* 53 (1990): 31-39.

⁵²Luke described the ship as falling upon a place "of two seas" (διθάλασσον). F. F. Bruce (*Commentary on the Book of Acts*, NIC [Grand Rapids: Eerdmans, 1977], 518) takes this as a reference to the narrow channel between Malta and a small island that shelters St. Paul's Bay on the northwest. There is some evidence in the classical literature for the term meaning *a shoal or sandbar*, and the NIV takes it in that sense. For the debate whether the ship ran aground on the western or on the eastern beach of St. Paul's Bay, see W. Cowan, "Acts xxvii. 39," *ExpTim* 27 (1915-16) ; G. A. Sim, "Acts xxvii.39," *ExpTim* 28 (1916-17): 187f.

⁵³The phrase "ran the ship aground" contains two classical words that are found only here in the NT: ναῦς and ἐπικέλλω. Both occur in Homer, *Odyssey* 9.145, 546.

the soldiers' plot to kill the prisoners. Luke explained that the centurion was primarily concerned with preserving *Paul's* life. So once again it was a Roman official who intervened to save the life of the apostle. Further, it is again evident that it was *Paul's* presence that was responsible for the preservation of the other voyagers—in this instance the other prisoners. With the dinghy gone, there was but one way the voyagers could flee the sinking ship and safely reach land—in the water. Those who could swim were ordered to jump in first (v. 43b). The rest made it to shore on planks or "pieces" from the ship's wreckage.[54] The phrase translated "pieces of the ship" in the NIV is ambiguous in Greek and could also be translated "on some people from the ship." The picture would be that of the non-swimmers being carried on the backs of those who could swim.

In either instance, *all* were able to reach shore safely (v. 44b). And the whole narrative from v. 23 on has made it clear that *Paul's* presence on the ship and God's protection of *him* was responsible for the remarkable deliverance of all 276 on board. In a real sense, it was something of a reversal of expectations. In many ancient shipwreck stories there is a motif in which a storm or shipwreck is attributed to the presence of one on board who has incurred the wrath of a god. The presence of the guilty party endangers the lives of all the voyagers.[55] In this instance the opposite took place. Paul's presence was in no sense responsible for the storm. Had his advice been followed, the ship would never have encountered the storm in the first place. On the contrary, Paul's presence was responsible for their *deliverance* from the storm. His God was with him, and because he was with the apostle, *all* were saved.

(8) Paul's Deliverance from the Viper (28:1-6)

[1]Once safely on shore, we found out that the island was called Malta. [2]The islanders showed us unusual kindness. They built a fire and welcomed us all because it was raining and cold. [3]Paul gathered a pile of brushwood and, as he put it on the fire, a viper, driven out by the heat, fastened itself on his hand. [4]When the islanders saw the snake hanging from his hand, they said to each other, "This man must be a murderer; for though he escaped from the sea, Justice has not allowed him to live." [5]But Paul shook the snake off into the fire and

---

[54]For rescue on planks in other sea narratives, cf. Homer, *Odyssey* 5.370f. and Achilles Tatius, *Leucippe and Clitiphon* 3.4, 5-6, 8).

[55]This was the case with Jonah. For examples in Greek and Roman literature, see G. B. Miles and G. Trompf, "Luke and Antiphon: The Theology of Acts 27-28 in the Light of Pagan Beliefs about Divine Retribution, Pollution, and Shipwreck," *HTR* 69 (1976): 259-67; D. Ladouceur, "Hellenistic Preconceptions of Shipwreck and Pollution as a Context for Acts 27-28," *HTR* 73 (1980): 435-49. Miles, Trompf, and Ladouceur argue that the main emphasis of the shipwreck narrative is to establish Paul's *innocence*. This motif, however, is implicit at best; the major emphasis certainly is God's providence in preserving the apostle for his *witness* before Caesar (v. 24).

suffered no ill effects. ⁶The people expected him to swell up or suddenly fall dead, but after waiting a long time and seeing nothing unusual happen to him, they changed their minds and said he was a god.

28:1 That Paul was under God's protection is further underscored by the first incident that occurred on Malta—the apostle's deliverance from the bite of a viper. This evidently took place soon after the entire party aboard the ship safely reached shore. They learned from the natives that they were on the island of Malta.[56] The ship's crew had been unable to ascertain their position because of the darkened sky in the storm's fury (27:20). Somewhat miraculously they had been delivered virtually on course for their final destination of Italy.

28:2-3 The simple natives of the island[57] did not share the fear and suspicion that one might have expected and showed the storm-weary voyagers "unusual kindness" (*philanthrōpian*), lighting a fire to warm them from the chilly breeze that followed the "northeaster" (v. 2). Paul did not consider it beneath his dignity to assist in the maintenance of the fire and gathered sticks up into a bundle and threw them on the blaze. The heat from the fire revived a snake from its cold-blooded stupor brought on by the chill. It had been concealed lifeless in Paul's bundle of twigs; and as the apostle threw the sticks on the fire, it struck and fixed itself to his hand.

The snake has provoked no end of discussion among scholars. Luke used a term (*echidna*) that generally denotes a "viper," a poisonous

---

[56]Because of the reference to "Adria" in 27:27 (see n. 33), there have been recurring attempts to place the site of Paul's shipwreck on the island of Melita, the modern Mljet, the southernmost of the Dalmatian islands in the Adriatic Sea. For a recent revival of this theory, see A. Acworth, "Where was St. Paul Shipwrecked? A Re-examination of the Evidence," *JTS* 24 (1973): 190-93, and O. F. A. Meinardus, "St. Paul Shipwrecked in Dalmatia," *BA* 39 (1976): 145-47. For a thorough rebuttal of this view, see Hemer, "Euraquilo and Melita," 100-111. Recently H. Warnecke has argued that the shipwreck took place on the island of Cephalonia further south in the Adriatic (*Die Tatsachliche Romfahrt des Apostels Paulus* [Stuttgart: Katholisches Bibelwerk, 1987]). For the implausibility of this suggestion, see B. Schwank, "Also doch Malta? Spurensuche auf Kefalonia," *BK* 45 (1990): 43-46, and J. Wehnert, "Gestrandet: Zu einer neuen These über den Schiffbruch des Apostels Paulus auf dem Wege nach Rom (Apg. 27-28)," *ZTK* 87 (1990): 67-99.

[57]Luke described the natives as "barbarians" (βάρβαροι). The term indicates a language difference and reflects Luke's Greek bias. For a Greek, anyone speaking a language other than Greek was denoted a "barbarian." The word is onomatopoetic, meaning that the foreign speech sounds to the Greek-speaker like "bar-bar-bar," meaningless babbling. (Cf. Paul's use of the term in precisely this sense in 1 Cor 14:11.) Ancient Maltese was a Punic dialect, deriving from the Phoenicians who colonized the island in the first millennium B.C. Inscriptions found on Malta in both Punic and Greek would indicate that these were the main languages used there in the first century; cf. H. J. Cadbury, *The Book of Acts in History* (New York: Harper, 1955), 24. Malta seems to have been under the administration of a Roman procurator in the first century (R. B. Rackham, *The Acts of the Apostles* [London: Methuen, 1901], 493).

snake; but it has been pointed out that today there are no poisonous snakes on Malta. Obviously the current situation on the island would have little to say about conditions there in the first century. Malta has been heavily populated through the centuries, and poisonous snakes would have had little chance for survival.[58] But the term *echidna* was not always used with precision, and it is possible that Paul's snake was not poisonous at all.[59] Whether or not that was the case is impossible to determine from the text.

28:4-5 What *is* clear from the text is the perception of the natives. They obviously saw the creature as venomous and expected Paul to die. Since they were native to the island and should have known their own species, their reaction probably is the best clue about how the narrative is to be taken. For them the serpent's bite was a sure sign that Paul was a fugitive from the gods and that divine retribution had finally caught up with him (v. 4).[60] In this they were reflecting a common ancient concept. The Romans, for instance, told the story of a fugitive who escaped a shipwreck but was killed by a snake that bit him as he lay recovering on the beach; and Jewish tradition told of the murderer who got his just deserts from the fangs of a viper.[61] But this was not the case with Paul. He simply shook the snake into the fire and suffered no ill effects from its bite (v. 5). Justice was not catching up with Paul. Quite the contrary—providence was *preserving* him.

28:6 It was remarkable how radically the islanders' opinion of Paul shifted. After waiting for a long time for the venom to take effect and waiting in vain, they drew the opposite conclusion. He was not a fugitive at all but rather a god (v. 6). One is surprised that Luke abruptly concluded the incident at this point. On an earlier occasion, when the natives of Lystra hailed Paul and Barnabas as gods, Paul quickly set them straight (14:11-15); and when Cornelius sought to worship Peter, the apostle cor-

---

[58]A. T. Robertson, *Word Pictures in the New Testament* (Nashville: Southern Baptist Sunday School Board, 1930) 3:478.

[59]A number of interpreters suggest that the snake may have belonged to the species *Coronella austriaca*, which is found in Malta today and which is a constrictor, thus fitting the picture of its clinging to Paul's hand (e.g., R. Pesch, *Apostelgeschichte* 2:298). This view is too influenced by the need to account for the absence of poisonous snakes in contemporary Malta and goes against the most natural reading of the text.

[60]Luke used the word δίκη to describe "justice." Δίκη was the name of the Greek goddess of justice, who was responsible for meting out to the guilty their just deserts. It is unlikely the Maltese "barbarians" venerated the Greek goddess Δίκη but likely that they had a similar concept in their own religion that Luke translated into the Greek equivalent.

[61]*Anthology Palatine* 7:290 and Tosepta, *Sanhedrin* 8:3. Perhaps the most interesting parallel is the tradition about the snake that bit the saintly rabbi Haninah ben Dosa and was later found dead at its hole. The saying then spread, "Woe to the man whom the snake meets, and woe to the snake whom Haninah ben Dosa meets" (Jerusalem Talmud, *Berakot* 5:1).

rected him immediately (10:25f.). The reader of Acts needs no reminder that the response of the Maltese was inappropriate. Rather, by ending on their acclamation, Luke emphasized another point altogether in this narrative—namely, that Paul was thoroughly under the protection of God. Whether a storm at sea or a viper on land, Paul was delivered against all expectations. Both were acts of divine providence; both were miraculous. Throughout Acts miracles are always shown to be in service to the word. They provide the occasion and opportunity for sharing the gospel. Luke gave no account of Paul's evangelizing Malta; but following the pattern of miracle and witness found throughout Acts, one would naturally assume that Paul seized this opportunity to share the gospel with the natives.

(9) The Hospitality of Publius (28:7-10)

[7]There was an estate nearby that belonged to Publius, the chief official of the island. He welcomed us to his home and for three days entertained us hospitably. [8]His father was sick in bed, suffering from fever and dysentery. Paul went in to see him and, after prayer, placed his hands on him and healed him. [9]When this had happened, the rest of the sick on the island came and were cured. [10]They honored us in many ways and when we were ready to sail, they furnished us with the supplies we needed.

28:7 The second incident Luke related from Paul's time on Malta deals with the hospitality of the natives and Paul's healing ministry on the island. It begins with the mention of Publius, who is designated as the "chief official" (*prōtos*) of the island. Inscriptions have been found on Malta that use this same title,[62] and Luke here may have used the precise designation borne by the main governing official of the island. Luke said that Publius welcomed "us" into his home and entertained "us" for three days "hospitably" (*philophronōs*, v. 7). Just who the "us" included is not clear. It may be that it concerned only the Christian group and not the entire 276 who were aboard ship.[63]

28:8-10 The stay in Publius's house afforded Paul the opportunity to reciprocate on his host's hospitality. Publius's father was sick with fever and dysentery. It may well be that this involved a sort of gastric fever caused by a microbe in goat's milk which was at one time so common on

---

[62]One inscription is in Greek and reads πρῶτος Μελιταίων καὶ Πάτρων (I. G. XIV.601). The other, in Latin, is badly mutilated. The reconstruction has (*munci*)*pi Meli*(*tensium*) *primus omni*(*um*) (C.I.L. X.7495). In both instances the πρῶτος/*primus* may not be an official title but a deferential appellation for rendering certain benefactions to the nation. See C. Hemer, "First Person Narrative in Acts 27-28," 100.

[63]There may be a shift in the "we" narrative beginning at 28:1, with the first-person plural being used more restrictively in 28:1-16 for the Christian group rather than the whole party aboard ship, as in chap. 27.

the island that the disorder was named "Malta fever."[64] Paul healed the man by laying his hands upon him and praying. This is the only time in Acts when both prayer and the laying on of hands accompany a healing.[65] The two acts are joined together in commissioning narratives (e.g., 6:6; 13:3), and Paul was healed of his blindness when Ananias laid his hands upon him; but prayer is not mentioned there (9:17). A similar practice is found in Jas 5:14, where prayer is combined with anointing in healing. Perhaps the closest parallel to Paul's healing of Publius's father is Jesus' healing of Peter's mother-in-law, who was also "oppressed" (*synechō*) with fever (Luke 4:38f.). In both instances word of the healing soon reached the surrounding neighborhood, and many came forth and were healed (Luke 4:40; Acts 28:9).[66] At Malta the natives responded by continuing their lavish hospitality. When the three winter months were over and the party was ready to resume its voyage, the Maltese furnished them amply with the food and provisions they would need (v. 10).

The emphasis on the Maltese hospitality is striking. It is recurrent throughout the account of Paul's stay on Malta: the Maltese welcomed the shipwrecked party with "unusual kindness" (v. 2); Publius received Paul's group and entertained them "hospitably" (v. 7); on their departure, the travelers were "honored" and amply fitted for their journey (v. 10).[67] It is the same sort of hospitality (*philanthrōpōs*) shown by the *Christians* of Sidon (27:3). Perhaps in this manner Luke was drawing attention to the fact that simple pagan "barbarians" like the Maltese have a genuine potential for becoming Christians. Their hospitality would in any event be in stark contrast with the reception Paul found from the Jews of Rome.

(10) The Final Leg to Rome (28:11-16)

[11]After three months we put out to sea in a ship that had wintered in the island. It was an Alexandrian ship with the figurehead of the twin gods Castor

---

[64]This is one of those passages where the "medical theory" has some basis, in the rather specific terminology employed—πυρετοῖς καὶ δυσεντερίῳ.

[65]A parallel is found in the Qumran literature in a midrash on Genesis where Abraham healed Pharaoh of a plague by praying and laying hands on him (1 QapGen 20:29). See W. Kirschslager, "Fieberheilung in Apg. 28 und Lk. 4," *Les Actes des Apôtres*, ed. J. Kremer (Gembloux: Duculot, 1979), 514f.

[66]Some interpreters have made a distinction between the two words used for healing, ἰάομαι (v. 8) and θεραπεύω (v. 9), arguing that the latter refers to Luke's healing through his medical practice, the former to Paul's miraculous healing. It should be noted that both words are used interchangeably in Luke 6:18 for Jesus' healings (Robertson, *WP* 3:481).

[67]It has been argued that the "honor" (τιμάς) heaped on the Christians (v. 10) actually consisted of honoraria, of fees paid for medical services. The word τιμή can certainly have the meaning of a payment or fee (cf. Acts 5:2; 1 Tim 5:17), but the emphasis is on the hospitality of the Maltese and on the divine healing ministry through Paul—not on Luke's practice of his medical profession.

and Pollux. [12]We put in at Syracuse and stayed there three days. [13]From there we set sail and arrived at Rhegium. The next day the south wind came up, and on the following day we reached Puteoli. [14]There we found some brothers who invited us to spend a week with them. And so we came to Rome. [15]The brothers there had heard that we were coming, and they traveled as far as the Forum of Appius and the Three Taverns to meet us. At the sight of these men Paul thanked God and was encouraged. [16]When we got to Rome, Paul was allowed to live by himself, with a soldier to guard him.

From his Damascus conversion on, Paul is depicted in Acts as continually on the move. In this passage his travels finally came to an end. More particularly, from 19:21 on, Paul's focus had been on Rome, the capital and hub of the empire. Now at last his vision was fulfilled as he reached the great city, the "ends of the earth." It was the fulfillment not just of Paul's vision but of the Lord's commission (cf. 1:8).

28:11 It was impossible to travel during the winter, and so those three months were spent on Malta, awaiting the favorable spring breezes.[68] Paul's ship had been wrecked, but another was located whose crew also had been wintering on Malta, perhaps up the coast at the major port of Valetta. Like the wrecked vessel, it was of Alexandrian registry, probably also a giant grain carrier. Luke said that its figurehead bore the images of the "twin gods" (NIV). Ships often carried the figurehead of these two gods, who were Castor and Pollux, the sons of Zeus and Leda. They were venerated as the protectors of seamen. When their constellation was viewed in the sky, this was always considered a favorable omen for a smooth voyage.[69]

28:12-13 The first leg of the renewed voyage took Paul to Syracuse, which was some ninety miles from Malta (v. 12). Syracuse, located on the eastern extremity of southern Sicily, had two harbors and was in the Roman period the capital city of the island. The party waited there for three days. The reason for the delay is not specified—perhaps the ship had business there or the winds were not favorable. The next leg of their voyage took them to Rhegium, a port at the southern tip of the boot of Italy, just opposite Sicily and at the entrance to the straits of Messina. It could be that the seventy-mile journey from Syracuse to Rhegium did not

---

[68]The ancient sources are somewhat at variance as to when the sea reopened for travel. Pliny (*Natural History* 2.122) placed the date early—on February 8. On the other hand, Vegetius (*Military Epitome* 4.39) stated that the seas were closed until March 10. If Luke's "three month" interval is precise, the earlier date would be the more likely for Paul's voyage. The shipwreck would have been at the latest in late October, allowing for November through January as the three months on Malta (see n. 19).

[69]D. Ladouceur ("Hellenistic Preconceptions," 444-46) documents the tradition that Castor and Pollux were viewed as the protectors of innocent seafarers and punishers of the guilty. He sees this detail as a further indicator that Luke wished to stress Paul's innocence.

go completely without difficulty. The majority text says that the party "sailed around" (*perielthontes*), which may indicate that they had to tack against the wind. (The NIV follows the variant reading, which has them "cutting anchor" and interprets this as indicating that they "set sail.")[70] The final leg of the journey took them from Rhegium through the straits of Messina up the west coast of Italy the 210 miles or so to Puteoli. Sailing was particularly good. There was a favorable south wind, and the voyage took only a day (v. 13). Puteoli in Paul's day probably was the main port for the grain fleet.[71] Modern Pozzuoli, it lay about eight miles northwest of Naples and approximately 130 miles by foot from Rome.

28:14a At Puteoli the Christian travelers found some "brothers" (meaning Christians) who prevailed upon them to spend a week with them (v. 14). It is remarkable how completely Julius and Paul's Roman guards have disappeared from the narrative since the end of chap. 27. Perhaps this indicates the great amount of freedom Paul enjoyed under his privileged custody and the high degree of trust he had established with his Roman guards. It should also be noted that a Christian community already was in Puteoli when Paul arrived there.[72] This should come as no surprise. The edict of Claudius, to which Luke referred in 18:2, dealt with a dispute in the Jewish community of Rome that seems to have involved Christ and is evidence that the gospel had already reached Italy by A.D. 49.[73] Paul's Letter to the Romans is perhaps the best evidence for the existence of a church there long before his own arrival.

28:14b In the present narrative word was evidently sent off to the Christians in Rome immediately upon Paul's arrival in Puteoli, and some of them intercepted him along the way (v. 15). Verse 14b seems premature and somewhat redundant with v. 16. Luke may have viewed Puteoli as belonging to "Rome" in the larger sense of the total area of Italian jurisdiction.[74] More likely, he simply wished to note that Paul's goal was

---

[70] The scribes evidently had problems with the verb in 13a. ℵ and B have περιελόντες, the term used in 27:40 for cutting the anchors; but that makes little sense in this context. The reading of the Byzantine text is περιελθόντες ("coming around"), which is still problematic. Does this mean *sailing about, tacking?*

[71] In a later day Ostia became the major port of Rome at the mouth of the Tiber. It was given to extensive silting and in Paul's day does not seem to have been sufficiently dredged to accommodate the large ships of the grain fleet.

[72] As in Rome, Christianity may have made its first inroads in the Jewish synagogues of Puteoli. There is known to have been an extensive Jewish community there. Josephus referred to it in *War* 2.104 and *Antiquities* 17.328. More debatable is whether there were Christian communities at nearby Herculaneum and Pompeii. See Hemer, *Acts in Hellenistic History*, 155, n. 156.

[73] Aquila and Priscilla may already have been Christians when they went to Corinth. See commentary on 18:2f.

[74] For the view that v. 14b refers to "greater Rome," see Ramsay, *St. Paul the Traveller*, 347.

now as good as attained. It had been a long and arduous route to Rome from Paul's first conception of the visit to the capital (19:21). He had to overcome angry mobs, endless legal proceedings, the fury of the sea, and long delays. Now at last his destination was as good as attained. In a real sense, v. 14b can be considered as the climax to the entire Book of Acts.[75]

28:15 Verse 15 is at best anticlimactic, going back and filling in the details of Paul's final steps to Rome. The route from Puteoli to Rome involved about 130 miles and took about five days by foot. It led to Capua by way of the Via Compana and then up the Via Appia to the capital. On the Appian Way, forty-three miles south of Rome, lay the stopping place known as Apii Forum, or "marketplace of Appius." It was there that a group of Christians from Rome intercepted the apostle, in the little town described by Horace as "crammed with boatmen and stingy tavern_keepers" (*Satires* 1.5.3). As the group of them proceeded another ten miles or so toward Rome, they encountered at the way station known as "Three Taverns" a second group of Christians who had come from the city to welcome the apostle. Probably there were several house churches in Rome, and the two groups represented different congregations. This is the only mention of the Roman Christians in Acts. They play no role in the narrative of Paul's witness in 28:17-31. Their presence here is significant. It assures the reader of the backing of a Christian community for the apostle's witness in the city. They served as a constant encouragement for him (v. 15b).

28:16 Verse 16 is transitional. It brings the long travel narrative to a close, and it opens the account of Paul's witness in Rome. Once again we are reminded that Paul was a prisoner because his military guard reappeared.[76] Still under free custody, he was granted considerable liberty, being allowed to live in his own rented house with only a single soldier to guard him (cf. v. 30). He was thus free to bear his witness; the subsequent narrative highlights this, but the presence of the soldier reminds us that it was a witness *in chains*.

---

[75]Robertson, *WP* 3:483.

[76]The Western text expands v. 16 considerably, indicating that the centurion gave the prisoners over to the *stratopedrarch* (στρατοπεδάρχῳ) and that Paul was allowed to stay "outside the barracks." This is almost certainly a later expansion of the text, but the question is raised whether it might accurately reflect the legal situation with prisoners like Paul from the provinces. If so, who was the "stratopedarch"? The experts are divided on this question as to whether this should be seen as the *praefectus praetorii* (the head of the praetorian guard), the *princeps perigrinorum* (the centurion over the detached foreign legionaries), or the *princeps castrorum* (the officer over the barracks for the legionaries to whom prisoners from the provinces would be delivered). On the whole question, see Hemer, *Acts in Hellenistic History*, 199f.

2. Paul's Witness in Rome (28:17-31)

The account of Paul's witness in Rome centers primarily on his testimony to the Jews of the city. This comes as something of a surprise because the narrative up to this point has prepared us for Paul's witness before Caesar. Nothing, however, is said of his trial before the emperor. Instead, the focus is on Paul's encounter with the Jewish community in Rome. A familiar pattern reappears, where Paul was first heard favorably by them, then was resisted, and finally turned to the Gentiles—a pattern that recapitulates Paul's experience with the Jews of Pisidian Antioch (13:42-48), of Corinth (18:5-7), and of Ephesus (19:8-10). It is not by accident that Luke ended his book on this note. The Jewish rejection of the gospel and the acceptance of the Gentiles has been a major theme throughout Acts. Indeed, the book opens with the question of Israel's place in God's kingdom (1:6). It closes on the same note.

The conclusion to Acts is carefully constructed.[77] It consists of an outer framework which focuses on Paul's situation in Rome, living in his own rented house and under military guard (vv. 16,30). In between are two scenes involving Paul's testimony to the Jews of Rome—an initial favorable encounter (vv. 17-22) followed by a second encounter in which the Jews reject Paul's message and the apostle turns to the Gentiles (vv. 23-28).

(1) First Meeting with the Jews (28:17-22)

[17]Three days later he called together the leaders of the Jews. When they had assembled, Paul said to them: "My brothers, although I have done nothing against our people or against the customs of our ancestors, I was arrested in Jerusalem and handed over to the Romans. [18]They examined me and wanted to release me, because I was not guilty of any crime deserving death. [19]But when the Jews objected, I was compelled to appeal to Caesar—not that I had any charge to bring against my own people. [20]For this reason I have asked to see you and talk with you. It is because of the hope of Israel that I am bound with this chain."

[21]They replied, "We have not received any letters from Judea concerning you, and none of the brothers who have come from there has reported or said anything bad about you. [22]But we want to hear what your views are, for we know that people everywhere are talking against this sect."

28:17 Paul's first conversation with the Jews of Rome occurred at his own initiative: he called together the Jewish leaders of Rome, and they

---

[77]For a detailed analysis of the structure of this section see H. J. Hauser, *Strukturen der Abschlusserzählung der Apostelgeschichte* (Apg. 28, 16-31), *AnBib* 86 (Rome: Biblical Institute, 1979); J. Dupont, "La conclusion des Actes et son rapport à l'ensemble de l'ouvrage de Luc," in *Les Actes*, 360-404.

came to him in his rented quarters (v. 17). There was an extensive Jewish community in Rome, but it does not seem to have been well-integrated but rather to have consisted of a number of separate synagogues. It is unclear exactly who these "leaders" of the Jewish community were—perhaps the ruling elders of the various Roman synagogues.[78] Paul set before them the circumstances that had brought him to Rome. His words summed up what is already familiar to the reader from the defense scenes of chaps. 22–26 and serve to underline one final time Paul's total innocence. He first pointed out that he had done nothing against the Jewish people or their ancestral customs. The Asian Jews in Jerusalem might quibble with this statement because they had charged him with exactly the opposite (cf. 21:28). Paul, however, had constantly pointed out that these charges were false and that he had been a law-abiding Jew in the strictest sense (cf. 22:3; 24:14; 26:4f.). Paul next described how he had been arrested in Jerusalem and "handed over" to the Romans (v. 17b). This is Paul's summary of the temple scene in which the Romans intervened, rescuing him from the angry Jewish mob and placing him under arrest (21:33). Paul's version to the Roman Jews brings out the parallel to Jesus, who was also "handed over" (*paredothēn*) to the Gentiles (cf. Luke 9:44; 18:32; 24:7).

28:18-20 Paul then pointed out to the Roman Jewish leaders that he was guilty of no crime deserving death (v. 18). The Roman officials had constantly affirmed this in his hearings before them (cf. 23:29; 25:25; 26:31). Paul's own version of his experience with the Roman officials is highly abbreviated and an interpretation of the events. The reference to their wanting to release him (v. 19a) is only explicitly borne out by Agrippa's comment after the appeal had been set in motion (26:32). Likewise, Paul's remark that he made his appeal because of the objection of the Jews is an interpretation. It was because Festus wished to do the Jews "a favor" that Paul had made his appeal (25:9). All of these things are familiar from the narrative of Acts 22–26. Paul's statement in 19b is a new emphasis and a new angle on his innocence: he had no charge to make against his people. He was a loyal Jew in every respect. Just as he was not guilty of any crime *against* the Jews, so he was innocent of any ill intent *toward* them. They had falsely accused *him*. He would make no accusations against *them*. He only wanted one thing from his fellow Jews—their commitment to Christ. It was ultimately because of "the hope of Israel" that Paul found himself in chains (v. 20). It was his testimony to the resurrection of Jesus, that Jesus is both Messiah and Lord,

---

[78]They are simply called "leaders" (πρῶτους). Inscriptions found at Rome designate the ruling elders as "gerousiarchs." See R. Penna, "Les Juifs à Rome au Temps de l'Apôtre Paul," *NTS* 28 (1982): 329f.

that constituted the real contention between him and the Jews. That was the *real* issue, and Paul had constantly focused on it in his defense speeches (23:6; 24:15; 26:8,23).

28:21 The response of the Roman Jews is somewhat surprising. First, they stated that they had received no official letters from Judea or even an oral report about Paul (v. 21). Some interpreters find this inconceivable.[79] Yet it may well be that because of winter travel conditions, no one from Palestine had arrived in Rome prior to Paul. It is also possible that the connections between Jerusalem and the synagogues of Rome were not very strong anyway.[80] Or it may possibly be that the Roman Jews were deliberately disassociating themselves from the trial of Paul, not wishing to be involved in a case that could eventually prove to be an embarrassment for the Jewish accusers.[81]

28:22 The second response of the Roman Jews is somewhat more puzzling. Their knowledge of the Christians did not seem to be very intimate, only a sort of hearsay acquaintance that "people everywhere are talking against this sect." Christians were well established in Rome. Paul had written an epistle to the church there, and Luke had just referred to the "brothers" who met Paul on his way to Rome (v. 15). The edict of Claudius seemed to have involved a dispute within the Jewish synagogue over Christ, and that only some ten years or so prior to this.[82] It is altogether likely that in the aftermath of Claudius's edict the Jewish synagogues kept themselves completely separate from the Christians,[83] but it seems equally likely that they would have had some acquaintance with the movement. Perhaps the Roman Jews were being "a model of diplomacy,"[84] maintaining as much distance as possible from the whole matter of Paul. In any event, their refusal to speak anything against Paul was in itself something of an indirect testimony to his innocence.

(2) Separation from the Jews (28:23-28)

23They arranged to meet Paul on a certain day, and came in even larger numbers to the place where he was staying. From morning till evening he explained and declared to them the kingdom of God and tried to convince them about Jesus from the Law of Moses and from the Prophets. **24**Some were convinced by what he said, but others would not believe. **25**They disagreed among themselves and

---

[79]E.g., R. Pesch, *Apostelgeschichte* 2:309.

[80]R. Penna ("Les Juifs à Rome, 336) points out that literary and inscriptional evidence reflects there was little interaction between the Roman Jews and Palestine.

[81]According to K. Lake and H. J. Cadbury (*Beginnings* 4:346), Roman law had severe penalties for prosecutors who brought poorly established cases.

[82]See commentary on 18:2.

[83]Rackham, *Acts*, 501.

[84]Bruce, *Acts:* NIC, 530.

began to leave after Paul had made this final statement: "The Holy Spirit spoke
the truth to your forefathers when he said through Isaiah the prophet:
  26" 'Go to this people and say,
  "You will be ever hearing but never understanding;
    you will be ever seeing but never perceiving."
  27For this people's heart has become calloused;
    they hardly hear with their ears,
    and they have closed their eyes.
  Otherwise they might see with their eyes,
    hear with their ears,
    understand with their hearts
    and turn, and I would heal them.'
  28"Therefore I want you to know that God's salvation has been sent to the
Gentiles, and they will listen!"

There is a close correspondence between the narratives of Paul's interaction with the Jews of Pisidian Antioch (13:14-50) and with those of
Rome (28:17-28). The former occurred at the beginning of Paul's wider
mission and the latter at its close. Both scenes involve an initial positive
response from the Jews who heard Paul's testimony and a request to hear
him further (13:42; 28:22). In both accounts a second hearing occurred on
a subsequent day (13:44; 28:23). In the course of the second meeting with
Paul, strong Jewish resistance to his witness developed (13:45; 28:24).
Thereupon Paul addressed them with a quote from the prophet Isaiah. At
Pisidian Antioch the text was from Isa 49:6 and pointed to the divine
imperative for a mission to the Gentiles (13:47). In Rome the text was Isa
5:9f. and highlighted the Jewish rejection of the divine message (28:26f.).
Together the two texts give the full picture—the witness to the Gentiles
and the rejection by the Jews. It was the Jewish rejection of the gospel
that gave impetus to the Gentile mission. Consequently, in both instances
Paul concluded his testimony to the Jews with an emphatic statement that
he was now turning to the Gentiles (13:46; 28:28).
    These two texts form a framework for all of Paul's missionary activity.
In between them the pattern of Jewish rejection and Gentile receptivity
regularly repeats itself. Paul never gave up. Rejected by the Jews of one
place, he always began his witness in a new town in the synagogue. The
question arises as to whether there is something final about Paul's rejection by the Roman Jews. In this instance there is no subsequent narrative
to show him in a new city, starting over once more with his witness to the
Jews there.
    28:23 As in Pisidian Antioch (13:44), Paul's second meeting with the
Roman Jews involved considerably larger numbers (28:23). In Rome, however, there was no Gentile contingent: the audience were solely Jews. Since
Paul was under guard, they came to him in his private rented quarters

(cf. vv. 16,30).[85] Paul devoted the entire day to presenting them with the gospel.[86] The content of his message is summarized in terms of the "kingdom of God" and "Jesus." The same two terms, "kingdom" and "Jesus," summarize his preaching in v. 31. They are twin concepts: Jesus stands at the center of God's sovereign rule; God's people are gathered around him. The Jews looked to the coming of the Messiah and the restoration of God's kingdom in a renewed Israel (cf. 1:6). The message of Acts has been that this has already occurred—in Jesus. This was what Paul set before them that day. He sought to convince them through an exposition of the Scriptures ("from the Law of Moses and from the Prophets"). Luke did not specify which texts Paul used to expound Jesus, but they were surely those which point to the necessity of the Messiah's suffering and to his resurrection—the texts Jesus set before the disciples after his resurrection (Luke 24:27,44-47), which Peter used to show Christ's messianic status to the Jews at Pentecost and in the temple square (Acts 2:17-36; 3:12-26) and which Paul himself expounded in the synagogue of Pisidian Antioch (13:32-39).[87]

28:24 The result was a sharp division among the Jews who heard Paul's witness—some being convinced, others refusing to believe him (v. 24). The reference to some being "convinced" (*epeithonto*) could mean no more than that some of the Roman Jews found Paul's arguments persuasive without implying their coming to a point of commitment to Christ. On the other hand, the picture of a divided synagogue is a constant of Acts—some believing, others resisting and violently opposing Paul. It is likely that the same pattern is to be seen here.[88] Some individual Jews believed, but "the Jews" as a whole, "the synagogue" in an official sense, did not accept Paul's witness to Christ. This had been the tragic story of the Jews in every community in which Paul had preached.

28:25 The divided Jews argued among themselves and began to disperse, but not before Paul had gotten in the last word—one final Old Testament testimony. This time it was not a prophecy regarding the Christ but rather one that applied to them and their refusal to hear the word of God. The text is introduced with particular emphasis—"well"

---

[85]H. J. Cadbury suggests that "place where he was staying" (ξενίαν) should be translated "guest table, hospitality" and should be seen as a reference to Paul's providing a "reception" for the Roman Jews ("Lexical Notes on Luke-Acts: III. Luke's Interest in Lodging," *JBL* 45 [1926]: 320).

[86]"From morning to evening" is an OT expression; cf. Exod 18:13; 1 Kgs 22:35; Sir 18:26.

[87]For the use of the messianic testimonia in these sermons, see the commentary on 2:17-36; 3:12-26; and 13:32-39.

[88]For the "believing" minority from synagogues that rejected Paul, see 13:43; 14:1; 17:4, 12; 18:8; 19:9. See also G. Krodel, *Acts*, PC (Philadelphia: Fortress, 1981), 499.

("the truth," NIV; *kalōs*) had the Holy Spirit uttered these words through Isaiah the prophet. The inspiration of the prophet's word is stressed through the reference to the Spirit's mediation. The Spirit is described as speaking the word of the prophecy. In every instance in Acts where a scriptural quote is introduced by a reference to the Spirit, the Spirit is described as having spoken (cf. 1:16; 4:25). In this manner the written Word is shown to be a dynamic, "living" Word.[89] Note that at this point Paul began to "distance" himself from the unbelieving Jews. Earlier he had addressed them as "my brothers" (v. 17). Now he spoke of "your" forefathers (v. 25b). Paul had not ceased being a Jew, but his faith in Christ sharply separated him now from his Roman brothers who refused the gospel message. Paul was *not* one with those hardhearted forefathers who had rejected God's word through Isaiah, who had resisted the Spirit in the past, and whose descendants were now so doing (cf. 7:51).

28:26-27 Verses 26-27 reproduce verbatim the Septuagint text of Isa 6:9f. In this Greek version the prophet's words constitute a prophecy of the people's obduracy. The three organs of perception are highlighted—the eyes, the ears, and the heart, the latter in Hebrew thought being considered the organ of understanding and will. The picture is that of a people who merely take in sensory perceptions but in no sense appropriate them. Their ears heard the sounds, but the hearing was without understanding. Their eyes took in the sights but without any insight because their hearts had become calloused; the message received by their eyes and ears was neither understood nor acted upon. Otherwise, they would have done something in response to God's message. If they had heard and understood the divine word, they would have turned from their ways in repentance (*epistrepsōsin*) and received God's healing.

The Jews of Rome had exemplified precisely this response. They had heard from Paul the message of God's salvation in Christ, but their hardness had made them unresponsive and resistant. The key concept in the narrative of Paul's encounter with the Jews of Rome is that of "hearing." The verb "to hear" (*akouō*) occurs five times and at key points. The first occurrence is when the Roman Jews expressed their desire to "hear" Paul's views (v. 22). But when they had heard his testimony, it became clear that they had not really "heard him" because they responded in disbelief and rejection. The quote from Isaiah refers to "hearing" three times, and its whole point is that hearing is not really hearing at all if the message is not acted upon. Finally, in v. 28, Paul referred to hearing one last time; and it is the last, emphatic word of the entire passage. The Gentiles would "hear"—they would "listen," would hear with receptive,

---

[89]F. Bovon, "'Schön hat der heilige Geist durch den Propheten Jesaja zu euren Vatern gesprochen' (Act. 28, 25)," *ZNW* 75 (1984): 226-32.

responsive hearts. The Jews had expressed their desire to hear Paul, but they were hardened to his message and really did not hear his word of salvation. It would be different with the Gentiles. They would hear and receive the gospel.[90]

Isaiah 6:9f. was a key Old Testament text for the early Christians as they sought to come to terms with the Jewish rejection of the gospel. It occurs in the Synoptic tradition among the sayings of Jesus with reference to the failure of the Jews to understand and appropriate the message of his parables (Matt 13:14f.; Mark 4:12; Luke 8:10). When in Rom 9–11 Paul wrestled with the riddle of the Jewish rejection of the gospel, he cited this same passage of Isaiah (Rom 11:8). Isaiah's words were seen as a real prophecy of the Jewish obduracy. They did not, however, explain it. It remained something of a riddle. In Rom 11 Paul suggested that perhaps the hardening was temporary, a time allowing for the message to be taken to the Gentiles, that finally in the mystery of God's plan of salvation there would be a great turning of his people to Christ. Here in Acts he provided no such solutions. The Jewish rejection was a reality and a riddle. To a great extent it remains so—how the gospel of God's salvation which was foreshadowed in the Jewish Scriptures, fulfilled in a Jewish Messiah, and first proclaimed by Jewish heralds like Paul would ultimately be embraced not by the Jews but primarily by Gentiles.

28:28 Now for the third, climactic time in Acts, Paul turned to the Gentiles (v. 28; cf. 13:46; 18:6). Paul saw his ministry as primarily to the Gentiles (cf. Gal 2:8), and his vision in the temple had confirmed this (Acts 22:21). Throughout Acts he has been depicted as having great success among the Gentiles. So Paul's directing his efforts to the Gentile mission was nothing new. The main question is whether at this point Paul's turning from the Jews to the Gentiles was final and definitive. Had Paul "given up" on the Jews? Many scholars feel that he had.[91] But there are significant clues in the text to indicate that such is not the case. All along, Luke has shown that there were some Jews who believed, even in those synagogues that rejected and persecuted Paul. The same pattern of acceptance and rejection appears in the present scene. In v. 30 Paul is said to have welcomed "all" who came to him. Elsewhere it is specified that Paul witnessed to both Jews and Gentiles (cf. 14:1; 18:4; 19:10), and there is no reason to believe that individual Jews have been

[90]For a full development of this theme of hearing, see J. Dupont, "La Conclusion des Actes," 372-76.

[91]This has been strongly stated recently by J. T. Sanders, *The Jews in Luke-Acts* (Philadelphia: Fortress, 1987). For a similar position see D. Slingerland, "'The Jews' in the Pauline Portion of Acts," *JAAR* 54 (1986): 305-21. E. Haenchen argues that for Luke the Jews are definitively rejected and the Gentiles alone become the people of the promise ("Judentum und Christentum in der Apostelgeschichte," *ZNW* 54 [1963]: 155-87).

excluded in this instance. Yet there is a sense in which the Jewish rejection is seen to be definitive. It had become clear that "official Judaism," the Jewish people as a whole, would not embrace Christ.

This rejection first became explicit at the martyrdom of Stephen. It repeated itself in every synagogue Paul entered. He was never able to remain in a single synagogue but always was forced to leave. The same was true in the present instance. The Jewish delegation in Rome was representative of official Judaism. It was the "leaders" (*prōtous*) of the Jews who came to Paul (v. 17). In Rome as in Jerusalem and the Diaspora synagogues, this official Judaism refused the gospel message. But everywhere individual Jews had come into the Christian fold, into "the way" within true Judaism, into the true people of God.[92] There is no reason to believe that the same pattern of a continued witness to Jews would not go on after this scene. Perhaps the wording of Paul's statement in v. 28 underscores this fact. Paul did not say that because the Jews had rejected his message he would turn to the Gentiles. Rather, he stated that God's salvation had already been sent to the Gentiles. The passage is thus not so much about Jewish exclusion as it is about Gentile inclusion in God's people. Acts is primarily the story of the inclusive gospel: God's salvation (*sōtērion*) has been sent to all.[93]

(3) Bold Witness to All (28:30-31)

[30]**For two whole years Paul stayed there in his own rented house and welcomed all who came to see him. [31]Boldly and without hindrance he preached the kingdom of God and taught about the Lord Jesus Christ.**

28:30-31[94] With vv. 30-31 Acts comes to a rather abrupt ending. In v. 30 Luke told us that Paul stayed in Rome for a period of two years,

---

[92]The opposite viewpoint to Sanders and Haenchen (n. 91) is espoused by J. Jervell, who argues that in Acts the only true Christianity is Jewish Christianity which represents the restored people of God. The question is not one of Gentile replacing Jew but rather of the mission of the (Jewish) people of God to the Gentiles ("Paulus . . . der Lehrer Israels," *NovT* 10 [1968]: 164-90). See also his book *Luke and the People of God* (Minneapolis: Augsburg, 1972). For a similar view see D. P. Moessner, "Paul in Acts: Preacher of Eschatological Repentance to Israel," *NTS* 34 (1988): 96-104. For the various viewpoints on the question of the Jews in Acts, see the collection of essays *Luke-Acts and the Jewish People*, ed. J. B. Tyson (Minneapolis: Augsburg, 1988).

[93]It should be noted that the neuter form (σωτήριον) occurs only in three places in Luke-Acts: here in 28:28 and in Luke 2:30; 3:6. In Luke 2:30 the context is Simeon's song in which God's salvation is described as "a light . . . for the Gentiles" and "glory to . . . Israel." Luke 3:6 is a quote from Isa 40:5 and is equally inclusive, speaking of "all flesh" seeing the salvation of God.

[94]Verse 29 is omitted from the text of the NIV on text-critical grounds. It is not found in the earliest witnesses (𝔓[74], ℵ, A, B, one Old Latin ms., Vulgate mss., the Syriac Peshitta, the

evidently living under free custody in his rented dwelling.[95] He graciously received "all" who came to visit him there, probably including Jews as well as Gentiles.[96] Verse 31 gives the content of his conversation with those who came to him. He "preached boldly" to them[97] in the power of the Holy Spirit—"without hindrance." This is perhaps a quasilegal term, meaning that the Romans put no obstacle in the way of his testimony to the gospel. This in itself would be significant, an implicit evidence to the fact that the Romans found nothing dangerous or subversive in his message.[98] Surely as F. Stagg has so convincingly demonstrated, this final word of the text of Acts points to even more—to the unbound gospel, triumphant over every barrier of superstition and of human prejudice.[99] The content of Paul's message forms the conclusion to the message of Acts. He preached "the kingdom of God" and taught about "the Lord Jesus Christ."[100] The two belong together: the good news of God's kingdom *is* the good news about Christ. This was the same message Paul shared with the Roman Jews (v. 23). It is ultimately the central message of Acts. The book begins with Jesus sharing the message of God's kingdom with his disciples (1:3). It quickly raises the burning question, "Are you at this time going to restore the kingdom to Israel?" (1:6). That question has now been answered. God has indeed restored his kingdom—in the Messiah, in Christ. And it is open to all who will receive him, Jew and Greek. In Christ, God's kingdom is realized as he

---

Coptic) and seems to have been a Western expansion added to round off the narrative, referring to the Jews continuing to argue among themselves as they departed: καὶ ταῦτα αὐτοῦ εἰπόντος ἀπῆλθον οἱ Ἰουδαῖοι, πολλὴν ἔχοντες ἐν ἑαυτοῖς συζήτησιν.

[95]Translations differ about the meaning of μισθώμα in v. 30. The word is a *hapax*, and its etymology would imply something earned. Hence the RSV renders it "at his own expense." But it is used with the word "to dwell" (ἐνέμεινεν) and the preposition ἐν, which seem to call for a dwelling place. Accordingly, the NIV renders "in his own rented house." See the debate between two German scholars on the subject: F. Saum, "Er lebte . . . von seinem eigenem Einkommen (Apg. 28, 30)," *BZ* 20 (1976): 226-29; E. Hansack, "'Er lebte . . . von seinem eigenem Einkommen' (Apg. 28, 30)," *BZ* 19 (1975): 249-53, and "Nochmals zu Apostelgeschichte 28, 30," *BZ* 21 (1977): 118-21.

[96]This assumption was evidently drawn quite early, as some Western witnesses have "Jews and Greeks" in addition to "all" in v. 30.

[97]In Acts the word "boldness" (παρρησία) seems to involve uncommon, inspired confidence in witness (cf. 2:29; 4:13). In 4:29 and 4:31 it is connected with the power of the Spirit.

[98]Perhaps ακωλύτως is a play on Paul's captive status. Though captive, he was "unbound" in his witness. Cf. the similar play on "fettered" (δέδεται) in 2 Tim 2:9.

[99]F. Stagg, *The Book of Acts: The Early Struggle for an Unhindered Gospel* (Nashville: Broadman, 1955). See also G. Delling, "Das letzte Wort der Apostelgeschichte," *NovT* 15 (1973): 193-204.

[100]Some Western witnesses add after "Jesus Christ": "saying that this is the Messiah, Jesus the son of God, by whom the whole world is to be judged."

comes to rule in the hearts of his people. The gospel proclaims the kingdom, and the gospel has triumphed. The final note of Acts is a triumphant one. The word of God has triumphed—but not Paul. Paul was still in chains, still a prisoner. Throughout Acts the triumph was never with the bearers of the gospel. They were rejected, beaten, reviled, imprisoned, and killed for their witness. But the gospel was unfettered, triumphant. Perhaps Luke deliberately ended on this note to remind his readers that with witness often comes suffering and trial. But when the witness is faithful, the gospel triumphs, the word of God's salvation strips all its bonds. And it is to that kind of witness we are called, even if, like Paul, the witness is in chains.

Still we are not satisfied with Luke's ending. How could he have led Paul through the endless hearings of chaps. 22–26 and the violent storm of chap. 27 and then left us in midair? We want to know what happened to Paul. It seems beside the point that Paul's situation probably was well known in the Christian communities that first read Acts. Still some scholars feel the abrupt ending of Acts is so unsatisfactory that they postulate Luke wrote Acts at this point, after two years of Paul's Roman custody and before his case came to trial.[101] The difficulty with this view is that it places Acts at an early date—even prior to the Gospel of Mark.[102] Others postulate that Luke may have intended a third volume which would have picked up at this point in his career.[103] A more radical solution is to argue that Paul received an unfavorable verdict and was executed and that Luke would not have wanted to mention this since it would detract from the favorable picture of the Roman officials which he had sought to portray.[104] It would seem, however, that Luke would not have portrayed the Romans in such a favorable light had they ultimately been responsible for Paul's death; and one wonders why Luke would not have developed the story of Paul's martyrdom as he did that of Stephen. One of the most ingenious solutions has been to argue that the "two years" of v. 30 refers to a set period of statutory limitations in Roman law. The first-century reader would thus know that if Paul did not appear before Caesar within

---

[101]E.g., Bruce, *Acts:* NIC, 536, n. 49; J. Munck, *The Acts of the Apostles*, rev. W. F. Albright and C. S. Mann, AB (Garden City, N.Y.: Doubleday, 1967), 260; Robertson, *WP* 3:489.

[102]See the discussion of the date of Acts in the Introduction.

[103]So T. Zahn, *Die Apostelgeschichte des Lucas* (Leipzig: Deichert, 1922), 1:16-18; Ramsay, *St. Paul the Traveller*, 351f.

[104]So Haenchen, *Acts*, 731f.; Schneider, *Die Apostelgeschichte*, HTKNT (Freiburg: Herder, 1980), 2:411; R. Pesch, *Apostelgeschichte* 2:306f. These interpreters feel that the reference to "seeing Paul's face no more" in the Miletus account (20:25,38) is a clear allusion to his martyrdom. Even if it is—and that is debatable—it need not be a reference to his martyrdom at the time of this first Roman imprisonment. In all likelihood Paul *had* been martyred by the time Luke wrote Acts.

this period he would have been set free.[105] Unfortunately the evidence for such a legal procedure is late and doesn't seem to apply to cases like Paul's.[106] All of these suggestions thus have problems, and it probably is best to see Luke as having ended at this point because he had accomplished his purposes in showing Paul in Rome preaching the gospel without hindrance.[107]

Whatever may have been the outcome of Paul's Roman imprisonment, Luke seems to have deliberately chosen to end his story where he did. He ended not on Paul but on the gospel, on the message of the kingdom. The word of God in Christ—not Peter, not Paul—is the real hero of Acts.[108]

---

[105]So K. Lake, "What was the End of St. Paul's Trial?" *The Interpreter* 5 (1908-09): 147-56; W. Ramsay, *The Teaching of Paul in Terms of the Present Day* (London: Hodder & Stoughton, 1914), 346-82.

[106]A. N. Sherwin White, *Roman Society and Roman Law*, 112-19. Sherwin-White argues that it is possible that Nero released Paul as a former prisoner under Claudius. There is precedent for the release of prisoners in cases that new emperors "inherited" from their predecessors.

[107]The question still remains as to what *did* happen to Paul. Written in the third century, Eusebius, *Church History* 2.22, cites a tradition (literally "word has it" [λόγος ἔχει]) that Paul was released after his first defense and went forth on a ministry of preaching and that subsequently he returned to Rome and suffered martyrdom under Nero. Eusebius cited 2 Tim 4:16 as evidence that Paul was released after his "first defense."

Indeed, the Pastoral Epistles are a key element in the whole question of Paul's Roman imprisonment. It is virtually impossible to fit the personal information of the Pastorals into the framework of Paul's ministry from the onset of his first missionary journey to the Roman imprisonment of Acts 28:30f. It is thus highly likely that the personal events related in the Pastorals date from a period after Paul's first Roman confinement and are thus themselves testimony to Paul's release and subsequent ministry. In this view Paul would have arrived in Rome sometime in 59 or 60 and been released in 61 or 62. His return to Rome, second imprisonment, and martyrdom would have taken place under the Neronic persecution of the Roman Christians in A.D. 64 or 65. According to early tradition, Paul was martyred under Nero, being taken about a mile outside the city walls along the Ostian Way and beheaded.

The earliest extracanonical reference that might indicate a release of Paul is 1 Clem 1:5, which speaks of his having reached the "limits of the west," possibly an allusion to his working in Spain. The Clementine tradition, however, may be nothing more than a conclusion drawn from Paul's own stated plans in Rom 15:24. For a discussion of the evidence for Paul's release, see R. P. C. Hanson, *The Acts*, NCB (Oxford: Clarendon, 1967), 28-35. Cf. F. F. Bruce, "St. Paul in Rome," *BJRL* 46 (1963-64): 326-45, 50 (1967-68): 262-79.

[108]Several suggestions regarding the ending of Acts are worth mentioning. C. H. Talbert (*Acts*, KPG [Atlanta: John Knox, 1984], 104) notes that in Acts a period involving two years is one of "special blessing" (Antioch, 11:26; Caesarea, 24:27; Corinth, 18:11; Ephesus, 19:10), which particularly highlights the witness to Christ. Tannehill (*Narrative Unity*, 2:356) notes that by not bringing the story of Paul to a close, Luke left the narrative open, with its ongoing threads pointing to the Gentile mission, the outreach to the further "ends of the earth," the Lord's return, and the abiding question of the mission to the Jews. Along similar lines Rackham (*Acts*, 502) notes that v. 31 is not really a conclusion but almost a new beginning: "the history of Christianity is a succession of beginnings."

Selected Subject Index[1]

---

[1]Indexes were prepared by Lanese Dockery.

Person Index

Scripture Index

559

Selected Bibliography

Books and Commentaries

Barrett, C. K. *A Critical and Exegetical Commentary on the Acts of the Apostles.* Vol. 1: *Preliminary Introduction and Commentary on Acts I–XIV.* ICC. Edinburgh: T & T Clark, 1994.

- ———. *Luke the Historian in Recent Study.* London: Epworth, 1961.

Bauckham, R., ed. *The Book of Acts in Its Palestinian Setting.* Vol. 4. *The Book of Acts in Its First Century Setting.* Grand Rapids: Eerdmans, 1995.

Black, M. *An Aramaic Approach to the Gospels and Acts.* 2d ed. Oxford: Clarendon, 1954.

Boice, J. M. *Acts: An Expositional Commentary.* Grand Rapids: Baker, 1997.

Bovon, F. *Luke the Theologian: Thirty-Three Years of Research (1950–1983).* Translated by K. McKinney. Allison Park, Penn.: Pickwick, 1987.

Brawley, R. L. *Centering on God: Method and Message in Luke–Acts.* Louisville: Westminster/John Knox, 1990.

Brown, R. E. *The Churches the Apostles Left Behind.* New York: Paulist, 1984.

Bruce, F. F. *The Acts of the Apostles: The Greek Text with Introduction and Commentary.* Third revised and enlarged edition. Grand Rapids: Eerdmans, 1990.

Bruce, F. F. *Commentary on the Book of Acts.* NICNT. Grand Rapids: Eerdmans, 1977.

Cadbury, H. J. *The Book of Acts in History.* New York: Harper & Brothers, 1955.

———. *The Making of Luke-Acts.* New York: Macmillan, 1927.

Carter, C. W. and R. E. *The Acts of the Apostles.* Grand Rapids: Zondervan, 1959.

Carver, W. O. *The Acts of the Apostles.* Nashville: Sunday School Board of the Southern Baptist Convention, 1916.

Cassidy, R. J. *Society and Politics in the Acts of the Apostles.* Maryknoll, N.Y.: Orbis, 1988.

Chase, F. H. *The Credibility of the Book of the Acts of the Apostles.* London: Macmillan, 1902.

Conzelmann, H. *Acts of the Apostles.* Trans. J. Limburg, A. T. Kraabel, and D. H. Juel. Hermeneia. Philadelphia: Fortress, 1987.

Davies, W. D. *Paul and Rabbinic Judaism.* London: SPCK, 1958.

Deissmann, A. *Paul.* Translated by R. M. Strachan and W. E. Wilson. New York: Doran, 1926.

Dibelius, M. *Studies in the Acts of the Apostles.* Edited by H. Greeven and translated by M. Ling. London: SCM Press, 1956.

Dix, G. *Jew and Greek: A Study in the Primitive Church.* Westminster: Dacre Press, 1953.

Dodd, C. H. *The Apostolic Preaching and Its Development.* London: Hodder & Stoughton, 1936.

Dunn, J. D. G. *The Acts of the Apostles.* Epworth Commentaries. London: Epworth, 1996.

Dupont, J. *The Salvation of the Gentiles: Essays on the Acts of the Apostles.* Translated by J. R. Keating. New York: Paulist, 1979.

———. *The Sources of Acts: The Present Position.* Translated by K. Pond. London:

Darton, Longman & Todd, 1964.

Easton, B. S. *Early Christianity: The Purpose of Acts and Other Papers.* Edited by F. C. Grant. London: SPCK, 1955.

Ehrhardt, A. *The Acts of the Apostles: Ten Lectures.* Manchester: Manchester University Press, 1969.

Esler, P. F. *Community and Gospel in Luke-Acts.* SNTS Monograph Series, 57. Cambridge: Cambridge University Press, 1987.

Evans, C. A. and J. A. Sanders. *Luke and Scripture: The Function of Sacred Tradition in Luke–Acts.* Minneapolis: Fortress, 1993.

Flender, H. *St. Luke: Theologian of Redemptive History.* Translated by R. H. and I. Fuller. Philadelphia: Fortress, 1967.

Foakes-Jackson, F. J. *The Acts of the Apostles.* MNTC. New York: Harper & Brothers, 1931.

Foakes-Jackson, F. J. and K. Lake, gen. eds. *The Beginnings of Christianity.* Part I: *The Acts of the Apostles.* London: Macmillan. In five volumes:

Vol. 1: *Prolegomena,* ed. Foakes-Jackson and Lake, 1920.

Vol. 2: *Prolegomena II and Criticism.* Edited by Foakes-Jackson and Lake, 1922.

Vol. 3: *The Text of Acts,* J. H. Ropes, 1926.

Vol. 4: *English Translation and Commentary,* K. Lake and H. J. Cadbury, 1933.

Vol. 5: *Additional Notes to the Commentary.* Edited by K. Lake and H. J. Cadbury, 1933.

Gaertner, B. *The Areopagus Speech and Natural Revelation.* Acta Seminarii Neotestamentici Upsaliensis xxi. Uppsala: C. W. K. Gleerup, 1955.

Gasque, W. W. and R. P. Martin, eds. *Apostolic History and the Gospel: Essays Presented to F. F. Bruce.* Grand Rapids: Eerdmans, 1970.

———. *A History of the Criticism of the Acts of the Apostles.* Grand Rapids: Eerdmans, 1975.

Gill, D. W. J. and C. Gempf, eds. *The Book of Acts in Its Graeco-Roman Setting.* Vol. 2 of *The Book of Acts in Its First Century Setting.* Grand Rapids: Eerdmans, 1994.

Goguel, M. *The Birth of Christianity.* Translated by H. C. Snape. London: Allen & Unwin, 1953.

Hackett, H. B. *Commentary on Acts.* Grand Rapids: Kregel, 1992. Reprint of 1882 edition.

Haenchen, E. *The Acts of the Apostles: A Commentary.* Translated by B. Noble and G. Shinn. Philadelphia: Westminster, 1971.

Hanson, R. P. C. *The Acts in the Revised Standard Version.* NCB. Oxford: Clarendon, 1967.

Harnack, A. *The Acts of the Apostles.* Translated by J. R. Wilkinson. New York: Putnam's, 1911.

———. *The Date of the Acts and of the Synoptic Gospels.* Translated by J. R. Wilkinson. New York: Putnam's, 1911.

———. *Luke the Physician: The Author of the Third Gospel and the Acts of the Apostles.* Translated by J. R. Wilkinson. Edited by W. D. Morrison. New York: Putnam's, 1907.

Harrison, E. *Interpreting Acts: The Expanding Church.* Grand Rapids: Zondervan, 1975.

Hemer, C. J. *The Book of Acts in the Setting of Hellenistic History.* Edited by C. Gempf. Tübingen: Mohr-Siebeck, 1989.

Hengel, M. *Acts and the History of Earliest Christianity*. Translated by J. Bowden. Philadelphia: Fortress, 1979.

Hengel, M. and A. M. Schwemer. *Paul between Damascus and Antioch: The Unknown Years*. Louisville: Westminster/John Knox, 1997.

Jeremias, J. *Jerusalem in the Time of Jesus*. Translated by F. H. and C. H. Cave. Philadelphia: Fortress, 1969.

Jervell, J. *The Theology of the Acts of the Apostles*. Cambridge: Cambridge University Press, 1996.

————. *The Unknown Paul: Essays on Luke-Acts and Early Christian History*. Minneapolis: Augsburg, 1984.

Johnson, L. T. *The Acts of the Apostles*. Sacra Pagina 5. Collegeville, Minn.: Liturgical Press, 1992.

Keathley, N. H., ed. *With Steadfast Purpose: Essays on Acts in Honor of Henry Jackson Flanders, Jr*. Waco: Baylor University, 1990.

Keck, L. E. and J. L. Martyn, eds. *Studies in Luke-Acts: Essays in Honor of Paul Schubert*. Nashville: Abingdon, 1966.

Kee, H. C. *Good News to the Ends of the Earth: The Theology of Acts*. Philadelphia: Trinity Press International, 1990.

Kistemaker, S. J. *Exposition of the Acts of the Apostles*. New Testament Commentary. Grand Rapids: Baker, 1990.

Knox, W. L. *The Acts of the Apostles*. Cambridge: Cambridge University Press, 1948.

Krodel, G. A. *Acts*. ACNT. Minneapolis: Augsburg, 1986.

Larkin, W. J. *Acts*. IVP New Testament Commentary. Downers Grove: InterVarsity, 1995.

Lenski, R. C. H. *The Interpretation of the Acts of the Apostles*. Minneapolis: Augsburg, 1961; reprint of 1934 edition.

Levinskaya, I. *The Book of Acts in Its Diaspora Setting*. Vol. 6 of *The Book of Acts in Its First Century Setting*. Grand Rapids: Eerdmans, 1996.

Luedemann, G. *Early Christianity according to the Traditions in Acts*. Translated by J. Bowden. Minneapolis: Fortress, 1987.

Maddox, R. L., Jr. *Acts*. Layman's Bible Book Commentary. Nashville: Broadman, 1979.

Maddox, R. *The Purpose of Luke-Acts*. Edinburgh: T & T Clark, 1982.

Marshall, I. H. *Acts: An Introduction and Commentary*. TNTC. Leicester, Eng.: InterVarsity Press, 1980.

————. *The Acts of the Apostles*. New Testament Guides. Sheffield, UK: JSOT Press, 1992.

Mills, W. E. *The Acts of the Apostles*. Bibliographies for Biblical Research. Lewiston, N.Y.: Mellen, 1996.

Moule, C. F. D. *A Chosen Vessel: Studies in the Acts of the Apostles*. New York: Association, 1961.

Munck, J. *Paul and the Salvation of Mankind*. Translated by F. Clarke. London: SCM Press, 1959.

Neil, W. *The Acts of the Apostles*. NCBC. Grand Rapids: Eerdmans, 1981.

Neyrey, J. H., ed. *The Social World of Luke-Acts: Models for Interpretation*. Peabody, Mass.: Hendrickson, 1991.

Norden, E. *Agnostos Theos*. Stuttgart: B. G. Teubner, 1956. Reprint of 1923 edition.

Parsons, M. C. and J. B. Tyson, eds. *Cadbury, Knox and Talbert: American Contribu-

tions to the Study of Acts. SBL Biblical Scholarship in North America. Atlanta: Scholars Press, 1992

Parsons, M. C. and R. I. Pervo. *Rethinking the Unity of Luke and Acts.* Minneapolis: Fortress, 1993.

Pervo, R. I. *Profit with Delight: The Literary Genre of the Acts of the Apostles.* Philadelphia: Fortress, 1987.

Pesch, R. *Die Apostelgeschichte.* 2 vols. Evangelisch-katholischer Kommentar zum Neuen Testament. Neukirchen-Vluyn: Neukirchener, 1986.

Rackham, R. B. *The Acts of the Apostles.* London: Methuen, 1901.

Ramsay, W. M. *The Cities of St. Paul: Their Influence on His Life and Thought.* Grand Rapids: Baker, 1979. Reprint of 1907 edition.

————. *St. Paul the Traveller and Roman Citizen.* Grand Rapids: Baker, 1978. Reprint of 1897 edition.

————. *The Teaching of St. Paul in Terms of the Present Day.* Grand Rapids: Baker, 1979. Reprint of 1913 edition.

Rapske, B. *The Book of Acts and Paul in Roman Custody.* Vol. 3 of *The Book of Acts in Its First Century Setting.* Grand Rapids: Eerdmans, 1994.

Reicke, B. *Glaube und Leben der Urgemeinde, Bemerkungen zu Apg. 1–7.* Zurich: Zwingli-Verlag, 1957.

Richard, E. ed. *New Views on Luke and Acts.* Collegeville, Minn.: Liturgical Press, 1990.

Robertson, A. T. *Luke the Historian in the Light of Research.* New York: Scribner's, 1920.

Roloff, J. *Die Apostelgeschichte.* Das Neue Testament Deutsch. Goettingen: Vandenhoeck & Ruprecht, 1981.

Sanders, J. T. *The Jews in Luke-Acts.* Philadelphia: Fortress, 1987.

Schille, G. *Die Apostelgeschichte des Lukas.* Theologischer Handkommentar zum Neuen Testament. Berlin: Evangelische Verlagsanstalt, 1983.

Schlatter, A. *Die Apostelgeschichte.* Stuttgart: Calwer Verlag, 1948.

Schmithals, W. *Die Apostelgeschichte des Lukas.* Zuercher Bibelkommentare. Zuerich: Theologischer Verlag, 1982.

Schneider, G. *Die Apostelgeschichte.* Herders Theologischer Kommentar zum Neuen Testament. 2 vols. Freiburg: Herder, 1980, 1982.

Simon, M. *St. Stephen and the Hellenists in the Primitive Church.* London: Longmans, Green, & Company, 1958.

Smith, J. *The Voyage and Shipwreck of St. Paul.* Fourth revised edition, 1880. Reprint. Grand Rapids: Baker, 1978.

Soards, M. L. *The Speeches in Acts: Their Content, Context, and Concerns.* Louisville: Westminster/John Knox, 1994.

Spencer, F. S. *The Portrait of Philip in Acts: A Study of Roles and Relations.* JSNTSup 67. Sheffield, UK: JSOT Press, 1992.

Stagg, F. *The Book of Acts: The Early Struggle for an Unhindered Gospel.* Nashville: Broadman, 1955.

Stott, J. R. W. *The Message of Acts: To the Ends of the Earth.* Bible Speaks Today. Leicester, UK: InterVarsity, 1990.

Talbert, C. H. *Acts.* Knox Preaching Guides. Atlanta: John Knox, 1984.

————. *Reading Acts: A Literary and Theological Commentary on the Acts of the Apostles.* Reading the New Testament. New York: Crossroad, 1997.

Tannehill, R. C. *The Narrative Unity of Luke-Acts: A Literary Interpretation.* Vol. 2: *The Acts of the Apostles.* Minneapolis: Fortress, 1990.

Torrey, C. C. *The Composition and Date of Acts.* Harvard Theological Studies, 1. Cambridge: Harvard University Press, 1916.

Van Unnik, W. C. *Sparsa Collecta: The Collected Essays of W. C. Van Unnik.* Part 1: *Evangelica, Paulina, Acta.* Supplements to Novum Testamentum, xxix. Leiden: Brill, 1973.

Wikenhauser, A. *Die Apostelgeschichte.* Regensburger Neues Testament. Dritte Auflage: Regensburg: Verlag Friedrich Pustet, 1956.

Wilcox, M. *The Semitisms of Acts.* Oxford: Clarendon Press, 1965.

Williams, C. S. C. *The Acts of the Apostles.* Harper's New Testament Commentaries. New York: Harper & Brothers, 1957.

Williams, D. J. *Acts.* New International Biblical Commentary, 5. Peabody, Mass.: Hendrickson, 1990.

Willimon, W. H. *Acts.* Interpretation. Atlanta: John Knox, 1988.

Winter, B. W. and A. D. Clarke, eds. *The Book of Acts in Its Ancient Literary Setting.* Vol. 1 of *The Book of Acts in Its First Century Setting.* Grand Rapids: Eerdmans, 1993.